Disparate Regimes

Nativist Politics, Alienage Law, and Citizenship Rights in the United States, 1865–1965

BRENDAN A. SHANAHAN

OXFORD
UNIVERSITY PRESS

Oxford University Press is a department of the University of Oxford.
It furthers the University's objective of excellence in research, scholarship,
and education by publishing worldwide. Oxford is a registered trade mark of
Oxford University Press in the UK and in certain other countries.

Published in the United States of America by Oxford University Press
198 Madison Avenue, New York, NY 10016, United States of America.

© Brendan A. Shanahan 2025

All rights reserved. No part of this publication may be reproduced, stored in a retrieval system, transmitted, used for text and data mining, or used for training artificial intelligence, in any form or by any means, without the prior permission in writing of Oxford University Press, or as expressly permitted by law, by license or under terms agreed with the appropriate reprographics rights organization. Inquiries concerning reproduction outside the scope of the above should be sent to the Rights Department, Oxford University Press, at the address above.

You must not circulate this work in any other form
and you must impose this same condition on any acquirer

Preassigned Control Number is on file at the Library of Congress.

ISBN 9780197660539 (hbk.)
ISBN 9780197660546 (pbk.)

DOI: 10.1093/9780197660577.001.0001

Printed by Marquis, Canada

OUP and the author gratefully acknowledge the assistance given by
the Frederick W. Hilles Publication Fund of Yale University.

Disparate Regimes

For Sarah, Claire, and Xavier

Acknowledgments

Writing this section is both a joyful and a daunting task. I first submitted an initial iteration of this book's Chapter 6 as a graduate seminar paper in 2012. Since then, this project has loomed large in my life. I owe a wealth of thanks to so many people who have helped me develop it—from idea to dissertation, from manuscript to book—over the course of a decade (plus). It is not possible to fully articulate the gratitude I hold for the teachers, colleagues, archivists, librarians, students, friends, and family who have directly and indirectly aided in *Disparate Regime*'s development. Here I do my best, knowing all too well that these few paragraphs could never fully measure up to the task.

This book project began in graduate school at the University of California, Berkeley. At Cal, I had three wonderful dissertation advisors. I thank Robin Einhorn, Mark Brilliant, and Irene Bloemraad for their counsel, encouragement, advocacy, and exhortation to always strive to improve my project. I also extend my appreciation to other UC Berkeley faculty, past and present. In the History Department, I especially thank Margaret Chowning, Brian DeLay, Sandra Eder, David Henkin, Stephanie Jones-Rogers, Rebecca McLennan, Mark Peterson, Daniel Sargent, and James Vernon. Outside the History Department, I recognize G. Cristina Mora, Rita Ross, Karen Tani, and Leti Volpp. I am especially indebted to Cybelle Fox for inspiring my interests in the history of US citizenship in her classes, scholarship, and mentorship.

My dissertation-turned-book was immeasurably improved by the sage advice I received sharing my work before numerous interdisciplinary workshops at UC Berkeley. I particularly acknowledge the Berkeley–France Fund Conference, the Canadian Studies Program, the Department of History's Legal History Workshop, the Interdisciplinary Immigration Workshop, Mark Brilliant's graduate student working group, and the Women's and Gender History Group. I am very grateful to my then–grad school peers who shared their time and advice at these venues, most especially Ryan Acton, Aparajita Basu, Dani Carrillo, Andy Chang, Esther Cho, Joe Duong, Maggie Jane Elmore, Giulia Fabini, Sheer Ganor, Alberto Garcia, Grace Goudiss, Anthony Gregory, Aaron Hall, Alexandra Havrylyshyn, Jae Yeon Kim, Sunmin Kim, Erica Lee, Rachel Martin, Sarah Gold McBride, Robert Nelson, Ivón Padilla-Rodríguez, Giuliana Perrone, Christian Phillips, Robin Savinar, Alicia Sheares, Sarah Stoller, Jennifer Robin Terry, and Brandon Williams. Christopher Casey, Trevor

viii ACKNOWLEDGMENTS

Jackson, Joseph Kellner, and Daniel Kelly read numerous iterations of several of my chapters; I thank them for their suggestions and patience.

For providing a stimulating and supportive intellectual home at Yale University, I am extremely grateful to the MacMillan Center for International and Area Studies, most notably its Center for the Study of Representative Institutions and Canadian Studies Committee, and the Department of History. I extend particular thanks to Jay Gitlin, Isaac Nakhimovsky, and Steven Smith for serving as great mentors and colleagues and to Hira Jafri, Sarah Hopkins, and Mark Roland for all their guidance and support at the MacMillan Center.

It is impossible to fully enumerate and thank everyone at Yale who has directly and indirectly improved my thinking, research, and writing about American federalism, alienage law, nativist politics, and citizenship rights. They include, but are certainly not limited to, Lauren Benton, Kate Birkbeck, John Dearborn, Beverly Gage, Martha Guerrero Badillo, Gabriel Lee, Mordechai Levy-Eichel, Mark Peterson (again), Stephen Pitti, Cristina Rodríguez, Noah Rosenblum, Stephen Skowronek, Erin Trahey, Patrick Weil, John Witt, and Emily Yankowitz.

I am very grateful for the research assistance of Leila Rock, who provided crucial aide identifying marital expatriate naturalization petitions alongside me at NARA–San Bruno (with the financial support of UC Berkeley's Graduate Division graduate mentor–undergraduate mentee research program) throughout the summer of 2013. Many thanks also go to Emily Lowe for supporting my research at NARA–Waltham. At Yale, Lucia Olubunmi Momoh has provided exceptional direction and assistance in the incorporation of images into *Disparate Regimes*, a subject hitherto unfamiliar and intimidating to me. I continue to learn from my students, past and present, at both Yale and UC Berkeley. I am very thankful for that opportunity and privilege.

The Center for the Study of Representative Institutions generously hosted a manuscript workshop for my book in 2021. I am especially grateful to Kunal Parker, Alexandra Filindra, Christopher Capozzola, and Julie Suk for leading each of its sessions and for their very helpful suggestions. I also thank all other attendees (each recognized in paragraphs above or below) for their concrete recommendations.

I am indebted to countless scholars who generously offered feedback or advice on my in-progress work at various times during this book's development. I especially thank Kerry Abrams, Margo Anderson, Ashley Johnson Bavery, Candice Bredbenner, Carl Bon Tempo, Dan Bouk, Elisa Camiscioli, Sarah Coleman, Sara Egge, Jennifer Elrick, Russell Fehr, Rachel Gunter, Ron Hayduk, Hidetaka Hirota, Pippa Holloway, Romain Huret, Franca Iacovetta, Jessica Barbata Jackson, Khalil Anthony Johnson, Linda Kerber, Alexander Keyssar, Kathryn Kish Sklar, Erika Lee, Beth Lew-Williams, Julian Lim, Rosina Lozano, Audrey Macklin, Martha Menchaca, Mae Ngai, Ann Marie Nicolosi,

Polly Price, Greg Robinson, Rachel Rosenbloom, Lucy Salyer, Dorothee Schneider, Emma Teng, Allison Brownell Tirres, Andrew Urban, Monica Varsanyi, and Roger Waldinger. Hardeep Dhillon and Debbie Kang merit special recognition for their extensive advice on, generous time spent aiding, and encouragement for *Disparate Regimes.*

While this book project began in graduate school, it would not have been possible without the support and guidance of numerous historians and teachers who taught me long before I attended Cal. Leonard Moore and John Zucchi encouraged me to consider graduate school as an undergraduate at McGill University and have continued to serve as exceptional mentors. Leslie Choquette at Assumption University in Worcester, Massachusetts, and Ray Bacon and Anne Conway at the Museum of Work & Culture in Woonsocket, Rhode Island, took me under their wings in the summers of 2009 and 2010 and taught me about primary-source research. I also thank my teachers at Tahanto Regional Middle/High School and Boylston Elementary School. I especially recognize Irene Barry, Patrick Minihan, and Steven Pacheco for stimulating my passion for (North) American immigration and citizenship history.

I am also deeply indebted to a wide array of librarians and archivists, first and foremost those at UC Berkeley and Yale. At Cal, I particularly thank the staff of the UC Berkeley Moffitt and Gardner Libraries, Interlibrary Borrowing Services office, Berkeley Law Library, and Bancroft Library. I am similarly grateful to the staff of the Sterling Memorial Library, Bass Library, and Beinecke Rare Book & Manuscript Library and to the teams at Manuscripts and Archives and Interlibrary Loan at Yale University. I especially recognize James Kessenides and Bill Landis at Yale for their unceasing assistance, time, and wise counsel.

Federal archivists, historians, and librarians played a similarly key role in the development of *Disparate Regimes.* I particularly thank Marian Smith and Zack Wilske of the US Citizenship and Immigration Services History Office for their repeated guidance and aide. I also recognize Bill Creech of the National Archives and Records Administration (Washington, DC) for his timely assistance. The support and patience of archivists at NARA branches in San Bruno, California; Waltham, Massachusetts; and Fort Worth, Texas, made much of the research for Chapter 6 of this book possible. I especially thank Joan Gearin, Meg Hacker, Sean Heyliger, Charles Miller, Jean Nudd, Barbara Rust, Joseph Sanchez, Ketina Taylor, and Nathaniel Wiltzen.

I am similarly indebted to library and archival professionals at numerous other institutions. I especially recognize the staff of the California State Archives, Massachusetts Commonwealth Archives, Nebraska State Archives, New York State Archives, Texas State Archives, and Wisconsin State Historical Society. I also thank all the professionals who aided me at the Center for Migration Studies Archive; Dallas Public Library; George Meany Memorial AFL–CIO Archive at

X ACKNOWLEDGMENTS

the University of Maryland, College Park; Harvard Law Library; Immigration and History Research Center Archives of the University of Minnesota; Library and Archives Canada; Mendocino County Historical Society; Southern Methodist University Law Library; University of Texas at Arlington Archives; Worcester Law Library; and Worcester Public Library. I particularly acknowledge Alyssa Ballard, Dominique Barrault, Mary Brown, Martha Clark, Jennifer Eidson, Jim Folts, Lee Grady, Caitlin Jones, Gayla Koerting, Gayle Martinson, Daniel Necas, Molly Ogrodnik, Michelle Pearse, and Laura Schnitker.

My book would not have been possible without the financial assistance of many fellowships, grants, and institutions. I thank McGill University's Philip F. Vineberg Travelling Fellowship for the support I received during my first academic year at UC Berkeley. UC Berkeley's Center for Race and Gender Travel Grant, Graduate Division Dissertation Completion Fellowship, the History Department's Graduate Student Fellowship and Research Fellowship, and the Institute of Governmental Study's Fred Martin Award and Mike Synar Graduate Research Fellowship enabled me to conduct research trips to archives across the country. I also thank the University of California at San Diego's Center for Comparative Immigration Studies—California Immigration Research Initiative Fellowship, William Nelson Cromwell Foundation Early Career Scholar Fellowship, Immigration and Ethnic History Society, Jack Miller Center, the Whitney and Betty MacMillan Center for International and Area Studies, and the Frederick W. Hilles Publication Fund of Yale University for their financial support, which variously enabled the completion of my dissertation and its transformation into a book.

I additionally thank *Law and History Review* and Cambridge University Press for their permission to incorporate and adapt components of my 2021 article, "A 'Practically American' Canadian Woman Confronts a United States Citizen–Only Hiring Law: Katharine Short and the California Alien Teachers Controversy of 1915," within *Disparate Regimes*. I am also deeply grateful to *Law and History Review*'s editor in chief, Gautham Rao, and the peer reviewers of that article for improving its interventions, which, in turn, sharpened the arguments of this book.

Susan Ferber was an exceptional editor of *Disparate Regimes*. I learned so much from her in this profoundly collaborative process of developing and editing a book. I also benefited from Susan's remarkably keen eye as a copy editor. I additionally recognize the anonymous peer reviewers for their deeply constructive and productive feedback on *Disparate Regimes*. Finally, I thank the whole editorial and production teams at Oxford University Press for their assistance. I am especially grateful to Susan Brown, Vasuki Ravi Chandran, and Cathryn Steele for helping me navigate the treacherous stage of production and for their very hard work on it.

ACKNOWLEDGMENTS   xi

I cannot adequately express how much I have learned from and been supported by my friends and family as *Disparate Regimes* took form. Many generously opened their homes to me as I conducted research on a tight budget. Others have shared practical advice, inspired my research, offered technical assistance, and served as (very patient) sounding boards for this project. Thanks go to all my aunts, uncles, cousins, and in-laws who unfailingly asked, "How's the dissertation/book going?" in the most positive way possible. Thank you for indulging me when I replied with an excited impromptu lecture; thanks also for your understanding when I could not even muster an answer. I especially thank Patrick Giguere, Jim and Terri Horan, Donna and Craig Kenyon, Patrick Lowe, Sandra MacKay and Paul Johnson, Dan and Laura MacIsaac, Cathy McIsaac, Eileen McIsaac, Gregory McIsaac, Patrick McIsaac, Tom and Lisa McIsaac, Brenda McNee, Cynthia Mitchell, Paul Shanahan, and Courtney Zientek.

I could not have wrestled this project into a book were it not for all of my McGill, Berkeley, and Yale friends. Among my fellow McGillians, I especially thank Jeremy Gold, Carly Kenyon, Liam Kimble, Arantxa Lewis, Aiya McNee, Kyriakos Moditis, Leigh Sadler, Eugénie Samson, and Megan Smeaton. In addition to Cal Bears recognized above, I additionally thank Bay Area friends and colleagues Liz Alspach, Olivia Benowitz, Matt Brennan, Angelo Matteo Caglioti, Liz Chadwick, Gillian Chisolm, Beki Cohen, Sophie Fitzmaurice, Anna Gallagher, Katherine Harper, Andrea Horbinski, Daniel Kelly, Elizabeth Kovats, Trevor Jackson, J. T. Jamieson, Brandon McKane, Ivana Mirkovic, Emina Mušanović, John Olmsted, Alicia Orta, Jason Rozumalski, Kerry Shannon, Julia Shatz, David Tamayo, Melissa Turoff, Mirjam Voerkelius, Julia Wambach, Drew Weber, Sam Wetherell, and Tim Wright. Since moving to the New Haven area, I have had the great fortune to make many wonderful friends, often fellow parents. While we tend not to "talk shop" in our few spare moments of uninterrupted conversation with young children running around, my work has benefited—both directly and indirectly—from your perspective.

To those I have inadvertently failed to include here by name, my apologies. Of course, all errors contained herein are my own.

Last, but certainly not least, I recognize how much my book has been shaped by the love, wisdom, and support of my immediate family: my parents-in-law, Brian MacKay and Maysa Dahan; my brother and sister-in-law, James Shanahan and Aleksandra Kuznetsova; and my parents, Joan and Dan Shanahan. Thank you for your encouragement, for opening your homes, and for sharing the joys and pains that come with writing a book.

To my best friend, partner, and spouse: thank you, Sarah. Thank you for the incalculable ways you have helped make this book a reality, your support and patience, and, above all, your unconditional love. This book is dedicated to you.

xii ACKNOWLEDGMENTS

To Claire and Xavier, you have improved this book in more ways than you will ever know. Years from now, you may or may not remember us playing and working on the couch together during COVID day care closures and your frequent drawing on my chapter drafts. Though I have not incorporated all your suggested edits (because every page would then be full of pictures of rainbows and clocks), you have served as veritable coauthors of *Disparate Regimes*. Your love, curiosity, and joy have inspired me to persevere in writing on good days and on bad. I also dedicate this book to both of you with my deepest appreciation, love, and hopes for your future.

Contents

Credits	xv
Note on Terminology	xvii
Introduction: Citizenship Rights as Citizen-Only Rights in American History	1

PART I. CONTESTING DISPARATE REGIMES OF CITIZENSHIP RIGHTS IN THE POLITICAL ECONOMY

1. Creating Disparate Regimes in the Polity: Noncitizens, Political Rights, and Nineteenth-Century State Constitutional Politics	11
2. Disputing Disparate Regimes in Employment: Blue-Collar Nativist State Hiring Laws in the Late Gilded Age and Progressive Era	35

PART II. INVENTING CITIZENSHIP RIGHTS AS CITIZEN-ONLY RIGHTS IN THE POLITY

3. Making Voters Citizens: Repealing Alien Suffrage via State Constitutional Amendment Campaigns, 1894–1926	67
4. Who Counts in the Polity? Noncitizens, Apportionment, and Representation in the Early to Mid-Twentieth Century	95

PART III. CONCRETIZING CITIZENSHIP RIGHTS AS CITIZEN-ONLY RIGHTS

5. Learning Citizenship Matters: Immigrant Professionals and State Anti-alien Hiring and Licensure Laws, 1917–52	119

xiv CONTENTS

6. Embedding American Citizenship and Citizenship Rights: Marital
   Repatriation Law from the Women's Suffrage Movement to
   the Cold War   144

   Conclusion: A "Lost Century," a Reboot, or an Uninterrupted
   Struggle? Citizenship Rights as Citizen-Only Rights   168

Endnotes   173
Works Cited   253
Index   291

Credits

1.1. Oren W. Weaver, *The Census System of Massachusetts* (Boston: Albert J. Wright, State Printer, 1876), 139. State Library of Massachusetts Special Collections Department.   24

2.1. "Foreigners Rush to Obtain Papers," *Philadelphia Inquirer*, June 29, 1897, 3. [The cartoon is captioned "Scene in the Corridor of the Post Office."] Image provided courtesy of Newspapers.com.   44

2.2. "Wachusett Dam, Largest of Its Kind, Now Completed," *Boston Globe*, November 5, 1905, SM4. Image published with permission of ProQuest LLC. Further reproduction is prohibited without permission. Image produced by ProQuest LLC as part of ProQuest® Historical Newspaper Product and UMI microfilm.   49

2.3. "I'll Take my Medicine—Crane," *New York American*, reproduced in *The Bulletin of the General Contractors Association*, vol. 6, no. 3 (March 1915), 67. The University Library, University of Illinois at Urbana–Champaign, Q. 690.6 GE.   56

3.1. "The Result of the Detroit City and State of Michigan Elections, 1892," *Patriotic American*, reproduced in Frederick Neal, *The A.P.A. and C.P.A. Exposed, or, Why They Exist* (Sandwich, ON, 1893), 21. Beinecke Rare Book and Manuscript Library, Yale University.   75

3.2. Reverend Olympia Brown, 1919. Library of Congress, Prints & Photographs Division, photograph by Harris & Ewing, LC-DIG-hec-12319.   81

3.3. *Tägliche Omaha Tribüne*, November 7, 1918, 1. Courtesy of the University of Nebraska–Lincoln Library and History Nebraska.   88

3.4. "Nicht-Bürger Fönnen Nicht Wählen [Noncitizens Cannot Vote]," *Tägliche Omaha Tribüne*, November 7, 1918, 5. Courtesy of the University of Nebraska–Lincoln Library and History Nebraska.   88

4.1. "Kelly Miller, LL.D.; Professor of Mathematics, Howard University, Washington, D.C.; Corresponding Secretary, National Sociological Society; Member of the Commission on the Race Problem, Sociological Society." Schomburg Center for Research in Black Culture, Jean Blackwell Hutson Research and Reference Division, The New York Public Library. New York Public Library Digital Collections, b11583854. https://digitalcollections.nypl.org/items/510d47df-b747-a3d9-e040-e00a18064a99.   107

4.2. Professor Ruth Silva, 1957. From "Will Lecture at Highacres Tonight," *Hazleton Standard–Sentinel*, March 22, 1957, 19. Reproduced with

xvi CREDITS

permission of the *Hazleton Standard–Speaker*. Provided Courtesy of the
State Library of Pennsylvania. Image published with permission of
ProQuest LLC. Further reproduction is prohibited without permission.
Image produced by ProQuest LLC as part of ProQuest® Historical
Newspaper Product and UMI microfilm.   115

5.1. "Mr. and Mrs. Thomas T. Sashihara are obtaining internal employment
clearance from Haruko Fujita to clear all government property before
leaving the Heart Mountain Relocation Center for outside employment,
1944." Photographer: Iwasaki, Hikaru. War Relocation Authority
Photographs of Japanese American Evacuation and Resettlement, UC
Berkeley: Bancroft Library and Archives/Online Archives of California.   135

5.2. Dr. Manuel Garcia-Godoy, c. 1974. University of Texas at El Paso Library,
Special Collections Department, *El Paso Herald–Post* Records, M5348.   138

6.1. Federal District Court, San Francisco Marital Expatriate Naturalization
Petitions Filed, FY 1923–1940; Petition and Record of Naturalization,
1903–1991, SF, RG 21; NARA–Pacific (San Bruno).   148

6.2. Federal District Court, Rhode Island Marital Expatriate Naturalization
Petitions Filed, FY 1923–1940; Petition and Record of Naturalization,
1842–1991, RI; RG 21; NARA–Northeast (Waltham).   149

6.3. Federal District Court, San Antonio Marital Expatriate Naturalization
Petitions Filed, FY 1923–1940; Petition and Record of Naturalization,
SA; RG 21; NARA–Southwest (Fort Worth).   150

6.4 and 6.5. Petition of Naturalization #5435. Alfhild Johanna Blumer, June
27, 1923. Petition and Record of Naturalization, 1903–1991, SF, Vol. 51,
Box 27; RG 21; NARA–Pacific (San Bruno).   152

6.6. Marital Repatriation Oaths Administered in Federal District Court, San
Francisco: FY, 1937–1969; Applications for Repatriation, 1936–1969;
SF; RG 21; NARA–Pacific (San Bruno).   161

6.7. Marital Repatriation Oaths Administered in Federal District Court, San
Antonio: FY 1937–1971; Applications to Regain Citizenship and
Repatriation Oaths, 1937–1970; SA; RG 21; NARA–Southwest (Fort Worth).   162

Note on Terminology

Alien, Alienage, Anti-alien, and Noncitizen

In recent years, immigrant rights advocates have urged writers and policymakers to use the noun *noncitizen* instead of *alien* to describe immigrants who have not completed the naturalization process. Viewing the latter term to be archaic and pejorative, many journalists, scholars, and political entities have adopted this approach. This book largely does so as well, though there are trade-offs with this new convention.[1]

While all immigrant "aliens" have been and continue to be noncitizens under federal law, not all noncitizens have been immigrants and/or aliens in policy or in popular understanding in American history. The (state and federal) citizenship status of free and enslaved African Americans remained a major subject of political and legal contestation in the antebellum United States, most notably in the *Dred Scott* case.[2] Many Native Americans remained noncitizens under US citizenship law as late as 1924 and were treated under federal treaties, the US Constitution, and federal jurisprudence as variously not subject to the jurisdiction of the United States, as members of separate but subordinate nations, and as wards of the national government.[3] Meanwhile, many residents of territories annexed during and around the time of the Spanish–American War were afforded not American citizenship, but instead the less robust legal status of US national.[4]

Just as it is important not to anachronistically project present-day meanings of citizenship onto early eras of American history, it is equally essential not to read noncitizen backward as a perfect synonym for alien.[5] The latter must be understood as one iteration of the former, albeit the version that has recently been most associated with noncitizenship.

While the adjectives *nativist* and *xenophobic* are often accurate descriptors of restrictive "alienage" laws, they are not perfect synonyms either. Nativist and xenophobic attitudes, movements, and policies sometimes target foreign-born noncitizens and naturalized immigrants irrespective of citizenship status. For those reasons, this book employs the term noncitizen in lieu of alien as a noun.[6] However, *alienage* (as a noun and adjective), alien (as an adjective), and *anti-alien* (as an adjective) are retained since alienage law is a distinct domain of US policymaking and jurisprudence that governs the rights of noncitizen immigrants owing to their citizenship status.

Nativism, Nativists, and Xenophobia

For more than half a century, US immigration historians have grappled with the definition of nativism. But a standardization in terminology and definitions has proved elusive. Few political actors explicitly self-identify as nativist (or xenophobic). Instead, the term nativist was first used by and has largely continued to be employed by foes of anti-immigrant legislation to describe their opponents. By contrast, those who seek to curtail immigrants' rights have instead variously claimed to be pro-American, nationalists, and/or patriots. Political actors espousing anti-immigrant sentiment have also often differed among themselves. Not every politician or voter who fought to adopt one alienage policy sought the passage of another proposed anti-alien law. Conversely, some political actors who advocated anti-alien measures did so to specifically target certain groups of noncitizen immigrants, often on the basis of religion, class, gender, and especially race. At times, such proponents were the children of immigrants or even naturalized immigrants themselves.[7]

Despite this complexity and slipperiness in definitions, this book describes political actors and actions aiming to restrict the rights of noncitizen immigrants via alienage law as nativist and as forms of nativism because they are the most literal expression of historian John Higham's classic formulation of the term: "intense opposition...on the ground of...foreign (i.e., 'un-American') connections."[8] For these reasons, the various individuals and policies that sought to transform access to key domains of the American political economy into citizen-only rights are best characterized as part of the nativist US political tradition.

Introduction

Citizenship Rights as Citizen-Only Rights in American History

In 1897, a noncitizen immigrant laborer living in the United States would have enjoyed or been denied a variety of rights depending on his state of residence. If he lived in Illinois, for instance, he may have found himself subjected to a state law stipulating that only US citizens and immigrants who had filed their "first papers" to begin the naturalization process were permitted to work on public and publicly funded jobsites. In Wisconsin, he would not have encountered an equivalent blue-collar nativist state hiring law. There, he would have been eligible to vote before becoming a US citizen if he possessed his first papers. Conversely, as a noncitizen in Massachusetts, he would have had to contend with a growing number of nativist state laws. He may have encountered one of several recent state laws restricting his employment on public construction projects, he would have been barred from voting, and he would have literally been counted out of the population for the purposes of apportioning state legislative seats.

A half century later, a noncitizen immigrant nurse would have likely confronted even more pervasive state anti-alien restrictions. If she lived in Colorado, she would not have been able to vote prior to her naturalization in 1947. There, and in many other states, women's suffrage activists had been at the forefront of repealing noncitizen voting rights laws during the Progressive and World War I eras. Meanwhile, if she lived in New York, she may have been ensnared by one or more of the state's many anti-alien public employment and licensure laws. She also would not have been counted as part of New York's polity when seats were apportioned to the state legislature.[1]

Of course, these policies governing the rights of noncitizen immigrants—formally known as state alienage laws—did not arise on their own and were not enforced in a vacuum. From the time of the Civil War through the civil rights era, a range of political actors—immigration restrictionists, blue-collar nativists, professional association lobbyists, and reform movement leaders like women's suffragists—fought to transform access to the polity and many forms of work into exclusive rights of US citizenship. Immigrants and their allies just

2   DISPARATE REGIMES

as fiercely challenged the ethics, efficacy, and constitutionality of these measures in court, on the job, in the press, via diplomacy, and especially in the political arena. Difficult to implement and inconsistently enforced in practice, such laws frequently reproduced or exacerbated broader patterns of immigrants' marginalization owing to race, sex, and class. Out of this contested maelstrom over the passage, administration, and constitutionality of nativist state alienage laws, many American citizenship rights were invented and concretized as citizen-only rights from the late nineteenth to the mid-twentieth centuries. *Disparate Regimes* recovers this often-overlooked history.

* * *

The evolution of US citizenship rights between 1865 and 1965 ranks among the most studied topics in American history. Looming largest are the changes that took place during the Civil War and Reconstruction, which produced nothing short of a revolution in American citizenship rights. Union military victory ended the abomination of slavery in the United States; federal constitutional revision during Reconstruction redefined the meaning of American citizenship as a legal status and many of its rights. The Fourteenth Amendment's equal protection clause confirmed the primacy of national citizenship in federal constitutional law vis-à-vis state and other forms of allegiances. Its birthright clause, in turn, recognized all who were born in the country as American citizens so long as they were "subject to the jurisdiction" of the United States. Combined, the three Reconstruction amendments transformed "voting and earning, as they have emerged out of the stress of inherited inequalities, especially the remnants of black chattel slavery" into the key markers of American citizenship and its constituent rights, as political theorist Judith Shklar argues in a widely read treatise.[2]

The countless betrayals of these constitutional reforms and the long-standing denial of equal rights to a majority of the nation's inhabitants undergird most histories of citizenship rights in the late-nineteenth- to mid-twentieth-century United States. African Americans were subjected to widespread physical assaults across the South, while state and local segregation laws made a mockery of the protections for equal citizenship rights ostensibly provided by the Reconstruction amendments to the federal constitution.[3] Asian Americans and Latino Americans faced similar racism and violence across the West and Southwest.[4] American citizenship was not immediately extended (if it ever was) to the residents of territories annexed by the United States amid imperial expansion at the turn of the twentieth century.[5] Many Native Americans were not recognized as US citizens until the passage of the federal Indian Citizenship Act of 1924.[6] Barred from naturalizing under racist federal nationality law, most East and South Asian immigrants were cast as "aliens ineligible to citizenship" until the mid-twentieth century.[7] Married American women remained tethered to the doctrine of coverture—which denied them full independence and economic standing—long after the Nineteenth Amendment's ratification.[8] Hundreds of thousands of native-born women even lost their US citizenship upon marriage to noncitizen men in the first decades of the twentieth century.[9]

In remedying many of these inequities, the federal victories won by an array of civil rights activists in the courtroom and in Congress during the mid- to late twentieth century have rightly been remembered as a Second Reconstruction.[10] Civil rights litigation led the Supreme Court to bar whites-only primary elections and to overturn the racist "separate but equal" doctrine by the mid-1950s, thereby revitalizing many dormant citizenship rights provisions under the federal constitution. Continued activism and political pressure engendered the passage of new federal laws, most notably the Civil Rights Act of 1964 and the Voting Rights Act of 1965. Together, these statutes recognized the equal voting and employment rights of Americans irrespective of race, sex, religion, and national origin and empowered the national government to investigate, correct, and punish violations thereof.[11] Though their promises have not been wholly fulfilled and their implementation has met numerous countervailing setbacks, the national reforms of the civil rights era nevertheless continue to embody and safeguard many of the foremost inclusive rights of American citizenship both in popular perception and under federal law.[12]

Immigrants are sometimes included in these histories of American citizenship rights. The efforts of marginalized noncitizens, particularly women and nonwhite immigrants, to overcome de facto hurdles and de jure bans to obtain US citizenship status have been interwoven into narratives of the development of American citizenship rights.[13] That the decades-long campaign to repeal the infamous federal immigration quota laws succeeded just as the civil rights movement achieved its greatest victories has also been widely observed.[14] By contrast, how citizenship rights have "functioned 'negatively' vis-à-vis resident aliens," in legal historian Kunal Parker's words, has received much less attention.[15]

In fact, scholars of American citizenship rights have often ignored this negative juxtaposition or argued for its marginality. Given their outsized weight, racism and sexism have generally trumped alienage as the dominant categories of analysis in studies of the history of US citizenship rights.[16] Indeed, many scholars have highlighted numerous instances in which white noncitizen men often obtained benefits and rights denied to nonwhite and/or female American citizens.[17] Others have described how Latino Americans and Asian Americans were often racialized as de facto foreigners by their white peers.[18] Comparatively low rates of immigration and a declining noncitizen population during the early to mid-twentieth century, in turn, have fueled claims then and since that

4   DISPARATE REGIMES

alienage was of decreasing value to the development of modern American citizenship rights.[19]

State governments' comparatively limited powers in several key areas of late-nineteenth- to mid-twentieth-century immigration and citizenship law have likewise kept state alienage policies sidelined in most accounts of US immigration history. From the time of the American Revolution until the Reconstruction era, state authorities had driven many important immigration policymaking matters (in the form of anti-pauper laws and immigrant settlement schemes) and enforced citizenship law (through the administration of naturalization paperwork and proceedings).[20] Ascendant federal immigration lawmaking and jurisprudence largely neutered state lawmakers' jurisdiction in the domain of exit–entry policy during the late nineteenth century. State jurists and bureaucrats similarly ceded much of their control over the implementation of naturalization law in the early twentieth century.[21] By contrast, the repeal of the federal immigration quota system in 1965 and the Supreme Court's recognition of alienage as a suspect class in 1971 have often been portrayed as inaugurating a new era of heightened immigrant rights federalism in recent American immigration history.[22]

To be sure, some forms of late-nineteenth- to mid-twentieth-century nativist state politics and alienage law have been better remembered than others. The passage and implementation of anti-alien land laws by western states targeting East and South Asian immigrants because of their status as "aliens ineligible to citizenship," for instance, have been well studied.[23] The causes behind the demise of noncitizen voting rights laws, in turn, have been a subject of scholarly investigation for nearly a century.[24] But these and other state-level disputes over nativist politics and alienage law have rarely been synthesized and foregrounded in most accounts of the evolution of US citizenship rights. This book places them at the center of the story.

* * *

Disparate Regimes studies the contestation, invention, and concretization of many political and economic rights as de jure citizen-only rights under state law from the time of the Civil War to the civil rights era. This approach hones in on one of the central challenges inherent to the study of citizenship: identifying how, why, when, where, and for whom its possession and its rights have or have not truly counted in discrete contexts and how this has changed over time.[25] Demonstrating how nativist state politics and alienage laws were prominently contested highlights both the wide variation of noncitizens' de jure rights on a state-by-state basis from the late nineteenth to the mid-twentieth centuries and the importance of that disparity to American politics, jurisprudence, and the lives of noncitizen immigrants. Illustrating how frequently citizenship rights were invented as citizen-only rights underscores that efforts to expand political rights and equal access to workplaces for some US citizens often intersected with and/or came at the expense of noncitizens' rights. Finally, exploring how alienage laws became embedded as citizen-only rights in law and in practice over time and across states highlights the ever-evolving, always relative, but generally increasing value of US citizenship between 1865 and 1965.

Disparate Regimes employs—but flips—Shklar's famous contention that the primary markers of American citizenship have become the right to vote and the right to be paid for one's labor to examine noncitizen immigrants' access to these rights on a state-by-state-basis.[26] It therefore unearths, compares, and contextualizes a range of state-level debates over noncitizen voting rights, anti-alien apportionment provisions, blue-collar nativist hiring policies, and anti-alien professional licensure laws. It ends by investigating the nebulous legal status of hundreds of thousands of US-born women who lost their nationality upon marriage to noncitizen men in the early to mid-twentieth century to illustrate the impact of these state developments on both federal understandings and popular perceptions of American citizenship and its rights.

Throughout, this book recognizes that alienage was never the only or always the primary lens through which US citizenship rights were debated and created. Indeed, it examines how and when alienage played a subordinate role to and/or operated in conjunction with other hierarchies—particularly various expressions of racism and sexism—in the making of American citizenship rights as citizen-only rights.

To do so, *Disparate Regimes* builds on a growing corpus of interdisciplinary scholarship about immigration federalism that challenges the characterization of the late nineteenth to the mid-twentieth centuries as a time when state authorities played, at most, a peripheral role in the laws and politics governing the lives and livelihoods of noncitizen immigrants.[27] This book describes the breadth and depth of ever-evolving state alienage laws governing noncitizens' political and employment rights as disparate regimes of citizenship rights.[28] To track and contextualize the proliferation of these policies, it draws on regionally distinct case studies, often from California, Massachusetts, Nebraska, New York, Texas, and Wisconsin.

Part I, "Contesting Disparate Regimes of Citizenship Rights in the Political Economy," explicates how and why states adopted widely different laws governing the inclusion or exclusion of noncitizens from the polity and their right to work in public and publicly funded employment from the mid-nineteenth to the early twentieth centuries. As Chapter 1 demonstrates, the politics of nineteenth-century state and statehood constitutional conventions proved central to the development of highly distinct and evolving regimes of citizenship

6 DISPARATE REGIMES

rights in the polity via the adoption, amending, and repeal of noncitizen voting rights and anti-alien apportionment provisions. Chapter 2 shows how public and/or publicly funded employment became a citizen-only right in many heavily immigrant–populated states during the late Gilded Age and the Progressive Era owing to the passage of numerous blue-collar nativist state hiring statutes. It further explores the highly inconsistent implementation and questionable permissibility of such policies—often lax in good economic conditions and suddenly resuscitated during hard times—before the unequivocal upholding of their constitutionality by the US Supreme Court in 1915.

Part II, "Inventing Citizenship Rights as Citizen-Only Rights in the Polity," interrogates how and why disparate regimes of citizenship rights and suffrage rights became disentangled during the early twentieth century, a time when all surviving noncitizen voting rights laws were repealed. However, the possession of US citizenship was only decoupled from "being counted" for the purposes of apportionment to state legislatures nationwide in the late 1960s and 1970s. While these chapters emphasize the importance of state-specific partisan and factional politics to the outcome of these disputes, they underscore how constitutional mechanics—especially the relative difficulty or ease of amending state constitutions—greatly shaped their timing. Chapter 3 underscores the crucial role played by both partisan and nonpartisan activists such as elite immigration restrictionists and self-styled election reformers in roughly a dozen discrete state constitutional amendment campaigns to repeal alien suffrage between 1894 and 1924. Women's suffragists, who claimed voting as the foremost exclusive right of American citizenship, grew increasingly central to these efforts. Chapter 4 identifies logistical and constitutional hurdles as key to the success or the failure of efforts to adopt, amend, or repeal anti-alien apportionment schemes in the early to mid-twentieth century before the ultimate demise of all remaining provisions in the late civil rights era as they proved unpopular and ineffective amid national redistricting reform.

Part III, "Concretizing Citizenship Rights as Citizen-Only Rights," illuminates how a range of historical actors—most notably state bureaucrats, federal immigration authorities, and, above all, noncitizens themselves—viewed exclusive rights of US citizenship to be increasingly tangible and powerful legal realities from the time of World War I until the 1960s. Chapter 5 explores the proliferation of, litigation over, and contested enforcement of hundreds of state anti-alien employment measures to demonstrate how citizen-only rights played out on jobsites, in noncitizens' persistent attempts to obtain work, and in state authorities' increasingly coercive efforts to implement anti-alien professional licensure laws. It contextualizes late civil rights–era federal litigation that overturned many, but far from all, such laws. Chapter 6 traces the efforts of thousands of US-born women to regain their stolen nationality from the time of the women's suffrage movement until the early Cold War years. It highlights a failed attempt by the Immigration and Naturalization Service to have such marital expatriates universally recognized as "citizens without citizenship rights" by decree in the 1940s to illustrate how significantly state-level disputes over noncitizen immigrants' political and economic rights had welded US citizenship rights to citizen-only rights in both law and popular understanding.

This book thus contends that the meaning and weight of US citizenship rights as citizen-only rights were principally contested not at the level of the national polity from the late nineteenth to the mid-twentieth centuries, but within dozens of different state polities. In 1890, noncitizen voting rights were deeply entrenched in roughly a dozen state constitutions. At the same time, anti-alien apportionment provisions were embedded in the constitutions of several major immigrant-destination states, like Massachusetts and New York. Proponents of turning voting into a citizen-only right and supporters of decoupling apportionment from the exclusive rights of citizenship eventually won out across the nation because of their determined, persistent political action to amend their respective state constitutions. While national partisan politics, federal constitutional reform, and US Supreme Court decisions sometimes influenced and intersected with these debates, they played a supporting role.

Debates over the restriction or barring of noncitizen immigrants from both professional licensure and publicly funded employment were also primarily contested in the domain of state politics during this era. Noncitizen workers, professionals, and their allies proved dexterous in challenging them—in courtrooms, before state licensing boards, on the job, and via diplomatic action— across levels and layers of government. But since federal jurisprudence afforded state lawmakers wide discretion in these matters until the late civil rights era, noncitizens and their advocates often found greater success when lobbying state lawmakers and rallying allies to defend immigrants' employment rights via state legislative action.

In sum, noncitizen immigrants grappled with disparate regimes of citizenship rights in the political arena and the workplace on a state-by-state basis in the century between the close of the Civil War and the apogee of the civil rights era. Those disparate regimes narrowed in the realm of political rights as suffrage was claimed and invented in tandem both as a de jure right of American citizenship and as a citizen-only right in the early twentieth century, even as most nonwhite Americans remained barred from the franchise in practice. State anti-alien apportionment provisions experienced a slower demise, but eventually converged in the direction of separating representation from the exclusive rights of US citizenship by the late 1960s and early 1970s. Noncitizens' access to public and publicly funded employment and to professional licensure likewise differed widely on a state-by-state basis well into the civil rights era.

8   DISPARATE REGIMES

This powerful strain of nativist politics and the proliferation of state anti-alien laws it produced dramatically transformed both the meaning and the relative weight of American citizenship rights. Their development propelled and empowered the idea that such rights were—or at least could be—identifiable, definable, and restricted to US citizens.

Disparate Regimes: Nativist Politics, Alienage Law, and Citizenship Rights in the United States, 1865–1965.
Brendan A. Shanahan, Oxford University Press. © Brendan A. Shanahan 2025.
DOI: 10.1093/9780197660577.003.0001

PART I

CONTESTING DISPARATE REGIMES OF CITIZENSHIP RIGHTS IN THE POLITICAL ECONOMY

1
Creating Disparate Regimes in the Polity
Noncitizens, Political Rights, and Nineteenth-Century State Constitutional Politics

When delegates assembled as a convention in the autumn of 1821 to rewrite New York's constitution, they were not lacking for subjects to debate. The Empire State's population, particularly in New York City, was rapidly growing. Slavery was set to be outlawed statewide in 1827. Amid these profound societal changes, convention delegates fiercely battled over who should participate in and count as part of their state's polity.[1] Under the existing 1777 constitution, only wealthy and middling-class men who owned significant amounts of property or met substantial taxpaying obligations could vote. Seats to both chambers of the state legislature were, in turn, apportioned on the basis of their electorates.[2]

While some delegates wanted to retain high class-based barriers to the franchise and apportionment, most sought to reduce or repeal such requirements, at least for some New Yorkers. Many proponents of removing taxpaying and property ownership qualifications for white working-class men also sought to bar wealthy and middling-class Black men from voting. Others still wanted to exclude noncitizen immigrants from the polity altogether.[3]

Eventually, convention delegates reached a compromise. Taxpaying and property ownership suffrage requirements were effectively repealed for white men (provided they were not paupers). Nonpauper white citizen men, women, and children would henceforth be included in apportionment calculations. However, noncitizen immigrants, paupers, and most free African Americans would remain excluded. In future, the only free Black men who would count for the purposes of representation were the wealthy few who met new—overtly racist—property ownership and taxpaying requirements to vote.[4]

Such debates were not unique to the Empire State. Most states repealed taxpaying and property ownership suffrage requirements for white men in the early nineteenth century. Conversely, property-owning and taxpaying free Black men lost the right to vote in all but a handful of northeastern states in those same years, while women were barred from the franchise nationwide.[5] Legislative reapportionment policies were also frequently disputed at state constitutional conventions prior to the Civil War.[6]

12 DISPARATE REGIMES

Immigrants' citizenship status was seldom a primary topic of these conflicts, however. In fact, rarely were the rights of noncitizen immigrants the focus of antebellum debate when delegates battled over whether political rights should be defined as "rights of citizenship." Instead, arguments over the proper role of noncitizen immigrants in the polity were usually considered alongside the rights and legal status of married women, Native Americans, and especially free Black persons. Nevertheless, several antebellum states chose to bar noncitizen immigrants from the franchise and exclude them from representation, other states opted for the opposite approach, and others still split the difference. Out of this maelstrom emerged disparate regimes of citizenship rights in the polity on a state-by-state basis.

This chapter examines the explosion of such regimes in the late antebellum period, their transformation during Reconstruction, and their tenuous continuation in the late nineteenth century.[7] It identifies the convening of state and statehood constitutional assemblies as crucial to the development of these disparate regimes.[8] Nineteenth-century American federalism and constitutional jurisprudence afforded states wide latitude to determine the exclusive political rights of US citizenship vis-à-vis noncitizen immigrants. Conflicts over alien suffrage laws and anti-alien apportionment schemes were therefore most often contested at or in the aftermath of state constitutional assemblies. The major exception to this pattern—national constitutional reform during Reconstruction—proves the broader rule. Only when redefining American citizenship did nineteenth-century federal lawmakers seriously consider and reject restricting political rights nationwide on the basis of alienage. This chapter thus illustrates how state constitutional politics made and reshaped disparate regimes of citizenship rights in the polity in the nineteenth-century United States.

The Rise of Disparate Regimes of Citizenship Rights in Antebellum Polities

Voting was not a right of citizenship in the era of the early republic. Many conservative politicians feared linking suffrage with the language of rights at all, preferring to frame voting as a privilege or obligation of property-owning men. The federal constitution of 1787 neither defined voting as a right of national citizenship nor specified who could vote. Instead, the founders granted states wide latitude to demarcate their respective electorates.[9]

Most early republican state lawmakers opted to significantly restrict access to the polls. American women (except single, property-owning women in New Jersey until 1807) were denied the franchise in all states and territories. Conversely, white noncitizen men could often vote provided they met all other taxpaying or property ownership requirements. But such alien suffrage provisions were never ubiquitous, and many proved short-lived.[10]

Eastern states often repealed their noncitizen voting rights laws at constitutional conventions during or following times of war, recession, or heightened xenophobia. By the eve of the Civil War, no Atlantic seaboard state enfranchised noncitizen white men. Some northeastern states, most notably Massachusetts and New York, adopted onerous registration requirements to hinder naturalized immigrants' access to the franchise.[11]

These nativist suffrage restrictions did not appear in isolation. Racist suffrage barriers were erected across the upper South, mid-Atlantic, and Midwest amid the so-called Jacksonian expansion of the franchise to white, male citizens. By the 1850s, only five states—all in the Northeast—recognized the equal suffrage rights of free Black men.[12] Northern African American civic organizations fiercely protested these restrictions, claiming suffrage as a right of citizenship and manhood, but they failed to block the onslaught of racist voting barriers.[13]

Though these patterns of disfranchisement abetted the demise of alien suffrage in the East, the ideology of universal white manhood suffrage actually buttressed the voting rights of noncitizen white men in the Midwest and West. No antebellum polity embodied these tendencies more than Wisconsin, where, following a failed convention in 1846, delegates reassembled in the winter of 1847–48 to draft a statehood constitution and fiercely debated a plan to enfranchise noncitizen men who had begun the naturalization process.[14]

Supporters contended that white immigrant men in Wisconsin who had declared their intention to become US citizens—then a required first step to naturalize—should be allowed to vote.[15] Several advocates stressed that the practice in Wisconsin Territory, and the Midwest more broadly, dated back to the Northwest Ordinance of 1787. Delegate H. T. Sanders, a Democrat from Racine (part of southeastern Wisconsin), contended that "at the close of the revolution there was no question of *foreigners*." As citizens and noncitizens "had all fought side by side," he maintained that "the fathers of the confederacy" had wisely "desired that rights and privileges should be equally extended to them, in the Northwest Territory."[16] Fellow Democrat and Fond du Lac delegate Samuel Beall similarly argued, "This question of suffrage was not a new one, nor was the question now under discussion, a new one. It was older than the constitution of the United States."[17]

Other proponents emphasized that white, male noncitizen voters were needed in Wisconsin's expanding, rural settler colonial society. Delegate John L. Doran, a Milwaukee Democrat, contended that alien suffrage was especially important because of the large, growing immigrant population. He contrasted Wisconsin with neighboring and more heavily populated Illinois, which was then in the process of rescinding alien suffrage rights. Doran

14   DISPARATE REGIMES

claimed the loss of such rights in Wisconsin would be even more foolish. "With so much land still to be located, much already purchased by foreigners for friends about to come to the territory," Doran argued that "it is rather too soon for us to begin to practice our exclusiveness."[18] Others went further. Delegate Peter D. Gifford, a Democrat from southeastern Waukesha County, warned that a majority of white men in Wisconsin might be disfranchised in the near future if immigration rates among "hardy foreigners from Europe" continued to grow. Alien suffrage was a necessary bulwark for democracy, he maintained, that would prevent "thr[owing] the whole power into the hands of a minority of the people."[19]

Opponents charged that pro-alien suffrage delegates were nakedly trying to bolster their own partisan interests or regional power. Critics of noncitizen voting rights, often Whigs, highlighted that support was concentrated among Democrats and delegates representing the heavily immigrant–populated regions of eastern and southern Wisconsin.[20] Delegate William Richardson of rural, southwestern Grant County, for instance, alleged that proponents had come to the simple conclusion that "we want their votes" and "we need their votes."[21] Delegate Alfred L. Castleman of Waukesha pointed to states that had recently repealed or were in the process of rescinding alien suffrage provisions as proof that "the experiment" in noncitizen voting "had been tried and failed."[22]

Opponents also rejected the notion that immigrants' declaration of intention entailed any commitment to or belonging in the polity. They emphasized that taking out "first papers" did not impose any obligations of citizenship on those who filed them. "I deny that such declaration makes them liable for the imposition of any burdens which they were not liable to without such declaration," Richardson argued, "for the plain reason that their relation to the government is not changed, as far as the liability for the imposition of burdens is concerned." Noncitizens, in his opinion, "were residents before such declaration, and they are nothing but residents after."[23] Delegate Charles Dunn of Lafayette County, a Democrat serving as the chief justice of the Wisconsin Territorial Supreme Court, similarly argued that "a declaration of intention . . . amounts to nothing, unless followed by consummation."[24]

These views proved to be in the minority. Most delegates voted in support of a first papers suffrage policy. Voters ratified the constitution and Congress admitted Wisconsin as the nation's thirtieth state in 1848. It is hardly surprising that first papers suffrage rights proved popular in Wisconsin, where more than one-third of all residents had been born abroad.[25] Though the new constitution incorporated thousands of noncitizen voters, it also denied the franchise to female and free Black residents.[26]

CREATING DISPARATE REGIMES IN THE POLITICAL ECONOMY   15

The states of Indiana, Kansas, Michigan, Minnesota, and Oregon also adopted first papers suffrage laws in the late antebellum era. Six territories likewise enfranchised white noncitizen immigrant men shortly before or during the Civil War.[27] Similar patterns of white, male inclusion and female, nonwhite exclusion emerged in these polities. Most Native Americans were not incorporated as voters in the states and territories they had long inhabited. But some antebellum polities did recognize the voting rights of persons of both Native and white ancestry and/or enfranchised individual Native Americans who were judged to have left tribal communities and thereby become US citizens.[28]

Although not all states in the Midwest and West adopted alien suffrage policies, none singled out noncitizens for exclusion from the population for apportionment purposes. Delegate William Richardson even contrasted his fervent opposition to alien suffrage with his support for the inclusion of noncitizens in apportionment provisions. He "den[ied] that aliens who are among us are not represented unless they are voters" because, under Wisconsin's "broad principle of representation, the basis is not the number of electors, but the number of inhabitants."[29] Thus, he maintained that noncitizens formed an integral, nonvoting component of Wisconsin's polity. In the Northeast, antebellum state politicians often came to a far more restrictive conclusion.[30]

* * *

Although the antebellum national constitution was silent on suffrage rights, it did strictly define federal apportionment policies. At the 1787 Philadelphia Constitutional Convention, the founders fiercely battled over whether each state should receive an equal number of seats in the new Congress or if seats should be apportioned on the basis of population (and, if so, whether enslaved persons should be counted in those calculations). The "Great Compromise" ultimately apportioned each state's number of seats in the House of Representatives on the basis of its total "free population" plus a three-fifths ratio of its enslaved population while excluding "Indians not taxed" from the count. Each state was reserved two seats in the Senate.[31]

Like Congress, antebellum state legislatures often had different bases of apportionment for their lower and upper chambers. Politicians from less-populated regions often fought successfully to require each county and/or municipality to receive a minimum degree of representation in one or both legislative chambers irrespective of their populations, thereby inflating the weight of rural white male residents' votes in state legislative elections. State lawmakers also wrestled over who counted as part of the population.[32]

Some of the first state constitutions adopted following the Declaration of Independence, such as New York's 1777 document, apportioned one or both

16 DISPARATE REGIMES

state legislative chambers on the basis of their electorate(s). Such schemes barred most noncitizen immigrants—and the majority of the state's residents, for that matter—from apportionment calculations owing to widespread early republican property ownership and/or taxpaying suffrage requirements.[33]

When Maine split from Massachusetts to enter the Union as the nation's twenty-third state in 1820, it became the first to explicitly exclude noncitizen immigrants by name from representation. Its new constitution predicated apportionment to the state's lower chamber on the basis of "the number of inhabitants" residing in Maine, "exclusive of foreigners not naturalized, and Indians not taxed."[34] New York delegates followed suit the following year by counting noncitizen immigrants out of the polity when revising apportionment policy for both chambers of their state legislature at their own constitutional convention.[35]

Twenty-five years later, delegates reconvened to discuss the New York constitution and again clashed over the issue. At the 1846 constitutional convention, Democratic delegates representing New York City argued that noncitizens should be included in apportionment calculations because they were residents of the state. Upstate Whigs and many rural Democrats countered that inclusion in the polity, however indirect, should be reserved for citizens. The latter position prevailed as delegates voted to retain the 1821 anti-alien apportionment provision in the state's new constitution.[36] Similar partisan, regional, and factional divisions over apportionment policy would soon prove even more pronounced in neighboring Massachusetts.

Mass Irish Catholic immigration thrust matters of apportionment to the fore of Bay State politics in the late 1840s and early 1850s. At a state constitutional convention held in 1853, small-town Yankee delegates offered a range of apportionment proposals aiming to bolster the standing of their communities in the Massachusetts General Court (the state legislature).[37] They did so in the hopes of offsetting the influence of politicians from Boston, who were growing even more empowered by the city's rapidly swelling noncitizen immigrant population. In the end, a plan to augment the number of seats assigned to small towns vis-à-vis cities was adopted by the convention. Though the scheme did not outright exclude noncitizens, many supporters made clear that they hoped it would reduce the weight of immigrants in state politics. To become part of the state's constitution, the policy had to be ratified by voters in the 1853 autumn elections. To widespread surprise, the reapportionment proposal was defeated at the polls by a 51.9 percent to 48.1 percent margin.[38]

Many Yankee voters—regardless of political party—accused Boston's Protestant Whig elite of colluding with the city's growing Irish Catholic immigrant, heavily Democratic population to defeat the amendment. Support for the new anti-immigrant Know-Nothing Party (formally the American Party)

CREATING DISPARATE REGIMES IN THE POLITICAL ECONOMY 17

exploded across the state.[39] In a remarkable landslide, 99 percent of seats in the state legislature were won by the upstart party in the 1854 fall elections.[40]

Henry Gardner, the state's new Know-Nothing governor, soon launched an ambitious nativist agenda. He and his allies enacted legislation surveilling and harassing Irish Catholic immigrant communities while expanding the state's deportation powers.[41] The Know-Nothings also embedded provisions into the commonwealth's highest law that forced would-be voters take a literacy test and required immigrant men wait two years after naturalization before voting.[42]

As part of that process, Know-Nothing lawmakers used their numbers to entrench anti-alien apportionment provisions in the commonwealth's constitution, overcoming significant structural hurdles in the absence of a convention. In 1856, they proposed two constitutional amendments that would base apportionment in both legislative chambers on the number of "legal voters" in the state.[43] These passed the House and Senate by two-thirds majority margins in back-to-back years, as required by the state constitution. The measures were then ratified by Bay State voters by huge majorities in 1857.[44] Backing for the anti-alien apportionment provisions was not limited to Know-Nothing partisans. In July 1857, the *Worcester Palladium*, an advocate for the new Republican Party, reasoned that only citizen-voters should be counted, "as the *political power* is in the hands of the *legal voters*."[45]

A few other antebellum polities also restricted some noncitizens from state legislative apportionment calculations. Kentucky, Tennessee, and (the upper legislative chamber in) Texas adopted electorate-based standards. Many southern states and some midwestern and western states restricted apportionment to white residents.[46] Proposals to count or exclude enslaved persons for the purposes of state legislative apportionment were often fiercely debated as powerful planters (who benefited from their inclusion) battled with smallholding white farmers (who were often underrepresented in state legislatures).[47] But it was in the Northeast where overtly nativist apportionment laws most influenced state politics and played a key role in determining the boundaries of both inclusive and exclusive citizenship rights. During Reconstruction, such debates would proliferate, become increasingly entangled, and grow in prominence as federal lawmakers contested the rights of US citizenship in the national polity.

Reconstructing American Citizenship and Defining the Political Rights of Citizens

In the aftermath of the Civil War, northern congressmen and senators fiercely debated what national citizenship should mean in the renewed republic. Some northern and Border South "moderate" Republicans, along with all Democrats,

18   DISPARATE REGIMES

sought to restrict federal constitutional reform to the Thirteenth Amendment, which banned slavery and involuntary servitude across the United States in 1865. But president Andrew Johnson's lax commitment to Reconstruction in the face of rising white supremacist terrorism and the enactment of discriminatory Black Codes by southern state legislatures led most northern Republicans to support broader constitutional reform to ensure federal protections for African Americans' civil rights. As in late antebellum state constitutional debates, whether citizenship rights should function as citizen-only rights rarely became the central focus of these Reconstruction conflicts. But these questions were nevertheless intimately connected to them.[48]

When northern members of Congress hammered out what would become the Fourteenth Amendment, they especially struggled over southern states' future congressional representation. As apportionment to the federal House of Representatives would no longer be based on the infamous Three-Fifths Compromise following the ratification of the Thirteenth Amendment, south-ern states were poised to gain seats in the US Congress. Since southern African American men remained disfranchised, that meant that whites in the states of the former Confederacy were perversely set to gain power in the Reconstruction Congress.[49] Northern Republicans refused to countenance such develop-ments.[50] One obvious solution—the enfranchisement of Black men—seemed unlikely to succeed in the immediate future. African American men were denied voting rights throughout most of the North, not just in the South. Many midwestern and mid-Atlantic states had voted down or were in the process of rejecting referenda on Black male suffrage rights in the immediate aftermath of the Civil War.[51]

In this context, representative Thaddeus Stevens, leader of the Radical Republicans, strongly backed a legal voter standard as the basis of apportion-ment to the nation's lower legislative chamber. Under Stevens's plan, the num-ber of federal House districts assigned to each state would be based on how many residents were eligible to vote. Stevens hoped that his scheme would induce white southerners to extend suffrage rights to former slaves or face the consequences of reduced representation in Congress.[52]

Foes of African American voting rights in Congress, both Democrats and some moderate Republicans, often opposed a legal voter basis of apportion-ment on explicitly racist grounds. But some Radical Republicans—fervent sup-porters of Black suffrage rights among them—resisted a national legal voter apportionment basis for a different reason.[53]

Radical Republican congressman James Blaine of Maine argued that a legal voter basis threatened the clout of northeastern states in Congress because of their large immigrant and female populations. He emphasized that western states—with their larger ratios of men to women—would significantly gain

CREATING DISPARATE REGIMES IN THE POLITICAL ECONOMY   19

representation at the expense of northeastern states.[54] Blaine chastised his fellow Radical Republicans for overlooking the "incidental evils" that Stevens's plan "would inflict on a large portion of the loyal states." Instead, he wanted states that disfranchised men on racist grounds to receive fewer seats. Blaine also advocated for voting to become a citizen-only right. He warned that a legal voter apportionment basis would "cheapen suffrage everywhere" and lead to "an unseemly scramble" among states to lower barriers to ensure their power in Congress. "Foreigners would be invited to vote on a mere preliminary 'declaration of intention,'" he decried, "and the ballot, which cannot be too sacredly guarded, and which is the great and inestimable privilege of the American citizen, would be demoralized and disgraced everywhere."[55] Blaine thus only wanted noncitizens to be counted for the purposes of representation. He did not envision them as full members of the polity.

He was not alone. Senator Henry Wilson, a Massachusetts Republican, also criticized electorate-based apportionment proposals on the grounds that northeastern states would lose power in Congress. Wilson was livid that a legal voter basis threatened to count the large noncitizen populations of northeastern states, like his own, out of the House's apportionment policy.[56] He sarcastically mused that it might "be best to make this sacrifice" and (by his estimation) "take fifteen Representatives from the loyal States and add them to the strength of the rebel States." But he warned that if his colleagues voted to do just that, "it will be whispered in the ears of the immigrants from the Old World that for the sake of the negro we have counted them out of the basis of representation."[57] The powerful senator thus played to nativists' fears. Notably, neither Blaine nor Wilson mentioned that their home states' constitutions counted noncitizens out of the population for the purposes of apportioning seats to their own legislatures.[58]

To mitigate the concerns of northeastern Republicans, several proponents of Stevens's plan—most notably Ohio representative Robert Schenck—offered to specifically exclude noncitizen voters residing in alien suffrage states from apportionment calculations.[59] Despite such efforts, electorate-based apportionment proposals were rejected in congressional debate. But Stevens's aims were not entirely defeated. The Fourteenth Amendment ultimately included a penalty provision, similar to Blaine's proposal, reducing the number of House seats assigned to states if they disfranchised Black freedmen made birthright citizens by the amendment's first clause. Section 2 of the Fourteenth Amendment commands that if states disfranchise male US citizens for reasons other than crime or rebellion, their number of seats in the federal House of Representatives should be reduced proportionally. The provision has never been enforced.[60]

In this manner, Reconstruction federal constitutional reapportionment reform transformed and built onto antebellum-era disparate regimes of citizenship

20 DISPARATE REGIMES

rights in the polity. Federal politicians rarely claimed representation as an inclusive or exclusive "right of citizenship." Their rhetoric far more often discussed the potential impact of a legal voter apportionment basis nationwide on regional and partisan power. Nevertheless, a proposal to count most noncitizens out of the national polity was seriously considered and rejected. And penalties were ultimately directed at states if they disfranchised not all men, but male US citizens.

Federal battles over suffrage rights continued in the late 1860s. Advocates of Black voting rights pressed for a federal guarantee of "universal manhood" suffrage irrespective of race. Women's suffragists also fought to be included in this national constitutional revision. During congressional deliberations over what would become the Fifteenth Amendment, policymakers especially debated whether suffrage should be an affirmative national right (and for whom) or whether states should be prevented from denying the franchise (and on what basis). Alien suffrage once more became entwined in battles over whether voting should become a national, exclusive right of citizenship.[61]

With even most Radical Republican leaders opposed or lukewarm to their cause, women's suffragists like Elizabeth Cady Stanton and Susan B. Anthony were fighting an uphill struggle during Reconstruction.[62] Some Republican leaders, such as Massachusetts's Senator Wilson, advocated enacting and ratifying an affirmative national right to vote for American men.[63] His ally, Pennsylvania senator Simon Cameron, argued that broad suffrage protections were needed "because it invites into our country everybody; the negro, the Irishman, the German, the Frenchman, the Scotchman, the Englishman, and the Chinaman."[64] But expanding immigrant voting rights—especially to Chinese migrants—was anathema to most other members of Congress. When Massachusetts senator Charles Sumner proposed eliminating any reference to citizenship in the Fifteenth Amendment, several of his colleagues launched into racist diatribes about its purported dangers, alleging that it would lead to mass immigration from China.[65]

Ultimately, the Fifteenth Amendment was written to prohibit explicitly racist suffrage restrictions. As with the Fourteenth Amendment's apportionment provisions, it incorporated a citizenship qualification that barred state or federal lawmakers from denying the voting rights of "citizens of the United States . . . on account of race, color, or previous condition of servitude."[66] While the Fifteenth Amendment thus dramatically expanded the number of US citizens eligible to vote, suffrage became neither an inclusive nor an exclusive right of citizenship nationwide.

States' disparate regimes were further buttressed by federal constitutional jurisprudence. In 1875, Virginia Minor, a Missouri women's suffragist, contended before the US Supreme Court that voting was an inherent right of all American citizens. Pointing to the country's history of sexist suffrage laws and the text of the Fifteenth Amendment, the court rejected her argument, determining that voting was not "one of the necessary privileges of a citizen of the United States." Though states and territories could extend suffrage rights to women, the court ruled that they were not required to do so. The high court also reasoned in *Minor v. Happersett* that voting was not an exclusive right of citizenship either, pointing to a growing number of laws that enfranchised noncitizen men (and occasionally women) in many US states and territories.[67]

* * *

The victory of the Union in the Civil War put the political rights of noncitizen immigrants on the agenda of many state constitutional conventions held across the newly liberated South. Alien suffrage proved popular at many of them. Four states of the former Confederacy (Arkansas, Florida, Georgia, and Texas) and the Border South state of Missouri adopted noncitizen voting provisions prior to 1877. Georgia repealed its policy at a convention organized in 1877 by white Democratic "Redeemers." But Louisiana would join the ranks of alien suffrage states at its own 1879 Redeemer convention.[68]

Southern states enacted alien suffrage provisions in large part to attract foreign laborers in a region with few immigrant workers. The 1870 census identified roughly one of every seven residents in the United States (14.4 percent of the population) as foreign-born. But the spread of immigrants across regions was uneven. While 20.5 percent of northeasterners and 18 percent of midwesterners hailed from abroad in 1870, a paltry 3.3 percent of southerners were immigrants.[69]

Many territories and states across the West also enforced alien suffrage laws as a means of encouraging white settler colonialism. By 1877, four states (Colorado, Kansas, Nebraska, and Oregon) and four territories (Dakota, Montana, Washington, and Wyoming) had granted white noncitizen men the right to vote.[70] Unlike the states of the former Confederacy, immigrants amounted to 31.6 percent of inhabitants residing in western states and territories in 1870, as counted by the federal census (which excluded "Indians not taxed" on its main enumeration).[71]

Alien suffrage was not always the central focus of Reconstruction-era territorial and statehood debates. At the 1875–76 constitutional convention in Colorado, where roughly one of every five residents had been born abroad, little debate was recorded over the topic of noncitizen voting. A majority of delegates serving on the Rights of Suffrage and Elections committee recommended a first papers suffrage policy, and this language was swiftly incorporated into the draft constitution.[72]

However, supporters of women's suffrage in Colorado argued fervently for US citizenship to be the primary qualification for political rights. They made a concerted push to try to make Colorado—which bordered the nation's only two

22 DISPARATE REGIMES

territories (Wyoming and Utah) that then enfranchised female voters—the country's first women's suffrage state.[73] But even one of their ostensible supporters, the *Colorado Free Springs* newspaper, warned that it would be "a serious calamity, if by means of the incorporation of a woman suffrage clause" the electorate rejected the whole draft constitution. Urging women's suffragists to be patient, the paper predicted, "It cannot be many years, before what you ask will be granted."[74] The committee ultimately voted to oppose adding a women's suffrage guarantee into the constitution.

Republican delegates H. P. H. Bromwell, a leading voice of Grange-backed rural reforms, and Agapito Vigil, a representative of the Hispano community, offered a blistering dissent to the committee's majority report.[75] They argued that just as racial requirements for voting had rightly been "expunged from thirty-seven Constitutions to the same charnel house of ancient abuses," so too should "the one word 'male'...be stricken out" proactively from Colorado's highest law.[76] They declared voting to be the "principal and real badge of citizenship" and likened the denial of women's suffrage to felon disfranchisement.[77] Hardly lacking their own prejudices, Bromwell and Vigil also claimed it was undignified for white women's demand for voting rights to be "coolly fl[u]ng . . . aside as though it came from the Cheyenne Indians."[78]

Despite the proliferation of alien suffrage laws, such policies were not adopted at all state constitutional conventions held during Reconstruction. When delegates assembled in Ohio to rewrite their state's constitution in 1873 and 1874, some sought to adopt a noncitizen voting rights law.[79] A leading supporter of the proposal, delegate R. P. L. Baber, contended that noncitizens who had served the country in war had earned the right to vote.[80] But he was not above appealing to the prejudices of his fellow delegates. Baber claimed that "a little more infusion of the honest German and foreign element" would help the state "confront and control the carpet-baggers and scalawags now enthroned in place and office by means of this degraded colored element, who are being used as the mere serfs of centralized power."[81] Opponents fought back with xenophobic rhetoric and had a ready reply to Baber's appeal to white male solidarity. They contended that it would be unfair to enfranchise noncitizen men while continuing to deny the suffrage to half of the citizenry: American women.[82] Delegate Lewis Campbell, a former US congressman, declared that if he had "ten thousand votes, I would give nine thousand nine hundred and ninety-nine to woman before I would give one to aliens."[83] While some delegates debated whether alien suffrage served to encourage or deter the naturalization of immigrants, most often they clashed over the suitability of noncitizen men to vote vis-à-vis other populations. Ultimately, the right would remain confined to American men in the Buckeye State.[84]

CREATING DISPARATE REGIMES IN THE POLITICAL ECONOMY   23

Other states were becoming even more restrictive. North Carolina began counting noncitizens out of the population for state legislative reapportionment calculations following its 1868 constitutional convention.[85] Tennessee lawmakers considered—but did not adopt—provisions extending suffrage rights to noncitizen men in 1867. Three years later, they voted to exclude noncitizens from the population for the purposes of representation.[86] These provisions were mainly symbolic in southern states that were home to few immigrants. North Carolina's foreign-born population (a mere 0.3 percent of the state's total) was the smallest—per capita and overall—of any state or organized territory in the nation in 1870.[87]

By contrast, post–Civil War anti-alien apportionment policies and politics reached their nadir in California, where more than one-third of the population hailed from abroad. The rapid rise of the racist-populist Workingmen's Party, which campaigned for the exclusion of Chinese immigrants and incited widespread violence against Chinese American communities, led to the convening of a state constitutional assembly in 1878–79. The Workingmen's Party appealed to native-born and immigrant white Californians alike. It was led by an Irish-born demagogue, Denis Kearney, who concluded his rallies with the racist diatribe "The Chinese Must Go."[88]

Though not the focus of the convention's discussions, delegates did debate anti-Chinese apportionment provisions. As they battled over regional control of the state legislature, many rural delegates sought to limit the total number of seats that could be assigned to San Francisco.[89] Proponents of this scheme claimed that San Franciscans would unfairly benefit from the city's large Chinese population in future rounds of apportionment without such a cap. "Your party cry is that the 'Chinese must go,'" stressed delegate W. J. Tinnin of the sparsely populated Trinity County in far northern California. And yet, Tinnin calculated that "there are four or five representatives" apportioned to (Workingmen's Party–dominated) San Francisco in the State Assembly owing to the city's large Chinese population.[90] San Francisco Workingmen's Party delegate Patrick Wellin defended including Chinese San Francisco residents in apportionment calculations, reasoning, "You count them in the interior" as well.[91] But Wellin's view was not universal among Workingmen's Party members at the convention. Delegate Charles C. O'Donnell, though an ostensible promoter of an equal population basis of state legislative apportionment, clarified, "We don't mean the Chinese." The San Franciscan reiterated bluntly, "We count them more as chattels or stock."[92]

Delegates ultimately adopted and the electorate ratified an exclusion of "persons who are not eligible to become citizens of the United States" from state legislative apportionment, in addition to many other explicitly racist provisions

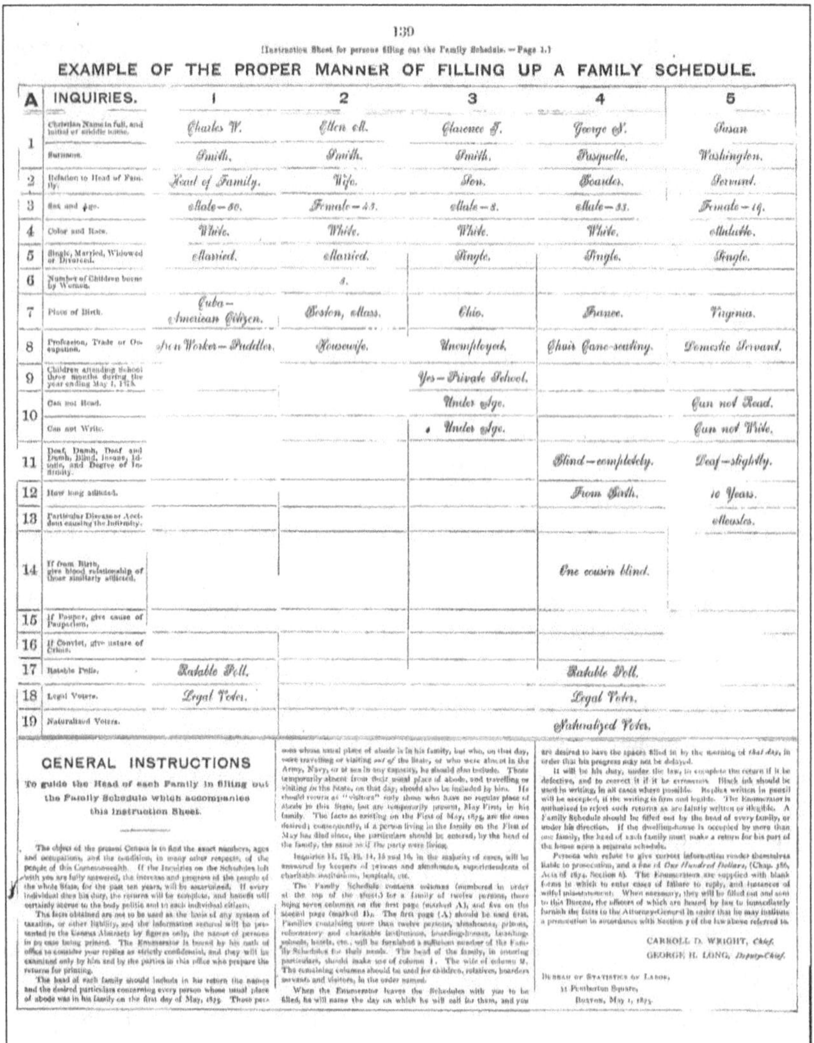

139

[Instruction Sheet for persons filling out the Family Schedule.—Page 1.]

EXAMPLE OF THE PROPER MANNER OF FILLING UP A FAMILY SCHEDULE.

A	INQUIRIES.	1	2	3	4	5
1	Christian Name in full, and initial of middle name.	Charles W.	Ellen M.	Clarence J.	George S.	Susan
	Surname.	Smith.	Smith.	Smith.	Pasquelle.	Washington.
2	Relation to Head of Family.	Head of Family.	Wife.	Son.	Boarder.	Servant.
3	Sex and Age.	Male—50.	Female—43.	Male—8.	Male—33.	Female—19.
4	Color and Race.	White.	White.	White.	White.	Mulatto.
5	Single, Married, Widowed or Divorced.	Married.	Married.	Single.	Single.	Single.
6	Number of Children borne by Women.		4.			
7	Place of Birth.	Cuba—American Citizen.	Boston, Mass.	Ohio.	France.	Virginia.
8	Profession, Trade or Occupation.	Iron Worker—Puddler.	Housewife.	Unemployed.	Chair Cane-seating.	Domestic Servant.
9	Children attending School three months during the year ending May 1, 1875.			Yes—Private School.		
10	Can not Read.			Under Age.		Can not Read.
	Can not Write.			Under Age.		Can not Write.
11	Deaf, Dumb, Deaf and Dumb, Blind, Insane, Idiotic, and Degree of Infirmity.				Blind—completely.	Deaf—slightly.
12	How long afflicted.				From Birth.	10 Years.
13	Particular Disease or Accident causing the Infirmity.					Measles.
14	If from Birth, give blood relationship of those similarly afflicted.				One cousin blind.	
15	If Pauper, give cause of Pauperism.					
16	If Convict, give nature of Crime.					
17	Ratable Polls.	Ratable Poll.			Ratable Poll.	
18	Legal Voters.	Legal Voter.			Legal Voter.	
19	Naturalized Voters.				Naturalized Voter.	

GENERAL INSTRUCTIONS

To guide the Head of each Family in filling out the Family Schedule which accompanies this Instruction Sheet.

The object of the present Census is to find the exact numbers, ages and occupations, and the condition, in many other respects, of the people of this Commonwealth. If the Inquiries on the Schedules left with you are fully answered, the increase and progress of the people of the whole State, for the past ten years, will be ascertained. If every individual does his duty, the returns will be complete, and benefit will certainly accrue to the body politic and to each individual citizen.

The facts obtained are not to be used as the basis of any system of taxation, or other liability, and the information secured will be presented in the Census Abstracts by figures only, the names of persons in no case being printed. The Enumerator is bound by his oath of office to consider your replies as strictly confidential, and they will be examined only by him and by the parties in this office who prepare the returns for printing.

The head of each family should include in his return the names and the desired particulars concerning every person whose usual place of abode was in his family on the first day of May, 1875. Those persons whose usual place of abode is in his family, but who, on that day, were travelling or visiting *out of* the State, or who were absent in the Army, Navy, or at sea in any capacity, he should also include. Those temporarily absent from their usual place of abode, and travelling or visiting *in* the State, on that day, should also be included by him. He should return as "visitors" only those who have no regular place of abode in this State, but are temporarily present, May First, in his family. The facts as existing on the First of May, 1875, are the ones desired; consequently, if a person living in the family on the First of May has died since, the particulars should be entered, by the head of the family, the same as if the party were living.

Inquiries 11, 12, 13, 14, 15 and 16, in the majority of cases, will be answered by keepers of prisons and almshouses, superintendents of charitable institutions, hospitals, etc.

The Family Schedule contains columns (numbered in order at the top of the sheet,) for a family of twelve persons, there being seven columns on the first page (marked A), and five on the second page (marked B). The first page (A) should be used first. Families containing more than twelve persons, almshouses, prisons, reformatory and charitable institutions, boarding-houses, boarding-schools, hotels, etc., will be furnished a sufficient number of the Family Schedules for their needs. The head of the family, in entering particulars, should make use of column 1. The wife of column 2. The remaining columns should be used for children, relatives, boarders servants and visitors, in the order named.

When the Enumerator leaves the Schedules with you to be filled, he will name the day on which he will call for them, and you are desired to have the spaces filled in by the morning of *that day*, in order that his progress may not be delayed.

It will be his duty, under the law, to complete the return if it be defective, and to correct it if it be erroneous. Black ink should be used in writing, in all cases where possible. Replies written in pencil will be accepted, if the writing is firm and legible. The Enumerator is authorized to reject such returns as are faintly written or illegible. A Family Schedule should be filled out by the head of every family, or under his direction. If the dwelling-house is occupied by more than one family, the head of each family must make a return for his part of the house upon a separate schedule.

Persons who refuse to give correct information render themselves liable to prosecution, and a fine of *One Hundred Dollars*, (Chap. 186, Acts of 1874, Section 6). The Enumerators are supplied with blank forms in which to enter cases of failure to reply, and instances of wilful misstatement. When necessary, they will be filled out and sent to this Bureau, the officers of which are bound by law to immediately furnish the facts to the Attorney-General in order that he may institute a prosecution in accordance with Section 7 of the law above referred to.

CARROLL D. WRIGHT, *Chief*.
GEORGE H. LONG, *Deputy-Chief*.

BUREAU OF STATISTICS OF LABOR,
33 Pemberton Square,
BOSTON, May 1, 1875.

Figure 1.1 Oren W. Weaver, *The Census System of Massachusetts* (Boston: Albert J. Wright, State Printer, 1876), 139. State Library of Massachusetts Special Collections Department.

targeting Chinese immigrants and Chinese Americans. Many of the latter provisions would be struck down by the courts as usurpations of federal immigration power and/or as violations of the Fourteenth Amendment. But omitting persons "ineligible to citizenship" from the population would survive.[93]

While California legislators relied on federal census data to reapportion their own legislature, lawmakers in Massachusetts and New York ordered the taking of their own censuses. In 1875, statistician Carroll D. Wright, chief of the Massachusetts Bureau of Statistics of Labor, designed and controlled a vast state census machine.[94] Employing 529 enumerators, 6 supervisors, and a large but numerically unidentified (often female) clerical staff, state employees compiled a massive three-volume, 2,852-page report on the commonwealth's population.[95] Though it analyzed an array of demographic and economic data, the state's "legal voter" apportionment basis was of paramount concern. The census distinguished immigrants from native-born residents and separated naturalized citizens from noncitizens, while prominently identifying residents who were legal voters for apportionment purposes.[96] Authorities in New York similarly highlighted the state constitution's apportionment provisions as the preeminent reason for their own 1875 census, breaking down the state's resident noncitizen population on a town-by-town and county-by-county basis.[97]

In sum, during and immediately after Reconstruction, national constitutional reform made neither voting nor apportionment the exclusive domain of American citizens. But lawmakers and voters did restrict federal suffrage protections to US citizen men. Meanwhile, states and territories continued to move in even more disjointed directions. Some adopted new alien suffrage provisions, while others counted all or some noncitizens out of the polity for the purposes of apportionment.

Creating Citizen-Only Polities at Gilded Age and Jim Crow Constitutional Conventions

Despite their recent proliferation, many alien suffrage laws would prove precarious during the Gilded Age and early Jim Crow years. While noncitizen voting rights policies were operative in seventeen states and territories in 1876, they could be found in only eleven polities by the end of 1901. Ten states and territories actually repealed their alien suffrage laws during that quarter century. Of those ten, four were states of the Deep South and another three were territories of the Mountain West petitioning for statehood.[98]

Battles over alien suffrage laws in the Deep South and the West were far from identical. The repeal of noncitizen voting rights was often a tangential part of broader white supremacist Jim Crow suffrage restriction campaigns in southern states, where relatively few immigrants resided. Alien suffrage policies were usually a larger topic of debate in western territories, where immigrants made up a far greater percentage of the population. There, women's suffrage rights (or the lack thereof) sometimes served as a rationale to disfranchise noncitizen men.

In both regions, noncitizen voting rights became a subject of debate largely because delegates were unable to avoid the topic as suffrage laws were written

26 DISPARATE REGIMES

or rewritten as a matter of course at these assemblies. Only at two conventions, those of North and South Dakota, did noncitizen voting rights survive into statehood. Most alien suffrage states that did not call constitutional conventions, by contrast, retained such policies into the Progressive Era.

As southern white Democrats regained power and overthrew Reconstruction-era state governments, they often moved to call constitutional conventions in the Redeemer (1870s–1880s) and Jim Crow (1890s–early 1900s) periods to further entrench their power. At these sites, delegates also often rescinded alien suffrage provisions that had been adopted in the wake of the Civil War. Georgia (1877), Louisiana (1898), and Alabama (1901) all repealed noncitizen voting rights via constitutional convention. Florida was the only southern state in the late nineteenth century to repeal its alien suffrage provisions via statute (in 1895).[99]

The primary aim of these three conventions was to drastically reduce African American political participation and head off the threat of Republican and third-party competition. As racist white Democrats agreed that Black disfranchisement was their goal, much debate centered on how grandfather clauses, poll taxes, and literacy tests would reduce the participation of poor white voters.[100] In both Georgia and Alabama, where immigrants represented less than 1 percent of each state's population, the repeal of alien suffrage was not controversial.[101]

By contrast, in Louisiana—where 49,747 immigrants represented 4.4 percent of the state's population in 1890—alien suffrage emerged as a much greater topic of dispute.[102] In 1879, delegates to Louisiana's first post-Reconstruction Redeemer constitution had made all male inhabitants of the state, irrespective of citizenship status, potential voters.[103] Amid rising calls for stricter, racist suffrage restrictions in the 1890s, noncitizen voting frequently came under attack in Louisiana. In New Orleans, at a December 1893 meeting of the elite Jefferson Democratic Club, Harvard- and Princeton-educated Frank Zacharie denounced noncitizen voting in Louisiana by pointing to its absence in northeastern states like New York that possessed much larger immigrant populations.[104] In March 1894, local New Orleans Knights of Labor members endorsed a ban on alien suffrage. The *New Orleans Picayune* echoed this call, editorializing that "further restraints must be laid on the importation of foreigners, and the making of them into voters even before they become citizens."[105] The *Baton Rouge Truth*, in turn, claimed that adopting a citizen-only suffrage policy would still be "a liberal concession" because it would "require of foreigners the probation of only a few years" before voting.[106]

Nevertheless, delegates meeting at Louisiana's constitutional convention in 1898 faced two unique challenges compared to their counterparts in other southern alien suffrage states. Many native-born white voters in southwest

Louisiana were francophones who could not speak, let alone read or write, English. And New Orleans, the state's largest city, possessed a sizeable immigrant, largely Italian, population.[107] Since different factions of the Democratic Party stood to benefit or be harmed by the disfranchisement of one or both groups, delegates battled fiercely over suffrage policies impacting these communities.[108] While they broadly agreed that grandfather clauses and poll tax measures were needed to ensure, in the words of delegate T. J. Kernan of East Baton Rouge, "the Democratic doctrine of universal manhood suffrage for white men," they often clashed over whether one needed to speak English to vote and/or whether noncitizen men should continue to be permitted to vote on their first papers.[109] Many delegates from the predominantly French-speaking southwestern part of the state and supporters of immigrant voting rights like former New Orleans mayor John Fitzpatrick fought to ensure that white men could register to vote in their native language and access interpreters during the registration process.[110] Opponents launched vituperative attacks against these plans. Just seven years after the mass lynching of eleven Italian immigrants in New Orleans, opponents slandered these proposals as a "Privileged Dago clause."[111] Kernan, a prominent lawyer and staunch advocate of non-English-speaking white, male voting rights, retorted by asking, "Who are we, I may ask, but foreigners, one or two degrees removed?"[112]

Ultimately, the convention's suffrage committee drafted an omnibus measure that provided voter registration assistance for non-English speakers and naturalized immigrants while repealing alien suffrage. Delegates were required to vote on the compromise in its entirety.[113]

Some embraced this approach while others only tolerated it as a necessary concession for their favored (anti-Black) grandfather clauses and poll taxes. Delegate Walter James Burke of the heavily French-speaking Iberia Parish argued that since the compromise "w[ould] take in many thousands of white citizens of Southwest Louisiana, it becomes incumbent on me to vote for" it. Burke clarified, however, that he was personally "opposed to the foreigner clause."[114] Delegate C. A. Presley of Natchitoches Parish, another largely francophone community, also voted for the compromise because "many worthy and good white men . . . could not register otherwise."[115]

Others claimed the measure unfairly favored francophones and immigrants over native-born and English-speaking whites. Ascension Parish delegate Paul Leche voted nay, grumbling that the proposal was "unfair in giving naturalized foreigners an advantage over native citizens," and warned that its registration provisions were "not sufficiently safe guarded against fraud." Delegate William Hart of New Orleans also voted against the deal, incorrectly stating that it "made electors" of "persons not citizens of the United States."[116]

28 DISPARATE REGIMES

Kernan, the most outspoken supporter of the agreement, challenged them, arguing, "Don't you know . . . that the illiterate Dago voter, who has come here in the last ten years, is excluded by the provision requiring him to have perfected his naturalization prior to the 1st of January, 1898?"[117] Kernan's views won out and the measure was adopted. These suffrage provisions became the basis for the mass disfranchisement of Black Louisianians in the age of Jim Crow.[118]

Many Democratic and Republican newspapers both within Louisiana and beyond its borders denounced noncitizen voting in the Bayou State and/or applauded its repeal. While supporters of Black voting rights in the Virginia-based *Tazwell Republican* decried efforts to disfranchise African Americans en masse in Louisiana, the newspaper did not endorse voting rights for all. What was needed, it argued, was the effective prevention of "illiterate Italian voters," not the wholescale disfranchisement of African American citizens.[119] The Republican-supporting *Philadelphia Inquirer*, in turn, denounced Louisiana's constitutional suffrage compromise for aiding in the registration of Cajun and immigrant voters. "The alien is thus raised," the *Inquirer* claimed, "not only above the illiterate negro, but above the ignorant white who is not a property-holder."[120] The *Banner–Democrat* of Lake Providence, Louisiana, counted alien suffrage among several "mistake[n]" voting experiments of the post–Civil War era that included the ratification of the Fifteenth Amendment and the rise of women's suffrage in the West. Pointing to a recent, successful repeal effort of alien suffrage in Minnesota, the paper encouraged politicians to ban noncitizen voting in the Bayou State, where it had "worked as badly here as in Minnesota."[121]

When the *Banner–Democrat* encouraged Louisiana to join the ranks of states rescinding noncitizen voting rights in 1897, it mentioned neighboring Texas. If an amendment to repeal alien suffrage were put to the voters of the Lone Star State, an "overwhelming" number would support it, the paper contended; however, noncitizen voting rights would not be removed from the Texas state constitution until 1921.[122] Similar noncitizen voting rights provisions would survive into the 1920s in two upper/Border South states—Arkansas and Missouri—as well.

Alien suffrage was not without its detractors in Texas. Populists mobilized against the practice in the mid-1890s, alleging that Democratic Party leaders in South Texas were bribing and coercing nonresident Mexican laborers to file first papers in return for votes. Though they were unsuccessful in repealing noncitizen voting rights outright, Texas Populists managed to negotiate the passage and secure the ratification of a watered-down constitutional amendment requiring that noncitizen men file their first papers at least six months before voting.[123]

Logistical and constitutional hurdles were higher for opponents of noncitizen voting rights in Missouri, Arkansas, and Texas than in most other southern

CREATING DISPARATE REGIMES IN THE POLITICAL ECONOMY   29

alien suffrage states. None of the three was entirely part of the Deep South, the epicenter of anti-Black mob lynchings and state violence during the Jim Crow era. Between 1890 and 1902, white elites prioritized codifying voting restrictions into the constitutions of states like Alabama, Louisiana, Mississippi, and South Carolina—particularly via conventions—where African Americans comprised close to or more than half of the population. By contrast, planter elites often found it more difficult to call conventions in states where white voters comprised a larger share of the population. The absence of constitutional conventions did not prevent de jure and de facto assaults on African Americans' access to the polls through literacy tests, poll taxes, grandfather clauses, and widespread white supremacist terror in such states, however.[124]

Significant immigrant populations in Texas and Missouri also impacted the electoral calculus of alien suffrage debates. In 1890, nearly 7 percent of Texas residents were immigrants. In Missouri, almost 9 percent of immigrants had been born abroad.[125] Politicians in Missouri and Texas had to determine whether repealing alien suffrage was in their own interests. Since both states possessed large German populations, which often fiercely opposed prohibition, brewing interests and anti-prohibition politicians had strong incentives to support alien suffrage laws.[126] Most entrenched white, Democratic lawmakers in Texas and Missouri opted to avoid raising the issue during the Gilded Age and Progressive Era if they could.

But the relative size of states' immigrant populations does not fully explain the longevity or brevity of alien suffrage laws. Arkansas, where barely over 1 percent of the state's population was born abroad in 1890, might have seemed like a prime candidate to rescind noncitizen voting rights amid Jim Crow constitutional developments. Politicians in Arkansas had little to lose by banning noncitizens from voting. If lawmakers in Florida, where roughly 6 percent of the population was foreign-born, could repeal alien suffrage with relatively little difficulty (as they did in 1895), why not Arkansas?[127] The reason lies in the high barriers then required to amend the Arkansas constitution. Aye votes had to outweigh both nays and abstentions for constitutional amendments to achieve ratification in Arkansas at a time when low voter participation on such measures was the norm.[128] Sustained white supremacist pressure succeeded in restricting African Americans' access to the ballot via constitutional amendment in Arkansas. But no similar movement arose to demand the repeal of alien suffrage. Not forced to confront the topic at a constitutional convention, state politicians and voters continued to permit the few noncitizen men living in Arkansas to vote until 1926.[129]

Just as four states of the Deep South repealed noncitizen voting rights via constitutional convention, alien suffrage emerged as a matter of debate at several western statehood assemblies. While noncitizen voting rights laws could

30 DISPARATE REGIMES

be found in most regions of the country outside the Northeast, nowhere were they more prevalent than in the West. In 1875, three western states (Kansas, Nebraska, and Oregon) and six future states (Colorado, Montana, the then-unified Dakotas, Washington, and Wyoming) enfranchised noncitizen men.[130]

The widespread practice of noncitizen voting rights in many Pacific Northwest, Rocky Mountain, and Plains states and territories might make the broader American West appear to have been uniquely open to pluralistic forms of democracy in the late nineteenth century. After all, full voting rights for women first became law in Wyoming Territory in 1869. Women's suffrage also spread much more rapidly in western states and territories than in polities found in other regions of the country.

But "the West" was not democratic or representative for all inhabitants. From widespread organized violence inflicted on Chinese immigrants to laws constricting East and South Asians' political and economic rights, the American West was one of the most inhospitable regions in the country for nonwhite immigrants.[131] Native Americans, subjected to ongoing state-directed violence and repression, remained formally excluded from the polity and US citizenship unless they "assimilated" into so-called white American norms of private land ownership.[132] Meanwhile, most states and territories with large Mexican-origin populations—Arizona, California, and New Mexico—barred noncitizen immigrants from voting.[133] Western alien suffrage laws thus primarily served as an inducement for and a tool of white settler colonialism.

Debates over noncitizen voting rights erupted intermittently in the West, particularly as territories were admitted to statehood. That process, often timed to national elections, frequently unfolded in rapid succession during the late nineteenth century whenever white settler colonials assumed a clear majority of the population. Sparsely populated Nevada was admitted as a state just in time to aid in president Abraham Lincoln's re-election in 1864. Colorado's statehood began mere months before the razor-thin presidential election of 1876, providing three critical Electoral College votes that helped Republican candidate Rutherford B. Hayes win the White House. Finally, between November 1889 and July 1890, the sparsely populated territories of Idaho, Montana, Washington, and Wyoming were all admitted to statehood, and Dakota Territory was divided into two states. Republicans, who held narrow majorities in both chambers of Congress, admitted these Mountain West states to boost their numbers in the US House and especially the Senate.[134] Arizona and New Mexico Territories, with their large Mexican-origin populations, were denied statehood until 1912.[135]

Though western territories had much smaller overall populations than southern states, immigrants made up a much larger percentage of the former's

CREATING DISPARATE REGIMES IN THE POLITICAL ECONOMY   31

residents. Immigrants represented about one of every four Wyoming inhabitants enumerated on the 1890 national census. In Montana, they numbered close to one of every three.[136] With immigrant voters so numerous, repealing alien suffrage laws could significantly harm or aid the electoral interests of convention delegates.

Noncitizen voting rights debates became especially fierce at Montana's constitutional convention. Some supporters warned that if Montana did not retain its alien suffrage law, immigrants might relocate to somewhere they could vote. Delegate Martin Maginnis, a Democrat who had long served as the nonvoting representative of Montana Territory in Congress, held that "in an old and settled state, I might take a different view of it, but I look upon it that we are all here in a new country."[137] Fellow Democratic delegate C. R. Middleton of sparsely populated Custer County likewise argued that "the qualification of requiring a man to be a full citizen of the United States . . . does not seem to me to be conducive to that kind of immigration that we want to have. . . . We should extend the hand of welcome and say to them, 'As soon as you are in this territory twelve months and have declared your intention to become a citizen you shall have a voice and vote in our elections.'"[138]

Two opponents from Silver Bow County, by contrast, both hailing from the mining city of Butte, claimed that noncitizen voters were easily bought and poorly educated. Democratic delegate Joseph Hogan, a twenty-seven-year-old miner, alleged he had "seen men that had been in the country for several years . . . and they had never even taken out their first papers; but they happened to be working for some corporation that wanted their vote, and they went up like so many cattle to suit the favor of their employers."[139] Fellow Democrat George Stapleton, a well-known lawyer who had served in the territorial legislature, objected that a foreigner who had been in the country for only one year could "kill the vote of the best man in Montana territory—a man who has made a lifetime study of the spirit and intention of our institutions."[140] An 1889 editorial in the *Helena Weekly Herald* similarly argued that suffrage required "higher qualifications for citizenship." A naturalized immigrant, the *Herald* claimed, "must regard citizenship as a very cheap thing when, after years of study and effort to become familiar with our institutions, he sees others just landed enjoying equal privileges."[141]

Other opponents of alien suffrage were far more overt in their anti-immigrant hostility. Charles Warren, a Republican delegate from heavily Democratic Butte, specifically targeted Italian immigrants as unwanted voters and compared them unfavorably to previous immigrant groups. Warren charged that Italian migrants were willing to sell their votes in Montana en masse before moving to other states to do the same. He slandered Italian

32 DISPARATE REGIMES

immigrants by publicly reading from a "little article" that a "friend" had "called [his] attention to," which read, "It is somewhat uncomfortable to reflect that a citizen of intelligence, property, good moral character, and a keen sense of the responsibilities and dignities of his duties as an American citizen, may have his ballot offset by an Italian Lazzarone, exuding garlic at every pour [*sic*] of his otherwise unpleasant body, whose intelligence does not equal that of the monkey for whom he grinds the organ, and upon whose sense, industry and honesty he depends for his maintenance and macaroni."[142] Warren's speech was met with "laughter and applause."[143]

Noncitizen voting was hotly contested in Montana because its repeal was proposed as a deal between delegates who wanted to pass a strict literacy test for would-be voters and those opposed to such educational requirements. A ban on alien suffrage won out while a literacy test was rejected. A five-year delay before the repeal went into effect allowed resident white immigrants to naturalize before losing the franchise.[144]

That noncitizen men—but not American women—possessed full suffrage rights did not go unnoticed in Montana. Vermont-born delegate Francis Sargent, representing Silver Bow County, stressed that "half of our own native born people are disfranchised." Sargent argued that he "fail[ed] to understand why members are so sensitive about the proposition that foreign-born residents shall remain in our country long enough at least to acquire some liberal knowledge of our institutions before being permitted the right to vote."[145] Although women's suffrage was remarked on, it did not become the central focus of consideration over whether suffrage should be restricted to citizens.

Similar debates played out in neighboring Wyoming at its 1889 constitutional convention. There, the subject of alien suffrage became entangled with—and even more subsumed by—battles over proposed educational requirements to vote.[146] Proponents of restricting voting rights in Wyoming employed language similar to their peers in Montana, with delegate C. W. Holden arguing that ignorant, foreign-born men in Wyoming were too often "unable to read the ballot," yet they were "rounded up" by unscrupulous government officials and "voted like so many cattle."[147] By contrast, Holden averred that he was certain his constituents believed that if women's suffrage rights were not protected by Wyoming's statehood constitution, "we would rather remain in a territorial condition throughout the endless cycles of time."[148]

Wyoming delegates ultimately voted to retain US citizen women's suffrage rights, but repealed their polity's noncitizen voting rights policy.[149] Delegates of the soon-to-be state of Washington also repealed their polity's alien suffrage law at their 1889 constitutional assembly.[150] The practice only survived statehood conventions in the former Dakota Territory where immigrants numbered roughly one of every four enumerated inhabitants of South Dakota and more than two of every five residents in North Dakota.[151]

Conversely, three states in the upper Midwest would go out of their way to repeal noncitizen voting provisions outside the context of a constitutional convention in the mid-1890s. Michigan and Minnesota overturned long-standing alien suffrage provisions via constitutional amendments in 1894 and 1896, respectively. North Dakota joined their ranks in 1898, rescinding a policy adopted at its statehood constitutional convention only nine years earlier.[152]

Those three campaigns were significant (and are addressed in Chapter 3). But they proved relative outliers among late-nineteenth-century efforts to repeal alien suffrage laws. Noncitizen men could vote on the basis of first papers in ten midwestern, southern, and western states at the dawn of 1902. Among them, only South Dakota had debated and retained noncitizen voting rights provisions at a late-nineteenth-century constitutional convention.[153]

* * *

The proliferation of both noncitizen voting rights laws and anti-alien apportionment policies during the antebellum era created disparate regimes of citizenship rights in the American polity on a state-by-state basis. Those differing regimes informed and were transformed by federal constitutional reform during Reconstruction. The repeal of several alien suffrage laws in the late Gilded Age heralded a retreat—but not the disappearance—of such regimes.

State constitutional conventions served as the primary sites of contestation over the political rights of noncitizens in the nineteenth century. Indeed, their convening—or lack thereof—played an outsized role in the adoption, embedding, and/or repeal of alien suffrage laws and anti-alien apportionment provisions. In the late nineteenth century, the demise of alien suffrage policies in the Deep South was often a tangential casualty of white supremacist voter restrictions arising at Jim Crow state constitutional conventions. Noncitizen voting rights often emerged as a more central topic of contention at western statehood constitutional conventions, with delegates increasingly debating the rights of American citizenship via their exclusion to noncitizens. Noncitizen voting rights escaped as part of the constitutions of only two of those new states. By contrast, such rights survived in a clear majority of late-nineteenth-century alien suffrage polities that did not convene state or statehood constitutional assemblies.

It is perhaps surprising that state constitutional provisions governing the political rights of American citizenship vis-à-vis noncitizen immigrants were rarely argued in the courtroom during the nineteenth century. That is because, under the prevailing federal constitutional order, states retained wide latitude to determine what were exclusive rights of citizenship in their polities under their own constitutions. Federal jurists largely deferred to them when determining whether suffrage and apportionment would be confined to (some) US citizens. By contrast, judges became more directly involved in disputes over the employment rights of noncitizen immigrants.

Disparate Regimes: Nativist Politics, Alienage Law, and Citizenship Rights in the United States, 1865–1965.
Brendan A. Shanahan, Oxford University Press. © Brendan A. Shanahan 2025.
DOI: 10.1093/9780197660577.003.0002

2

Disputing Disparate Regimes in Employment

Blue-Collar Nativist State Hiring Laws in the Late Gilded Age and Progressive Era

In mid-February 1915, public schoolteacher Katharine Short was shocked to learn that she would soon lose her job. California attorney general Ulysses S. Webb had just announced that school boards across the Golden State were required to enforce a long-forgotten 1901 law banning noncitizens from all forms of state, county, and local public employment. A Canadian national, Short was among hundreds of noncitizen teachers whose livelihoods were suddenly thrown into jeopardy across California. She was also among a particularly unlucky few denied outstanding pay by local officials. In response, Short appealed to Canadian authorities to defend her contractual rights, challenged her local school board and district attorney to issue her salary, and lobbied state lawmakers to alter the law that had ensnared her. She also shaped news coverage of this escalating international dispute, which drew in leading politicians and diplomats of the era, from the governor of California and the US secretary of state to the British ambassador in Washington, DC, and the governor general of Canada.[1]

Although the conflict over this California statute proved especially fiery, it was only one in a series of debates and controversies over the enactment and enforcement of state anti-alien public and/or publicly funded employment laws during the late Gilded Age and Progressive Era. Between 1889 and 1914, at least ten states adopted similar laws.[2] Like California, most states approving such measures—including Illinois, Massachusetts, New York, New Jersey, and Pennsylvania—were major immigrant-destination polities.[3]

Rather than being aimed at teachers, such laws were foremost targeted at noncitizen "common" laborers seeking construction work on public and publicly funded jobs.[4] Ever-expanding infrastructure demands on state and local governments presented numerous opportunities for building trade unionists to complain of competition from ostensibly "temporary" noncitizen immigrant workers.[5] Ambitious lawmakers seeking the support of the former were more than

36 DISPARATE REGIMES

happy to demand the passage and enforcement of state anti-alien public and publicly funded hiring laws, especially during economic downturns.[6] Meanwhile, prevailing constitutional jurisprudence afforded states significant police powers to restrict noncitizens' employment rights.[7] In fact, after first enacting anti-alien public and/or publicly funded employment laws, state law-makers in Pennsylvania (in 1897) and Arizona (in 1914) adopted even broader anti-alien tax and hiring laws, respectively, which aimed to discourage the hiring of noncitizens in all lines of work.[8] While both the Pennsylvania and the Arizona measures were rapidly and unequivocally struck down in the courtroom as unconstitutional, the legitimacy of anti-alien public and publicly funded employment policies under both state and federal constitutional law was much less clear. As such, their ethics, efficacy, and constitutionality were frequently contested in state legislatures, newspaper columns, lower courts, and jobsites from the late 1880s until 1915, when the US Supreme Court upheld state anti-alien public and publicly funded employment laws.

To be sure, late Gilded Age and Progressive Era blue-collar nativist state hiring laws were often less potent than other contemporaneous forms of economic discrimination, especially those based on race.[9] Nevertheless, this chapter demonstrates that state anti-alien public and publicly funded employment policies were still highly significant to the building trade unionists and blue-collar nativists who lobbied for them, the state and local politicians who sought to curry favor with such voters, the communities and employers disrupted by the enforcement of these measures, the national lawmakers and diplomats drawn into ensuing controversies, and the noncitizen workers whose livelihoods were imperiled by them. Moreover, it reveals how the inconsistent implementation of these laws frequently impacted immigrant populations differently owing to inequalities of race, gender, and class.

To measure the relative weight and meaning of blue-collar nativist state hiring laws, this chapter examines disputes over their adoption, enforcement, and adjudication in states across the country. It explores how they drew inspiration from West Coast anti-Chinese nativism and arose directly out of anti–temporary immigrant labor battles in the 1880s and early 1890s, particularly at the behest of building trade unionists. This chapter further demonstrates how these employment laws significantly expanded in scope and power during the Depression of the mid-1890s as native-born white laborers demanded access to hitherto undesirable public construction jobs. It then illustrates how they became widely perceived to be "dead letters" on the job and in lower courts when the economy improved. It finally explicates their abrupt resuscitation and upholding by the highest court in the land amid national and international controversies over their implementation during the recession of 1914–15. Overall, this chapter argues that clashes over anti-alien public and publicly funded hiring laws created increasingly disparate regimes of citizenship rights in key domains of employment on a state-by-state basis.

From West Coast Anti-Chinese Politics to Anti–Temporary Immigrant Worker Laws

State alienage laws restricting or expanding noncitizens' economic rights long predated the Gilded Age. Many states, especially in the Northeast, significantly constrained the ability of noncitizen immigrants to own, bequeath, and/or inherit property as a legacy of British common law prior to the Civil War. By contrast, beginning in the mid-nineteenth century, many midwestern and western states and territories adopted relatively inclusive noncitizen property ownership policies to encourage white settler colonial immigration.[10]

The power of blue-collar nativist organizations and movements to shape state politics similarly varied across the country. The United Order of American Mechanics, a blue-collar nativist society that called on employers to hire only white, Protestant, US citizen workers, achieved significant strength in mid-nineteenth-century Pennsylvania.[11] The Know-Nothing political movement of the 1850s achieved a broad national scope, particularly finding success in the Northeast, mid-Atlantic, and Border South. But whether blue-collar nativists could graft employment grievances onto broader state policies excluding, criminalizing, or even deporting poor immigrants from within their borders fluctuated within Atlantic seaboard states.[12]

The most powerful strain of antebellum blue-collar nativist politics and policies emerged in the form of West Coast anti-Chinese nativism. Anti-alien hiring and licensure laws were particularly common and pernicious in California. In the 1850s, state lawmakers repeatedly enacted legislation forcing noncitizens to pay hefty monthly fees to work as miners, disproportionately targeting and impacting Chinese immigrants.[13] During the Civil War and Reconstruction years, local and state laws were passed explicitly denying employment rights to Chinese immigrants in California. Such measures, which aimed to restrict the hiring and/or licensing of Chinese-born residents or individuals counted as members of the "Chinese" (sometimes "Mongolian") "race," became even more onerous during and in the wake of the Depression of the mid-1870s. In fact, revisions to the state constitution backed by the Workingmen's Party included provisions barring private companies from hiring Chinese immigrants, criminalizing the public employment of Chinese workers, and calling for the exclusion and deportation of Chinese immigrants.[14]

Chinese workers, merchants, business owners, and community leaders successfully challenged many of these racist hiring and licensure policies as

38 DISPARATE REGIMES

violations of their due process, equal protection, and/or treaty rights guaranteed under the federal constitution. State efforts to exclude and deport Chinese immigrants en masse were similarly defeated as unconstitutional efforts to usurp federal immigration powers. And in 1886, the US Supreme Court struck down an ostensibly race-neutral San Francisco laundry shop ordinance as a violation of the Fourteenth Amendment's equal protection clause owing to the city's racially discriminatory implementation of that policy in the *Yick Wo v. Hopkins* case.[15]

Nevertheless, the employment rights of East (and later South) Asian immigrants remained under attack. Chinese laborers were repeatedly subjected to violent vigilante campaigns and expelled from mining towns and smaller cities across the West. With the enactment of the Chinese Exclusion Act in 1882 (which prohibited the immigration of Chinese laborers for ten years), the Scott Act of 1888 (barring the re-entry of hitherto resident Chinese laborers to the United States from abroad), and the Geary Act in 1892 (which extended the Chinese Exclusion Act and required all resident Chinese immigrants and Chinese Americans to carry identification cards to distinguish them from unauthorized immigrants), resident Chinese workers were increasingly identified and racialized as undocumented immigrants.[16]

Racist local and state labor politics powered this nineteenth-century campaign to bar Chinese immigrants from working and living in the West.[17] White laborers in California especially asserted that Chinese immigrants posed a threat to their livelihoods and living standards. They and allied politicians framed Chinese laborers, overwhelmingly male, as "unfree coolies" (an orientalized depiction of indentured contract laborers), strikebreakers who undercut "white family" wage standards, and temporary "sojourners." Chinese laborers were thereby subordinated as "forever foreigners" by the racist politics and policies of western states and by federal immigration and citizenship law.[18]

As these developments reached a fever pitch on the West Coast, Carroll D. Wright, head of the Massachusetts Bureau of Statistics of Labor, launched into a vituperative assault on "the Chinese of the Eastern States." In an 1881 report, Wright argued that efforts to improve working conditions and reduce the average hours of work in Massachusetts were constantly being undercut by this "horde of industrial invaders." He further complained that such migrants "do not come to make a home among us" since "their purpose is merely to sojourn a few years as aliens." Wright did allow that they were "indefatigable workers, and docile." But this was a backhanded compliment. The "Chinese of the Eastern States" often "live[d] in the most beggarly way so that out of their earnings they may spend as little for living as possible," he claimed, so as "to carry out of the country what they can thus save."[19]

Wright's rhetoric was widely reported and soon provoked international protests. But it was not Chinese authorities who demanded an apology. Instead, French Canadian immigrants and Canadian officials—especially lawmakers in Quebec—decried his allegation that "with some exceptions the Canadian French are the Chinese of the Eastern States."[20]

Wright was not unique in making such analogies. Late-nineteenth-century blue-collar nativists and upper-class immigration restrictionists frequently compared various migrant populations to Chinese laborers, attacking and stigmatizing other East and South Asian immigrants alongside Mexican, sometimes Canadian, and often "new" southern and eastern European immigrants as strikebreakers, "contract laborers," and temporary competitors. Among European immigrants, southern Italians—disproportionately male and working-class—were especially analogized to Chinese laborers.[21] Often tied to seasonal labor cycles and prone to return migration, they were frequently termed "birds of passage" by their contemporaries.[22]

While analogies between the discrimination experienced by Chinese immigrants and European and Canadian migrants should not be overread, they mattered a great deal to the development of blue-collar nativist politics and policies. Indeed, immigration restrictionists embraced the lessons of and aimed to build on the success of West Coast anti-Asian politics.[23]

The political success of anti-Chinese West Coast nativism, in turn, empowered labor unionists and blue-collar nativists to seek the passage and enforcement of federal immigration legislation restricting competition from other ostensibly unfree or temporary immigrant workers. Just three years after the Chinese Exclusion Act became law, the Knights of Labor successfully lobbied Congress to enact the Foran Act of 1885 to prohibit the entry of "alien contract laborers." The American Federation of Labor, "patriotic" societies, and immigration restrictionists subsequently obtained amendments to the Foran Act, strengthening its enforcement mechanisms. But they still viewed the law as insufficient and ineffective.[24]

As early as 1888, a congressional investigation into violations of the Foran Act spurred demands for a federal ban on temporary laborers from entering the United States altogether. The committee's majority report proposed admitting only blue-collar immigrant laborers who would promptly begin the naturalization process by filing their "first papers." The committee's chairman, Democratic congressman Melbourne Ford, was particularly vicious in his characterization of Italian immigrant laborers. He especially bemoaned the recruitment of temporary immigrant workers by "padroni," much-maligned transnational labor contractors of foreign, often Italian, origin.[25] But the Michigan congressman also hoped his legislation would prevent Canadians from commuting to work in the United States.[26]

40 DISPARATE REGIMES

Though Ford's first papers–only immigration proposal did not become law, late–Gilded Age blue-collar nativist-allied politicians continued to complain of labor market competition from birds-of-passage immigrant workers and Canadian commuters. In the early 1890s, Democratic congressman John Chipman of Detroit routinely introduced legislation aiming to ban all noncitizens who were "non-resident of the United States" from any form of "work at any mechanical trade or in any manual labor."[27] In 1896, his successor, Republican congressman John Corliss, introduced similar legislation that sought to bar temporary immigrants and commuting workers from entering the country. Corliss's bill, incorporated as an amendment to senator Henry Cabot Lodge's literacy test immigration restriction legislation, came the closest to enactment. Though it passed both chambers of Congress, the Lodge–Corliss bill was vetoed by president Grover Cleveland in early 1897. Among other misgivings, Cleveland objected to the legislation's potential harm to US–Canadian relations and to American workers and employers operating on both sides of the border.[28]

Blue-collar nativists and allied lawmakers like John Corliss may have failed to enact federal legislation excluding temporary immigrant laborers and border-crossing commuters, but they knew that immigration law was not their only tool to punitively instrumentalize American citizenship. One of the few elements of the Lodge–Corliss bill that Cleveland did not object to in his veto message was a clause inserted by Corliss to ban "the employment of aliens upon any public works of the United States," which the lame duck president concluded was "in line with other legislation of a like character."[29]

Indeed, in 1886, the House of Representatives had actually passed legislation, later rejected by the Senate, which sought to restrict hiring on federal public works projects to US citizens and immigrants who held first papers.[30] Three years later, New York lawmakers enacted a statute giving preferential employment on public works in the state to its citizens.[31] Three other states—Illinois, Idaho, and Wyoming—enacted hiring policies that same year, restricting public and publicly funded construction jobs to US citizens and immigrants who held first papers.[32]

The passage and selective implementation of the 1889 Illinois statute is particularly instructive. Its sponsor, state senator D. C. Hagle, argued that his "Bill Against Public Employment of Aliens" was needed given "a large and increasing population growing up about us who do not and will not become citizens" and "cause labor troubles like those that take place in large cities like Chicago."[33] Hagle, a Republican from rural southern Illinois, was supported by both Chicago's building trade unionists and the state's Republican governor, Joseph Fifer. Fifer promptly signed the bill into law after its overwhelming passage in the legislature.[34] While it threatened steep penalties for noncompliant employers, just "how the authorities could be informed as to who were or were not aliens seemed difficult," as the *Chicago Tribune* pointed out. Consequently, city officials announced that "the statement of the contractor" would be accepted as evidence of compliance, though they promised to investigate alleged violations of the law.[35]

In early 1891, just as hundreds of out-of-town laborers—many of them Italian immigrants—began arriving in Chicago seeking construction work for the massive Columbian Exposition that the city would host two years later, building trade unionists weaponized that investigation process. Amid a series of strikes and negotiations with leading contractors, they demanded the strict implementation of Hagle's 1889 anti-alien public works employment law.[36] Violent protests against the hiring of Italian laborers even led one company, the McArthur Brothers, to briefly halt World's Fair work in mid- to late February.[37] Feeling pressure from both union members and local and state politicians, the leaders of the exposition publicly committed to trying to enforce an anti-alien hiring policy for all related construction projects. But fair president Lyman Gage made clear that it would be difficult to do so in practice since "it may be that certain parts of the work cannot be done by naturalized citizens."[38]

Rather than put their livelihoods at risk, many Italian immigrants declared their intention to become US citizens en masse in courtroom filings. Armed with these first papers, they would be able to work as low-paid, "common" laborers.[39] Nevertheless, Hagle's bill remained in force, serving as both a potential tool to be wielded in future labor conflicts and a tangible reminder to immigrant workers of the precarity of their employment.[40] In fact, in mid-March 1891, immigrant laborers working on an unrelated municipal project abruptly lost their jobs following a complaint about their hiring. After a brief investigation, their boss was told by Chicago authorities to fire his workers or "forfeit his pay."[41] Calls for the adoption of even more restrictive blue-collar nativist state hiring laws and their firm application soon grew louder as anti–temporary immigrant worker rhetoric and building trade unionist tactics merged with the politics of unemployment.

The Politics of Unemployment

The Panic of 1893 and its ensuing depression wrought massive devastation on the American economy. Charity officials and municipal and state authorities reported an explosion in unemployment during its first winter in 1893–94. But the financial crisis persisted for years. As late as 1897, roughly one of eight workers was unemployed across the country.[42] Building trade workers, common laborers, farm workers, and others dependent on seasonal hiring cycles were particularly vulnerable to joblessness.[43]

42 DISPARATE REGIMES

In response, unemployed laborers and union leaders pressed elected officials to expand hiring on and funding for public works programs. Jacob Coxey guided an "army" of the unemployed in a peaceful march on Washington, DC, in an unsuccessful effort to pressure President Cleveland and Congress to invest half a billion dollars in public construction projects to put the jobless to work.[44] In Massachusetts, Morrison I. Swift led major demonstrations on the Boston Common to demand the state government expand public works projects and hiring.[45] Around the country, city halls and state legislatures came under pressure to hire or contract with private employers to alleviate the crisis.[46]

Politicians responded by touting their commitment to combat unemployment. Democratic governor Roswell Flower of New York, for instance, claimed that he had done all in his power to ensure state contracts were issued to expedite hiring on state construction and canal work.[47] He was not alone. Economist Carlos Closson found during the winter of 1893–94 that "employment has been provided in a considerable number of cities by means of an increase in the amount of public work, paid for by special loans or appropriations. In some cities new public works have been begun or anticipated with the object of furnishing work. In others existing public works have been pushed forward at a somewhat augmented rate." But Closson astutely noted that "the amount . . . of such special public employment . . . has not been so large as might have been expected."[48] Governor Flower explicitly rejected proposals to dramatically expand public works projects in his state. He warned that such action would set a "dangerous precedent for the future, justifying paternal legislation of all kinds and encouraging prodigal extravagance." More emphatically, he argued, "In America the people support the government; it is not the province of the government to support the people."[49]

Though Flower rejected public works relief programs as a means of alleviating mass unemployment, he did sign a law restricting hiring on all public and publicly contracted state and municipal construction work to US citizens in 1894.[50] Lawmakers in other states followed suit.

The Panic of 1893 struck Pennsylvania first and hit the state hard.[51] In and around Pittsburgh, authorities and employers estimated that between 19,000 and 26,000 laborers had lost their jobs by the start of winter in 1893. In Philadelphia, relief officials calculated that roughly 75,000 workers had become unemployed.[52]

As in New York, Pennsylvania politicians debated whether to expand public works projects and/or to restrict hiring on public construction jobs to US citizens. Invoking the rhetoric of "America for Americans," blue-collar nativists especially fought to privilege or mandate the hiring of US citizens.[53] Supporters of such restrictions, like Allegheny city councilman Arthur Kennedy, argued in the autumn of 1893 that the city should "give citizens a chance" to find work, "instead of filling the streets with Hungarians and Italians."[54]

Opponents decried these schemes for their symbolic cruelty. Philadelphia councilman Franklin Harris blasted a municipal anti-alien hiring proposal in 1893 as "a meaningless, flippant appeal to the masses for purposes of empty sentiment."[55] A year later, Philadelphia councilman Henry Clay reminded his colleagues, "Of old it was 'no Irish need apply.'" He denounced anti-alien employment proposals as an effort to scapegoat "the degraded Italian," criticizing such measures as "un-American."[56]

Other politicians tried to have it both ways by supporting such policies in theory while balking at their adoption in practice. Some felt sweeping citizen-only hiring proposals were too rushed or too broad.[57] Others doubted whether they could or would be enforced in practice.[58] Still others questioned the constitutionality of these schemes.[59]

As the Depression wore on, support for nativist hiring legislation grew in Pennsylvania. In June 1895, state lawmakers restricted employment on all public and publicly contracted construction projects throughout Pennsylvania to US citizens.[60] In December 1896, the Philadelphia City Council banned noncitizens from additional forms of municipal employment.[61] The following year, John Fahy, a United Mine Workers leader from northeastern Pennsylvania's anthracite coal region, successfully lobbied the state legislature to pass the so-called Alien Tax Act of 1897.[62] That law required all employers in the state to pay a three-cent daily tax to county authorities for every male noncitizen worker over the age of twenty-one on their payroll, a cost employers were empowered to pass on to their workers.[63]

Employers soon began investigating the citizenship status of their workers to comply with the Alien Tax Act's requirements.[64] Some announced that they would henceforth only hire US citizens, while others began discharging noncitizen workers. One distraught long-resident German immigrant explained to the *Philadelphia Inquirer* that "for the next three years I will be compelled to pay something over $9 a year to the State, and at the same time run the chance of not getting any employment, on account of the trouble and expense incurred by employers, who have to see that the money is paid." By contrast, the *Inquirer* reported that blue-collar nativists in Philadelphia, especially mill workers, were "feeling jubilant" about "the effect the bill is expected to have" because it was widely viewed as "aid[ing] the American born wage-earners in securing places heretofore held by aliens." Of immigrants struggling to hold their jobs, the *Inquirer* coldly observed that "there is no doubt that the action of the Legislature is having the desired effect."[65]

Immigrants rushed to courthouses across Pennsylvania and even sought aid at courtrooms in neighboring states to naturalize en masse to avoid wage deductions and company layoffs.[66] Two days before the law came into effect, immigrants in Philadelphia broke the record for the most citizenship petitions filed in a single day in the city's history.⁶⁷ Chinese immigrants challenged the constitutionality of the law for its disproportionate harm on "aliens ineligible to citizenship" in court.⁶⁸ And at a trilingual (English-, German-, and Italian-language) rally in Philadelphia against the law, Socialist Labor Party speakers denounced business owners who "scour[ed] Europe for immigrants to beat down wages" while "taking advantage of native prejudice born of the struggle for existence to lay a heavy tax on the starvation wages of aliens." They argued that its "real purpose" was to "refill a plundered treasury and placate native Americans, foolish enough to think it will give them all work at good wages."⁶⁹

Figure 2.1 "Foreigners Rush to Obtain Papers," *Philadelphia Inquirer*, June 29, 1897, 3. The cartoon is captioned "Scene in the Corridor of the Post Office." Image provided courtesy of Newspapers.com.

The biggest collective pushback took place in northeastern Pennsylvania's anthracite coal communities, where eastern European workers walked off the job to protest low wages and dangerous, abusive working conditions made worse by the Alien Tax Act. Amid these protests, on September 10, 1897, Luzerne County sheriff James Martin and his deputies shot and killed nineteen striking immigrant laborers and wounded scores more in the brutal Lattimer Massacre.[70]

While some employers were violently clashing with their workers, others challenged the law's constitutionality in court. In a series of cases filed in 1897 and 1898, employer lawsuits successfully halted and later overturned the Alien Tax Law as a violation of both the federal Fourteenth Amendment's equal protection clause and the "uniform" tax requirements of the state constitution.[71] Immigrant workers flooded the *Philadelphia Inquirer* with questions about ongoing court rulings. They especially wanted to know if they were entitled to back pay for wages withheld by their employers under the Alien Tax Act. They were.[72]

Pennsylvania lawmakers' broad efforts in 1897 to discourage the employment of noncitizens across all lines of work via tax policy proved unique.[73] But blue-collar nativist state hiring laws were nevertheless becoming more pervasive during and following the Depression of the mid-1890s. In 1895, as cities and towns debated their own anti-alien hiring measures, the Massachusetts General Court restricted hiring on state highway construction work to "citizens of this Commonwealth."[74] A year later, Massachusetts state lawmakers enacted a US citizen preference law for all other forms of public and publicly funded construction work.[75] New Jersey legislators, by contrast, adopted a strict US citizen–only hiring law for all public and publicly funded construction work in 1899.[76] And after quietly blocking several building trade union–supported citizen-only public works hiring bills in previous years, California lawmakers banned noncitizens from all forms of public employment at the state, county, and municipal levels in 1901. Notably, they did not exclude noncitizens from publicly funded construction projects.[77]

To be sure, such laws were not ubiquitous or all-powerful. Major immigrant destination states with extant alien suffrage laws—like Texas and Wisconsin—did not adopt such measures during the Progressive Era. And many state anti-alien hiring policies were described as impotent by reporters, politicians, and even labor leaders. Rather than being repealed, blue-collar nativist state hiring laws were increasingly rendered moribund by lower courts and on the job.

Becoming Dead Letter Laws in Court and on the Job

Almost as soon as New York's strict citizen-only public works hiring law took effect in 1894, unions complained of widespread violations to the state's Bureau

46 DISPARATE REGIMES

of Statistics of Labor. Some emphasized corruption in their grievances. The New York City Brotherhood of Carpenters and Joiners Local No. 382, for instance, charged collusion between "public officers" and "unscrupulous employers and contractors" who "violate the statute law every day."[78] Other unions bemoaned the purported impact of failures to enforce the Alien Labor Law on local labor markets. In Ithaca, the Tin, Sheet Iron and Cornice Makers' Union Local No. 26 claimed that 300 "Poles and Italians" were working on a sewer project while there were "good men—plenty of them—here and in the county that are American citizens that would work" on the project (if wages were raised from $1.20 to $1.50 per day).[79] Other unions still, like the Auburn Iron Workers' Knights of Labor Assembly No. 1858, concluded the statute was no more than "a dead-letter law."[80]

The law was further hobbled when Henry Warren, a supervisor for the Barber Asphalt Paving Company, appealed his conviction under the Alien Labor Law to the New York Superior Court of Buffalo in 1895. Warren openly admitted to hiring Italian nationals to work on a city-contracted paving project, arguing that the law violated the contractual rights of employers and employees guaranteed by the federal and state constitutions. The court agreed and overturned his conviction. Judge Truman C. White reasoned that lawmakers could bar noncitizens from public employment but could not compel contractors on publicly funded projects to do the same. Once authorities contracted with a private firm, he argued, "the state surrenders its public and government functions" and "exercises no dominion over the property or control over the employment of laborers upon the work being done."[81] White also ruled that the law violated federal treaty obligations to Italian nationals who possessed "the same rights and privileges in respect to their person and property as are secured to our own citizens."[82]

White's ruling went unnoticed by most unions at the time, but they took note the following year when other cases alleging violations of the Alien Labor Law were thrown out in court because of the precedent set by *People v. Warren*. In September 1896, union leaders demanded a hearing before the state Court of Appeals, only to learn that they had missed their window to file an appeal. Granite Cutter union leader William J. O'Brien, who served as president of the Workingmen's State Trade Assembly, claimed that the Barber Asphalt Paving Company "ha[d] stolen a march on organized labor" by having their agent "quietly arrested and arraigned...in order to test the constitutionality of the law."[83] Enraged, the ostensibly nonpartisan New York Central Labor Union called on its members to oppose a Democratic judge who had concurred in White's ruling in the upcoming fall elections.[84]

O'Brien's anger over the judicial overturning of the 1894 New York Alien Labor Law was not uncommon among Irish Americans in the building trades.

At that time, Irish American workers denounced and sometimes physically attacked Italian laborers who dared to enter the construction industry, a domain long dominated by Irish immigrants and their children. While Italian immigrants came to outnumber Irish-origin laborers on public works projects in New York City as early as the 1880s, Irish American political leaders largely retained patronage power through their dominance of Tammany Hall and union leadership positions within building trade unions. In fact, many second-generation Irish Americans obtained higher-paid skilled positions as Italian "common laborers" came to dominate pick-and-shovel work. Nevertheless, Irish American laborers continued to complain that Italian immigrants' growing industry presence and employment as strikebreakers reduced their own bargaining power.[85]

As public construction in New York City boomed at the turn of the century, building trade union leaders and allied politicians invoked citizen-only hiring demands to shape perceptions of who should be hired for such work and for what wages. For instance, in 1900, Democratic state assembly member Maurice Minton bemoaned that Italian workers employed on tunnel projects "carry away from this State and Nation to Italy a large amount of the money paid out in wages, to the loss and disadvantage of the State of New York." Those construction jobs, Minton argued, should go "to our native-born citizens and to our Irish-American and German-American citizens."[86] Few Progressive Era lawmakers and even fewer building trade union leaders demanded equal employment opportunities on these jobsites for African American workers as an inclusive right of citizenship.[87]

Amid this ongoing interethnic labor strife, building trade unionists successfully lobbied lawmakers in New York to enact additional anti-alien hiring laws restricting employment to US citizens on public works projects in 1897, 1902, and 1909.[88] As in *People v. Warren*, however, state judges sometimes struck down or limited the scope of these laws under the prevailing laissez-faire "freedom of contract" doctrine.[89] And, in practice, the vast majority of common laborers employed on Progressive Era New York City construction projects were Italian nationals.[90] But when thousands of Italian subway workers under the leadership of laborer and organizer Tito Pacelli struck against their bosses in 1903 for higher wages and safer working conditions, most (heavily Irish) American building trade unionists failed to come to their aid. One such individual refused to support striking Italian subway laborers in part because "these men are not American citizens."[91]

As had been the case in Chicago a decade earlier, building trade unionists in New York wielded complaints over purported violations of citizen-only hiring laws as weapons in labor disputes with employers. In 1904, for instance, the New York Department of Labor received 430 complaints of alleged violations

48   DISPARATE REGIMES

of the state's public works employment laws. Many were filed by New York City asphalt workers amid a labor conflict over contractors' alleged breaches of the Alien Labor Law and the state's eight-hour-workday policy on public construction jobs.[92] In response, city authorities empowered local inspectors to "stop work whenever they discovered violations of law," halted payments to some contractors, and canceled contracts with others.[93] Probing the records of companies employing 6,300 laborers on municipally funded jobsites, state Labor Department investigators concluded that more than two-thirds of workers were noncitizens and found that 121 of 125 contracts examined violated the state's anti-alien hiring provisions.[94] Throughout the conflict, "work, however, did not stop."[95]

In September 1904, New York City Corporation counsel John Delaney issued a legal opinion clarifying that most noncitizen laborers working on publicly funded jobs, especially Italian nationals, "enjoy[ed] treaty rights of which they can not be deprived by a statute of the state."[96] Delaney insisted that henceforth, if anyone complained to city authorities about a potential violation of the anti-alien hiring clause, "it would be necessary to know whether the alien employed has the protection of a treaty before it could be established whether the complaint is good."[97] This essentially put an end to filings. The following year, the state Department of Labor received just one complaint about the hiring of noncitizens on public works jobs. The department found that this was "no doubt . . . due," in part, "to the doubtful constitutionality" of the law "relating to employment of aliens on public works."[98]

As in New York, the Illinois public works hiring law restricting jobs to citizens and immigrants who held first papers, first adopted in 1889, was struck down by state jurists in *City of Chicago v. Hulbert* in 1903.[99] In his widely read 1900 treatise, legal scholar Christopher Tiedeman exaggeratingly argued that "in each case" whereby "States . . . have by legislation undertaken to protect native labor against alien labor," the courts had struck down such laws as "an invasion of the jurisdiction of the United States government and an unconstitutional interference with the rights of resident aliens."[100] However, the US Supreme Court would not rule on the constitutionality of state anti-alien public and/or publicly funded employment laws for another fifteen years. Implementing blue-collar nativist hiring laws was another matter entirely, however, as residents of Massachusetts would learn all too well.

On March 24, 1898, Boston city councilor Daniel McIsaac proposed a citywide policy of hiring "only citizens of the United States" for municipal employment and ensuring "that preference shall be given to residents of Boston." McIsaac claimed that he had recently investigated hiring practices in the city and discovered that in one unnamed department "there were as many aliens as citizens employed." He argued that it was not "fair to employ aliens and nonresidents" for municipal work at a time when "more than 1000 men" recently "stood in line throughout a whole night for the privilege of registering in the civil service." McIsaac's proposal won the unanimous approval of his peers on the city council.[101]

Less than two years later, however, McIsaac, serving as a state representative, opposed a bill sponsored by fellow Irish American Democrat David Walsh to launch a special committee to investigate, among other topics, alleged violations of the state's "citizen preference" publicly funded hiring laws.[102] McIsaac's about-face can be explained by intense turn-of-the-century water resource battles that split state politics along regional divides as much as partisan and ethnic ones. Urban (largely Irish American) Democrats like McIsaac and suburban (largely Yankee) Republicans in Greater Boston were then tenuously allied in a fight to rapidly expand the water supply to the city and its environs.[103]

In 1895, the state Metropolitan Water Board had selected Walsh's central Massachusetts hometown of Clinton to serve as the fulcrum of the future Wachusett Reservoir and Dam to store and provide drinking water for Greater Boston.[104] Most residents of Clinton, along with those of neighboring Boylston, Sterling, and West Boylston, had fiercely opposed the project. Its nearly decade-long construction entailed the loss of more than six and a half square miles of land and the displacement of 1,700 residents along with their homes, workplaces, and halls of worship. When completed in 1905, the dam claimed the title (albeit briefly) as the largest in the world.[105]

Figure 2.2 "Wachusett Dam, Largest of Its Kind, Now Completed," *Boston Globe*, November 5, 1905, SM4. Image published with permission of ProQuest LLC. Further reproduction is prohibited without permission. Image produced by ProQuest LLC as part of ProQuest® Historical Newspaper Product and UMI microfilm.

50 DISPARATE REGIMES

During construction, local residents often came into conflict with contractors, Italian immigrant laborers, and the Water Board.[106] In November 1899, Clinton residents elected Walsh—who promised to challenge the power of the Water Board—to his first term in the legislature.[107] The following year, he swiftly secured passage of a bill to launch a special legislative investigative committee into the Water Board's activities on the Wachusett project.[108] Amid the ensuing twenty-six days of hearings, Walsh charged, among other allegations, that contractors and the Water Board "directly and indirectly" breached "the law which gives preference to citizens."[109] Like many of his contemporaries, Walsh did not specify whether he was referring to 1895 "Massachusetts citizen" or 1896 "US citizen" preference hiring laws.[110]

Some central Massachusetts residents embraced Walsh's rhetoric to demand the strict enforcement of citizen preference hiring requirements in an effort to press contractors to increase wages. At a mass meeting of 1,200 residents of Clinton led by the town's Businessmen's Association on March 30, 1900, residents denounced the supposed "great injustice to citizen laborers, in that aliens have been employed instead of citizens, and that large sums paid for labor have been sent out of the state and also out of this country." They also denounced the poor working conditions laborers were forced to endure.[111] Rather than creating a local cross-class alliance with labor unions and immigrant workers, the businessmen were far more interested in wielding violations of the state's citizen preference hiring policies as weapons in their public relations battle with construction firms, labor contractors, and the Water Board. Most laborers working on the project in 1900 bought their food, drink, and supplies from contractors at company stores. Clinton shop owners wanted access to them as customers.[112]

The hearings—especially claims of drunken worker violence, disruptions to these small communities, and abusive padroni activities—dominated state newspaper headlines for months.[113] But there was never any doubt that construction firms mostly employed nonlocal, noncitizen workers. Indeed, contractors and Water Board representatives admitted as much. Nathan Brock, co-owner of a major construction firm working on the Wachusett project, Nawn and Brock, claimed that he "always desired to give the preference to citizens" and even paid them a cent and a half more per hour than noncitizens. But he contended that it was "practically impossible to carry on public works without Italian laborers."[114] J. H. Benton, the Water Board's lawyer, similarly argued that "a good many people misunderstood" the meaning of the state's citizen preference hiring laws. He believed such policies only required employers to consider hiring (state and/or US) citizens if "the citizen is willing to work at the same price as any foreigner, work under the same conditions under which the foreigner is willing to work," and "is willing to stand on an even keel with the foreigner." Benton

DISPUTING DISPARATE REGIMES IN EMPLOYMENT   51

further warned that if wages were raised to the rate sought by local laborers, the project would cost taxpayers millions of dollars more.[115]

On July 10, 1900, the joint legislative investigative committee issued its findings. It substantiated claims of widespread violations of state liquor laws and found numerous examples of contractors coercing laborers to shop at company stores and live in their shantytowns. But in the matter of whether preference was required to be given to citizens in hiring, the *Boston Herald* found that "this law is a dead letter so far as work on the Wachusett reservoir is concerned." Indeed, the committee's own majority report concluded that, "in general, citizens will not submit to many of the conditions of life provided by contractors for public work, or work for the wages paid by such contractors. The only solution of the problem, if the state really means to provide for an actual and not merely theoretical preference of citizens, is to let the contracts at such figures as will enable the contractors to pay a wage large enough to attract citizen labor and compel the payment of such a wage."[116]

Likely preparing for public blowback from the committee's findings, just three days before the report came out, the Water Board "instructed" its "Chief Engineer . . . to employ citizens only for day labor in connection with the construction of the Wachusett Dam."[117] A week later, the board ordered the firing of a foreman from the Nawn and Brock firm who refused to hire a local citizen who had applied to work for the same common labor wages as immigrant laborers but refused to live in the contractors' shantytown.[118] These actions were exceptions to broader hiring and enforcement patterns on the Wachusett project, however.[119] An estimated 65 to 70 percent of the more than 4,000 total workers on the Wachusett Dam project were Italian nationals. Several hundred African American laborers, many originally from Virginia, were recruited to work on the project, often for especially dangerous jobs like laying dynamite. Not the citizens Walsh had in mind when he demanded citizen preference in hiring, Black workers were confined to low-paying common labor jobs.[120]

Though anti-alien public works policies in Massachusetts were largely dead letters in practice, demands for their adoption and strict implementation boosted the careers of at least two politicians. Daniel McIsaac's pleas in 1898 to restrict hiring to US citizens in Boston municipal employment earned the young city councilor front-page coverage in the *Boston Globe*.[121] He would go on to serve in both chambers of the state legislature and as assistant district attorney and corporation counsel of Boston.[122] For David Walsh, the Wachusett controversy launched his lengthy political career and eventual rise to the governorship and US Senate.[123]

Meanwhile, Progressive Era politicians in other states sometimes sought to curry favor with blue-collar nativists and building trade unionists by pushing

52 DISPARATE REGIMES

for the passage of new anti-alien public and publicly funded hiring laws. Lawmakers in Louisiana (1908) and Arizona (1912) both adopted such measures.[124]

In other states, opportunistic politicians demanded the vigorous implementation of extant policies. In March 1897, the Philadelphia City Council reported it had received "numerous complaints" about "the employment of alien labor on public work" despite state and municipal policies restricting such jobs to US citizens. In response, the council ordered the city's director of public works to ensure that his subordinates and contractors thoroughly apply a citizen-only hiring policy.[125] A few months later, city coroner Samuel Ashbridge garnered favorable press coverage upon receiving the plaudits of a local chapter of the "Sons of America" patriotic society for demanding the rigorous exclusion of noncitizens from employment "upon city contracts."[126]

Despite this rhetoric, the implementation of anti-alien public and publicly funded employment laws remained sporadic during the Progressive Era. Newspapers and union officials sometimes reported allegations of purported violations of these laws.[127] Less commonly, they commented on their enforcement.[128] But as late as 1913, these policies were most frequently wielded by building trade labor representatives as tools in negotiations with contractors or by ambitious politicians seeking the attention of blue-collar nativist voters. They were hardly ever the central focus of union organizing or political campaigning.

In fact, politicians sometimes came to regret having adopted strict citizen-only public hiring policies. On February 16, 1899, the Philadelphia City Council debated a resolution to officially authorize payments to noncitizens already working at the Municipal Hospital in violation of the city's anti-alien hiring policies. The *Philadelphia Inquirer* reported that the hospital had hired many noncitizen women "at $16 or $17 a month" because they were "the only ones [the hospital] could get to do the scrubbing." In passing, the paper noted that councilman Edward Patton, "the father of a good deal" of anti-alien employment legislation, was the sponsor of this very proposal. Rather than criticize Patton's about-face, the reporter remarked that it reflected "one of the comical things about alien labor legislation."[129]

It is unlikely that the immigrant women whose livelihoods were imperiled by the rediscovery of this policy viewed the precarity of their low-paid employment, the hypocrisy of Councilman Patton, or the city's citizen-only hiring provisions as "comical." A decade and a half later, amid another recession-induced unemployment crisis, many more immigrants would similarly feel the sudden and unexpected weight of the resuscitation of such dead letter laws.

DISPUTING DISPARATE REGIMES IN EMPLOYMENT   53

Reviving Dead Letter Laws during Hard Times

Between October and December 1914, John Gill, leader of the Bricklayers' and Masons' Union of New York City, came before the New York Public Service Commission alleging numerous violations of the state's public works hiring laws by contractors working on a massive subway expansion project.[130] Gill, like many union leaders before him, complained that construction firms undercut union wages by illegally employing noncitizen workers, mostly Italian immigrants. In a letter to the editor of the *New York Times*, he noted that "the enforcement of the law will cost the contractors more money," but argued that such wages were better off in "the pockets of American citizens instead of" noncitizen laborers "who take it back to foreign countries with them and spend it there." Shortly after bringing his complaints, Gill proudly pointed to reports of New York City naturalization courts being "flooded" with "applications for citizenship" as proof that his provocations were having an immediate impact.[131]

The New York General Contractors Association, by contrast, viewed the law as a "menace."[132] In its monthly *Bulletin*, the association claimed that "few men who were born in this country, or who have lived here long enough to become citizens, are willing to do pick and shovel work," so "there must always be a class of men that will tackle the roughest and dirtiest kind of work without flinching." In the eyes of the association, it was not possible to "recruit that kind from the ranks of ex-city employees or citizens."[133] Seeking to settle the matter once and for all, the head of the Contractors Association, Clarence A. Crane, coordinated his own pro forma arrest with authorities to serve as a test case of the constitutionality of the New York Alien Labor Law in state court. Meanwhile, his ally, William Heim, filed a taxpayer civil lawsuit seeking to injunct the law's implementation.[134]

The New York Subway Hiring Controversy, which threatened a huge expansion project that employed up to 20,000 workers at any time and cost about $2 million per week, proved particularly intense.[135] Between flouting the law and trying to hire only US citizen workers, contractors were beset by numerous work slowdowns and stoppages.[136] On February 25, 1915, in an opinion written by justice Benjamin Cardozo, the New York State Court of Appeals unexpectedly upheld the Alien Labor Law. This news ground subway construction work to a chaotic halt; thousands of noncitizen workers were abruptly laid off.[137]

State lawmakers, under pressure for months from contractors, the Chamber of Commerce, the Italian government, and most New York newspapers, hastily debated whether to repeal the legislation. At the behest of leading Democratic state senator Robert Wagner, legislators instead replaced the state's citizen-only public works hiring statute with a citizen-preference employment law in mid-March 1915.[138] This enabled subway construction to resume.[139]

54   DISPARATE REGIMES

While this dispute echoed many previous Progressive Era anti-alien employment conflicts, the context in which it was fought proved quite different. The city and country were then in the throes of a significant recession brought about by the Panic of 1913.[140] But unlike during previous Progressive Era economic downturns, the outbreak of World War I and German submarine warfare had dramatically decreased transatlantic return migration among blue-collar immigrants.[141] Republican New York City mayor John Mitchel made sure to tie his response to mounting unemployment among US citizens as war raged in Europe. Though construction delays were regrettable, Mitchel emphasized that he "certainly agree[d] with the labor unions in believing that Americans should be employed on all work where it is possible to get them." While many US citizens would have preferred other forms of employment, Mitchel maintained "that many of them would be willing to do almost anything in these hard times."[142]

The New York Subway Hiring Controversy of 1914–15 also overlapped with a growing number of other state, national, and international anti-alien employment disputes. In California, the Grange, alongside western nativist organizations such as the Native Sons of the Golden West, had successfully campaigned to limit the property rights of Japanese (and other East and South Asian) immigrant farmers with the passage of the state's Alien Land Act of 1913, which barred persons ineligible to citizenship from owning land. Though it precipitated a major international controversy—with the Japanese Embassy strongly objecting to state lawmakers and the US State Department alike—the California measure spawned several imitators in other western states, including Arizona. But blue-collar nativists in Progressive Era Arizona did not limit their legislative agenda to their own explicitly racist anti-Asian land law.[143]

In the early statehood era, Anglo (i.e., non-Hispanic white) blue-collar nativists—especially unionized miners—were especially powerful in Arizona politics. In the early 1910s, fears among Anglo miners of growing competition from southern and eastern European immigrants and refugees fleeing the Mexican Revolution rose precipitously. In the 1914 fall elections, they pressed for and won a state referendum campaign to require all private businesses in the state employing five or more individuals to retain a workforce in which US citizens comprised at least 80 percent of all workers. Italian and British representatives swiftly protested this "80 percent" citizen hiring law, alleging treaty violations. Meanwhile, anti-labor activist and restaurant owner Billy Truax's likely coordinated firing of his noncitizen cook Mike Raich in the mining town of Bisbee provided an opportunity to test the law's constitutionality in federal court (which speedily halted its implementation via injunction).[144]

The New York conflict, therefore, was fought alongside several other major state anti-alien hiring controversies. It also increasingly intersected with them

DISPUTING DISPARATE REGIMES IN EMPLOYMENT   55

in media coverage, diplomacy, jurisprudence, and politics.[145] Disputes surrounding the California Alien Land Law, the New York Subway Hiring Controversy, and the Arizona 80 percent citizen hiring law each became major national media stories and remained so for months.[146] News accounts and editorials of one dispute sometimes referenced or directly compared it to another.[147]

Owing to growing international protests and disruptions emanating from these controversies, some lawmakers and commenters proposed adopting federal legislation to clarify the economic rights of noncitizens across the United States. The Wilson administration rejected the idea, maintaining that individuals who believed their constitutional or treaty rights had been violated could file suit in court.[148] Many did. As a result, the US Supreme Court agreed to take up both cases emanating from the New York Subway Hiring Controversy and litigation arising from Arizona's 80 percent law during the same term in 1915.[149]

Amid all this media attention, immigrant workers were seldom the focus of news coverage in major English-language newspapers. When papers subtly or overtly critiqued the impact of blue-collar nativist state hiring laws, they generally emphasized the harm such policies posed to employers, the economy, and/or US diplomatic relations.[150] In one instance, the *New York American* went so far as to print a drawing of Crane, founder and secretary of the New York General Contractors Association, sitting dejected in a small jail cell awaiting his chance to test the constitutionality of the Alien Labor Law in court.[151] In fact, Crane, the New York Public Service Commission, and prosecutors had arranged his arrest to enable a test case. At his arraignment, Crane posted a $300 bail. Upon receiving his sought-after conviction, he opted to pay a $50 fine rather than spend ten days in jail.[152]

While press coverage of the supposed plight of contractors sometimes crossed into hagiography, newspapers did accurately identify one paradoxical feature of the New York Subway Hiring Controversy: the power the Alien Labor Law had gained precisely owing to its long-standing weakness. Warning that building trade unionists had identified "a fighting weapon" in demanding the strict implementation of a hitherto dead letter law, the *New York Journal of Commerce* called for the repeal of the Alien Labor Law at the outset of the dispute in November 1914.[153] And when Judge Cardozo issued his opinion upholding the constitutionality of the Alien Labor Law in February 1915, the *New York Times* emphasized the chaotic predicament "subway contractors f[ou]nd themselves in" owing to "the sudden enforcement of the long-dormant law."[154] Hitherto widespread views that these laws were weak, "long-dormant," and dead letters had actually increased their power to wreak havoc by disrupting and even shutting down work entirely, albeit briefly, as building trade unions successfully pressed for their enforcement amid heightened unemployment.

Figure 2.3 "I'll Take my Medicine—Crane," *New York American*, reproduced in *The Bulletin of the General Contractors Association*, vol. 6, no. 3 (March 1915), 67. The University Library, University of Illinois at Urbana–Champaign, Q. 690.6 GE.

At the very same time that work momentarily ground to a halt in New York, another controversy was breaking out in California over teachers who learned that their jobs had been thrown into jeopardy owing to the rediscovery of California's long-"forgotten" 1901 citizen-only public employment law.[155] As in other states, high joblessness in the winter of 1914–15 led to growing attacks on noncitizens' public employment in California. In December 1914, Kern County supervisors demanded that all county departments strictly enforce the state's 1901 citizen-only public hiring law. Upon discovering that the director of the county's high school farm was a noncitizen, county officials asked state superintendent of public instruction Edward Hyatt if the law applied to teachers. Hyatt sought counsel from the office of state attorney general Ulysses S. Webb, which deemed that the law applied to all public employees, including teachers and support staff.[156]

Neither Webb nor Hyatt spelled out how to administer the policy, so local and county authorities scrambled to implement the law on the fly. Most school superintendents, including those of Los Angeles and San Francisco, continued to employ and pay noncitizen teachers while awaiting further instructions.[157] Others, fearing heavy fines, took a more restrictive approach. In Kern County, authorities announced plans to fire English immigrant W. E. Sutherst as the head of Bakersfield's high school farm. Sutherst quit in protest and left the country.[158] In Santa Barbara and Mendocino Counties, noncitizen teachers were even deprived of their salaries for past work. However, some of those teachers continued to work while hoping for retroactive compensation if the law was later altered or struck down.[159]

Denying pay for past work was too extreme for Hyatt, who warned of "chaos ahead for the schools . . . if school trustees continue to refuse to pay aliens." He knew that "hundreds of teachers w[ould] refuse to teach and the school term w[ould] be badly disrupted" if they were not paid.[160] He hoped that school districts would permit noncitizen teachers—whom he estimated to number roughly 250 to 300 in total—to continue to work until the end of the school year.[161] But Hyatt refused to issue an order to that effect, maintaining that "trustees cannot be forced to pay if they are unwilling to take the chance" of being punished for breaking the law.[162]

Amid this growing precarity, teachers fought to keep their jobs. Just days after the citizen-only hiring policy was announced, twelve teachers wrote to Hyatt "asking what they can do to hold their positions."[163] P. J. Conway, a Canadian national and schoolteacher in the Mendocino County town of Ukiah, asked University of California president Benjamin Ide Wheeler to become involved in "the cause" of lobbying lawmakers to repeal the 1901 anti-alien public employment law.[164] Meanwhile, many immigrant teachers hastily filed paperwork to become US citizens. In Sonoma County, the local *Press Democrat* reported that "several young women school teachers . . . recently filed their declarations of intentions to become American citizens." The paper claimed that most had previously "failed to declare their intentions because of sentimental reasons or uncertainty as to their future plans. Now that it has been brought home to them," the *Press Democrat* continued, "most of the aliens are taking the first steps toward becoming American citizens."[165] Other newspapers told of similar naturalization upticks.[166]

Meanwhile, in Los Angeles, two self-described allies of noncitizen teachers adopted very different approaches to mitigate the impact of the law's sudden reapplication. Anna Stewart, a longtime history teacher, rallied members of the Southern Council of the California Teachers' Association to denounce the

58 DISPARATE REGIMES

"undeserved hardship" and "grave injustice" done to noncitizen teachers while calling for the passage of relief legislation.[167] Los Angeles school superintendent Mark Keppel proposed a highly unusual and coercive option for some teachers to keep their jobs: shotgun weddings. Noting that (most) immigrant women who wed US citizen men automatically and immediately became citizens themselves, Keppel encouraged the approximately one hundred noncitizen women teachers working in his city's schools to promptly marry American men.[168] The *Los Angeles Herald* viewed this as a "happy solution of the problem," an opinion few teachers shared.[169]

Conflicting and coercive laws of marriage, citizenship, and employment affected more than immigrant women involved in the Alien Teachers Controversy. Since the passage of the federal Expatriation Act of 1907, any US-born woman who subsequently married a foreign man had automatically lost her US citizenship.[170] Many of these marital expatriate teachers wrote to the state attorney general to ask what could be done. Without exception, they were told "that they t[ook] the nationality of their husbands."[171] Noncitizen faculty members and instructors at the University of California worried that they, too, would lose their jobs in March 1915.[172] The tortuous enforcement of and growing disputes over the rediscovered hiring law ensured that this storm would continue to rage in California politics. An international campaign against it launched by one Canadian teacher, however, dramatically reshaped the controversy's scope.

Katharine Short, an Ontario-born Canadian and British subject, had been teaching in California for nearly ten years. Upon learning that Mendocino school officials would refuse to pay her salary following the attorney general's announcement, Short fought back. She pointed to her year-long teaching contract to demand her salary and reminded her supervisors that they had been aware that she "was a Canadian and not naturalized" when they hired her. A recent homeowner, Short was anxious for a rapid solution to the controversy since she was in danger of defaulting on her mortgage. On February 28, she wrote to her father, William Short, in Ontario to ask him to implore Canadian authorities to intervene to "help to protect the contract rights of its citizens." She claimed that the state's newly enforced citizen-only teacher policy "affects about 1500 people in the state, the large majority of whom are Canadians."[173] She and nearby P. J. Conway also threatened a lawsuit against local school trustees to try to obtain their paychecks.[174]

Katharine Short was well suited to lead this campaign. A family friend, William Gray, had recently been elected to Canada's national Parliament.[175] William Short asked Gray to advocate on his daughter's behalf to influence "public opinion" in Canada, particularly "when California is asking Canadians and other foreigners to visit the Panama Exhibition," a massive international exposition in San Francisco that was held alongside a rival world fair in San

DISPUTING DISPARATE REGIMES IN EMPLOYMENT 59

Diego to celebrate the opening of the Panama Canal.[176] Gray, who happened to hold major oil and mining investments in California, readily agreed.[177]

By mid-March, newspapers across Ontario were reporting on the plight of Canadian teachers in California and on Gray's advocacy on behalf of their contractual rights.[178] News of the dispute was soon found in papers across the United States and abroad.[179] Gray also lobbied the Canadian Ministry of Justice and Department of External Affairs to intervene in the controversy.[180] On March 18, he raised the matter directly in the House of Commons, calling on his fellow governing Conservatives to pressure American authorities to redress "this gross injustice" and see that the "jug handled Act" in California be "wiped off the statute book."[181] Prime minister Robert Borden's administration proved eager to help. Its most ardent supporters—Anglo-Canadian nationalists and British imperialists (often one and the same)—were already suspicious of and perceptive to American slights and threats toward Canada.[182]

While Canadian officials in Ottawa investigated and briefed Sir Cecil Spring Rice, the United Kingdom's ambassador to the United States, on the matter, the British crown's representative in Canada, governor general Prince Arthur, a son of Queen Victoria, took a personal interest in this dispute. On April 1, he privately wrote to Spring Rice to argue that a travel advisory for Canadians living in or headed to California might be necessary. He contended that "if the circumstances are as represented by Miss Short, it would seem to be of the utmost importance that representations should be made at once to the Federal Government, or, at any rate, that Canadians should be aware of the conditions they are likely to meet with in the State of California and the disabilities to which they will be exposed there."[183]

Though not ready to issue such a warning, Spring Rice wrote to US secretary of state William Jennings Bryan, imploring him to intervene to ensure Canadian teachers like Short were paid.[184] The ambassador reminded Bryan that the Borden administration "ha[d] joined whole heartedly in the Panama Exhibition and one of the Ministers ha[d] left his Parliamentary duties in order to assist at the opening ceremonies." He especially protested the sudden enforcement of the law and warned of its harm to US–Canadian relations, arguing that "it is evident that such a measure, enforced in such a manner, and at such a time, by which innocent persons, many of them women, are made to suffer in such a way, is calculated, if it should appear to be correctly reported, to arouse public opinion in Canada to a most unfortunate degree."[185]

In response to this diplomatic pressure, Bryan telegraphed California governor Hiram Johnson, urgently requesting a "statement of facts." He also "suggest[ed] . . . whether it would not be advisable to seek to obtain some prompt legislative action for the relief of those aliens who have rendered services for which they are unable to obtain payment."[186] Johnson, who had rejected

60 DISPARATE REGIMES

Japanese diplomatic pressure to veto anti-alien land legislation two years earlier, was stirred to act in response to the growing US–Canadian controversy
and State Department pressure.[187] He informed Bryan that a bill to alter the
state's citizen-only public employment requirement was already working its
way through the legislature, and he was confident of its success. Johnson
promptly launched an investigation into the implementation of the law.[188] The
following day, he reported that preliminary results had found only 4 noncitizen
teachers—not 1,500—who had lost their jobs, while identifying "approximately
two hundred others who are ineligible under the law" but continued to work
and receive pay. Johnson also pointed to the existence of a law that required
British subjecthood to work as a public schoolteacher in Katharine Short's
home province of Ontario, questioning on what grounds British and Canadian
officials sought redress from authorities in California.[189]

Though this latter discovery threw a wrench in Katharine Short's campaign,
her broad strategy of pressing her case locally, appealing to newspapers, and
lobbying officials in California and Canada proved unstoppable.[190] Teachers
ensnared by the state's citizen-only public schoolteacher policy were generally
portrayed sympathetically by the press. The *Mendocino Beacon*, for instance,
reported that "Miss Short is said to be a very popular and very competent
teacher and her pupils and friends sincerely hope that she will hold her position."[191] Other columns emphasized the dispute's growing harm to California's
international reputation. The (Santa Barbara) *Morning Press* argued in an April
editorial that "if treaties are involved, and international relations at stake,
California cannot afford to make so small a matter an issue." The paper further
argued that "there is a difference . . . in countries. It is said there are many
American teachers in Canada; but Canada is part of America, and the lines of
separation from the United States is little more than imaginary. There is less
objection to Canadians teaching in the schools of the American states than
there would be to teachers from countries more widely separated from the
United States."[192] Unfavorable nationwide and international press coverage of
the dispute—just when the state sought to attract business investment and
tourism—further increased pressure on lawmakers to alter the state's public
employment law.[193]

Short's case was further bolstered by the persistent support of Canadian
authorities and the US State Department's desire to bring about a speedy resolution to the controversy. The Canadian Ministry of Justice insisted (with considerable sleight of hand) throughout months-long correspondence with the
British Embassy in Washington that Ontario's anti-alien public schoolteacher
policy was not comparable to the California law.[194] By contrast, in mid-April,
Secretary of State Bryan's close advisor, Robert Lansing, wrote to Johnson to
lobby the governor to alter his state's public employment law, arguing that a

citizen-only teacher policy seemed to be "of comparatively little advantage to the citizens of your State, while its provisions might easily lead to ill-feeling on the part of foreign governments."[195]

A bill to change the state's citizen-only public employment provisions rapidly advanced in the state legislature.[196] Its lead sponsor, state senator Herbert Jones, went so far as to argue that "the great majority of these foreign-born teachers are Canadian girls who have come here when very young and are practically American in education, training and sentiment." It was unfair that a "forgotten . . . dead letter" law, he argued, could suddenly strike at immigrants' livelihoods "like a clap of thunder."[197]

After Jones's bill sailed through the legislature in April, Johnson signed it into law in mid-May. It retroactively validated the payment of salaries to noncitizen teachers like Short.[198] On May 25, she was finally paid her long-overdue salary.[199]

Short was wise to have launched a multipronged campaign. Had she followed President Wilson's advice and solely sought redress in the courts, she would have almost certainly failed. Later that fall, the US Supreme Court did strike down Arizona's 80 percent citizen hiring law in all lines of work in the *Truax v. Raich* case as both a violation of noncitizens' Fourteenth Amendment rights and a usurpation of federal immigration powers (viewing the law to be an attempt to render most immigrants inadmissible by denying them access to work in Arizona). But the court came to the opposite conclusion in litigation arising out of the New York Subway Hiring Controversy. The high court upheld the constitutionality of legislation banning or limiting the hiring of noncitizens in public and publicly contracted lines of work as a legitimate exercise of state police powers and the right of lawmakers to circumscribe who could receive public funds. The court further rejected the contention that federal treaty obligations required states like New York to exempt foreign nationals, especially Italian workers, from anti-alien hiring bans in these two joined cases: *Heim v. McCall* and *People v. Crane*. Noncitizen public schoolteachers, like Short, would have fallen under the latter umbrella of jurisprudence.[200]

Unfortunately for other public employees in California, the new law that emerged from Katharine Short's campaign proved limited in scope. It clarified that faculty of the state university system or "specialist[s] or expert[s] temporarily employed" faced no citizenship requirements. Women born in the United States who had lost citizenship via marriage would also be allowed to work as public schoolteachers. Immigrants, however, would have to file a declaration of intention to naturalize and become citizens within six months of eligibility to teach in California's public schools. All other types of state, county, and municipal employment remained closed to noncitizens.[201] The law, therefore, did not challenge the nativist ideology behind citizen-only employment policies. It instead carved out narrow exceptions for (some) educators.

62 DISPARATE REGIMES

Not all immigrant teachers were even eligible to work under the new policy. In 1915, only unmarried, divorced, or widowed women could file independently to become US citizens. Immigrant women married to noncitizens could not work as teachers unless their husbands promptly naturalized.[202] East and South Asian immigrants were racially barred from citizenship owing to the Naturalization Act of 1870 (which held that only white or Black immigrants could become citizens) and therefore could not become public schoolteachers even after the enactment of Jones's bill.[203] And while most Mexican nationals were then recognized as "white by law" under federal naturalization policies, racist discrimination in practice contributed to dramatically lower naturalization rates among Mexican immigrants compared to other groups eligible for citizenship.[204]

Publicity surrounding the controversy had even heightened pressure on some local and county officials to enforce oft-forgotten citizen-only hiring requirements in other lines of work. As early as February, the San Luis Obispo–based *Morning Tribune* reminded its readers that noncitizens were not allowed to do "any county work" under the state law and encouraged "roadmasters and others employing all classes of labor" to "bear this matter in mind and thus, perhaps, later save themselves considerable inconvenience" by hiring only US citizens.[205] By April, noncitizen immigrant janitors in Redondo Beach and city road and parks workers in Riverside had lost their jobs.[206]

In Riverside, city officials acted in response to a petition signed by "42 working men" who demanded the immediate firing of all noncitizens employed by the city. Their leader, G. J. Gatliff, specifically targeted Mexican immigrants and elided (Anglo) whiteness with citizenship. The *Riverside Daily Press* reported that he "protest[ed] against the employment of 'cholo' labor in the street department, particularly during a year when so many white men and citizens were out of employment."[207] Gatliff got his wish. Within weeks, twelve Mexican immigrants were fired by the Riverside Street Department and two were dismissed by the city Park Board. One Light Department employee was permitted a leave of absence to complete his naturalization paperwork and resume working in a few months. Unlike the other fired noncitizen employees, he was not described as "Mexican."[208] No alteration to the state's public employment policy or exception from its application arose in response to the sudden loss of their livelihoods. Unlike Katharine Short, they were not viewed by lawmakers or the press as "practically American."

* * *

In some ways, the intervention of the highest court in the land into blue-collar nativist state hiring disputes in 1915 changed everything. On the one hand, by finally taking on—and thoroughly rejecting—a challenge to the constitutionality of state anti-alien public and publicly funded hiring laws, the US Supreme Court gave its blessing to the increasingly disparate regimes of citizenship rights that pervaded the nation in blue-collar construction work and public employment. Such a determination was not preordained. This was, after all, the same high court that routinely struck down other state labor laws—such as maximum hour legislation, minimum wage statues, and even Arizona's 80 percent law—as violations of federal contract rights.[209] And the high court's joint rulings in *Heim v. McCall* and *Crane v. New York* augured major ramifications in subsequent decades for noncitizen immigrants' employment and licensure rights.

On the other hand, courts usually only proved to be decisive players in shaping the development of blue-collar nativist state hiring laws when striking down their most draconian iterations, such as those trying to bar noncitizens from all forms of employment. By contrast, battles over the passage, enforcement, and possible amending of state anti-alien public and publicly funded employment laws were most prominently, repeatedly, and decisively fought in the political arena. From lobbying for the adoption of such measures and demanding their stringent implementation to garnering newspaper headlines and responding to recession-induced unemployment crises, building trade unionists, blue-collar nativists, and ambitious politicians paved the way for these interconnected yet disparate regimes of citizenship rights across the nation. After all, the two largest disputes arising from the implementation of state anti-alien public and/or publicly funded employment laws in 1915 had actually been resolved months prior to the high court's rulings owing to intense public relations, diplomatic, legal, and political campaigns in New York and California. Those ultimately successful efforts rendered neither citizen-only hiring rhetoric impotent nor the surviving blue-collar nativist hiring laws toothless. Lawmakers in both New York and California opted not to jettison their states' anti-alien public and publicly funded employment policies entirely, instead mitigating the impacts of distinct controversies arising from their implementation while retaining their broader architecture and ideology. In so doing, they further embedded disparate regimes of citizenship rights on a state-by-state basis into the American political economy in law, politics, and popular perception.

Disparate Regimes: Nativist Politics, Alienage Law, and Citizenship Rights in the United States, 1865–1965.
Brendan A. Shanahan, Oxford University Press. © Brendan A. Shanahan 2025.
DOI: 10.1093/9780197660577.003.0003

PART II
INVENTING CITIZENSHIP RIGHTS AS CITIZEN-ONLY RIGHTS IN THE POLITY

3

Making Voters Citizens

Repealing Alien Suffrage via State Constitutional Amendment Campaigns, 1894–1926

In early 1918, Carrie Chapman Catt, president of the National American Woman Suffrage Association (NAWSA), believed that she had found a powerful rallying cry to help propel the women's suffrage movement to nationwide success: concomitantly campaigning to disfranchise male noncitizen voters.[1] Catt had considered these men to be powerful and incorrigible opponents of the women's suffrage cause for years.[2] With so many American men away at war, she argued that those same voters had become a unique national security threat. Not only did Catt believe it to be "undeniably inconsistent, unjust and tyrannical" for seven states to grant noncitizen men the vote while only one of them enfranchised American women in April 1918, but also she and her organization protested that alien suffrage laws enabled a large number of "enemy alien" Germans to have a say at the ballot box.[3]

Many other women's suffragists had long battled—and continued to fight—to repeal alien suffrage laws alongside Catt. "Equal suffrage states ha[d] been first" in recent years "to take up the problem of the alien voting on first papers," the *Woman Citizen*, a national publication of the NAWSA, proudly contended in April 1918.[4] By July of that same year, the *Woman Citizen* would argue that making "full citizenship" the "basis for suffrage...for men and women without discrimination" across the country was needed to ensure the "standardization" of voting as a de jure right of only American citizens.[5]

In so doing, the NAWSA denounced the disparate regimes of citizenship rights in the polity that had pervaded the United States throughout the nineteenth century. At the same time, middle- and upper-class white suffragists' calls to homogenize voting rights and citizenship rights were often belied by their failure to fight for nonwhite Americans' access to the ballot and, in some cases, their active opposition to multiracial democracy.[6] But Catt had also correctly read the pulse of much of the country. All remaining state alien suffrage laws would be repealed during and shortly after World War I.[7]

This chapter explores how and why roughly a dozen state constitutional amendment campaigns succeeded in dismantling these laws from the late

68   DISPARATE REGIMES

Gilded Age to the World War I era. It illustrates how opponents denounced noncitizen voting rights as a national outrage requiring nationwide reform, but nevertheless centered their efforts on state-specific matters prior to World War I. In turn, it shows how adversaries of alien suffrage laws channeled wartime nationalism and postwar nativism to collaborate in ever more intersecting, yet still distinct, state campaigns during and in the aftermath of the global conflict.

Constitutional mechanics and state-specific partisan and interest group politics played outsized roles in anti-alien suffrage campaigns. From lobbying for the passage of amendments in legislatures to rallying support for their ratification, partisan institutions and civic organizations often provided the logistical and institutional support necessary to repeal alien suffrage laws as stand-alone ballot measures. They cultivated and marshaled a broad opposition that increasingly relied on national organizations—from the NAWSA and its successor, the League of Women Voters, to various allied "patriotic" groups—to argue that alien suffrage weakened the nation and imperiled its security.[8]

It was far from a foregone conclusion that lawmakers and voters—without court order or federal mandate—would defy long-standing practice and repeal noncitizen voting rights via the adoption and ratification of thirteen late-nineteenth- and early-twentieth-century state constitutional amendments. These ballot measures and the campaigns that propelled them transformed state politics and constitutional law. They amounted to a significant retreat from the disparate regimes of citizenship rights in the polity that had prevailed in the nineteenth century on a state-by-state basis. They also greatly helped to standardize voting into the foremost de jure citizenship right as citizen-only right in the United States.

Elite Opposition to Disparate Regimes of Citizenship Rights in the Polity

Elite immigration restrictionists, largely Anglo-Protestant Republicans, were among the most vocal opponents of immigrants' suffrage rights in the late nineteenth and early twentieth centuries. Decrying the culture, religion, and ethno-racial origin of "new" immigrants, they warned of an allegedly nefarious and growing power of foreign-born voters. Along with other self-styled election "reformers," immigration restrictionists frequently claimed that immigrant voters were a major source of urban political machine–orchestrated voter fraud.[9] For instance, Massachusetts business executive A. S. Muirhead, a fierce critic of Tammany Hall, alleged that in the 1890s, "it was not difficult to make a citizen;

in fact they made them so freely that the party which prevailed in New York was usually Tammany, because they made them citizens before they touched the American shore."[10] Though exaggerated, Muirhead's claims were echoed by other immigration restrictionists and elite election reformers in American newspapers and current affairs journals.[11]

Congress responded to accusations of pervasive voter and naturalization fraud by passing the omnibus Naturalization Act of 1906. Transforming the process by which racially eligible immigrant men and unmarried immigrant women could petition to become US citizens, the law systematized and federalized naturalization documents, set a seven-year limit on the validity of "first papers" in naturalization proceedings, and transferred much of the administration and adjudication of citizenship petitions to federal officers and judges.[12]

In addition to these federal developments, elite immigration restrictionists and self-styled election reformers also aimed to further reduce the power of immigrants in American politics via state legislative action. They crafted and rallied support for a range of state laws designed to shrink the suffrage rights of poor and working-class residents, often specifically targeting blue-collar foreign-born voters. Among other measures, they campaigned for Australian-style private (unilingual) ballots, educational prerequisites to access the polls, and strict voter residency and registration requirements. Lawmakers in midwestern, western, and especially northeastern states often acceded to some or all of these demands, just as southern lawmakers embedded poll tax and literacy test voter restrictions into their Jim Crow state constitutions. Some states obliged immigrant voters to wait several months after becoming US citizens and/or required proof of naturalization to cast a ballot.[13] Evidence of the latter could be hard to produce around the turn of the twentieth century, especially if an immigrant derived citizenship from the naturalization of his or her husband or father.[14]

Amid their broader attacks on the voting rights of poor, working-class, and foreign-born US citizens, Gilded Age and Progressive Era immigration restrictionists and their allies were, unsurprisingly, among the most vociferous opponents of noncitizen voting rights. One such critic, J. Chester Lyman, took to the pages of the widely circulated highbrow journal the *North American Review* to both highlight the importance of state alien suffrage laws and denounce the persistence of disparate regimes of citizenship rights in the late-nineteenth-century American polity. In his 1887 article, "Our Inequalities of Suffrage," Lyman claimed it was a scandal that a "wood-chopper of Michigan, who has been in the country but one year," possessed "just as much power in the selection of a President of the United States as the resident of Kentucky who, in order to vote, must be a citizen of the United States and have lived in the State two years."[15] This disparity was not just outrageous, Lyman argued, but also

70　DISPARATE REGIMES

downright dangerous. While he admitted that some immigrants "rank among our most intelligent men," Lyman claimed that most "lower[ed] the average of our moral and mental powers." Enfranchising recent European migrants, he alleged, threatened American democracy and republican institutions, owing to their "individual ignorance, want of acquaintance with our laws and customs, and absence of American ideas."[16] While Lyman endorsed draconian educational and registration requirements to bar a range of "undesirable" individuals from casting ballots, he was especially perturbed by the practice of noncitizen voting. Nothing short of federal constitutional reform was needed, according to Lyman, to restrict suffrage access to ensure that "only *duly qualified* citizens shall vote" in national elections.[17]

Other elite opponents of alien suffrage focused their efforts on specific state campaigns. In 1894, legal scholar Henry Chaney wrote a short treatise for the Michigan Political Science Association in which he critiqued noncitizen voting rights just as Michiganders prepared to go to the polls to vote on that very subject. Chaney conceded "that some of the evils that were feared from alien suffrage have not, in this State at least, developed."[18] But he claimed that noncitizens had no reason to naturalize if they already possessed the franchise and warned of the dangers posed by immigrants who "vote as they are told, ignorantly and corruptly."[19] Pointing to persistent, but recently heightened ethnoreligious tensions across the border, Chaney also argued that "the strong race feeling of the French inhabitants has been so strengthened and kept in countenance...that Canadian progress under British rule has always been half paralyzed in consequence." If noncitizens continued to be permitted to vote in the United States, he warned, then the country risked becoming as divided and in danger of civil strife as Canada.[20]

Major East Coast newspapers—located in polities where alien suffrage laws were not in force—sometimes offered similarly exaggerated warnings about the alleged threats of alien suffrage to American democracy. The *Philadelphia Press* contended in 1896 that certainly "no other country in the civilized world gives such a right to those who still owe allegiance to some other government."[21] The following year, the *Philadelphia Inquirer* negatively juxtaposed states with extant alien suffrage laws to Pennsylvania, where "the franchise is accorded, as it should be everywhere, to citizens only."[22] The *Washington Post* put it more forcefully in 1902. "Men who are no more fit to be trusted with the ballot than babies are to be furnished with friction matches" were too often allowed to vote before becoming citizens, according to the *Post*.[23]

Opponents brought the subject to the masses when convening a "suffrage congress" at the Chicago World's Fair in August 1893. They included "state laws permitting aliens to vote" among "the most vital questions in current politics." In so doing, they explicitly elevated them to the level of debate over women's

MAKING VOTERS CITIZENS 71

suffrage, the direct election of US senators, the abolition of the Electoral College, direct democracy reforms, and, in their words, "the limitation and regulation of the suffrage in communities having mixed races."[24]

Despite the breadth of these critiques, few nationwide institutions or national political actors were as vocal as the women's suffrage movement in denouncing alien suffrage. Leading native-born Anglo-American women's suffragists often viewed immigrant voters as powerful opponents of their cause. Susan B. Anthony, for instance, believed that noncitizen men had contributed to the defeat of a women's suffrage campaign in Colorado in 1877. At an 1880 congressional hearing, Anthony embraced racist and xenophobic tropes in an effort to convince federal lawmakers that her movement had been beaten by disreputable forces in Colorado. She alleged that while "native-born white men, temperance men, cultivated, broad, generous, just men, men who think" had supported women's voting rights, they were outnumbered by a less desirable "class of voters" in Colorado, largely of Mexican and German origin.[25]

Similar accusations were heard following the defeat of an 1890 women's suffrage campaign in South Dakota. Suffragists had been beaten by roughly a two-to-one margin and 23,790 votes in total. The contemporaneous NAWSA-sponsored *History of Woman Suffrage*, coauthored by Anthony, bemoaned that "30,000 Russians, Poles, Scandinavians and other foreigners" were permitted to vote in the state and claimed that "most" had "opposed woman suffrage."[26] Reverend Olympia Brown, a leading suffragist in the upper Midwest, was among those who increasingly portrayed opponents of the women's suffrage movement as a nefarious alliance of antisuffragist leaders, brewing interests, and foreign-born, especially noncitizen, voters.[27]

In an attempt to sway public opinion, late–Gilded Age and Progressive Era suffragists and their outlets often argued that "intelligent," white American women would serve the republic far better as voters than recent immigrant men. The *Woman's Tribune*, for instance, called it a "degradation" in 1896 to "b[e] governed by ignorant aliens." It was unjust to deny "the most highly educated woman in the land" access to the ballot box, the publication asserted, while "ignorant" noncitizen men could vote in many states across the nation.[28]

Women's suffrage leaders also claimed that the practice of noncitizen voting increased risks of fraud. In a 1904 address delivered during her first term as president of the NAWSA, Carrie Chapman Catt presciently called for major federal naturalization reforms, arguing that rules were too lax and "ma[de] possible the forging of certificates, and the addition to the voting lists of men who have not yet remained the necessary five years in our land."[29] Her criticism of recent immigrants casting ballots in American elections only grew over time.

72 DISPARATE REGIMES

"When we first began to work for suffrage, there were fifteen states in which men might vote without being citizens," she reflected a decade and a half later. The "worst sinner," in her eyes, had been Michigan. "Before an election men were colonized from Canada, and when they came over to Detroit and lived ten days they had a vote," Catt alleged. Such practices amounted to, she claimed, a "flagrant...political crime."[30]

Women's suffragists further attacked alien suffrage laws to make the affirmative case that voting should be a right of—and only of—US citizens, irrespective of gender. For instance, Alice Stone Blackwell's *Woman's Column* blasted the hypocrisy that "not one" state that enfranchised noncitizen men in 1892 "allow[ed] an American woman, however intelligent, responsible and public-spirited," the right to vote.[31] The *Women's Tribune* tied these two subjects together even more directly in 1896. It called on American women across the country to "unite in demanding not only that the arbitrary sex line should be removed but that the States should not so violate the letter and spirit of the Federal Constitution as to make their resident aliens voters before they are citizens of the United States." The *Tribune* claimed federal constitutional reform was needed to repeal alien suffrage laws because "no political party is so bold as to dare to risk the loss of the foreign vote by demanding a change or by challenging the alien vote when cast" in states where noncitizen voting remained law in 1896.[32]

The *Tribune's* prediction proved incorrect, however. While partisan competition for votes occasionally helped to keep alien suffrage laws on the books into the new century, that was usually not the case. On the contrary, local interest group engagement and state-specific partisan politics helped spell the demise of these policies in the upper Midwest and West.

The Progressive Era Retreat of Noncitizen Voting in the Upper Midwest and West

Immigrants were numerous in each of the six states of the West and upper Midwest that repealed their alien suffrage laws via constitutional amendment during the late Gilded Age and Progressive Era. They were also well represented in Nebraska, which held a failed anti-alien suffrage constitutional amendment campaign in 1910.

Colorado and Oregon, though relatively thinly inhabited, with 539,700 and 413,536 residents, respectively, possessed significant immigrant populations at the dawn of the twentieth century. In fact, the percentage of residents born abroad in Colorado (16.9 percent) and Oregon (15.9 percent) in 1900 ranked slightly above the national average of 13.6 percent. The repeal of noncitizen voting rights threatened to transform electoral politics even more in the upper

Midwest, where roughly 1 of every 4 residents of Michigan, Minnesota, and Wisconsin had been born abroad. The large and growing populations of each of these three states—which ranged from 1.75 million to 2.42 million inhabitants—were increasingly anchored on the fast-expanding metropoles of Detroit, Minneapolis, and Milwaukee, all of which ranked among the twenty most populous cities in the nation by 1900. In the medium-sized state of Nebraska, 1 of every 6 of the state's 1.07 million residents had been born abroad. And in sparsely populated North Dakota—home to 319,146 enumerated inhabitants in 1900—more than 1 of every 3 residents were foreign-born. In no other state did immigrants represent as large a percentage of all inhabitants (see Table 3.1).[33]

It was thus far from predetermined that noncitizen voting rights would be repealed in a half-dozen states between 1894 and 1914 or that state politicians, partisan-affiliated organizations, and interest groups would take the lead in opposing alien suffrage. No campaign better illustrates these dynamics than the battle over noncitizen voting in late–Gilded Age Michigan.

Gilded Age state lawmakers were particularly brazen in altering suffrage, redistricting, and reapportionment laws to maximize partisan advantage after an election transferred control of the legislature and the governor's mansion from one party to another. By gerrymandering state legislative districts, adopting new bases of apportionment, and/or significantly altering voting rights in the wake of an electoral victory, partisan legislators sought to entrench recent victories into future advantages.[34] Michigan was no exception to this trend.

Like most upper Midwest states during this period, the state's electorate generally favored the Republican Party.[35] Grand Old Party (GOP) presidential nominees won Michigan, and thus all of its Electoral College votes, in every

Table 3.1 Populations of Six Upper Midwestern and Western States in 1900 Repealing Alien Suffrage via Progressive Era Constitutional Amendment

State	Percent Foreign-Born	Foreign-Born Population	Total Population	Date Alien Suffrage Repealed
Michigan	22.4	541,653	2,420,982	1894
Minnesota	28.9	505,318	1,751,394	1896
North Dakota	35.4	113,091	319,146	1898
Colorado	16.9	91,155	539,700	1902
Wisconsin	24.9	515,971	2,069,042	1908
Oregon	15.9	65,748	413,536	1914

Note: On population figures, see Campbell J. Gibson and Emily Lennon, "Nativity of the Population, for Regions, Divisions, and States: 1850 to 1990," in *Historical Census Statistics on the Foreign-Born Population of the United States: 1850–1990*, https://www.census.gov/population/www/documentation/twps0029/twps0029.html; *Twelfth Census of the United States*. See also notes throughout the chapter for specific dates of repeal.

74 DISPARATE REGIMES

contest held between 1856 and 1888.[36] But Democrats usually remained competitive and even won control of both legislative chambers and the governor's mansion in the 1890 midterm elections.[37]

Once in power in early 1891, Democratic lawmakers capitalized on their brief total control in Michigan by altering how the state assigned presidential electors to the Electoral College. The Miner Law (named after its sponsor, state representative John Miner) allocated electors to presidential candidates based on the number of congressional districts they carried. Because no Democratic presidential nominee had carried the state in forty years, Michigan Democrats hoped the scheme would help boost their standard-bearer's electoral vote count. The plan worked. Former president Grover Cleveland won five of Michigan's fourteen electors despite losing the statewide vote en route to his national victory in 1892. But those five electoral votes came at a cost.[38]

Michigan Republicans retook the state legislature and the governorship at those same 1892 elections. Upon regaining power in Lansing, they promptly repealed the Miner Law, once more allocating all presidential electors to the winner of the statewide popular vote. They also moved to repeal alien suffrage via constitutional amendment, finding ready allies outside the legislature.[39]

W. J. H. Traynor, the head of the American Protective Association (APA), a virulently anti-Catholic organization, lived in Michigan and published his widely circulated paper, *The Patriotic American*, from Detroit.[40] While Traynor articulated numerous anti-Catholic diatribes, he especially argued that Catholics could not be trusted with political power owing to their alleged dual allegiances to the country and to the papacy.[41] Traynor and his organization called on Protestant Americans to oppose Catholic candidates and defeat Catholic voters at the polls. Though an immigrant from Canada himself, Traynor made a certain kind of anti-immigrant politics central to his agenda.[42] The APA warned hysterically that immigrants, "under the direction of certain ecclesiastical institutions, had become so dominant a factor in politics as to virtually control it."[43]

Despite this demagoguery, neither Traynor nor the APA was confined to the fringes of state or national politics. Traynor published numerous columns in the highbrow *North American Review*. APA members regularly lobbied GOP state and national lawmakers to enact anti-Catholic legislation. They also ran for office themselves.[44] The association reached its zenith in the early to mid-1890s when membership may have numbered as high as 100,000 nationwide.[45] Members were especially numerous in midwestern states like Michigan. Its staunchest backer in national politics, Republican congressman William S. Linton, hailed from Saginaw.[46]

When the GOP returned to power in Lansing in early 1893, the repeal of noncitizen voting rights was high on its agenda. Despite its significant

Figure 3.1 "The Result of the Detroit City and State of Michigan Elections, 1892," *Patriotic American*, reproduced in Frederick Neal, *The A.P.A. and C.P.A. Exposed, or, Why They Exist* (Sandwich, ON, 1893), 21. Beinecke Rare Book and Manuscript Library, Yale University.

majorities in both chambers, the party was not assured of victory in or out of the state legislature. The GOP needed to stay united or win over some Democratic lawmakers to meet the state's constitutional requirement that an amendment receive at least a two-thirds majority approval from both chambers before being sent to voters for ratification.[47]

Though the amendment sailed through the Senate, it met stiffer resistance in the House.[48] There, Democratic representative Thomas Barkworth of Jackson County, himself a naturalized English immigrant, fought to prevent the amendment's adoption.[49] Knowing that his Republican colleagues were eager to wrap up the legislative session, Barkworth repeatedly forced procedural votes in an effort to defeat or delay the amendment.[50] The Republican majority responded by "rushing partisan measures." Barkworth failed to prevent a final vote on the amendment in the House, which was adopted by a 70–20 majority.[51] The amendment would therefore be put to voters in the fall of 1894.

The passage of the amendment by state lawmakers in early 1893 did not receive much press attention at the time. In an article published the day after the Michigan House approved the amendment, the *Detroit Free Press* devoted greater attention to Barkworth's staunch advocacy of universal women's suffrage

76 DISPARATE REGIMES

rights in a separate exchange than to his delaying tactics in the alien suffrage battle.[52] In fact, the *Free Press* failed to mention that the amendment proposed to repeal Michigan's long-standing alien suffrage law at all. Instead, it framed the measure as an effort to extend residency requirements before inhabitants could register to vote.[53] This was not entirely wrong. By continuing to enfranchise long-resident noncitizen men already holding first papers, the amendment mostly proposed to restrict the suffrage rights of future immigrants.[54] Once the ratification campaign entered high gear the following year, however, the Democratic-supporting *Free Press* would take the matter much more seriously.

With the midterm elections approaching in the autumn of 1894, the *Detroit Free Press* fought to mobilize opposition to the anti-alien suffrage constitutional amendment. It denounced the measure as "Republican in its origin" and an effort "to disfranchise a large number of foreign-born voters." Arguing that the state GOP had "always been distrustful of the foreign-born voter because it has been unable to secure his support except to a very limited extent," the paper warned that the party "would gladly disfranchise them all, no doubt, if that were practicable." Rallying immigrants and "the native-born citizen who believes in fair play," the *Free Press* called on Michiganders across the state "to oppose the amendment."[55]

Other Democratic-supporting papers and Democratic politicians also blasted the measure in the lead-up to the 1894 midterm elections. The *Bay City Times* offered inflated estimates that the amendment "would deprive 75,000 persons of the right of suffrage in this state." The paper warned that it represented "a part of the scheme of the American plutocrats to reduce labor to a condition of serfdom." While it denounced "cheap labor" immigration, the paper defended noncitizen voting rights as a necessary bulwark against workers' "serfdom and dependence." It also ominously warned that the measure represented the beginning of a "movement for the disfranchisement of labor...in Michigan."[56]

While the *Bay City Times* denounced efforts to repeal alien suffrage in class terms, James O'Hara, the Democratic nominee for state attorney general, claimed that the "real purpose" of the measure—which he estimated would disfranchise around 25,000 voters across the state—was "to secure the A.P.A. vote." By endorsing the amendment, O'Hara argued, "the republican party has yielded to the A.P.A. eatred [sic] of foreigners and would facrfice [sic] the latter's vote to keep the former." O'Hara also pointed to the state GOP platform, which endorsed the total repeal of alien suffrage, to warn that the amendment represented just a first step in the party's plans for disfranchisement.[57]

Meanwhile, one GOP-supporting newspaper took pains to downplay the party's platform. The *L'Anse Sentinel* omitted the entire section that endorsed the repeal of alien suffrage in its news coverage of the party's state convention.[58] This Republican-backing small-town paper, which circulated in the heavily immigrant–populated Upper Peninsula, probably suspected that advertising the GOP's opposition to alien suffrage would do more harm to the party's electoral prospects than good in the region.[59]

In other parts of the state, Republicans showed no such hesitancy. A leading Detroit Republican organization, the Alger Club, actively campaigned in favor of the amendment in the lead-up to the 1894 midterms.[60] The *True Northerner*, a Republican-supporting newspaper based in the western Michigan town of Paw Paw, argued that the anti-alien suffrage amendment was "the most important question to be submitted to the people of the state of Michigan for their approval or disapproval." It decried the state's long-standing noncitizen voting rights law as "grossly unjust, in that it places the ignorant alien of two years and a few months' residence on the same footing with the most intelligent American-born citizen."[61]

Despite their opposite stances, the *Detroit Free Press* and the *True Northerner* agreed that abstentions threatened to torpedo the will of the people. The *Free Press* accurately noted that frequently the "questions at the bottom of the official ballots are slighted," with most Michiganders "neglecting to pay any attention to them."[62] Warning that the GOP was hoping constituents would forget to vote nay, the paper exhorted readers to crush the amendment "by so decisive a majority as to teach the Republican party in Michigan that it cannot hoodwink the people."[63] The GOP-backing *True Northerner* expressed confidence that most Michiganders supported the amendment, but feared that the measure "may be defeated through the oversight of those who would vote for it but, in their hurry to get back to their places of business, forget to do so."[64]

The midterm elections of 1894 produced sweeping victories for Republicans across much of the country—especially in the industrial Northeast and Midwest—amid mass dissatisfaction with the Cleveland administration's handling of the economic crisis wrought by the Panic of 1893.[65] Michigan Republican governor John Rich scored a landslide re-election in 1894 (winning 237,215 votes to his Democratic opponent's 130,823).[66] While less than half of all Michiganders who voted in the gubernatorial election cast ballots for or against the amendment, it nevertheless won by a huge margin (receiving 117,088 votes in favor against 31,537 opposed).[67]

The *Detroit Free Press* conceded that the measure had proved more popular than anticipated. Even the city's districts "where there are many foreign-born citizens" failed to produce "considerable opposition" to the amendment at the polls.[68] However, the *Free Press* argued that the underlying mechanics governing how Michigan's constitution could be amended were too lax, pointing out that "most of the amendments which have been adopted in the last quarter of a

78 DISPARATE REGIMES

century have been carried by a ridiculously small fraction of the vote polled at the same time on state or other officers." To achieve ratification, an amendment should be forced to meet "some decent minimum of votes," the paper contended.[69]

The *Free Press* was not alone in arguing that states' constitutional amendment ratification procedures should be made more difficult. In response to similar concerns, voters and lawmakers in nearby Minnesota altered their state constitution in 1898 to require that a majority of all voters participating in an election cast ballots affirmatively in favor of an amendment for it to achieve ratification (i.e., ayes would henceforth have to outnumber nays and abstentions). This adjustment would subsequently stifle the ratification of most amendments submitted to Minnesotans during this period because of continued low voter participation on such questions.[70] But that change appeared two years too late to preserve the state's long-standing alien suffrage law.

The midterm elections of 1894 were particularly fortuitous for Republicans in Minnesota. That fall, they easily re-elected GOP governor Knute Nelson and won landslide majorities in both legislative chambers against a divided Populist and Democratic opposition.[71] Once the new legislature convened in 1895, Republican lawmakers adopted and submitted a proposed constitutional amendment to the electorate to repeal alien suffrage via ballot measure in the autumn of 1896. The amendment aimed to ban all noncitizens from voting in Minnesota upon ratification, with no loophole for noncitizen voters already residing there.[72]

As had been the case in Michigan, most Minnesota voters abstained on the anti-alien suffrage constitutional amendment. While 337,229 voters cast ballots in the 1896 gubernatorial race, only 150,434 Minnesotans opted to vote aye or nay on the anti-alien suffrage amendment. But since roughly 45,000 more Minnesotans voted to repeal alien suffrage than endorsed the retention of such rights, the amendment was ratified.[73]

Newspapers as far away as Louisiana, South Carolina, and Pennsylvania applauded voters in Minnesota for the ratification of the anti-alien suffrage amendment. The (Lake Providence) *Banner–Democrat* pointed to its success to argue that other states enfranchising noncitizen men—like Louisiana— should cease being "too liberal in granting the franchise to foreigners before they could possibly have acquainted themselves with American institutions."[74] The *Philadelphia Press* likewise "hoped that the example of Minnesota will be followed all over the union and American citizenship be invested with a new dignity."[75] The (Kingstree, South Carolina–based) *County Record* claimed that since "few States have so large a percentage of foreign-born citizens as Minnesota, the adoption of this amendment indicates that real foreign-born citizens do not favor alien voting."[76]

Gunder Halverson, a supporter of alien suffrage who resided in the small town of Lyle in southern Minnesota, disagreed. He denounced it as "an insult to the foreign born people" of the state and evidence of a "knownothingism craze." Halverson believed that those who had voted for the amendment had "d[one] so believing that it had reference only to foreigners hereafter applying to citizenship."[77] The *Minneapolis Times*, by contrast, jocularly reported that the election results suggested that some "men will vote to disfranchise themselves." The Twin Cities–based People's Party organ, *The Representative*, went even further. It argued that Republican partisanship was so engrained among a large segment of Minnesota voters that "there are a great many good, honest men in Minnesota who, if the Republican party submitted an amendment to the Constitution to their votes, providing that they should be themselves hung, would cheerfully vote for it, if it only had the stamp of the G.O.P. upon it."[78]

While it is unclear whether any meaningful number of noncitizen voters cast ballots in support of the amendment, the repeal of alien suffrage certainly had a significant impact on the composition of the state's electorate. Shortly after the amendment's ratification was confirmed, newspapers and political parties repeatedly encouraged noncitizen men to petition for citizenship if they were eligible to do so.[79] Despite such efforts, tens of thousands of immigrants who held first papers remained disfranchised. Approximately 40,000 fewer Minnesotans voted in the midterm elections of 1898 than had done so four years earlier.[80]

While the repeal of noncitizen voting in Minnesota in 1896 was widely reported as a significant development in national press outlets, a successful attempt to rescind alien suffrage rights in neighboring North Dakota two years later went largely ignored in state and national media.[81] In 1897, legislators in this similarly Republican-dominated state adopted legislation that put a constitutional amendment seeking to both repeal alien suffrage and institute an educational requirement for all would-be voters before the electorate in the fall 1898 elections.[82] The results proved closer in North Dakota than had been the case in Michigan and Minnesota just a few years earlier. A total of 21,177 North Dakota voters casting ballots on the question (56.5 percent) supported the repeal effort, while a significant 16,329 (43.5 percent) opposed it.[83]

Although the desire of Republican lawmakers to strengthen their partisan advantage played a central role in each of these three 1890s constitutional amendment campaigns, support for and opposition to the repeal of alien suffrage did not always map perfectly onto partisan lines in the upper Midwest. In fact, shortly after the ratification of North Dakota's amendment in the fall of 1898, Republican state representative Ormsby McHarg sought to have it

80   DISPARATE REGIMES

disqualified. McHarg implored the state attorney general to issue an opinion declaring the measure "null and void" on the grounds that it had violated the state constitution's requirement that propositions be voted on "separately" by combining two distinct changes to the state's suffrage provisions into one amendment. His efforts, however, were unsuccessful.[84]

McHarg was a rare GOP state politician who criticized the methods used to repeal noncitizen voting rights. In Wisconsin, by contrast, the Democratic-backing *Sheboygan Daily Press* applauded the state's electorate in 1908 for ratifying an anti-alien suffrage constitutional amendment. The paper claimed that the measure represented "a blow at the big corporations and trusts who have been intimidating foreigners by weired [*sic*] tales of 'shut downs' if the democratic party got in power." Amid an uptick in unemployed foreign-born laborers returning to their home countries in the wake of the Panic of 1907, the *Daily Press* argued that "suffrage should never be allowed to foreigners who may be here today, and tomorrow on the way back to their native land."[85]

As had been the case in North Dakota a decade earlier, the Wisconsin anti-alien suffrage amendment did not dominate news coverage during the fall elections of 1908. In a lukewarm endorsement of the measure, the *La Crosse Tribune* went so far as to state that "the amendment is not of vital importance."[86] Most voters agreed. While over 450,000 Wisconsinites cast ballots for president in 1908, barely over a quarter of them expressed an opinion on whether to repeal alien suffrage. Nevertheless, the measure was ratified by a large margin of 86,576 votes in favor and only 36,773 opposed.[87] Its disfranchisement provisions did not come into immediate effect for most noncitizen voters residing in Wisconsin because the amendment gave immigrant men possessing first papers four years to complete their naturalization.[88]

Shortly before that grace period was set to expire, another voting rights amendment was put to the electorate in Wisconsin. After years of organizing and lobbying by suffragist leaders such as Olympia Brown of the Wisconsin Woman's Suffrage Association and Ada Lois James of the Political Equality League, a women's suffrage amendment was sent to the state electorate in November 1912.[89] Voter participation on this amendment was high. Of the nearly 400,000 Wisconsin men who cast ballots in the presidential election that year, fewer than 40,000 abstained on the women's suffrage question. By over 90,000 votes, the proposed amendment was decisively defeated.[90]

Brown claimed that Wisconsin lawmakers had significantly undercut their chances of winning by changing the mechanics of voting in advance of the women's suffrage measure. "Heretofore constitutional amendments have received slight attention and have been carried by a few votes of those most intelligent and most interested," she maintained, in a report written shortly after the amendment's rejection. She argued that because of "the varied character of our population...the only hope of carrying our measure lay in not attracting the attention of the lower orders to the subject." Unfortunately for suffragists, the legislature had adopted new ballot rules designed to boost electoral participation, leading many voters to cast highly visible "separate pink ballot[s]" specific to the women's suffrage amendment. "WE WERE BEATEN BY THE PINK BALLOT," Brown thundered, in her after-action report.[91]

Ida Lois James and her competing suffragist organization, the Wisconsin Political Equality League, disagreed significantly on strategy and tactics toward immigrant voters. The organization had campaigned hard to convert blue-collar and immigrant voters to the women's suffrage cause through sustained working-class and multilingual outreach. Yet it was not above selectively employing anti-German rhetoric to mobilize support for their cause. After all, brewing interests and German American associations tied to the beer industry were indeed significant opponents of women's suffrage in Wisconsin.[92]

Despite the defeat in Wisconsin and a broader series of setbacks in the upper Midwest, Progressive Era women's suffragists were finding greater success farther west.[93] In two western states, anti-immigrant sentiment actually became directly intertwined with victorious efforts to enfranchise US citizen women

Figure 3.2 Reverend Olympia Brown, 1919. Library of Congress, Prints & Photographs Division, photograph by Harris & Ewing, LC-DIG-hec-12319.

82　DISPARATE REGIMES

and embed such rights into their respective state constitutions by making voting both a citizenship right and a citizen-only right.

* * *

Colorado, which had affirmed noncitizen voting rights at its 1875–76 statehood convention, would be one of the first states to witness a coordinated, two-pronged campaign to enfranchise American women and disfranchise noncitizen men. Susan B. Anthony, who had fought hard for women's suffrage in the state during an unsuccessful 1877 constitutional amendment campaign, spoke for many suffragists in blaming immigrant men for the defeat.[94]

Colorado suffragists would not forget the alleged role played by immigrants in this 1877 dispute. While women's equal suffrage rights had become law in Colorado in 1893, this provision had not become part of the state constitution at that time.[95] In 1902, an amendment was submitted to the electorate to insert female voting rights into the state's highest law. Women's suffragists and their supporters made sure to incorporate the repeal of alien suffrage onto the same measure. The ballot read, "That every person over the age of twenty-one years" who "shall be a citizen of the United States" would henceforth have equal voting rights. If the measure passed, no noncitizen would be allowed to vote. For those who supported both women's suffrage and alien suffrage (or neither policy), there was no way to disentangle the two. Women's suffragists won the day by a large margin (35,372 ayes against only 20,087 nays).[96]

A similar, and even more complicated, story played out in Oregon a decade later. When Oregon was admitted as a state in 1859, its constitution permitted white, male immigrants possessing first papers to vote, while barring African Americans and persons of East Asian origin. Though the federal Fifteenth Amendment voided race-based restrictions for male US citizens, the requirement that noncitizens file first papers continued to disfranchise East Asian immigrant men in Oregon owing to their ineligibility to naturalize.[97]

While the process of filing for first papers was often a relatively simple task for most white, noncitizen men (if they could afford to pay the associated costs), it was an impossible challenge for married women. Under prevailing federal nationality laws, married women could not file such declarations because their citizenship was inextricably tied to that of their spouses. A married immigrant woman could only derive US nationality through her husband's naturalization, while any native-born woman who married a foreign man following the passage of the Expatriation Act of 1907 automatically lost her American citizenship.[98]

Following the success of a 1912 women's suffrage referendum in Oregon, local election authorities soon found themselves at a loss as to which categories of married women could and should be permitted to register to vote.[99] State attorney general Andrew Crawford offered legal guidance in March 1913, declaring that neither marital expatriates nor immigrant women married to noncitizen husbands who held first papers would be allowed to vote. Since married noncitizen women could not hold first papers in their own names, he announced that they would be ineligible to vote unless and until their husbands naturalized (and thereby such women themselves became US citizens via derivation). "A difference in the state and federal constitutions causes this variance to exist," Crawford claimed, according to the *Coos Bay Times*.[100]

Crawford's legal opinion failed to silence all questions on the matter. Less than a week after the attorney general delivered his announcement, the *East Oregonian* reported that this "peculiar slip in our election laws" had been "causing trouble" within one family in Portland where "the wife [was] a suffragette but her husband [was] opposed to votes for women." Already a voter on the basis of his first papers, the husband refused to naturalize and thereby enable his wife to vote as a US citizen. She, in turn, threatened that "if he continues that attitude she w[ould] secure a divorce and thus obtain the right of franchise" independently.[101]

Shortly thereafter, Crawford altered his opinion. He reasoned that married women derived their intent to become US citizens—and thereby gained suffrage rights—if their noncitizen husbands possessed first papers.[102] This amended policy also proved unpopular with many Oregonians, especially women's suffragists. They mobilized alongside other opponents of alien suffrage and called on voters to ratify a state constitutional amendment to repeal noncitizen voting rights that had already been circulating in the state legislature.[103]

Supporters of the amendment harnessed nativist fears and denounced the state's alien suffrage law as outdated to buttress their cause. A group of state lawmakers supporting the measure argued that its ratification would protect women's voting rights and bring Oregon into broader alignment with most other states' suffrage provisions. They also ominously warned that the completion of the Panama Canal risked opening the state to a large number of undesirable "immigrants of a new kind" who could "be easily led by the unscrupulously [sic] to vote vicariously."[104] The *Morning Register* of Eugene similarly noted that by 1914 just "nine of the 48 states now permit aliens to vote on their first papers." The paper maintained that "Oregon's popular form of government makes such safeguards as this amendment is designed to provide particularly necessary."[105]

This sentiment proved popular with Oregon's voters. Roughly 80 percent of the more than 200,000 ballots cast on the question were marked as ayes in November 1914.[106] US-born women married to noncitizen men continued to be denied the vote in Oregon, along with all other states that had adopted women's suffrage laws but required American citizenship to vote.[107]

84　DISPARATE REGIMES

This lopsided margin and high rate of voter turnout was unusual for late–Gilded Age and Progressive Era state anti-alien suffrage ballot measures. In fact, one proposed amendment put to voters in Nebraska in 1910 was not adopted owing to a high number of abstentions. While 100,450 Nebraskans voting on the anti-alien suffrage question supported it (far outnumbering 74,878 nays), 68,062 voters abstained, and the measure failed the state constitution's amendment requirements.[108] Undeterred by this defeat, opponents soon sought to neuter the state's surviving alien suffrage law via administrative means. As in Oregon, the meaning of immigrants' first papers under state and federal law became the subject of contention in Nebraska.

One of the provisions of the federal 1906 Naturalization Act specified that if an immigrant had not become a US citizen within seven years of filing his or her first papers, he or she would have to restart the naturalization process and file a new declaration of intention.[109] As that date approached in early 1913, numerous immigrants in Nebraska holding old declarations hastened to complete their petitions for citizenship.[110] They had good reason to hurry. In September of that same year, the election commissioner of Douglas County moved to prevent noncitizen men whose first papers were seven years old or more from registering to vote.[111]

Election commissioner Harley Moorhead must have known that his announcement would be controversial. His office had been created earlier that year by a bipartisan coalition of self-styled election reformers in the state legislature in response to allegations that the longtime Democratic and political machine–backed mayor of Omaha, James Dahlman, was benefiting from electoral fraud. Moorhead, an anti-machine Democrat, had been appointed by Nebraska's governor to investigate and prevent such alleged activities.[112] He got fast to work rewriting the city's voter registration policies, which his detractors denounced for circumscribing residents' access to the rolls and for allegedly outright disfranchising other eligible voters.[113]

Though generally supportive of Moorhead's "reforms," Republican state attorney general Grant Martin rebuffed his attempt to bar noncitizen men from voting on old first papers via administrative fiat.[114] Martin issued an opinion ruling that those documents still held meaning in Nebraska, even if they were invalid in the eyes of the federal government for the purposes of naturalization. Martin contended foremost that "the right of suffrage comes from the state and not from the federal government." While the Fifteenth Amendment barred "states…from discriminating against any citizen of the United States," Martin argued that the federal government "has never pretended" to order "who should be the voters in the respective states." He concluded that "whether or not [alien declarants] complete their naturalization is a matter to which the constitution of the state of Nebraska apparently is indifferent."[115]

MAKING VOTERS CITIZENS   85

Thus, while opponents of noncitizen voting rights were both numerous and powerful in Nebraska, its long-standing alien suffrage policy remained entrenched in and protected by the state's highest law throughout the Progressive Era. A half-dozen other states also retained such laws as late as 1918. Significant de jure constitutional and/or de facto logistical barriers had helped to embed noncitizen voting rights in each of their respective constitutions as well. To overcome such hurdles, activists would need to foment or benefit from a significant disruption to the underlying dynamics of their states' politics or to their constitutional mechanics. World War I would prove to be that catalyst.

Standardizing Citizenship Rights as Citizen-Only Rights in Wartime and Reaction

The entry of the United States into World War I in early 1917 dramatically transformed the de jure and de facto rights of noncitizens—especially those of enemy aliens—residing in the country. Amid a dramatic upsurge in wartime nationalism and anti-German sentiment, nationals of imperial Germany became subject to federal registration and were restricted as to where they could live and work.[116] Many had their assets frozen and held by a federal alien property custodian.[117] At the state level, formal "councils of defense" and ad hoc "vigilance" associations frequently surveilled and harassed German-origin communities.[118]

Many American citizens were outraged that noncitizens, especially enemy aliens, might vote in seven states during wartime. Women's suffrage organizations made common cause with patriotic politicians and organizations to end the practice during and shortly after the war. In so doing, they harnessed an increasingly national, nativist sentiment while also arguing that US women represented a necessary bulwark to protect American democracy and national security.

Voters in Kansas, Nebraska, and South Dakota would repeal their states' alien suffrage laws via successful wartime constitutional amendment campaigns by massive margins in high-turnout elections. Anti-German sentiment was particularly prominent in these midwestern Plains states where German American communities had long exerted significant political power. In four states of the upper South and lower Midwest, the repeal of alien suffrage laws would take longer. In Texas, a joint woman's suffrage–noncitizen disfranchisement amendment was actually rejected at the polls in 1919. Noncitizen voting rights would only be fully repealed there in 1921, after US citizen women (largely white, Anglo Texans in practice) had gained the right to vote. In Arkansas, Indiana, and Missouri, where barriers to the ratification of state constitutional

86 DISPARATE REGIMES

amendments were especially high, campaigns to repeal noncitizen voting rights ultimately succeeded after the war. There, former suffragists allied with nativists, broader state constitutional reformers, and veterans' organizations in multiyear anti-alien suffrage campaigns (see Table 3.2).[119]

Women's suffragists had long waged an unsuccessful battle in Nebraska. There, opponents of the women's suffrage cause—frequently led and funded by those involved in the brewing industry or in liquor sales—often argued that suffragists were a front for the prohibition movement. Although prohibitionists often did support female voting rights, women's suffrage leaders in Nebraska labored mightily to distinguish the two movements. Yet the state's large German-origin population formed a formidable bloc of opposition to both prohibition and women's suffrage at the polls. Precincts with large German-origin populations voted overwhelmingly against a narrowly defeated women's suffrage measure in 1914 (with roughly 90 percent opposed) and against a successful prohibition amendment in 1916 (with around 85 percent opposing the measure).[120]

War with Germany transformed the political landscape in the state overnight. The Nebraska Council of Defense was especially fierce in surveilling German American communities. It regularly encouraged residents to report on

Table 3.2 Demographic Contrast of Seven States Repealing Alien Suffrage in the World War I Era, 1920

State	Foreign-Born Population	German-Born Population	Germans Largest?[a]	Year(s) Anti-alien Suffrage Amendment Succeeded
Kansas	6.3% (110,967)	23,380	Yes	1918
Nebraska	11.6 % (150,665)	40,969	Yes	1918
South Dakota	13.0% (82,534)	15,674	No	1918
Indiana	5.2% (151,328)	37,377	Yes	1921
Texas	7.8% (363,832)	31,062	No	1921 (for general elections)[b]
Missouri	5.5% (186,835)	55,776	Yes	1922 and 1924
Arkansas	0.8% (14,137)	3,979	Yes	1926 (ruling on 1920 amendment)

Note: On population figures, see Campbell J. Gibson and Emily Lennon, "Nativity of the Population, for Regions, Divisions, and States: 1850 to 1990," in *Historical Census Statistics on the Foreign-Born Population of the United States: 1850–1990,* https://www.census.gov/population/ www/documentation/twps0029/twps0029.html; *Fourteenth Census of the United States,* 306–11. See also notes throughout the chapter for specific dates of repeal.

[a] Yes, if residents born in Germany represent the state's largest immigrant population.
[b] The Texas legislature had repealed noncitizen voting rights for primary elections in 1918.

their neighbors for any alleged utterances contrary to the war effort. Serving as prosecutor, judge, and jury of individuals hauled before them, the council often demanded that suspects purchase liberty bonds as proof of contrition for an alleged act of defeatism or disloyalty.[121]

Cognizant of the sudden political vulnerability of German Americans, in early 1917, leading Nebraska women's suffragists sought to come to an accommodation with their erstwhile foes.[122] They agreed to oppose efforts to ban German-language instruction in Nebraska's schools in return for the support of German American lawmakers for the passage of a partial women's suffrage law. After the 1917 anti–German language bill was stymied in the legislature, state senator John Mattes, a leading German American lawmaker, betrayed women's suffragists by organizing a signature-collection campaign to launch a referendum against the recently enacted partial women's suffrage law. Though suffragist leaders soon proved that fraudulent signatures had been used to initiate the referendum, Mattes's scheme succeeded in preventing the partial suffrage law from taking effect until after the 1918 midterms.[123]

Outraged, women's suffragists redoubled their efforts to harness rising anti-German sentiment in Nebraska to advance their cause. In one August 1917 issue alone, the NAWSA's *Woman Citizen* ran two articles that repeated long-standing claims that a powerful civic association in the state, the German–American Alliance, was a front for liquor interests, while adding the new argument that the group represented a disloyal organization in wartime.[124] A year later, the outlet contended that true "Nebraskans are indignant because their soldiers in the army are denied the right to vote while the country's enemies are entitled to participate in the government." The *Woman Citizen* further claimed that conscription data indicated "that approximately 20,000 men were claiming exemption from service" owing to alienage in the state. Such men, the publication reminded its readers, could still vote in Nebraska.[125] The *St. Louis Post–Dispatch* concurred that too many noncitizens, and enemy aliens in particular, were "taking advantage of their lack of second papers" to avoid the draft while "giving no indication of their intent to forego their voting privilege."[126]

In January 1918, the Nebraska Council of Defense endorsed repealing the state's alien suffrage law via constitutional amendment.[127] The council opposed efforts by women's suffragists to tack a female enfranchisement clause onto the same measure, however. Instead, a stand-alone anti-alien suffrage amendment was approved by state lawmakers and was submitted to the electorate for ratification in the fall.[128]

Democratic governor Keith Neville strongly backed the measure. In one of many speeches endorsing a ban on the use of German in schools and attacking "little Germanies," Neville turned his fire on the state's long-standing alien suffrage law. Far too often, he claimed, "the alien enemy and many other aliens"

Tägliche Omaha Tribüne

35. Jahrgang. Omaha, Neb., Donnerstag, den 7. November 1918 8 Seiten —Nr. 205.

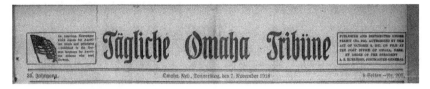

Figure 3.3 *Tägliche Omaha Tribüne*, November 7, 1918, 1. Courtesy of the University of Nebraska–Lincoln Library and History Nebraska.

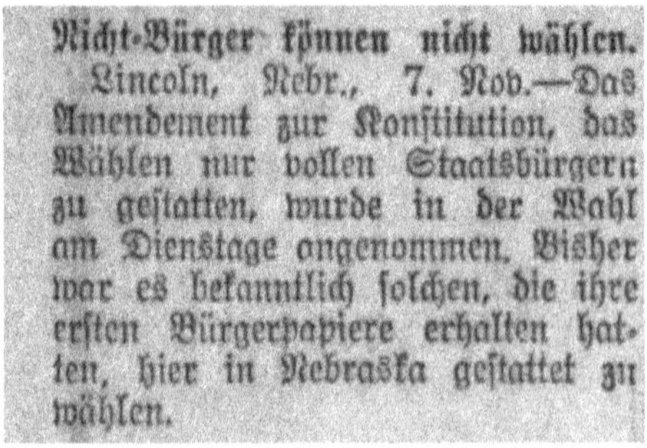

Nicht-Bürger können nicht wählen.

Lincoln, Nebr., 7. Nov.—Das Amendement zur Konstitution, das Wählen nur vollen Staatsbürgern zu gestatten, wurde in der Wahl am Dienstage angenommen. Bisher war es bekanntlich solchen, die ihre ersten Bürgerpapiere erhalten hatten, hier in Nebraska gestattet zu wählen.

Figure 3.4 "Nicht-Bürger Fönnen Nicht Wählen [Noncitizens Cannot Vote]," *Tägliche Omaha Tribüne*, November 7, 1918, 5. Courtesy of the University of Nebraska–Lincoln Library and History Nebraska.

took advantage of "every privilege of citizenship" while "evad[ing] military service." At a time when the country was "plunged into war" and its very "existence [was] at stake," he maintained voting should be restricted to US citizens.[129]

Nebraskans agreed. On November 7, 1918, the German-language *Tägliche Omaha Tribüne* reported that henceforth "Nicht-Bürger fönnen nicht wählen [Noncitizens Cannot Vote]."[130] The amendment had carried with 123,292 votes in favor and only 51,600 opposed (plus roughly 50,000 abstentions), thereby surmounting the state constitution's high hurdles to achieve ratification.[131]

A similar situation played out in Kansas, where the NAWSA supported an anti-alien suffrage amendment in the fall of 1918. The *Woman Citizen* claimed that it was no coincidence that Kansas, where women already possessed the ballot, was "first among the states" to view "the alien as a war problem." It applauded state legislators for submitting an amendment to the state's electorate aiming to repeal noncitizen voting rights soon "after war was declared."[132] Voters in Kansas ratified the measure by large margins in the fall of 1918. Over 235,000 Kansans voted in favor of the amendment while roughly 90,000 opposed it.[133] Though equal voting rights were not on the ballot in Kansas and Nebraska, state and national women's suffrage leaders directly tied their cause to the repeal of alien suffrage in both Plains states. Elsewhere, that connection was made even more concrete.

Some supporters of women's suffrage in Congress, including Republican senator Joseph Frelinghuysen of New Jersey and Democratic senator Thomas Gore of Oklahoma, proposed incorporating an alien suffrage ban into the wording of what would become the Nineteenth Amendment.[134] The NAWSA endorsed this approach in a front-page *Woman Citizen* article in July 1918. Believing noncitizen voting to be a relic of bygone times, it argued that "the urgent need of American democracy at this hour is standardization, and the keystone of that standardization in America, as President Wilson has pointed out, is the settlement of the woman suffrage question. With the settlement of that question a common ground of full citizenship as a basis for suffrage should be found for men and women without discrimination."[135] Such proposals to turn voting into an exclusive federal right of US citizenship were not adopted, but a similar effort was already underway at the state level in South Dakota.[136]

South Dakota, home to many German immigrants and German-descended Russian migrants, had long been a major disappointment to women's suffragists. Six previous women's suffrage campaigns had come up short in the state.[137]

As in other Plains states, South Dakota suffragists took advantage of the wartime situation. When the South Dakota legislature voted to tie American women's enfranchisement and noncitizen disfranchisement together on the same amendment, state suffragists made the repeal of alien suffrage central to their ratification campaign.[138] The NAWSA expressed confidence in April 1918 that "only the alien will vote against" the amendment.[139] Throughout the ensuing summer and fall campaign, South Dakota women's suffragists embraced this line, arguing, in the words of one local leader, that voters should "safeguard their homes by giving the ballot to the women of the state who are wholeheartedly with their country in its aims and purposes, and by taking political privilege from men who still admit their loyalty to the Kaiser."[140] As in neighboring Nebraska, opponents of noncitizen voting rights in South Dakota had an ally residing in their state's gubernatorial mansion. Republican governor Peter Norbeck argued that it was "high time to make citizenship a requirement for suffrage" in the few states, like South Dakota, that "at this time, unfortunately," continued to enfranchise noncitizen men.[141]

The South Dakota women's suffrage–alien disfranchisement measure was ratified by a roughly 20,000-vote majority.[142] Catt and other NAWSA officials were ecstatic. The *Woman Citizen* ran an article on the successful South Dakota campaign entitled, "How to Win a State," praising suffragists in the state for their strategy.[143] Catt and her colleagues would soon attempt to redeploy it in Texas.

The two largest immigrant communities in Texas were especially vulnerable at the time.[144] Germans and German Americans had come under widespread

90 DISPARATE REGIMES

surveillance during wartime and lost many partners in state politics. Mexican immigrants and Mexican Americans had even fewer Anglo allies. Their political and civil rights had been increasingly restricted in Jim Crow Texas, while many had borne witness to or been victims of white supremacist terror and state violence amid cross-border spillover conflicts during the Mexican Revolution.[145]

In January 1918, Texas attorney general B. F. Looney announced that all enemy aliens—including immigrants who possessed first papers—would be barred from voting while the United States was at war with their nation.[146] That same year, state legislators barred noncitizens from voting in primary elections while simultaneously granting that right to American women. But they would need a state constitutional amendment to extend this policy to general elections.[147]

Because no southern state had yet enfranchised women on an equal basis to men, Texas suffragists were reluctant to launch a state constitutional amendment campaign for women's equal voting rights. Their ostensible allies in the legislature nevertheless thrust one upon them following the 1918 midterm elections. Seeking to boost participation on a forthcoming prohibition ballot measure in 1919, Texas legislators voted to send a state constitutional amendment proposing to enfranchise US citizen women and to disfranchise noncitizen men to the electorate at the same time. Women's suffragists, who had struggled for decades to create distance between their own movement and that of prohibitionists, fought in vain to block the joint amendment behind the scenes.[148] State and national women's suffrage leaders placed their hopes in trying to replicate their peers' success in South Dakota by attempting to sway native-born, white men—even those who had long resisted women's equal suffrage rights—to vote in favor of the measure.[149]

During the ensuing campaign, many white, middle-class suffragists and their supporters attacked Germans and German Americans as agents of an enemy power while arguing that the amendment was necessary to reduce the weight of voters of Mexican origin, whom they frequently described as uneducated and racially inferior. Shortly before the end of the war, the *Woman Citizen* had declared that "Texas women urgently appealed for the vote" because the "state does not permit its soldiers to vote, even when in camp in Texas," though it allowed for noncitizen voting.[150] Catt later described this as intolerable since "men in sympathy with our enemy country in time of war...could actually decide" the state's fate.[151] The *El Paso Herald* claimed that lawmakers "whose pockets bulge with poll tax receipts to be distributed among ignorant Mexican voters doubtless will lead the opposition to suffrage. The intelligent votes of American women they can't control."[152] The men of Texas delivered a stinging defeat to suffragists, rejecting the joint women's suffrage–anti-alien suffrage amendment by roughly 25,000 votes (while the prohibition measure was adopted).[153]

Fortunately for the women's suffrage cause, within weeks, Texas voters approved the federal Nineteenth Amendment, becoming the first southern state to do so. Consequently, noncitizen men would go to the polls alongside (in practice, overwhelmingly white) women for the first time in a Jim Crow Texas general election in 1920. It would also be the last. Armed with the franchise, women's suffragists appealed to their allies in the legislature to put another amendment before voters to repeal the state's alien suffrage law for good. State and national suffrage leaders, most Texas politicians, and an increasingly anti-immigrant press in Texas exhorted voters to repeal noncitizen voting during a summer campaign in 1921. The amendment was ratified, albeit narrowly, with just under 52 percent of ballots cast in favor.[154]

Three other states would repeal alien suffrage laws in the 1920s: Arkansas, Indiana, and Missouri. Noncitizen voting rights had long endured in these states, in large part owing to their particularly high bars for constitutional reform. When *Everybody's Magazine*, a public affairs publication, asked politicians from these states in November 1918 what, if anything, they were doing to repeal noncitizen voting rights, Indiana governor James P. Goodrich replied that he would take action if he could. But he bemoaned the fact that it would take "at least four years to change the constitution."[155] Goodrich was not exaggerating. Indiana's constitution required that back-to-back sessions of both chambers of the legislature approve a constitutional amendment before it could be sent to the electorate for ratification.[156] For its part, the Arkansas constitution required aye votes to outnumber nays and abstentions on such ballot measures.[157] Meanwhile, in Missouri, an alliance of self-styled election reformers had fought unsuccessfully throughout the Progressive Era to convene a constitutional assembly to alter their state's highest laws.[158]

Missouri had a modest immigrant presence in 1920. A total of 5.5 percent of the state's residents—186,835 individuals—were foreign-born. Germans were the most numerous among them.[159] As in Texas, the Missouri attorney general unilaterally declared in 1918 that enemy alien men were ineligible to vote notwithstanding their possession of first papers.[160] The Missouri Council of Defense spread word of this ruling widely, sending 5,000 posters announcing the ban to polling places throughout the state.[161] The St. Louis Board of Elections even threatened to indict any local official who permitted an enemy alien to vote in the 1918 midterms.[162]

Despite an ensuing dramatic drop in the number of noncitizen voters casting ballots in Missouri, some state politicians remained hesitant to support the total repeal of noncitizen voting rights. Missouri governor Frederick Gardner only indicated that an amendment to the state constitution to end alien suffrage

92　DISPARATE REGIMES

was part of his long-term agenda.[163] Women's suffragists were unimpressed. They claimed that leading Missouri politicians, especially US senator James Reed, opposed the women's suffrage cause owing to their reliance on German votes.[164]

Election reformers in Missouri finally succeeded in their quest to organize a constitutional assembly in 1921. While the ensuing 1922–23 convention did not produce a new state constitution, the electorate was asked to vote on a flurry of constitutional amendments arising from it. One such measure put to voters in November 1922 sought to eliminate the state constitution's now-obsolete suffrage clause restricting voting rights to "males." Most newspapers at the time failed to notice that this amendment sponsored by the League of Women Voters—later ratified by a sizeable majority of roughly 84,000 votes—seemed poised to repeal noncitizen voting rights in Missouri.[165] While the ballot itself only informed voters that the amendment would "eliminate[] the requirement that a voter must be a 'male' citizen of the United States," the full text of the measure also removed all previous state constitutional "reference to voting upon the declaration of intention to become a citizen." As the *St. Louis Post–Dispatch* wrote a month after the election, "The effects of the amendment will be more far-reaching than is indicated by the caption on the Constitutional ballot."[166]

The impacts of the measure were indeed sweeping. The following February, St. Louis elections officials asked the state attorney general's office to issue a ruling on whether the amendment had disfranchised voters who held first papers. Emma Bobb, the chief elections clerk in St. Louis, estimated that if this were the case, approximately 25,000 voters would lose suffrage rights in the city alone. Although most voters had not known that they were casting ballots on whether to repeal alien suffrage the previous year, state assistant attorney general Merrill Otis issued an opinion that the measure had done just that.[167]

A year later, opponents of noncitizen voting rights sought to reiterate that Missouri had indeed become a citizen-only suffrage state. At a special election organized in February 1924, Missourians cast ballots on twenty-one additional proposed amendments. One sought to enact numerous changes to and clarifications of the state's election laws. Its provisions included banning "insane" persons from voting, empowering the state legislature to enact voter registration requirements, and allowing for the inspection of ballots in the case of suspected fraud. The measure would also make explicit that only US citizens could vote in Missouri elections. This second amendment was ratified, with 53.5 percent of votes cast in favor (175,589) and 46.5 percent of ballots opposed (152,713).[168]

While the League of Women Voters had supported the amendment that ultimately repealed noncitizen voting rights in Missouri, the organization played a more overt role in Indiana. Critics of alien suffrage laws like Progressive Era scholar Hattie Plum Williams, election reformer Ross Franklin Lockridge Sr., and US vice president Thomas Marshall (a former state governor) had often pointed to low naturalization rates in Indiana to claim that noncitizen voting rights actively hindered the incorporation of immigrants into the state and national polity.[169] Though immigrants made up only about one in every twenty residents of Indiana in 1920, the state's arduous constitutional amendment process had helped stymie multiple previous efforts by state legislators to repeal alien suffrage rights.[170]

Despite those defeats, state authorities unilaterally banned enemy aliens from voting in the midterm elections of 1918. US attorney L. Ert Slack threatened to arrest any such person who tried to cast a ballot.[171] Two years later, state authorities pointed to the continued absence of a formal peace treaty with Germany to retain that unilateral ban. By that point, a constitutional amendment aiming to prevent all noncitizens from voting in future elections had been approved for the first time by state legislators. Following the swift reapproval of the measure in 1921 by the subsequent legislature, the amendment was sent to the state's electorate for ratification.[172]

Opponents of noncitizen voting rights, most notably the state branch of the League of Women Voters, campaigned in support of the amendment, which also removed the state constitution's now defunct provisions restricting suffrage rights to men. Asking Indianans, "Shall Citizens of Indiana or Aliens Make Our Laws?" the league launched "a systematic campaign of education for the amendment." The campaign concluded with a "'Bill Board Saturday'…when flag-decorated automobiles filled with men and women dashed from place to place putting up posters" and canvassing voters. One league leader argued that it had "been left to two groups—the women and the soldiers—to push this amendment. To the soldier, citizenship and the right to be an American is something he has pledged his life for. It is a definite and tangible thing to be protected and developed. To the women who were so long disfranchised, the right to vote takes its true place as the most prized gift of citizenship—its crown and seal."[173] The state Chamber of Commerce also staunchly backed the amendment, while the *Indianapolis Star* ran numerous opinion pieces and editorials in support of it.[174]

By a majority of nearly 50,000 (130,242 votes in favor to 80,574 ballots opposed), in September 1921, Indiana voters repealed their state's long-standing alien suffrage law.[175] In the aftermath of their victory, League of Women Voters activists pressed GOP and Democratic leaders and local and state election authorities to ensure that noncitizens were promptly removed from voter registration rolls and barred from access to the ballot at future elections.[176] Over the coming months and years, Indiana would become the epicenter of the reborn nativist Ku Klux Klan of the 1920s.[177]

State alien suffrage laws ultimately died an anticlimactic death in the United States a few years later. Arkansans had voted on an amendment to repeal alien suffrage rights in 1920. While this measure received far more ayes than nays

94 DISPARATE REGIMES

(87,237 to 49,757), so many Arkansans opted not to vote on the question that the measure did not surmount the state constitution's requirement that the amendment receive a majority of all ballots cast at the election. In 1926, the Arkansas Supreme Court ruled that constitutional amendments voted on since 1910 were no longer bound by that requirement. The 1920 measure was retroactively declared ratified. Suddenly, in a polity where fewer than one of every hundred residents was an immigrant, the last remaining state alien suffrage law was rescinded in the United States.[178]

* * *

The overturning of noncitizen voting rights by thirteen state constitutional amendment campaigns dramatically transformed the meaning and weight of citizenship rights as citizen-only rights in the United States. The repeal of these long-standing alien suffrage laws helped turn voting into the preeminent right exclusive to American citizens. To be sure, the demise of alien suffrage had minimal effects on the politics of Arkansas or the overall size of the electorate in Indiana. But successful efforts to repeal noncitizen voting rights did significantly impact the polities of and political life within many midwestern, southern, and western states. The restriction of suffrage rights to (some) US citizens across the country also amounted to a significant retreat—but not total overturning—of the disparate regimes of citizenship rights in the polity on a state-by-state basis that had proliferated in the nineteenth-century United States.

The end of noncitizen voting rights across the country was not a foregone conclusion. It was the result of discrete state-by-state political disputes over the meaning of US citizenship and voting rights. National political actors—particularly elite immigration restrictionists, election reformers, and women's suffragists—often helped put a spotlight on and encouraged the repeal of state noncitizen voting laws during the late Gilded Age and Progressive Era. But these campaigns centered on the partisan, interest group, and ethno-racial politics of the state electorates debating such amendments. During and shortly after World War I, the rhetoric and focus of those campaigns shifted as women's suffragists and their successors increasingly took the lead, arguing for the standardization of voting rights nationwide. But even in the context of wartime nationalism and postwar nativism, opponents of noncitizen voting rights in states like Nebraska, South Dakota, Texas, Missouri, and Indiana had to battle hard to invent suffrage as a de jure citizenship right and a citizen-only right within their respective polities.

Disparate Regimes: Nativist Politics, Alienage Law, and Citizenship Rights in the United States, 1865–1965.
Brendan A. Shanahan, Oxford University Press. © Brendan A. Shanahan 2025.
DOI: 10.1093/9780197660577.003.0004

4

Who Counts in the Polity?

Noncitizens, Apportionment, and Representation in the Early to Mid-Twentieth Century

When a new year dawned in January 1893, New York Democrats were feeling optimistic. They were entering their eleventh consecutive year in control of the gubernatorial mansion in Albany, and one of their own, Grover Cleveland, a former Buffalo mayor and past state governor, would return to the White House after winning the 1892 presidential election. Democrats had done so well in recent elections that they had managed to overcome the state constitution's apportionment provisions—which overrepresented small, Grand Old Party (GOP)–friendly, upstate counties to the detriment of New York City's largely Democratic boroughs—to achieve rare majorities in both chambers of the state legislature. Cognizant that this was a unique opportunity to amend those apportionment provisions, New York Democratic lawmakers swiftly maneuvered to hold a state constitutional convention in 1894. The timing proved inauspicious.[1]

Following the onset of the Panic of 1893, New York voters swung hard against the governing Democrats in elections held later that autumn. The GOP regained control of the legislature and won a majority of delegates for the upcoming constitutional convention.[2] There, Republican delegates passed new egregious malapportionment schemes, granting a minimum representation to all counties in the State Assembly and capping the total number of seats allocated to urban centers in the Senate.[3] As depression set in, New York voters jettisoned all remaining Democratic statewide officeholders in the 1894 midterms while ratifying the GOP-backed constitution and an apportionment-specific amendment by sizeable majorities.[4]

Despite significant news coverage of apportionment battles in New York, little attention was paid to one feature the new constitution retained: an anti-alien clause that counted noncitizens out of the population for the purposes of representation.[5] Fighting a rearguard retreat against the GOP's broader malapportionment plans, Democratic delegates barely even mustered symbolic opposition to this long-standing nativist provision.[6] But state Democrats would long encounter its full weight. While New York City was home to more than

96 DISPARATE REGIMES

half of the state's total population in 1910, its hundreds of thousands of noncitizens were not counted for the purposes of apportionment. The city thus received nowhere near half the seats of either chamber of the legislature.[7] The anti-alien clause, in combination with the state's other malapportionment provisions, helped transform the Democratic Party into a near-permanent legislative minority. As Democratic governor Al Smith would later observe, the legislature of the nation's most populous state had become "constitutionally Republican."[8]

While battles over state anti-alien apportionment schemes had been debated in all regions of the country during the nineteenth century, they grew more acute in the early twentieth century. By the 1920s, roughly a dozen states— ranging from those with some of the smallest immigrant populations in the country (North Carolina) to those with the largest (New York)—counted some or all noncitizens out of the population for the purposes of apportionment.[9] One related federal dispute became so heated that Congress failed to reappor- tion at all after the 1920 census for the first and only time in US history.[10]

Anti-alien schemes were not the only forms of early- to mid-twentieth- century state legislative malapportionment. Like New York, many other states made political units, such as counties or municipalities, the key basis for allo- cating seats to their legislatures. In Rhode Island, every town and city received one state senator, regardless of population, until 1928. Such policies could pro- duce truly egregious inequities in representation. In 1900, the 606 residents of West Greenwich held the same sway in the Rhode Island State Senate as did the 175,597 residents of Providence.[11] Alternatively, once in power, majority party lawmakers often brazenly flouted state constitutional obligations to reappor- tion their legislatures on a regular basis. New York state lawmakers, for instance, unconstitutionally retained the same apportionment between 1917 and 1943.[12] Other states went far longer. As legal scholar Hugh Bone bemoaned in 1952, "Despite the fact that all but a half dozen states call for reapportionment every 10 years or less, only 11 states...can be said to have partially or fully complied with this time requirement since 1930."[13]

Mid-twentieth-century trade unions, opposition parties, middle-class "good government" organizations, and scholar-activists challenged these types of malapportionment, both in the courtroom and in the court of popular opinion. Their efforts largely succeeded in the "redistricting" cases of the 1960s, wherein the Warren-era Supreme Court ruled that the federal constitution required states to regularly reapportion their legislatures and mandated a roughly equal population basis of apportionment for those districts.[14]

Disputes over the adoption, repeal, and/or implementation of nativist provi- sions have usually been portrayed as tangential to the history of redistricting and reapportionment reform. This chapter, by contrast, underscores both their centrality to the gradual unwinding of disparate regimes in the American polity on a state-by-state basis and their importance to the invention of citizenship rights as citizen-only rights in US history.[15] To do so, it recounts fierce debates over these policies at several World War I–era state constitutional conventions and explains how and why they triggered considerable state and federal reapportionment gridlock in the early to mid-twentieth century. It then shows how surviving state anti-alien apportionment provisions finally met their end in the mid- to late twentieth century owing to their tortuous enforcement and redundancy amid broader, national redistricting and reapportionment reforms.

The combination of logistical and constitutional mechanics and sectional and factional politics greatly shaped the evolution, longevity, and ultimate demise of nativist state apportionment policies. While lawmakers who embraced inclusive immigrant rights rhetoric were sometimes able to defeat proposed anti-alien schemes when they benefited from high constitutional hurdles, such arguments generally proved insufficient when they tried to repeal extant nativist apportionment policies from the time of World War I to the civil rights era. Instead, partisan, intraparty, and sectional rivalries more often collided with anti-alien apportionment schemes to produce sustained gridlock. Supporters of including noncitizens in apportionment policies, in turn, increasingly emphasized the convoluted, impractical, and arcane enforcement of such provisions as part of a broader redistricting and reapportionment reform movement in the mid- to late twentieth century. They ultimately succeeded in court and even more so at the ballot box during the civil rights era, when all surviving state anti-alien apportionment provisions were repealed via constitutional amendment or fell into desuetude.

Debating Citizenship Rights as Citizen-Only Rights in the World War I–Era Polity

The first quarter of the twentieth century was a time of significant constitutional reform in the United States. After a forty-three-year-long hiatus since the ratification of the last federal amendment in 1870, the national constitution was amended four times in rapid succession between 1913 and 1920. State constitutional reform was also heightened during these years. Lawmakers and voters took up a variety of amendments, ranging in subject from direct democracy reforms (empowering the electorate to initiate laws, veto bills, and/or recall sitting lawmakers) to nativist public policy measures (such as California's infamous anti-Japanese Alien Land Law of 1920).[16] Meanwhile, seventeen states launched constitutional conventions between 1896 and 1923. Three even held

98 DISPARATE REGIMES

multiple such assemblies during that narrow time span.[17] State legislative reapportionment policies were often a major reason for convening them.[18]

Anti-alien apportionment policies emerged as an especially significant topic of debate at three World War I–era assemblies. In Massachusetts, leading Boston Democrats blasted their state's long-standing "legal voter" apportionment policy as nativist and outdated. In New Hampshire, small-town GOP delegates sought to adopt a new nativist apportionment scheme for their state legislature's lower chamber. In Nebraska, proposals to exclude noncitizens became tied to a broader, powerful strain of nativism during and in the aftermath of World War I. Constitutional mechanics—which usually favored delegates seeking to retain existing policies—would prove crucial to the success or failure of those proposals. Of the three, only Nebraska, where anti-German sentiment reached its greatest expression in the nation during the late 1910s, altered its apportionment policy vis-à-vis noncitizens.

Reapportioning the lower chamber of the Massachusetts General Court proved to be a complicated affair in the early twentieth century. The state constitution stipulated that the 240 seats of the Massachusetts House of Representatives had to be reapportioned every ten years "equally, as nearly as may be," on the basis of the "relative numbers of legal voters" residing in the state. While municipalities were theoretically responsible for identifying the number of legal voters residing within their jurisdiction, the General Court had, in practice, transferred that work to the state Bureau of Statistics of Labor in the mid- to late nineteenth century. Local and county officials still retained significant power in the adoption and administration of apportionment policies, however. While the state census determined how many seats each county would receive, it was local and county officials who delegated them to various subdivisions (i.e., towns and city wards) within their jurisdiction.[19]

As chairman of the Suffolk County Apportionment Commission in 1916, James Brennan possessed considerable power to influence how many House seats would be allocated to each of Boston's twenty-six wards and those of the neighboring Winthrop, Chelsea, and Revere.[20] Brennan, a leading Democratic powerbroker and former state senator, lobbied his fellow commissioners to adopt an apportionment policy favorable to himself and to his partisan and factional allies, most notably Democratic state representative Martin Lomasney, the well-known "ward boss" of Boston's West End neighborhood.[21] Under Brennan's leadership, the commission allocated two House seats to Brennan's own Ward 3 (home to 4,854 legal voters) and three seats to Lomasney's Ward 5 (which contained 7,946 legal voters). Conversely, it assigned just one seat to Ward 23 (home to 5,596 legal voters and the city's GOP leader Herman Hormet) and apportioned only two seats to Ward 6 (home to a rival Democratic leader, city clerk James Donovan, and 8,618 legal voters).[22] These were but the

WHO COUNTS IN THE POLITY? 99

most blatant of several violations of the state constitution's apportionment provisions. GOP leaders filed multiple lawsuits contesting the (state) constitutionality of these reapportionment plans. Brennan's opponents even threatened to pursue criminal charges against those responsible for what they viewed as a blatantly fraudulent plan.[23]

Brennan offered numerous extraconstitutional reasons for assigning extra seats to his own and Lomasney's wards. In court, he cited high levels of commercial development and important business interests in Wards 3 and 5 to support his contention that they were rapidly growing in population compared to other city neighborhoods. He also argued that because Lomasney's Ward 5 was one of "the most cosmopolitan communit[ies] in the country" and home to "every European Nation," it especially merited an additional seat.[24] But in an interview with the *Boston Globe*, Brennan implied that his commission was merely responding in kind to gerrymandering and malapportionment by small-town and suburban Republican officials elsewhere in the commonwealth, which, he argued, unfairly turned Democratic statewide electoral majorities into legislative minorities.[25] Unsurprisingly, Brennan's explanations did not hold up in state courtrooms. Twice the Massachusetts Supreme Judicial Court ordered Suffolk County officials to amend their reapportionment plans to comply with the commonwealth's constitutional requirements.[26]

Despite Brennan's scattershot efforts to justify his commission's apportionment plans, he chose not to center his arguments on one glaring inequity built directly into the state constitution: the state's legal voter apportionment basis itself. Both Brennan's and Lomasney's wards contained large noncitizen (and thus nonvoting) populations that were not counted for the purposes of representation. Though the recent state census enumerated only 7,946 legal voters in Lomasney's Ward 5, its total population was 77,573. In fact, Ward 5's enumerated population (which critics alleged was inflated by nonresident "mattress voters") outnumbered the city's second most populous district, Ward 2, by 35,669 residents.[27]

Brennan likely avoided this subject because, as the chairman of Suffolk County's Apportionment Commission, he was powerless to change the state constitution's legal voter apportionment clause and the inequalities in representation it produced in 1916. But that would change when he assumed a new position the following year.

In 1917, hundreds of delegates descended on Boston to participate in the commonwealth's first constitutional convention in over half a century. Brennan and Lomasney were both there, serving as prominent members of the Democratic caucus.[28] At the convention, they maintained that incorporating noncitizens into the state constitution's apportionment provisions was both a matter of fair play and an important means of recognizing immigrants' rights

100 DISPARATE REGIMES

and standing within the community. Brennan reminded his colleagues that the commonwealth's "forefathers" had, after all, "fought against taxation without representation."[29] Both pointed to the history of the Know-Nothing Party and argued that the legal voter basis was an odious relic of that nativist era.[30] Lomasney specifically argued that "the history of the country" since the 1850s should "convince you that you can trust the alien."[31] He did not mince words. Comparing supporters of an electorate-based apportionment standard to slave owners of the antebellum era, Lomasney warned his opponents to "not deceive" themselves into thinking that their "unfair opposition to the aliens will be successful forever."[32]

Lomasney and Brennan's lofty rhetoric did not sway Republican delegates (who were in the majority) and some small-town Democrats. Proponents of retaining the state's long-standing apportionment provisions pointed to wartime conscription policy whereby immigrant men who had not filed or withdrew their declarations of intention to become citizens were not subject to the draft (though they would be henceforth barred from naturalization if they did so).[33] Surely such men should not be counted, argued GOP delegate Charles Underhill of Somerville, who believed that this exemption had been used "altogether too frequently, to my mind and according to the reports of the drafting boards."[34] Republican delegate William Kinney of Boston expressed similar sentiments. "If ever there was an hour in the history of Massachusetts when an argument to take away from" citizens' "influence and transfer it to an alien population not subject to such civic obligations, should not be entertained," he maintained, "I think it is this."[35]

Opponents also resorted to blunt regional and/or xenophobic language. Delegate Timothy Quinn from the small town of Sharon argued against his fellow Democrats' proposal, countering that it "would be very unfair to the districts which have a small and stable population and would be advantageous to those populous centers, manufacturing centers, which have a large floating population."[36] Underhill, in turn, warned that while "the Irish race have made good citizens," he was less sure of other, more recent, immigrants. "Let us differentiate between aliens and aliens," he cautioned.[37]

Though Massachusetts lawmakers would not adopt an egregious malapportionment scheme akin to those found in neighboring Connecticut, Rhode Island, and New York (each of which explicitly overrepresented rural communities), Lomasney and Brennan were unable to convince their peers to do away with the commonwealth's legal voter standard.[38] The convention rejected their proposal by a nearly two-to-one margin.[39] Familiar battles were also fought in New Hampshire, but there it was nativists who sought to alter their state constitution's existing policy.

While it was far from the nation's most populous or urbanized state, New Hampshire experienced similar divisions between its small-town (heavily

Yankee Protestant) communities and its urban, industrial (often Catholic immigrant–origin) populations.[40] The State Senate's seats, unique among early-twentieth-century legislative chambers, were allocated on the basis of the amount of taxes paid by residents of each county. While the lower chamber employed a total population basis, its mechanics of reapportionment were also complex. Every town possessing at least 600 inhabitants was guaranteed a full-time representative. Municipalities with fewer than 600 residents received a part-time representative. By contrast, larger towns and cities were only assigned additional seats per 1,200 inhabitants.[41]

Not only did this policy unfairly favor rural residents over inhabitants of mill towns and cities, but also it produced a highly unwieldly chamber. Its huge, unfixed membership usually numbered around 400. Many Progressive Era commentators and lawmakers in New Hampshire pressed for a state constitutional convention. Upon receiving permission from voters in 1916, delegates met intermittently between 1918 and 1921 to debate numerous subjects, foremost among them reforming apportionment policy for the state's House of Representatives.[42]

Such was the context when Republican delegate Curtis Childs, from the small town of Henniker, "propose[d] to change the basis of our representation" to find a way to count noncitizens out of the state constitution's apportionment provisions. He specifically maligned southern and eastern European immigrants who mostly inhabited manufacturing cities like Manchester, to the detriment of his own country town. "Now, why should citizens of Turkey or Russia or Germany, and the gypsies of Austria-Hungary, have 30 or 40 representatives in our House?" he thundered.[43] Delegate James Lyford, a leading GOP politician from the state's relatively small capital city of Concord, supported a scheme to base apportionment on the number of votes cast in past elections. He admitted that "there will be a larger reduction from the manufacturing centers... owing to the[ir] alien population." But Lyford maintained that immigrants' "education and Americanization" was the proper "cure" for this problem.[44] Democrat Henry H. Metcalf, also of Concord, believed rural citizens were better people. "Cities are made up...largely of alien population, who have no interests in common with the average intelligent New Hampshire voter," he contended. Therefore, Metcalf insisted that "they are not entitled to the same consideration as the people in these little country towns upon which we must depend."[45]

As in Massachusetts, New Hampshire delegates who supported including noncitizens in apportionment provisions were fighting against a rising tide of wartime and postwar xenophobia. But several still staunchly defended the inclusion of all residents in apportionment policies as an affirmative right. Delegate Jeremiah Doyle, a leading Democrat and former mayor of the state's

102 DISPARATE REGIMES

second most populous city, Nashua, blasted claims that recent migrants were inferior to previous immigrants. "It was but a short time ago," Doyle reminded his nativist peers, that they had "referred to foreigners as the Irish and the French." Only presently did they "find fault with the Greeks, and...criticize the cities because the Greeks come there, and other nationalities." He also emphasized that immigrants paid taxes, performed military service, and created jobs. Doyle judged that his peers "ought to be ashamed of [them]selves to come here and be afraid of any foreigner, whatever country he may come from."[46] GOP delegate John Cavanaugh of Manchester, an Irish American Catholic, similarly implored his colleagues to "not speak too harshly of the alien" and asked them how their ancestors had come to live in the United States.[47]

Delegates did vote to marginally reduce the size of the state's lower legislative chamber (to between 300 and 325 members) and base apportionment on the number of ballots cast at presidential elections (thereby indirectly excluding noncitizens).[48] To achieve ratification, the measure had to receive a two-to-one margin of victory at the polls. Though a sizeable majority of New Hampshire voters supported the amendment's ratification at the 1920 fall elections, it narrowly failed to become part of the constitution by a 37 percent to 63 percent margin.[49] Thus, while constitutional mechanics in Massachusetts hindered efforts to repeal a long-standing nativist apportionment provision, in New Hampshire they played a crucial role in narrowly stymieing the adoption of a proposed similar scheme.

Votes-cast apportionment proposals were not unique to New Hampshire. Indiana and Illinois voters would reject similar constitutional measures in 1921 and 1922, respectively.[50] Votes-cast provisions either remained or became part of apportionment policies in Arizona, Idaho, and Kansas in the early to mid-twentieth century.[51] But nowhere did debates over such schemes so rapidly transform state constitutional law and politics as they did in Nebraska.

Though holding a constitutional convention had long been a goal of progressive reformers in Nebraska, its timing was not favorable to their cause. When it opened in late 1919, conservative policymakers significantly outnumbered their progressive peers.[52] Earlier that same year, Nebraska legislators had enacted the Siman Act, which banned almost all forms of instruction in languages other than English in public and private schools throughout the state. Delegates embraced similar policies at the convention, adopting amendments declaring English to be the state's official language and restricting the property ownership rights of noncitizens.[53]

In this xenophobic atmosphere, delegates in Nebraska also debated whether to amend the state constitution's total population apportionment basis. As in

WHO COUNTS IN THE POLITY? 103

New Hampshire, several delegates proposed adopting a votes-cast standard of apportionment to reduce the political power of Nebraska's immigrants.[54] Some, like Democrat Earl Marvin, hailing from the small town of Beatrice, wanted to go further. He proposed imposing a hard cap on the number of seats apportioned to heavily populated counties, especially Douglas County, home to Omaha.[55] Marvin argued it was necessary to "reduce some of the representations of these alien elements, and the third ward controlled vote, and the gang that is delivered in blocks of five and that sort of thing."[56]

Unlike convention debates in Massachusetts and New Hampshire, few delegates rose to oppose nativist proposals in Nebraska. One delegate, Isaiah Lafayette Albert, might have been expected to lead the opposition. A distinguished former judge and past Democratic state senator, Albert would play a crucial role in ultimately successful litigation to overturn the Siman Act.[57] He would later write in the pages of the *North American Review* that most of the so-called "'alien element'" in Nebraska had "been swift to adopt our manners and customs, to identify itself with our institutions and to educate its children in English."[58] However, at the convention, Albert actually served as the initial author of the votes-cast reapportionment proposal.[59] He maintained that it was necessary to exclude residents who had "no settled interest in the state or the community" from Nebraska's "basis of representation."[60]

The most powerful adversary of a votes-cast apportionment basis, delegate A. R. Oleson, supported its principles but feared its possible unintended consequences far more. Oleson, a former Republican state senator from sparsely populated Cuming County, warned fellow rural delegates that it might inadvertently empower politicians in heavily populated Douglas County, since Omaha possessed a large "floating population" of single, voting-eligible, young men.[61] To mitigate this danger, he suggested counting noncitizens out of the population instead. Oleson's peers incorporated this language into a broader proposed reapportionment amendment, which the convention approved by a three-to-one margin.[62]

This proposal still had to receive the support of the state's electorate to achieve ratification. To ensure that delegates' work would not be stymied by abstentions, a special election was organized in September 1920.[63] Few voters turned out at the polls. While more than 380,000 Nebraskans would participate in the presidential election that November, less than 100,000 voted in September. Nevertheless, most who did vote cast affirmative ballots for all amendments. Each attained ratification. The anti-alien apportionment amendment won by a comfortable three-to-one margin.[64] In the span of less than two years, Nebraska lawmakers and voters disfranchised noncitizen immigrants and promptly counted them out of the polity altogether.

104   DISPARATE REGIMES

Malapportioned Gridlock in the States and in Congress

Like many states, Congress had long found reapportionment policy for its lower chamber to be a challenge. In the nineteenth century, congressmen often battled over various methods of calculating proper ratios of representation. When faced with reducing a state's delegation, Congress generally found it expedient to add extra seats for other states. In this manner, the House would grow from 65 members in 1789 to 435 in the reapportionment that followed in the wake of the 1910 census.

Decennial reapportionment continued to befuddle Congress in the early to mid-twentieth century. After the 1920 enumeration, politicians from states that were set to lose seats and their allies in Congress protested their impending loss of power. Pointing to census results that showed, for the first time, that most of the nation's population lived in urban centers, they transformed debates over reapportionment into a major struggle between rural and urban interests. They soon identified counting noncitizens out of the national population for the purposes of federal apportionment policy as their strongest pretext to cling to power.[65]

Most of the states that were going to lose seats—such as Alabama, Indiana, and Nebraska—had recently experienced lower-than-average rates of immigration and/or witnessed significant outmigration. Politicians from these states argued it was unfair that their proportionally large native-born, US citizen populations would lose power at the expense of growing noncitizen immigrant populations in states like California, Michigan, and New York.[66] As early as January 1921, legislation was introduced in Congress to keep noncitizens out of the next reapportionment.[67] Though some Republican congressional leaders (who controlled an enormous majority in 1921 and 1922) were amenable to such a policy, this approach threatened to split their caucus, and that of the Democratic Party, along sectional and urban–rural lines. No federal reapportionment legislation became law in time for the 1922 midterms. A lengthy stalemate then ensued. Throughout the 1920s, Congress remained apportioned on the basis of the 1910 enumeration.[68]

Many members of Congress who wanted to exclude noncitizens from representation could not contain their fury at the thought of their states' ceding power in national politics to states whose noncitizen immigrant populations had grown since the 1910 census. Republican senator Frederic Sackett of Kentucky wanted to know why a "great body of aliens who make no effort to become citizens should have a voice in determining the representation of native-born citizens."[69] Senator Hugo Black, a Democrat from Alabama, turned his ire on undocumented immigrants when protesting the inclusion of noncitizens in congressional reapportionment.[70] Democratic congressman John Rankin of Mississippi, an especially noxious white supremacist, claimed that California, which was poised to gain "nine additional seats" after the 1930 enumeration, unfairly benefited from the inclusion of "thousands of Mexicans and oriental aliens" in the count.[71] GOP representative Homer Hoch of Kansas was likewise irate that his "state [would] lose one member and New York gain four members through inclusion of thousands of unnaturalized aliens."[72]

But it was not just rural legislators who protested. The New York State Women's Republican Club endorsed the exclusion of noncitizens from the next round of congressional reapportionment. The *New York Times* reported in 1929 that the organization's treasurer, E. M. Dickinson, backed such provisions since she believed "crime could be traced in most instances to alien criminals and that hospitals for the insane are filled mostly with aliens and children of aliens." In Dickinson's words, congressmen should place "their political plums second to patriotism."[73] Other conservative activists, especially prohibition supporters, fought vociferously for a citizen-only apportionment policy.[74] Southern Methodist bishop James Cannon Jr. argued that this was "the most important legislative proposition before the country." Without its adoption, he feared that federal prohibition would be gravely wounded owing to the composition of the next Congress.[75]

Though proponents of excluding noncitizens were often quite explicit in their eugenicist views, ideological commitments, and partisan or sectional interests, some claimed their scheme was also needed to invent citizenship rights as citizen-only rights. Congressman Hoch insisted that he was not "attack[ing]" noncitizens or trying "to take any rights away from" them, but instead defending the rights of American citizens. If an immigrant chose not to naturalize, "in fairness," Hoch asked, "should [he or she] be counted"? Hoch also accused fellow GOP representative Fiorello La Guardia of New York—who adamantly fought for the inclusion of noncitizens in federal reapportionment policy—of hypocrisy, pointing out that New York's state legislature had long excluded noncitizens in its own reapportionment provisions.[76]

Proponents of including noncitizens in congressional reapportionment fought back hard against this onslaught. Pointing to the growing inequalities in representation wrought by the prolonged stalemate, Republican representative James Beck of Pennsylvania accused his colleagues of "virtually" effecting "a coup d'état."[77] The *Chicago Tribune* argued in December 1928 that the continued failure to reapportion the House since the 1920 census was the equivalent of disfranchising 10 million Americans.[78]

Some advocates also staunchly defended noncitizen immigrants' inclusion in the count as an indirect form of representation that rightly belonged to them.[79] Republican congressman John Schafer of Wisconsin decried anti-alien proposals as "taxation without representation." They were especially unjust, he contended,

106 DISPARATE REGIMES

given that many noncitizens had answered the recent call to arms.[80] For his part, Beck averred that a noncitizen "from my district is a constituent of mine," since he or she must "obey the laws which I help to make." As his constituents, Beck believed they were owed representation.[81]

Immigrant rights defenders also had an ace up their sleeve. Throughout the 1920s, the National Association for the Advancement of Colored People (NAACP) and allied northern politicians, led by Massachusetts Republican congressman George Tinkham, clamored for the enforcement of the Fourteenth Amendment's "penalty clause" whereby states were supposed to lose seats in Congress if they disfranchised American citizens. When southern Democratic politicians insisted on excluding noncitizens from reapportionment, Tinkham demanded that their states lose House seats owing to the mass disfranchisement of African Americans across the South.[82]

To break the gridlock, in 1929 Republican senator Arthur Vandenberg of Michigan, a proponent of including noncitizens, suggested taking reapportionment away from Congress altogether. He proposed legislation to empower the US Census Bureau to determine how many seats should be allocated to each state. GOP congressional leaders craftily maneuvered to pass Vandenberg's legislation without penalizing southern states. They combined two competing reapportionment measures—one barring noncitizens from the count and the other requiring the enforcement of the Fourteenth Amendment's penalty clause—as a joint amendment to Vandenberg's bill. GOP leaders knew that many members supported one of the two provisions, but few supported both. As expected, the joint amendment was defeated. Shortly thereafter, the original apportionment bill including noncitizens in the count proceeded to a final vote, was adopted, and was signed into law on June 19, 1929.[83]

Opponents of counting noncitizens would continue to fight on. They even succeeded in having bills favorably reported out of committee as late as 1931.[84] But Vandenberg called their bluff, announcing that he would be amenable to an exclusion of noncitizens if federal reapportionment policy were set to the number of actual votes cast in recent elections. Owing to a dramatic drop in voter registration and electoral participation across the South following the onset of Jim Crow suffrage restrictions, Vandenburg's counterproposal threatened to reduce the representation of both Mississippi and Alabama in the House from eight to two seats.[85] Though they continued to protest, southern Democrats and rural Republicans furtively folded their increasingly weak hand. When the House was reapportioned following the 1930 census, noncitizens were included in the tally. They have been ever since.[86]

Republican congressional leaders, particularly House majority leader John Tilson of Connecticut, were given credit for shepherding the apportionment bill through the "Alien and Negro" controversy, as it was described at the time.[87]

Nearly three decades later, scholar Orville Sweeting published a fawning article depicting Tilson as a hero, highlighting quotations from the congressman where he implored his colleagues to "lay aside petty differences on immaterial things" and instead "pass through the House a census bill and an apportionment bill, a duty...too long delayed."[88] Many reporters' coverage of the debate tacitly concurred.[89]

Writing in the African American paper the *New York Amsterdam News*, scholar and civil rights activist Kelly Miller offered a rare rebuke. Having already fiercely challenged the Census Bureau over what he believed to be a

Figure 4.1 "Kelly Miller, LL.D.; Professor of Mathematics, Howard University, Washington, D.C.; Corresponding Secretary, National Sociological Society; Member of the Commission on the Race Problem, Sociological Society." Schomburg Center for Research in Black Culture, Jean Blackwell Hutson Research and Reference Division, The New York Public Library. New York Public Library Digital Collections, b11583854. https://digitalcollections.nypl.org/items/510d47df-b747-a3d9-e040-e00a18064a99.

108   DISPARATE REGIMES

widespread undercount of African Americans, Miller admitted that he found the idea of counting noncitizens out of the population to be reasonable because they were not required to perform military service.[90] But he correctly asserted that the entire dispute had been a farce since the "Federal Constitution...places the basis of representation upon the number of persons in the several states." By treating nativist federal reapportionment proposals as legitimate, Miller pointed to an obvious but oft-unspoken reality. Advocates of Vandenberg's reapportionment bill were conceding to an approach whereby "the South would let the North observe the Constitution," only if "the North, in turn, would let the South violate it" by disfranchising African Americans but benefiting from their numbers for the purposes of representation. "As always, the Negro is made the football, to be kicked back and forth between parties, interests, and sections," Miller ruefully concluded.[91]

Though anti-alien proposals would reappear in subsequent federal apportionment legislation, such nativist bills never came as close to passage as they had in 1929.[92] Politicians articulating immigrant rights claims could thus be successful in rearguard reapportionment battles in the early to mid-twentieth century. But such rhetoric would prove insufficient ammunition to overcome entrenched nativist provisions in force in states like New York.

* * *

When Kansas representative Homer Hoch rose in 1928 to accuse fellow Republican congressman Fiorello La Guardia of hypocrisy for his position on federal reapportionment, their colleagues must have known that he was taking a cheap shot at La Guardia's expense. La Guardia nevertheless opted to clarify that "up-State people trying to cut down the representation from New York City" were responsible for the inclusion of an anti-alien clause in his state's constitution and that he was "ashamed of it."[93] A few months later, another congressman from New York City, Democrat Emanuel Celler, also argued in favor of repealing the provision from the New York constitution. He stressed that the policy led to dramatic inequities in the relative power of New York City's residents in the state legislature compared to inhabitants of Upstate New York. Moreover, since noncitizens paid taxes (and, as he noted, more than two-thirds of the state's taxes came from New York City), Celler argued that the clause essentially meant immigrants were being "taxed without representation."[94]

Pleas by La Guardia and Celler for apportionment reform largely fell on deaf ears in Albany during the winter of 1928–29. Though state legislative districts had not been reallocated since 1917—in defiance of New York's constitutional requirement of a decennial reapportionment—upstate GOP state lawmakers were content to benefit from the gridlock. Though Democrats held uninterrupted control of New York's gubernatorial mansion between 1923 and 1942, the GOP usually controlled both chambers of the state legislature. Democratic statewide victories only translated into legislative majorities if the party won by huge margins in New York. Since Republicans remained competitive in statewide elections in New York during the late 1920s, the electoral conditions necessary for reapportionment reform seemed distant.[95]

The stock market crash of 1929 and the ensuing Great Depression dramatically altered the electoral calculus in New York. Governor Franklin Roosevelt, who had bested the GOP nominee by less than 1 percent of the vote in 1928, was re-elected by a gargantuan twenty-four-point margin in 1930.[96] Two years later, Roosevelt was elevated to the White House, and New York Democrats won all statewide elections and gained control of the State Senate for the first time in ten years. Buoyed by the New Deal's popularity, in 1934, Democrats won a narrow majority of seats in the State Assembly for the first time in more than two decades.[97] Despite these electoral victories, reforming the state's apportionment policy would not be easy.

While intraparty battles between Tammany Hall and "independent" factions of the New York Democratic Party were not new, they became particularly pronounced in the early New Deal years. Tammany-backed Democrats battled with powerful "independent" Democrats such as New York secretary of state Edward Flynn (the Democratic "boss" in the Bronx), Roosevelt, and his gubernatorial successor, Herbert Lehman, for control over nominations, patronage, and the allocation of relief and public works funds. This infighting grew so pronounced that competing Tammany and anti-Tammany candidates split Democrats' ballots in New York City's 1933 mayoral election, enabling a progressive Republican, La Guardia, to capture the office.[98]

These intraparty battles among Democrats could not have come at a worse time for supporters of state legislative reapportionment reform in New York. Following their midterm victories in 1934, Democratic leaders eagerly discussed ambitious reapportionment reform proposals and hoped to repeal the anti-alien clause. As the *New York Times* reported, they accurately recognized the provision as one of the constitution's several "limitations which ma[de] it difficult to elect a Democratic Senate and almost impossible, except in a landslide, to elect a Democratic Assembly."[99] But Democratic lawmakers would have little room for error when the new legislature convened in January 1935. Despite Governor Lehman's massive 1934 re-election victory over his GOP rival, Robert Moses, Democrats would possess only a four-seat majority in the lower chamber owing to the malapportionment of the state legislature.[100]

This narrow margin gave Tammany Hall leaders significant leverage to shape or outright defeat apportionment legislation. They soon concluded that virtually any reapportionment would represent a net loss to their power since Manhattan's population had ceased growing while New York City's outer

110   DISPARATE REGIMES

boroughs were rapidly gaining inhabitants. Locked out of power in New York City Hall and faced with an additional loss of clout in Albany, Tammany bosses refused Lehman's many entreaties to support reapportionment legislation in 1935. Democratic assemblymen James Stephens and William Andrews of Harlem—the lone African American members of the chamber—also fiercely protested reapportionment plans drawn up by their party's leadership that threatened to combine their districts. If the Republican minority remained united in opposition to the governor's reapportionment plans, rebellious Democratic assemblymen had the votes to stymie any bill.[101] GOP lawmakers were more than happy to do their part.

To justify their support for continued reapportionment gridlock, New York Republican leaders bemoaned a recent, seemingly minor, administrative change to the implementation of the state constitution's anti-alien apportionment clause. In 1931, New York voters had approved a constitutional amendment to empower the secretary of state's office to employ population statistics compiled by the federal census as the basis of any future reapportionment. Though this reform had been adopted as a result of dissatisfaction with the quality of data provided by the state's own census, plans to use US Census Bureau records soon proved controversial because federal enumerators in 1930 did not ask all residents about their nationality. Critics further alleged that even this incomplete federal data were not compiled to a sufficient degree of local specificity to accurately calculate apportionment figures.[102]

In response, Lehman and Flynn called on the federal government for help. The Roosevelt administration obliged, ordering employees of the Civil Works Agency and the Census Bureau to aid the New York secretary of state's office in the task of identifying noncitizens on a block-by-block basis in New York City. But this additional work, especially that of Civil Works Agency officials, also came under criticism for alleged inaccuracies.[103]

Republicans could hardly contain their glee as these developments unfolded. The anti–New Deal *Chicago Tribune* accused Flynn and his allies of trying to "gerrymander" themselves into power, a criticism that New York Democrats had so frequently (and accurately) lobbed at Republicans. The paper also noted that it certainly looked like Roosevelt was intervening to help anti-Tammany Democrats, like his close ally, Flynn, gain control over the Democratic Party in New York once and for all.[104] It was hard to miss the irony of leading New York Democrats—including the president of the United States—going to such lengths to count noncitizens out of the population for state legislative apportionment, when only a few years earlier New York City's mostly Democratic congressional delegation had vocally opposed an identical federal nativist scheme. Meanwhile, New York Republicans continued to denounce the quality of citizenship data that Democratic leaders sought to employ to reapportion the legislature.[105]

They succeeded in blocking all reapportionment proposals introduced by Democratic leaders throughout 1935.[106] When the GOP once again took control of the lower legislative chamber the following year, the window for action had closed.

The state would not be reapportioned until 1943 when the GOP—once more fully in control in Albany following the gubernatorial victory of Republican Thomas Dewey—stacked the deck to its own advantage. With New York City's outer boroughs and suburbs continuing to grow in population, Republicans redrew and reapportioned districts to capture these voters. When some upstate and Manhattan Republicans protested that these plans threatened to disempower them, GOP leaders plowed ahead. State authorities again contracted with the US Census Bureau to provide data on the state's noncitizen population. This time, they used it. Democrats would not win control of both legislative chambers in Albany again until 1964.[107]

Anti-alien Apportionment Policies amid "One Man, One Vote" Reforms

Disputes over the adoption and implementation of state malapportionment policies, including nativist schemes, did little to strengthen public trust in representative democracy. In response, a growing number of middle-class, civil society reformers challenged them in the 1950s and 1960s. Reform proponents included concerned scholars, labor unions, elements of both political parties stuck in opposition in their respective state legislatures, and, most especially, "good government" nonpartisan groups such as the National Municipal League. These groups highlighted the various ways in which widespread malapportionment made a mockery of the basic democratic principle of equal representation and harmed public policy.[108]

In 1953, president Dwight D. Eisenhower launched the Commission on Intergovernmental Relations to study and propose solutions to problems plaguing federal–state relations. The president appointed most of its participants (naming scholars, advisors, and businessmen, including its chairman, Meyer Kestnbaum), and congressional leaders appointed members from their own chambers. The final report targeted state legislative malapportionment for significant criticism. The Kestnbaum Commission argued that inequalities in representation had actually weakened the power of states by forcing cities to turn to the federal government as a negotiating partner in the absence of representative and responsive state governments.[109]

The commission and other critics of malapportionment blasted state governments for going decades, sometimes as much as half a century, without

112 DISPARATE REGIMES

reallocating districts, deeming this a disregard for basic republican governance. They also argued that states should no longer employ "geographic" units (usually counties) as their primary metric of apportionment. Instead, reformers contended that population figures should be the foremost basis of representation. But unless their party had recently won an unexpected victory, state politicians in power were unlikely to favor these proposals. In response, reformers took their battle to the courts.[110]

By the early 1960s, Hugo Black was no longer a US senator from Alabama opposing the inclusion of noncitizens in federal apportionment policies. Instead, he was an associate justice of the federal Supreme Court, having been appointed to his seat in 1937 by president Franklin D. Roosevelt. In a fateful twist, Black would become a crucial vote in favor of decisions requiring state governments to apportion legislative districts on the principle of one man, one vote.[111] In response to the Tennessee state legislature's refusal to reapportion for more than sixty years, the Supreme Court announced in *Baker v. Carr* (1962) that it would hear challenges to policies that claimants believed were in violation of the federal constitution's Fourteenth Amendment equal protection clause. Two years later, in *Reynolds v. Sims* (1964), the high court ordered state legislatures to regularly reapportion into roughly equally populated districts.[112]

These "redistricting" cases set a firm precedent and had major impacts on state politics and governance. In several northeastern states, many GOP strongholds rapidly became Democratic majorities as rural Republicans lost power in state politics. The transformation was often slower in the South, because most white voters remained members of the Democratic Party for at least another generation. This reapportionment reform nevertheless enabled suburban, white Republicans to make inroads in legislatures across the Sun Belt, from which they would grow their party into the dominant force of southern state politics.[113]

Chief justice Earl Warren had good reason to believe, as the *New York Times* later paraphrased, that these cases represented the "most significant" rulings of the court under his leadership. Redistricting and reapportionment reform, Warren argued, were necessary to ensure that "everyone in this country" possessed "an opportunity to participate in his government on equal terms with everyone else."[114]

Despite Warren's inclusive rhetoric and the very tangible results of his court's opinions, the redistricting rulings did not specify precisely who should be counted as part of the population. In fact, the high court upheld a temporary "registered voter" apportionment basis adopted by Hawaii lawmakers in *Burns v. Richardson* (1966) owing to the disproportionately large military population living in and around Honolulu, most of whom formally resided out of state. The court declared that it would accept a temporary apportionment standard for Hawaii only "so long as it produce[d] a distribution of legislators not substantially different from that which would result from use of a permissible population basis."[115] But it also clarified that "neither in *Reynolds v. Sims* nor in any other decision has this Court suggested that the States are required to include aliens, transients, short-term or temporary residents, or persons denied the vote for conviction of crime in the apportionment base by which their legislators are distributed and against which compliance with the Equal Protection Clause is to be measured."[116]

Nevertheless, the high court's rulings had a rapid impact on long-standing nativist legislative apportionment schemes in some states. In 1967, the Massachusetts Supreme Judicial Court issued an advisory opinion about the commonwealth's legislative apportionment policy. Pointing to the differing number of representatives who would be allocated to counties under "total population" and legal voter standards, the jurists concluded that the state constitution's basis of apportionment violated the "not substantially different" requirements set forth by *Burns*.[117] Three years later, voters approved a constitutional amendment to base representation in the General Court on the commonwealth's total number of inhabitants.[118]

Unlike in Massachusetts, advocates and lawmakers in New York did not launch an effort to repeal their state constitution's anti-alien clause in response to court prodding. New Yorkers would, however, increasingly reject their constitution's long-standing nativist apportionment provisions in the 1960s as overly complex and redundant.

Mid-twentieth-century proponents of reapportionment reform could point to an additional reason to repeal extant state anti-alien clauses. Owing to low levels of immigration and high rates of naturalization in previous decades, noncitizens had dropped to less than one of every twenty residents of the country by 1940.[119] One intergovernmental advisory commission, led by Francis Bane, the former executive director of the Social Security Board, noted in 1962 that most experts had concluded that "the nation's alien population ha[d]" so "diminished since the immigration acts of the 1920's ... that it [was] no longer of significance in the overall picture."[120] Though some scholars and advocates conceded that it may have made sense to count noncitizens out of the population for purposes of apportionment in an earlier era, many argued that continuing to exclude them from state populations in the 1960s was at best superfluous and at worst counterproductive. Political scientist and reapportionment reform advocate Gordon Baker articulated these sentiments in a 1960 National Municipal League pamphlet, contending that "the exclusion of aliens (or specification of citizen population or legal voters) does not yield a much different basis from total population except in a few key places. At the height of the immigration wave it did make a substantial difference, especially in New York City, and probably still does there to some extent. One original purpose of excluding aliens in earlier days was to keep down the representation of

114   DISPARATE REGIMES

immigrant-laden urban areas. Today the exclusion has little practical effect except for a few localities."[121]

Fellow political scientist Ruth Silva, a longtime Pennsylvania State University professor, was more direct in her support for citizen-only policies in theory, but not in practice. Silva was arguably the foremost participant in New York's reapportionment battles in the 1960s as both a consultant to the state government and an indefatigable commentator on the subject for both scholarly and general audiences.[122] In a series of articles published in law reviews, political science journals, and even the popular magazine *Scientific American*, she argued in favor of streamlining state legislative reapportionment in New York. As part of that process, she maintained that removing the constitution's anti-alien clause would have a negligible effect on the drawing of state legislative seats, but would save time and money while eliminating a major administrative headache.[123] Likely trying to nudge wary suburban GOP lawmakers, Silva noted in one publication that "the number of aliens has declined more rapidly in the City than" elsewhere and that "no county's population included more than 6.7 per cent aliens."[124] In another, she stressed that because "the ratio between citizens and non-citizens is now approximately the same in every county, the inclusion of aliens in the apportionment base is a matter of no practical consequence."[125]

There was one more, very practical, reason that several scholars and advocates like Silva argued in favor of repealing anti-alien provisions: US Census Bureau leaders had dropped the citizenship question from the main 1960 enumeration.[126] It would therefore be very difficult, if not impossible, for most states to distinguish citizens from noncitizens when drawing legislative districts. However, in New York, the state government had proactively sought the aid of the Census Bureau in the lead-up to the 1960 census, even paying the federal agency to ask all New York residents about their nationality.[127]

Ultimately, unlike many prior apportionment disputes in New York, the inclusion or exclusion of noncitizens did not dominate legislative or litigation battles in the 1960s. In the wake of the *Baker* and *Reynolds* rulings, governor Nelson Rockefeller and his GOP allies struggled mightily to avoid fully surrendering their party's now unconstitutional advantages. They responded by drafting numerous reapportionment plans, each seeking to minimize the impact of the redistricting revolution on GOP control of the state legislature. Such schemes, however, were repeatedly rejected in court, most notably by the US Supreme Court in *WMCA, Inc. v. Lomenzo* (1964), for failing to comply with new precedents.[128]

Amid continued reapportionment gridlock and litigation, New York voters approved a call to convene a constitutional assembly in 1967 to revise the state's highest law. Democratic delegates, who controlled a majority at the convention, adopted several measures to revise the state constitution's apportionment

Figure 4.2 Professor Ruth Silva, 1957. From "Will Lecture at Highacres Tonight," *Hazleton Standard-Sentinel*, March 22, 1957, 19. Reproduced with permission of the *Hazleton Standard-Speaker*. Provided Courtesy of the State Library of Pennsylvania. Image published with permission of ProQuest LLC. Further reproduction is prohibited without permission. Image produced by ProQuest LLC as part of ProQuest® Historical Newspaper Product and UMI microfilm.

provisions. One clause provided that henceforth the legislature would be reapportioned on a total population basis, using data provided by the decennial federal census. After the convention's revisions were rejected en masse by the New York electorate, reformers introduced a constitutional amendment in the legislature seeking to make a total population reapportionment standard part of the supreme law of the land in the Empire State.[129]

In the fall of 1969, New Yorkers were asked to vote on that measure. In an aptly titled editorial, "Odd Road to a Good End," the *New York Times* strongly endorsed the amendment. Echoing Silva's arguments, the *Times* claimed that it "would save the state at least $1 million," noted that "most good governmental groups" supported it, and emphasized that "the number of aliens is now so small…that the political consequences of the change would be nil."[130] New York voters agreed, ratifying the amendment by a 70 percent to 30 percent margin.[131]

Around the same time, nativist clauses were repealed with relatively little fanfare in Arizona, North Carolina, and Tennessee, as well as other states.[132]

116 DISPARATE REGIMES

Similar provisions in Texas, Nebraska, and Maine were deemed unconstitutional and/or were rendered inoperative in practice.[133] Rare were cases like Oregon, where a campaign to overturn an arcane racist and nativist state apportionment clause arose for explicit reasons of equality.[134] Thus, by the end of the civil rights era, state legislative anti-alien apportionment provisions, common a half century earlier, were no longer in force in any state of the land.

* * *

Nativist apportionment schemes and the citizenship rights as citizen-only rights claims that buttressed them remained powerful in state and national politics from the time of World War I until the civil rights era. To be sure, opponents did win crucial rearguard battles that prevented their expansion into new states in the early twentieth century. They also decisively defeated an attempt to enact federal anti-alien legislation that would have governed apportionment for the US House of Representatives in the 1920s. But foes of these schemes were generally unable to overturn long-standing, potent nativist state apportionment policies during the early to mid-twentieth century. Instead, most anti-alien clauses were only repealed, struck down, or rendered moot amid broader redistricting and reapportionment reforms in the mid- to late twentieth century. And even in the civil rights era, opponents of these nativist provisions had to fight hard to achieve those victories.

Nevertheless, their ultimate success represents a crucial development in the invention of many citizenship rights as citizen-only rights in American history. The previous chapter illustrated how the repeal of many state alien suffrage laws in the late Gilded Age and Progressive Era remade voting into an exclusive right of (some) US citizens across the nation by the early twentieth century. The history of nativist reapportionment policies, by contrast, demonstrates how a political right previously restricted to American citizens in many states became disassociated from US citizenship throughout the country by the mid- to late twentieth century. Together, they illuminate how a host of political actors marshaled the mechanism of state constitutional politics to overturn the disparate regimes of citizenship rights in the polity that had prevailed in the nineteenth-century United States. These state-level actors did not simply respond to national politics and jurisprudence. Nor was the ultimate convergence in state laws governing the rights of noncitizen immigrants in the polity predetermined. Instead, these developments were above all contingent on discrete legal, constitutional, and especially political battles fought within the states.[135]

Disparate Regimes: Nativist Politics, Alienage Law, and Citizenship Rights in the United States, 1865–1965.
Brendan A. Shanahan, Oxford University Press. © Brendan A. Shanahan 2025.
DOI: 10.1093/9780197660577.003.0005

PART III
CONCRETIZING CITIZENSHIP RIGHTS AS CITIZEN-ONLY RIGHTS

5

Learning Citizenship Matters

Immigrant Professionals and State Anti-alien Hiring and Licensure Laws, 1917–52

By all accounts, Theresa Oglou was an ideal California public schoolteacher. The eldest child of a large Italian immigrant family and a graduate of the University of California, Berkeley, Oglou began her long service as a popular Italian and Spanish instructor at Galileo High School in San Francisco's North Beach neighborhood in 1925. But her employment became gravely imperiled in the late 1930s. Though Oglou had long believed herself to be a native-born US citizen, she had actually been born in Italy. As a noncitizen, she had inadvertently run afoul of California's public employment law of 1915, which required that immigrant schoolteachers file their "first papers" to obtain work and promptly naturalize upon eligibility to retain their jobs.[1]

Oglou later testified that she began the naturalization process as soon as she learned of her alienage in 1936, just as she left the country for an extended study of dance in Germany. Upon her return to California to resume teaching, however, local and state education officers began receiving anonymous letters alleging that Oglou had lied about her citizenship status. A subsequent investigation found she had listed four different birthdates on official documents. Though concerned by these inconsistencies, the state Department of Education granted her a temporary teaching license while she pursued her petition for citizenship. Oglou made a crucial error on her naturalization application by listing "dancer" as her occupation, not "teacher." Believing this amounted to an attempt to mislead federal authorities, naturalization examiner Stanley B. Johnson recommended denying her application for a lack of "good moral character."[2]

But Oglou would not be denied her job without a fight. On November 2, 1940, she challenged Johnson in a heated naturalization hearing. Oglou firmly maintained that she had no memories of her early childhood in Italy and had genuinely believed herself to be a US citizen. Fellow instructors and her lawyer spoke to her integrity, teaching abilities, and devotion to her students. Major Joseph Nourse, the superintendent of San Francisco's public schools and a former principal of Galileo High School, vouched for her ability to instill loyalty to the United States among her largely immigrant and second-generation students.[3]

120   DISPARATE REGIMES

Oglou had to challenge Johnson's often-hostile claims in person as he sought to catch her inadvertently admitting to intent to commit fraud.[4] She also employed a patronizing personal attorney who relied on sexist tropes to beg the court for mercy.[5] And she had little time to spare. Not only was her temporary teaching license set to expire the following spring, but also, if she did not naturalize by December 26, 1940, she would have to register as a noncitizen at her local post office to comply with the terms of a new federal law: the Alien Registration Act of 1940. Her persistence paid off. On Christmas Eve 1940, US District Court judge Martin Walsh declared her inconsistencies to be immaterial to her petition and granted her citizenship immediately.[6]

While a courtroom victory for a noncitizen immigrant teacher represented a rare resolution to an anti-alien employment dispute in 1940, the blue-collar nativist state hiring law, professional licensure barriers, and administrative complications Oglou encountered were far from unique. In the two and a half decades after the US Supreme Court unambiguously upheld their constitutionality in 1915, several states adopted new and/or strengthened long-standing anti-alien public and publicly funded employment laws. Federal lawmakers ultimately followed suit, enacting policies that impeded and later barred noncitizen immigrants from many New Deal jobs programs during the so-called Roosevelt recession of the mid- to late 1930s. As in the late Gilded Age and Progressive Era, however, these laws often functioned as "dead letters" in good economic times before they were abruptly resuscitated during unemployment crises. They also continued to primarily target working-class immigrants and to disproportionately harm nonwhite foreign-born laborers.[7] But blue-collar nativist state hiring laws could also ensnare noncitizen professionals, especially women like Oglou, working in two female-dominated fields. Teachers and nurses, along with virtually all other immigrant professionals, then confronted a growing maze of state licensing requirements and/or overtly nativist restrictions on their licensure as well.

The late nineteenth and early twentieth centuries had witnessed an explosion in the types of employment—such as accounting, engineering, nursing, and teaching—that were widely recognized in policy and in practice as professions. Along with "old" professions like law and medicine, they became increasingly distinguished from other lines of work by their growing social status and governance by autonomous state or state-authorized licensing boards in the early decades of the twentieth century.[8] Supporters argued that these licensing boards protected the public by ensuring practitioners met basic standards. Critics countered that they were often "captured" by professional organizations to the detriment of consumers, patients, and prospective licensees, especially those from marginalized backgrounds.[9]

LEARNING CITIZENSHIP MATTERS   121

Licensure barriers also restricted immigrants' access to the professions. Universities frequently discriminated against immigrants in admissions, especially nonwhite, female, and/or Jewish foreign-born applicants.[10] State licensing boards likewise regularly refused to recognize degrees issued by foreign universities or failed to grant "reciprocal licenses" to experienced immigrant professionals.[11] But the most pervasive state licensure barriers immigrant professionals encountered in the early to mid-twentieth century were citizenship requirements. Anti-alien professional licensing laws could be found in all states during the early to mid-twentieth century, but they became especially ubiquitous in the Northeast and West.[12] Unlike blue-collar nativist state hiring laws, anti-alien licensure measures frequently sailed through legislatures at the behest of professional interest groups with little to no news coverage. Though immigrant rights activists struggled to keep track of their spread, by 1946, no fewer than 495 state anti-alien professional and occupational licensure laws were in force across the country.[13]

Enforcing state anti-alien licensure laws also proved difficult. State licensing board members tasked with implementing them generally had little expertise in immigration and citizenship law. They often responded by crafting harsh ad hoc documentation requirements and applied them unsparingly when marginalized noncitizens—East and South Asian immigrants, women, and/or refugees—sought licensure. Immigrant professionals and their allies countered by doggedly resisting anti-alien licensure laws in court, by challenging their draconian administration before licensing boards, and, less commonly, by appealing to the public and policymakers for redress.[14]

This chapter examines the proliferation of early- to mid-twentieth-century state anti-alien professional employment policies, their contestation in court, and, above all, their convoluted implementation. It contextualizes how these battles sometimes grew out of and frequently unfolded alongside working-class nativist employment disputes. But unlike blue-collar nativist state hiring laws, anti-alien professional licensure policies rarely became dead letters when unemployment rates were low. Indeed, this chapter stresses how state professional licensing board members generally tried to strictly apply such laws regardless of economic conditions. Above all, it argues that the growing ubiquity and tortuous enforcement of state anti-alien hiring and licensure measures increasingly concretized citizenship rights as citizen-only rights in professional employment during the early to mid-twentieth century.

Contextualizing the Origins of Anti-alien Licensure Policies

Prior to World War I, state anti-alien licensure laws mostly governed access to skilled and semiskilled occupations. Lawmakers in New York, for instance,

122 DISPARATE REGIMES

restricted or banned the licensure of noncitizen pawnbrokers (1883), plumbing inspectors (1892), liquor dealers (1896), and private investigators (1909).[15] Some states only issued hunting or fishing permits to US citizens; others imposed hefty fees on noncitizens.[16] Immigrant peddlers, often eastern European Jews or Middle Eastern migrants, sometimes encountered similar impediments.[17]

Though less common, early anti-alien professional licensure laws were not unheard of. The Empire State's citizen-only attorney policy dated to at least 1871. Noncitizens in New York were later denied licensing as certified public accountants (1896) and architects (1915).[18] By contrast, state lawmakers usually balked at barring noncitizen teachers from licensure and/or employment in public schools during the Progressive Era. California lawmakers even voted to exempt most noncitizen teachers from a strict statewide citizen-only public employment policy in 1915.[19] But US entry into World War I threatened to abruptly alter such attitudes.

In the spring of 1917, lawmakers in New York debated legislation seeking to ban noncitizens from serving as public schoolteachers across the state. Though this particular bill was not adopted, immigrant teachers, especially foreign-language instructors, remained under suspicion.[20] In the winter of 1917, John Hulshof, head of foreign-language instruction in New York City's public schools, felt compelled to reassure the public that students were receiving a patriotic education. He announced that only citizens and immigrants who had begun the naturalization process were permitted to work under his supervision. Defending his own employment, this German-born official emphasized that "he ha[d] been an American citizen for thirty-two years." He also noted that he personally vetted foreign-language textbooks and made sure to purge views that did "not conform to American ideals."[21]

Such assurances were not enough for New York state lawmakers amid growing wartime xenophobia. In early 1918, a new anti-alien public schoolteacher bill was introduced in the legislature and swiftly enacted into law.[22] Although patronage from Tammany Hall–aligned Democrats had helped make Irish-origin women— immigrants from Ireland and their more numerous US-born daughters—the largest bloc of public schoolteachers in New York City, only the Socialist Party's delegation of state lawmakers forcefully objected to this legislation.[23]

Though especially pronounced, debates over the employment of noncitizen teachers were not unique to wartime New York. California education authorities announced in May 1918 that they would seek to "refus[e] to grant credentials to alien enemies." They also planned to investigate the status of teachers' naturalization petitions to "ascertain whether . . . the proper time had elapsed" for them to become citizens in compliance with the 1915 law. If no "attempt had been made to complete" the citizenship petitions of those eligible to naturalize, education authorities planned to cancel their credentials.[24]

LEARNING CITIZENSHIP MATTERS   123

The conclusion of the war did not stop the *Los Angeles Times* from warning that foreign teachers were "poison[ing]" the minds of American students. Editorializing in the autumn of 1919, the paper encouraged school boards across the state to investigate allegations that communist, socialist, and other "radical" teachers were spreading "the seeds of hate, rebellion, anarchy and murder" among students. Though an otherwise conservative and staunchly anti-union publication, the paper went so far as to argue that "if inadequate pay facilitates the employment of alien plotters in our schools and colleges by failing to attract the best type of American educator, then the pay should be raised to any level, however high."[25] In the eyes of the *Los Angeles Times*, war and fear of radical immigrants had dramatically increased the potential danger posed by noncitizen teachers in California.

The paper's fears of subversive, noncitizen workers were far from exceptional in the aftermath of World War I. Some private employers declared that they would henceforth only hire American citizens as the first Red Scare swept the nation in 1919.[26] And in Wisconsin, state lawmakers adopted a 1923 blue-collar nativist hiring law restricting noncitizen immigrants' access to some public works jobs during severe economic downturns.[27]

Much to the dismay of blue-collar nativists and their allies, such policies did not become the norm for public or private employment in the Roaring Twenties.[28] In Texas, legislators debated and rejected a statewide anti-alien public works hiring proposal in 1919.[29] And as industrial relations scholar William Leiserson noted in 1924, while private employers may have feared noncitizens as enemy agents or subversives during wartime and amid the postwar antiradical hysteria, few proved willing to permanently limit their pool of potential workers to US citizens.[30] But the lobbying of blue-collar nativists was finding much greater success on another front in the early 1920s: immigration restriction politics.

The Rise of Nativist Professional Licensure Laws in an Age of Immigration Quotas

World War I emboldened and empowered immigration restrictionists. They achieved a long-sought aim in 1917 when Congress overrode president Woodrow Wilson's veto to enact the Literacy Test Act. Not satisfied, they clamored for even more coercive legislation to curtail immigration in the war's aftermath.[31] Backed by "patriotic" organizations like the newly formed American Legion, eugenicists like Madison Grant, and the Ku Klux Klan, they lobbied Congress to enact the Emergency Quota Act of 1921 and the even more draconian Johnson–Reed Act of 1924. The latter drastically reduced immigration

124 DISPARATE REGIMES

from southern and eastern Europe and effectively cut it off from East and South Asia altogether. Southwestern growers, building contractors, and allied politicians argued that Mexican noncitizen laborers performed essential but low-paid farm labor and construction work eschewed by white Americans. They succeeded in exempting immigrants hailing from countries within the Americas from the quota system.[32]

Though these changes to federal immigration law led to a significant overall decline in the number of immigrants entering the United States during the 1920s, the number of professionals grew as a percentage of all migrants admitted to the country. While they had comprised less than 1 percent of the nation's immigrants in 1912, they numbered more than 3.5 percent by 1926. But many found it hard to work in their respective fields. As Marian Schibsby of the Foreign Language Information Service (FLIS) noted in real time, immigrant professionals were increasingly ensnared by new onerous state professional licensure obligations.[33]

Born in World War I as a branch of the federal government's Committee on Public Information (the Wilson administration's wartime propaganda machine), the FLIS proved popular among social workers as a useful clearinghouse of information and as a resource for foreign-language newspapers.[34] After a temporary takeover by the Red Cross, it became an independent immigrant advocacy organization and functioned as an "early think tank" during the interwar years, with access to and influence at the highest levels of the federal government.[35]

Just a year after the passage of the Johnson–Reed Act in 1924, the organization began warning that a growing number of highly educated immigrants were unable to work in their professions. In its monthly journal, *The Interpreter*, the FLIS implored readers in November 1925 to recognize a growing "influx of" immigrants from "the middle classes" of Europe who were struggling to find professional employment.[36] It warned that too often Americans "assum[ed] that the immigrant's economic condition is invariably improved by coming to America."[37] That belief, *The Interpreter* maintained, blinded Americans to the plight of immigrants like an anonymous Austrian physician who had moved to the United States to rebuild his life and practice after losing his savings in World War I. Upon relocating across the Atlantic, "he learned that his European degrees did not entitle him to practice medicine. He would have to study English and pass a series of examinations before our authorities would grant him a license. Too old to start all over again, he has taken a job as a bus boy in a lunch room."[38]

The FLIS worked hard to combat these developments. Four years later, an *Interpreter* article similarly argued that it was necessary to confront widespread "anti-alien propaganda" that well-educated "immigrants come here only to reap the fruits of American prosperity" by emphasizing the skills they brought to the country. The FLIS even pointed to the comments of secretary of labor James Davis, a fervent immigration restrictionist, who advocated for professional immigrants' entry as part of a "flexible and more highly selective immigration policy."[39] Since so few people knew about state anti-alien licensure policies, the FLIS touted in 1925 that it shared "articles on the professions" throughout the "foreign language press."[40] In another publication, the organization encouraged new immigrants to promptly "inquire about the license regulations of the[ir] community," since breaking these laws "generally me[ant] arrest and fine" as "ignorance of the law d[id] not prevent punishment."[41]

Such anti-alien licensure "regulations" were indeed growing increasingly prevalent. In her 1927 *Handbook for Immigrants to the United States*, Schibsby found that twenty-eight states required US citizenship of lawyers and another nine mandated that immigrants file declarations of intention to become citizens for admission to the bar.[42] To practice medicine, Schibsby identified eleven states that required American citizenship as a condition of licensure, while another fifteen issued licenses to immigrants only if they possessed first papers.[43] She also found that states occasionally required citizenship or first papers as a condition of licensure in the fields of dentistry, nursing, and pharmacy.[44]

Schibsby recognized that other logistical factors posed major barriers for professional immigrants seeking licensure, noting that they often struggled to demonstrate English-language proficiency or provide sufficient evidence of their educational credentials.[45] Failure to produce or verify documentation for state licensing boards in the 1920s was not always the fault of immigrants. The refusal of the US government to establish diplomatic relations with the new Soviet Union during the 1920s, for instance, made it impossible for most migrants from the former Russian Empire to turn to consular officers to confirm their educational and professional credentials.[46] The actions of the California Board of Pharmacy illustrate the inconsistent and at times draconian approaches of state licensing boards to these challenges of documentation.

In January 1924, the Board of Pharmacy voted to be generous to Peter Goolin, a graduate of the Imperial Military Medical Academy of Petrograd. Though unable to verify his documents with consular officials, the board determined that Goolin's "affidavits on experience were satisfactory" and his "oral examination sufficient" to grant him a full license. Three and a half years later, when another pharmacist, A. Kamalian, presented his "affidavits on experience and proof of registration in Russia" before the same board, its members determined that they could not authenticate Kamalian's documents because "their translations had not been made by a consul." Though they gave him a temporary permit, Kamalian was ordered to "have the Polish or other qualified consul verify the translations" in order to receive a permanent license.[47]

126   DISPARATE REGIMES

The board's efforts were further complicated when state lawmakers adopted a first papers requirement for immigrant pharmacists in April 1927.[48] Thereafter, petitioners for pharmacy licenses in California would have to provide sufficient proof of American citizenship or of their formal declaration of intention to naturalize. Board members, though highly educated and leading representatives of their profession, were not experts in US nationality law and soon found this new task overwhelming. By July of that same year, the board instructed its assistant to meet with the state attorney general's office to learn relatively basic information, such as whether an immigrant could "file papers for citizenship immediately after arriving in the United States or must such persons wait until residing for one year in this State."[49]

The California Board of Pharmacy also faced more practical challenges. In April 1928, Russian-born pharmacist David Kruger "presented papers showing citizenship in the United States" at a board meeting, but he understandably refused to surrender his naturalization papers "for the Board's records." Board members, in turn, instructed him "to send in a photostatic copy" of them. Though he met all other requirements, the board refused to grant him a license until he submitted such a copy for their record keeping.[50] Two years later, however, board members were warned that it was a violation of federal law "to make any kind of copy of such papers."[51] In response, the board ultimately dropped its demand that individuals turn over (original or copied) citizenship papers when applying for a license.[52]

The passage and bungled administration of the 1927 California anti-alien pharmacy licensure law were not widely discussed in the press. As legal scholar Milton Konvitz noted in 1946, such legislation was "always being introduced in state legislatures." But "such acts [were] not sponsored by public-spirited persons or groups." Nor were they debated broadly by politicians in the public sphere. Instead, such restrictions were usually "offered and 'pressured' by the organized business, profession, or calling. If the bill passes, it means that the pressure group was considered worthy of attention; if it fails, it means that the pressure group did not amount to much in terms of prestige, voting strength, or financial contributions to political campaigns. Such laws are directed to the elimination of competition from aliens qualified to engage in the callings."[53]

In fact, anti-alien licensure lobbying campaigns were sometimes unknown to members of professional associations that privately advocated for them. Even though twenty-six states required either US citizenship or a declaration of intention to practice medicine by 1927, the American Medical Association (AMA) had not taken a policy of publicly supporting those measures. But that did not prevent prominent AMA leaders like Dr. N. P. Colwell from privately lobbying state boards of medicine for citizenship requirements. Colwell, head of the AMA's national Council on Medical Education in the mid-1920s, wrote to the Texas Board of Medicine in the spring of 1924 to ask its members if "it was about time for the state boards of the country to adopt citizenship as a qualification for license." Shortly before formally reading Colwell's letter into the record at a June 1924 meeting, the board voted to restrict doctors' licenses in Texas to US citizens and to immigrants who held first papers.[54]

Though the AMA did not launch an overtly nativist campaign to restrict all medical licenses to citizens during the Roaring Twenties, in 1926 its Council on Medical Education did warn of a "rather serious situation" resulting from an "influx of physicians from abroad," which "ha[d] increased from 138 in 1919 to 731 in 1924." The council cautioned that it was becoming increasingly difficult to confirm the "credentials" and "identity" of doctors hailing from "certain countries abroad, especially from Russia." To ostensibly mitigate against potential fraud, it encouraged state licensing boards to "carefully investigat[e] . . . the credentials of all foreign candidates."[55]

Although the AMA council noted that immigrant doctors were "entering a field already seriously crowded," it did not openly endorse a strict citizen-only licensure policy. "No undue obstacles," it further argued, "should be placed in the way of the foreign physician of known qualifications who desires particularly to secure graduate medical education in this country." Though Colwell had privately lobbied Texas officials for a citizenship requirement just two years earlier, publicly his council proclaimed that it was only concerned about verifying the quality of foreign doctors' education, experience, and training.[56] A similar process was underway at many American medical schools where Jewish applicants were increasingly denied admission. Though some administrators like Harvard College president A. Lawrence Lowell publicly supported creating "Jewish quotas" for their universities, more often medical schools required "personal interview[s]" of applicants that were used as proxy to deny Jews admission.[57]

While proponents of anti-alien professional licensing restrictions like Colwell usually preferred to lobby lawmakers and board members behind the scenes, advocates of blue-collar nativist hiring laws were generally far more eager to publicly promote their cause.[58] Their demands for the passage and strict implementation of such measures would rise to a fever pitch following the stock market crash of 1929.[59]

"Where Shall the Alien Work" during the Great Depression?

Lawmakers in many states adopted new or reinforced old anti-alien public and/ or publicly funded employment laws in the early years of the Great Depression.

128   DISPARATE REGIMES

In 1931 alone, new blue-collar nativist hiring policies were enacted in the major immigrant-destination states of California, Massachusetts, and Texas.[60] By the end of the following year, anti-alien public and/or publicly funded employment laws could be found in eighteen states that were home to just over two-thirds of the nation's noncitizen immigrant population.[61] Local authorities frequently responded to popular pressure by vigorously implementing these measures amid the spiraling unemployment crisis of the early 1930s.[62]

Blue-collar nativists similarly tried to bar noncitizen immigrants from new federal public and/or publicly funded jobs programs upon Democratic nominee Franklin Roosevelt's victory in the 1932 presidential election. While the Roosevelt administration stymied most such demands in the early New Deal years, it increasingly gave ground to nativists as the thirties wore on, particularly after the midterm elections of 1938 delivered a sharp rebuke to the president.[63] Most notably, in 1939, Congress passed and Roosevelt signed legislation barring noncitizens from employment on the largest New Deal public works program: the Works Progress (later Projects) Administration. Around 45,000 noncitizens lost their jobs in the ensuing purge.[64]

As in previous economic downturns, state anti-alien public and/or publicly funded employment laws most impacted marginalized immigrant laborers. From illiterate, non-English-speaking migrants in Massachusetts to Mexican-born construction workers in California, state blue-collar nativist hiring policies especially harmed already vulnerable immigrants in the early years of the Great Depression.[65] Thousands of out-of-work and precariously employed Mexican nationals and their US citizen family members were deported or coerced to "repatriate" on ostensible public grounds charges, often due to the collaboration of local and state officials with federal immigration authorities.[66] Colorado governor Ed Johnson, a firm proponent of citizen-only public works hiring policies, even declared martial law and deployed the National Guard in an attempt to bar noncitizens from his state in 1936. Johnson and his associates nakedly embraced anti-Mexican racial profiling and ensnared numerous US citizens in their cruel, brief, and ultimately aborted campaign.[67] In this manner, such attacks formed part of a larger assault on the employment of nonwhite and/or married female workers during the 1930s.[68]

Though not their primary targets, noncitizen professionals could also be harmed by the passage of new and resuscitation of dormant blue-collar nativist hiring laws during the Great Depression. Immigrant women—particularly those who worked in the heavily female and comparatively less remunerative professions of nursing and teaching—were especially susceptible to their weight.[69] Disputes over the enforcement of a 1931 Massachusetts citizen-preference public employment law in city and state hospitals across the commonwealth serve as a case in point.[70]

LEARNING CITIZENSHIP MATTERS   129

In August 1931, Boston city councilor John F. Dowd pressed his colleagues on the council and mayor James Michael Curley to fire all noncitizen nurses employed at the municipal hospital. The *Boston Globe* reported that Dowd "argued that it was unfair to employ nurses who were aliens, even if they had first papers, when there were citizen registered nurses unemployed."[71] Despite expressing his "sincere regret" and dismay at "the severity of the punishment" an anti-alien purge would impose, Mayor Curley announced that a legal opinion issued by the city attorney compelled him to fire all—eighteen, mostly Canadian—noncitizen nurses employed at Boston City Hospital.[72] In nearby Quincy, nine noncitizen nurses were laid off, while five others quit to protest their impending dismissal.[73] Authorities in several other Bay State cities similarly came under pressure to fire noncitizen nurses at their municipal hospitals.[74] Meanwhile, Boston Finance Commission chairman Frank Goodwin, a powerful Republican politician, lobbied state hospital officials to discharge noncitizen nurses working under their supervision.[75]

Though the real and prospective firing of noncitizen nurses across Massachusetts did not metastasize into a full-blown diplomatic crisis in 1931, the news was nevertheless received with indignation by many Canadians.[76] The *Boston Globe* reported that hospital officials and nurses in Canadian cities like "Toronto, Montreal, St. John [New Brunswick], and Halifax [Nova Scotia]" were variously "much concern[ed]" or outraged by the developments. A representative of McGill University's Royal Victoria Hospital scoffed that "Montreal hospitals put good nursing before any petty qualifications of nationality," while Toronto General Hospital superintendent C. J. Decker denounced the move as "unfair." Officials in Canada's poor, eastern Maritime provinces were especially alarmed since so many of the nurses hailed from "these Down East Provinces."[77]

Canadian noncitizen nurses had some powerful allies in Massachusetts politics. Authorities in some cities, notably those of Haverhill, refused to fire noncitizen nurses.[78] State health commissioner Dr. George H. Bigelow similarly backed their continued employment in state hospitals. His position was supported by Democratic governor Joseph Ely, who had brought the state's citizen-preference law into force. Ely argued that the new law was designed to shape future hiring practices, not to bring about a purge of hospital staff.[79]

In an editorial at the height of the controversy aptly titled "Is It Wise?" the *Boston Globe* took a different tactic to criticize the firing of immigrant nurses in Massachusetts. While the paper conceded that the dismissals were "doubtless justified by the strict observance of the statutes," it pointed out that firing eighteen staff members "at one swoop" would undoubtedly harm the operations of and care provided by Boston's public hospital and threatened to "reduc[e]" a venerable profession to "the status of 'job' or patronage."[80] Such warnings

130 DISPARATE REGIMES

proved prescient. One state away, noncitizen nurses would soon be ensnared by a similar, even larger purge.

On Christmas Eve 1931, the *New York Times* reported that the commissioner of New York City's twenty-six public hospitals, Tammany Hall–backed Dr. J. G. William Greeff, had just announced that "only citizens and applicants for citizenship" would subsequently be hired to work as "graduate nurses," hospital "attendants," or even "student nurses" at no pay under his supervision. Greeff's scheme—which the *Times* recognized as an attempt "to halt the employment of aliens"—posed a real threat to many nurses' jobs. At that time, roughly one in five graduate nurses employed by city hospitals were noncitizens. Eighty-three, almost all of whom came from Canada, had not yet begun the process of becoming citizens. Since so many nurses then resided in hospital housing, their room and board were at risk along with their jobs. Unconcerned by their plight, Greeff affirmed that inquiries "from nurses eager to serve . . . show that there are more than enough citizens to fill the entire nursing staff."[81]

One New York City noncitizen nurse, Karin Mueller, wrote to the FLIS to express her fear about such developments. She stressed that immigrant nurses such as herself disproportionately worked in "contagious diseases" wards because "native nurses [had] preferred private duty" prior to the Depression. While Mueller noted that immigrant nurses were "hop[ing] to avoid discrimination with the help of our foreign consuls," they remained "threatened" by the potential "discharge of all aliens from city employment."[82] She was right to worry.

In early December 1932, shortly before $1.5 million in budget cuts to the city's public hospitals were to take effect, Greeff began to fire hundreds, possibly over a thousand, noncitizen workers under his supervision.[83] In a front-page *New York Times* interview, Greeff asked rhetorically, aside from "the necessity for economy, we have got to take care of our own first, haven't we?" He conceded that "those who are affected probably will not like it." To their concerns, he heartlessly retorted, "But what can they do?"[84]

Greeff dramatically understated the outrage then mustering to oppose his scheme. The *New York Herald* reported on December 16 that Greeff and his assistant had to "t[ake] refuge in an uptown hospital" to escape "protests and pleas coming into the main office" in response to the rolling layoffs of noncitizen hospital staff. Outrage at Bellevue Hospital, "which ha[d] the largest share of alien employees," grew so pronounced that five police officers were called in owing to "rumors that there might be trouble."[85] The following day, the *New York Times* issued an editorial denouncing Greeff for "Dismiss[ing] to the Breadline" 400 noncitizen hospital workers and planning to "release 700 more before the end of the year." It argued that Greeff's position was based on "a distorted meaning for 'aliens.'" While a citizen-only employment policy might be

LEARNING CITIZENSHIP MATTERS   131

justified in a time of mass unemployment if the country had a policy of "unrestricted immigration," the *Times* argued that it was unjust to purge noncitizen hospital workers who "ha[d] been living a number of years in this country," for they were, in effect, "citizen[s] in the making." The paper also contended that while suffrage was rightly an exclusive political right of citizenship, it was "absurd to argue that we are as justified in withholding from [noncitizens] the right to earn" pay from hard, necessary hospital work.[86]

Such objections were not enough to force a reversal of Greeff's policy. The Boston-based *Jewish Advocate* and the FLIS would later find that 1,415 noncitizens were ultimately fired from New York City public hospitals in the winter of 1932–33.[87]

Despite these purges, distinguishing citizens from noncitizens often proved difficult for employers and authorities alike. Numerous immigrants then derived American citizenship from the naturalization of a parent or spouse and struggled to provide proof of their US nationality. Many American citizens, in turn, had been born before all states required the issuance of birth certificates. Some US-born women had earlier lost their American citizenship upon marriage to noncitizen immigrant men, but often had no documentation to that effect either.[88]

Blue-collar nativists therefore lobbied state lawmakers to establish increasingly coercive immigrant identification practices to ostensibly aid in the implementation of anti-alien hiring policies. In 1931, Michigan lawmakers enacted legislation aiming to create a mandatory system of state identification documentation for resident noncitizens to theoretically distinguish them from citizens and undocumented immigrants alike. But that Michigan statute, and a subsequent similar Pennsylvania law, were struck down in court as unconstitutional attempts to usurp federal powers.[89] Blue-collar nativists and allied politicians bemoaned that such rulings weakened the effectiveness of (state and federal) anti-alien public and publicly funded employment laws. They, in turn, fought for analogous federal legislation throughout the 1930s. But only following the outbreak of World War II in Europe and the fall of France to Nazi Germany did such a federal bill—the Alien Registration Act of 1940—come into law.[90]

Advocates of anti-alien licensure policies, on the other hand, often harnessed immigrants' limited access to documentation to deny them professional certification during the Great Depression. For instance, in 1938, New York lawmakers adopted a statute requiring immigrant nurses to produce proof of US citizenship or first papers to obtain licensure. To retain their licenses, nurses in possession of first papers were further required to naturalize within seven years of filing those declarations.[91] Shortly after the law's passage, Ethel Prince, president of the New York State Nurses Association, spread word of the new policy

132   DISPARATE REGIMES

while noting that German consular officials often refused to help locate or verify the credentials of Jewish refugee nurses. Prince did not, however, advocate exempting refugee nurses fleeing the Nazi regime from these growing restrictions. Instead, she sought to publicize the new requirements under the guise of warning Jewish nurses that their employment prospects would be highly tenuous in Depression-era New York.[92] Many other noncitizen immigrant professionals were also learning that access to licensure was increasingly becoming a citizen-only right in states across the nation.

* * *

State lawmakers proved receptive to demands by professional associations to erect barriers to the licensure of immigrants during the Great Depression.[93] Whereas FLIS researcher Marian Schibsby had discovered that twenty-eight states required citizenship for admission to the bar and another nine compelled first papers from lawyers in the mid-1920s, by 1933, immigrant rights advocate and scholar Harold Fields found that thirty-five states required citizenship of attorneys and another eight mandated at least their declarations of intention to naturalize. Schibsby had only mentioned scattered citizenship requirements for pharmacists in her 1927 *Handbook*, but Fields identified eight states that maintained a citizen-only policy in 1933 and another three that required first papers for pharmacists.[94] While nativist hiring statutes could be found in some form in every state, Fields emphasized that in general "the number of such laws is proportional to the alien or foreign-born population of each state." Accordingly, "in the New England and Middle Atlantic States the greatest number of such laws is to be found." However, he also underscored that "in Western and Southern border states," marginalized Mexican and Asian immigrant populations experienced "discriminatory laws out of proportion to their alien population." Fields believed that state anti-alien employment and licensure laws, along with broader nativist hiring practices, had grown so pervasive that he titled his most famous publication on the subject, "Where Shall the Alien Work?"[95]

While the FLIS had waged a lonely struggle to call public attention to the weight and scope of noncitizen professional restrictions during the 1920s, Fields was far from the only scholar trying to take stock of anti-alien professional licensure laws during the Great Depression.[96] In 1934, the *Pennsylvania Law Review* published Leonard Helfenstein's note on the "Constitutionality of Legislative Discrimination against the Alien in His Right to Work." This article aimed to identify and contextualize a growing "body of new legislation" that was "making citizenship a requisite for employment in public projects and in many professions and trades" across the country.[97] Similarly, in his massive 1938 comparative study, *American Family Laws*, legal scholar Chester Vernier devoted an entire section to identifying and comparing state legislation related to noncitizens' "Rights of Employment and Labor." In it, Vernier sought to demonstrate how state policies toward noncitizens "ha[d] not been as liberal as the common law" since all states and territories in the nation "ha[d] adopted statutory or constitutional provisions" limiting their access to licensure and employment.[98] Though these scholars agreed that citizenship requirements were growing in number during the Great Depression, their exact figures and means of calculation sometimes differed.[99]

Legal scholars often wrote about anti-alien licensing restrictions to identify means to overturn them, both in the courtroom and in the court of popular opinion. Because the US Supreme Court had ruled anti-alien public and publicly funded employment laws to be constitutional in 1915, continued litigation against such policies was rare.[100] Lawsuits against state anti-alien professional licensure laws were comparatively more common. In courtroom filings and hearings against such measures, noncitizens' claims most often rested on treaty obligations and equal protection grounds.[101] These arguments usually met with little success, however, because jurists generally upheld the constitutionality of anti-alien professional licensure laws under the police powers of state lawmakers to govern their constituents' "health, safety, morals, and welfare."[102]

With challenges to state anti-alien licensure laws coming up short in court, scholars increasingly criticized their inhumanity and irrationality in appeals to lawmakers and the broader public. Monsignor John A. Ryan, a staunch pro-immigrant labor rights activist, professor, and priest at the Catholic University of America, used the platform of an FLIS-sponsored "Conference on the Alien in America" in 1936 to preach that "discriminations against the alien in the matter of employment are at least ninety per cent unwarranted, foolish and unjust."[103]

Five years later, at a March 1941 address for the *New York University Law Quarterly Review*, attorney Basil O'Connor took a more measured approach in asking his audience to ponder a hypothetical analogy. Should the courts uphold a law denying "a red-headed man" the right to work as an elevator operator even though everyone knew "that there is no correlation between the color of a man's hair" and such work? Obviously not, he contended.[104] By that same logic, O'Connor argued that when "an alien is excluded from employment," it was readily apparent that "it is not because his distinguishing characteristics make him unsafe . . . but for some other reason," such as "a dislike of aliens or a desire to prevent them from competing with citizens for jobs." Such prejudice, he argued, "d[id] not meet the principle of . . . equal treatment for all persons." But O'Connor was compelled to admit that "the courts have frequently ignored this principle" when deciding anti-alien licensure cases.[105]

Political scientist David Fellman, by contrast, sought to distinguish justifiable licensing restrictions from those he considered arbitrary. In a 1938 law review article, he argued that anti-alien attorney policies were understandable because a "lawyer is an officer of the court, and has an unusually close connection with the laws of the land." However, that rationale did not "justify

134   DISPARATE REGIMES

exclusion from medicine, engineering, [and] accountancy." Like O'Connor, Fellman rhetorically asked "what public interest" was served "by requiring citizenship of doctors and embalmers" or if a citizen was "likely to be a better pharmacist or engineer or accountant than an alien."[106] He concluded, however, that amid "the stringencies of the depression, aliens . . . have been a convenient and rather hapless target of discriminatory legislation."[107]

Sometimes state authorities found fault with their own anti-alien licensure laws. The Massachusetts Division of Immigration and Americanization offered thinly veiled critiques of the many citizenship requirements for employment and licensure in force across the Bay State during the Great Depression. The division noted in 1930 that such provisions had "usually been placed upon the statute books because of pressure in some occupational group, labor union and profession." This lobbying had led to "sometimes rather anomalous situations" wherein "different standards have been set for somewhat similar occupations." The division confessed that it could find no inherent logic in making citizenship a necessity for "registration as pharmacist, druggist or embalmer," while "no such requirement is made for registration as physician, surgeon or nurse."[108] Eight years later, the division warned that while "citizenship should be, perhaps, a precious privilege to be earned," it was too frequently becoming a "requirement for livelihood."[109] But not all immigrant professionals could expeditiously earn or were even eligible to obtain that "precious privilege" in the 1930s.

Racially marginalized immigrants, especially "aliens ineligible to citizenship" like Makhan Singh Sandhu, disproportionately bore the burden of state antialien licensure laws. Sandhu, who hailed from India, applied to take his qualifying exam to become a registered pharmacist in California in July 1931. While the Golden State's requirement that immigrant pharmacists possess first papers posed a seemingly impenetrable barrier to his licensure, Sandhu had found a court that allowed him to make a formal declaration of intention to become a US citizen. Board members were stumped on how to proceed. While they recognized that he had provided them with legitimate documents, they did not know if it was in their power to grant a license to a "party . . . not eligible for citizenship."[110] Though the board learned from naturalization officials that Sandhu had not violated federal law, it ultimately decided that he was "unable to qualify" for a pharmacy license and denied his application.[111]

Meanwhile, in the fall of 1931, Japanese national Shigeo Kato, who had received an entry-level "assistant" pharmacy license before the state required first papers, petitioned to upgrade to a full license. Kato's plea was supported by Japanese American civil rights activist Sei Fujii, himself a trained lawyer who was barred from practicing in the state because of California's anti-alien attorney policy. The board denied Kato's application.[112] In October 1932, the board went so far as to formally recommend that the state legislature amend the California pharmacy licensure law so that only persons "eligible to citizenship" could receive licenses.[113] State lawmakers ignored their request.

The following autumn, three Japanese pharmacists working under assistant-level licenses were also denied in their attempts to receive full licensure. In response, Thomas Sashihara, Fusuichi Fukushima, and Kesanosuke Sakuda filed suit against the board.[114] After a defeat in lower court, their lawyer, Maurice Norcop, argued on appeal that the first papers requirement was both an

Figure 5.1 "Mr. and Mrs. Thomas T. Sashihara are obtaining internal employment clearance from Haruko Fujita to clear all government property before leaving the Heart Mountain Relocation Center for outside employment, 1944." Photographer: Iwasaki, Hikaru. War Relocation Authority Photographs of Japanese American Evacuation and Resettlement, UC Berkeley: Bancroft Library and Archives/Online Archives of California.

136 DISPARATE REGIMES

infringement of federal treaty obligations with Japan and an equal protection violation of the Fourteenth Amendment. The California Court of Appeal for the Second District rejected his arguments in June 1935. In its ruling in *Sashihara et al. v. California State Board of Pharmacy*, the court conceded that the Treaty of Commerce and Navigation guaranteed Japanese nationals equal access to the "trade[s]," but it distinguished pharmacy licensure from them. The court also dismissed Norcop's equal protection argument. Since pharmacists handled "chemicals and poisons" and could cause great "harm" in their work, the court ruled that the profession fell under the state's police powers. If the state determined that noncitizens—even immigrants ineligible to naturalize— should be denied access to these professions, the court reasoned that "it is obvious from these facts and others that there may be a reasonable basis for the existence of the discrimination against" them.[115] Though Sashihara would persevere to create both a successful pharmacy practice and his own five-and-dime business, he and his family would be forcefully removed from California and incarcerated by their own government in World War II.[116]

East and South Asian immigrants continued to be ensnared by state antialien licensing laws as the Depression wore on. In Wisconsin, most European- and Canadian-born accountants could meet their state's first papers requirement provided they had the economic means. But M. A. Rauf, who hailed from India, could not. Without any debate about the ethics, practicality, or constitutionality of barring aliens ineligible to citizenship, the Wisconsin Board of Accountancy rejected his application for licensure in August 1934.[117]

The California Board of Pharmacy grew increasingly exasperated with having to enforce the state's first papers requirement and deal with matters of citizenship. In October 1939, after denying a Chinese immigrant's application for licensure, board members voted to contact "the Deans of the colleges of pharmacy" across the state to reiterate the importance of "the citizenship requirement in the Pharmacy Law so that alien students in the future may be advised of the fact that they are not eligible for examination unless they can become citizens."[118]

Migrant Jewish doctors, especially those fleeing Nazi Germany, were also targeted by a growing number of licensure restrictions in the mid- to late 1930s as the AMA embraced unabashed nativism. At its annual convention in 1935, the AMA Board of Trustees complained that an "influx of foreign physicians" to the country was continuing unabated despite the drastic drop in overall immigration during the Great Depression. Noting that total immigration to the United States had "diminished from 279,678 in 1929 to 29,470 in 1934," it lamented that foreign doctors continued to move to the United States at rates similar to those seen in years prior to the stock market crash in 1929 (398 immigrant physicians entered the country in 1929; 353 arrived in 1934). In that same period, the number of doctors moving to the United States from Germany had grown "from 22 in 1929, to 160 in 1934." The board grumbled that under the quota system, "there seems at present no practicable way of limiting" the entry of refugee doctors moving to the United States. But it ominously remarked that "whether such physicians may or may not" work in their new homes "depends primarily on their ability to meet the requirements of the laws of the several states."[119]

Three years later, California physician William R. Molony introduced a resolution at the 1938 AMA Annual Convention calling for the adoption of citizen-only licensure policies for doctors throughout the country. While Molony vaguely alluded to citizenship requirements for medical licenses that he claimed were pervasive in other countries as justification for his proposal, he especially bemoaned the "increasing numbers" of "foreign graduates" who were "seeking admittance to the practice of medicine in these United States." Molony also dressed his nativism in the language of loyalty, arguing that "a period of residence" was needed for immigrant doctors to gain "a full and satisfactory knowledge of the American conception of patriotism and of ethical ideas of medicine."[120] The AMA House of Delegates adopted Molony's resolution, making it the formal policy recommendation of the organization.[121]

The timing could not have been worse for refugee doctors. Shortly after the outbreak of war in Europe, the *Journal of the American Medical Association* admitted that "difficult situations have been created" owing to the proliferation of anti-alien licensure laws, even recognizing that "physicians from Germany and the nations it has taken over" were likely to be harmed by them. But the AMA did not rethink its support for such policies.[122] Instead, it sought their indiscriminate application, as the travails of immigrant doctors in Texas illustrate.

In June 1938, the Texas Board of Medical Examiners voted to deny licenses to twenty-one noncitizen physicians. Among them were "17 Germans who have sought refuge in this country," the *Austin Statesman* reported. The board claimed that "Europe was in such a chaotic state it had been impossible to ascertain whether schools from which the alien candidates graduated met the standards set by the Texas board."[123] In October, the board convened a special meeting to address challenges posed by "the political and social rejustments [*sic*] taking place in the educational institutions of Central Europe." It ultimately voted to inform numerous immigrant doctors that they could not take the upcoming state medical licensure exams owing to "the tardiness of foreign nations in furnishing the required information in time."[124] When several of them showed up to take the tests in November anyway, the board, after significant internal debate, voted to permit some—deemed to "have reasonably completed their credentials and forms"—to seek licensure via examination.[125]

The following year, Texas state lawmakers enacted a strict citizen-only physician licensing law.[126] One immigrant doctor denied access to licensure under the provisions of the new statute, Mexican national Manuel Garcia-Godoy, strenuously challenged it in court.[127] In *Manuel Garcia-Godoy v. Texas State Board of Medical Examiners*, the District Court of Travis County upheld the policy. Garcia-Godoy's case did succeed in enabling noncitizen doctors to pursue their licensure applications if they had applied prior to the adoption of the 1939 citizen-only licensing law. Unfortunately for Garcia-Godoy, the board also refused to recognize his medical degree from the National University of Mexico. As an apt symbol of their overlapping protectionist interests, the Texas Board of Medicine forwarded its bills arising from Garcia-Godoy's lawsuit ($43.55) to the state AMA branch.[128] The national AMA's Bureau of Legal Medicine and Legislation, in turn, applauded the Texas branch for pursuing and winning this case, which it believed to be "the first time ... that a citizenship requirement in relation to medical licensure ha[d] been squarely before a court."[129]

Figure 5.2 Dr. Manuel Garcia-Godoy, c. 1974. University of Texas at El Paso Library, Special Collections Department, *El Paso Herald–Post* Records, M5348.

By the end of the 1930s, therefore, professional organizations like the AMA were becoming more overt in their support for anti-alien licensure laws and less reticent about publicity surrounding controversies over their implementation. American entry into World War II and its concomitant rise in both wartime nativism and acute labor shortages would alter that equation in contradictory ways.

Conflicting Directions during World War II and the Early Cold War

Few senior members of the Roosevelt administration knew more about the effects of anti-alien hiring and licensure restrictions on the eve of the country's participation in World War II than Earl Harrison. A longtime immigrant rights advocate and lawyer, Harrison supervised the massive federal effort to enroll millions of noncitizens nationwide in 1940. Harrison used his platform as director of the federal Alien Registration program to challenge nativist employment and licensure barriers, contending that they both harmed immigrants' livelihoods and impeded the nation's war mobilization plans.[130] For instance, in a June 1941 address, Harrison implored Americans to recognize that owing to restrictive national immigration laws and growing naturalization rates, the country's noncitizen population was fast declining. He reasoned that it was therefore "patently absurd to place the blame for such national ills as unemployment on the aliens."[131] Harrison also called on his fellow citizens to recognize that anti-alien employment policies "tend[ed] to impede our National Defense program."[132] In a series of presentations and announcements, he and his allies regularly argued that employment discrimination against noncitizens ran counter to American values.[133]

Following his promotion to commissioner of the Immigration and Naturalization Service shortly after US entry into the war, Harrison continued to urge the public to reject employment discrimination against noncitizens. In a 1943 address, he argued that "everyone knows that our armed forces are filled with boys of Italian and German extraction who are just as loyal and just as eager for our victory as the rest." He went so far as to applaud the American public for opposing mass "witch-hunt[s]" against individuals solely because of their nationality or ethnicity.[134] Harrison conspicuously failed to note the incarceration of Japanese nationals and Japanese Americans among the pressing problems that needed to be rectified.[135] Instead, he stressed that "there are so many states which have laws and regulations excluding aliens from services usually granted to citizens. There are too many states which preclude aliens from operating certain types of business enterprises or practicing in certain

140 DISPARATE REGIMES

professions." Harrison proudly noted that the Immigration and Naturalization Service was trying to mitigate the effects of these anti-alien licensing restrictions by "provid[ing] for more expeditious consideration of naturalization petitions filed by doctors and surgeons." With opponents alleging "that 'the alien doctors' will steal the practices of those who have gone into the Army and the Navy," he urged Americans to recognize "that there is plenty of work for all and there will continue to be," for both citizens and noncitizens alike.[136] Not all public servants were of the same opinion.

Owing to fears of subversion, job loss, and labor shortages, state politicians and licensing officials often articulated conflicting and even contradictory approaches toward noncitizens' employment and licensure during World War II. For instance, only three months after the attack on Pearl Harbor, members of the California Teacher Preparation and Licensing Commission debated how to better enforce the state's requirement that only US citizens or immigrants in the process of becoming citizens could work as public schoolteachers. The commission initially decided that all teachers would henceforth have to provide documentation of citizenship or first papers when applying for their credentials. But before implementing such a policy, the commission turned to the office of state attorney general Earl Warren for advice.[137]

Warren's deputy, T. A. Westphal Jr., strongly urged California education authorities not to demand citizenship papers from all teachers since there were no explicit stipulations for such documentation requirements in the state's labor or education statutes. In a memo to the licensing commission (signed by Warren), Westphal concluded that it would be best to continue the policy of "accepting the applicant's statement of citizenship, unless circumstances appear to warrant a further examination of the claim."[138] The commission's aborted efforts were soon made temporarily moot. Owing to a shortage of teachers, in 1943, the California state legislature authorized the issuance of "emergency credentials" to noncitizen teachers (provided they were not "enemy aliens") that would automatically expire upon the war's conclusion.[139]

The Texas Board of Medical Examiners was moving in similarly contradictory directions. Acknowledging a growing need for doctors in Texas as physicians entered military service, the board voted to waive several examination and experience requirements for the "graduates of the English Speaking Schools of our Allied Countries" as early as November 1941. Nevertheless, at that same meeting and at another convened in January 1944, board members did not consider ignoring the citizenship requirement, nor did they lobby lawmakers to amend the state's anti-alien physician licensure law.[140] Meanwhile, the board continued to deny credentials to most graduates of the Universidad Nacional Autónoma de México. Only the prodding of governor Beauford H. Jester in 1947 prompted the board to consider the universal recognition of degrees from the preeminent university in Mexico (which it acceded to after its own "investigation" two years later).[141]

Such developments were not unique to California and Texas. Despite the passage of wartime fair employment laws by some northern state legislatures, anti-alien licensure policies were rarely repealed or struck down as unconstitutional in the aftermath of World War II.[142] In fact, state lawmakers actively expanded their number and scope, adopting no fewer than sixty-nine new anti-alien occupational and professional licensure statutes between 1940 and 1957.[143]

Since most noncitizens had to reside in the United States for five years before they could naturalize, anti-alien licensure laws especially harmed recent refugees during and following World War II. Sociologist Donald Peterson Kent found in 1953 that noncitizen doctors were naturalizing at a greater and faster rate than other migrant professionals, with teachers and lawyers following close behind.[144] He further observed that "refugee physicians," in particular, had "tended to concentrate in the few states that are most liberal in their licensing policies."[145]

State licensing boards also frequently adopted more stringent mechanisms to enforce long-standing citizenship requirements as servicemen returned home from the war. For instance, in 1947, the Texas Board of Public Accountancy adopted new rules to implement the state's "Proof of Citizenship" requirement, henceforth compelling foreign-born accountants to submit their own naturalization documents to state officials in Austin. Though the board recognized that this was a significant demand, it insisted in correspondence with immigrant accountants that "there is no way of establishing proof of citizenship without submitting your actual citizenship papers." The board assured them, however, that their papers would be promptly returned after the verification process had been completed.[146]

Immigrant dentists in Massachusetts likewise encountered more restrictive licensing regulations in the immediate postwar years. In June 1946, the Massachusetts Board of Dentistry wrote to already-licensed immigrant dentists to demand that they promptly submit proof of citizenship or first papers before the board's next meeting a month later. Those who failed to submit such paperwork, the board warned, would have their licenses immediately suspended. The following month, the board voted to suspend the licenses of twelve immigrant dentists on these grounds. One of them, Yohei Noji, a Japanese national, protested the revocation of his license because he could not file for his first papers. The board referred his grievance to the state attorney general's office, which ruled in Noji's favor.[147] Japanese professionals in other states were usually not so fortunate.

In his pathbreaking 1946 legal monograph, *The Alien and the Asiatic in American Law*, Milton Konvitz criticized policymakers and members of the

142 DISPARATE REGIMES

public who made excuses for or dismissed the importance of the unequal rights afforded to East and South Asian immigrants under state and federal jurisprudence. Writing just a year after the end of both the Holocaust and Japanese American internment, Konvitz urged readers to remember that, although "Jews constituted only 1 per cent of" Germany's population in the early 1930s, their small numbers "did not save them from the wrath of the Nazis."[148] While noting that fourteen citizen-only licensing policies in New York harmed all noncitizens, he underscored that first papers requirements in thirteen other professions and occupations posed impenetrable barriers for many East and South Asian migrants owing to their status as racially ineligible to citizenship.[149]

Meanwhile, East and South Asian immigrants and civil rights organizations continued to challenge the constitutionality of restrictions on the basis of "ineligibility to citizenship" in court. The US Supreme Court haltingly, but increasingly, overturned such policies in the late 1940s. In January 1948, the high court ruled in *Oyama v. California* that key elements of the California Alien Land Acts were unconstitutional. Later that same year, in *Takahashi v. Fish & Game Commission*, the court struck down a similar ban on Japanese immigrants' access to fishing licenses. But to completely rid California and the nation of their effects, explicitly racist federal naturalization laws would have to be repealed.[150]

Chinese immigrants, first targeted for anti-alien legislation in California during the gold rush era, became eligible for American citizenship in wartime. To bolster cooperation with Chinese allies, Congress repealed the infamous Chinese Exclusion Act in 1943. Since the world's most populous country was afforded only a token annual immigration quota, the legislation had a far greater immediate impact on the lives of Chinese nationals residing in the United States, who—provided they met all other requirements—could finally become US citizens.[151] The dismantling of the Chinese Exclusion Act also signaled that long-standing racist naturalization bans on other immigrants from East and South Asia could someday be repealed.

When Congress overrode president Harry S. Truman's veto of the McCarran–Walter Immigration and Nationality Act of 1952, the last remaining federal naturalization restrictions on the basis of race—then targeting Japanese immigrants—were finally overturned. Though would-be migrants from Asia were often denied entry into the United States owing to paltry national quotas, the act finally dismantled the category of aliens racially ineligible to citizenship. With its destruction, no longer would East and South Asian immigrants be perpetually barred from a range of professions under state anti-alien licensure laws.[152]

* * *

LEARNING CITIZENSHIP MATTERS 143

The passage of the McCarran–Walter Act did not bring about an end to state anti-alien hiring and licensure laws, of course. In fact, the US Supreme Court was loath to overturn them on equal protection grounds under the leadership of chief justice Earl Warren from 1953 until 1969. But the high court largely reversed course in the years following his retirement, increasingly recognizing alienage as a suspect class.[153] In *Sugarman v. Dougall* (1973), In re *Griffiths* (1973), and *Examining Board v. Flores de Otero* (1976), the court struck down citizenship requirements for most civil service jobs, attorneys, and "common occupations," like engineering and architecture.[154]

But the high court did not overturn all anti-alien employment laws or nativist state licensure regimes. In *Ambach v. Norwick* (1979), the US Supreme Court upheld New York's long-standing requirement that noncitizen immigrant public schoolteachers naturalize upon eligibility.[155] Meanwhile, state lawmakers and licensing boards were turning to other mechanisms to restrict the licensure of immigrant professionals, especially graduates of foreign medical schools.[156]

The proliferation of state anti-alien professional employment and licensure measures in the early to mid-twentieth century thus left a significant impact and legacy. Foremost, the explosion of such laws boosted the material weight of the possession of US citizenship for resident immigrants. It also led a host of historical actors—from noncitizen professionals and their advocates to licensing board members and judges—to increasingly encounter citizenship rights as citizen-only rights in their lives and livelihoods.

To be clear, such laws neither ensured nor grew out of efforts to afford equal employment rights to all US citizens from the Progressive Era to the early Cold War period. These years were marred by the institutionalization of Jim Crow legal regimes in the South, widespread employment and educational prejudice against women, and many other forms of de jure and de facto economic discrimination directed at marginalized American citizens. Indeed, nativist state employment policies often intersected with and actively exacerbated discriminatory measures against marginalized Americans. But state anti-alien hiring and licensure laws, in particular, also forced immigrant rights advocates, licensing authorities, and, above all, noncitizens themselves to learn about matters of citizenship and how much citizenship could matter.

Disparate Regimes: Nativist Politics, Alienage Law, and Citizenship Rights in the United States, 1865–1965.
Brendan A. Shanahan, Oxford University Press. © Brendan A. Shanahan 2025.
DOI: 10.1093/9780197660577.003.0006

6

Embedding American Citizenship and Citizenship Rights

Marital Repatriation Law from the Women's Suffrage Movement to the Cold War

Ethel Mackenzie (née Coope) was outraged. After campaigning hard for the successful 1911 California women's suffrage referendum, Mackenzie learned that she would still be denied the right to vote. Though born a US citizen, she had lost her American nationality upon marrying Scottish singer Gordon Mackenzie in 1909 under the provisions of the federal Expatriation Act of 1907. Believing that law to be in violation of the Fourteenth Amendment's birthright citizenship clause, Mackenzie challenged its constitutionality before the highest court in the land. The US Supreme Court ruled against Mackenzie in 1915, reasoning that her marriage "with a foreigner [was] tantamount to voluntary expatriation."[1]

Marital expatriation would not long survive the women's suffrage revolution in the United States, however. Following the ratification of the Nineteenth Amendment, Congress adopted several statutes in the 1920s and the early 1930s that recognized the independent citizenship status of women henceforth marrying spouses of different nationalities. These laws also increasingly allowed marital expatriates to regain US citizenship as immigrants in their native-born country if they met all other eligibility provisions, paid the associated fees, and passed a naturalization test. For some women, those requirements were insurmountable.[2]

Rebecca Shelley, a pacifist, repeatedly tried and failed to regain her native-born US citizenship in the 1930s. Since she refused to swear an oath promising to defend the nation, Shelley's petition was opposed by Immigration and Naturalization Service (INS) officers and repeatedly stymied in federal court.[3] A July 1940 amendment to the federal Repatriation Act of 1936, which aimed to simplify and accelerate the process whereby marital expatriates could apply for and regain their American citizenship, soon gave Shelley hope.[4]

Construing the amendment extremely broadly, INS leaders interpreted it to mean that all permanently resident marital expatriates, like Shelley, had been automatically "deemed" to be US citizens by decree. But INS administrators

EMBEDDING AMERICAN CITIZENSHIP AND CITIZENSHIP RIGHTS   145

announced at the same time that such women would not possess the "rights of citizenship" unless and until they took an oath of allegiance in court.[5] Overnight, Shelley had seemingly become an American citizen again without violating her pacifist values. But when she tried to take the oath of allegiance and regain her citizenship rights, Shelley was again denied because she would not promise to defend the United States. The US Court of Appeals in Washington, DC, in turn, ruled that Shelley could not take the oath and regain her citizenship rights because she was not a US citizen at all. It rejected the view "that Congress [had] created a class of so-called 'citizens' from whom, although they had committed no offense, it withheld all the rights of citizens," effectively declaring the INS interpretation of federal repatriation law to be null and void within its jurisdiction.[6]

This chapter explores and contextualizes the efforts of thousands of US-born women like Mackenzie and Shelley to regain their birthright American citizenship and its accompanying rights in the courtroom during the early to mid-twentieth century. It extrapolates from regional case studies to estimate that between 80,000 and 130,000 women likely applied to regain their stolen citizenship nationwide via naturalization between fiscal year (FY) 1923 and FY 1940 and that somewhere between 32,000 and 63,000 additional marital expatriates probably took the oath of allegiance under federal repatriation law between FY 1936 and FY 1975.[7] Judges usually approved marital expatriates' applications to regain their US citizenship and citizenship rights. But some petitioners were denied. Adverse rulings in the 1920s and 1930s, often spurred on by federal naturalization officials who construed citizenship law restrictively, disproportionately harmed young marital expatriates, mothers raising children, and, most especially, women of color.

INS leaders dramatically changed course in 1940 to declare all permanently resident marital expatriates to have been deemed to be "citizens without citizenship rights" just as two other major federal statutes—the Alien Registration Act and the Nationality Act of October 14, 1940—came into law and sharpened distinctions between citizenship and alienage on the eve of American entry into World War II.[8] Though many jurists initially acceded to the INS's broad interpretation of federal repatriation law, as the 1940s wore on, they increasingly rejected the claim that US citizenship status could be formally separated from American citizenship rights. With the Supreme Court never ruling on the subject, INS leaders continued to affirm the validity of their approach. By the early 1950s, however, marital expatriates who had not taken an oath of allegiance were generally treated in administrative practice as noncitizens.

This chapter examines the obstacles marital expatriates often encountered in their persistent efforts to regain American citizenship, highlighting the generally increasing relative value of its exclusive rights over time.[9] It argues that the failure

146 DISPARATE REGIMES

of INS leaders to have permanently resident marital expatriates unilaterally and universally recognized as citizens without the rights of citizenship illustrates how embedded the idea of US citizenship rights as citizen-only rights had become in both law and popular perception by the middle of the twentieth century.

"Food for Thought": Repatriation as Naturalization (1922–36/1940)

Hundreds of thousands of US-born women lost their citizenship upon marriage following the passage of the Expatriation Act of 1907.[10] Under its terms, if an American-born woman married a noncitizen immigrant, she automatically lost her nationality.[11] If her husband naturalized, she became a US citizen again. Otherwise, she had to obtain a divorce or wait until he died to regain her birthright.[12] Following the ratification of the Nineteenth Amendment, women's rights organizations—most notably the new League of Women Voters—successfully lobbied for the passage of the Cable Act in 1922, which disentangled the nationality of most US-born women who subsequently married noncitizen men.[13] American women who married men ineligible for citizenship (i.e., East and South Asian men) continued to lose their nationality until the passage of a 1931 amendment to the Cable Act ended that overtly racist policy.[14]

Marital expatriates did not automatically regain their stolen American citizenship and its rights following the passage of the Cable Act in 1922 and its subsequent amendments. Instead, the vast majority who sought to become US citizens once more during the 1920s and 1930s had to naturalize in court as immigrants in their native-born country.

Amalia Bertha Stratton was one such woman. Born in 1882 in Fountain City, Wisconsin, Stratton lost her US nationality when she married Harry D'Arcy Stratton, a Canadian. On December 28, 1922, she appeared before a clerk of the federal district court in San Francisco to file her naturalization petition. Two US citizens accompanied her to verify her long-standing residency in California. A federal judge signed off on her petition on April 2, 1923. That same day, she took an oath of allegiance to the United States, abjured all loyalty to Great Britain and Canada, and became an American citizen once more.[15]

Stratton likely followed the same naturalization process that most marital expatriates went through to regain her citizenship during the 1920s and 1930s. Either immediately before she filed her petition with the clerk or shortly thereafter, Stratton would have had to submit to a background check by Bureau of Naturalization officials stationed in San Francisco. In addition to confirming her identity, naturalization examiners would have (prior to 1930) ensured her residency credentials, verified her racial qualifications, and probably quizzed

EMBEDDING AMERICAN CITIZENSHIP AND CITIZENSHIP RIGHTS   147

her on her English-language skills and on questions that could appear on an upcoming citizenship test administered by a naturalization judge at her final hearing. She would have also had to appear in court with two witnesses.[16] The judge could have questioned her about her "knowledge of the history, geography, government, and law of the country," her literacy and competency in English, and her intention to reside permanently in the United States.[17] Although the judge had the right to overrule a naturalization examiner's supportive recommendation, it would have been very unusual for him to do so.[18]

In San Francisco, marital expatriates like Amalia Stratton represented a sizeable number of all noncitizens—male and female—petitioning for citizenship in the four years following the passage of the Cable Act. Between FY 1923 and 1926, a total of 149 US-born women applied to regain citizenship at the federal district court in San Francisco. They comprised 7.8 percent, 4.5 percent, 5.0 percent, and 4.1 percent of all naturalization petitioners during those four fiscal years, respectively. Of them, 140 were successfully naturalized (one was told she was already a citizen).[19]

All told, between FY 1923 and FY 1940, a total of 1,373 marital expatriates filed to regain their citizenship under the provisions of the Cable Act in San Francisco's federal court (representing 2.99 percent of 45,945 naturalization petitioners). In the late 1920s and again in the late 1930s, marital expatriate petitioners regularly numbered over 100 per year. Despite an overall drop in marital expatriate petitions during the early years of the Great Depression, Asian American women flocked to apply for citizenship after the Cable Act was amended in 1931 to permit their naturalization. Twenty-three women whose husbands were Japanese, Chinese, or Indian immigrants regained their native-born American citizenship in FY 1932. They amounted to nearly one-third of all (73) marital expatriates who reacquired citizenship in federal court in San Francisco that year.[20] Similar patterns unfolded further west, in Hawaii. Given the islands' demographics, Asian American women represented a majority of marital expatriates petitioning for naturalization in Honolulu's federal district court in FY 1931 and FY 1932.[21]

A different story unfolded in the nation's smallest state. Rhode Island had attracted tens of thousands of immigrants to work in its factories during the late nineteenth and early twentieth centuries, becoming the country's most densely populated state. By 1920, immigrants and their children—particularly those of Irish, Italian, Portuguese, and Canadian heritage—made up a majority of the state's population.[22] But when ninety-three marital expatriates petitioned to regain US citizenship in the federal district court of Rhode Island between FY 1923 and FY 1926, they represented a smaller proportion of all naturalization petitioners than their peers in San Francisco during their four initial years of eligibility (peaking at 2.5 percent in FY 1925).[23]

148 DISPARATE REGIMES

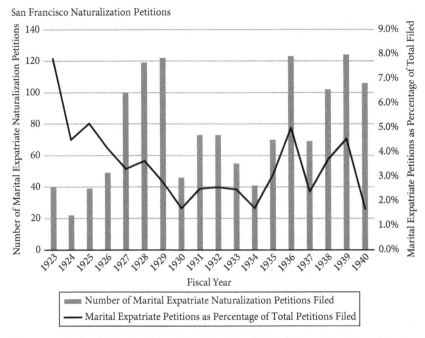

Figure 6.1 Federal District Court, San Francisco Marital Expatriate Naturalization Petitions Filed, FY 1923–1940; Petition and Record of Naturalization, 1903–1991, SF, RG 21; NARA–Pacific (San Bruno).

Marital expatriates rushed to regain citizenship in Rhode Island in FY 1928, likely as part of a broader naturalization and voter registration drive among northeastern Catholics when New York Democratic governor Al Smith became the first major-party Catholic nominee for president.[24] While just 24 expatriates applied to regain citizenship in FY 1927, in FY 1928 that number jumped to 95.[25] Naturalization rates among Rhode Island marital expatriates dropped in the early 1930s, likely due to increased costs imposed on would-be applicants by the Hoover administration during the early Depression years, before increasing once more in the late 1930s.[26] Ultimately, 618 marital expatriates petitioned to naturalize in the federal district court of Rhode Island, representing roughly 1 of every 39 applicants for citizenship (2.59 percent) between FY 1923 and FY 1940.[27]

In the federal courts of Texas, marital expatriates often represented an even larger percentage of petitions filed between FY 1923 and FY 1940. In Houston, marital expatriates represented 4.05 percent (120 of 2,963) of all naturalization petitions.[28] In the border city of Laredo, they numbered 1 of every 12 noncitizens—male and female—applying for citizenship (45 of 535).[29]

EMBEDDING AMERICAN CITIZENSHIP AND CITIZENSHIP RIGHTS   149

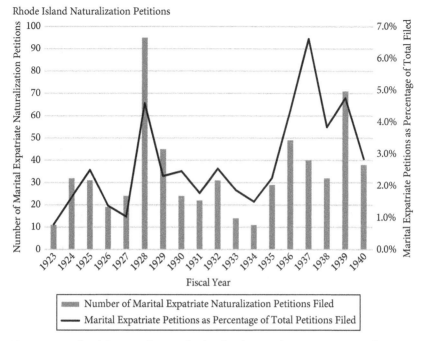

Figure 6.2 Federal District Court, Rhode Island Marital Expatriate Naturalization Petitions Filed, FY 1923–1940; Petition and Record of Naturalization, 1842–1991, RI; RG 21; NARA–Northeast (Waltham).

Though Houston and Laredo contained vastly different populations, San Antonio—one of the state's largest cities and home to sizeable Anglo-American, Mexican American, and Mexican immigrant populations in the 1920s and 1930s—offers a unique cross-section of the state's demographics.[30] There, 139 (4.10 percent) of all 3,391 petitions for naturalization between FY 1923 and FY 1940 were filed by marital expatriates, a higher percentage than in San Francisco or Providence.[31] Rates of rejection were also higher in San Antonio. Ten marital expatriate petitioners in total were stymied in San Antonio's federal district court (another 3 were told that they were already US citizens).[32] All but 1 rejected petitioner was of Mexican origin.[33]

Since the Bureau of Naturalization (and later the INS) did not distinguish marital expatriates from foreign-born immigrants in their annual reports, it is impossible to determine exactly how many former American women reacquired their citizenship through naturalization. These case studies allow for reasonable estimates, however. Between FY 1923 and FY 1940, a total of 3,163,218 noncitizens across the country filed petitions to acquire American citizenship. If the rate of marital expatriates in Providence petitioning for citizenship

150   DISPARATE REGIMES

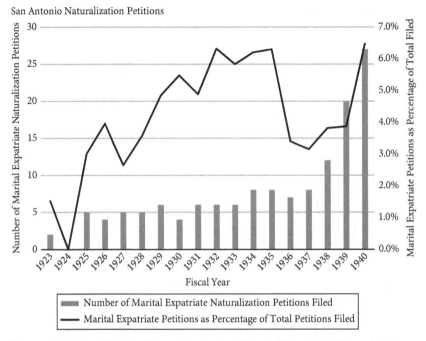

Figure 6.3 Federal District Court, San Antonio Marital Expatriate Naturalization Petitions Filed, FY 1923–1940; Petition and Record of Naturalization, SA; RG 21; NARA–Southwest (Fort Worth).

(2.59 percent of the total) is indicative of national patterns, then roughly 81,811 of those noncitizens were marital expatriates. If San Francisco's figures are typical (2.99 percent), the estimated number of marital expatriates petitioning to naturalize rises to 94,528. If the San Antonio numbers are representative (4.10 percent), then roughly 129,663 marital expatriates petitioned for citizenship. It is thus likely that marital expatriates filing to naturalize numbered at least in the high tens of thousands nationwide.[34]

Moreover, if patterns in San Francisco, Providence, and San Antonio are indicative, a large majority of marital expatriates were successful in their petitions during the interwar decades. But what of those who were denied?

In both San Francisco and Providence, "failure to prosecute" (to appear before a naturalization judge and complete the petition) was a common reason for denial, particularly in the four years following the passage of the Cable Act in 1922.[35] Judges and naturalization examiners in San Francisco proved much quicker to throw out a woman's petition than officials in Providence, however. Helen Mercedes Gilliand, for instance, petitioned to regain her citizenship in San Francisco on December 14, 1922. Just eleven months later, at the request of the local naturalization examiner, judge John S. Partridge denied her petition

EMBEDDING AMERICAN CITIZENSHIP AND CITIZENSHIP RIGHTS 151

citing failure to prosecute.[36] Gilliand's case was far from unusual in San Francisco, where marital expatriates' petitions were often thrown out after roughly a year of inactivity.[37] By contrast, Anna Patricia McKeen of Pawtucket, Rhode Island, filed her petition in Providence on May 7, 1924, and waited over three years before returning to the court, but she regained her citizenship without ever having to ask for an extension.[38] Between FY 1923 and FY 1926, only three marital expatriates had their cases denied in Providence owing to the failure-to-prosecute provision. Two of those petitions were almost four years old when they were dismissed.[39]

Use of this failure-to-prosecute provision by San Francisco naturalization examiners and judges could greatly hinder the efforts of mothers raising young children. Alfhild Johanna Blumer, a Bay Area resident, managed to file her petition for naturalization on June 27, 1923. She was subsequently notified that she had until January 5, 1925, to pass her citizenship exam and take the oath of allegiance. Raising an infant and giving birth to a second child had prevented Blumer from reappearing before the court. Worried that she might not make it back in time, she wrote to the clerk's office in December 1924 and informed the court that it was "just as difficult as ever to get away with a 1 and 2 year old but I want my citizenship." On January 4, 1925, she again implored the clerk for an extension because one of her witnesses had been admitted to the hospital. On the recommendation of the San Francisco Naturalization Office, her petition was denied the following day. Just two days later, however, federal district court judge Frank Kerrigan overruled that decision, granting Blumer a much-needed extension. On October 5, 1925, she swore the oath of allegiance and became an American citizen once more.[40]

Ernestine Welden was not so fortunate. She, too, was raising a toddler when she petitioned to regain her native-born citizenship in San Francisco's federal district court in October 1923. Like Blumer, Welden was given until January 5, 1925, to complete her naturalization. When she was unable to do so, Welden's petition was dismissed.[41]

Though mothers were not overtly banned owing to the Bureau of Naturalization's interpretation of the Cable Act, wives under twenty-one years of age often were. On December 27, 1923, US-born Dorothy Chamorro filed a petition for naturalization in San Francisco.[42] At her final hearing before Judge Kerrigan on May 5, 1924, M. R. Bevington, chief examiner of the San Francisco Naturalization Office, moved to dismiss eighteen-year-old Chamorro's case.[43] Although her lawyer implored the judge to consider that a denial would render his client stateless, Kerrigan rejected Chamorro's petition.[44] While the judge conceded that "it may seem harsh to classify a native born applicant, with one of foreign birth," Kerrigan maintained that the Cable Act was clear that a marital expatriate "*shall be naturalized upon full and complete compliance with all*

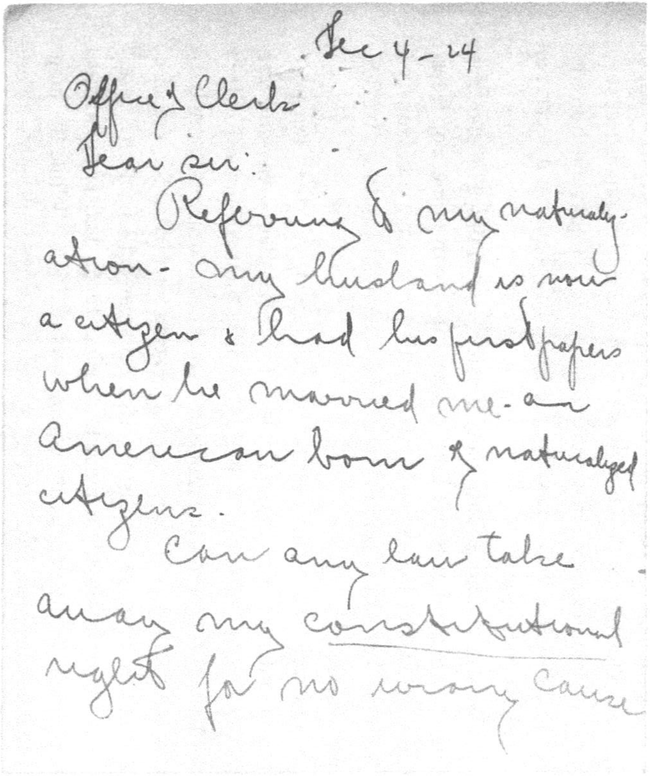

Dec 4-24

Office of Clerk

Dear sir:

Referring to my naturaliz-ation - my husband is now a citizen & had his first papers when he married me - an American born of naturalized citizens.

Can any law take away my constitutional right for no wrong cause

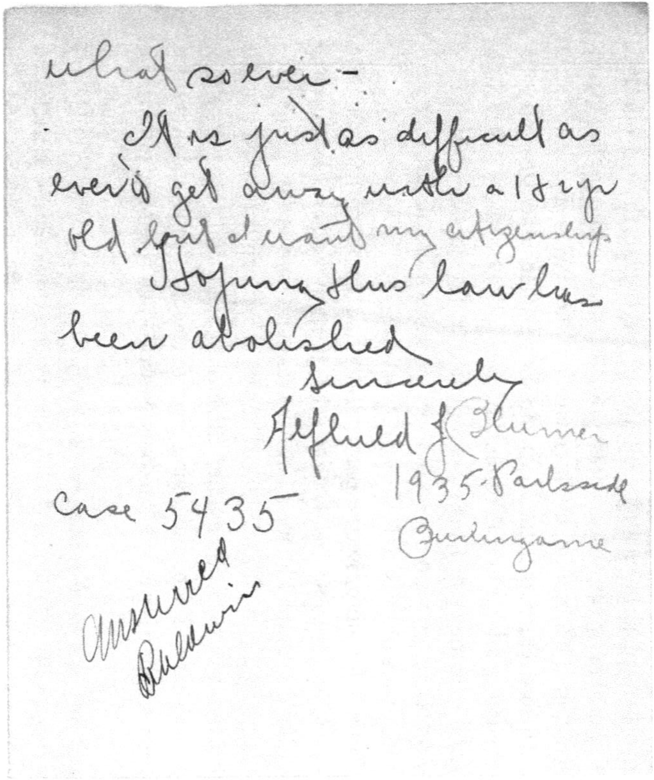

what so ever -

It is just as difficult as ever to get away with a 1 & 2 yr old but I want my citizenship

Hoping this law has been abolished

Sincerely

Alfhild J Blumer

1935 Parkside

Burlingame

Case 5435

Answered

Baldwin

Figures 6.4 and 6.5 Petition of Naturalization #5435. Alfhild Johanna Blumer, June 27, 1923. Petition and Record of Naturalization, 1903–1991, SF, Vol. 51, Box 27; RG 21; NARA–Pacific (San Bruno). In her note, Blumer emphasized that "my husband is now a citizen & had his first papers when he married me—an American born of naturalized citizens." She demanded to know "can any law take away my constitutional right for no wrong cause what so ever" while emphasizing, "It is just as difficult as ever to get away with a 1 & 2 yr old but I want my citizenship."

EMBEDDING AMERICAN CITIZENSHIP AND CITIZENSHIP RIGHTS   153

the requirements of the naturalization laws," including the prerequisite "that the petitioner shall have reached the age of twenty-one years."[45] On June 29, 1926, marital expatriate Molly Di Rita of Cranston, Rhode Island, a mere five months shy of turning twenty-one, was also denied her petition of naturalization.[46]

Residency requirements also complicated the efforts of many marital expatriates. Social work scholar Sophonisba Breckinridge noted in 1931 that one of the greatest "hardship[s]" that many marital expatriates faced in their efforts to regain citizenship was proving compliance with all federal residency conditions.[47] Prior to 1930, marital expatriates were required to provide proof of continuous residency for at least one year in the United States. But Congress had not clearly defined the meaning of residency via statute, forcing judges and naturalization officials to interpret whether a marital expatriate had satisfied such prerequisites on their own.[48]

Marital expatriate Jeanette Anderson Haas encountered the full frustrations of such unclear residency requirements. A native of San Francisco, Haas had married her Swiss husband in 1912 and proceeded to live with him in Mexico. Crossing the border at El Paso, the couple returned to the United States in 1923 and received certificates of arrival marked "for temporary purposes."[49] When Haas petitioned to regain her US citizenship in March 1929, those three words would cause her a great deal of trouble.[50] Paul Armstrong, the district director of the San Francisco Naturalization Office, opposed Haas's petition on the grounds that she was not a legal permanent resident and "had not come within the quota provisions of the Act of 1921."[51] Undeterred, Haas challenged this ruling in court. Her three attorneys successfully demonstrated that the residency requirements of the Cable Act said nothing about how marital expatriates entered the country and prevailed in court. On July 24, 1929, Haas swore an oath of allegiance to the United States and became an American citizen once more.[52]

In San Antonio, denials of naturalization petitions overwhelmingly targeted and harmed one population: Mexican American women. Between FY 1935 and FY 1940, federal judges in San Antonio rejected the petitions of nine marital expatriates, all of them Mexican Americans. While failure to prosecute or "absence" was sometimes cited as grounds for refusal, the rejections were usually paired with other rationales. "Lack of knowledge" and/or supposed inability to speak English were enumerated as a justification to bar six petitioners. Cecilia Chavez Gonzalez was even denied in 1939 because of her purported "lack of good moral character." Though a San Antonio assistant district attorney served as one of her witnesses, the thirty-nine-year-old mother of six was denied her petition and not given an opportunity to return at a later point to reapply.[53] Though Chavez Gonzalez theoretically could have challenged the ruling before a higher court, she did not. Given the deep economic recession and pervasive racism African American and Mexican American women

154 DISPARATE REGIMES

encountered in Jim Crow Texas, she would have likely found little recourse in a costly appeal.[54]

As the experiences of Blumer, Chamorro, and Chavez Gonzalez demonstrate, how examiners and judges interpreted federal citizenship statutes could be just as important as the language of the law itself. Their cases also illustrate that perseverance played an equally important role in shaping the outcome of marital expatriate naturalization petitions. Determined women who faced administrative obstacles frequently fought back with the means at their disposal to ensure that they had their best possible chance to regain citizenship. Women with sufficient funds often hired lawyers to challenge unfavorable recommendations and highlighted their American identity and patriotism in their courtroom pleas.[55] For Mexican American women in Texas during the 1930s, applying to regain citizenship—and proving one's supposed linguistic, civic, and moral "fitness"—was a battle in and of itself.

Uneven access to information about evolving federal women's independent citizenship laws also likely impacted marital expatriates' naturalization patterns. The Massachusetts Division of Immigration and Americanization reported in 1924 that it had received "a growing number of inquiries from women on naturalization matters" following the adoption of "the Cable Act and the amendment allowing women to vote."[56] The following year, however, the division noted that most women who were "seeking citizenship . . . are of English speaking stock."[57] These naturalization rates largely mirrored contemporaneous voter registration patterns because middle-class Anglo-American women often signed up faster than their working-class immigrant-origin peers in the years following the ratification of the Nineteenth Amendment.[58]

While many women discovered and contested their expatriation when they sought to register to vote, others felt its weight upon their exclusion from work or social services by nativist state alienage laws.[59] The *Woman Citizen* warned in October 1921 that one marital expatriate in New York was about to lose her job as a schoolteacher under the state's new citizen-only public educator hiring law. Since she could not locate her noncitizen immigrant husband for a divorce, she had no legal recourse to naturalize and retain her job.[60] Though the passage of the Cable Act the following year might have ultimately saved her employment, the *New York Times* reported in June 1925 that working-class noncitizen women in New York City—immigrants and marital expatriates alike—were often "ignorant" of the new married women's nationality law until a personal "tragedy" was made worse owing to their alienage, such as state legislation denying widows' pensions to noncitizens.[61] Marital expatriates most harmed by the loss of their US citizenship and its rights—from Asian American women who became "aliens ineligible for citizenship" to economically precarious women—sometimes struggled to re-enter the United States and even risked deportation from the country of their birth.[62]

EMBEDDING AMERICAN CITIZENSHIP AND CITIZENSHIP RIGHTS   155

Despite these inequities, the leadership of the Bureau of Naturalization/INS continued to endorse a restrictive interpretation of citizenship law vis-à-vis marital expatriates during the 1920s and the 1930s.[63] Congress had extended explicit fast-track repatriation provisions to former US citizen men who had joined the armies of the Entente powers prior to American entry into World War I. All they had to do was go before a naturalization court, explain why they lost their citizenship, and take an oath of allegiance.[64] Although federal natural-ization commissioner Raymond Crist recognized that marital expatriates across the country wanted to know why they were "not . . . accorded the same privilege," he declined to forcefully advocate for extending repatriation provi-sions to these women in 1923. Such considerations were, quite literally in his opinion, "food for thought" for the nation's legislators.[65] INS leaders were equally clear that native-born marital expatriates were not to be considered American citizens until they had taken the oath of allegiance.[66] Indeed, the INS would continue to interpret citizenship law restrictively for marital expatriates, even as a limited number were made eligible for expeditious repatriation pro-ceedings beginning in 1936.

Creating a Shortcut: Repatriation via Oath (1936–40)

On June 25, 1936, president Franklin Roosevelt signed into law a new federal Repatriation Act that promised to facilitate the efforts of thousands of marital expatriates to regain their birthright nationality. It stipulated that a marital expatriate whose marriage had ended "shall be deemed to be a citizen of the United States" upon taking an oath of allegiance to the United States in court. No longer would she have to petition for naturalization. She could appear before a judge in court, prove her eligibility, and promptly regain her citizen-ship. Qualified women residing abroad would also henceforth be permitted to repatriate at a US embassy or an American consulate.[67]

The INS soon learned that implementing this law would be harder than expected. The legislation simply stated that a woman "whose marital status with such alien has or shall have terminated" could take the oath of allegiance and regain her citizenship.[68] Clearly, widows and divorcées were covered under this law. The eligibility of other women was less clear-cut. Just two weeks after the passage of the act, Fred Schlotfeldt, district director of the Chicago INS office, wrote to his superiors in Washington, DC, to inquire whether a woman whose husband had naturalized in the years following the enactment of the Cable Act could repatriate. Since she was no longer married to a noncitizen, it seemed plausible that she could regain her citizenship under the Repatriation Act's provisions.[69] INS commissioner D. W. MacCormack's legal advisors favored such an interpretation.[70] However, solicitor Charles Gregory, the top

156 DISPARATE REGIMES

legal advisor in the Labor Department, which then housed the INS, disagreed.[71] Gregory's position won out and such women were determined to be ineligible.[72] Puerto Rican women born before 1917 were not recognized by the INS as native-born citizens, so marital expatriates from the island were denied access to the Repatriation Act's provisions as well.[73]

While the INS Central Office in Washington, DC, was interpreting this new law restrictively for tens of thousands of US-born women, it made sure to expand its benefits to a smaller group of men: the husbands of remarried marital expatriates. The 1934 federal Equal Nationality Act had waived the prerequisite that petitioners file "declarations of intention" prior to naturalization for immigrant men married to American women. It also reduced their residency requirement from five to three years.[74] As early as August 1936, INS administrators were asked whether a woman who had regained her citizenship under the provisions of the Repatriation Act could help expedite her second husband's naturalization petition. In this circumstance, semantics mattered. To accelerate her husband's naturalization petition, a woman had to be a native-born or naturalized US citizen. But were marital repatriates either?[75]

INS administrators debated whether a marital expatriate had forfeited her status as a native-born citizen and, if so, whether her repatriation was an act of naturalization. The INS Board of Legal Review ruled that marital expatriates had indeed abandoned their native-born status.[76] The INS Central Office later confirmed that "the resumption of citizenship by the wife . . . constitute[d] a 'naturalization.'" Hence, second husbands of marital repatriates were eligible to make use of the expedited naturalization provisions of the Equal Nationality Act of 1934.[77] Thus, while thousands of marital expatriates were prohibited from making use of the provisions of the 1936 Repatriation Act owing to a restrictive reading of the law, the INS made sure that a small number of immigrant men could indirectly benefit from the same statute.

That strict interpretation undoubtedly contributed to the limited number of women who employed the Repatriation Act in the initial years following its passage. Between FY 1937 and FY 1940, 140 women regained their birthright citizenship in San Francisco's federal district court via repatriation.[78] Far more marital expatriates—400 in total—made use of the Cable Act's provisions to naturalize during those four fiscal years in the same court.[79]

As early as the summer of 1936, Solicitor Gregory theorized that the "publicity that will possibly ensue" owing to confusion related to the language of the Repatriation Act "may result in the enactment of amendatory legislation that will clarify the meaning of the law, and, perhaps, the extension of its provisions" to marital expatriates still married to their immigrant husbands.[80] But he did not press the issue. As Commissioner Crist had let the matter drop in 1923, so too did Gregory. The plight of marital expatriates was simply not a priority for

EMBEDDING AMERICAN CITIZENSHIP AND CITIZENSHIP RIGHTS 157

leading federal immigration and naturalization authorities in the interwar years. That attitude would abruptly change in the summer and fall of 1940 when an amendment to the Repatriation Act sponsored by freshman Democratic congressman Thomas D'Alesandro of Maryland unexpectedly collided with two other new federal nationality and alienage laws adopted that same year.

Shifting Course: Repatriation by Decree (1940–52)

First elected to Congress as a staunch New Deal Democrat in the 1938 midterms, D'Alesandro quickly made a name for himself as a leading champion of federal immigrant rights legislation. Attuned to the challenges many immigrants encountered when trying to acquire US citizenship, he sponsored numerous bills aimed at accelerating or otherwise facilitating their naturalization.[81] One of D'Alesandro's proposed reforms sought to amend the Repatriation Act of 1936 to expand its reach to most marital expatriates.[82] In addition to marital expatriates whose marriages to noncitizens had terminated, those "who ha[d] resided continuously in the United States since the date of such marriage" would be eligible to regain citizenship under the terms of his legislation.[83] On July 2, 1940, Roosevelt signed D'Alesandro's bill into law.[84]

D'Alesandro's 1940 measure should have been far easier for federal administrators and marital expatriates alike to construe than the 1936 law it amended. It stood to reason that eligible women whose marriages to noncitizens had ended and/or had always lived in the United States could henceforth take the oath of allegiance, repatriate, and regain their native-born American citizenship and citizenship rights. That was certainly how many of D'Alesandro's constituents understood the policy. The *Baltimore Sun* reported that "102 women who had lost their citizenship through marriage to foreigners" had been "restored to American citizenship" en masse in the city's federal district court on November 18, 1940.[85] It further reported that D'Alesandro, who attended the proceedings, "got all the credit for his work."[86]

The 102 women seeking to repatriate in Baltimore on the same day in late 1940 were not an anomaly. Just six weeks after the passage of the amendment, the New York City INS office reported that 2,000 women had applied to regain citizenship via repatriation.[87] Marital expatriates and their supporters across the country routinely implored the INS Central Office and local branches to speed up the repatriation process. However, when INS officials in Washington, DC, distributed forms, so many women applied that several local branches ran out. This delay did not sit well with marital expatriates and their supporters. Sixty-nine residents of Highland Park, Michigan, sent a petition to US solicitor general Francis Biddle urging him to intervene on November 25, 1940.[88] On December 4, 1940,

158 DISPARATE REGIMES

the *Detroit Free Press* reported that local courts were processing the requests of about 3,000 women to take the oath of allegiance. In response, they organized mass repatriations for hundreds of marital expatriates at a time.[89]

Such logistical challenges grew even more acute as 1940 drew to a close. On December 20, 1940, justice Henry Kimball of the New York Supreme Court wrote to US attorney general Robert Jackson to warn that an INS officer had recently claimed "that his district had 5000 applications for repatriation which could not be taken care of by reason of the lack of forms." "Surely," argued Kimball, "the rights of these married women entitled to be repatriated under the law now in effect should not be rendered valueless to them by mere lack of simple printed forms."[90]

The adoption of two other major federal laws in 1940 magnified the importance of citizenship and alienage for marital expatriates and their advocates. The first, the Alien Registration Act, was adopted in June 1940 amid the fall of France to the German blitzkrieg.[91] It tasked the INS with the massive job of identifying and registering nearly all noncitizens in the country by December 26, 1940. Under its terms, the vast majority of resident noncitizens above the age of fourteen were required to submit to fingerprinting and provide considerable information about themselves to federal authorities (including their physical description, manner of entry into the country, and civic associations). A clarion warning to the roughly 5 million noncitizens in the United States that they were not full members of the nation's body politic, it was no coincidence, as the *Chicago Tribune* observed, that naturalization petitions shot up right "after passage of the bill."[92]

Many marital expatriates became deeply aware of the tangible consequences of their loss of citizenship amid the registration drive. Naomi Gresser corresponded with INS officials and congressman Emanuel Celler during the summer of 1940 to determine whether she, a marital expatriate, had to register if she was unable to take an oath of repatriation by Christmas. Citing the service's play-it-safe policy, Donald R. Perry, the assistant director of the INS registration program, responded affirmatively.[93] That autumn, Charles Muller, assistant INS district director in New York, informed his superiors that his office had received numerous similar queries. He did not know how to respond.[94]

At the same time, the passage of the federal Nationality Act of 1940 seemingly made it even harder for marital expatriates to regain US citizenship. Aiming to tie together diverse statutes related to American citizenship "into a comprehensive nationality code," Roosevelt signed an omnibus naturalization and nationality bill into law on October 14, 1940.[95] Its text carried forward the provisions of the original Repatriation Act of 1936 without including D'Alesandro's recent amendment. Since the 1940 Nationality Act repealed all prior naturalization legislation not explicitly included in it, the new nationality

EMBEDDING AMERICAN CITIZENSHIP AND CITIZENSHIP RIGHTS 159

code seemed to have inadvertently revoked the Baltimore congressman's amendment adopted just ten weeks earlier. There was a brief grace period since the Nationality Act would not take effect until January 13, 1941.[96]

The Nationality Act's presumed repeal of D'Alesandro's amendment caused significant consternation among marital expatriates, INS officials, and judges. INS leaders came under pressure to rapidly distribute repatriation forms in the autumn and winter of 1940 precisely as a result of fears that thousands of women would miss their window to repatriate before January 13, 1941.[97] INS district officers felt the strain of this situation firsthand. On December 6, 1940, Henry Nicolls of the Boston INS branch informed his superiors that his office had received so many "applications for repatriation" that it would be difficult for "them [to] appear in court prior to January 11, 1941."[98] INS officers in New York and St. Paul, Minnesota, likewise reported similar challenges processing repatriation requests at the end of 1940.[99]

INS administrators thus faced two imminent deadlines as they interpreted rapidly changing federal nationality and alienage laws. Virtually all noncitizens in the country had to register with federal authorities by December 26, 1940. And INS administrators, judges, and marital expatriates would have to work as quickly as possible to process repatriation applications before January 13, 1941, if it was determined that marital expatriates still married to noncitizens would not be allowed to repatriate after that date under the new Nationality Act.

In this context, INS leaders dramatically reversed course and interpreted federal naturalization and repatriation law extremely broadly. In October 1940, the INS Central Office announced that all US-born marital expatriates who had continuously resided in the country would not have to register as noncitizens because they had been, automatically, repatriated by D'Alesandro's legislation earlier that year.[100] The INS came to this novel interpretation by stretching the meaning of the original Repatriation Act of 1936, which stated that a marital expatriate who was no longer married to a noncitizen husband "shall be deemed to be a citizen of the United States to the same extent as though her marriage to said alien had taken place on or after September 22, 1922." However, it also stipulated that "no such woman shall have or claim any rights as a citizen of the United States until she have duly taken the oath of allegiance."[101] INS leaders had previously understood this language to mean that women had to take the oath of allegiance to regain American citizenship. By contrast, when deputy commissioner T. B. Shoemaker announced in October 1940 that the INS leadership was reconstruing this language to have deemed all marital expatriates eligible under the terms of the Repatriation Act of 1936 and its 1940 amendment to be US citizens once more by decree, he underscored that such women would not possess citizenship rights if they did not take the requisite oath of allegiance.[102]

160 DISPARATE REGIMES

INS administrators never explicitly stated why they reinterpreted federal repatriation law just as Congress was adopting the Nationality Act of 1940. There is no doubt, however, that it—and the Alien Registration Act—weighed heavily on their minds. In his memo, Shoemaker made sure to add that "this construction of the statute by the Service will be uniform in its applicability to all branches, including Registration."[103] Just two days later, the *New York Times* assured eligible marital expatriates that they need not register.[104] INS leaders would have likely balked at the thought of enforcing penalties—including a fine of up to $1,000 or a prison sentence of up to six months—on American-born women who refused or failed to register (had they been required to). Widespread confusion and fear of punishment drove many marital expatriates to register with federal authorities anyway.[105]

Thus, INS leaders opted to reverse administrative policy and interpret repatriation law broadly at the very moment when the agency would have been responsible for forcing marital expatriates to reckon with the consequences of their alienage. The INS did not even bother to specify which rights would be denied to them.[106]

Many marital expatriates refused to accept this precarious legal status. On January 14, 1941, the *New York Times* reported that 3,000 marital expatriates "ha[d] just filed applications for repatriation" in New York City.[107] The *Washington Post*, which kept track of the names of marital expatriates who took the oath of allegiance in its local articles on naturalizations, also noted an uptick in repatriation requests in the nation's capital city. On October 2, 1940, the *Post* reported that marital expatriates numbered 15 of 72 (20.8 percent) total citizenship oaths administered in the city's federal district court the day before.[108] A month later, they numbered 18 of a total 68 (26.5 percent).[109] And 19 marital expatriates declared the oath of allegiance of a total of 98 men and women (19.4 percent) on January 7, 1941.[110]

Such "floods" of women rushing to take the oath of repatriation were not unusual for this era.[111] In both the San Francisco Bay Area and southern and western Texas, marital expatriates mobilized in significant numbers to regain their citizenship rights in FY 1941, FY 1942, and FY 1943. A total of 21.2 percent (204 of 962) of marital expatriates who took the repatriation oath of allegiance in San Francisco's federal district court between FY 1937 and FY 1975 did so in those three fiscal years alone.[112] In San Antonio's federal district court, 288 of 496 total repatriation oaths were taken by marital expatriates in that same three-year time span (58.1 percent).[113] In El Paso, of 228 repatriation oaths taken in the federal district court between FY 1937 and FY 1969, 86 took place on just two days alone: December 19 and 20, 1940, barely a week before the Alien Registration Act took effect.[114]

EMBEDDING AMERICAN CITIZENSHIP AND CITIZENSHIP RIGHTS   161

The INS only began tallying the number of repatriation oaths administered to marital expatriates nationwide in FY 1944. Its annual reports ultimately counted 21,047 repatriation oaths taken by marital expatriates across the country between FY 1944 and FY 1975.[115] While it is impossible to determine precisely how many women regained their US citizenship (rights) prior to FY 1944, oaths administered in San Francisco and San Antonio can serve as a basis for a low estimate (11,736) and high approximation (42,157), respectively, of national repatriation rates between FY 1937 and FY 1943.[116] Thus, at least 10,000 marital expatriates across the United States, and very possibly many more, probably took an oath of repatriation shortly before and during the country's participation in World War II (see Table 6.1).

American citizenship thus acquired greater weight in wartime for many marital expatriates. One woman who took the Repatriation Act's oath in January 1942 explained in an interview with the *Atlanta Constitution* that she had been unaware she would lose her citizenship upon marriage. But Marjorie Levick (née Pugh) maintained that even if she had known about the Expatriation Act's provisions when she wed her English husband in 1907, it would have made little difference to her. "That was before women even had the right to vote and citizenship didn't carry so many privileges for us as it does now," she noted. Reporter Celestine Sibley underscored that women like Levick had increasingly encountered the effects of their expatriation because they were "not entitled

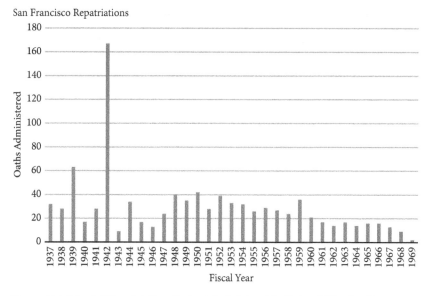

Figure 6.6 Marital Repatriation Oaths Administered in Federal District Court, San Francisco: FY, 1937–1969; Applications for Repatriation, 1936–1969; SF; RG 21; NARA–Pacific (San Bruno).

162   DISPARATE REGIMES

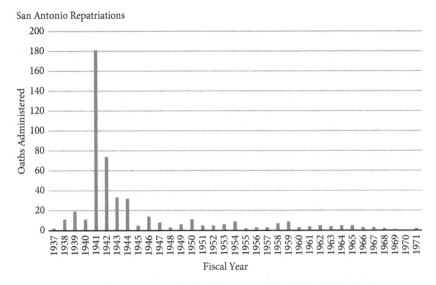

Figure 6.7 Marital Repatriation Oaths Administered in Federal District Court, San Antonio: FY 1937–1971; Applications to Regain Citizenship and Repatriation Oaths, 1937–1970; SA; RG 21; NARA–Southwest (Fort Worth).

Table 6.1 Estimated Number of Repatriation Oaths Administered Nationally to Marital Expatriates, Fiscal Years 1937–75

	Federal District Court, San Francisco	Federal District Court, San Antonio
Total oaths taken in federal district court 1937–43 (a)	344	331
Total oaths taken in federal district court 1937–75 (b)	962	496
Oaths taken 1937–43/total oaths taken (a/b) = (c)	35.8%	66.7%
1944–75 percentage of total (1 − c) = (d)	64.2%	33.3%
National total oaths taken 1944–75 = (e)	21,047	21,047
High and low estimations of national repatriation oaths taken 1937–75 = (e)/(d) = (f)	32,783	63,204
High and low estimations of national repatriation oaths taken 1937–43 = (f) − (e) = (g)	11,736	42,157

Note: INS Annual Reports, Fiscal Years 1944–75; Applications for Repatriation, 1936–1969, US District Court for the Southern (San Francisco) Division of the Northern District of California, RG 21, NARA–Pacific (San Bruno); Applications to Regain Citizenship and Repatriation Oaths, 1937–1970, US District Court for the Western (San Antonio) District of Texas, RG 21, NARA–Southwest (Fort Worth).

EMBEDDING AMERICAN CITIZENSHIP AND CITIZENSHIP RIGHTS   163

to vote, to hold government jobs, to travel with an American passport or to enjoy any of the privileges enjoyed by their neighbors." However, the global conflict was "the principal reason Mrs. Levick started thinking seriously of the privileges and cares of being an American." As Levick herself explained, "the condition the world is in makes us all think of such things" and made her "want to be a complete citizen."[117] In this, marital expatriates like Levick shared much in common with the 1.5 million immigrants—many of them long-resident, middle-aged women—who naturalized following the passage of the Alien Registration Act and during US participation in World War II.[118]

INS Deputy Commissioner Shoemaker should have been happy. His novel interpretation of federal repatriation law had seemingly solved a series of thorny logistical problems for his agency and opened the door for tens of thousands of American-born women to regain their rights as US citizens. But he and his colleagues in INS leadership soon faced a major problem: not all federal courts agreed that marital expatriates in the country had become American citizens without the rights of citizenship by decree.

Several federal judges began taking exception to the INS's new understanding of federal repatriation law as early as 1941. Pacifist Rebecca Shelley's 1941 case was the most famous and prominent example. Not only was her petition contested soon after the INS had announced its new reading of federal repatriation law, but also it was argued before the second highest court in the nation: the US Court of Appeals in Washington, DC.[119] That court's strongly worded condemnation of what it saw as the INS's deliberate misinterpretation of federal repatriation and naturalization law rejected Shelley's contention that she was a citizen without the rights of citizenship and threatened to upend the citizenship status of thousands of US-born women.[120]

Following the *Shelley* ruling, the INS district director in Kansas City, Missouri, wrote to his superiors in Washington, DC, to ask if a reinterpretation of federal repatriation policy was forthcoming. Shoemaker responded with an unequivocal no. INS administrators pressed on with their expansive view of the Repatriation Acts of 1936 and 1940.[121]

In March 1942, judge William C. Coleman paused the repatriation proceedings of all marital expatriates who were still married to their husbands in the US District Court of Maryland while he studied the matter further.[122] Shortly thereafter, Coleman concluded that the omnibus Nationality Code had indeed repealed D'Alesandro's 1940 measure. In response, the Baltimore congressman lobbied his colleagues in an unsuccessful effort to enact additional federal legislation "to reaffirm the right to simplified repatriation" for continuously resident women who were still married to their foreign-born husbands.[123] With this political defeat, marital expatriates' citizenship status remained foremost a subject of legal contestation.

164   DISPARATE REGIMES

Occasionally, INS leaders' broad interpretation of federal repatriation law won outright in court. One Chicago federal district court judge went so far as to determine in 1941 that a permanently resident marital expatriate "is a citizen of the United States," and therefore "it is unnecessary for her to take an oath of allegiance or repatriation." However, "as tangible evidence of the existence of her rights of citizenship," he ordered that "she should be permitted to take the oath and to receive certification of that fact."[124] In many other federal district courts, this question simply never arose. There, marital expatriates continued to take the oath of allegiance under the terms of the Repatriation Acts of 1936 and 1940 without hindrance.[125]

The citizenship status of marital expatriates most often became the subject of courtroom debate when their husbands sought to benefit from expedited naturalization privileges only available to the spouses of American citizens. INS leaders long maintained that these men could make use of such provisions—even if their wives had not taken the oath of allegiance—because such women were already US citizens.[126] In 1944, a federal district court judge in Pennsylvania concurred, approving the expedited naturalization of an immigrant man from Wales married to a marital expatriate who had yet to take an oath of repatriation.[127]

In several other similar federal cases, however, this position came under withering judicial criticism. Judges who opposed the INS's repatriation policy usually argued that the agency was willfully misconstruing the meaning of federal law and/or inventing a new category of citizenship. Between 1944 and 1946, three men married to marital expatriates appeared before federal district courts in Pennsylvania and Oregon only to have their petitions for expedited naturalization denied. Citing *Shelley*, judge Harry Kalodner twice ruled that there was no such thing as a citizen without citizenship rights in his Pennsylvania courtroom.[128] In Oregon, judge James A. Fee found the same. He also took the opportunity to condemn the INS for "persist[ing] in recommending such persons for citizenship" after the *Shelley* decision. In Fee's view, naturalization officers were abusing the good faith that he and other judges placed in their opinions by asking jurists to "overrul[e] what is the plain intention of Congress."[129] Though both Kalodner and Fee found the marital expatriates in question to be noncitizens, neither ruled that they were ineligible to take the repatriation oath. On the contrary, their husbands were denied an expedited naturalization procedure precisely because these women had not yet taken that oath.

In Hawaii, many marital expatriates were told that they had missed their window to repatriate. Federal district court judge Frank McLaughlin denied Shee Mui Chong Yuen's 1944 request to take an oath of repatriation. "We have,

EMBEDDING AMERICAN CITIZENSHIP AND CITIZENSHIP RIGHTS   165

and have always had, in our country but one class of citizens, namely, full fledged citizens," he contended. Citing the 1940 Nationality Act, he concluded that the petitioner had "by inaction . . . lost the opportunity of acquiring citizenship" under "this now extinct method" of repatriation.[130] When INS officials tried to get around McLaughlin's restrictions, they were stymied by Hawaii's territorial governor, Ingram Stainback, who refused to allow such women to obtain American passports.[131] Fortunately for this applicant, not all avenues to citizenship were closed to her. McLaughlin suggested that she naturalize under the provisions of the Nationality Act of 1940. He even went as far as to state that "if the Naturalization Service refuses, as it has in the past, to permit applicant and others to file petitions under the Nationality Act because that Service says she and they are already citizens, under proper application this Court will order the Service to allow the filing of such petitions."[132] Persistent in his findings, just three years later, McLaughlin ordered that marital expatriate Yuen Loo Wong be naturalized, not repatriated.[133]

McLaughlin's strident opposition to the INS interpretation of federal repatriation law was a harbinger of things to come. On July 23, 1948, Ernest A. Gross, legal advisor to US secretary of state George Marshall, wrote to attorney general Thomas Clark and informed him that the State "Department is impressed by the reasoning" of judges who opposed the INS interpretation of repatriation law, "particularly that of the Circuit Court of Appeals in the *Shelley* case." Since other departments generally deferred to the Justice Department on overlapping jurisdictional matters dealing with the construction of immigration and naturalization law, Gross asked the attorney general if his office was open to reinterpreting federal repatriation policy.[134] In deference to McLaughlin's conclusions in Hawaii, that same year, a federal judge in northern California informed San Francisco naturalization examiners that all repatriation applications of marital expatriates still married to their husbands would be rejected in his court.[135]

A month after the Justice Department received the State Department request, the INS responded with a sixteen-page memorandum defending its policy.[136] INS administrators also wrote a seven-page sample brief defending Shoemaker's interpretation of repatriation law, sent it to San Francisco naturalization officers, and told them to defend it in court.[137] This brief, highlighting the two US district court cases that had ruled in the INS's favor, was used successfully on at least three occasions.[138]

INS officials' interpretation of repatriation law, under attack for years, was effectively upended with the passage of the Immigration and Nationality Act on June 27, 1952. Marital expatriates were not left out of this statute. Unlike earlier legislation, however, the new law did away with the confusing language of deeming persons to be citizens and instead used more explicit terminology. Section

166   DISPARATE REGIMES

324 stipulated that an eligible marital expatriate had the right to repatriate (or naturalize) and that "from and after" she would be considered a US citizen. This terminology seemed to clarify that no oath meant no citizenship.[139]

The INS would nevertheless continue to publicly insist that such persons had been repatriated and remained citizens without the rights of citizenship.[140] In a front-page 1956 article in the *New York Herald Tribune*, reporter Judith Crist sought to bring attention to the numerous native-born women who had lost citizenship upon marriage decades earlier and were "still unaware of their anomalous situation" under American nationality laws. While her investigation centered on the practical challenges such women encountered, Crist noted that they were technically citizens in the eyes of the INS, though they did not possess "'first class' citizenship rights, such as voting or obtaining a passport."[141]

Nevertheless, over the next decade, the INS made seemingly minor adjustments that indicated a de facto change in policy. Though the INS had long maintained that marital expatriates need not register under the provisions of the Alien Registration Act, many women had done so. Some included that number in their repatriation paperwork as early as 1941. By the mid-1950s, it was common to find such a number on the margins of repatriation files. Around 1960, the INS even added a line for marital expatriates' noncitizen registration numbers on the repatriation form itself.[142] INS leaders, recognizing the de facto failure of their legal interpretation to retain sway, thus tacitly acknowledged that women they considered citizens without the rights of citizenship were widely viewed under the law and understood in practice to be noncitizens.

* * *

Between September 1922 and July 1940, Congress steadily expanded and facilitated marital expatriates' access to regain their native-born American citizenship. Somewhere between 80,000 and 130,000 women likely naturalized as immigrants in their own country during that eighteen-year span. Whether they wanted to vote, work as public schoolteachers, leave and re-enter the country, or simply regain their birthright, thousands of US-born women fought to reclaim their American citizenship and its rights. Marginalized women—Asian Americans, Mexican Americans, nonresidents, poor women, and young mothers—faced higher legal and practical barriers when trying to regain their stolen citizenship and were more likely to be outright denied. By contrast, some other marital expatriates went decades without knowing that they had lost it. Throughout the 1920s and 1930s, federal naturalization officials generally viewed the alienage of these US-born women to be an administrative nuisance, rather than a grave injustice. The adoption of the Repatriation Act of 1936 and an amendment to it in 1940 initially augured more of the same.

The passage of the federal Alien Registration Act and Nationality Act in 1940, however, abruptly changed that calculus in the eyes of INS leaders. They responded by trying to administratively invent a new de jure category of citizenship for permanently resident marital expatriates: citizens without citizenship rights. Amid conflicting court rulings over the constitutionality of such a category, thousands of marital expatriates hastened to regain their native-born citizenship rights during and following World War II by taking a repatriation oath of allegiance. While the INS formally stood behind its interpretation of federal repatriation law for decades thereafter (and its successor entity, the Department of Homeland Security, technically continues to do so), in practice, INS officials increasingly treated such women as noncitizens.

The failure of INS leaders to have their invented category of citizens without the rights of citizenship unambiguously and universally recognized in federal court was of great significance to the lives of marital expatriates. It also testified to a broader ascendance of the idea that American citizenship should be tied to identifiable, exclusive citizenship rights in law, politics, and popular understanding by the time of World War II. In 1875, the US Supreme Court had wholeheartedly accepted a distinction between citizenship status and citizenship rights by unanimously ruling that American women's citizenship had no bearing on their disfranchisement.[143] As late as 1915, the same high court ruled that the marriage of a US-born woman to a noncitizen immigrant man constituted an affirmative act of voluntary expatriation.[144] By 1944, however, a federal judge could write, in earnest, that "we have, and have always had, in our country but one class of citizens, namely, full fledged citizens."[145]

Of course, the exercise of citizenship rights would remain illusory for many Americans in 1944 and thereafter. Indeed, Japanese American citizens were then interned by their own government en masse that very same year. And African Americans across the Deep South confronted Jim Crow laws that made a mockery of the promise of equal citizenship rights under the federal constitution. Nevertheless, the proliferation of state alienage laws from the late nineteenth century until the mid-twentieth century had helped to invent and concretize many citizenship rights as citizen-only rights in the American political economy. The growing preeminence of the idea that citizenship rights were coextensive with citizen-only rights in law and popular perception, in turn, made it increasingly untenable to formally recognize thousands of American-born women as citizens without the rights of citizenship in federal jurisprudence.

Disparate Regimes: Nativist Politics, Alienage Law, and Citizenship Rights in the United States, 1865–1965.
Brendan A. Shanahan, Oxford University Press. © Brendan A. Shanahan 2025.
DOI: 10.1093/9780197660577.003.0007

Conclusion

A "Lost Century," a Reboot, or an Uninterrupted Struggle? Citizenship Rights as Citizen-Only Rights

Noncitizen immigrants navigated disparate regimes of citizenship rights on a state-by-state basis from the late nineteenth to the mid-twentieth centuries. Whether they could vote, access public and publicly funded employment, or simply be counted as part of the population for the purposes of representation varied greatly from the time of the Civil War until the late Gilded Age. Several states confined one or more of these "rights" to (some) American citizens. Others did not. At no time, however, were disparate regimes of citizenship rights static.

On the contrary, they were transformed by the proliferation of state laws restricting noncitizens' political and employment rights from the turn of the century until the early Cold War years. Opponents of noncitizen voting rights overcame numerous state constitutional hurdles to redefine voting into the premier exclusive, de jure right of citizenship in the United States by successfully campaigning to repeal all hitherto remaining alien suffrage laws during the first quarter of the twentieth century. State lawmakers likewise adopted a range of blue-collar nativist hiring measures and hundreds of anti-alien licensure policies throughout the early to mid-twentieth century. Meanwhile, in their increasingly coercive efforts to enforce these provisions and to distinguish US citizens from noncitizens, lawmakers, jurists, and administrators at all levels of government helped to invent and concretize many citizenship rights as citizen-only rights in law, practice, and popular understanding.

But immigrant rights advocates, allied politicians, and above all noncitizens themselves never ceased to challenge nativist state hiring and licensure laws alongside newly proposed and long-standing anti-alien apportionment provisions on the job, via diplomacy, in the courtroom, and, most especially, in the realm of state politics. Blue-collar nativist state hiring laws and anti-alien professional licensure measures were occasionally amended or repealed to mitigate controversies arising from their implementation from the late Gilded Age to the World War II era. Others were sporadically struck down in court or became

CONCLUSION 169

ineffective in practice. Proposed anti-alien apportionment schemes for the New Hampshire state legislature and the US House of Representatives were even thwarted before becoming law in the 1920s. But these rearguard successes failed to halt a broader onslaught of nativist state lawmaking in the early to mid-twentieth century. Immigrant rights forces achieved far more lasting victories during the late civil rights era as all remaining nativist apportionment provisions and most (but not all) state anti-alien hiring and licensure laws were repealed, overturned, or rendered inoperative.

Given these developments, it may be tempting to read *Disparate Regimes* as a story of the creation, evolution, and close of a "lost century" of nativist politics and state alienage law in American history. Much as legal scholar Gerald Neuman unearthed a range of state-level migration policies adopted between the American Revolution and Reconstruction to dispel the "myth" that there were few US immigration laws prior to the passage of national Chinese exclusion legislation, this book has recovered a surfeit of state alienage laws enacted between the Civil War and the civil rights era to demonstrate their continued power and powers long after federal authorities assumed supremacy in the domain of immigration law.[1]

But a lost-century framing nestles uncomfortably alongside the breadth and importance of recent and ongoing battles over immigration federalism in the United States since the civil rights era. As early as the 1970s, policymakers in major immigrant-destination states like California and New York moved to restrict or ban undocumented immigrants from a range of social assistance programs. That same decade, lawmakers in Texas tried (and failed) to bar undocumented children from attending public schools in their state.[2] While US Supreme Court rulings handed down in the late 1960s and the early 1970s continue to prevent the adoption of sweeping anti-alien hiring and licensure laws akin to those of the early twentieth century, the "political function" exception carved out by those precedents has afforded state lawmakers significant latitude to restrict noncitizens' access to several lines of work if they so choose.[3] Moreover, though no state has enforced an anti-alien apportionment scheme for decades, the Trump administration's narrowly defeated effort to add a citizenship question to the 2020 census would have provided allied state lawmakers the means to (try to) do so.[4]

Immigrant rights advocates and allied state lawmakers have fought just as hard to defend and expand noncitizens' rights over the past half century. From lawmakers in Massachusetts and sixteen other states authorizing the issuance of driver's licenses to undocumented residents to policymakers in California declaring the Golden State to be a "sanctuary" polity in 2017, many states have recently extended protections to noncitizens, including undocumented immigrants, residing within their jurisdiction.[5] Several cities in progressive states—from Takoma

170 DISPARATE REGIMES

Park, Maryland, to San Francisco, California—have enfranchised noncitizen voters in some or all local elections.[6]

Given their scope, how should recent and ongoing disputes over noncitizen voting rights, anti-alien apportionment schemes, and nativist state employment laws be understood vis-à-vis similar, prior conflicts? Are modern-day debates best seen as part of an uninterrupted continuation of long-standing battles over disparate regimes of citizenship rights on a state-by-state basis since the time of the Civil War? Or do they herald, to adapt social scientist Monica Varsanyi's framing of the history of noncitizen voting rights, the "rise and fall and rise" again of such disparate regimes in the American political economy?[7]

On the one hand, contemporary debates over noncitizens' standing in the polity rhetorically rhyme a great deal with previous disputes. Much as their predecessors did more than a century ago, current supporters of alien suffrage policies frequently argue that disfranchisement amounts to taxation without representation and that expanding voting rights to noncitizen immigrants would better incorporate them into the political community. Contemporary detractors of noncitizen voting rights likewise reproduce arguments marshaled by earlier opponents, often contending that alien suffrage cheapens citizenship or invites fraud.[8] The reasoning of present-day proponents and foes of anti-alien apportionment schemes, recently articulated in *Evenwel v. Abbott* (a 2016 Texas state legislative redistricting and reapportionment case brought before the US Supreme Court), similarly echoes many of the arguments of prior debates over "who counts" in the polity.[9] Meanwhile, the continued disfranchisement of many US citizens, most notably ex-felons, underscores that even those rights most commonly portrayed as exclusive rights of citizenship remain rarely—if ever—universally accessible to all Americans.[10]

Despite these rhetorical similarities, compared to their predecessors, state lawmakers in the early twenty-first century do not possess the same levels of autonomy and relative power to shape the outcome of contemporary debates over noncitizen voting rights and anti-alien apportionment schemes. Though a growing number of municipalities have enfranchised noncitizen voters in local elections, no state has (re)adopted a policy of universal noncitizen voting rights. Even if a state were to do so, since 1996, federal law has barred noncitizens from voting in national elections.[11] Conversely, while federal Republican policymakers may well try again to add a citizenship question to a future census in the hopes of enabling the crafting of new state anti-alien apportionment schemes, there is no guarantee that such gambits would prove successful. After all, it has been more than half a century since the prevailing redistricting cases of the 1960s ruled tangentially on the inclusion of noncitizens in state legislative apportionment provisions. It has been even longer since the census has questioned all the nation's residents about their citizenship status or since states

CONCLUSION 171

have conducted their own enumerations to aid in the implementation of anti-alien apportionment schemes. Critics of a citizenship question and foes of state anti-alien apportionment schemes retain numerous avenues to challenge them as unconstitutional in the courtroom and to fight against them in state and federal politics.[12] Past and present conflicts over noncitizens' rights in the polity therefore should not be understood as continuous owing to the profound differences between early-twentieth- and early-twenty-first-century iterations of American federalism.

By contrast, modern-day state anti-alien hiring and licensure laws offer some clearer evidence of continuity with past nativist employment measures. State governments retain wide latitude to restrict or ban noncitizens from public and publicly funded employment and/or licensure in lines of work—such as teaching in public schools—deemed by the US Supreme Court to possess a sufficient "political function." And just as early- to mid-twentieth-century anti-alien hiring and licensure policies most harmed noncitizens who were least able to naturalize owing to racism, sexism, and poverty, current nativist employment laws disproportionately impact the largest category of "aliens ineligible to citizenship" in modern America: undocumented immigrants.[13]

Despite these similarities, current state anti-alien employment and licensing laws operate in a fundamentally different legal context than that which existed prior to the civil rights era. Unlike Progressive Era cases contested before the US Supreme Court like *Heim v. McCall* and *People v. Crane* (which upheld the constitutionality of state anti-alien public and publicly funded employment laws in 1915) or interwar conflicts decided by state courts such as *Sashihara et al. v. California State Board of Pharmacy* (which affirmed the legality of most state bans on noncitizens' access to professional licensure in 1935), present-day jurisprudence over nativist state employment laws remains heavily informed by federal precedent set in the late 1960s and early 1970s recognizing noncitizens as a suspect class.[14] Additionally, the sheer breadth of anti-alien public and publicly funded hiring laws and nativist licensure policies that have been struck down, rendered inoperative, or repealed since that time amounts to a different paradigm of state alienage laws in kind and in scale.[15] In fact, some states like California that once enforced a host of anti-alien hiring and licensure laws have moved in the opposite direction in recent years by recognizing immigrants' licensure rights—irrespective of citizenship or legal status—for a range of occupations and professions.[16]

Moreover, state laws distinguishing the employment rights of US citizens vis-à-vis noncitizens are no longer the primary de jure means by which immigrants' employment rights are curtailed. Instead, noncitizens—as legal permanent residents, H-1B visa holders, persons with temporary protected status, recipients of Deferred Action for Childhood Arrivals, and undocumented

172 DISPARATE REGIMES

migrants, among other categories—work in an age largely governed by differing levels of alienage, set mostly by federal law, that afford distinct degrees of employment rights.[17] States have exercised and continue to retain significant latitude to expand or constrain protections for millions of noncitizens by participating in or rejecting collaboration with the federal E-Verify program or by otherwise joining or opposing federal efforts to identify undocumented workers.[18] But the legacies of late–civil rights era jurisprudence, the contemporary preeminence of noncitizens' legal and/or visa status, and the growing ascendence of federal law in shaping immigrants' access to and protections at work greatly distinguish contemporary blue-collar nativist hiring laws and anti-alien professional licensure measures from those of prior eras.

Thus, there are more differences than continuities between historical and ongoing debates over noncitizen voting rights, anti-alien apportionment schemes, and nativist hiring measures. But contemporary inhabitants of the United States are not witnessing a warmed-over reboot of a lost century of disparate regimes of citizenship rights either. Twenty-first-century debates about what should and should not be exclusive "rights of American citizenship" largely operate on the premise that citizenship rights as citizen-only rights are real, carry weight, and can be—at least theoretically—defined.

These presumptions were not paramount or settled in American politics, law, or common perception at the time of the Civil War. Nor was their ascendance by the civil rights era inevitable. Rather, they were in large measure produced by a multitude of debates over the rights of noncitizens in the American political economy waged primarily in the realms of nativist state politics and alienage law between the late nineteenth and the mid-twentieth centuries.[19] Thus, while those of us who reside in the United States no longer inhabit an era of disparate regimes of citizenship rights on a state-by-state basis, we do continue to live in an age of citizenship rights as citizen-only rights.

Disparate Regimes: Nativist Politics, Alienage Law, and Citizenship Rights in the United States, 1865–1965.
Brendan A. Shanahan, Oxford University Press. © Brendan A. Shanahan 2025.
DOI: 10.1093/9780197660577.003.0008

Endnotes

Note on Terminology

1. For a discussion of these trade-offs, see, especially, Beth Lew-Williams, *The Chinese Must Go: Violence, Exclusion, and the Making of the Alien in America* (Cambridge, MA: Harvard University Press, 2018), 8.
2. See, among many others, James Kettner, *The Development of American Citizenship, 1608–1870* (Chapel Hill: University of North Carolina Press, 1978); and Martha S. Jones, *Birthright Citizens: A History of Race and Rights in Antebellum America* (New York: Cambridge University Press, 2018).
3. Among other works, see Earl M. Maltz, "The Fourteenth Amendment and Native American Citizenship," *Immigration and Nationality Law Review* 22 (2001): 625–46; T. Alexander Aleinikoff, *Semblances of Sovereignty: The Constitution, the State, and American Citizenship* (Cambridge, MA: Harvard University Press, 2009); and Michael J. Witgen, *Seeing Red: Indigenous Land, American Expansion, and the Political Economy of Plunder in North America* (Chapel Hill: University of North Carolina Press, 2022).
4. See, especially, among many others, Sam Erman, *Almost Citizens: Puerto Rico, the U.S. Constitution, and Empire* (New York: Cambridge University Press, 2018); and Christopher Capozzola, *Bound by War: How the United States and the Philippines Built America's First Pacific Century* (New York: Basic Books, 2020).
5. On the importance of not imposing contemporary views of terms like citizenship and citizenship rights onto earlier eras of US history, see, especially, William J. Novak, "The Legal Transformation of Citizenship in Nineteenth-Century America," in *The Democratic Experiment: New Directions in American Political History*, ed. Meg Jacobs, William J. Novak, and Julian E. Zelizer (Princeton, NJ: Princeton University Press, 2009), 85–87, 109–12.
6. This book does employ alien as a noun if it appears within an original quotation.
7. John Higham, *Strangers in the Land: Patterns of American Nativism, 1860–1925* (New York: Atheneum, 1963), 3–11.
8. Quotation in main text from Higham, 4. Higham's definition is among the most famous of the word, but it has not been universally accepted. Higham later questioned and doubted the utility of the term in his own subsequent scholarship. See Linda S. Bosniak, "'Nativism' the Concept: Some Reflections," in *Immigrants Out! The New Nativism and the Anti-immigrant Impulse in the United States*, ed. Juan F. Perea (New York: New York University Press, 1996), 281–83, 292–95nn9, 13, 17, 19. Historian Erika Lee has made xenophobia the central unit of her analysis— in juxtaposition to nativism—viewing the former to be a more capacious term for different forms of "fear and hatred of foreigners" than the latter (7). See Erika Lee, *America for Americans: A History of Xenophobia in the United States* (New York: Basic Books, 2019), 7–12.

Introduction

1. Each of these state laws is discussed at length and cited in the chapters.
2. Quotation in main text from Judith Shklar, *American Citizenship: The Quest for Inclusion* (Cambridge, MA: Harvard University Press, 1991), 101. While Shklar's claim is grounded in political theory, three classic histories of American citizenship rights argue that the Civil War and Reconstruction were central to the evolution of modern US citizenship. James Kettner asserts that the Union's victory in the Civil War produced "a consistent doctrine of citizenship" for the first time (10). Federal constitutional reform enacted in its wake, he maintains, defined national citizenship and recognized its primacy vis-à-vis state allegiances (334–51). See Kettner, *Development of American Citizenship*, 10, 334–51. Historians William Novak and Eric Foner contend likewise in, respectively, Novak, "Legal Transformation of Citizenship," 85–119; and Eric Foner, *The Second Founding: How the Civil War and Reconstruction Remade the Constitution* (New York: W. W. Norton, 2019).

174   NOTES TO PAGES 2–3

3. J. Morgan Kousser, *The Shaping of Southern Politics: Suffrage Restriction and the Establishment of the One-Party South, 1880–1910* (New Haven, CT: Yale University Press, 1974); Michael Perman, *Struggle for Mastery: Disfranchisement in the South, 1888–1908* (Chapel Hill: University of North Carolina Press, 2001); Ira Katznelson, *When Affirmative Action Was White: An Untold History of Racial Inequality in Twentieth-Century America* (New York: W. W. Norton, 2005); Stephen Kantrowitz, *More Than Freedom: Fighting for Black Citizenship in a White Republic, 1829–1889* (New York: Penguin Press, 2012); Paul E. Herron, *Framing the Solid South: The State Constitutional Conventions of Secession, Reconstruction, and Redemption, 1860–1902* (Lawrence: University Press of Kansas, 2017).

4. Alexander Saxton, *The Indispensable Enemy: Labor and the Anti-Chinese Movement in California* (Berkeley: University of California Press, 1971); Gwendolyn Mink, *Old Labor and New Immigrants in American Political Development: Union, Party, and State, 1875–1920* (Ithaca, NY: Cornell University Press, 1986); George Sánchez, *Becoming Mexican American: Ethnicity, Culture, and Identity in Chicano Los Angeles, 1900–1945* (New York: Oxford University Press, 1993); Evelyn Nakano Glenn, *Unequal Freedom: How Race and Gender Shaped American Citizenship and Labor* (Cambridge, MA: Harvard University Press, 2002); Erika Lee, *At America's Gates: Chinese Immigration during the Exclusion Era, 1882–1943* (Chapel Hill: University of North Carolina Press, 2003); Stephen J. Pitti, *The Devil in Silicon Valley: Northern California, Race, and Mexican Americans* (Princeton, NJ: Princeton University Press, 2004); Monica Muñoz Martinez, *The Injustice Never Leaves You: Anti-Mexican Violence in Texas* (Cambridge, MA: Harvard University Press, 2018); Lew-Williams, *The Chinese Must Go*.

5. Bartholomew H. Sparrow, *The Insular Cases and the Emergence of American Empire* (Lawrence: University Press of Kansas, 2006); Erman, *Almost Citizens*; Robert C. McGreevey, *Borderline Citizens: The United States, Puerto Rico, and the Politics of Colonial Migration* (Ithaca, NY: Cornell University Press, 2018); Capozzola, *Bound by War*.

6. Maltz, "Fourteenth Amendment"; Cathleen D. Cahill, *Recasting the Vote: How Women of Color Transformed the Suffrage Movement* (Chapel Hill: University of North Carolina Press, 2021); Ned Blackhawk, *The Rediscovery of America: Native Peoples and the Unmaking of U.S. History* (New Haven, CT: Yale University Press, 2023).

7. Lee, *At America's Gates*; Hiroshi Motomura, *Americans in Waiting: The Lost Story of Immigration and Citizenship in the United States* (New York: Oxford University Press, 2006); Dorothee Schneider, *Crossing Borders: Migration and Citizenship in the Twentieth-Century United States* (Cambridge, MA: Harvard University Press, 2011); Lew-Williams, *The Chinese Must Go*; Hardeep Dhillon, "The Making of Modern US Citizenship and Alienage: The History of Asian Immigration, Racial Capital, and US Law," *Law and History Review* 41, no. 1 (February 2023): 1–42.

8. Linda K. Kerber, *No Constitutional Right to Be Ladies: Women and the Obligations of Citizenship* (New York: Hill and Wang, 1998); Suzanne Mettler, *Dividing Citizens: Gender and Federalism in New Deal Public Policy* (Ithaca, NY: Cornell University Press, 1998); Alice Kessler-Harris, *In Pursuit of Equity: Women, Men, and the Quest for Economic Citizenship in 20th-Century America* (New York: Oxford University Press, 2001); Nancy F. Cott, *Public Vows: A History of Marriage and the Nation* (Cambridge, MA: Harvard University Press, 2002); Rebecca DeWolf, *Gendered Citizenship: The Original Conflict over the Equal Rights Amendment, 1920–1963* (Lincoln: University of Nebraska Press, 2021).

9. Candice Lewis Bredbenner, *A Nationality of Her Own: Women, Marriage, and the Law of Citizenship* (Berkeley: University of California Press, 1998); Martha Gardner, *The Qualities of a Citizen: Women, Immigration, and Citizenship, 1870–1965* (Princeton, NJ: Princeton University Press, 2005); Leti Volpp, "Divesting Citizenship: On Asian American History and the Loss of Citizenship through Marriage," *UCLA Law Review* 53, no. 2 (December 2005): 405–83.

10. The political and legal gains of the mid-century African American civil rights movement, in particular, have long been described as a Second Reconstruction. See, among others, C. Vann Woodward, "The Political Legacy of Reconstruction," *The Journal of Negro Education* 26, no. 3 (1957): 231–40; Joe R. Feagin and Harlan Hahn, "The Second Reconstruction: Black Political Strength in the South," *Social Science Quarterly* 51, no. 1 (1970): 42–56; Eric Foner, "Reconstruction Revisited," *Reviews in American History* 10, no. 4 (1982): 82–100; Manning Marable, *Race, Reform and Rebellion: The Second Reconstruction in Black America, 1945–1982*

NOTES TO PAGE 3   175

(Jackson: University Press of Mississippi, 1984); and Ari Berman, *Give Us the Ballot: The Modern Struggle for Voting Rights in America* (New York: Picador, 2015).

11. See, broadly, Kerber, *No Constitutional Right*; Kessler-Harris, *In Pursuit of Equity*; John David Skrentny, *The Minority Rights Revolution* (Cambridge, MA: Harvard University Press, 2002); Laughlin McDonald, *A Voting Rights Odyssey: Black Enfranchisement in Georgia* (New York: Cambridge University Press, 2003); Charles L. Zelden, *The Battle for the Black Ballot: Smith v. Allwright and the Defeat of the Texas All White Primary* (Lawrence: University Press of Kansas, 2004); Nancy MacLean, *Freedom Is Not Enough: The Opening of the American Workplace* (Cambridge, MA: Harvard University Press, 2006); Thomas J. Sugrue, *Sweet Land of Liberty: The Forgotten Struggle for Civil Rights in the North* (New York: Random House, 2008); and Michael Waldman, *The Fight to Vote* (New York: Simon & Schuster, 2016).

12. On these limits in practice, see, among many others, Thomas J. Sugrue, *The Origins of the Urban Crisis: Race and Inequality in Postwar Detroit* (Princeton, NJ: Princeton University Press, 1996); Robert O. Self, *American Babylon: Race and the Struggle for Postwar Oakland* (Princeton, NJ: Princeton University Press, 2005); MacLean, *Freedom Is Not Enough*; and Risa L. Goluboff, *The Lost Promise of Civil Rights* (Cambridge, MA: Harvard University Press, 2007).

13. Reed Ueda, "The Changing Path to Citizenship: Ethnicity and Naturalization during World War II," in *The War in American Culture: Society and Consciousness during World War II*, ed. Lewis A. Erenberg and Susan E. Hirsch (Chicago: University of Chicago Press, 1996), 202–16; Ian Haney-López, *White by Law: The Legal Construction of Race* (New York: New York University Press, 1996); Kerber, *No Constitutional Right*; Bredbenner, *Nationality of Her Own*; Gardner, *Qualities of a Citizen*; Motomura, *Americans in Waiting*; Schneider, *Crossing Borders*; Cindy I-Fen Cheng, *Citizens of Asian America: Democracy and Race during the Cold War* (New York: New York University Press, 2013); and Cybelle Fox and Irene Bloemraad, "Beyond 'White by Law': Explaining the Gulf in Citizenship Acquisition between Mexican and European Immigrants, 1930," *Social Forces* 94, no. 1 (September 2015): 181–207.

14. Desmond King, *Making Americans: Immigration, Race, and the Origins of the Diverse Democracy* (Cambridge, MA: Harvard University Press, 2000); Daniel Tichenor, *Dividing Lines: The Politics of Immigration Control in America* (Princeton, NJ: Princeton University Press, 2002); Mae Ngai, *Impossible Subjects: Illegal Aliens and the Making of Modern America* (Princeton, NJ: Princeton University Press, 2004); Catherine Lee, *Fictive Kinship: Family Reunification and the Meaning of Race and Nation in American Migration* (New York: Russell Sage Foundation, 2013); Danielle Battisti, *Whom We Shall Welcome: Italian Americans and Immigration Reform, 1945–1965* (New York: Fordham University Press, 2019); Maddalena Marinari, *Unwanted: Italian and Jewish Mobilization against Restrictive Immigration Laws, 1882–1965* (Chapel Hill: University of North Carolina Press, 2020).

15. Kunal Parker, *Making Foreigners: Immigration and Citizenship Law in America, 1600–2000* (New York: Cambridge University Press, 2015), 233.

16. Shklar, for instance, contends that despite "the importance of nationality" and "ungenerous and bigoted immigration and naturalization policies...their effects and defects pale before the history of slavery and its impact upon our public attitudes." Shklar, *American Citizenship*, 14. Historian C. Vann Woodward makes similar arguments in "Political Legacy of Reconstruction," 238. Works of immigration history that describe state anti-alien public and/or publicly funded employment laws, in particular, as of only marginal importance in the late nineteenth and early twentieth centuries include Higham, *Strangers in the Land*, 46–47, 72–73, 183–84; and Mink, *Old Labor*, 123.

17. See, especially, Glenn, *Unequal Freedom*; Ngai, *Impossible Subjects*; Katznelson, *When Affirmative Action*; Cybelle Fox, *Three Worlds of Relief: Race, Immigration, and the American Welfare State from the Progressive Era to the New Deal* (Princeton, NJ: Princeton University Press, 2012); and Natalia Molina, "Deportable Citizens: The Decoupling of Race and Citizenship in the Construction of the 'Anchor Baby,'" in *Deportation in the Americas: Histories of Exclusion and Resistance*, ed. Kenyon Zimmer and Cristina Salinas (College Station: Texas A&M University Press, 2018), 164–91.

18. See, among others, Sánchez, *Becoming Mexican American*; Claire Jean Kim, "The Racial Triangulation of Asian Americans," *Politics & Society* 27, no. 1 (1999): 105–38; Glenn, *Unequal Freedom*; Pitti, *Devil in Silicon Valley*; and Mae M. Ngai, "Birthright Citizenship and the Alien Citizen," *Fordham Law Review* 75, no. 5 (2007): 2521–30.

176 NOTES TO PAGE 4

19. Sometimes advocates of immigrant rights made this point themselves to advance their own political agenda. Several state legislative reapportionment debates in the 1960s serve as a case in point. See, among others, Gordon E. Baker, *State Constitutions: Reapportionment* (New York: National Municipal League, 1960); Ruth C. Silva, "The Population Base for Apportionment of the New York Legislature," *Fordham Law Review* 32, no. 1 (October 1963): 1–50; and Ruth C. Silva, "Reapportionment and Redistricting," *Scientific American* 213, no. 5 (1965): 20–27. On the relative marginalization of the category of alienage during major federal civil rights political developments in the mid-twentieth century, see, especially, Monica W. Varsanyi, "The Rise and Fall (and Rise?) of Non-citizen Voting: Immigration and the Shifting Scales of Citizenship and Suffrage in the United States," *Space and Polity* 9, no. 2 (2005): 113–34.

20. See, especially, among others, Gerald L. Neuman, "The Lost Century of American Immigration Law (1776–1875)," *Columbia Law Review* 93, no. 8 (1993): 1833–901; Kunal M. Parker, "State, Citizenship, and Territory: The Legal Construction of Immigrants in Antebellum Massachusetts," *Law and History Review* 19, no. 3 (Fall 2001): 583–643; Anna O. Law, "Lunatics, Idiots, Paupers, and Negro Seamen—Immigration Federalism and the Early American State," *Studies in American Political Development* 28, no. 2 (October 2014): 107–28; Hidetaka Hirota, *Expelling the Poor: Atlantic Seaboard States and the Nineteenth-Century Origins of American Immigration Policy* (New York: Oxford University Press, 2017); and Christina A. Ziegler-McPherson, *Selling America: Immigration Promotion and the Settlement of the American Continent, 1607–1914* (Santa Barbara, CA: Praeger, 2017).

21. On state lawmakers' considerable powers to shape exit–entry immigration policy until the late nineteenth century and the continued importance of state judges and bureaucrats in the administration of naturalization law until the early twentieth century, see Rogers Smith, *Civic Ideals: Conflicting Visions of Citizenship in U.S. History* (New Haven, CT: Yale University Press, 1997); Motomura, *Americans in Waiting*; Schneider, *Crossing Borders*; Patrick Weil, *The Sovereign Citizen: Denaturalization and the Origins of the American Republic* (Philadelphia: University of Pennsylvania Press, 2013); and Hirota, *Expelling the Poor*.

22. On growing attention to the importance of immigration federalism in the decades following the 1960s, see, among others, Hiroshi Motomura, *Immigration Outside the Law* (New York: Oxford University Press, 2014); Pratheepan Gulasekaram and S. Karthick Ramakrishnan, *The New Immigration Federalism* (New York: Cambridge University Press, 2015); Cybelle Fox, "'The Line Must Be Drawn Somewhere': The Rise of Legal Status Restrictions in State Welfare Policy in the 1970s," *Studies in American Political Development* 33, no. 2 (October 2019): 275–304; Allan Colbern and S. Karthick Ramakrishnan, *Citizenship Reimagined: A New Framework for States Rights in the United States* (New York: Cambridge University Press, 2020); and Sarah Coleman, *The Walls Within: The Politics of Immigration in Modern America* (Princeton, NJ: Princeton University Press, 2021).

23. Milton Konvitz, *The Alien and the Asiatic in American Law* (Ithaca, NY: Cornell University Press, 1946); Karen Isaksen Leonard, *Making Ethnic Choices: California's Punjabi Mexican Americans* (Philadelphia: Temple University Press, 1992); Mark Kanazawa, "Immigration, Exclusion, and Taxation: Anti-Chinese Legislation in Gold Rush California," *Journal of Economic History* 65, no. 3 (September 2005): 779–805; Motomura, *Americans in Waiting*; Daniel Martinez HoSang, *Racial Propositions: Ballot Initiatives and the Making of Postwar California* (Berkeley: University of California Press, 2010); Mark Brilliant, *The Color of America Has Changed: How Racial Diversity Shaped Civil Rights Reform in California, 1941–1978* (New York: Oxford University Press, 2010); Gabriel J. Chin, "A Nation of White Immigrants: State and Federal Racial Preferences for White Noncitizens," *Boston University Law Review* 100, no. 4 (2020): 1271–314.

24. Leon Aylsworth, "The Passing of Alien Suffrage," *American Political Science Review* 25, no. 1 (1931): 114–16; A. Elizabeth Taylor, "The Woman Suffrage Movement in Arkansas," *The Arkansas Historical Quarterly* 15, no. 1 (1956): 17–52; Paul Kleppner, *Continuity and Change in Electoral Politics, 1893–1928* (New York: Greenwood Press, 1987); Alexander Keyssar, *The Right to Vote: The Contested History of Democracy in the United States* (New York: Basic Books, 2000); Ron Hayduk, *Democracy for All: Restoring Immigrant Voting Rights in the United States* (New York: Routledge, 2006); Martha Menchaca, *Naturalizing Mexican Immigrants: A Texas History* (Austin: University of Texas Press, 2011); Sara Egge, *Woman Suffrage and Citizenship in the Midwest, 1870–1920* (Iowa City: University of Iowa Press, 2018); Jessica Barbata Jackson, *Dixie's Italians: Sicilians, Race, and Citizenship in the Jim Crow Gulf South* (Baton Rouge:

NOTES TO PAGES 4–5   177

Louisiana State University Press, 2020); Rachel Michelle Gunter, "Immigrant Declarants and Loyal American Women: How Suffragists Helped Redefine the Rights of Citizens," *The Journal of the Gilded Age and Progressive Era* 19, no. 4 (October 2020): 591–606.

25. On the importance of and difficulties inherent in addressing these questions, see, especially, Irene Bloemraad, "Does Citizenship Matter?" in *The Oxford Handbook of Citizenship*, ed. Ayelet Shachar et al. (New York: Oxford University Press, 2017), 524–50. See also Linda Bosniak, *The Citizen and the Alien: Dilemmas of Contemporary Membership* (Princeton, NJ: Princeton University Press, 2006).

26. Shklar, *American Citizenship*, 101.

27. Other works arguing for the continued importance of state governments in immigration federalism from the late nineteenth to the mid-twentieth centuries include Luis Plascencia, Gary P. Freeman, and Mark Setzler, "The Decline of Barriers to Immigrant Economic and Political Rights in the American States: 1977–2001," *International Migration Review* 37, no. 1 (2003): 5–23; Irene Bloemraad, "Citizenship Lessons from the Past: The Contours of Immigrant Naturalization in the Early 20th Century," *Social Science Quarterly* 87, no. 5 (2006): 927–53; Motomura, *Americans in Waiting*; Alexandra Filindra, "E Pluribus Unum? Federalism, Immigration and the Role of the American States" (PhD diss., Rutgers University, 2009); Christina A. Ziegler-McPherson, *Americanization in the States: Immigrant Social Welfare Policy, Citizenship, & National Identity in the United States, 1908–1929* (Gainesville: University Press of Florida, 2009); Michael Cornelius Kelly, "A Wavering Course: United States Supreme Court Treatment of State Laws Regarding Aliens in the Twentieth Century," *Georgetown Immigration Law Journal* 25, no. 3 (Spring 2011): 701–40; Thomas Romero, "A War to Keep Alien Labor out of Colorado: The 'Mexican Menace' and the Historical Origins of Local and State Anti-immigration Initiatives," in *Strange Neighbors: The Role of States in Immigration Policy*, ed. Carissa Byrne Hessick and Gabriel J. Chin (New York: New York University Press, 2014), 63–96; Parker, *Making Foreigners*; Robin Dale Jacobson, Daniel Tichenor, and T. Elizabeth Durden, "The Southwest's Uneven Welcome: Immigrant Inclusion and Exclusion in Arizona and New Mexico," *Journal of American Ethnic History* 37, no. 3 (Spring 2018): 5–36; Peter Catron, "The Citizenship Advantage: Immigrant Socioeconomic Attainment in the Age of Mass Migration," *American Journal of Sociology* 124, no. 4 (January 2019): 999–1042; Chin, "Nation of White Immigrants"; Ashley Johnson Bavery, *Bootlegged Aliens: Immigration Politics on America's Northern Border* (Philadelphia: University of Pennsylvania Press, 2020); Monica W. Varsanyi, "Hispanic Racialization, Citizenship, and the Colorado Border Blockade of 1936," *Journal of American Ethnic History* 40, no. 1 (2020): 5–39; Colbern and Ramakrishnan, *Citizenship Reimagined*; Robin Dale Jacobson and Daniel Tichenor, "States of Immigration: Making Immigration Policy from Above and Below, 1875–1924," *Journal of Policy History* 35, no. 1 (January 2023): 1–32; and Allison Brownell Tirres, "Exclusion from Within: Noncitizens and the Rise of Discriminatory Licensing Laws," *Law & Social Inquiry* 49, no. 3 (2024): 1783–811.

28. In adopting this terminology, this book especially borrows from the insights of Canadian political scientist Jane Jenson, her collaborators, and scholars working in her tradition who analyze citizenship as a regime. Viewing citizenship as more than a legal status or bearer of rights, those belonging to this school emphasize its relational nature, its constant evolution, and similarities, convergences, and differences in citizenship policies among polities. Political scientists Aude-Claire Fourot, Nora Nagels, and Mireille Paquet, in particular, describe a citizenship regime as a "political construct that is contingent upon historical heritage, and generated by political and social forces, without being deterministic of all social relations or inalterable by actors." See Mireille Paquet, Nora Nagels, and Aude-Claire Fourot, "Introduction: Citizenship as a Regime," in *Citizenship as a Regime: Canadian and International Perspectives*, ed. Mireille Paquet, Nora Nagels, and Aude-Claire Fourot (Montreal, QC: McGill-Queen's University Press, 2018), 8. More broadly, see Jane Jenson, "Fated to Live in Interesting Times: Canada's Changing Citizenship Regimes," *Canadian Journal of Political Science/Revue canadienne de science politique* 30, no. 4 (1997): 627–44; Jane Jenson and Susan Phillips, "Redesigning the Canadian Citizenship Regime: Remaking the Institutions of Representation," in *Citizenship, Markets, and the State*, ed. Colin Crouch, Klau Eder, and Damian Tambini (New York: Oxford University Press, 2000), 69–89; and Jane Jenson, "Afterword: Thinking about the Citizenship Regime Then and Now," in *Citizenship as a Regime*, 255–70. Other scholars of immigration federalism who employ the term *regime* include Jacobson and Tichenor, "States of Immigration."

178   NOTES TO PAGES 11-12

Chapter 1

1. Debates at New York's 1821 constitutional convention over suffrage rights and apportionment provisions have been studied by numerous scholars. See James A. Henretta, "The Rise and Decline of Democratic Republicanism: Political Rights in New York and the Several States, 1800–1915," *Albany Law Review* 53, no. 2 (1989): 357–402; Laura-Eve Moss, "Democracy, Citizenship and Constitution-Making in New York, 1777–1894" (PhD diss., University of Connecticut, 1999), 41–97; Laura E. Free, *Suffrage Reconstructed: Gender, Race, and Voting Rights in the Civil War Era* (Ithaca, NY: Cornell University Press, 2015), 16–33; and David A. Bateman, *Disenfranchising Democracy: Constructing the Electorate in the United States, the United Kingdom, and France* (New York: Cambridge University Press, 2018), 68–73, 126–33.

2. Moss, "Democracy, Citizenship," 53–54, 88–92.

3. See, broadly, Moss, "Democracy, Citizenship," 41–97; Free, *Suffrage Reconstructed*, 16–33; Bateman, *Disenfranchising Democracy*, 68–73, 126–33.

4. Moss, "Democracy, Citizenship," 41–97; Free, *Suffrage Reconstructed*, 16–33; Bateman, *Disenfranchising Democracy*, 68–73, 126–33.

5. Keyssar, *Right to Vote*, 26–76; Free, *Suffrage Reconstructed*, 9–54; Bateman, *Disenfranchising Democracy*, 75–200.

6. As political scientist John Dinan has shown, aside from the statehood itself, "No issue has been more important in generating conventions on a regular basis than legislative reapportionment" (314). See John Dinan, "Explaining the Prevalence of State Constitutional Conventions in the Nineteenth and Twentieth Centuries," *Journal of Policy History* 34, no. 3 (July 2022): 297–335.

7. Other key works of scholarship on the history of state alien suffrage laws include Gerald M. Rosberg, "Aliens and Equal Protection: Why Not the Right to Vote?" *Michigan Law Review* 75, no. 5–6 (May 1977): 1092–136; Gerald L. Neuman, "'We Are the People': Alien Suffrage in German and American Perspective," *Michigan Journal of International Law* 13, no. 2 (Winter 1992): 259–335; Jamin B. Raskin, "Legal Aliens, Local Citizens: The Historical, Constitutional and Theoretical Meanings of Alien Suffrage," *University of Pennsylvania Law Review* 141, no. 4 (April 1993): 1391–470; Virginia Harper-Ho, "Noncitizen Voting Rights: The History, the Law and Current Prospects for Change," *Immigration and Nationality Law Review* 21 (2000): 477–528; Keyssar, *Right to Vote*; Varsanyi, "Rise and Fall"; Hayduk, *Democracy for All*; Stanley Renshon, *Noncitizen Voting and American Democracy* (New York: Rowman & Littlefield, 2009); Sarah Song, "Democracy and Noncitizen Voting Rights," *Citizenship Studies* 13, no. 6 (December 2009): 607–20; Aziz Rana, *The Two Faces of American Freedom* (Cambridge, MA: Harvard University Press, 2010); Menchaca, *Naturalizing Mexican Immigrants*; Monica W. Varsanyi, "Fighting for the Vote: The Struggle against Felon and Immigrant Disfranchisement," in *Beyond Walls and Cages: Prisons, Borders, and Global Crisis*, ed. Andrew Burridge, Jenna M. Loyd, and Matthew Mitchelson (Athens, GA: University of Georgia Press, 2013), 266–76; Zornitsa Keremidchieva, "The Congressional Debates on the 19th Amendment: Jurisdictional Rhetoric and the Assemblage of the US Body Politic," *Quarterly Journal of Speech* 99, no. 1 (January 2013): 51–73; Egge, *Woman Suffrage and Citizenship*; Arturo Castellanos Canales, "The Right of Suffrage of Shosics (Noncitizens) in the United States" (JSD diss., Cornell University, 2020); Gunter, "Immigrant Declarants"; Jackson, *Dixie's Italians*; and Alan H. Kennedy, "Voters in a Foreign Land: Alien Suffrage in the United States, 1704–1926," *Journal of Policy History* 34, no. 2 (April 2022): 245–75. Less voluminous studies on nineteenth-century state anti-alien apportionment provisions include Hugh A. Bone, "States Attempting to Comply with Reapportionment Requirements," *Law and Contemporary Problems* 17, no. 2 (Spring 1952): 387–416; Robert B. McKay, *Reapportionment: The Law and Politics of Equal Representation* (New York: Simon & Schuster, 1970); and Moss, "Democracy, Citizenship."

8. Others who emphasize the importance of state constitutional conventions to these developments include Keyssar, *Right to Vote*, 167; and John J. Dinan, *The American State Constitutional Tradition* (Lawrence: University Press of Kansas, 2006), 3.

9. Smith, *Civic Ideals*, 115–36; Keyssar, *Right to Vote*, 11–14; Parker, *Making Foreigners*, 50–80; Helen Irving, *Citizenship, Alienage, and the Modern Constitutional State: A Gendered History* (New York: Cambridge University Press, 2016), 48–55; Allan J. Lichtman, *The Embattled Vote in America: From the Founding to the Present* (Cambridge, MA: Harvard University Press, 2018), 8–35.

NOTES TO PAGES 13-14   179

10. Judith Apter Klinghoffer and Lois Elkis, "'The Petticoat Electors': Women's Suffrage in New Jersey, 1776–1807," *Journal of the Early Republic* 12, no. 2 (1992): 159–93; Keyssar, *Right to Vote*, 32–33; Parker, *Making Foreigners*, 65. As Kunal Parker emphasizes, the poor laws of ante-bellum Massachusetts—which governed access to local "settlement"—greatly complicated the development of distinct citizenship rights in the state. See Parker, "State, Citizenship, and Territory."

11. See, especially, Keyssar, *Right to Vote*, 32–33; 82–87. See also Rosberg, "Aliens and Equal Protection"; Neuman, "We Are the People"; Raskin, "Legal Aliens, Local Citizens"; Harper-Ho, "Noncitizen Voting Rights"; and Varsanyi, "Rise and Fall."

12. Keyssar, *Right to Vote*, 55–60; Free, *Suffrage Reconstructed*, 9–54; Lichtman, *Embattled Vote in America*, 46–63.

13. See, especially, Free, *Suffrage Reconstructed*, 33–54; and, broadly, Jones, *Birthright Citizens*; and Bateman, *Disenfranchising Democracy*.

14. Other key works that examine Wisconsin constitutional debates over alien suffrage rights and their entanglement with other disputes (particularly over noncitizen property rights) include Ray A. Brown, "The Making of the Wisconsin Constitution," *Wisconsin Law Review*, no. 4 (July 1949): 648–94; and Allison Brownell Tirres, "Ownership without Citizenship: The Creation of Noncitizen Property Rights," *Michigan Journal of Race & Law* 19 (Fall 2013): 1–52.

15. *Journal of the Convention to Form a Constitution for the State of Wisconsin: With a Sketch of the Debates, Begun and Held at Madison, on the Fifteenth Day of December, Eighteen Hundred and Forty-Seven* (Madison, WI: Tenney, Smith, and Holt Printers, 1848). On the rights and status of immigrants holding "first papers" in broader US history, see, especially, Motomura, *Americans in Waiting*; Chin, "Nation of White Immigrants."

16. Quotation in main text from *Journal of the Convention to Form a Constitution for the State of Wisconsin, 1847*, 170 (emphasis in the original). On delegate biographical information, see *Journal of the Wisconsin Constitutional Convention*, 4; and "Proceedings of the Democratic District Convention at Waterford, July 15, 1852," *Kenosha Democrat*, September 16, 1852, 2.

17. Quotation in main text from *Journal of the Convention to Form a Constitution for the State of Wisconsin, 1847*, 167. On delegate biographical information, see "Democratic Ticket," *Wisconsin Democrat* [Green Bay], September 22, 1849, 2; and "Wisconsin Legislature. In Senate," *Wisconsin Democrat* [Green Bay], January 12, 1850, 1.

18. Main text quotation from *Journal of the Convention to Form a Constitution for the State of Wisconsin, 1847*, 177. On delegate biographical information, see *Journal of the Wisconsin Constitutional Convention*, 4; and "Correspondence," *Daily Free Democrat* [Milwaukee], October 22, 1850, 2. Supporters of noncitizen voting rights also rallied their colleagues to adopt some of the most expansive (state) constitutional protections for noncitizens' property rights in the country. See, especially, Tirres, "Ownership without Citizenship."

19. Quotation in main text from *Journal of the Convention to Form a Constitution for the State of Wisconsin, 1847*, 152. On delegate biographical information, see *Journal of the Wisconsin Constitutional Convention*, 5; and "Waukesha County Board," *Milwaukee Daily Sentinel*, April 15, 1853, 2.

20. On this political context, see Frederic L. Paxson, "A Constitution of Democracy—Wisconsin, 1847," *Mississippi Valley Historical Review* 2, no. 1 (1915): 3–24; Louise P. Kellogg, "The Alien Suffrage Provision in the Constitution of Wisconsin," *Wisconsin Magazine of History* 1, no. 4 (June 1918): 422–25; and R. Lawrence Hachey, "Jacksonian Democracy and the Wisconsin Constitution," *Marquette Law Review* 62, no. 4 (1979): 485–530.

21. Quotation in main text from *Journal of the Convention to Form a Constitution for the State of Wisconsin, 1847*, 166. Delegate biographical information from *Journal of the Wisconsin Constitutional Convention*, 4.

22. Quotation in main text from *Journal of the Convention to Form a Constitution for the State of Wisconsin, 1847*, 168. On delegate biographical information, see *Journal of the Wisconsin Constitutional Convention*, 5; and "Death of Dr. A. L. Castleton [sic]," *Wisconsin State Journal* [Madison], September 1, 1877, 1.

23. Quotation in main text from *Journal of the Convention to Form a Constitution for the State of Wisconsin, 1847*, 165. During the Civil War, however, alien declarant men were deemed draft eligible. Men possessing first papers who refused to participate in the draft were ordered to leave the country (and those who had already voted were determined to have already missed that opportunity). See Candice Lewis Bredbenner, "A Duty to Defend? The Evolution of Aliens'

180 NOTES TO PAGES 14–16

Military Obligations to the United States, 1792 to 1946," *Journal of Policy History* 24, no. 2 (April 2012): 230–34.

24. Quotation in main text from *Journal of the Convention to Form a Constitution for the State of Wisconsin, 1847*, 149. For delegate biographical information, see, especially, "Dunn, Charles, 1799–1872," *Wisconsin Historical Society, Dictionary of Wisconsin History*, https://www.wisconsin history.org/Records/Article/CS7222.

25. Keyssar comes to this figure from the 1850 census. See Keyssar, *Right to Vote*, 33.

26. See also Henry A. Chaney, "Alien Suffrage," *Michigan Political Science Association* 1, no. 2 (1894): 130–39; Paxson, "Constitution of Democracy"; Kirk Harold Porter, *A History of Suffrage in the United States* (Chicago: University of Chicago Press, 1918), 119–21; Kellogg, "Alien Suffrage Provision"; Brown, "Making of the Wisconsin Constitution"; Hachey, "Jacksonian Democracy"; Neuman, "We Are the People," 297–98; and Keyssar, *Right to Vote*, 33.

27. Scholars frequently differ on the precise number of alien suffrage polities at any given time because of scarce—and sometimes competing—sources. By my count, the territories adopting alien suffrage policies in the late antebellum years and during the Civil War were Colorado, Dakota, Idaho, Nebraska, Nevada, and Washington (though Nevada dropped its alien suffrage policy upon gaining statehood in 1864). See Rosberg, "Aliens and Equal Protection," 1098; Neuman, "We Are the People," 298–99; Raskin, "Legal Aliens, Local Citizens," 1407–8; Keyssar, *Right to Vote*, 371–73; and Varsanyi, "Rise and Fall," 119. Battles over these provisions were not confined to the state or territorial level. Federal lawmakers sometimes clashed over alien suffrage rights (among other topics) when debating the admission of new states, such as Oregon, into the Union. See, especially, Jacki Hedlund Tyler, *Leveraging an Empire: Settler Colonialism and the Legalities of Citizenship in the Pacific Northwest* (Lincoln: University of Nebraska Press, 2021), 229–82.

28. Keyssar, *Right to Vote*, 32–33, 54–60; Jameson Sweet, "Native Suffrage: Race, Citizenship, and Dakota Indians in the Upper Midwest," *Journal of the Early Republic* 39, no. 1 (2019): 99–109; Witgen, *Seeing Red*, 273–326.

29. *Journal of the Convention to Form a Constitution for the State of Wisconsin, 1847*, 166.

30. Keyssar aptly contrasts antebellum state and territorial policymakers' views on (white) noncitizen voting rights on the basis of their attitude toward urban "worker" immigrants in the Northeast (largely exclusionary) and rural "settlers" in the Midwest (relatively inclusive). See Keyssar, *Right to Vote*, 82–87.

31. See, broadly, Jack N. Rakove, *Original Meanings: Politics and Ideas in the Making of the Constitution* (New York: Vintage Books, 1997); and Peter H. Argersinger, "The Value of the Vote: Political Representation in the Gilded Age," *Journal of American History* 76, no. 1 (1989): 59–90.

32. See, especially, Douglas Keith and Eric Petry, "Apportionment of State Legislatures, 1776–1920," Brennan Center for Justice (New York: New York University School of Law, September 25, 2015).

33. Moss, "Democracy, Citizenship"; Keith and Petry, "Apportionment of State Legislatures."

34. *The Debates and Journal of the Constitutional Convention of the State of Maine, 1819–'20* (Augusta: Maine Farmers' Almanac Press, 1894), 11. For broader context, see Peter Neil Berry, "Nineteenth Century Constitutional Amendment in Maine" (master's thesis, University of Maine, 1965); McKay, *Reapportionment*, 336–38; and Marshall J. Tinkle, *The Maine State Constitution* (New York: Oxford University Press, 2013).

35. Moss, "Democracy, Citizenship," 41–97; Henretta, "Rise and Decline"; Free, *Suffrage Reconstructed*, 16–33; Bateman, *Disenfranchising Democracy*, 68–73, 126–33.

36. Silva, "Population Base for Apportionment," 7–9; Henretta, "Rise and Decline," 372–74; Moss, "Democracy, Citizenship," 35, 92–94.

37. Massachusetts lawmakers and voters had only recently adopted a total inhabitant basis of apportionment for the state legislature's lower chamber via constitutional amendment in 1840. See Charles F. Gettemy, *An Historical Survey of Census-Taking in Massachusetts: Including a Sketch of the Various Methods Adopted from Time to Time since 1780 for Determining and Apportioning the Membership of the House of Representatives and the Senate and the Council (1919–22)* (Boston: Wright & Potter, State Printers, 1919), 113 (and 102–34 more broadly). Held in Massachusetts Commonwealth Archives, Boston, MA, Secretary of the Commonwealth Records, Labor Bureau Statistics, 788 X 312 HH 57 3113. On convention debates over various reapportionment proposals, see *Journal of the Constitutional Convention of the Commonwealth*

NOTES TO PAGES 16–19   181

of Massachusetts, 1853 (Boston: White and Potter, Printers to the Convention, 1853), 157–58, 174–79, 197–208, 364–68, 394–96.

38. The convention ultimately merged several proposed "reforms"—including the apportionment proposal—into one combined amendment. The campaign over the omnibus amendment, however, centered on its apportionment provisions. See Samuel Shapiro, "The Conservative Dilemma: The Massachusetts Constitutional Convention of 1853," *The New England Quarterly* 33, no. 2 (1960): 207–24; Dale Baum, "Know-Nothingism and the Republican Majority in Massachusetts: The Political Realignment of the 1850s," *Journal of American History* 64, no. 4 (1978): 959–86; and Thomas H. O'Connor, "Irish Votes and Yankee Cotton: The Constitution of 1853," *Proceedings of the Massachusetts Historical Society* 95 (1983): 88–99.

39. O'Connor recognizes that other scholars have demonstrated that the "Irish" vote was not inordinately large in rejecting the amendment. Far more important, argues O'Connor, was that many Massachusetts voters, even "contemporary Bostonians believed these charges to be true" (99). See O'Connor, "Irish Votes," 98–99.

40. While the party gained significant support in the mid-1850s across northeastern, Border South, and mid-Atlantic states amid the collapse of the Whig Party over slavery and rising anti-immigrant and anti-Catholic sentiment, nowhere was its growth as dramatic as in Massachusetts. See, among others, Baum, "Know-Nothingism," 959–60; Hirota, *Expelling the Poor*, 101–2; and Luke Ritter, "Immigration, Crime, and the Economic Origins of Political Nativism in the Antebellum West," *Journal of American Ethnic History* 39, no. 2 (Winter 2020): 62–91.

41. On the draconian Know-Nothing legislative agenda, see, especially, Hirota, *Expelling the Poor*, 100–28.

42. This two-year voting ban was far shorter than initial Know-Nothing plans. Upon coming to power in 1855, they variously proposed a lifelong suffrage ban and twenty-one- and fourteen-year waiting periods. See Keyssar, *Right to Vote*, 86; and Baum, "Know-Nothingism," 973–75. This two-year waiting period was later repealed in 1863 by Bay State voters years after the demise of the Know-Nothings. See Lawrence M. Friedman and Lynnea Thody, *The Massachusetts State Constitution* (New York: Oxford University Press, 2011), 174, 209.

43. Gettemy, *Historical Survey*, 122, 133.

44. A total of 31,227 voters supported and only 6,282 opposed the House amendment. A total of 32,971 voters approved and only 4,342 voters opposed the Senate "legal voter" reapportionment amendment. See Gettemy, *Historical Survey*, 122, 133.

45. "Census of Voters," *Worcester Palladium*, July 8, 1857, 2 (emphasis in original).

46. See John Cornyn, "The Roots of the Texas Constitution: Settlement to Statehood," *Texas Tech Law Review* 26, no. 4 (1995): 1143, 1145–51; and Evenwel v. Abbott, 578 U.S. ___ (Docket No. 14–940) (2016). Oregon's first constitution adopted an explicitly racist "white voters" apportionment basis in 1859, thereby targeting both free Blacks and Chinese immigrants. See Gordon E. Baker, "Reapportionment by Initiative in Oregon," *Western Political Quarterly* 13, no. 2 (1960): 508–19; and Keith and Petry, "Apportionment of State Legislatures."

47. Mario Chacón and Jeffrey Jensen, "Direct Democracy, Constitutional Reform, and Political Inequality in Post-colonial America," *Studies in American Political Development* 34, no. 1 (April 2020): 148–69.

48. See, among other works, George David Zuckerman, "A Consideration of the History and Present Status of Section 2 of the Fourteenth Amendment," *Fordham Law Review* 30, no. 1 (October 1961): 93–136; Garrett Epps, *Democracy Reborn: The Fourteenth Amendment and the Fight for Equal Rights in Post–Civil War America* (New York: Holt Paperbacks, 2007); Free, *Suffrage Reconstructed*; and Foner, *Second Founding*.

49. See, especially, Epps, *Democracy Reborn*, 89–120; and Zuckerman, "Consideration of the History," 93–107.

50. Epps, *Democracy Reborn*, 104.

51. Keyssar, *Right to Vote*, 89.

52. Zuckerman, "Consideration of the History," 96; Epps, *Democracy Reborn*, 103–4; Free, *Suffrage Reconstructed*, 114.

53. See, broadly, Zuckerman, "Consideration of the History," 93–107; Epps, *Democracy Reborn*, 102–20; and Free, *Suffrage Reconstructed*, 114–18.

54. Zuckerman, "Consideration of the History," 95; Free, *Suffrage Reconstructed*, 116; Foner, *Second Founding*, 61.

182   NOTES TO PAGES 19–21

55. *Congressional Globe of the Thirty-Ninth Congress* (Washington, DC: Blair & Rives, January 8, 1866), 141.
56. Zuckerman, "Consideration of the History," 100.
57. *Congressional Globe of the Thirty-Ninth Congress*, March 8, 1866, 1256.
58. Maryland Democratic senator Reverdy Johnson charged Radical Republicans with hypocrisy, arguing that they claimed to represent northern (disfranchised) women, noncitizens, and children while threatening to reduce southern representation if the region continued to disfranchise Black men. See *Congressional Globe of the Thirty-Ninth Congress*, June 8, 1866, 3029.
59. Zuckerman, "Consideration of the History," 95–98.
60. See, broadly, Zuckerman, "Consideration of the History"; and Epps, *Democracy Reborn*.
61. Keyssar, *Right to Vote*, 93–104; Free, *Suffrage Reconstructed*, 78–132; Lichtman, *Embattled Vote in America*, 79–92; Foner, *Second Founding*, 93–123.
62. Free, *Suffrage Reconstructed*, 78–111; Foner, *Second Founding*, 109–15.
63. Keyssar, *Right to Vote*, 95.
64. *Congressional Globe of the Fortieth Congress* (Washington, DC: Blair & Rives, February 9, 1869), 1036. As first quoted in Keyssar, *Right to Vote*, 97.
65. Neuman, "We Are the People," 307; Raskin, "Legal Aliens, Local Citizens," 1425–28; Harper-Ho, "Noncitizen Voting Rights," 280, 292; Keyssar, *Right to Vote*, 102; Lichtman, *Embattled Vote in America*, 84.
66. Keyssar, *Right to Vote*, 93–104.
67. Minor v. Happersett, 88 U.S. 21 Wall. 162, quotation from 170 and, more broadly, passim (1875). See also "An Important Decision: Mrs. Virginia L. Minor's Suit Settled," *St. Louis Dispatch*, March 31, 1875, 4. Other scholars who have examined the *Minor* case as a contest over suffrage rights and the definition of citizenship rights include Motomura, *Americans in Waiting*, 117; Rebecca Mead, *How the Vote Was Won: Woman Suffrage in the Western United States, 1868–1914* (New York: New York University Press, 2006), 37; Zornitsa Keremidchieva, "The Gendering of Legislative Rationality: Women, Immigrants, and the Nationalization of Citizenship, 1918–1922" (PhD diss., University of Minnesota, 2007), 39–40; Ron Hayduk, "Political Rights in the Age of Migration: Lessons from the United States," *Journal of International Migration and Integration* 16, no. 1 (2015): 114; and Gunter, "Immigrant Declarants."
68. This chapter employs Michael Perman's definition and periodization of "Three Phases in the History of Black Suffrage": (1) Reconstruction (1867 to early 1870s), (2) Redemption (mid-1870s to mid-1890s), and (3) Restoration (or Jim Crow) (1890–1908). Perman characterizes the Redeemer era as a time of growing white Democratic power, voter manipulation, and attacks on Black voters. By contrast, Perman defines the Jim Crow era as a time of mass (constitutionally imposed) Black disfranchisement and white supremacist violence. See Perman, *Struggle for Mastery*, 11. For a slightly different framework and periodization, see Herron, *Framing the Solid South*, 13. On dates of the passage (and/or repeal) of these state alien suffrage laws, see Neuman, "We Are the People," 299; Keyssar, *Right to Vote*, 371–73; and Hayduk, *Democracy for All*, 19–22.
69. The percentage of southerners born abroad was lower in most states of the former Confederacy. Immigrants tended to be (slightly) more numerous in the Border South states of Delaware, Kentucky, Maryland, West Virginia, and Washington, DC. (Missouri is counted by the Census Bureau as a Midwestern state, though it, too, had a higher-than-average immigrant population). The only former Confederate states to have immigrant populations larger than the region's 3.3 percent average in 1870 were Louisiana (8.5 percent) and Texas (7.6 percent). See, especially, Campbell J. Gibson and Emily Lennon, "Nativity of the Population, for Regions, Divisions, and States: 1850 to 1990," in *Historical Census Statistics on the Foreign-Born Population of the United States: 1850–1990* (working paper: POP-WP029, February 1999), https://www.census.gov/population/www/documentation/twps0029/twps0029.html.
70. See, especially, Hayduk, *Democracy for All*, 19–22. Often misidentified, historian Alexander Keyssar correctly notes the repeal of alien suffrage in Idaho Territory during Reconstruction within the main text of his book. Keyssar, *Right to Vote*, 138, 371–73. See also *Laws of the Territory of Idaho, 1874–1875*, "An Act Relative to Elections," 683–95.
71. Of the eight western alien suffrage polities, immigrants ranged from a low of 12.8 percent (Oregon) to a massive 38.7 percent (Montana) of their respective populations. See Gibson and Lennon, "Nativity of the Population."
72. Though a full record of debate was not saved, future Colorado Supreme Court chief justice Henry C. Thatcher seems to have proposed a first papers suffrage policy as a stand-alone

NOTES TO PAGES 22–3   183

measure on February 7, 1876. Though Thatcher's proposal was rejected by his peers, the following day, the majority report of the convention's Committee on Rights of Suffrage and Elections included noncitizen voting rights within its much broader suffrage provisions. See *Proceedings of the Constitutional Convention Held in Denver, December 20, 1875, to Frame a Constitution for the State of Colorado Together with the Enabling Act* (Denver, CO: Smith-Brooks Press, 1907), 256, 265. Of Colorado's 194,327 enumerated residents in 1880, a total of 39,790 were foreign born. See Gibson and Lennon, "Nativity of the Population." On Thatcher, see "Judge Henry C. Thatcher," Wilbur Fisk Stone, ed., *History of Colorado Illustrated*, vol. 2 (Chicago: S. J. Clark, 1918), 64–68.

73. See, among others, "Territorial and Otherwise," *Canon City Avalanche*, February 10, 1876, 1; "The Colorado Constitution," *Minneapolis Tribune*, February 13, 1876, 1; and "Colorado Items," *Chicago Daily Tribune*, February 13, 1876, 16.

74. "Women Suffrage and the New Constitution," *Colorado Free Press*, January 15, 1876, 2.

75. On these lawmakers' background and their importance in this debate, see Gordon Morris Bakken, *Rocky Mountain Constitution Making, 1850–1912* (New York: Greenwood Press, 1987), 87; Howard Roberts Lamar, *The Far Southwest, 1846–1912: A Territorial History*, rev. ed. (Albuquerque: University of New Mexico Press, 2000), 251–53; Amy Bridges, *Democratic Beginnings: Founding the Western States* (Lawrence: University Press of Kansas, 2015), 70, 159n29; and Susan Wroble, "Agapito Vigil," in *Colorado Encyclopedia*, https://coloradoencyclopedia.org/article/agapito-vigil.

76. *Proceedings of the Constitutional Convention Held in Denver*, 271.

77. *Proceedings of the Constitutional Convention Held in Denver*, 267.

78. *Proceedings of the Constitutional Convention Held in Denver*, 271.

79. See also Keyssar, *Right to Vote*, 136–38.

80. *Official Report of the Proceedings and Debates of the Third Constitutional Convention of Ohio: Assembled in the City of Columbus, on Tuesday, December 2, 1873 Volume II—Part 2* (Cleveland, OH: W. S. Robison, 1874), 1851.

81. Quotation in main text from *Official Report of the Proceedings and Debates of the Third Constitutional Convention of Ohio*, 1928. Baber was, in turn, a staunch Lincoln Republican, an opponent of Radical Republicans during Reconstruction, and finally a Democrat. See E. L. Taylor, "Richard Plantaganet Llewellyn Baber," *Ohio History Journal* 19, no. 4 (October 1910): 370–81.

82. Keyssar, *Right to Vote*, 137.

83. Quotation in main text from *Official Report of the Proceedings and Debates of the Third Constitutional Convention of Ohio*, 1802. For delegate biographical information, see "Campbell, Lewis Davis 1811–1882," in *Biographical Directory of the United States Congress*, https://bioguide.congress.gov/search/bio/C000096. Keyssar also finds Campbell to have been a key opponent of alien suffrage at the Ohio convention. See Keyssar, *Right to Vote*, 137.

84. Keyssar uses the Ohio convention as his primary example to explore later alien suffrage battles, finding it to be "prolonged and colorful" but concluding that "there was nothing unusual about either its content or the outcome of the vote" (138). He finds that economic downturns, rising immigration rates, accompanying xenophobia, and nationalism during World War I were leading causes of the demise of alien suffrage. See Keyssar, *Right to Vote*, 136–38. Political scientist Ron Hayduk similarly finds that these Ohio debates provide key "insights about ethnic prejudices of the day" in battles over noncitizen voting. See Hayduk, *Democracy for All*, 32; and *Official Report of the Proceedings and Debates of the Third Constitutional Convention of Ohio*.

85. *Constitution of the State of North-Carolina: Together with the Ordinances and Resolutions of the Constitutional Convention, Assembled in the City of Raleigh, Jan. 14th, 1868* (Raleigh, NC: Joseph W. Holden, Convention Printer, 1868). See also Elizabeth Durfee, "Apportionment of Representation in the Legislature: A Study of State Constitutions," *Michigan Law Review* 43, no. 6 (1945): 1109; and Keith and Petry, "Apportionment of State Legislatures."

86. "Tennessee Legislature: Senate," *Republican Banner*, March 2, 1867, 1; *Journal of the Proceedings of the Convention of Delegates Elected by the People of Tennessee, to Amend, Revise, or Form and Make a New Constitution, for the State* (Nashville, TN: Jones, Purvis, Printers to the State, 1870); Durfee, "Apportionment of Representation," 1111.

87. In 1870, a mere 3,029 of North Carolina's 1,071,361 residents hailed from abroad. Tennessee's immigrant population was not as drastically small (19,316 foreign-born residents were enumerated that year in Tennessee: 1.5 percent of the state's population). However, this was still below the (already paltry) southern regional average of 3.3 percent foreign-born residents. See, especially, Gibson and Lennon, "Nativity of the Population."

184 NOTES TO PAGES 23-6

88. Joseph Grodin, Calvin Massey, and Richard Cunningham, *The California State Constitution: A Reference Guide* (Westport, CN: Greenwood Press, 1993), 351–53. See, broadly, Saxton, *Indispensable Enemy*; Mink, *Old Labor*; and Lew-Williams, *The Chinese Must Go*. Of 560,247 California residents in 1870, a total of 209,831 (37.5 percent of all residents) were born abroad. The US Census specifically identified 49,310 "Chinese" residents in California (though it did not distinguish Chinese immigrants from US-born Chinese Americans). See Gibson and Lennon, "Nativity of the Population"; and "Table I. Population, 1870–1790, by States and Territories, in Aggregate, and as White, Colored, Free Colored, Slave, Chinese, and Indian," in *Ninth Census of the United States of America* (Washington, DC: US Government Printing Office, 1872), 1–8.

89. *Debates and Proceedings of the Constitutional Convention of the State of California, Convened at the City of Sacramento, Saturday, September 28, 1878*, vol. 3 (Sacramento, CA: J. D. Young, Supt. State Printing, 1881), 1248–51.

90. Quotation in main text from *Debates and Proceedings of the Constitutional Convention of the State of California*, 3:1249. For delegate biographical information, see "Judge W. J. Tinnin, Pioneer, Crosses the Divide," *Fresno Morning Republican*, November 25, 1910, 12.

91. *Debates and Proceedings of the Constitutional Convention of the State of California*, 3:1249. On delegate partisan affiliation, see Winfield J. Davis, *History of Political Conventions in California: 1849–1892* (Sacramento: California State Library, 1893), 390–92.

92. *Debates and Proceedings of the Constitutional Convention of the State of California, Convened at the City of Sacramento, Saturday, September 28, 1878*, vol. 2 (Sacramento, CA: J. D. Young, Supt. State Printing, 1881), 755. On delegate partisan affiliation, see Davis, *History of Political Conventions*, 390–92.

93. See, broadly, *Debates and Proceedings of the Constitutional Convention of the State of California*. See also Noel Sargent, "The California Constitutional Convention of 1878–9," *California Law Review* 6, no. 1 (1917): 1–22; Ralph Kauer, "The Workingmen's Party of California," *Pacific Historical Review* 13, no. 3 (1944): 278–91; and Harry N. Scheiber, "Race, Radicalism, and Reform: Historical Perspective on the 1879 California Constitution," *Hastings Constitutional Law Quarterly* 17, no. 1 (Fall 1989): 35–80.

94. To comply with the state constitution's requirements that each town and city count its number of legal voters, local officials technically had to sign off on enumerators assigned to their jurisdictions. See "General Introduction," *1875 Census of Massachusetts* (Boston: Albert J. Wright, State Printer, 1876), xviii–xix. Wright would build on his experience in Massachusetts, later serving as the inaugural federal commissioner of labor and supervising the 1890 national census. See Horace Wadlin, "Carroll Davidson Wright: A Memorial," *Fortieth Annual Report on the Statistics of Labor, 1909* (Boston: Wright & Potter Printing, State Printers, 1911), 359–404.

95. *1875 Census of Massachusetts* Volumes 1–3 and Compendium (Boston: Albert J. Wright, State Printer, 1876–77).

96. Legal voters were defined as any male citizen "who has reached the age of 21 years, not an idiot, pauper nor convict." See Oren W. Weaver, *The Census System of Massachusetts* (Boston: Albert J. Wright, State Printer, 1876), 140.

97. *Census of the State of New York for 1875* (Albany, NY: Weed, Parsons, 1877), vii, 14–29.

98. Seventeen minus ten did not equal seven in alien suffrage math. Between 1876 and 1901, Louisiana adopted and then repealed an alien suffrage law. North Dakota and South Dakota emerged from Dakota Territory with both new states initially retaining noncitizen voting rights. But in 1898, North Dakota voters repealed their alien suffrage law via state constitutional amendment. Oklahoma Territory (created in 1890) also was an alien suffrage polity prior to statehood. See Rosberg, "Aliens and Equal Protection," 1098; Kleppner, *Continuity and Change*, 166; Neuman, "We Are the People," 298–99; Raskin, "Legal Aliens, Local Citizens," 1407–8; Keyssar, *Right to Vote*, 371–73; Varsanyi, "Rise and Fall," 119; and Hayduk, *Democracy for All*, 19–22.

99. Keyssar, *Right to Vote*, 371–73; Hayduk, *Democracy for All*, 19–22.

100. See, broadly, Kousser, *Shaping of Southern Politics*; Perman, *Struggle for Mastery*; and Herron, *Framing the Solid South*.

101. *Journal of the Constitutional Convention of the People of Georgia, Held in the City of Atlanta in the Months of July and August, 1877* (Atlanta, GA: Jas. P. Harrison, 1877); *Journal of the Proceedings of the Constitutional Convention of the State of Alabama, Held in the City of Montgomery, Commencing May 21st, 1901* (Montgomery, AL: Brown Printing, 1901); Kousser, *The Shaping of Southern Politics*, 61, 165–71; Perman, *Struggle for Mastery*, 193. On

NOTES TO PAGES 26–8   185

the foreign-born populations of both states in 1890, see Gibson and Lennon, "Nativity of the Population."

102. Gibson and Lennon, "Nativity of the Population."

103. *Official Journal of the Proceedings of the Constitutional Convention of the State of Louisiana, Held in New Orleans, Monday, April 21, 1879* (New Orleans, LA: Jas. H. Cosgrove, 1879).

104. Zacharie warned, "If the great state of New York...had, like this state of Louisiana, a law giving the right of franchise to any foreigner declaring his intention to become a citizen, what a state of things would result." Pointing to frequently narrow electoral margins in New York, Zacharie mused on the dangers "if 1000 Canadians were imported to change the political destiny of that great state." See "Elective Franchise and Ballot Reform," *New Orleans Picayune*, December 3, 1893, 12. See also "Qualifications for Suffrage," *New Orleans Picayune*, November 20, 1893, 4; Helen P. Trimpi, *Crimson Confederates: Harvard Men Who Fought for the South* (Knoxville: University of Tennessee Press, 2010), 358–62; and "Colonel Francis 'Frank' Charles Zacharie (1839—1910)," *Louisiana Digital Library*, https://louisianadigitallibrary.org/islandora/object/lasc-nonjusticesportraits:58.

105. "For Ballot Reform," *New Orleans Picayune*, March 12, 1894, 4.

106. This editorial was reproduced in the *Picayune*'s roundup of statewide newspapers' opinion pieces. See "Louisiana Opinions," *New Orleans Picayune*, August 7, 1893, 6.

107. *Official Journal of the Proceedings of the Constitutional Convention of the State of Louisiana: Held in New Orleans, Tuesday, February 8, 1898. And Calendar* (New Orleans, LA: H. J. Hearsey, 1898); Kousser, *Shaping of Southern Politics*, 152–65; Perman, *Struggle for Mastery*, 124–47.

108. See, especially, Jackson, *Dixie's Italians*, 71–97.

109. *Official Journal of the Proceedings of the Constitutional Convention of the State of Louisiana*, 144.

110. Perman, *Struggle for Mastery*, 140–47.

111. Matthew Frye Jacobson, *Whiteness of a Different Color: European Immigrants and the Alchemy of Race* (Cambridge, MA: Harvard University Press, 1998), 56–62; Jackson, *Dixie's Italians*, 43–70.

112. Quotation in main text from *Official Journal of the Proceedings of the Constitutional Convention of the State of Louisiana*, 122. Delegate biographical information from "Hon. T. J. Kernan Smitten Suddenly," *Times–Democrat* [New Orleans], January 10, 1911, 6.

113. See also, on the role of the suffrage committee, Perman, *Struggle for Mastery*, 140.

114. Quotation in main text from *Official Journal of the Proceedings of the Constitutional Convention of the State of Louisiana*, 143. Delegate biographical information from "The Convention," *Times–Democrat* [New Orleans], February 9, 1898, 1.

115. Quotation in main text from *Official Journal of the Proceedings of the Constitutional Convention of the State of Louisiana*, 144. Delegate biographical information from "The Convention," 1.

116. Quotations in main text from *Official Journal of the Proceedings of the Constitutional Convention of the State of Louisiana*, 144. Delegate biographical information from "The Convention," 1.

117. *Official Journal of the Proceedings of the Constitutional Convention of the State of Louisiana*, 122.

118. African American voter registration fell by roughly 90 percent when these provisions took effect. See Kousser, *Shaping of Southern Politics*, 49; and Perman, *Struggle for Mastery*, 147.

119. The paper credited the *Philadelphia Press* with first publishing this article. See "Tampering with the Suffrage," *Tazwell Republican*, March 17, 1898, 2.

120. The *Inquirer* was particularly harsh in its characterization of Louisiana's Cajun community. It alleged that "a great deal of romance has surrounded the Acadians, but many of their descendants in Louisiana, although they are thrifty and industrious, are densely ignorant, and cannot be said to have moved with the times." See "Suffrage in Louisiana," *Philadelphia Inquirer*, April 1, 1898, 8.

121. "Limitation of the Suffrage," *Banner–Democrat*, January 2, 1897, 2.

122. This *Banner–Democrat* article was first published by the *New Orleans Times Democrat*. See "Limitation of the Suffrage," 2. Historian Jessica Barbata Jackson similarly shows how this New Orleans paper argued that Louisianians were falling behind their peers elsewhere in the country by retaining noncitizen voting rights into the mid-1890s in Jackson, *Dixie's Italians*, 76 and 180n24.

186 NOTES TO PAGES 28–30

123. See, broadly, Gregg Cantrell, "'Our Very Pronounced Theory of Equal Rights to All': Race, Citizenship, and Populism in the South Texas Borderlands," *Journal of American History* 100, no. 3 (December 2013): 663–90.

124. See, broadly, Kousser, *Shaping of Southern Politics*; Perman, *Struggle for Mastery*; Dinan, *American State Constitutional Tradition*; and Herron, *Framing the Solid South*. For demographic data, see United States, *Eleventh Census of the United States, 1890* (Washington, DC: US Government Printing Office, 1896), 395–97.

125. See Gibson and Lennon, "Nativity of the Population."

126. Opponents of alien suffrage (particularly women's suffragists) often criticized what they saw as an unholy alliance between anti-(women's) suffragists, German-origin immigrants, and brewing interests. See, among many others, Charles E. Neu, "Olympia Brown and the Woman's Suffrage Movement," *Wisconsin Magazine of History* 43, no. 4 (Summer 1960): 277–87; Frederick Luebke, "The German–American Alliance in Nebraska, 1910–1917," *Nebraska History* 49, no. 2 (Summer 1968): 165–86; Patricia O'Keefe Easton, "Woman Suffrage in South Dakota: The Final Decade, 1911–1920," *South Dakota History* 13, no. 3 (Fall 1983): 206–26; Menchaca, *Naturalizing Mexican Immigrants*, 206–59; Egge, *Woman Suffrage and Citizenship*; and Gunter, "Immigrant Declarants."

127. On demographic data, see Gibson and Lennon, "Nativity of the Population." On repeal dates, see: Keyssar, *Right to Vote*, 371–73; Hayduk, *Democracy for All*, 19–22.

128. Indeed, only when the Arkansas Supreme Court ruled that this provision no longer applied was alien suffrage repealed in the state. See, especially, Aylsworth, "Passing of Alien Suffrage." Arkansas was not alone. In Nebraska, an anti-alien suffrage proposal received a wide plurality of votes cast on the measure in 1910. But it did not surmount a similar total vote majority standard. See Burton W. Folsom, "Tinkerers, Tipplers, and Traitors: Ethnicity and Democratic Reform in Nebraska during the Progressive Era," *Pacific Historical Review* 50, no. 1 (February 1981): 69; see also Hattie Plum Williams, "The Road to Citizenship," *Political Science Quarterly* 27, no. 3 (September 1912): 399–427; and Keyssar, *Right to Vote*, 371–73. On comparative state policies governing constitutional amendment requirements, see, broadly, Dinan, *American State Constitutional Tradition*; Hayduk, *Democracy for All*, 19–22; and Gunter, "Immigrant Declarants."

129. The more numerous noncitizen men in the Sunshine State, by contrast, abruptly lost that right via legislative statute in 1895 because Florida's erstwhile alien suffrage law was not protected under the state constitution. See "An Act to Provide for the Registration of All Legally Qualified Voters in the Several Counties of the State, and to Provide for General and Special Elections and for the Returns of Elections," Pub. L. No. Chapter 4328 No. 7, Florida Statutes—Fifth Regular Session 56 (1895); see also Kousser, *Shaping of Southern Politics*, 91–103, 123–30; Perman, *Struggle for Mastery*, 59–69; and Herron, *Framing the Solid South*, 220.

130. Keyssar, *Right to Vote*, 138, 371–73; Hayduk, *Democracy for All*, 19–22.

131. See, especially, Higham, *Strangers in the Land*; Saxton, *Indispensable Enemy*; Mink, *Old Labor*; and Lew-Williams, *The Chinese Must Go*.

132. Even the formal possession of US citizenship did not guarantee access to suffrage rights, in practice, for many Native Americans well into the mid-twentieth century. See, among others, N. D. Houghton, "The Legal Status of Indian Suffrage in the United States," *California Law Review* 19, no. 5 (1931): 507–20; and Willard Hughes Rollings, "Citizenship and Suffrage: The Native American Struggle for Civil Rights in the American West, 1830–1965," *Nevada Law Journal* 5, no. 1 (Fall 2004): 126–40.

133. Raskin, "Legal Aliens, Local Citizens"; Varsanyi, "Rise and Fall."

134. On late-nineteenth-century statehood constitutional conventions in the West, see, especially, Bakken, *Rocky Mountain Constitution Making*; and Bridges, *Democratic Beginnings*. On statehood admission and Republican national political considerations, see Daniel Wirls, "Regionalism, Rotten Boroughs, Race, and Realignment: The Seventeenth Amendment and the Politics of Representation," *Studies in American Political Development* 13, no. 1 (April 1999): 1–30.

135. These two territories were long denied statehood owing to Anglo fears that Mexican nationals and Mexican Americans would acquire significant power if these territories became states. See, broadly, Linda C. Noel, *Debating American Identity: Southwestern Statehood and Mexican Immigration* (Tucson: University of Arizona Press, 2014). See also Jacobson, Tichenor, and Durden, "Southwest's Uneven Welcome"; Rosina Lozano, *An American*

NOTES TO PAGES 31–5   187

Language: The History of Spanish in the United States (Berkeley: University of California Press, 2018).

136. Gibson and Lennon, "Nativity of the Population."

137. Quotation in main text from *Proceedings and Debates of the Constitutional Convention: Held in the City of Helena, Montana, July 4th, 1889, August 17th, 1889* (Helena, MT: State Publishing Company, 1921), 353. Maginnis elaborated on these views at greater length later in debate. See also pp. 356–57. For delegate biographical information, see "Maginnis, Martin 1841–1919," in *Biographical Directory of the United States Congress*, https://bioguide.congress.gov/search/bio/M000050.

138. Main text quotation from *Proceedings and Debates of the Constitutional Convention: Held in the City of Helena, Montana*, 352. For delegate biographical information, see "Montana's Solons," *Livingston Enterprise*, January 19, 1889, 6.

139. Quotation in main text from *Proceedings and Debates of the Constitutional Convention: Held in the City of Helena, Montana*, 354. Delegate biographical information from "Our Law-Givers," *Daily Independent* [Helena, MT], August 4, 1889, 2.

140. Quote in main text from *Proceedings and Debates of the Constitutional Convention: Held in the City of Helena, Montana*, 356. Delegate biographical information from "Death of George W. Stapleton Pioneer of State of Montana," *Anaconda Standard*, April 26, 1910, 6.

141. "Citizenship," *Helena Weekly Herald*, August 1, 1889, 5.

142. Quotation in main text from *Proceedings and Debates of the Constitutional Convention: Held in the City of Helena, Montana*, 359. On delegate biographical information, see "Stalwart Son of the West Passes over Last Long Trail," *Butte Miner*, April 14, 1921, 1, 8.

143. *Proceedings and Debates of the Constitutional Convention: Held in the City of Helena, Montana*, 359.

144. Bakken, *Rocky Mountain Constitution Making*, 88–90, 149–50.

145. Quotation in main text from *Proceedings and Debates of the Constitutional Convention: Held in the City of Helena, Montana*, 357; "Honored Son of Peacham Dies in Washington," *Caledonian–Record* [St. Johnsbury, VT], December 17, 1927, 7.

146. See, especially, *Journal and Debates of the Constitutional Convention of the State of Wyoming, Begun at the City of Cheyenne on September 2, 1889, and Concluded September 30, 1889* (Cheyenne, WY: Daily Sun, 1893), 69, 396–97, 434–35.

147. See *Journal and Debates of the Constitutional Convention of the State of Wyoming*, 375.

148. See *Journal and Debates of the Constitutional Convention of the State of Wyoming*, 350.

149. Keyssar, *Right to Vote*, 371–73; Hayduk, *Democracy for All*, 19–22.

150. As historian Susan VanBurkleo describes, Washington Territory's alien suffrage law had been greatly complicated by the enfranchisement and then subsequent disfranchisement of women in the territory during the 1880s. See Sandra F. VanBurkleo, *Gender Remade: Citizenship, Suffrage, and Public Power in the New Northwest, 1879–1912* (New York: Cambridge University Press, 2015), 47–48. On the repeal of the alien suffrage law upon Washington's statehood, see *Constitution for the State of Washington* (1889) Article VI, Section 1.

151. *Journal of the Constitutional Convention for North Dakota Held at Bismarck, Thursday, July 4 to Aug. 17, 1889* (Bismarck, ND: Tribune, State Printers and Binders, 1889); *Journal of the Constitutional Convention of South Dakota, July, 1889* (Sioux Falls, SD: Brown and Saenger, Printers and Binders, 1889). Though Oklahoma was an alien suffrage territory under federal law in 1890, it, too, would repeal that policy at its 1907 statehood constitutional convention. See Neuman, "We Are the People," 298; and Hayduk, *Democracy for All*, 19–22. On demographic data, see Gibson and Lennon, "Nativity of the Population."

152. On the often-missed repeal of North Dakota's alien suffrage law in 1898, see Kleppner, *Continuity and Change*, 166. For other dates, see Keyssar, *Right to Vote*, 371–73; and Hayduk, *Democracy for All*, 19–22.

153. Kleppner, *Continuity and Change*, 166; Keyssar, *Right to Vote*, 371–73; Hayduk, *Democracy for All*, 19–22.

Chapter 2

1. This draws on Brendan A. Shanahan, "A 'Practically American' Canadian Woman Confronts a United States Citizen-Only Hiring Law: Katharine Short and the California Alien Teachers Controversy of 1915," *Law and History Review* 39, no. 4 (November 2021): 621–48.

188   NOTES TO PAGES 35–7

2. I have found Gilded Age and Progressive Era anti-alien public and/or publicly funded employment laws in ten states. Many later enacted additional blue-collar nativist hiring laws and/or amended their initial statutes. I cite the year of the initial passage of such a law here: Arizona (1912), California (1901), Idaho (1889), Illinois (1889), Louisiana (1908), Massachusetts (1895), New York (1889), New Jersey (1899), Pennsylvania (1895), and Wyoming (1889). Citations to each statute follow in the notes to this chapter below.

3. Battles over anti-immigrant hiring restrictions were not confined to state alienage laws governing public and publicly funded employment in the late nineteenth and early twentieth centuries, of course. Some unions adopted de facto barriers or even outright bans on the membership of noncitizens. Chinese immigrants were especially harmed by these—among other explicitly racist—bans. On overt anti-alien union membership rules, see, especially, French Eugene Wolfe, *Admission to American Trade Unions* (Baltimore: Johns Hopkins University Press, 1912); and Robert Asher, "Union Nativism and the Immigrant Response," *Labor History* 23, no. 3 (1982): 325–48. State lawmakers sometimes enacted anti-alien occupational and professional licensure laws in the Gilded Age and Progressive Era as well. See, among others, Leonard Helfenstein, "Constitutionality of Legislative Discrimination against the Alien in His Right to Work," *University of Pennsylvania Law Review* 83, no. 1 (November 1934): 74–82; and Plascencia, Freeman, and Setzler, "Decline of Barriers."

4. As historian David Montgomery writes, "unemployed craftsmen" generally only tried to obtain so-called common labor jobs "during hard times." See David Montgomery, *The Fall of the House of Labor: The Workplace, the State, and American Labor Activism, 1865–1925* (New York: Cambridge University Press, 1989), 65. In many circumstances, those who toiled on backbreaking public and/or publicly contracted road work were coerced, unpaid convict laborers in this era. On the intersection of immigrant workers and convict laborers, see Kelly Lytle Hernández, *City of Inmates: Conquest, Rebellion, and the Rise of Human Caging in Los Angeles, 1771–1965* (Chapel Hill: University of North Carolina Press, 2017), 57–63. On convict leasing more broadly, see Douglas A. Blackmon, *Slavery by Another Name: The Re-enslavement of Black Americans from the Civil War to World War II* (New York: Anchor Books, 2009); and Pippa Holloway, *Living in Infamy: Felon Disfranchisement and the History of American Citizenship* (New York: Oxford University Press, 2013).

5. Jon Teaford, *The Unheralded Triumph: City Government in America, 1870–1900* (Baltimore: Johns Hopkins University Press, 1984); Steven Erie, *Rainbow's End: Irish-Americans and the Dilemmas of Urban Machine Politics, 1840–1985* (Berkeley: University of California Press, 1990).

6. Higham, *Strangers in the Land*; Samuel T. McSeveney, *The Politics of Depression: Political Behavior in the Northeast, 1893–1896* (New York: Oxford University Press, 1972).

7. Kelly, "Wavering Course"; Filindra, "E Pluribus Unum?"

8. Higham, *Strangers in the Land*, 72–73, 183.

9. Two leading historians of American nativism, John Higham and Gwendolyn Mink, both describe late-nineteenth- and early-twentieth-century state anti-alien hiring laws as weak owing to their selective enforcement and multiple defeats in lower courts. Of state anti-alien hiring laws adopted in the 1880s and 1890s, Higham argues that they were "far from common, and fear of direct economic competition from immigrants must have affected only limited groups and regions." He likewise argues (a bit too broadly) that usually "the courts...held such statutes contrary to the Fourteenth Amendment" prior to 1915 (73). He does, however, identify growing pressure for such anti-immigrant measures as part of the "Summit of Prewar Nativism" in 1914 and 1915 (183). See Higham, 46–47, 72–73, 183–84. Mink is more explicit than Higham and argues that these laws were generally not effective. She writes that "these statutes were mostly symbolic: under laissez-faire capitalism they could limit immigrant opportunities only with respect to *public* employment." See Mink, *Old Labor*, 123.

10. See, among others, Parker, "State, Citizenship, and Territory"; Tirres, "Ownership without Citizenship"; and Ziegler-McPherson, *Selling America*.

11. The order's better-known successor "junior" organization would achieve a much greater national reach and degree of power in the Gilded Age. Higham, *Strangers in the Land*, 57; Michael Feldberg, "Urbanization as a Cause of Violence: Philadelphia as a Test Case," in *The Peoples of Philadelphia: A History of Ethnic Groups and Lower-Class Life, 1790–1940*, ed. Allen F. Davis and Mark H. Haller (Philadelphia: University of Pennsylvania Press, 1998), 53–70; Thomas Keil and Jacqueline M. Keil, *Anthracite's Demise and the Post-coal Economy of Northeastern Pennsylvania* (New York: Rowman & Littlefield, 2014), 31–32; Parker, *Making Foreigners*, 101–4.

NOTES TO PAGES 37–9   189

12. See, especially, Hirota, *Expelling the Poor*; Law, "Lunatics, Idiots, Paupers"; and Ritter, "Immigration, Crime."
13. Kanazawa, "Immigration, Exclusion, and Taxation."
14. *Debates and Proceedings of the Constitutional Convention of the State of California*; Kauer, "Workingmen's Party of California"; Saxton, *Indispensable Enemy*; Mink, *Old Labor*, 71–112; Scheiber, "Race, Radicalism, and Reform"; Tomás Almaguer, *Racial Fault Lines: The Historical Origins of White Supremacy in California* (Berkeley: University of California Press, 1994), 178–80; Mae Ngai, *The Lucky Ones: One Family and the Extraordinary Invention of Chinese America* (Boston: Houghton Mifflin Harcourt, 2010), 24–40; Lew-Williams, *The Chinese Must Go*.
15. On this legal history, see, especially, Charles J. McClain, *In Search of Equality: The Chinese Struggle against Discrimination in Nineteenth-Century America* (Berkeley: University of California Press, 1994); and Thomas Wuil Joo, "New Conspiracy Theory of the Fourteenth Amendment: Nineteenth Century Chinese Civil Rights Cases and the Development of Substantive Due Process Jurisprudence," *University of San Francisco Law Review* 29, no. 2 (Winter 1995): 353–88. See also Konvitz, *Alien and the Asiatic*, 172–74; Saxton, *Indispensable Enemy*; Motomura, *Americans in Waiting*, 64–70; and Ngai, *Lucky Ones*, 44–45.
16. On anti-Chinese vigilante violence, see, especially, Lew-Williams, *The Chinese Must Go*. On Chinese exclusion, undocumented immigration, and the creation of a federal identification regime for all Chinese and Chinese American residents in the United States following the Geary Act of 1892, see, among others, Lee, *At America's Gates*; Ngai, *Impossible Subjects*; and Hernández, *City of Inmates*, 64–91.
17. Few mid- to late-nineteenth-century white laborers were "native" to western states like California, however. The vast majority had recently migrated from states (or Canadian provinces) "back east" or from Europe. See Francis Amasa Walker, *A Compendium of the Ninth Census* (Washington, DC: US Government Printing Office, 1872), 392–37, 400–401. See also Michael Kazin, *Barons of Labor: The San Francisco Building Trades and Union Power in the Progressive Era* (Urbana: University of Illinois Press, 1988), 21–22.
18. In this context, Chinese immigrants became, in historian Alexander Saxton's phrase, "the indispensable enemy" against whom white workers, union leaders, and politicians rallied and organized. See Saxton, *Indispensable Enemy*. See also Mink, *Old Labor*, 71–112; Almaguer, *Racial Fault Lines*, 153–82; Erika Lee, "The Chinese Exclusion Example: Race, Immigration, and American Gatekeeping, 1882–1924," *Journal of American Ethnic History* 21, no. 3 (Spring 2002): 36–62; and Justin F. Jackson, "Labor and Chinese Exclusion in US History," *Oxford Research Encyclopedia of American History* (November 29, 2021), https://oxfordre.com/americanhistory/view/10.1093/acrefore/9780199329175.001.0001/acrefore-9780199329175-e-545.
19. Massachusetts Bureau of Statistics of Labor, "Twelfth Annual Report of the Massachusetts Bureau of Statistics of Labor" (Boston: Rand, Avery, Printers to the Commonwealth, January 1881), 469–70.
20. Quotation in main text from Massachusetts Bureau of Statistics of Labor, 469. On the "Wright Affair" in French Canadian immigration historiography, see, among many others, Normand Lafleur, *Les «Chinois» de l'Est ou la vie quotidienne des Québécois émigrés aux États-Unis de 1840 à nos jours* (Montréal, QC: Leméac, 1981); Pierre Anctil, "L'identité de l'immigrant québécois en Nouvelle-Angleterre. Le rapport Wright de 1882," *Recherches Sociographiques* 22, no. 3 (1981): 331–59; Yves Roby, *Les Franco-Américains de la Nouvelle-Angleterre: Rêves et réalités* (Sillery, QC: Septentrion, 2000), 61–79; and FlorenceMae Waldron, "Gender and the Quebecois Migration to New England, 1870–1930: A Comparative Case Study" (PhD diss., University of Minnesota, 2003), 100–121. On the episode in broader US immigration history, see, among others, Lee, "Chinese Exclusion Example," 47–48; Roger Daniels, *Coming to America: A History of Immigration and Ethnicity in American Life* (New York: Perennial, 2002), 258–59; and David Roediger, *Working toward Whiteness: How America's Immigrants Became White: The Strange Journey from Ellis Island to the Suburbs* (New York: Basic Books, 2005), 51.
21. See, especially, Rudolph Vecoli, "Chicago's Italians prior to World War I: A Study of Their Social and Economic Adjustment" (PhD diss., University of Wisconsin, 1963); Lee, "Chinese Exclusion Example"; Donna Gabaccia, "The 'Yellow Peril' and the 'Chinese of Europe': Global Perspectives on Race and Labor, 1815–1930," in *Migration, Migration History, History: Old Paradigms and New Perspectives*, ed. Leo Lucassen and Jan Lucassen (New York: Peter Lang, 1997), 177–96; Jacobson, *Whiteness*; and Roediger, *Working toward Whiteness*.

190 NOTES TO PAGES 39–40

22. Historians continue to debate whether these analogies were employed to racialize southern and eastern Europeans as nonwhite, as occupying some liminal status between whiteness and non-whiteness, or as white but nevertheless negatively racialized within a broader category of white-ness vis-à-vis native-born Yankees and northern and western Europeans. Works of scholarship in the latter camp, to which this book subscribes, often emphasize that southern and eastern Europeans were viewed as white under federal immigration and naturalization law and by the US Census. Among many other works of scholarship that engage these debates, see Jacobson, *Whiteness*; David Roediger and James Barrett, "Making New Immigrants 'Inbetween': Irish Hosts and White Panethnicity, 1890 to 1930," in *Not Just Black and White: Historical and Contemporary Perspectives on Immigration, Race, and Ethnicity in the United States*, ed. Nancy Foner and George M. Fredrickson (New York: Russell Sage Foundation, 2004), 167–96; Thomas A Guglielmo, *White on Arrival: Italians, Race, Color, and Power in Chicago, 1890–1945* (New York: Oxford University Press, 2003); Roediger, *Working toward Whiteness*; Victoria Hattam, *In the Shadow of Race: Jews, Latinos, and Immigrant Politics in the United States* (Chicago: University of Chicago Press, 2007); Nell Irvin Painter, *The History of White People* (New York: W. W. Norton, 2010); Brendan A. Shanahan, "Enforcing the Colorline and Counting White Races: Race and the Census in North America, 1900–1941," *American Review of Canadian Studies* 44, no. 3 (2014): 293–307; Fox and Bloemraad, "Beyond 'White by Law'"; Stefano Luconi, "Black Dagoes? Italian Immigrants' Racial Status in the United States: An Ecological View," *Journal of Transatlantic Studies* 14, no. 2 (2016): 188–99; Joel Perlmann, *America Classifies the Immigrants: From Ellis Island to the 2020 Census* (Cambridge, MA: Harvard University Press, 2018); and Jackson, *Dixie's Italians*.
23. Historian Erika Lee famously articulates and demonstrates how subsequent immigration restrictionists employed West Coast anti-Asian politics as "their dominant model" following the passage of federal Chinese exclusion legislation. See Lee, *At America's Gates*, 32. See also, more broadly, Lee, "Chinese Exclusion Example."
24. On the political development of and efforts to enforce the Alien Contract Labor Law, see, among others, Charlotte Erickson, *American Industry and the European Immigrant, 1860–1885* (Cambridge, MA: Harvard University Press, 1957); Catherine Collomp, "Unions, Civics, and National Identity: Organized Labor's Reaction to Immigration, 1881–1897," *Labor History* 29, no. 4 (1988): 450–74; Gunther Peck, *Reinventing Free Labor: Padrones and Immigrant Workers in the North American West, 1880–1930* (New York: Cambridge University Press, 2000); and Mark Wyman, *Round-Trip to America: The Immigrants Return to Europe, 1880–1930* (Ithaca, NY: Cornell University Press, 2018), 34–35, 102–9.
25. On the Ford Committee, see, among others, Peck, *Reinventing Free Labor*, 88–89; and Paul Moses, *An Unlikely Union: The Love–Hate Story of New York's Irish and Italians* (New York: New York University Press, 2015), 73–81. On the rise (and critiques) of "padronism," see, additionally, Robert F. Harney, "Montreal's King of Italian Labour: A Case Study of Padronism," *Labour/Le Travail* 4 (January 1979): 57–84; and Bruno Ramirez, *On the Move: French-Canadian and Italian Migrants in the North Atlantic Economy, 1860–1914* (Toronto, ON: McClelland & Stewart, 1991), 96–110.
26. Ford brought his committee to Detroit to highlight and investigate allegations that employers in Michigan were advertising for prospective Canadian workers to move to the state and/or commute from border cities like Windsor (neighboring Detroit) and Sarnia (next to Port Huron). See "Frauds in Immigration," *Detroit Free Press*, December 27, 1888, 5.
27. Quotation in main text from "The Alien Labor Bill," *Detroit Free Press*, January 26, 1894, 8. See also "The Senate on Wool," *Philadelphia Inquirer*, August 31, 1890, 5; and "Will Put Up the Bars," *Pittsburgh Commercial Gazette*, December 9, 1892, 1.
28. "Cleveland's Veto," *Philadelphia Inquirer*, March 3, 1897, 2. On the Lodge–Corliss bill more broadly, see, among others, Higham, *Strangers in the Land*, 104–5; Thomas A. Klug, "Residents by Day, Visitors by Night: The Origins of the Alien Commuter on the U.S.–Canadian Border during the 1920s," *Michigan Historical Review* 34, no. 2 (2008): 77–80; Mink, *Old Labor*, 128n29; Aristide R. Zolberg, *A Nation by Design: Immigration Policy in the Fashioning of America* (New York: Russell Sage Foundation, 2006), 227; and Wyman, *Round-Trip to America*, 103–4.
29. "Cleveland's Veto," 2.
30. Higham, *Strangers in the Land*, 46.
31. "An Act to Regulate the Rate of Wages on All Public Works in This State, and to Define What Laborers Shall be Employed Thereon," New York—112nd Legislature (1889), Ch. 380: 508.

NOTES TO PAGES 40–1   191

32. "Aliens: To Protect the Labor of Native and Naturalized American Citizens," Illinois—36th General Assembly (1889), Regular Session: 19–216; Article XIII, Section 5 of Constitution of the State of Idaho: Adopted by a Constitutional Convention Held at Boise City in the Territory of Idaho, August 6, 1889 (Caldwell, ID, 1907); Article XIX, "Miscellaneous" and "Labor on Public Works," Sections 1–2: Constitution of the State of Wyoming: Adopted by the People at a General Election Held November 5th, 1889 (Laramie, WY, 1908). Higham identifies the 1889 anti-alien hiring laws in Idaho, Illinois, and Wyoming, but not New York; see Higham, *Strangers in the Land*, 46. As historian Amy Bridges highlights, anti-alien hiring restrictions in both Idaho and Wyoming arose as part of broader (often extrajudicial) attacks on Chinese workers. See Bridges, *Democratic Beginnings*, 96–97.
33. "To Protect American Labor," *Chicago Daily Tribune*, March 28, 1889, 9.
34. Historian Rudolph Vecoli credits Chicago's trade union movement, which "resented most strongly the employment of Italian laborers on public works" as the key backers of the bill. Vecoli importantly emphasizes that "the purpose of the law's proponents was to exclude from public employment the 'birds of passage.'" See Vecoli, "Chicago's Italians prior to World War I," 418–19. On Hagle's biography and district, see *Journal of the Senate of the Thirty-Sixth General Assembly* (Springfield, IL: Phillips Brothers, State Printer, 1889), 2; and *Journal of the Senate Special Session of the Fortieth General Assembly of the State of Illinois* (Springfield, IL: Phillips Brothers, State Printer, 1898), 167–68. See also "To Protect American Labor," 9; "State Capitol Notes," *Chicago Daily Tribune*, May 4, 1889, 9; and "Striking Brickmakers," *Chicago Daily Tribune*, June 21, 1889, 8.
35. Quotation in main text from "Striking Brickmakers," 8. The law restricted hiring on public and publicly funded construction projects to US citizens and immigrants possessing first papers. Immigrants possessing those papers were required to naturalize within three months upon eligibility to retain their jobs. Officials and contractors found to have paid wages to ineligible immigrant workers were "personally liable" for the equivalent costs. See "Aliens: To Protect."
36. The Chicago World's Fair of 1893 is arguably the most famous international exposition of all time. It ultimately counted 27.5 million entrants. The classic text on the fair is Erik Larson, *The Devil in The White City* (New York: Vintage Books, 2003), 5. More broadly, on blue-collar nativist labor conflicts during construction for the Chicago World's Fair, see Vecoli, "Chicago's Italians," 418–22; Richard Schneirov and Thomas J. Suhrbur, *Union Brotherhood, Union Town: The History of the Carpenters' Union of Chicago, 1863–1987* (Carbondale: Southern Illinois University Press, 1988), 44–60; and Robert B. Ross, "Scales and Skills of Monopoly Power: Labor Geographies of the 1890–1891 Chicago Carpenters' Strike," *Antipode* 43, no. 4 (2011): 1281–304.
37. "Work Has Been Stopped," *Chicago Daily Tribune*, February 14, 1891, 8; "No Foreigners Need Apply," *Chicago Daily Tribune*, February 20, 1891, 6; "Principal Events of the Week," *Chicago Daily Tribune*, February 28, 1891, 9. See also Vecoli, "Chicago's Italians," 419; and Ross, "Scales and Skills," 1297.
38. Gage further noted that the legislature had passed a resolution in 1890 calling on directors to implement the 1889 anti-alien hiring law on World's Fair sites. Gage stated that "the directors are disposed to give the weight and consideration to the resolution which it deserves." But he emphasized that the "resolution…is not a law" (1). Quotation in main text also from "Senators and Directors Confer," *Chicago Daily Tribune*, March 3, 1891, 1. Pressure from lawmakers was significant. State representative Henry Carmody, a Chicago Democrat, demanded that his peers launch a formal investigation into alleged violations of the state's anti-alien public construction hiring law. While Carmody's proposal was adopted by the House, it was narrowly defeated in the Senate. The upper chamber did agree to send members to meet with the World's Fair directors and the McArthur Brothers, however. See "To Investigate the Fair," *Chicago Daily Tribune*, February 21, 1891, 1; and "Debate on the Labor Question," *Chicago Daily Tribune*, February 26, 1891, 6. Municipal politicians in Chicago also created a (short-lived) "special-Aldermanic, eight-hours-a-day, non-alien-labor investigating committee." See "Makes Two Concessions," *Chicago Daily Tribune*, March 7, 1891, 2.
39. "Senators and Directors Confer," 1; "Makes Two Concessions," 2; "No More to Be Granted," *Chicago Daily Tribune*, March 15, 1891, 6; Vecoli, "Chicago's Italians," 421–22; Ross, "Scales and Skills," 1298. For broader labor context, see Schneirov and Suhrbur, *Union Brotherhood, Union Town*, 48–53.
40. As historian Rudolph Vecoli notes, World's Fair jobsites were, quite literally, marked by "No Aliens Need Apply" signs. See Vecoli, "Chicago's Italians," 421.

192   NOTES TO PAGES 41–3

41. "Cannot Employ Aliens," *Chicago Daily Tribune*, March 12, 1891, 6.
42. Carlos C. Closson, "The Unemployed in American Cities," *Quarterly Journal of Economics* 8, no. 2 (January 1, 1894): 168–217; Leah Hannah Feder, *Unemployment Relief in Periods of Depression: A Study of Measures Adopted in Certain American Cities, 1857 through 1922* (New York: Russell Sage Foundation, 1936), 76–85; Christina Romer, "Spurious Volatility in Historical Unemployment Data," *Journal of Political Economy* 94, no. 1 (February 1986): 31.
43. Alexander Keyssar, *Out of Work: The First Century of Unemployment in Massachusetts* (New York: Cambridge University Press, 1986), 39–76; Timothy J. Hatton and Jeffrey G. Williamson, "Unemployment, Employment Contracts, and Compensating Wage Differentials: Michigan in the 1890s," *Journal of Economic History* 51, no. 3 (September 1991): 607–18.
44. Udo Sautter, *Three Cheers for the Unemployed: Government and Unemployment before the New Deal* (New York: Cambridge University Press, 1991), 99.
45. Keyssar, *Out of Work*, 225–31.
46. See, among others, Feder, *Unemployment Relief in Periods of Depression*, 168–88; Samuel Rezneck, "Unemployment, Unrest, and Relief in the United States during the Depression of 1893–97," *Journal of Political Economy* 61, no. 4 (August 1953): 324–45; and Sautter, *Three Cheers*, 94–110.
47. McSeveney, *Politics of Depression*, 34. On demands for work relief to counteract unemployment during the mid-1890s and their broader context, see Closson, "Unemployed in American Cities"; Feder, *Unemployment Relief*, 98–125, 168–88; Rezneck, "Unemployment, Unrest, and Relief"; Keyssar, *Out of Work*; Sautter, *Three Cheers*, 94–99; and Joan Waugh, "'Give This Man Work!': Josephine Shaw Lowell, the Charity Organization Society of the City of New York, and the Depression of 1893," *Social Science History* 25, no. 2 (2001): 217–46.
48. Closson, "Unemployed in American Cities," 216–17.
49. As quoted in Rezneck, "Unemployment, Unrest, and Relief," 332. In the words of historian Udo Sautter, so small in scale were adopted measures that "the dreadful misery of the 1890s passed without any state or federal authorities trying out the public works tool" as part of a broader work relief strategy (99). See Sautter, *Three Cheers*, 98–99. See also McSeveney, *Politics of Depression*, 34–35.
50. "An Act to Amend Chapter 385 of the Laws of 1870, entitled 'An Act to Regulate the Hours of Labor of Mechanics, Workingmen and Laborers in the Employ of the State, or Otherwise Engaged on Public Works,'" New York—117th Legislature (1894), Ch. 622: 1569. See also Rezneck, "Unemployment, Unrest, and Relief," 327, 332; Higham, *Strangers in the Land*, 72–73; and Mink, *Old Labor*, 123.
51. The financial panic's immediate impetus is generally credited to the bankruptcy of the Philadelphia and Reading Railroad in February 1893. See, among others, Douglas Steeples and David O. Whitten, *Democracy in Desperation: The Depression of 1893* (Westport, CT: Greenwood Press, 1998), 32.
52. Closson, "Unemployed in American Cities," 180–81.
53. One such Philadelphia proposal was called "the 'America for Americans' bill." See "The City Fathers in an Uproar," *Philadelphia Inquirer*, March 9, 1894, 8. This rhetoric was a common rallying cry for different anti-immigrant movements in US history. See Dale T. Knobel, *America for the Americans: The Nativist Movement in the United States* (New York: Twayne, 1996); and Lee, *America for Americans*.
54. "Work for Citizens," *Pittsburgh Commercial Gazette*, October 20, 1893, 2. Allegheny City (annexed by Pittsburgh in 1907) should not be confused with the eponymous county. See Dan Peterson and Carol Rooney, *Allegheny City: A History of Pittsburgh's North Side* (Pittsburgh, PA: University of Pittsburgh Press, 2013).
55. "The City Fathers Hold Short Sessions," *Philadelphia Inquirer*, March 10, 1893, 7. Harris may have had additional motivations to oppose the proposed anti-alien hiring policy. He owned a construction company that "engaged in the construction of some of the largest buildings in and around Philadelphia." See Leland M. Williamson et al., eds., *Prominent and Progressive Pennsylvanians of the Nineteenth Century*, vol. 2 (Philadelphia: Record Publishing Company, 1898), 237.
56. "City Fathers in an Uproar," 8.
57. The *Philadelphia Inquirer* reported in March 1893 that select councilman James Miles "thought that while [an anti-alien hiring] bill had many commendable features, there was no time to perfect it so late in the session." See "All Trolley Bills Pass Select Council," *Philadelphia Inquirer*,

NOTES TO PAGES 43–4   193

March 22, 1893, 8. That same spring, Councilman Clay expressed "his willingness to go a great ways to bring about the exclusion of aliens from public work." The *Inquirer* reported, however, that "he felt the proposed measure was too sweeping." See "City Fathers Hold Short Sessions," 7.

58. In Philadelphia, Councilman Harris emphasized this point. He "doubted if Americans could be obtained to do some of the city labor for which foreigners were employed." See "City Fathers Hold Short Sessions," 7. Allegheny councilman John A. Born likewise warned that "now it was possible to get American labor on the streets, but when the mills and factories start again this will not be the case. Then the resolution might cause trouble." See "Work for Citizens," 2.

59. Allegheny councilman C. W. Gerwig "was in sympathy with the spirit of the resolution, but he doubted if it was legal. He asked that the resolution be sent to the city solicitor." "Work for Citizens," 2. More boldly, Councilman Clay of Philadelphia argued that the proposal ran afoul of the state constitution. See "City Fathers in an Uproar," 8.

60. "Providing that none but citizens of the United States shall be employed in any capacity in the erection, enlargement or improvement of any public building or public work within this Commonwealth," Pennsylvania—General Assembly, Regular Session (1895), Act No. 182: 269.

61. "Lines of Local News," *Philadelphia Inquirer*, December 18, 1896, 7. Only two members of the City Council's thirty-member upper chamber opposed the policy. One was Henry Clay. Franklin Harris, who had denounced a similar bill in 1893, voted in favor. See *Journal of Select Council of the City of Philadelphia, from October 1, 1896 to April 1, 1897*, vol. 2 (Philadelphia: George F. Lasher, Printer and Binder, 1897), 130–31.

62. Other scholars of the Pennsylvania Alien Tax Act of 1897 include Higham, *Strangers in the Land*, 72–73; Victor Greene, *The Slavic Community on Strike: Immigrant Labor in Pennsylvania Anthracite* (Notre Dame, IN: University of Notre Dame Press, 1968), 111–51; Michael Novak, *Guns of Lattimer* (New York: Basic Books, 1978); Perry K. Blatz, *Democratic Miners: Work and Labor Relations in the Anthracite Coal Industry, 1875–1925* (Albany: SUNY Press, 1994), 45–63; Melvyn Dubofsky, "The Lattimer Massacre and the Meaning of Citizenship," *Pennsylvania History* 69, no. 1 (Winter 2002): 52–57; Paul A. Shackel and Michael Roller, "The Gilded Age Wasn't So Gilded in the Anthracite Region of Pennsylvania," *International Journal of Historical Archaeology* 16, no. 4 (December 2012): 761–75; Michael P. Roller, "Rewriting Narratives of Labor Violence: A Transnational Perspective of the Lattimer Massacre," *Historical Archaeology* 47, no. 3 (2013): 109–23; and Paul A. Shackel, *Remembering Lattimer: Labor, Migration, and Race in Pennsylvania Anthracite Country* (Urbana: University of Illinois Press, 2018).

63. "An Act Regulating the Employment of Foreign Born Unnaturalized Male Persons over Twenty-One Years of Age, and Providing a Tax on the Employers...," Pennsylvania—General Assembly, Regular Session (1897), Act No. 139: 166–68.

64. The *Inquirer* reported that in Shamokin, "The new alien labor law levying three cents per day upon foreigners is being rigidly enforced throughout the anthracite regions. Clerks at mines are now engaged in making lists of all such workmen as possess naturalization papers." See "Searching Mines for Aliens," *Philadelphia Inquirer*, July 8, 1897, 2. Likewise, the paper reported Philadelphia mill foremen were tasked with asking workers about their citizenship status. See "Foreigners Rush to Obtain Papers," *Philadelphia Inquirer*, June 29, 1897, 3.

65. "Foreigners Rush," 3.

66. The *Inquirer* reported 127 naturalizations and 172 first papers issued that day by Philadelphia's courts. See "Foreigners Rush," 3. A month later, the *Inquirer* advised readers when courts in Camden (New Jersey) would hold naturalization hearings, noting that "there's a rush of aliens who are making application for citizenship to evade payment of the Pennsylvania alien tax." See "Over in Camden," *Philadelphia Inquirer*, July 3, 1897, 3. The *Inquirer* later reported that 3,593 first papers had been issued in Philadelphia courts between July 15 and September 3, noting, "The rush began immediately following the passage of the Alien Tax law." See "Rush for First Papers," *Philadelphia Inquirer*, September 3, 1897, 10.

67. The *Inquirer* reported that "so many applications were never before received on a single day." See "Foreigners Rush," 3.

68. The paper reported that "preparations are already being made to carry the case of Toy Chee, a young man learning the construction of locomotives at Baldwin's, into court as early as possible." See "Chinamen Will Resist," *Philadelphia Inquirer*, July 23, 1897, 10. Chee's Pennsylvania courtroom prospects were not entirely without hope in 1897. As historian Beth Lew-Williams has recently stressed, the 1900 US Census actually counted 8,415 Chinese immigrants as

194 NOTES TO PAGES 44–5

naturalized American citizens despite long-standing racist federal bans against their naturalization (522). Whereas state and local courts in the western states "repeatedly defined the Chinese as nonwhite" in the Civil War era and Gilded Age, Lew-Williams finds that "in the East, South, and Midwest, where the Chinese were few and scattered, their racial status was never as pressing or obvious." Chinese petitioners in states like Pennsylvania therefore sometimes succeeded in overcoming racist naturalization bans in the mid- to late nineteenth century (524). See Beth Lew-Williams, "Chinese Naturalization, Voting, and Other Impossible Acts," *The Journal of the Civil War Era* 13, no. 4 (2023): 515–36.

69. "Against the Alien Tax," *Philadelphia Inquirer*, July 22, 1897, 10.

70. See Higham, *Strangers in the Land*, 72–73; Greene, *Slavic Community on Strike*, 111–51; Novak, *Guns of Lattimer*; Blatz, *Democratic Miners*, 45–63; Dubofsky, "Lattimer Massacre"; Shackel and Roller, "Gilded Age"; Roller, "Rewriting Narratives"; and Shackel, *Remembering Lattimer*.

71. Key cases included Juniata Limestone Co. v. Fagley, 187 Pa. 193 (1898); Juniata Limestone Co. v. Blair County Commissioners, 7 D.R. 201 (1898); Fraser v. McConway & Torley Co., 6 D.R. 555 (1897); and Ade v. County Commissioners, 20 Pa. C.C. 672 (1898). See George Wharton Pepper and William Draper Lewis, *A Digest of the Laws of Pennsylvania from 1897 to 1901* (Philadelphia: T. & J. W. Johnson, 1903), cxxi; and Frank Marshall Eastman, *The Law of Taxation in Pennsylvania* (Newark, NJ: Soney & Sage, 1909), 587. News coverage included "Rush for First Papers," 10; "Alien Law Tangle in Blair," *Philadelphia Inquirer*, March 31, 1898, 6; "Tax for Aliens," *Philadelphia Inquirer*, March 26, 1898, 6; and "Upholds Judge Acheson," *Pittsburgh Commercial Gazette*, July 22, 1898, 4.

72. At the outset of the conflict, immigrants often asked whether first papers represented sufficient compliance (they did not). "Answers to Correspondents," *Philadelphia Inquirer*, July 15, 1897, 7; "Answers to Correspondents," *Philadelphia Inquirer*, August 16, 1897, 6. Once courts began ruling against the law, readers especially asked whether they could recoup withheld wages. See "Answers to Correspondents," *Philadelphia Inquirer*, October 17, 1897, 6; "Answers to Correspondents," *Philadelphia Inquirer*, February 11, 1898, 8; and "Answers to Correspondents," *Philadelphia Inquirer*, February 14, 1898, 9.

73. The most similar attempt was an Idaho statute seeking to require that all employers hire only US citizens and immigrants who possessed first papers. It, too, was overturned. See *Ex parte* Case, 20 Idaho, 128, 116 Pac. 1037 (1911). Higham, *Strangers in the Land*, 72. See also Helfenstein, "Constitutionality of Legislative Discrimination," 75.

74. "An Act Relative to the Construction of State Highways," Massachusetts General Court—Acts and Resolves, January Session (1895), Act No. 347: 389–90. Disputes over the hiring of noncitizens (and sometimes out-of-state or out-of-town laborers) arose in Malden, Winchester, and Boston, among other municipalities. See "Employ Citizens First," *Boston Daily Globe*, March 20, 1895, 6; "Only Citizens Wanted," *Boston Daily Globe*, April 12, 1895, 3; and "Council Opposed," *Boston Daily Globe*, April 3, 1896, 3.

75. "An Act Relative to the Employment of Mechanics and Laborers on Public Works," Massachusetts General Court—Acts and Resolves, January Session (1896), Act No. 494: 492. The "preference" law was a far cry from what the Boston Central Labor Union sought. In 1895, the Central Labor Union endorsed a citizen-only bill for all public works hiring in the state. See "Will Oppose It," *Boston Daily Globe*, February 4, 1895, 2. Similar legislation was debated the following year as well. See "A Bill to Require the Employment of United States Citizens Only as Mechanics, Workingmen and, on Public Works, 85," Massachusetts General Court, Senate, *Journal of the Senate for the Year 1896* (Boston: Commonwealth of Massachusetts, 1896).

76. "An Act Respecting the Employment of Mechanics and Laborers upon the Public Work of This State and the Municipalities within the Same," New Jersey Legislature—123rd Session (1899), Chapter 202: 524–25. See also "Work of the New Jersey Legislature," *Philadelphia Inquirer*, March 27, 1899, 6.

77. "An Act to Secure to Native-Born and Naturalized Citizens of the United States the Exclusive Right to Be Employed in any Department of the State, County, City and County, or Incorporated City or Town in This State," California Legislature—34th Session (1901), Ch 185: 589. For press coverage of this and previous legislation (often highlighting labor support), see "No Alien May Do Public Work: The California Labor Convention Favors American Citizens," *San Francisco Call*, October 26, 1896, 12; "Labor Convention Adjourns Sine Die," *San Francisco Chronicle*, March 22, 1897, 11; "Over Two Hundred New Bills in the Assembly," *San Francisco Chronicle*, January 12, 1901, 2; and "Bills Signed by Governor," *Los Angeles Times*, March 29,

NOTES TO PAGES 46–8   195

1901, 3. Previous, defeated anti-alien hiring legislation included AB 575: "An Act to Secure to Native-Born and Naturalized Citizens of the United States the Exclusive Right to Labor on Public Works in this State." *Journal of the Assembly, 32nd Session, State of California* (Sacramento, CA: State Printing Office, 1897), 225; and AB 393: "An Act to Secure to Native Sons and Naturalized Citizens of the United States the Exclusive Right to Labor on Public Works in this State," *Journal of the Senate, 33rd Session, State of California* (Sacramento, CA: State Printing Office, 1899), 1113.

78. "Thirteenth Annual Report of the New York Bureau of Statistics of Labor for the Year 1895, Vol. 1" (Albany, NY: Wynkoop Hallenbeck Crawford, State Printers, 1896), 539.

79. "Thirteenth Annual Report of the New York Bureau of Statistics of Labor 1895, Vol. 1," 542.

80. "Thirteenth Annual Report of the New York Bureau of Statistics of Labor 1895, Vol. 1," 543.

81. People v. Warren, 13 Misc. 615, 34 N.Y.S. 942, 944 (1895).

82. People v. Warren, 943.

83. Quotation in main text from "Favors Alien Laborers," *New York Times*, September 27, 1896, 2. While union leaders considered asking for a review by the state attorney general, the *Times* reported that "the building trades were somewhat at a loss" concerning "what to do in the matter." See "To Take Legal Counsel," *New York Times*, September 28, 1896, 8. See also "Rather Hazy," *New York Times*, September 29, 1896, 4; and "After Judge White," *Buffalo Evening Herald*, September 28, 1896, 1.

84. "Politics in the C.L.U.," *New York Tribune*, October 5, 1896, 8; "Rushes into Politics," *New York Times*, October 5, 1896, 5; "Losing Faith in Tammany," *New York Times*, October 12, 1896, 2. Despite the Central Labor Union's efforts, justice Robert C. Titus was reported to be serving on the New York Eighth District Court of Appeals the following year. See *New York Supplement Volume 45, May 27, 1897–July 22, 1897* (St. Paul, MN: West Publishing, 1897), v. Gwendolyn Mink also notes the Central Labor Union's opposition to Titus as a result of *People v. Warren* in Mink, *Old Labor*, 123n17.

85. See, among others, Nancy Foner, *From Ellis Island to JFK: New York's Two Great Waves of Immigration* (New Haven, CT: Yale University Press, 2000), 81, 88; James R. Barrett, *The Irish Way: Becoming American in the Multiethnic City* (New York: Penguin Books, 2013), 145; Moses, *Unlikely Union*, 82–99; Tyler Anbinder, *City of Dreams: The 400-Year Epic History of Immigrant New York* (New York: Mariner Books, 2016), 396–400; and Wyman, *Round-Trip to America*, 49, 53.

86. "No Alien Labor on the Tunnel," *New York Times*, January 23, 1900, 9.

87. As sociologist Nancy Foner emphasizes, Black workers were disproportionately ejected "from trades where they had previously been accepted" and were increasingly "confin[ed] to the most menial, least attractive jobs" amid labor competition with "new" European immigrants at the turn of the century. See Foner, *From Ellis Island*, 89.

88. See "An Act in Relation to Labor, Constituting Chapter Thirty-Two of the General Laws," New York—120th Legislature (1897), Ch. 415: 461–502; "An Act to Amend the Labor Law, Relative to the Employment of Labor on Public Works," New York—125th Legislature (1902), Ch. 454: 1098–1099; and "An Act Relating to Labor, Constituting Chapter Thirty-One of the Consolidated Laws," New York—132nd Legislature (1909), Ch. 36: 2037–2106 (see §14, 2044).

89. Key cases included Meyers v. City of New York, 58 App. Div. 534, 69 N.Y.S. 529 (1901); and People ex rel. Rodgers v. Coler, 166 N.Y. 1, 59 N.E. 716 (1901). See also William McKinney, ed., *McKinney's Consolidated Laws of New York Annotated* (Northport, NY: Edward Thompson, 1917), 45–47.

90. See, among others, Moses, *Unlikely Union*, 82–99.

91. As Paul Moses finds, this union official also embraced nakedly discriminatory anti-Italian language. As quoted in Moses, 94.

92. "Fourth Annual Report of the New York Commissioner of Labor" (Albany, NY: Brandow Printing, 1905), 15–17.

93. Quotation in main text from "Fourth Annual Report of the New York Commissioner of Labor," 16; more broadly, see 15–17.

94. "Fourth Annual Report of the New York Commissioner of Labor," 18.

95. "Fourth Annual Report of the New York Commissioner of Labor," 17.

96. "Fourth Annual Report of the New York Commissioner of Labor," 18.

97. "Fourth Annual Report of the New York Commissioner of Labor," 157.

98. Complaints also fell that year as courts struck down a state law mandating an eight-hour day on publicly funded projects. See "Fifth Annual Report of the New York Commissioner of Labor" (Albany, NY: Brandow Printing, 1906), II 20.

196 NOTES TO PAGES 48–50

99. City of Chicago v. Hulbert, 205 Ill. 346, 68 N.E. 786 (1903). See Lindley Clark, "Labor Laws Declared Unconstitutional," *Bulletin of the Bureau of Labor* 21, no. 91 (November 1910): 933. See also William E. Forbath, *Law and the Shaping of the American Labor Movement* (Cambridge, MA: Harvard University Press, 2009), 188.

100. Christopher Gustavus Tiedeman, *A Treatise on State and Federal Control of Persons and Property in the United States: Considered from both a Civil and Criminal Standpoint* (St. Louis, MO: F. H. Thomas Law Book, 1900), 331. Higham largely relies on Tiedeman's analysis for his own framing of the relative weakness of blue-collar nativist state hiring laws in the courtroom during the late Gilded Age and early Progressive Era. See Higham, *Strangers in the Land*, 73 and 346n12. On Tiedeman's influence, see, among many others, David N. Mayer, "The Jurisprudence of Christopher G. Tiedeman: A Study in the Failure of Laissez-Faire Constitutionalism," *Missouri Law Review* 55, no. 1 (Winter 1990): 93–162.

101. "No Pictures," *Boston Daily Globe*, March 25, 1898, 2.

102. McIsaac did vote in favor a substitute bill that would have directed already existing House committees to inquire into such allegations, but not launch a formal separate investigation. See Massachusetts General Court, House of Representatives, *Journal of the House of Representatives for the Year 1900* (Boston: Commonwealth of Massachusetts, 1900), 104–5, 116–20.

103. See, especially, Sarah S. Elkind, *Bay Cities and Water Politics: The Battle for Resources in Boston and Oakland* (Lawrence: University Press of Kansas, 1998), 79–117.

104. Wachusett Reservoir and Dam disputes—both over the selection of its location and struggles among employers, (largely immigrant) laborers, and local residents—have been studied by many others. They include Glenn F. Anderson, "The Social Effects of the Construction of the Wachusett Reservoir on Boylston and West Boylston," *Historical Journal of Massachusetts* 3, no. 1 (Spring 1974): 51–58; Jill Lepore, "Resistance, Reform, and Repression: Italian Immigrant Laborers in Clinton, 1896–1906," in *Labor in Massachusetts: Selected Essays*, ed. Kenneth Fones-Wolf and Martin Kaufman (Westfield, MA: Westfield State College, 1990), 138–67; Sarah S. Elkind, "Building a Better Jungle: Anti-urban Sentiment, Public Works, and Political Reform in American Cities, 1880–1930," *Journal of Urban History* 24, no. 1 (1997): 53–78; Elkind, *Bay Cities*, 99–117; Eamon McCarthy Earls, *Wachusett: How Boston's 19th Century Quest for Water Changed Four Towns and a Way of Life* (Franklin, MA: Via Appia Press, 2012); and Jean Innamorati, Dennis DeWitt, and Tracy Lindboe, "Workers of Wachusett," *Journal of the New England Water Works Association* 133, no. 3 (September 2019): 159–67.

105. As the *Boston Globe* reported upon the dam's opening, "It is the largest dam in the world. . . . There are dams which are longer, and there are others which are higher, but there is none to compare with it in both length and width." See "Wachusett Dam Largest of Its Kind, Now Completed," *Boston Globe*, November 5, 1905, SM4. More broadly, see Lepore, "Resistance, Reform, and Repression," 140–41; Elkind, "Building a Better Jungle," 60–62; and Innamorati, DeWitt, and Lindboe, "Workers of Wachusett," 162–65.

106. Anderson, "Social Effects"; Lepore, "Resistance, Reform, and Repression," 151–55; Elkind, "Building a Better Jungle," 60–62; Elkind, *Bay Cities and Water Politics*, 111–13.

107. Lepore, "Resistance, Reform, and Repression," 155.

108. Walsh was sworn in as a state representative on January 4, 1900. On January 25 of that year, the House approved his proposal and rejected a watered-down investigation by a narrow margin of 102–99. The Senate then adopted Walsh's proposal (slightly amended) by a vote of 16–13. In the news coverage of this legislation, the freshman legislator was widely recognized as not just the sponsor of, but also the driving force behind, the bill. See Massachusetts General Court, House of Representatives, *Journal of the House of Representatives for the Year 1900*, 10, 116–20, 1512; "Many Charges Made," *Boston Herald*, January 26, 1900, 12; "Walsh's Order," *Boston Daily Globe*, January 26, 1900, 3; and "Senate Joins House," *Boston Herald*, February 1, 1900, 12.

109. Quotation in main text from "Walsh Explains," *Boston Daily Globe*, February 28, 1900, 2. On the length of the hearings, see Lepore, "Resistance, Reform, and Repression," 153.

110. Critics sometimes named the 1895 law that had created the Metropolitan Water Commission and required preference be given to "Massachusetts citizens" on its projects in their complaints. Rarely did they mention or seem to know of a (seemingly superseding) law enacted the following year requiring that preference be given to US citizens on all public works projects in the state. See "An Act to Provide for a Metropolitan Water Supply," Massachusetts

NOTES TO PAGES 50–2   197

General Court—Acts and Resolves, January Session (1895), Act No. 488: 565–82; see also "Walsh Explains"; "Hearings End," *Boston Daily Globe*, May 5, 1900, 6; "Claims of Counsel," *Boston Herald*, May 7, 1900, 12; and "Board Scored," *Boston Daily Globe*, July 11, 1900, 6.

111. "Denunciation: Clinton Citizens Condemn Water Board," *Boston Daily Globe*, March 31, 1900, 4.

112. Indeed, as Lepore finds, one of the leaders of the Businessmen's Association, Thomas Tate, overtly admitted under testimony that he was roused to action because he found the padroni system to be "injurious to the business interests of Clinton" (156). Lepore, "Resistance, Reform, and Repression," 154–58.

113. For examples, see "Denunciation: Clinton Citizens Condemn," 4; "In Commissary Shanties," *Boston Daily Globe*, March 8, 1900, 9; "Obliged to Use Italians," *Boston Daily Globe*, March 16, 1900, 14. See also Lepore, "Resistance, Reform, and Repression," 156–59; and Elkind, *Bay Cities*, 112.

114. Quotation in main text from "Obliged to Use Italians," 14. Brock might have felt able to admit to hiring mostly noncitizens because his partner, Harry Nawn, was a leading Boston politician (though Nawn himself had come under fire for similar employment practices in Boston a year earlier). See "Only Citizens of Boston," *Boston Daily Globe*, September 11, 1899, 6; and James J. Connolly, *The Triumph of Ethnic Progressivism: Urban Political Culture in Boston, 1900–1925* (Cambridge, MA: Harvard University Press, 2009), 36–37.

115. Quotation in main text from "Claims of Counsel," 12. On Benton's frequent allusions to possible additional costs, see also Lepore, "Resistance, Reform, and Repression," 159.

116. The minority report disagreed, arguing that even at the going rate of "$1.50 or $1.75 per day," contractors could have found, in the words of the *Boston Herald*, "a sufficient number of citizen mechanics and laborers" to work. See "Water Board Blamed," *Boston Herald*, July 11, 1900, 10.

117. See "Metropolitan Water Board Minutes," July 7, 1900, 433, Massachusetts Commonwealth Archives, Environmental Affairs, MDC 2092X 313 N 119 T, Box 2: "1896–1901."

118. See Henry Sprague to Hiram A. Miller, July 14, 1900, "Chairman's Outgoing Correspondence," Massachusetts Commonwealth Archives, Environmental Affairs, MDC 2095X 313 N 119 T; and "Metropolitan Water Board Minutes," July 14, 1900, 445–446, Massachusetts Commonwealth Archives, Environmental Affairs, MDC 2092X 313 N 119 T, Box 2: "1896–1901."

119. An examination of the records of the Water Board (particularly its minutes and correspondence) produced few other discussions of citizen preference legislation. In August 1900, the Water Board revised and clarified the language it employed on future contracts with construction firms related to the state's multiple citizen preference hiring laws. The new contracts would henceforth specify that "the contractor, in the construction of the work, shall give preference in employment to citizens of the Commonwealth, and in the employment of mechanics and laborers, where citizens of the Commonwealth are not available, shall give preference to citizens of the United States who are not citizens of the Commonwealth." And in May 1901, it once more received reports of violations of these requirements by the firm Nawn and Brock. See Henry Sprague to Attorney General H. M. Knowlton, August 16, 1900, "Chairman's Outgoing Correspondence," Massachusetts Commonwealth Archives, Environmental Affairs, MDC 2095X 313 N 119 T; and "Metropolitan Water Board Minutes," May 15, 1901, 104, Massachusetts Commonwealth Archives, Environmental Affairs, MDC 2093X 313 N 120 T, Box 1: "1901–1905."

120. Lepore, "Resistance, Reform, and Repression," 143–48, 163–64; Innamorati, DeWitt, and Lindboe, "Workers of Wachusett," 161.

121. "No Pictures," 1–2.

122. "D. V. McIsaac Dies, Prominent Lawyer," *Boston Daily Globe*, April 3, 1931, 19; "Last Tribute Paid Daniel V. McIsaac," *Boston Daily Globe*, April 5, 1931, A32. See also Damien Murray, *Irish Nationalists in Boston: Catholicism and Conflict, 1900–1928* (Washington, DC: Catholic University of America Press, 2018), 66.

123. As historian Joseph Huthmacher emphasizes, Walsh was the most successful Democrat to consistently win statewide office in this erstwhile Republican stronghold before the New Deal era. See, especially, J. Joseph Huthmacher, *Massachusetts People and Politics, 1919–1933* (New York: Atheneum, 1969), 117–49.

124. Not coincidentally, the Louisiana law was adopted in the aftermath of the Panic of 1907. See "An Act Requiring That Mechanics Employed on All State or Public Buildings or Public

198 NOTES TO PAGES 52–3

Works in Cities Exceeding Ten Thousand (10,000) Population throughout the State, Shall Be Citizens of the State, Except under Certain Circumstances...," Louisiana—General Assembly (1908), Act No. 271: 398–99. The 1912 Arizona law restricted "any State, County or municipal works or employment" to US citizens, "wards" (Native Americans), and immigrants in possession of first papers. See "An Act Relating to the Construction, Maintenance, and Improvement of State Roads and Bridges...," Arizona—1st State Legislature, Special Session (1912), Ch. 66: 188–194.

125. "Pittsburg Would Not Be Welcome," *Philadelphia Inquirer*, March 26, 1897, 3.

126. "Sons of America," *Philadelphia Inquirer*, June 20, 1897, 37. Two years later, "Stars and Stripes Sam," as the Republican politician was known, was elected mayor (215). Muckraking journalist Lincoln Steffens would lambast Ashbridge for "br[eaking] through all the principles of moderate grafting" that had preceded him in the city (216). See Lincoln Steffens, *The Shame of the Cities* (New York: McClure, Phillips, 1904), 215–18.

127. Frank Gordon, a supervisor for the Pittsburgh-based Booth and Flinn contracting company, estimated that 50 of 400 laborers working under his direction on an 1897 road improvement project were noncitizens. He acknowledged that they "had no legal right to do so," owing to Pennsylvania's 1895 citizen-only public works hiring law. But he argued "it was either employ them or let the work stand, as he could not get enough residents or citizens." See "Work on County Roads: The Contracting Firms Are Obliged to Employ Aliens," *Pittsburgh Commercial Gazette*, October 15, 1897, 5. The *New York Times* likewise reported on the 1905 state Labor Department's investigation into the widespread hiring of noncitizens on public works contracts despite the state's citizen-only hiring policy. See "City Contract Labor Sixty Per Cent. Alien," *New York Times*, April 18, 1905, 6.

128. The *Stockton Independent* reported in March 1909 that the San Joaquin County Highway Commission sought to dispel any "fear that aliens may be given employment on some of the good road work to be done," promising to strictly implement the 1901 California statute "prohibit[ing] the employment of certain aliens on public works." See "No Aliens Will Work on Good Roads," *Stockton Independent*, March 10, 1909, 2. Two years later, an Idaho American Federation of Labor organizer reported that some "street work and some Government contract work" had "[been] done by alien labor." The organizer stressed that "this is in violation of State law, and one contractor was recently arrested and will be prosecuted." See "What Our Organizers Are Doing," *The American Federationist* 18 (July 1911): 551.

129. "Councils in Session," *Philadelphia Inquirer*, February 17, 1899, 3. Fortunately for the imperiled workers, this legislation authorizing the payment of their salaries was rapidly enacted. See *Journal of the Common Council, of the City of Philadelphia, from October 6, 1898 to March 30, 1899*, vol. 2 (Philadelphia: Dunlap Printing, 1899), 382, 461.

130. "Report of the Public Service Commission for the First District of the State of New York for the Year Ending December 31, 1914" (Albany, NY: New York Public Service Commission, 1915), 92–94.

131. Quotations in main text from John Gill, "The New York Alien Law: Mr. Gill Tells Why Subway Contractors Should Be Held to It," *New York Times*, November 21, 1914, 12; Gill was not exaggerating. The *New York Times* reported in December that "records were broken last month at the Naturalization Bureau of the County Clerk's office when 4,143 men applied for papers admitting them to citizenship. This was the largest number of applicants in any one month in this county. This rush for citizenship was due to the steps taken to enforce the law providing that only citizens shall be employed on public work, thus barring aliens from employment on the new subway construction." See "Big Rush of Aliens to Become Citizens," *New York Times*, December 13, 1914, 11.

132. "Contractors' Statement on the Alien Labor Difficulty," *The Bulletin of the General Contractors Association* 5, no. 11 (November 1914): 339.

133. "Contractors' Statement," 341.

134. The two cases were thus People v. Crane, 214 N.Y. 154, 108 N.E. 427 (1915); and Heim v. McCall, 239 U.S. 175 (1915). See "Criminal Case Test of Alien Labor Act," *New York Times*, November 25, 1914, 7; "Alien Labor Law Might Bring Chaos," *New York Times*, December 5, 1914, 8. See also "Prohibition of Employment of Aliens in Construction of Public Works," *Columbia Law Review* 15, no. 3 (March 1915): 263–65; Thomas Reed Powell, "The Right to Work for the State," *Columbia Law Review* 16, no. 2 (February 1916): 99–114; Motomura, *Americans in Waiting*, 69–70; Kelly, "Wavering Course."

NOTES TO PAGES 53–4   199

135. "Alien Labor Ban May Tie Up All Transit Work," *New York Tribune*, November 18, 1914, 1; "Give Hearing Today on Alien Repeal," *New York Times*, March 3, 1915, 8. Other scholars who examine the controversy include Higham, *Strangers in the Land*, 183–84; Catron, "The Citizenship Advantage," 1005.
136. "Alien Labor Ban May Tie Up All Transit Work," 1; "Will Dig Subways, but Fight Alien Act," *New York Times*, November 19, 1914, 1; "The New York Alien Labor Law," *New York Times*, November 19, 1914, 10; "Unions Want a Part in Labor Law Test," *New York Times*, November 20, 1914, 18; "Grout Seeking Test of Alien Labor Law," *New York Times*, November 21, 1914, 6; "Give Hearing Today on Alien Repeal," 8.
137. The future US Supreme Court justice's role in shaping this decision was widely recognized in the press. See "Court Upholds Alien Labor Law," *New York Times*, February 26, 1915, 1, 5; and "Alien Law Decision Halts New Subways," *New York Times*, February 27, 1915, 5.
138. "Contractors to Fight to Keep Alien Laborers," *New York Tribune*, November 19, 1914, 1, 5; "The Unions' Case Not Clear," *New York Tribune*, November 19, 1914, 8; "Repeal the Alien Labor Law!" *New York Tribune*, February 27, 1915, 8; "Whitman to Urge Alien Act Repeal," *New York Times*, February 28, 1915, 1, 8; "Whitman Plans Alien Law Relief," *New York Times*, March 2, 1915, 1; "Give Hearing Today on Alien Repeal," 8; "Checks Alien Law Repeal," *New York Times*, March 5, 1915; "Alien Law Repeal Passes the Senate," *New York Times*, March 9, 1915, 1; "Satisfactory to All," *New York Tribune*, March 11, 1911, 8. The amended law, which took effect on March 11, 1915, was "An Act to Amend Section Fourteen of the Labor Law, Relating to Preference in Employment of Persons upon Public Works, and Authorizing the Validation and Modification of Contracts for Public Improvements Affected by Said Section," New York—138th Legislature (1915), Ch. 51: 101–3. See also "The Alien Labor Decision," *The Bulletin of the General Contractors Association* 6, no. 3 (March 1915): 67–68.
139. Though the Contractors Association critiqued the future US senator (Wagner was then senate minority leader in the state legislature) for preventing a complete repeal of the act, it was relieved that under the new preference system "the danger of actual forfeiture of contract is very much minimized" (68). See "The Amended Alien Labor Law," *The Bulletin of the General Contractors Association* 6, no. 3 (March 1915): 68–70. Contractors also secured a favorable opinion from the state attorney general, stipulating that if a US citizen applied for the same job and pay as an already-employed noncitizen worker at a later date, the contractor had no obligation to discharge the noncitizen. See "May Keep Aliens on Subway Work," *New York Times*, April 5, 1915, 9.
140. On unemployment during the winter of 1914–15, see Feder, *Unemployment Relief*, 224–31; Keyssar, *Out of Work*, 235–36, 262–78; Sautter, *Three Cheers*, 100–106; and Daniel Amsterdam, "Before the Roar: US Unemployment Relief after World War I and the Long History of a Paternalist Welfare Policy," *Journal of American History* 101, no. 4 (2015): 1128.
141. As historian Neil Larry Shumsky finds, amid the Panic of 1907 "and its attendant depression and unemployment, immigrants began leaving the United States as never before" (62). Return migration surpassed 395,000 in fiscal year 1908 alone. But the war years witnessed "a major falloff" in outbound migration (from over 303,000 in fiscal year 1914 to just under 130,000 in fiscal year 1916) (63). See Neil Larry Shumsky, " 'Let No Man Stop to Plunder!' American Hostility to Return Migration, 1890–1924," *Journal of American Ethnic History* 11, no. 2 (1992): 62–63.
142. "Contractors to Fight," 1.
143. See, among many others, Herbert LePore, "Prelude to Prejudice: Hiram Johnson, Woodrow Wilson, and the California Alien Land Law Controversy of 1913," *Southern California Quarterly* 61, no. 1 (1979): 99–110; Leonard, *Making Ethnic Choices*; Masao Suzuki, "Important or Impotent? Taking Another Look at the 1920 California Alien Land Law," *Journal of Economic History* 64, no. 1 (March 2004): 125–43; Motomura, *Americans in Waiting*, 69–70, 75–76; and Erika Lee, *The Making of Asian America: A History* (New York: Simon & Schuster, 2015), 132.
144. On the 80 percent law, see, among others, Astrid J. Norvelle, "80 Percent Bill, Court Injunctions, and Arizona Labor: Billy Truax's Two Supreme Court Cases," *Western Legal History* 17, no. 2 (Summer/Fall 2004): 163–210; Motomura, *Americans in Waiting*, 68–70; Eric V. Meeks, *Border Citizens: The Making of Indians, Mexicans, and Anglos in Arizona* (Austin: University of Texas Press, 2007), 79; Katherine Benton-Cohen, *Borderline Americans: Racial Division and Labor War in the Arizona Borderlands* (Cambridge, MA: Harvard

200   NOTES TO PAGES 55–7

University Press, 2011), 200–205; Allison Brownell Tirres, "Property Outliers: Non-citizens, Property Rights and State Power," *Georgetown Immigration Law Journal* 27 (2012): 103–4; Jacobson, Tichenor, and Durden, "Southwest's Uneven Welcome," 12–13; and Jacobson and Tichenor, "States of Immigration," 18–20.

145. Not all anti-alien conflicts grabbed national headlines during the Depression of 1914–15. In Tucson, a contractor was fined fifty dollars upon pleading guilty to violating the state's anti-alien public works hiring law. See "Wingett Fined for Alien on State Job," *Tucson Citizen*, August 27, 1914, 1. In Massachusetts, newly elected governor David Walsh signed two bills into law strengthening the state's citizen preference hiring provisions for both public and pub-licly funded employment. See "An Act Relative to the Wages of Mechanics Employed in the Construction of Public Works," Massachusetts General Court—Acts and Resolves (1914), Ch. 474: 413–14; and "An Act to Authorize the Giving of Preference in Appointment and Employment to Citizens," Massachusetts General Court—Acts and Resolves (1914), Ch. 600: 546. Critics, however, charged that they were insufficient. See, among others, "Boston's 70-Cent Gas Bill Favored," *Boston Daily Globe*, April 14, 1915, 11; and "Martin H. Shannahan Arrested in Lynn," *Boston Daily Globe*, July 10, 1915, 7.

146. See, for instance, for national coverage of the California Alien Land Act, "New Alien Bill Is Anti-Japanese," *New York Times*, April 30, 1913, 1; and "California Is Not Inclined to Heed Wilson," *Arizona Republican*, May 3, 1913, 1, 7. On the New York Subway Hiring Controversy, see "Arrogance of Labor Trust," *Los Angeles Times*, December 20, 1914, VI3; "Will Use U.S. Labor," *Pittsburgh Gazette Times*, February 27, 1915, 2. On the Arizona 80 percent law, see "Arizona Law a Boomerang," *Los Angeles Times*, December 21, 1914, I7; and "Stirred by Alien Law," *Washington Post*, December 5, 1914, 1, 3.

147. See, among others, "Anti-Alien Laws," *San Francisco Chronicle*, December 14, 1914, 6; and "Alien Labor Complications," *New York Times*, December 14, 1914, 10.

148. See, for instance, "General Alien Laws Opposed by President," *St. Louis Post–Dispatch*, December 15, 1914, 3; "Can't Stop Anti-Alien Laws," *New York Times*, December 16, 1914, 10; and "Alien Treaty Rights Discussed by Wilson," *The Atlanta Constitution*, December 16, 1914, 14.

149. Motomura, *Americans in Waiting*, 69–70; Kelly, "Wavering Course," 704–8.

150. See, among many others, "Arizona Law a Boomerang," 17; "Labor Suit Ties Up $12,000,000 in Work," *New York Times*, December 29, 1914, 4; "Alien Labor Law Might Bring Chaos," 8; and "Repeal the Alien Labor Law!" 8.

151. "I'll Take my Medicine—Crane," *New York American*; reproduced in "Alien Labor Decision," 67.

152. "Latest Subway News," *The Bulletin of the General Contractors Association* 5, no. 11 (November 1914): 335–38; "Status of the Alien Labor Cases," *The Bulletin of the General Contractors Association* 5, no. 12 (December 1914): 367–68; "Our Annual Dinner," *The Bulletin of the General Contractors Association* 5, no. 12 (December 1914): 401–4.

153. This article was reproduced in the business-friendly *Los Angeles Times* as part of the paper's coverage of the New York Subway Hiring Controversy. See "Will Stop Four Big Contracts," *Los Angeles Times*, November 29, 1914, VI3.

154. "Alien Law Decision Halts," 5.

155. "State Quizzed on Subject of Alien Teachers," *San Francisco Chronicle*, April 1, 1915, 17.

156. Hiram Johnson to William Jennings Bryan, April 6, 1915, 2–3, Bancroft Library and Archives, Berkeley, CA, Hiram Johnson Papers, MSS C-B 581 Part II, Box 3, "Letters from Johnson, April 1914–July 1915" (hereafter BANC, "Letters from Johnson"); "Teachers Aroused by Webb Ruling," *Daily Colusa Sun*, February 10, 1915, 1.

157. Los Angeles superintendent Mark Keppel informed the press that he was "not going round with a magnifying glass lookig [sic] for alien teachers." See "Alien Teachers Ask Hyatt for Warrants," *Los Angeles Herald*, March 19, 1915, 12. San Francisco superintendent Alfred Roncovieri believed state authorities had overreacted to a situation that "must have arisen from spite work against some individual teacher." See "Alien Teachers in Law Trouble," *San Francisco Chronicle*, March 20, 1915, 7.

158. "Alien Teacher Out," *Los Angeles Times*, February 15, 1915, I16; "School Disrupted by Alien Teacher," *Sacramento Union*, April 2, 1915, 12.

159. "Alien Teachers Appeal to Hyatt," *Daily Colusa Sun*, March 19, 1915, 1; "Alien Teacher Salaries Held in Santa Barbara," *Los Angeles Times*, April 2, 1915, I7.

NOTES TO PAGES 57–9   201

160. "Alien Teachers' Salaries Held Up by the Trustees," *San Francisco Chronicle*, March 19, 1915, 1.
161. "Many Teachers in State Ineligible," *Sacramento Union*, February 19, 1915, 8.
162. "Alien Teachers Appeal," 1.
163. "Alien Teachers Ask How to Hold Place," *Los Angeles Herald*, February 18, 1915, 10.
164. P. J. Conway to Benjamin Ide Wheeler, February 27, 1915, BANC/Office of the University President Records, CU-5 Series 2, Box 8, 1915: Folder 8:3, 469: "Alien Teachers Bill."
165. "Teachers Are to Be Citizens," *Press Democrat* [Santa Rosa], March 17, 1915, 6.
166. "Will Naturalization Make Teachers More Honest or Competent?" *Sacramento Union*, April 24, 1915, 1; "Alien Teachers Getting Papers Naturalization," *Red Bluff Daily News*, April 27, 1915, 4.
167. Quotation in main text from Anna Stewart to Benjamin Ide Wheeler, Resolution 2, March 2, 1915. See also Stewart to Wheeler, February 19, 1915, BANC/Office of the University President Records, CU-5 Series 2, Box 8, 1915: Folder 8:3, 469: "Alien Teachers Bill."
168. "100 Teachers Must Wed to Keep Jobs," *Los Angeles Herald*, February 19, 1915, 9. Under the Naturalization Act of 1855, immigrant women automatically assumed US citizenship upon their marriage to American citizens or the naturalization of their noncitizen husbands with one key exception: women racially ineligible for citizenship (i.e., East and South Asian women). See, especially, Marian Smith, "'Any Woman Who Is Now or May Hereafter Be Married...': Women and Naturalization, ca. 1802–1940," *Prologue* 30, no. 2 (Summer 1998): 146–53.
169. Quotation in main text from "100 Teachers Must Wed," 9. Just four days after Keppel proposed his "solution," the *Los Angeles Herald* advised its readers that one hundred local female immigrant teachers were supposedly in desperate need of husbands. The *Herald* published a letter written by an anonymous, self-described "One of the Imperiled 100." After listing her requirements for a prospective shotgun husband ("brunet," tall, and at least "35 or 40" years of age), she reiterated her desire for autonomy by noting her openness to a husband from the East Coast, "in case a 'leave of absence' should sometime be desirable." See "100 Men Wanted to Qualify as Able to Wed," *Los Angeles Herald*, February 23, 1915, 9.
170. See, among others, Bredbenner, *Nationality of Her Own*; and Gardner, *Qualities of a Citizen*.
171. "Alien Teachers in Law Trouble," 7.
172. The university's leadership strenuously challenged the notion that the law applied to noncitizen faculty members and continued to employ and pay noncitizen professors' salaries. See "Alien Teachers in State Are Denied Money Is Charge," *San Francisco Chronicle*, March 16, 1915, 3; and "Alien Teachers in Law Trouble," 7.
173. Katharine Short to William Short, February 28, 1915, Library and Archives Canada/Bibliothèque et Archives Canada RG 25 Vol. 1161, File 671, "Employment of Aliens in California—State Law" (hereafter LAC/BAC, "Employment of Aliens in California").
174. "Suit Threatened over Alien Teacher Trouble," *Ukiah Dispatch Democrat*, February 26, 1915; "Alien Teachers Appeal to Hyatt," 1.
175. "William Gray," Parliament of Canada, https://lop.parl.ca/sites/ParlInfo/default/en_CA/People/Profile?personId=13112.
176. Quotation in main text from William Short to William Gray, March 10, 1915, LAC/BAC, "Employment of Aliens in California." On the 1915 California exhibitions, see Carolyn Peter, "California Welcomes the World: International Expositions, 1894–1940 and the Selling of the State," in *Reading California: Art, Image, and Identity, 1900–2000*, ed. Stephanie Barron, Sheri Bernstein, and Ilene Susan Fort (Berkeley: University of California Press, 2000), 69–84.
177. Hiram Johnson to William Jennings Bryan, April 6, 1915, 5, BANC, "Letters from Johnson."
178. "Dominion Asked to Secure Rights for Canadians," *Free Press* [London, ON], March 10, 1915, LAC/BAC, "Employment of Aliens in California"; "Canadian Teachers Classed as Aliens," *Ottawa Citizen*, March 15, 1915, 6; "Salaries Refused to Alien Teachers," *The Globe* [Toronto, ON], March 16, 1915, 13; "Refusing to Pay Canadians," *Ottawa Citizen*, March 19, 1915, 3.
179. See, among others, "Canadians' Pay Withheld," *Rochester Democrat and Chronicle*, March 16, 1915, 2; "Says Canadians Not Paid," *Boston Daily Globe*, March 16, 1915, 13; "Education Bill Causes a Row," *Los Angeles Times*, March 18, 1915, 15; "Californian Law," *The Scotsman*, March 18, 1915, 5; and "Alien Teachers in California," *South China Morning Post*, April 17, 1915, 6.
180. E. L. Newcombe to Joseph Pope, March 15, 1915; Gray to Pope, March 16, 1915, LAC/BAC, "Employment of Aliens in California."
181. *House of Commons Debates*, 12th Parliament, 5th Session, Vol. 2: March 18, 1915, 1190.

202 NOTES TO PAGES 59-61

182. Borden's Conservative Party (of which Gray was a member) had defeated their rival Liberals for the first time in fifteen years in the federal election of 1911 on a strong wave of anti-American sentiment. During the campaign, Borden and his allies had successfully framed a negotiated, but not-yet-ratified US–Canada trade agreement as a threat to Canada's economic interests and national security. See, especially, John Herd Thompson and Stephen J. Randall, *Canada and the United States: Ambivalent Allies* (Athens, GA: University of Georgia Press, 2002), 87–92; Simon J. Potter, "The Imperial Significance of the Canadian–American Reciprocity Proposals of 1911," *The Historical Journal* 47, no. 1 (March 2004): 81–100; and Kendrick A. Clements, "Manifest Destiny and Canadian Reciprocity in 1911," *Pacific Historical Review* 42, no. 1 (1973): 32–52.

183. Quotation in main text from Prince Arthur to Spring Rice, April 1, 1915, LAC/BAC, "Employment of Aliens in California." Official US–Canadian diplomatic communications ran through the British Embassy in Washington, DC, until 1927. See Stephen Azzi, *Reconcilable Differences: A History of Canada–US Relations* (New York: Oxford University Press, 2014), 105. During his lifetime, Prince Arthur was also widely referred to by his title of peerage: the Duke of Connaught.

184. Formal Correspondence of Spring Rice to Bryan, March 24, 1915, 1–2; Personal Correspondence of Spring Rice to Bryan, March 24, 1915, 1–3, LAC/BAC, "Employment of Aliens in California."

185. Personal correspondence, March 24, 1915, 2, LAC/BAC, "Employment of Aliens in California."

186. Bryan to Johnson, March 29, 1915, 1–2. BANC Hiram Johnson Papers, MSS C-B 581 Part II, Box 34, "Letters to Johnson, UI-VZ," Folder, "U.S. State Department, January–December 1915."

187. LePore, "Prelude to Prejudice."

188. Johnson to Bryan, March 30, 1915, 1–3. BANC, "Letters from Johnson."

189. Quotation in main text from Johnson to Bryan, March 31, 1915, 1; more broadly, see 1–2, BANC, "Letters from Johnson." See also "Alien Enemies in Public Positions," *Canada Law Journal* Vol. LI, No. 1 (January 1915): 5. Found in LAC/BAC, "Employment of Aliens in California."

190. I discuss the vicissitudes of Short's campaign in greater detail in "'A Practically American' Woman Confronts a United States Citizen–Only Hiring Law."

191. Quotation in main text from "Regarding Alien Teachers," *Mendocino Beacon*, February 27, 1915. In Santa Barbara County, the *Lompoc Journal* lambasted the state's citizen-only policy for leading to the unwanted, abrupt firing of a popular school principal in the middle of the academic year. See "Alien Law Hits Local School Teacher," *Lompoc Journal*, March 13, 1915, 1.

192. "Why Alien Teachers?" *Morning Press* [Santa Barbara, CA], April 4, 1915, 4.

193. "Teachers Affected by California Law," *Ottawa Citizen*, April 3, 1915, 5; "Forgotten Law Is Invoked to Oust Teachers," *Arizona Republican*, April 1, 1915, 1, 5; "Protests Dismissal of Canadians in California," *Detroit Free Press*, April 3, 1915, 9; "California Bill Aids Alien Teachers," *Christian Science Monitor*, April 2, 1915, 7. To be sure, some news columns and opinion pieces defended the state's citizen-only schoolteacher policy. See "No Alien School Teachers," *Sacramento Union*, February 7, 1915, 4; "Surprising Ignorance," *Riverside Daily Press*, May 28, 1915, 4; and "The Naturalization of School Teachers," *Los Angeles Herald*, May 31, 1915, 6.

194. Only at the very end of the dispute did deputy minister of justice E. L. Newcombe clarify that Ontario did indeed have a similar citizen-only public schoolteacher law. However, he claimed that unlike officials in Mendocino, local authorities in Ontario would have paid the salary of a noncitizen teacher who had been mistakenly hired. See Newcombe to Pope, April 14, 1915; Newcombe to Pope, May 22, 1915, LAC/BAC, "Employment of Aliens in California."

195. Lansing would soon replace Bryan as US secretary of state. Quotation in main text from Robert Lansing to Johnson, April 20, 1915, 2. "U.S. Department of State, January–December 1915," BANC Hiram Johnson Papers MSS C-B 581, Part II, Box 34, "Letters to Johnson, UI-VZ," Folder, "U.S. State Department, January–December 1915."

196. The bill received the unanimous approval of the Senate Judiciary Committee in late March. See "Johnson Is Opposed to Speeders," *Hanford Journal*, March 28, 1915, 1. The whole Senate passed the legislation in early April. See "Bill to Aid Alien Teachers Approved," *San Francisco Chronicle*, April 2, 1915, 3.

197. "Would Relieve Alien Teachers," *Los Angeles Times*, March 28, 1915, I7.

NOTES TO PAGES 61-8   203

198. "Assembly Approves Exemption of Aliens," *San Francisco Chronicle*, April 20, 1915, 1; "First Papers Entitle Aliens to Teach in Public Schools," *Sacramento Union*, May 17, 1915, 10.
199. Katharine Short to Ministry of Justice, May 26, 1915. LAC/BAC, "Employment of Aliens in California."
200. Kelly, "Wavering Course," 704-8; Motomura, *Americans in Waiting*, 69; Kerry Abrams, "Plenary Power Preemption," *Virginia Law Review* 99, no. 3 (2013): 619-21.
201. "An Act to Secure to Native-Born and Naturalized Citizens of the United States the Exclusive Right to be Employed in Any Department of the State, County, City and County, and City Government in This State, Except in Certain Schools" California Legislature—41st Session (1915), Ch. 417: 690-91. See also "Employment of Aliens in Academic Positions," December 20, 1946, BANC/Office of the University President Records, CU-5, Ser. 3, Box 30, Folder 277, "Alien Employment Policy, 1915-57."
202. See Smith, "'Any Woman Who Is'."
203. See, especially, Haney-López, *White by Law*.
204. Menchaca, *Naturalizing Mexican Immigrants*; Patrick D. Lukens, *A Quiet Victory for Latino Rights: FDR and the Controversy Over "Whiteness"* (Tucson: University of Arizona Press, 2012); Fox and Bloemraad, "Beyond 'White by Law.'"
205. "Cannot Employ Aliens," *Morning Tribune* [San Luis Obispo, CA], February 24, 1915, 1.
206. "Alien Janitors Barred from School Service," *Sacramento Union*, April 15, 1915, 9; "Old Alien Labor Law to Get Riverside into Spot Light," *Riverside Daily Press*, April 26, 1915, 6; "Native Laborers Replacing Aliens," *Riverside Daily Press*, May 1, 1915, 2.
207. "Old Alien Labor Law," 6.
208. "Native Laborers Replacing Aliens," 2.
209. Scholarship on *Lochner*-era court labor legislation and the ideology behind and jurisprudence governing "right to contract" law is vast. Key works include Forbath, *Law and the Shaping*; Amy Dru Stanley, *From Bondage to Contract: Wage Labor, Marriage, and the Market in the Age of Slave Emancipation* (New York: Cambridge University Press, 1998). On previous (successful) invocations of federal contract rights in court by immigrant rights advocates, see, especially, Joo, "New Conspiracy Theory"; and McClain, *In Search of Equality*. On the jurisprudential impact of the 1915 anti-alien cases, notably the *Truax* decision, see Motomura, *Americans in Waiting*; and Kelly, "Wavering Course."

Chapter 3

1. Carrie Chapman Catt, "The Citizen and the Vote," *The Woman Citizen*, April 6, 1918, 366.
2. For additional context for Catt's views on alien suffrage, see, among others, "Hearings before House Committee," *The Woman Citizen*, January 12, 1918, 130-31, 136-37; and Carrie Chapman Catt, "The Carrie Chapman Catt Citizenship Course: How the Vote Came to Men," *The Woman Citizen*, October 30, 1920, 610-13.
3. Quotation in main text from Catt, "Citizen and the Vote," 366. See also "Southern Suffragists Roused over Slacker Vote," *The Woman Citizen*, January 12, 1918, 132, 137; "Citizenship in Nebraska," *The Woman Citizen*, February 2, 1918, 189; "South Dakota's Citizenship Measure," *The Woman Citizen*, July 20, 1918, 148, 158; Alice Stone Blackwell, "Alice Stone Blackwell's Page," *The Woman Citizen*, August 31, 1918, 272; and "Catching Up with Indiana Women," *The Woman Citizen*, December 14, 1918, 592.
4. "The Alien in Equal Suffrage States," *The Woman Citizen*, April 27, 1918, 438.
5. "Amending the Amendment," *The Woman Citizen*, July 13, 1918, 125.
6. Recent works on the persistent efforts of women of color to fight for the ballot alongside and/ or in conflict with white suffragists include Martha S. Jones, *Vanguard: How Black Women Broke Barriers, Won the Vote, and Insisted on Equality for All* (New York: Basic Books, 2020); and Cahill, *Recasting the Vote*.
7. For dates of the repeal of state alien suffrage laws, this chapter largely relies on and offers minor corrections to Keyssar, *Right to Vote*, 371-73; and Hayduk, *Democracy for All*, 19-22.
8. This chapter joins in a long line of scholarship exploring the causes of, in the words of political scientist Leon Aylsworth, "The Passing of Alien Suffrage." Many scholars who examine the rise and fall of alien suffrage laws or situate them within wider histories of American voting rights have argued that broad ideological and/or demographic factors best explain their late-nineteenth- and early-twentieth-century repeals. Such reasons include the "close of the frontier" and its accompanying white settler colonial incorporation schemes, the development of

204   NOTES TO PAGES 68–71

southern Jim Crow suffrage regimes, and a rise in broader voting restrictions targeting "new" southern and eastern Europeans and Mexican nationals. See Rosberg, "Aliens and Equal Protection"; Neuman, "We Are the People"; Raskin, "Legal Aliens, Local Citizens"; Harper-Ho, "Noncitizen Voting Rights"; Keyssar, *Right to Vote*, 136–38; Varsanyi, "Rise and Fall"; Hayduk, *Democracy for All*, 25–30; Renshon, *Noncitizen Voting*, 71–73; Song, "Democracy and Noncitizen Voting"; Varsanyi, "Fighting for the Vote"; Lichtman, *Embattled Vote in America*, 140–41; and Kennedy, "Voters in a Foreign Land." Historians who examine discrete campaigns against noncitizen voting rights laws and/or explore their increasingly close connections with efforts to enfranchise American women have often been more closely attuned to the acute causes behind the demise of these policies on a state-by-state basis. On the former, see, among others, Folsom, "Tinkerers, Tipplers, and Traitors"; Peter H. Argersinger, "Electoral Reform and Partisan Jugglery," *Political Science Quarterly* 119, no. 3 (2004): 499–520; Cantrell, "'Our Very Pronounced Theory'"; Ron Hayduk, Marcela Garcia-Castañon, and Vedika Bhaumik, "Exploring the Complexities of 'Alien Suffrage' in American Political History," *Journal of American Ethnic History* 43, no. 2 (2024): 70–118. On the latter, see, among others, A. Elizabeth Taylor, "The Woman Suffrage Movement in Texas," *The Journal of Southern History* 17, no. 2 (May 1951): 194–215; Neu, "Olympia Brown"; Sara Hunter Graham, *Woman Suffrage and the New Democracy* (New Haven, CT: Yale University Press, 1996); Judith N. McArthur and Harold L. Smith, *Minnie Fisher Cunningham: A Suffragist's Life in Politics* (New York: Oxford University Press, 2005); Menchaca, *Naturalizing Mexican Immigrants*; Egge, *Woman Suffrage and Citizenship*; and Gunter, "Immigrant Declarants."

9. See, especially, Hayduk, *Democracy for All*, 36–39; and, broadly, Keyssar, *Right to Vote*, 117–71.
10. Muirhead made these allegations years after the fact at a meeting of fellow business executives and social welfare experts in 1919. See *Proceedings of the National Conference on Americanization in Industries, Held at the Atlantic House, Nantasket Beach, Massachusetts, June 22, 23 and 24, 1919* (New York, 1919), 80.
11. See, broadly, Keyssar, *Right to Vote*, 117–46, 159–62; and Hayduk, *Democracy for All*, 28–40.
12. Schneider, *Crossing Borders*, 204–11; Keyssar, *Right to Vote*, 139–40.
13. See, broadly, Keyssar, *Right to Vote*, 117–71; and Hayduk, *Democracy for All*, 16–40.
14. Shane Landrum, "The State's Big Family Bible: Birth Certificates, Personal Identity, and Citizenship in the United States, 1840–1950" (PhD diss., Brandeis University, 2014); Craig Robertson, *The Passport in America: The History of a Document* (New York: Oxford University Press, 2012); Magdalena Krajewska, *Documenting Americans: A Political History of National ID Card Proposals in the United States* (New York: Cambridge University Press, 2017).
15. J. Chester Lyman, "Our Inequalities of Suffrage," *North American Review* 144, no. 364 (1887): 298.
16. Lyman, 299.
17. See Lyman, 305 (emphasis in original).
18. Chaney, "Alien Suffrage," 136. Other scholars who have employed Chaney's treatise in their own work include Neuman, "We Are the People"; Raskin, "Legal Aliens, Local Citizens"; and Harper-Ho, "Noncitizen Voting Rights."
19. Chaney, "Alien Suffrage," quotation in main text from p. 137; on naturalization patterns, see p. 136.
20. Quotation in main text from Chaney, 136–37. While Chaney's worries about the presumed dangers of civil strife in Canada were exaggerated, ethnolinguistic and religious conflicts in Canadian politics grew pronounced during the early to mid-1890s. They were also well covered by the American press and were often commented on by US political actors. See, among others, Brendan A. Shanahan, "The Late Nineteenth-Century North American Catholic Schools Question: Tangled Disputes over Catholic Public Education in Manitoba and Minnesota," *The Catholic Historical Review* 110, no. 1 (Winter 2024): 47–71.
21. "Suffrage Amendment: What the Philadelphia Press Says of Minnesota," *Minneapolis Journal*, December 9, 1896, 2.
22. "Answers to Correspondents," *Philadelphia Inquirer*, February 11, 1897, 6.
23. "For Intelligent Suffrage," *Washington Post*, July 29, 1902, 6. As quoted in Hayduk, *Democracy for All*, 28. This was not an aberration for the paper. As scholar Alan Kennedy-Shaffer emphasizes, the *Washington Post* frequently "crusaded against alien suffrage" in its pages. See Kennedy, "Voters in a Foreign Land," 266.
24. Quotation in main text from "Suffrage Convention," *St. Paul Daily Globe*, February 11, 1893, 1. When this "congress" did convene, Frederick Douglass, then seventy-five years old, attended to

NOTES TO PAGES 71–4   205

forcefully rebut the "ultra white supremacy arguments" of Stephen B. Weeks of North Carolina. See "How to Rule a City," *Chicago Daily Tribune*, August 10, 1893, 9.

25. Though Anthony viewed Mexican immigrants and US-born Mexican Americans alike as opponents of women's suffrage, she indirectly identified noncitizen voting rights as a factor that contributed to the 1877 defeat of Colorado suffragists when commenting on the ethno-racial origins, nativity, and citizenship of voters in a particular precinct she had campaigned in. See "Arguments of the Woman-Suffrage Delegates before the Committee on the Judiciary of the United States Senate," January 23, 1880, Senate Miscellaneous Document No. 74, 47th Congress, 1st Session, 17. Political scientist Alan Grimes devotes a page and a half of his text to block quote from Anthony's testimony (though he misidentifies the page numbers on which it appears in his citation). See Alan Pendleton Grimes, *The Puritan Ethic and Woman Suffrage* (New York: Oxford University Press, 1967), 87–88.

26. Quotation from Susan B. Anthony and Ida Husted Harper, *History of Woman Suffrage*, vol. 4 (New York: Fowler & Wells, 1902), 556–57. See also Grimes, *Puritan Ethic*, 86. Grimes also reproduces this quotation in his discussion of anti-immigrant sentiment in late-nineteenth-century women's suffrage referenda. However, he misidentifies the total number of the nay votes on the 1890 South Dakota ballot measure.

27. See, especially, Neu, "Olympia Brown," 281.

28. "Voters Who Are Not Citizens," *The Woman's Tribune*, January 25, 1896, 1.

29. Carrie Chapman Catt, "President's Annual Address Delivered by Mrs. Carrie Chapman Catt before the 36th Annual Convention of the National American Woman Suffrage Association Held in Washington, D.C. February 11 to 17, 1904, Inclusive," 17, Iowa State University: Archives of Women's Political Communication, https://awpc.cattcenter.iastate.edu/2018/03/03/presidents-annual-address-for-the-nawsa-feb-11-1904/.

30. Catt, "Carrie Chapman Catt Citizenship," 613.

31. "Aliens and Women," *The Woman's Column*, September 10, 1892, 4.

32. "Voters Who Are Not," 1.

33. In fact, political scientist Paul Kleppner has estimated that roughly one of every six eligible North Dakota voters in 1890 was a noncitizen man, the highest rate in the nation. They were also quite numerous in Minnesota and Wisconsin, numbering "about 8 percent" of their electorates as well. See Kleppner, *Continuity and Change*, 166. Demographic data drawn from Gibson and Lennon, "Nativity of the Population"; and "Table XXII—Population of Cities Having 25,000 Inhabitants or More in 1900, Arranged According to Population: 1880 to 1900," *Twelfth Census of the United States, 1900* (Washington, DC: US Government Printing Office, 1901), lxix.

34. See, especially, Mark Wahlgren Summers, *Party Games: Getting, Keeping, and Using Power in Gilded Age Politics* (Chapel Hill: University of North Carolina Press, 2005); and Peter H. Argersinger, *Representation and Inequality in Late Nineteenth-Century America: The Politics of Apportionment* (New York: Cambridge University Press, 2012).

35. On politics in Gilded Age Michigan and the upper Midwest more broadly, see, among others, Richard J. Jensen, *The Winning of the Midwest: Social and Political Conflict, 1888–1896* (Chicago: University of Chicago Press, 1971); Paul Kleppner, *The Cross of Culture: A Social Analysis of Midwestern Politics 1850–1900* (New York: Free Press, 1970); Paul Kleppner, *The Third Electoral System, 1853–1892: Parties, Voters, and Political Cultures* (Chapel Hill: University of North Carolina Press, 1979); Kleppner, *Continuity and Change*; and Argersinger, *Representation and Inequality*.

36. On results, see Donald Richard Deskins, Hanes Walton, and Sherman C. Puckett, *Presidential Elections, 1789–2008: County, State, and National Mapping of Election Data* (Ann Arbor: University of Michigan Press, 2010).

37. Argersinger, "Electoral Reform," 504.

38. Michigan's two final Electoral College votes (assigned because of the state's two US Senate seats) were divided into two megadistricts, as historian Peter Argersinger notes (505). More broadly, see Argersinger, "Electoral Reform," 505–15.

39. Jensen, *Winning of the Midwest*, 225–26; Argersinger, "Electoral Reform," 515–19.

40. See, especially, Higham, *Strangers in the Land*, 80–87; and Jensen, *Winning of the Midwest*, 232–37.

41. Put most succinctly, Traynor alleged that "the Papist places the church above the state, and canon law above civil law" (74). See W. J. H. Traynor, "The Aims and Methods of the A.P.A.," *North American Review* 159, no. 452 (July 1894): 67–76.

206   NOTES TO PAGES 74–7

42. While APA rhetoric was often similar to that of previous and subsequent nativist organizations—particularly its embrace of the language of "Americanism"—the APA's organizational traditions and anti-Catholicism drew largely from neighboring Canadian Protestant models. Traynor himself was also a leader in the anti-Catholic, pro-British imperialist Orange Order. See, succinctly, Higham, *Strangers in the Land*, 80–87; and Jensen, *Winning of the Midwest*, 232–37; and see, more broadly, Donald L. Kinzer, *An Episode in Anti-Catholicism: The American Protective Association* (Seattle: University of Washington Press, 1964); Cory D. Wells, "'Tie the Flags Together': Migration, Nativism, and the Orange Order in the United States, 1840–1930" (PhD diss., University of Texas, Arlington, 2018); and Shanahan, "Late Nineteenth-Century."

43. W. J. H. Traynor, "Policy and Power of the A.P.A.," *North American Review* 162, no. 475 (June 1896): 659.

44. Traynor, "Aims and Methods"; Traynor, "Policy and Power"; Higham, *Strangers in the Land*, 80–87.

45. The APA claimed it possessed roughly 2.5 million members in 1896 and alleged it could "influence at least 4,000,000 votes." See Traynor, "Policy and Power," 666. Such claims were grossly inflated. Historian Richard Jensen estimates that it is "generous to credit the society with 100,000 dues-paying members, nationwide, at its peak." See Jensen, *Winning of the Midwest*, 233.

46. Higham, *Strangers in the Land*, 80, on Linton; more broadly, see 80–87.

47. In the Senate, eleven Democrats narrowly prevented twenty-one Republicans from holding a supermajority. In the House, sixty-nine Republicans dramatically outnumbered twenty-nine Democrats (plus two third-party lawmakers) following the 1892 elections. See "Party Statistics," Michigan Legislative Biography, https://mdoe.state.mi.us/legislators/session/PartyStatistics?sortOrder=startDate&page=4. See also Article XX, "Amendment and Revision of the Constitution," Michigan Constitution (1850).

48. The amendment was approved in the Senate by a 22–4 vote. See *Journal of the Senate of the State of Michigan, 1893, Vol. 1* (Lansing, MI: Robert Smith, State Printers and Binders, 1893), 187–88; see also "The Legislature," *Detroit Free Press*, February 2, 1893, 2.

49. "Thomas Barkworth," Michigan Legislative Biography, https://mdoe.state.mi.us/legislators/Legislator/LegislatorDetail/3425.

50. See "Dilly-Dallied Too Long," *Detroit Free Press*, May 16, 1893, 3; and "Gone a Glimmering: The Republican Pretense of a Short Legislative Session," *Detroit Free Press*, May 20, 1893, 3.

51. Quotation in main text from "Gone a Glimmering," 3; *Journal of the House of Representatives of the State of Michigan, 1893, Vol. 3* (Lansing, MI: Robert Smith, State Printers and Binders, 1893), 1913–20.

52. When a Republican lawmaker proposed incorporating a strict educational test onto a bill that aimed to enfranchise women for local elections, Barkworth denounced the proposal as "class legislation of a most vicious nature." Barkworth countered with legislation to enfranchise all women in the state "to give women equal rights with men." Barkworth argued to applause that "an uneducated woman is no more dangerous to our institutions than an uneducated man, and should have equal right before the law." See "Gone a Glimmering," 3.

53. The paper described the amendment as "requir[ing] a residence of twenty days in the township or ward, and in this country two years and six months and a declaration of intention to become a citizen." It thus missed the key point that it proposed disfranchising future noncitizen residents. See "Gone a Glimmering," 3.

54. On its wording, see *Journal of the House of Representatives of the State of Michigan*, 3 (1893): 1919–20.

55. "The Suffrage Amendment," *Detroit Free Press*, November 5, 1894, 4.

56. "To Disfranchise Voters," *Bay City Times*, October 10, 1894, 4.

57. *Kalamazoo Gazette*, October 9, 1894, 4. Jensen also includes a quotation from O'Hara (drawing from a different newspaper's coverage that did not include these typos) in Jensen, *Winning of the Midwest*, 225–26.

58. "For a Second Term," *L'Anse Sentinel*, August 4, 1894, 4. For a comparative local newspaper that did include coverage of the state GOP's stance toward alien suffrage on its 1894 platform, see "Rich Will Run Again," *True Northerner*, August 3, 1894, 6.

59. See, for instance, Russell M. Magnaghi, *Upper Peninsula of Michigan: A History* (Marquette, MI: 906 Heritage Press, 2017).

60. On the Alger Club, see J. A. Matthews, *The Alger Republican Club: Our Trip to Washington: Including a Synopsis of the Organization, History and Object of the Alger Republican Club*

NOTES TO PAGES 77–80   207

(Detroit, MI, 1889). On its role in the constitutional amendment campaign, see "The Suffrage Amendment," November 5, 1894, 4.

61. "Local Department," *True Northerner*, November 2, 1894, 1.

62. "Those Amendments," *Detroit Free Press*, November 9, 1894, 5.

63. "The Suffrage Amendment," November 5, 1894, 4.

64. "Local Department," 1.

65. See, broadly, Kleppner, *Cross of Culture*, 179–268; McSeveney, *Politics of Depression*; and Jensen, *Winning of the Midwest*, 209–68.

66. Michigan Manual, "Summary of Vote for Governor, 1835–2006," http://www.legislature.mi. gov/documents/publications/MichiganManual/2009-2010/09-10_MM_IX_pp_08-12_ Votes4Gov.pdf.

67. "Those Amendments," 5; *Bay City Times*, December 15, 1894, 2.

68. Quotation in main text, "Those Amendments," 5. See also "Defeated!" *Detroit Free Press*, November 7, 1894, 1.

69. "The Suffrage Amendment," *Detroit Free Press*, November 8, 1894, 4.

70. As political scientists William Anderson and Albert James Lobb pointed out more than a century ago, "Had the amendment itself applied to this election, it would have failed of adoption by 55,866 votes" owing to widespread abstentions on that very same measure (147). See William Anderson and Albert James Lobb, *A History of the Constitution of Minnesota: With the First Verified Text* (Minneapolis: University of Minnesota, 1921), 147–52.

71. See, especially, "Minnesota Elections," 477. https://www.sos.state.mn.us/media/1364/chapter_ 10-minnesota_votes.pdf. See also John D. Hicks, "The People's Party in Minnesota," *Minnesota History Bulletin* 5, no. 8 (1924): 531–60; and Peter H. Argersinger, "'A Place on the Ballot': Fusion Politics and Antifusion Laws," *American Historical Review* 85, no. 2 (April 1980): 287–306.

72. Chapter 3, "An Act Proposing an Amendment to Section One (1) of Article Seven (7) of the Constitution of the State of Minnesota Which Relates to the Elective Franchise," *1895 Laws of Minnesota* (St. Paul, MN: 1895), 7–8.

73. The amendment was ratified by a vote of 97,980 ayes against 52,454 nays. See "Minnesota Elections," 477; and Anderson and Lobb, *History of the Constitution*, 180.

74. "Limitation of the Suffrage," 2.

75. As quoted in "Suffrage Amendment: What the Philadelphia Press Says of Minnesota," 2.

76. *The County Record* [Kingstree, SC], April 29, 1897, 7.

77. "The Citizenship Amendment," *Mower County Transcript*, January 20, 1897, 1.

78. The *Minneapolis Times* is quoted in "Disfranchising Themselves," *The Representative*, November 25, 1896, 3.

79. "Are You a Citizen?" *Princeton Union*, November 19, 1896, 1; "Naturalization Necessary," *Saint Paul Globe*, December 11, 1896, 4; "Eegin at Once [*sic*]," *Saint Paul Globe*, September 26, 1897, 4.

80. Anderson and Lobb, *History of the Constitution*, 180. See also J. W. Garner and Alpheus Snow, "Participation of the Alien in the Political Life of the Community," *Proceedings of the American Society of International Law* 5 (1911): 172–92; and Kleppner, *Continuity and Change*, 165–66.

81. Despite North Dakota's huge immigrant and noncitizen populations, the anti-alien suffrage measure hardly made any waves in the local press. Newspapers largely only mentioned the amendment in passing when including broader information about nominations for the upcoming elections. See "Proposed Amendment to the Constitution of the State of North Dakota," *Bismarck Weekly Tribune*, November 4, 1898, 2. Scholarship on the repeal of alien suffrage in the state has been rare (and often misidentifies its date). Kleppner, who correctly notes the amendment's ratification in 1898, offers a rare exception. See Kleppner, *Continuity and Change*, 166.

82. "Concurrent Resolution," in *Proposed Amendments to the Constitution, Laws Passed at the Fifth Session of the Legislative Assembly of the State of North Dakota* (Grand Forks, ND: Herald, State Printers and Binders, 1897), 349. On North Dakota's GOP-leaning electorate, see D. Jerome Tweton, "Considering Why Populism Succeeded in South Dakota and Failed in North Dakota," *South Dakota History* 22, no. 4 (1993): 330–44.

83. See "The Official Vote," *Bismarck Weekly Tribune*, December 23, 1898, 7.

84. "The Constitutional Amendment Question," *Bismarck Weekly Tribune*, January 13, 1899, 3.

85. Quotations in main text from "Amendment Is Passed," *Sheboygan Daily Press*, November 6, 1908, 1. On rising rates of return migration during the recession induced by the Panic of 1907, see Shumsky, "Let No Man Stop," 62.

208 NOTES TO PAGES 80–2

86. Ironically, this particular claim that "the amendment is not of vital importance" appeared in an article entitled "The Amendments Important," *La Crosse Tribune*, October 27, 1908, 3.

87. J. D. Beck, ed., *The Blue Book of the State of Wisconsin* (Madison, WI: Democrat Printing, State Printer, 1909), 263, 558.

88. "Amendment Is Passed," 1; John D. Buenker, *The History of Wisconsin: The Progressive Era, 1893–1914*, vol. 4 (Madison: Wisconsin Historical Society, 1998), 512.

89. On the Wisconsin women's suffrage movement and the 1912 amendment campaign, see, among others, Marilyn Grant, "The 1912 Suffrage Referendum: An Exercise in Political Action," *The Wisconsin Magazine of History* 64, no. 2 (1980): 107–18; Genevieve C. McBride, *On Wisconsin Women: Working for Their Rights from Settlement to Suffrage* (Madison: University of Wisconsin Press, 1993), 201–34; and Tracie Grube-Gaurkee, "Women Desire the Ballot: Wisconsin Woman Suffrage Association, World War I, and Suffrage as a War Measure" (master's thesis, University of Nebraska at Kearney, 2020).

90. The amendment was defeated by a vote of 135,736 in favor and 227,054 opposed. A total of 399,975 Wisconsin men had concomitantly cast ballots for president at the same election. See Industrial Commission, ed., *The Wisconsin Blue Book* (Madison, WI: Democrat Printing, State Printer, 1913), 214, 271.

91. See "Report of the Wisconsin Woman Suffrage Association for the Year Ending 1912, by the Retiring President, Rev. Olympia Brown," 2, Wisconsin Woman's Suffrage Association Files, Wis MSS HV, Box 26, Folder 2, "Reports, Minutes and Proceedings, Lists, Notes, and Memoranda, 1911–1919," Wisconsin Historical Society Archives, Madison (all caps in original). Other scholars who have emphasized the importance of the "pink ballots" to both suffragists' campaign strategy and postmortems on the amendment's defeat include McBride, *On Wisconsin Women*, 225, 229; and Grube-Gaurkee, "Women Desire the Ballot," 49–50.

92. See, for instance, "Did you come to this country as a stranger, one of many immigrants? If so do you remember how you were treated?," "Socialism Means Democracy in Government," and "Election Day Prediction" in Ada L. James Papers, Wis MSS OP, Box 24, Folder 3, "1912 Speeches, Articles, and Plan of Organization + N.D. Fragments," Wisconsin Historical Society Archives, Madison. On the German–American Alliance and the brewing industry's opposition to women's suffrage in Wisconsin, in particular, see McBride, *On Wisconsin Women*, 222–26.

93. On the women's suffrage movement in the upper Midwest during the Progressive Era, see, among many others, Grant, "1912 Suffrage Referendum"; McBride, *On Wisconsin Women*; Graham, *Woman Suffrage*; and Egge, *Woman Suffrage and Citizenship*.

94. Grimes, *Puritan Ethic*, 87–88.

95. The NAWSA's own historians noted the peculiarity of Colorado's suffrage laws. According to the organization, Colorado's original 1876 constitution provided only "School suffrage" for women. However, the constitution did enable legislators to "at any time submit a measure to the voters for the complete franchise, which, if accepted by the majority, should become law." Such a vote occurred in 1893, and "by a majority of 6,347," voters extended equal voting rights to women. Nearly a decade later, suffragists campaigned to ensure their voting rights were written into the state's constitution. NB: The original source inaccurately reports this amendment being ratified in 1901 (it was actually ratified the following year). See Elizabeth Cady Stanton et al., *History of Woman Suffrage*, vol. 6 (New York: Fowler & Wells, 1922), 59. On that November 1902 election, see *Colorado Springs Gazette*, November 2, 1902, 5; and "The Proposed Constitutional Amendments," *Colorado Springs Weekly Gazette*, November 6, 1902, 6. See also Hayduk, *Democracy for All*, 19.

96. Stanton et al., *History of Woman Suffrage*, 6:59–60.

97. Porter, *History of Suffrage*, 131.

98. See, among many others, Bredbenner, *Nationality of Her Own*; and Gardner, *Qualities of a Citizen*.

99. On the 1912 Oregon women's suffrage referendum, see Eileen L. McDonagh and H. Douglas Price, "Woman Suffrage in the Progressive Era: Patterns of Opposition and Support in Referenda Voting, 1910–1918," *American Political Science Review* 79, no. 2 (1985): 415–35; and Kimberly Jensen, "'Neither Head nor Tail to the Campaign': Esther Pohl Lovejoy and the Oregon Woman Suffrage Victory of 1912," *Oregon Historical Quarterly* 108, no. 3 (2007): 350–83. Examples of confusion in Oregon over the eligibility of married women to register to vote under federal nationality law include T. H. Crawford, "Rights of Women Defined: Does an

NOTES TO PAGES 83–5   **209**

Alien Woman upon Marrying a Citizen of the United States, Become a Citizen without Other Act on Her Part?" *La Grande Observer,* September 26, 1913, 1; and "Alien Wives Are Citizens," *La Grande Observer,* October 27, 1913, 2.

100. "Aliens' Wives Affected," *Coos Bay Times,* March 18, 1913, Evening edition, 2.

101. "A Cause of Strife," *East Oregonian,* March 21, 1913, 4.

102. "Crawford Modifies His Former Opinion," *East Oregonian,* March 29, 1913, 10; "Wives Can Vote on First Papers," *Evening Herald* [Klamath Falls, OR], March 31, 1913, 2. With confusion on this subject continuing to fester, the attorney general again clarified in late October 1913 that noncitizen women whose husbands possessed first papers could vote. See "Women Have Same Rights as Husbands," *Oregon Daily Journal,* October 25, 1913, 7.

103. "Alien in Equal Suffrage," 438. On the emergence of this proposed amendment early in the 1913 session of the Oregon legislature, see "Citizenship Resolution Has Passed Senate," *Oregon Daily Journal,* January 24, 1913, 11.

104. Originally in the *Portland Journal,* republished as "Study of Amendments," *Ashland Tidings,* September 28, 1914, 8.

105. "The Measures," *Morning Register* [Eugene, OR], September 30, 1914, 4.

106. The amendment carried, with 164,879 votes in favor and only 39,847 opposed. The anti-alien suffrage amendment received more aye votes than any of the other twenty-nine statewide direct ballot measures put before Oregonians that year. See Ben W. Olcott, *Blue Book and Official Directory: Oregon 1915–1916* (Salem, OR: State Printing Department, 1915), 145.

107. At the time of the repeal of alien suffrage in Oregon in 1914, eleven western states enfranchised women on an equal basis to men. Only one of those states, Kansas, also enfranchised noncitizen voters who held first papers. See Keyssar, *Right to Vote,* 371–73, 402; and Hayduk, *Democracy for All,* 19–22.

108. Burton W. Folsom, *No More Free Markets or Free Beer: The Progressive Era in Nebraska, 1900–1924* (Lanham, MD: Lexington Books, 1999), 69. See also Williams, "Road to Citizenship."

109. Schneider, *Crossing Borders,* 204–11; Marian Smith, "Immigration and Naturalization Service," in *A Historical Guide to the U.S. Government,* ed. George Kurian, 305–8 (New York: Oxford University Press, 1998).

110. "Rush for Second Papers," *Nebraska State Journal,* February 15, 1913, 4.

111. The *Omaha Daily Bee* devoted two articles to this subject on one day alone. See "Douglas Registration up to Attorney General," *Omaha Daily Bee,* September 18, 1913, 3; and "More Disfranchisement," *Omaha Daily Bee,* September 18, 1913, 6.

112. See, especially, Stephen Wiitala, "Election Law Turmoil in Nebraska" (master's thesis, University of Nebraska, Omaha, 1991), 2–3. More broadly on splits within the state Democratic Party, see Folsom, *No More Free Markets,* 52–70; and Laura McKee Hickman, "Thou Shalt Not Vote: The Struggle for Woman's Suffrage in Nebraska" (master's thesis, University of Nebraska, Omaha, 1997), 54–56.

113. See, among other articles, "Moorhead's Plans to Exclude Foreign Born," *Omaha Daily Bee,* August 7, 1913, 1; "Moorhead Changes Ruling," *Omaha Daily Bee,* August 8, 1913, 12; "Moorhead Shuts Out Many," *Omaha Daily Bee,* August 11, 1913, 3; "Unregistered Cannot Vote," *Omaha Daily Bee,* August 15, 1913, 6; and "Grant Martin Comes to the Defense of Harley Moorhead," *Omaha Daily Bee,* October 18, 1913, 16. See also Williams v. Moorhead, 96 Neb. 559, 148 N.W. 552 (1914).

114. See "Grant Martin Comes," 16.

115. Quotation in main text from "Moorhead Views Rejected: Attorney General Martin Rules on Who May Vote," *Omaha Daily Bee,* September 20, 1913, 1. See also, on widespread coverage of this ruling, "No Federal Statute Can Control Voting," *Lincoln Journal Star,* September 19, 1913, 1; and "Held First Papers Grant Citizenship Right in Nebraska," *O'Neil Frontier,* September 25, 1913, 6. Nebraska authorities were not alone in grappling with the challenge of conflicting meanings of first papers owing to state and federal law. Three years earlier, judge Arthur Fuller of Crawford County, Kansas, had similarly issued a decision separating the Naturalization Act of 1906—and the validity of first papers documents—from suffrage rights in his state. See "How Aliens May Vote: Judge Fuller of Pittsburg Renders an Important Decision," *Fort Scott Republican,* November 5, 1910, 2.

116. See, broadly, Christopher Capozzola, *Uncle Sam Wants You: World War I and the Making of the Modern American Citizen* (New York: Oxford University Press, 2008).

210 NOTES TO PAGES 85-8

117. Such laws even ensnared native-born women married to German husbands. See Sarah Galloway Kruse, "Independent Citizenship: Marriage, Expatriation, and the Cable Act, 1907–1936" (master's thesis, Texas Women's University, 1998); and Bredbenner, *Nationality of Her Own*, 68–73.
118. See, broadly, Christopher Capozzola, "The Only Badge Needed Is Your Patriotic Fervor: Vigilance, Coercion, and the Law in World War I America," *Journal of American History* 88, no. 4 (March 2002): 1354–82; and Capozzola, *Uncle Sam Wants You*.
119. For repeal dates (and minor corrections), see Kleppner, *Continuity and Change*, 166; Keyssar, *Right to Vote*, 371–73; and Hayduk, *Democracy for All*, 19–22.
120. On electoral results, see Folsom, "Tinkerers, Tipplers, and Traitors," 62. More broadly, see Williams, "The Road to Citizenship"; and Folsom, *No More Free Markets*.
121. On Nebraska, specifically, see Luebke, "German–American Alliance"; Louise Rickard, "The Politics of Reform in Omaha, 1918–1921," *Nebraska History* 53 (1972): 419–45; and Caleb Samuel Kociemba, "German Americans and the Nebraska Nonpartisan League: Links of Persecution and Loyalty" (master's thesis, University of Nebraska at Kearney, 2019). More broadly, see Frederick Luebke, *Bonds of Loyalty: German Americans and World War I* (DeKalb: Northern Illinois University Press, 1974); and Capozzola, *Uncle Sam Wants You*.
122. See, especially, McKee Hickman, "Thou Shalt Not Vote," 40–42.
123. For real-time accounts, see "Justice in Nebraska," *The Woman Citizen*, February 23, 1918, 249; and "To Get Back Beer," *The Woman Citizen*, June 15, 1918, 45. See also, specifically, McKee Hickman, "Thou Shalt Not Vote," 43–44, 86–87; and, more broadly, Thomas Chalmer Coulter, "A History of Woman Suffrage in Nebraska, 1856–1920" (PhD diss., The Ohio State University, 1967).
124. "The Teutonic Touch in Nebraska," *The Woman Citizen*, August 25, 1917, 230; Marion Woolworth Fairfield, "Correspondence," *The Woman Citizen*, August 25, 1917, 231.
125. Quotations in main text from "Citizenship in Nebraska," 189. While state governments increasingly enfranchised soldiers via absentee ballots during World War I (following a precedent set by the Civil War), federal protections for military voters were not established until World War II. Additionally, some states barred soldiers and sailors stationed on bases from qualifying as voters owing to residency restrictions. See, especially, Keyssar, *Right to Vote*, 150–51, 246–47, 429n20; see also, broadly, Gunter, "Immigrant Declarants."
126. Quotation in main text from "Alien Voter Slackers," *St. Louis Post-Dispatch*, January 13, 1918, 2. Other examples of news and editorial coverage along these lines include "Metcalfe Raps Court Decision," *Omaha Daily Bee*, January 29, 1918, 3; "Women Protest Lest They Lose the Ballot," *Plattsmouth Semi-Weekly Journal*, February 11, 1918, 6; and "The Suffrage Amendment," *North Platte Semi-Weekly Tribune*, November 1, 1918, 4.
127. Executive Committee of the Nebraska State Council of Defense, "Minutes of the Fourth Meeting, January 17, 1918," 1. Nebraska State Council of Defense Records, RG 23, S1 F3: "Records, 1917–19, Proceedings Nebraska State Council of Defense, May 1917–Jan 1919," Box 1, Nebraska Historical Society, Lincoln, NE: Preservations Office.
128. "Metcalfe Raps Court Decision," 3; "Nebraska to Vote on Alien Suffrage," *Evening Star* [Washington, DC], April 7, 1918, 7; "Nebraska Has Plans to Curb Seditionists: State Officials Believe New Law Will Put Stop to Disloyalty," *Bismarck Tribune*, April 22, 1918, 2. See also Kociemba, "German Americans," 65–66.
129. "Address Delivered in 1918 by Governor Keith Neville," 7. Governor Keith Neville Files, RG 1 SG 26 S4, F1: "Speeches, 1917–1919," Box 7, Nebraska Historical Society, Lincoln, NE: Preservations Office.
130. See front cover and "Nicht-Bürger Fönnen Nicht Wählen," *Tägliche Omaha Tribüne*, November 7, 1918, 1, 5.
131. Kate Heltzel, ed., *Nebraska Blue Book: 56th Edition* (Lincoln: Nebraska Legislature, 2022), 238. The measure received widespread support from native-born "Yankee" Protestants. But historian Burton Folsom estimates that up to one-third of German-origin and more than half of Czech- and Swedish-origin voters also probably supported it. See Folsom, "Tinkerers, Tipplers, and Traitors," 62, 70–73.
132. "Alien in Equal Suffrage," 438.
133. "Alien in Equal Suffrage," 438; "Finish the Count," *The Topeka State Journal*, November 20, 1918, 1–2; and "News Items from All over Kansas," *The Hays Free Press*, December 5, 1918, 6.

NOTES TO PAGES 89–91   211

134. On Gore's proposal, see "Amending the Amendment," 125. On Frelinghuysen's advocacy, see, broadly, Keremidchieva, "Congressional Debates."
135. "Amending the Amendment," 125.
136. Though a federal constitutional alien suffrage ban was defeated, like the Fifteenth Amendment before it, the Nineteenth Amendment ultimately banned suffrage restrictions on the basis of sex for "citizens of the United States." See, especially, Keremidchieva, "Gendering of Legislative Rationality"; and Keremidchieva, "Congressional Debates," 60–67.
137. See, among others, Neu, "Olympia Brown," 281; Dorinda Riessen-Reed, *The Woman Suffrage Movement in South Dakota* (Pierre: South Dakota Commission on the Status of Women, 1975); Easton, "Woman Suffrage"; and Egge, *Woman Suffrage and Citizenship*, 165–70.
138. "South Dakota's Citizenship Measure," 148; Stanton et al., *History of Woman Suffrage*, 6:591–52.
139. "South Dakota to the Fore," *The Woman Citizen*, April 6, 1918, 369.
140. Quotation in main text from "South Dakota's Citizenship Measure," 148. For another account of the South Dakota campaign, see also Stanton et al., *History of Woman Suffrage*, 6:592–93.
141. "The Governors Speak," *Everybody's Magazine* 39, no. 5 (November 1918): 4.
142. Egge, *Woman Suffrage and Citizenship*, 169.
143. "How to Win a State," *The Woman Citizen*, November 16, 1918, 508–9.
144. United States, *Fourteenth Census of the United States, 1920* (Washington, DC: US Government Printing Office, 1921), 306–11.
145. See, broadly, Evan Anders, *Boss Rule in South Texas: The Progressive Era* (Austin: University of Texas Press, 1979); Martinez, *Injustice Never Leaves You*; Gregg Cantrell, *The People's Revolt: Texas Populists and the Roots of American Liberalism* (New Haven, CT: Yale University Press, 2020); and Walter D. Kamphoefner, *Germans in America: A Concise History* (Lanham, MD: Rowman & Littlefield, 2021).
146. "Germans with First Papers Cannot Vote Is Looney's Opinion," *Austin Statesman*, January 19, 1918, 2.
147. As historian Rachel Gunter finds, the repeal of alien suffrage rights and women's enfranchisement in primary elections was intertwined with intra–Democratic Party disputes following the impeachment of governor James Ferguson and his attempts to regain the nomination from his successor, William Hobby. Hobby, in turn, sought to enfranchise women as a means to boost his own re-election efforts. See, especially, Gunter, "Immigrant Declarants," 596; Rachel Michelle Gunter, "More Than Black and White: Woman Suffrage and Voting Rights in Texas, 1918–1923" (PhD diss., Texas A&M University, 2017), 66–96. Other works on the women's suffrage movement in Texas and its intersection with anti-alien suffrage efforts include Taylor, "Woman Suffrage Movement"; Graham, *Woman Suffrage*, 132–63; McArthur and Smith, *Minnie Fisher Cunningham*, 79–83; and Menchaca, *Naturalizing Mexican Immigrants*, 206–59.
148. See, specifically, Gunter, "Immigrant Declarants," 596–97; and, broadly, Gunter, "More Than Black," 158–216.
149. Taylor, "Woman Suffrage Movement," 211–12; McArthur and Smith, *Minnie Fisher Cunningham*, 79; Menchaca, *Naturalizing Mexican Immigrants*, 229; Gunter, "Immigrant Declarants," 597.
150. "Texas's Women Voters," *The Woman Citizen*, July 20, 1918, 156.
151. Catt, "Carrie Chapman Catt Citizenship," 613.
152. "Prohibition and Suffrage Will Carry If Given Full Support," *El Paso Herald*, April 18, 1919, 6.
153. Menchaca, *Naturalizing Mexican Immigrants*, 231–32; Gunter, "More Than Black," 170–80, 216–18; Gunter, "Immigrant Declarants," 598–99.
154. The measure received 57,622 ballots cast in favor (51.7 percent) and 53,910 opposed (48.3 percent). See SJR 1, 37th Regular Session, *Legislative Reference Library of Texas* https://lrl.texas.gov/legis/billsearch/amendmentDetails.cfm?amendmentID=88&legSession=37-0&billTypedetail=SJR&billNumberDetail=1. More broadly, see "What Happened to Texas?" *The Woman Citizen*, August 27, 1921, 18; Taylor, "Woman Suffrage Movement," 215; Graham, *Woman Suffrage*, 135–36; McArthur and Smith, *Minnie Fisher Cunningham*, 82–84; Menchaca, *Naturalizing Mexican Immigrants*, 234–44; and Gunter, "Immigrant Declarants," 599.
155. "Governors Speak," 6.

212 NOTES TO PAGES 91–3

156. Article 16, "Amendments," *Constitution of the State of Indiana, 1851.*
157. Aylsworth, "Passing of Alien Suffrage," 114–16.
158. Isidor Loeb, then dean of the University of Missouri's School of Business and Public Administration, published widely on the topic and advocated for moderate reforms. See, for instance, Isidor Loeb, *Constitutions and Constitutional Conventions in Missouri* (Columbia: State Historical Society of Missouri, 1920); "Dr. Isidor Loeb Advises Caution in Drafting of New Constitution for State," *St. Louis Post-Dispatch*, February 25, 1922, 6; and Isidor Loeb, "Opportunity to Revise the Constitution Frequently Now a Fixed Missouri Policy," *St. Louis Post-Dispatch*, April 25, 1922, 13. See also, more broadly, on news coverage of proposed state constitutional reform, "Gardner's Plans Given in Message," *Fair Play* [St. Genevieve, MO], January 18, 1919, 4; "Constitutional Convention," *The Farmington Times*, February 14, 1919, 1; and "Missouri State News," *Potosi Journal*, November 9, 1921, 2.
159. United States, *Fourteenth Census of the United States, 1920*, 306–11. On Missouri German Americans during World War I, see, broadly, Luebke, *Bonds of Loyalty*; and Petra DeWitt, *Degrees of Allegiance: Harassment and Loyalty in Missouri's German-American Community during World War I* (Athens, OH: Ohio University Press, 2012).
160. "No Enemy Alien Voters," *St. Louis Post-Dispatch*, March 19, 1918, 16.
161. "Aliens Refused Vote at Primary," *Greenfield Vidette*, August 8, 1918, 5; "Aliens Refused Vote at Primary," *Lawrence Chieftain*, August 15, 1918, 7; "Aliens Refused Vote at Primary," *Cameron Sun*, August 8, 1918, 6.
162. "400 Enemy Aliens Here Are Barred from Voting," *St. Louis Post-Dispatch*, August 31, 1918, 1.
163. "Governors Speak," 6.
164. "William E. Borah," *The Woman Citizen*, October 26, 1918, 429.
165. The *St. Louis Post-Dispatch* indicated that the amendment had not just been sponsored, but also actually been drafted, by the Missouri League of Women Voters. See "Test for New Voting-Qualification Law," *St. Louis Post-Dispatch*, February 10, 1923, 3. The amendment was adopted by a vote of 383,499 in favor and 299,404 opposed. See David C. Valentine, "Constitutional Amendments, Statutory Revision and Referenda Submitted to the Voters by the General Assembly or by Initiative Petition, 1910–2010" (Columbia: Missouri Legislative Academy, December 2010), 5.
166. The *Post-Dispatch* maintained that the measure's text, which stipulated that "every citizen of the United States, who is over the age of 21 years, possessing the following qualifications, shall be entitled to vote at all elections by the people," seemed to have clearly repealed noncitizen voting rights. See "State Amendments to Be in Effect Soon: Acting Gov. Lloyd to Proclaim Two Passed Nov. 7—One Bars Voting by Aliens," *St. Louis Post-Dispatch*, December 11, 1922, 13.
167. The *St. Louis Post-Dispatch* extensively covered these postelection developments. See "Test for New Voting-Qualification Law," 3; "Status of Aliens at Spring Election under Discussion," *St. Louis Post-Dispatch*, February 11, 1923, 7; and "Registration for Primary March 9 to Be About 245,000," *St. Louis Post-Dispatch*, February 25, 1923, 19.
168. In their "explanation" of Amendment 9, lawmakers proposing these changes argued that the measure was required to ensure "only citizens of the United States" were enfranchised, on the seemingly erroneous basis that, without it, the "Constitution permits aliens to vote on first papers." See Charles Becker, *Official Manual of the State of Missouri 1923-1924: The Blue Book* (Columbia: Office of the Missouri Secretary of State, 1924), 534; and Valentine, "Constitutional Amendments, Missouri," 5. For broader context, see William F. Swindler, "Missouri Constitutions: History, Theory and Practice," *Missouri Law Review* 23, no. 1 (January 1958): 32–62; and William F. Swindler, "Missouri Constitutions: History, Theory and Practice (Continued)," *Missouri Law Review* 23, no. 2 (April 1958): 157–79.
169. Williams, "Road to Citizenship," 417–18; Ross Franklin Lockridge, *How Government Functions in Indiana: An Indiana Supplement to Thomas Harrison Reed's Form and Function of American Government* (Yonkers, NY: World Book Company, 1918), 20–21; Thomas Marshall, "Misunderstood America," *The Forum*, January 1918, 6.
170. On previous failed anti-alien suffrage legislation in Indiana during the Progressive Era, see Charles Kettleborough, *Constitution Making in Indiana Vol. 1: 1780-1851* (Fort Wayne: Fort Wayne Printing Company–Indiana Historical Commission, 1916), cxvi–cxvii; "New Constitution Theme of Pastors," *South Bend News-Times*, July 9, 1917, 10; "Suggests Change in Constitution," *South Bend News-Times*, July 9, 1917, 2; and "Seeks to Bar Alien Votes,"

NOTES TO PAGE 93–5   213

Indianapolis Star, January 21, 1919, 8. On the foreign-born population of Indiana in 1920, see Gibson and Lennon, "Nativity of the Population"; and United States, *Fourteenth Census of the United States, 1920*, 306–11.

171. "U.S. Warns against Any Illegal Voting: Vote Buying and Balloting by Alien Enemies Will Be Prosecuted by Government," *Indianapolis Star*, November 4, 1918, 1.

172. "Vote Is Denied Alien Enemies," *Indianapolis Star*, September 25, 1920, 20; Charles Kettleborough, *Constitution Making in Indiana Vol. 3: 1916–1930* (Indianapolis: Indiana Historical Bureau, 1930), 193–94.

173. Quotations in main text from "Should Aliens Vote?" *The Woman Citizen*, September 10, 1921, 18. For context, see also "Constitutional Amendments to Be Voted on Tomorrow," *Indianapolis Star*, September 5, 1921, 3.

174. "Notes of League of Women Voters," *Indianapolis Star*, August 1, 1921, 4; John B. Stoll, "From the Watch Tower," *Indianapolis Star*, August 10, 1921, 6; Robert W. McBride, "Aliens Should Not Be Voters," *Indianapolis Star*, August 14, 1921, 18; "Vote on the Amendment," *Indianapolis Star*, August 22, 1921, 6; B. R. Inman, "Views of the People: Would Shut Off Alien Voting," *Indianapolis Star*, September 6, 1921, 6.

175. Indiana also required ayes to outnumber nays and abstentions. However, because few voters abstained on the anti-alien suffrage measure, the amendment easily surmounted that obstacle as well in 1921. See Kettleborough, *Constitution Making in Indiana Vol. 3*, 229–30.

176. "Notes of League of Women Voters," *Indianapolis Star*, October 23, 1921, 42; "Women Ask about Steps to Prohibit Voting by Aliens," *Indianapolis Star*, October 27, 1921, 7.

177. More broadly, on this history in Indiana, see James H. Madison, *Indiana through Tradition and Change: A History of the Hoosier State and Its People, 1920–1945* (Indianapolis: Indiana Historical Society, 1982); Leonard J. Moore, *Citizen Klansmen: The Ku Klux Klan in Indiana, 1921–1928* (Chapel Hill: University of North Carolina Press, 1997); and James H. Madison, *The Ku Klux Klan in the Heartland* (Bloomington: Indiana University Press, 2020).

178. Aylsworth, "Passing of Alien Suffrage," 114–16; Taylor, "Woman Suffrage Movement," 51–52; Gunter, "Immigrant Declarants," 600–601. On the foreign-born population of Arkansas in 1920, see Gibson and Lennon, "Nativity of the Population"; and United States, *Fourteenth Census of the United States, 1920*, 306–11.

Chapter 4

1. For context on New York Gilded Age state politics in the leadup to the convention, see McSeveney, *Politics of Depression*, 3–31; and Edward Foley, *Ballot Battles: The History of Disputed Elections in the United States* (New York: Oxford University Press, 2015), 178–90. More broadly, see, Ruth C. Silva, "Legislative Representation: With Special Reference to New York," *Law and Contemporary Problems* 27, no. 3 (Summer 1962): 408–33; Silva, "Population Base for Apportionment," 1–50; and Moss, "Democracy, Citizenship and Constitution-Making." On New York legislative elections, see Michael J. Dubin, *Party Affiliations in the State Legislatures: A Year by Year Summary, 1796–2006* (Jefferson, NC: McFarland, 2015), 136.

2. McSeveney, *Politics of Depression*, 32–62; Foley, *Ballot Battles*, 190; Moss, "Democracy, Citizenship and Constitution-Making," 245.

3. Under the 1894 constitution, all New York counties (save the extremely sparsely populated Hamilton County) were to receive at least one Assembly seat. In the Senate, by contrast, no county was permitted to ever have more than one-third of all seats, while no two neighboring counties could ever hold a combined majority. The state constitution also boosted rural districts when apportioning new seats to the Senate. Political scientist Ruth Silva explores these debates and their implications at great length in her numerous publications, including Silva, "Legislative Representation," 409–12, 415–16; and Ruth C. Silva, "Apportionment of the New York Assembly," *Fordham Law Review* 31, no. 1 (October 1962): 1–72. See also, among others, McSeveney, *Politics of Depression*, 63–86; and Foley, *Ballot Battles*, 190–93.

4. The apportionment amendment carried by a vote of 404,335 in favor and 350,625 opposed. See Moss, "Democracy, Citizenship and Constitution-Making," 37. As McSeveney highlights, voter backlash against Democrats in the mid-1890s was so strong that the amendment, which "was specifically designed to discriminate against" New York City boroughs, scored a favorable majority in both New York and Kings Counties (82). See McSeveney, *Politics of Depression*, 63–86. See also Silva, "Legislative Representation," 410–12; Silva, "Apportionment of the New York Assembly"; Foley, *Ballot Battles*, 190–93; and Dubin, *Party Affiliations*, 136.

214 NOTES TO PAGES 95–6

5. News examples include "Partisan in Purpose: Republican Supremacy Sought by a New Apportionment," *New York Times*, July 23, 1894, 5; "Shrewd Political Scheme: Republicans Expect to Keep Themselves in Power for Years," *New York Times*, August 27, 1894, 1; and "To Serve Partisan Purposes: The Republican Apportionment Scheme Unfair to Cities," *New York Times*, September 6, 1894, 8. As political scientist Ruth Silva notes, the 1894 constitution did remove a (then-dormant) antebellum-era clause counting "persons of color not taxed" out of the population. See Silva, "Population Base for Apportionment," 9–10.
6. Both Moss and Silva highlight that opponents of a nativist legislative apportionment basis were especially sparse at the 1894 convention compared to previous state constitutional assemblies. See Silva, "Population Base for Apportionment," 6–10; and Moss, "Democracy, Citizenship and Constitution-Making," 88–96.
7. In 1910, there were more than 800,000 white immigrant men in New York City; more than half were noncitizens. See United States, *Thirteenth Census of the United States, 1910* (Washington, DC: US Government Printing Office, 1911), 1092.
8. Gus Tyler and David I. Wells, "New York 'Constitutionally Republican,'" in *The Politics of Reapportionment*, ed. Malcolm Edwin Jewell (New Brunswick, NJ: Transaction Publishers, 1962), 221.
9. State legislative anti-alien apportionment schemes were fairly common in the early to mid-twentieth century. Maine, New York, Nebraska, and North Carolina each ultimately explicitly counted noncitizen immigrants out of their populations. The state legislatures of Massachusetts, Tennessee, and Texas (in the latter case its upper chamber), in turn, based apportionment on their states' qualified voter populations. California counted "aliens ineligible to citizenship" out of the population, while Oregon (theoretically) excluded all nonwhite persons from the count for the purposes of apportionment (though the exclusion of nonwhite citizens was unconstitutional under the federal Fourteenth Amendment). Indiana based apportionment on their state's male population; Arizona, Idaho, and Kansas apportioned (at least in part) on the basis of the number of votes cast in recent elections. On these policies, their passage, and their ultimate demise, see, especially, Appendix to the States' Attorneys General Brief in Evenwel v. Abbott, App. 1–10; Valdimer Orlando Key, "Procedures in State Legislative Apportionment," *American Political Science Review* 26, no. 6 (December 1932): 1050–58; Charles W. Shull, "Legislative Apportionment and the Law," *Temple Law Quarterly* 18, no. 3 (1944): 388–405; Durfee, "Apportionment of Representation"; Bone, "States Attempting to Comply"; and Keith and Petry, "Apportionment of State Legislatures."
10. Federal reapportionment disputes have received more scholarly attention than their state-level counterparts. Works that examine the failure to reapportion the House of Representatives after the 1920 enumeration include Zuckerman, "Consideration of the History"; Margo Anderson, *The American Census: A Social History* (New Haven, CT: Yale University Press, 1988); Charles Eagles, *Democracy Delayed: Congressional Reapportionment and Urban–Rural Conflict in the 1920s* (Athens, GA: University of Georgia Press, 1990); M. L. Balinski and H. Peyton Young, *Fair Representation: Meeting the Ideal of One Man, One Vote* (Washington, DC: Brookings Institution Press, 2001); Charles A. Kromkowski, *Recreating the American Republic: Rules of Apportionment, Constitutional Change, and American Political Development, 1700–1870* (New York: Cambridge University Press, 2002); and Nicholas G. Napolio and Jeffery A. Jenkins, "Conflict over Congressional Reapportionment: The Deadlock of the 1920s," *Journal of Policy History* 35, no. 1 (January 2023): 91–117. Scholarship on attempts by the Trump administration to identify noncitizens via the census includes Pamela S. Karlan, "Reapportionment, Nonapportionment, and Recovering Some Lost History of One Person, One Vote," *William & Mary Law Review* 59, no. 5 (April 2018): 1921–60; Justin Levitt, "Citizenship and the Census," *Columbia Law Review* 119, no. 5 (June 2019): 1355–98; Thomas P. Wolf and Brianna Cea, "A Critical History of the United States Census and Citizenship Questions," *Georgetown Law Journal Online* 108, no. 1 (2019): 1–36; Amanda K. Baumle and Dudley L. Poston, "Apportionment of the US House of Representatives in 2020 under Alternative Immigration-Based Scenarios," *Population and Development Review* 45, no. 2 (June 2019): 379–400; Adriel I. Cepeda Derieux, Jonathan S. Topaz, and Dale E. Ho, "'Contrived': The Voting Rights Act Pretext for the Trump Administration's Failed Attempt to Add a Citizenship Question to the 2020 Census," *Yale Law and Policy Review* 38, no. 2 (Spring 2020): 322–59; and Teresa A. Sullivan, *Census 2020: Understanding the Issues* (Cham, Switzerland: Springer International, 2020).

NOTES TO PAGES 96–9   215

11. See *U.S. Census of Population and Housing, 1900: Vol. 1—Population of States and Territories* (Washington, DC: US Government Printing Office, 1901), 350. On Rhode Island's egregious malapportionment, see, among others, John D. Buenker, "The Politics of Resistance: The Rural-Based Yankee Republican Machines of Connecticut and Rhode Island," *New England Quarterly* 47, no. 2 (1974): 217; Argersinger, "Value of the Vote"; and Evelyn Savidge Sterne, *Ballots & Bibles: Ethnic Politics and the Catholic Church in Providence* (Ithaca, NY: Cornell University Press, 2004), 236–52.

12. Bone, "States Attempting to Comply" 401.

13. Bone, 388–89.

14. See, broadly, David O. Walter, "Reapportionment of State Legislative Districts," *Illinois Law Review* 37, no. 1 (1942): 20–42; Durfee, "Apportionment of Representation"; Bone, "States Attempting to Comply"; Commission on Intergovernmental Relations and Meyer Kestnbaum, "A Report to the President for Transmittal to the Congress" (Washington, DC, June 1955); Baker, "Reapportionment by Initiative"; Baker, *State Constitutions*; Ruth C. Silva, "One Man, One Vote and the Population Base," in *Representation and Misrepresentation: Legislative Reapportionment in Theory and Practice*, ed. C. Herman Pritchett and Robert A. Goldwin (Chicago: Rand McNally, 1968), 53–70; and McKay, *Reapportionment*.

15. Exceptions that do highlight the importance of state anti-alien schemes to the politics of reapportionment in US history include Silva, "One Man, One Vote"; Moss, "Democracy, Citizenship and Constitution-Making"; and Marta Tienda, "Demography and the Social Contract," *Demography* 39, no. 4 (November 2002): 587–616.

16. George Alan Tarr, "State Constitutional Politics: An Historical Perspective," in *Constitutional Politics in the States: Contemporary Controversies and Historical Patterns*, ed. George Alan Tarr (Westport, CT: Greenwood, 1996), 3–23; Todd Donovan and Shaun Bowler, "An Overview of Direct Democracy in the American States," in *Citizens as Legislators: Direct Democracy in the United States*, ed. Shaun Bowler, Todd Donovan, and Caroline J. Tolbert (Columbus: Ohio State University Press, 1998), 1–26; Thomas Goebel, *A Government by the People: Direct Democracy in America, 1890–1940* (Chapel Hill: University of North Carolina Press, 2003); Suzuki, "Important or Impotent?"

17. See Dinan, *American State Constitutional Tradition*, 8–10.

18. Dinan, "Explaining the Prevalence," 314.

19. The Massachusetts Senate was much smaller, comprising only forty members. While its basis of apportionment was also the legal voter population, its districts were apportioned and redistricted directly by the state legislature, as opposed to local and county officers. See, especially, Charles F. Gettemy, *An Historical Survey*, 122–23, 134. See also, broadly, Weaver, *Census System of Massachusetts*.

20. "City Apportionment Stirs Republicans," *Boston Globe*, August 1, 1916, 5.

21. On Lomasney, see, among others, Huthmacher, *Massachusetts People and Politics, 1919–1933*, 14–16; John D. Buenker, "The Mahatma and Progressive Reform: Martin Lomasney as Lawmaker, 1911–1917," *The New England Quarterly* 44, no. 3 (1971): 397–419; and Thomas H. O'Connor, *The Boston Irish: A Political History* (Boston: Back Bay Books, 1997), 122–26, 141–65.

22. See, among many other news articles, "City Apportionment Stirs Republicans," 5; "Brennan Says Hill Made Offer," *Boston Globe*, August 12, 1916, 1, 2; "Seek to Compel New Apportionment," *Boston Globe*, August 17, 1916, 6; "No Decision on Apportionment," *Boston Globe*, September 16, 1916, 9; and "To Meet for New Apportionment," *Boston Globe*, October 6, 1916, 12. On census figures for total and legal voter populations, see Charles Gettemy, *The Massachusetts Decennial Census, 1915* (Boston: Wright & Potter, State Printers, 1918), 46–47.

23. Legal scholar David O. Walter identifies the key cases as Attorney-General v. Suffolk County Apportionment Commissioners, 224 Mass. 598, 113 N.E. 581 (1916); Donovan v. Suffolk County Commissioners, 225 Mass. 55, 113 N.E. 740 (1916); and Brophy et al. v. Suffolk County Apportionment Commissioners, 225 Mass. 124, 113 N.E. 1040 (1916) in Walter, "Reapportionment," 27–28. On news coverage of this litigation, see, among others, "Apportionment a Poser for Court," *Boston Globe*, August 5, 1916, 8; "Brennan Says Hill Made Offer," 1; and "Apportionment to Full Bench," *Boston Globe*, September 19, 1916, 10.

24. "No Decision on Apportionment," 9.

25. "Brennan Says Hill Made Offer," 1–2.

216 NOTES TO PAGES 99–101

26. Brennan and his allies first sought to mitigate adverse court rulings by changing their apportionment schemes as minimally as possible. Their revised plans were also rejected by the court. Only their third plan was (narrowly) accepted as permissible. On news coverage, see, among others, "Again to Enjoin New Districts," *Boston Globe*, August 13, 1916, 13; "Seek to Compel New Apportionment," 6; and "Democrats Fight New Apportionment," *Boston Globe*, October 8, 1916, 18. See also Walter, "Reapportionment," 27–28.
27. Ward 2 possessed 41,904 residents, of whom 5,835 were legal voters. See "City Apportionment Stirs Republicans," 5; and Gettemy, *Massachusetts Decennial Census, 1915*, 46–47. Historian Russell Fehr suggests that figures for Lomasney's ward were likely deliberately inflated to aid in "his control of a narrow electorate in his ward, in which the Italian and Jewish residents did not vote and Irish from elsewhere (commonly called 'mattress voters') did." See Russell MacKenzie Fehr, "Anxious Electorate: City Politics in Mid-1920s America" (PhD diss., University of California, Riverside, 2016), 379n1412.
28. Among key works on the convention, see, especially, Augustus Peabody Loring, "A Short Account of the Massachusetts Constitutional Convention 1917–1919," *The New England Quarterly* 6, no. 1 (1933): 1–99; Henry L. Shattuck, "Martin Lomasney in the Constitutional Convention of 1917–1919," *Proceedings of the Massachusetts Historical Society* 71 (October 1953): 299–310; and John Allen Hague, "The Massachusetts Constitutional Convention: 1917–1919. A Study of Dogmatism in an Age of Transition," *The New England Quarterly* 27, no. 2 (1954): 147–67.
29. *Debates in the Massachusetts Constitutional Convention, 1917–1918*, vol. 3 (Boston: Wright and Potter, State Printers, 1920), 161.
30. *Debates in the Massachusetts Constitutional Convention, 1917–1918*, 3:161, 176.
31. *Debates in the Massachusetts Constitutional Convention, 1917–1918*, 3:177.
32. *Debates in the Massachusetts Constitutional Convention, 1917–1918*, 3:178.
33. On lengthy postwar political and legal battles over these provisions, see Bredbenner, "Duty to Defend?" 234–48.
34. Quotation in main text from *Debates in the Massachusetts Constitutional Convention, 1917–1918*, 3:182. On the future congressman's partisan affiliation, see "Underhill, Charles Lee," in *Biographical Directory of the United States Congress, 1774–Present*, https://bioguider-etro.congress.gov/Home/MemberDetails?memIndex=U000006.
35. Quotation in main text from *Debates in the Massachusetts Constitutional Convention, 1917–1918*, 3:176. Kinney was a longtime Boston GOP politician. See, for instance, "Republicans Undecided as to Campaigns," *Christian Science Monitor*, September 25, 1913, 5.
36. Quotation in main text from *Debates in the Massachusetts Constitutional Convention, 1917–1918*, 3:168. On Quinn's partisan affiliation, see *Number of Assessed Polls, Registered Voters, and Persons Who Voted in Each Voting Precinct at the State, City, and Town Elections, 1918* (Boston: Wright & Potter, State Printers, 1919), 347.
37. *Debates in the Massachusetts Constitutional Convention, 1917–1918*, 3:182.
38. In fact, by the mid-twentieth century, Massachusetts was often identified as having one of the more equitably apportioned legislatures in the country. See, especially, Bone, "States Attempting to Comply."
39. *Debates in the Massachusetts Constitutional Convention, 1917–1918*, 3:186.
40. See, among others, Tamara K. Hareven and Randolph Langenbach, *Amoskeag: Life and Work in an American Factory-City* (New York: Pantheon Books, 1978); and Mark Paul Richard, *Not a Catholic Nation: The Ku Klux Klan Confronts New England in the 1920s* (Amherst: University of Massachusetts Press, 2015), 58–69.
41. The length of time rural hamlets could send representatives was calculated on the basis of their population divided by six hundred (i.e., a town with three hundred inhabitants received representation for five of every ten years). See Norman Alexander, "New Hampshire—the State with the Largest Legislative Body," *National Municipal Review* 13, no. 5 (May 1924): 306–13; Durfee, "Apportionment of Representation," 1108; and Lawrence Friedman, *The New Hampshire State Constitution* (New York: Oxford University Press, 2015), 128–32, 144–45.
42. *State of New Hampshire Convention to Revise the Constitution June 5, 1918, January 13, 1920, January 28, 1921*, 3 vols. (Manchester, NH: John B. Clarke, 1921). See also, among others, Leonard D. White, "The New Hampshire Constitutional Convention," *Michigan Law Review* 19, no. 4 (1921): 383–94; Leonard D. White, "The Tenth New Hampshire Convention," *American Political Science Review* 15, no. 3 (August 1921): 400–403; Alexander, "New Hampshire"; and Friedman, *New Hampshire State Constitution*, 128–32.

NOTES TO PAGES 101–3   217

43. Quotation in main text from *State of New Hampshire Convention to Revise the Constitution*, vol. 2 (1920): 236. On Child's partisan affiliation, see *State of New Hampshire: Manual for the General Court, 1911 (No. 12)* (Concord, NH, 1911), 288.

44. Quotation in main text from *State of New Hampshire Convention to Revise the Constitution*, 2 (1920): 139. On Lyford's political power and partisan affiliation, see "James O. Lyford Declines Nomination to N.H. House," *Boston Globe*, September 17, 1924, 3.

45. Quotation in main text from *State of New Hampshire Convention to Revise the Constitution*, 2 (1920): 240. On Metcalf's background, see "Henry H. Metcalf, Editor, Dead at 90," *New York Times*, February 6, 1932, 17.

46. Quotation in main text from *State of New Hampshire Convention to Revise the Constitution*, 2 (1920): 252. On Doyle's background and partisan affiliation, see "Jeremiah J. Doyle: Ex-Nashua Mayor, Dean of N.H. Lawyers, at 87," *Boston Globe*, November 19, 1948, 6.

47. Quotation in main text from *State of New Hampshire Convention to Revise the Constitution*, 2 (1920): 267. On Cavanaugh's political career and background, see "Much-Needed Amendment in New Hampshire," *The Sacred Heart Review* 48, no. 20 (November 2, 1912): 308; and Harlan C. Pearson, *Biographical Sketches of the Members of the New Hampshire Constitutional Convention of 1912* (Concord, NH: T. J. Twomey, 1912), 33.

48. "Would Limit Number of Representatives," *Portsmouth Herald*, January 28, 1920, 3; "Will Submit 7 Amendments to the People," *Portsmouth Herald*, January 30, 1920, 3; "Discussion of Proposed Changes in the New Hampshire Constitution," *Portsmouth Herald*, October 18, 1920, 4.

49. The measure received 51,441 ayes and 29,639 nays. See *State of New Hampshire: Manual for the General Court, 1921 (No. 17)* (Concord, NH, 1921), 324. Writing in the pages of the *American Political Science Review*, scholar Leonard White viewed the defeat of a series of amendments that attracted broad popular support due to the state constitution's two-thirds majority ratification requirement to be "disastrous." See White, "Tenth New Hampshire Convention," 402.

50. Indiana retained an apportionment policy based on its male population into the early twentieth century. Efforts to replace it with a votes-cast policy were rejected by voters in 1921. On the amendment's defeat, see "Amendments and Purpose Set Forth by Bar Committee," *Indianapolis Star*, August 16, 1921, 16; and "Two Tax Amendments Are Defeated 4 to 1," *Indianapolis Star*, September 7, 1921, 1, 9. On the persistence of the state's male-only inhabitant apportionment policy into the mid- to late twentieth century, see Howard D. Hamilton, Joseph E. Beardsley, and Carleton C. Coats, "Legislative Reapportionment in Indiana: Some Observations and a Suggestion," *Notre Dame Law Review* 35, no. 3 (1960): 371–72; and William McLaughlin, *The Indiana State Constitution* (New York: Oxford University Press, 2011), 84–85. A votes-cast provision was included in a proposed new Illinois state constitution that was thoroughly rejected by voters in 1922. See *Journal of the Committee of the Whole of the Constitutional Convention, 1920–1922, of the State of Illinois. Convened at the Capitol in Springfield, January 6, 1920, and Adjourned Sine Die October 10, 1922* (Springfield: Illinois State Journal, 1922); *The Proposed New Constitution of Illinois, 1922 with Explanatory Notes and Address to the People: For Submission to the People at a Special Election on Tuesday, December 12, 1922*, 1922, 24–25; and Walter F. Dodd, "Illinois Rejects New Constitution," *American Political Science Review* 17, no. 1 (1923): 70–72.

51. See, broadly, Key, "Procedures in State Legislative"; Shull, "Legislative Apportionment"; Durfee, "Apportionment of Representation"; and Bone, "States Attempting to Comply."

52. Owing to strong factional politics within both major parties in early-twentieth-century Nebraska, delegates largely assembled into progressive and conservative blocs, irrespective of party. See, among others, Addison E. Sheldon, "The Nebraska Constitutional Convention, 1919–1920," *American Political Science Review* 15, no. 3 (1921): 391–400; Peter Longo and Robert Miewald, *The Nebraska State Constitution: A Reference Guide* (Westport, CT: Greenwood, 1993), 13–19.

53. Sheldon, "Nebraska Constitutional Convention"; Charles Kettleborough, "Amendments to State Constitutions 1919–21," *American Political Science Review* 16, no. 2 (May 1922): 257–59; Longo and Miewald, *Nebraska State Constitution*, 13–19; William G. Ross, *Forging New Freedoms: Nativism, Education, and the Constitution, 1917–1927* (Lincoln: University of Nebraska Press, 1994), 74–114.

54. See, especially, *Journal of the Nebraska Constitutional Convention: Convened in Lincoln December 2, 1919*, vol. 2 (Lincoln, NE: Kline Publishing, 1920), 2036–63.

55. *Journal of the Nebraska Constitutional Convention*, 2:2040–41, 2050–51. On Marvin's partisan affiliation, see "E. M. Marvin Dies; Longtime Sun Publisher," *Beatrice Daily Sun*, April 27, 1969, 1.

218   NOTES TO PAGES 103–4

56. *Journal of the Nebraska Constitutional Convention*, 2:2040.
57. G. W. Phillips, *Past and Present of Platte County, Nebraska: A Record of Settlement, Organization, Progress and Achievement Vol. II* (Chicago: S. J. Clarke Publishing, 1915), 43–44; Donald R. Hickey, Susan A. Wunder, and John R. Wunder, *Nebraska Moments*, 2nd ed. (Lincoln, NE: Bison Books, 2007), 202.
58. I. L. Albert, "English in Nebraska Schools," *North American Review* 216, no. 800 (July 1922): 143–44.
59. Delegate C. C. Flansburg informed the whole convention that it was Albert who suggested the reapportionment amendment in committee, which also contained provisions breaking up at-large citywide state legislative districts. Critics alleged that such districts empowered corrupt machine politicians from Omaha. See *Journal of the Nebraska Constitutional Convention*, 2:2040, 2051, 2053.
60. *Journal of the Nebraska Constitutional Convention*, 2:2051.
61. Quotation in main text from *Journal of the Nebraska Constitutional Convention*, 2:2042. On Oleson's longevity in Nebraska politics and stature within the state GOP, see "Big Fund for Education," *Omaha Daily Bee*, May 15, 1902, 3.
62. Unhappy with all the provisions that were combined as one proposed reapportionment amendment, Oleson actually voted against the measure that incorporated his anti-alien legislation at its final reading (2145–46). See also, broadly, *Journal of the Nebraska Constitutional Convention*, 2:2024, 2058, 2060–63, 2145–46.
63. Sheldon, "Nebraska Constitutional Convention"; Kettleborough, "Amendments to State Constitutions," 257–59; Longo and Miewald, *Nebraska State Constitution*, 13–19.
64. The anti-alien apportionment provisions received little press attention when adopted by the convention. See "Redistricting Measure Passes Second Reading," *Omaha Daily Bee*, March 12, 1920, 3; and "Redistricting Bill Favored by Convention," *Omaha Daily Bee*, March 11, 1920, 3. And they received virtually no mention in the actual election materials furnished by state authorities. On the sample ballot published by newspapers in advance of the election and in broader pamphlets distributed to the public, the measure (Amendment 5) was simply described as requiring single-member districts and broadly reforming the process of legislative apportionment. See "Sample Ballot," *Dakota County Herald*, September 16, 1920, 2; and "Proposed Amendments to the Constitution of the State of Nebraska as Adopted by the Constitutional Convention 1919–20," B2F6: "Research Materials and Publications, Nebraska Government, 1914–1934," Box 2, Leon Aylsworth Papers RG 12-19-10, Lincoln: University of Nebraska, Lincoln Library, Archives and Special Collections—Library Depository Retrieval Facility. On election results, see "New Laws Approved by Voters," *Omaha Daily Bee*, September 23, 1920, 1; "Proposed Constitutional Amendments Are Carried," *North Platte Semi-Weekly Tribune*, September 24, 1920, 5; Sheldon, "Nebraska Constitutional Convention," 398–99; and Deskins, Walton, and Puckett, *Presidential Elections, 1789–2008*, 320.
65. On these developments, see, among others, Zechariah Chafee, "Congressional Reapportionment," *Harvard Law Review* 42, no. 8 (June 1929): 1015–47; Hubert Searcy, "Problems of Congressional Reapportionment," *The Southwestern Social Science Quarterly* 16, no. 1 (June 1935): 58–68; Louis Charles Boochever, "A Study of the Factors Involved in the Passage of the 1929 Bill for Reapportionment of the House of Representatives" (master's thesis, Cornell University, 1942); Orville J. Sweeting, "John Q. Tilson and the Reapportionment Act of 1929," *Western Political Quarterly* 9, no. 2 (June 1956): 434–53; Anderson, *American Census*; Eagles, *Democracy Delayed*; Balinski and Young, *Fair Representation*; Kromkowski, *Recreating the American Republic*; and Napolio and Jenkins, "Conflict over Congressional Reapportionment."
66. See, especially, Boochever, "Study of the Factors"; and Napolio and Jenkins, "Conflict over Congressional Reapportionment."
67. This bill was sponsored by outgoing Upstate New York representative William Hill. Though New York as a whole stood to gain from the continued inclusion of noncitizens in federal reapportionment policy, the GOP congressman allied with representatives from states that were slated to lose representation. See "Bill to Keep Aliens out of Apportionment," *San Francisco Chronicle*, January 23, 1921, 3; and "House of Representatives Apportionment," *Wall Street Journal*, January 24, 1921, 7.
68. On the history of this lengthy congressional gridlock, see, particularly, Eagles, *Democracy Delayed*, 32–84. On factional, regional, and partisan voting patterns, see, especially, Napolio and Jenkins, "Conflict over Congressional Reapportionment."

NOTES TO PAGES 104–7   219

69. "Census Row on Alien Ban," *Los Angeles Times*, May 26, 1929, 1.
70. See Balinski and Young, *Fair Representation*, 57. Representative (and future Speaker of the House) William Bankhead, also of Alabama, likewise contended that undocumented immigrants (whom he vastly overestimated to number two to three million) should be counted out of the population. See Sweeting, "John Q. Tilson," 444.
71. "Redistricting Foes Prepare," *Los Angeles Times*, November 20, 1930, 3. Scholar Ira Katznelson describes Rankin as "one of the chamber's most unashamed racists," even for his era, and "something of a thug, openly anti-black, anti-Jewish, and anti-Catholic." See Katznelson, *When Affirmative Action*, 123.
72. "Klan Issue Raised on Apportionment," *New York Times*, December 16, 1928, 19.
73. "Curb on Aliens Urged by Republican Women," *New York Times*, January 9, 1929, 63.
74. See, for instance, "Klan Issue Raised on Apportionment," 19; "Exclusion of Alien in Census Urged to Boost Prohibition," *Washington Post*, February 4, 1929, 16; and "Cannon Urges Plan for Census Change," *Washington Post*, July 8, 1930, 1, 3.
75. "Cannon Urges Plan," 1.
76. "Klan Issue Raised," 19.
77. "J. M. Beck Flays Methodist Plan to Reapportion," *Chicago Daily Tribune*, November 28, 1930, 18.
78. Arthur Sears Henning, "Reapportioning Bill Debate to Bare Inequities," *Chicago Daily Tribune*, December 31, 1928, 1–2.
79. Indeed, as historian Charles Eagles highlights, Vandenberg's allies often attacked their opponents' nativism, defended inclusion in apportionment provisions as a right of all residents, and warned that if noncitizens were excluded, "others might try to bar additional groups" (77). See, especially, Eagles, *Democracy Delayed*, 77–78.
80. "Klan Issue Raised," 19.
81. "Alien Amendment before Committee," *Washington Post*, January 15, 1931, 3.
82. The NAACP, Tinkham, and allied politicians sought to utilize the results of the 1920 census to advance the cause of Black voting rights long before Vandenberg's legislation was debated in 1929. As early as 1920 and 1921, the NAACP and Tinkham had collaborated and lobbied lawmakers to use the results of the enumeration to enforce the Fourteenth Amendment's penalty provisions. See, for instance, "NAACP on Reapportionment Legislation, December 17, 1920–July 8, 1921," Papers of the NAACP, Part 11: Special Subject Files, 1912–1939, Series B: Harding, Warren G. through YWCA, Group I, Series C. See also, on Tinkham's decade-long efforts to raise the issue in the House, Eagles, *Democracy Delayed*, 34–37, 47–48, 52, 63, 71, 80.
83. See, especially, Sweeting, "John Q. Tilson"; Anderson, *The American Census*, 152–56; Eagles, *Democracy Delayed*, 63–84; and Balinski and Young, *Fair Representation*, 46–59.
84. For news coverage of these efforts, see "Redistricting Foes Prepare," 3; "J. M. Beck Flays Methodist Plan to Reapportion," 18; Kelly Miller, "Reapportionment," *New York Amsterdam News*, December 3, 1930, 20; Arthur Crawford, "Negro Vote Hits Plans of South to Reapportion," *Chicago Daily Tribune*, December 21, 1930, 4; "Capper Opposes Counting Aliens," *Los Angeles Times*, December 30, 1930, 1; "Alien Amendment before Committee," 3; "Alien Count Bill Reported," *New York Times*, February 18, 1931, 5; and "The Reapportionment Vote," *Los Angeles Times*, April 8, 1931, A4.
85. Crawford, "Negro Vote Hits Plans," 4.
86. Political scientists Nicholas G. Napolio and Jeffrey Jenkins have recently argued in their analysis of congressional voting patterns on 1920s reapportionment legislation that "although the rhetorical debates on the House floor in the 1920s were wide-ranging—with concerns about economy, demography, and political power—ultimately what mattered most on average for individual members' votes to reapportion was their own political self-interest. Those from states slated to lose seats—and some members from states that could not trust their state legislatures to redistrict in their favor—were unlikely to support reapportionment." See Napolio and Jenkins, "Conflict over Congressional Reapportionment," 112. See also, more broadly, Searcy, "Problems of Congressional Reapportionment"; Boochever, "Study of the Factors"; Sweeting, "John Q. Tilson"; Anderson, *American Census*, 152–56; Eagles, *Democracy Delayed*, 63–115; and Balinski and Young, *Fair Representation*, 46–59.
87. See, for instance, "Redistricting Foes Prepare," 3.
88. Quotation in main text from Sweeting, "John Q. Tilson," 450. Sweeting's fawning hagiography was largely drawn from his personal interactions with Tilson (434).

220 NOTES TO PAGES 107-9

89. Arthur Crawford, "House Votes to Reapportion Seats, 272–105," *Chicago Daily Tribune*, June 7, 1929, 1; "Census Bill Passed; Amendments Killed," *New York Times*, June 7, 1929, 1, 8.

90. Miller, "Reapportionment," 20. On Miller's critique of the 1920 count, see Kelly Miller, "Enumeration Errors in Negro Population," *The Scientific Monthly* 14, no. 2 (February 1922): 168–77. Two months later, the Census Bureau fired back at Miller in the same publication. See Le Verne Beales, "The Negro Enumeration of 1920: A Reply to Dr. Kelly Miller," *The Scientific Monthly* 14, no. 4 (April 1922): 352–60. On Miller's decades-long battles against Census Bureau undercounts of African Americans, see, especially, Dan Bouk, *Democracy's Data: The Hidden Stories in the U.S. Census and How to Read Them* (New York: Farrar, Straus and Giroux, 2022). More broadly, on Miller's prolific scholarly and popular writings, see, especially, Sylvie Coulibaly, "Kelly Miller, 1895–1939: Portrait of an African American Intellectual" (PhD diss., Emory University, 2006).

91. Miller, "Reapportionment," 20.

92. See "House Seats Bill Bars Alien Count," *New York Times*, March 13, 1940, 14; "House for Revision of Apportionment," *New York Times*, April 12, 1940, 14; and "House Seats Urged on Basis of Votes Cast," *The Washington Post*, January 20, 1941, 27. Scholars who note the 1940 debate include Howard A. Scarrow, "One Voter, One Vote: The Apportionment of Congressional Seats Reconsidered," *Polity* 22, no. 2 (Winter 1989): 253–68; Tienda, "Demography," 594–95; and Sarah K. Cowan, "Periodic Discordance between Vote Equality and Representational Equality in the United States," *Sociological Science* 2 (August 2015): 442–53.

93. Quotation in main text from "Klan Issue Raised on Apportionment," 19. Eagles also highlights this "audacious" exchange. See Eagles, *Democracy Delayed*, 70. By then, La Guardia was already a well-known advocate of immigrant rights. See, among others, Mason B. Williams, *City of Ambition: FDR, La Guardia, and the Making of Modern New York* (New York: W. W. Norton, 2013), 54–62.

94. Quotation in main text from "Asks New Apportionment," *New York Times*, February 10, 1929, 24. On Celler's subsequent, more famous, role as a major proponent and author of federal immigration policy reforms of the 1950s and 1960s, see Ngai, *Impossible Subjects*, 227–64; Battisti, *Whom We Shall Welcome*; and Marinari, *Unwanted*.

95. In 1931, the GOP-controlled legislature even tried to adopt reapportionment legislation (for the state's congressional delegation) via a concurrent resolution—as opposed to a statutory act—in an end run around Roosevelt's impending veto. This scheme, which embraced a proto-independent state legislature theory, ultimately failed when the US Supreme Court ruled it unconstitutional the following year. See "Redistricting Plan Fails in High Court," *New York Times*, December 31, 1931, 3; "New York Reapportionment Appeal," *Wall Street Journal*, February 27, 1932, 7; and "3 Redistricting Acts Held Void by High Court," *New York Herald Tribune*, April 12, 1932, 6. On electoral results, see Sean J. Savage, *Roosevelt: The Party Leader, 1932-1945* (Lexington: University Press of Kentucky, 2014), 7–10; and Dubin, *Party Affiliations*, 137.

96. As political scientist Sean Savage emphasizes, Tammany Hall–related scandals in New York City inhibited broader Democratic Party breakthroughs in Upstate New York even as Roosevelt carried the state by huge margins in 1930. See Savage, *Roosevelt*, 7–13. On electoral results, see Dubin, *Party Affiliations*, 137.

97. "Roosevelt's Lead in State 596,996," *New York Times*, December 10, 1932, 11; Savage, *Roosevelt*, 12–13; Dubin, *Party Affiliations*, 137.

98. On these dynamics, see, among others, Warren Moscow, *Politics in the Empire State* (New York: Alfred A. Knopf, 1948), 134–36; Erie, *Rainbow's End*, 114–15, 133, 138; Chris McNickle, *To Be Mayor of New York: Ethnic Politics in the City* (New York: Columbia University Press, 1993), 42–43; Williams, *City of Ambition*, 121–32; and Savage, *Roosevelt*, 68–75. On their impact on reapportionment disputes, in particular, see, especially, Bone, "States Attempting to Comply," 401–2; Silva, "Population Base for Apportionment," 11–12; and Conrad P. Rutkowski, "State Politics and Apportionment: The Case of New York" (PhD diss., Fordham University, 1971), 27.

99. "State Democrats Seek Firmer Hold," *New York Times*, November 13, 1934, 5.

100. James A. Hagerty, "State Ticket Wins," *New York Times*, November 7, 1934, 1; "Full Control of Legislature Enables Democrats to Enact Sweeping State Program," *New York Herald Tribune*, November 8, 1934, 10; Dubin, *Party Affiliations*, 137.

NOTES TO PAGES 110–11 221

101. See, among other news accounts, "Text of Governor Lehman's Message Containing Recommendations for Legislature," *New York Herald Tribune*, January 3, 1935, 8; James A. Hagerty, "Tammany Is Facing Shrinkage of Power," *New York Times*, March 10, 1935, E11; Hickman Powell, "Redistricting Bill Presented," *New York Herald Tribune*, March 14, 1935, 2; "Reapportionment," *New York Times*, March 15, 1935, 20; Hickman Powell, "Redistricting Bill Defeated by Assembly," *New York Herald Tribune*, March 22, 1935, 1, 4; "Finish Fight Urged on Redistricting," *New York Times*, March 31, 1935, 13; and "The Text of the Address by Governor Lehman Demanding Reapportionment," *New York Times*, April 8, 1935, 15. See also Bone, "States Attempting to Comply," 401–2; and Silva, "Apportionment of the New York Assembly," 26–27.

102. Though enumerators asked white, male immigrants if they had been naturalized, they did not ask nonwhite populations about their citizenship status. See, especially, Silva, "Population Base for Apportionment," 11–15. See also "Roosevelt Helps Reapportionment," *New York Times*, March 2, 1934, 1.

103. For press coverage, see "Roosevelt Helps Reapportionment," 1; "Roosevelt Aids Anti-Tammany Chief in Bronx," *Chicago Tribune*, March 3, 1934, 22; "State Democrats Seek Firmer Hold," 5; "Roosevelt Move Peril to Tammany," *New York Times*, March 3, 1934, 7; and "Finish Fight Urged on Redistricting," 13. Mid-century scholars and commissions that explored these efforts include Bone, "States Attempting to Comply," 401–2; Advisory Commission on Intergovernmental Relations, "A Commission Report: Apportionment of State Legislatures" (Washington, DC, December 1962), 20–21; and Silva, "Population Base for Apportionment," 11–15.

104. Quotation in main text from "Roosevelt Aids Anti-Tammany Chief in Bronx," 22. See also "Roosevelt Helps Reapportionment," 1. On the close relationship and political allegiances between Roosevelt and Flynn, see McNickle, *To Be Mayor*, 42–44; and Savage, *Roosevelt*, 68–75.

105. "Finish Fight Urged," 13; "Republican Explains Redistricting Fight," *New York Times*, March 24, 1935, N2.

106. Bone, "States Attempting to Comply," 401.

107. On news coverage of (ultimately overcome) friction among Republicans, see "Dewey Obtains Agreement on Redistricting: Sees Republican Chiefs on Legislative Revision," *New York Herald Tribune*, March 6, 1943, 10; "Redistricting Up in Albany: Republican Legislators Split on Dewey-Approved Plan for Reapportionment," *Baltimore Sun*, March 9, 1943, 15; and "Redistricting Upheld; City Gains Seats," *New York Herald Tribune*, November 19, 1943, 1, 18. For news coverage of the state government's negotiation with Census Bureau officials and subsequent use of federal citizenship data from the 1940 enumeration, see, among others, "Asks $20,000 for State Census," *New York Times*, March 15, 1940, 16; "State to Pay for Census Data," *New York Herald Tribune*, August 29, 1941, 17; and "Legislature Hopes to Act on Apportionment Plan," *New York Herald Tribune*, January 13, 1942, 10. More broadly, see Bone, "States Attempting to Comply," 401–2; Silva, "Population Base for Apportionment," 13–15; Rutkowski, "State Politics and Apportionment," 27; and Dubin, *Party Affiliations*, 137.

108. Good government reports included Baker, *State Constitutions*; Advisory Commission on Intergovernmental Relations, "Commission Report"; and David Wells, "Legislative Representation in New York State: A Discussion of Inequitable Representation of the Citizens of New York in the State Legislature and Congress" (New York: International Ladies' Garment Workers' Union, 1963). For contemporary scholarship on this reapportionment and redistricting reform movement, which often indirectly encouraged and/or directly intervened in it, see, among others, "Legislative Reapportionment," *Law and Contemporary Problems* 17, no. 2 (Spring 1952): 253–470; Baker, "Reapportionment by Initiative in Oregon"; "Symposium: Baker v. Carr," *Yale Law Journal* 72, no. 1 (November 1962): 7–106; Malcolm Jewell, ed., *The Politics of Reapportionment* (New York: Transaction Publishers, 1962); Silva, "Legislative Representation"; and McKay, *Reapportionment*.

109. Commission on Intergovernmental Relations and Kestnbaum, "A Report to the President for Transmittal to the Congress," ii–ix, 38–42. On the role of the Kestnbaum Commission and its successor, see Deil S. Wright, "The Advisory Commission on Intergovernmental Relations: Unique Features and Policy Orientation," *Public Administration Review* 25, no. 3 (September 1965): 196–97.

222   NOTES TO PAGES 112–14

110. See, broadly, Commission on Intergovernmental Relations and Kestnbaum, "Report to the President," 38–42; Baker, *State Constitutions*; Advisory Commission on Intergovernmental Relations, "Commission Report"; Wells, "Legislative Representation"; and McKay, *Reapportionment*.
111. Roger K. Newman, *Hugo Black: A Biography* (New York: Pantheon Books, 1994), 265, 517–20.
112. See, especially, McKay, *Reapportionment*, 59–146.
113. David Lublin and D. Stephen Voss, "Racial Redistricting and Realignment in Southern State Legislatures," *American Journal of Political Science* 44, no. 4 (October 2000): 792–810; Stephen Ansolabehere and James M. Snyder Jr., "Reapportionment and Party Realignment in the American States," *University of Pennsylvania Law Review* 153, no. 1 (November 2004): 433–58; Gary Miller and Norman Schofield, "The Transformation of the Republican and Democratic Party Coalitions in the US," *Perspectives on Politics* 6, no. 3 (September 2008): 433–50; Joseph Aistrup, *The Southern Strategy Revisited: Republican Top-Down Advancement in the South* (Lexington: University Press of Kentucky, 2015).
114. Alden Whitman, "For 16 Years, Warren Saw the Constitution as Protector of Rights and Equality," *New York Times*, July 10, 1974, 24.
115. Burns v. Richardson, 384 U.S. 73, 74 (1966).
116. Burns v. Richardson, 92. See also Robert Horwitz, "Reapportionment in the State of Hawaii—Considerations on the Reynolds Decision," in *Representation and Misrepresentation: Legislative Reapportionment in Theory and Practice*, ed. C. Herman Pritchett and Robert A Goldwin (Chicago: Rand McNally, 1968), 21–52.
117. Opinion of the Justices to the Senate, No. 353 (Massachusetts Supreme Judicial Court, 1967).
118. The Massachusetts Supreme Judicial Court offered this 1967 opinion in response to a political dispute. The state's Republican governor and attorney general both sought to retain the legal voter apportionment basis. Their opponents in the legislature denied its (federal) constitutionality following the recent US Supreme Court rulings. See Joseph Harvey, "2d Redistricting Suit Filed by Bottomly, Wife," *Boston Globe*, April 4, 1967, 1, 4; Cornelius Noonan, "House Votes to Revise Congressional and Legislative Districts," *Boston Globe*, July 14, 1967, 1, 6; and "Redistricting by the Book," *Boston Globe*, November 2, 1967, 18. The 1970 reapportionment amendment—ratified by voters—both did away with multimember districts and inscribed the new total population basis into the Massachusetts constitution. See "What Is a Referendum?" *Boston Globe*, October 20, 1970, A8; "Mass. Voters Also Deciding on 5 Referendum Questions," *Boston Globe*, November 2, 1970, 5; and "Final Nov. 3 Vote Recorded on 5 Referenda Questions," *Boston Globe*, December 4, 1970, 3. See also Friedman and Thody, *Massachusetts State Constitution*, 208–10.
119. See "Series B 237-278: Citizenship-Citizenship Status of the Population" in United States, *Historical Statistics of the United States, 1789-1945; a Supplement to the Statistical Abstract of the United States, Prepared with the Cooperation of the Social Science Research Council* (Washington, DC: US Government Printing Office, 1949), B32.
120. Advisory Commission on Intergovernmental Relations, "Commission Report," 30.
121. Baker, *State Constitutions*, 6.
122. In fact, as political scientist Conrad Rutkowski underscores, Silva's work helped launch reapportionment conflicts in New York at the dawn of the 1960s. In particular, he characterizes her official report to the state government on the topic as a "relatively complete, objective, and dispassionate account of the history and nature of apportionment practices within the state." He also emphasizes that "it was simultaneously a highly explosive political document" (85). See Rutkowski, "State Politics and Apportionment," 82–89, 139–40. Indeed, the *New York Times* reported in May 1962 that her findings were "long-suppressed" by state lawmakers seeking to stymie reapportionment reform. Conversely, her work was viewed as so valuable by reform proponents, like radio station WMCA leadership, that they pushed successfully for the report's public revelation amid litigation with the state government. See "Why Wait for the Courts?" *New York Times*, May 14, 1962, 28.
123. Among her voluminous writings in the 1960s on reapportionment reform in New York, see, especially, Ruth C. Silva, "Apportionment of the New York State Legislature," *American Political Science Review* 55, no. 4 (1961): 870–81; Silva, "Legislative Representation"; Silva, "Apportionment of the New York Assembly"; Silva, "Population Base for Apportionment"; Silva, "Reapportionment and Redistricting"; and Silva, "One Man, One Vote." Throughout her career, Silva never hesitated to combine her scholarly expertise with (bipartisan) policy

NOTES TO PAGES 114–16   223

advice and advocacy. She had previously advised progressive Democratic senator Paul Douglas of Illinois in the 1950s. But Silva was personally a Republican, who in 1964 staunchly opposed proposals to repeal the Electoral College system, arguing that it generally helped the GOP and her adopted state of Pennsylvania. See George Draut, "The Electoral College," *The Progress* [Clearfield, PA], November 25, 1964, 4; and Wolfgang Saxon, "Ruth Silva, 74, Political Scientist Who Advised on the Presidency," *New York Times*, April 6, 1995, D31.

124. Silva, "Population Base for Apportionment," 17.

125. To emphasize this fact, Silva repeated this exact point in the text and notes of her *American Political Science Review* article no fewer than three times. See Silva, "Apportionment of the New York State Legislature," quotation from 880; see also 870 (b), 876 (note to Table VIII). On broader efforts by reformers to link citizenship rights with civil rights in an era when relatively low numbers of noncitizens were residing in the country, see Varsanyi, "Rise and Fall," 125.

126. Since 1960, a citizenship question has only been asked of randomized respondents who fill out a longer-form survey. Its removal, as historian Margo Anderson describes, was part of a broader reform by the Census Bureau to ask only the most fundamental identification questions on the main form. See Anderson, *American Census*, 201 (and, broadly, 191–212).

127. Rutkowski, "State Politics and Apportionment," 139–43; Silva, "Population Base for Apportionment," 13–14.

128. WMCA, Inc. v. Lomenzo, 377 U.S. 633 (1964). McKay's appendix section enumerates the many court cases over reapportionment in New York during the 1960s. See McKay, *Reapportionment*, 380–90. McKay was himself deeply involved in those Empire State reapportionment debates. See Rutkowski, "State Politics and Apportionment," 408–11.

129. For a brief summary of this constitutional history, see Peter J. Galie and Christopher Bopst, *The New York State Constitution*, 2nd ed. (New York: Oxford University Press, 2012), 35–37. More broadly, see Henrik N. Dullea, *Charter Revision in the Empire State: The Politics of New York's 1967 Constitutional Convention* (New York: SUNY Press, 1997), 392.

130. "Odd Road to a Good End," *New York Times*, September 2, 1969, 46.

131. The amendment was ratified with 2,229,299 yeas against only 960,452 nays. See Department of State, "Votes Cast for and against Proposed Constitutional Conventions and also Proposed Constitutional Amendments," Excerpted from the *Manual for the Use of the Legislature of the State of New York* (Albany, NY, 2019): https://history.nycourts.gov/wp-content/uploads/2019/01/Publications_Votes-Cast-Conventions-Amendments-compressed.pdf. See also Clayton Knowles, "All 4 Amendments on the Ballot Appear Headed for Approval," *New York Times*, November 5, 1969, 34.

132. Arizona's "ballots-cast" basis, Tennessee's "qualified voter" standard, and North Carolina's explicit anti-alien clause were all repealed in the late 1960s and early 1970s following the US Supreme Court's redistricting rulings. See States' Attorneys General Brief in Evenwel v. Abbott, 3–5; and see Brennan Center Brief in Evenwel v. Abbott, 23nn7–8.

133. The Texas Senate's "qualified voter" apportionment basis was deemed unconstitutional by the state attorney general, while Maine and Nebraska's anti-alien clauses are no longer used. See States' Attorneys General Brief in Evenwel v. Abbott, 9n29, App. 4–5; and Brief for Appellees (State of Texas) in Evenwel v. Abbott, 23–24n7.

134. With little fanfare, middle-class Oregonian civic associations pushed to rescind the state's "archaic reference to 'white' population" in its apportionment clause amid a broader effort to reform the state legislature in 1952. See Baker, "Reapportionment by Initiative," 510. The California constitution's similarly racist and nativist apportionment clause, which specifically excluded immigrants "ineligible to citizenship," also became inoperative that same year owing to the passage of the federal Immigration and Nationality (McCarran–Walter) Act of 1952, which repealed explicit naturalization bans on the basis of race. On previous efforts to implement this policy in California, see "Chinese, Japanese, Hindoos in State Number 100,933," *San Francisco Chronicle*, January 23, 1921, C7; and "Reapportionment Vote," A4.

135. I am indebted to one of Oxford University Press's anonymous outside readers of the manuscript for clarifying this point about the unique utility of this chapter as the exception that proves the broader rule of *Disparate Regimes*.

224 NOTES TO PAGES 119-20

Chapter 5

1. *In re* Theresa Oglou, Petition Number 42709, November 2, 1940, Hearing before Designated Naturalization Examiner Stanley B. Johnson, Contested Naturalization and Repatriation Case Files, 1924–1992, US District Court for the Southern (San Francisco) Division of the Northern District of California, Box 4, RG 21, NARA–Pacific (San Bruno).
2. *In re* Theresa Oglou, P.N. 42709, November 2, 1940, Hearing before Stanley B. Johnson: 5–6, 29, Stanley B. Johnson, Report and Recommendation of Designated Naturalization Examiner, I. M. Peckham, Exceptions to Report and Recommendation of Naturalization Examiner: 4–5, Contested Naturalization and Repatriation Case Files, 1924–1992, SF, Box 4, RG 21, NARA–Pacific (San Bruno).
3. See, broadly, *In re* Theresa Oglou, P.N. 42709, November 2, 1940, Hearing before Stanley B. Johnson, Contested Naturalization and Repatriation Case Files, 1924–1992, SF, Box 4, RG 21, NARA–Pacific (San Bruno).
4. Oglou was careful to deny fearing the loss of her job when petitioning for citizenship, avoiding inadvertently confessing to fraudulent intent. She also withstood hostile questioning when Johnson began reading from a letter she had written about him in court. Oglou took pains to defuse the situation, emphasizing that she did not intend to "harm[]" Johnson (40). But she made clear that Johnson was "rather antagonistic against [her] and thought [he] would not give [her] a fair chance" (36). See *In re* Theresa Oglou, P.N. 42709, November 2, 1940, Hearing before Stanley B. Johnson: 36–41, Contested Naturalization and Repatriation Case Files, 1924–1992, SF, Box 4, RG 21, NARA–Pacific (San Bruno).
5. Her attorney, I. M. Peckham, patronized Oglou as a "girl" with "an abnormally poor memory." See *In re* Theresa Oglou, P.N. 42709, I. M. Peckham, Exceptions to Report and Recommendation of Naturalization Examiner: 3, Contested Naturalization and Repatriation Case Files, 1924–1992, SF, Box 4, RG 21, NARA–Pacific (San Bruno).
6. *In re* Theresa Oglou, P.N. 42709, December 24, 1940, Judge Martin Walsh, Opinion Order, Contested Naturalization and Repatriation Case Files, 1924–1992, SF, Box 4, RG 21, NARA–Pacific (San Bruno).
7. Debates over proposed and adopted federal blue-collar nativist hiring measures during the mid- to late New Deal era rank among the most studied de jure anti-alien public and publicly funded employment policies in US history. See, among others, Mary Anne Thatcher, *Immigrants and the 1930s: Ethnicity and Alienage in Depression and On-coming War* (New York: Garland, 1990); Fox, *Three Worlds of Relief*; and Bavery, *Bootlegged Aliens*. On the continued proliferation and strengthening of state anti-alien public and publicly funded employment laws in the quarter century after the Supreme Court's rulings on noncitizens' employment rights in 1915, see, among others, Harold Fields, "Where Shall the Alien Work?" *Social Forces* 12, no. 2 (1933): 213–21; and Chester Garfield Vernier, *American Family Laws: A Comparative Study of the Family Law of the Forty-Eight American States, Alaska, the District of Columbia, and Hawaii (to Jan. 1, 1937)* (Stanford, CA: Stanford University Press, 1938). On the disproportionate harm wrought by these laws on the lives and livelihoods of nonwhite immigrants, see, among others, Konvitz, *Alien and the Asiatic*; Sánchez, *Becoming Mexican American*, 210–11; Pitti, *Devil in Silicon Valley*, 82–87; Zaragosa Vargas, *Labor Rights Are Civil Rights: Mexican American Workers in Twentieth-Century America* (Princeton, NJ: Princeton University Press, 2013), 46; and Chin, "Nation of White Immigrants."
8. Though the "learned professions" of "medicine, law, and theology" had predated the founding of the American republic, economists Marc T. Law and Sukkoo Kim argue that it was in "the late nineteenth and the early twentieth centuries" that "modern-day professions" were born (723). See Marc T. Law and Sukkoo Kim, "Specialization and Regulation: The Rise of Professionals and the Emergence of Occupational Licensing Regulation," *Journal of Economic History* 65, no. 3 (September 2005): 723–56. On the rise of state boards of medicine as a marker of the field's broader professionalization, see Paul Starr, *The Social Transformation of American Medicine: The Rise of a Sovereign Profession and the Making of a Vast Industry* (New York: Basic Books, 1982); and Brenton D. Peterson, Sonal S. Pandya, and David Leblang, "Doctors with Borders: Occupational Licensing as an Implicit Barrier to High Skill Migration," *Public Choice* 160 (July 2014): 45–63. As legal scholar Richard Abel demonstrates, state governments often made bar associations de facto licensing agencies in the early to mid-twentieth century by "requir[ing] practitioners to join" them (46). See, more broadly, Richard Abel, *American Lawyers* (New York: Oxford University Press, 1989), 40–73. While scholars continue to

NOTES TO PAGES 120–1   225

disagree over which fields became professions (and when), sociologist Tracey Adams has persuasively argued that we should instead focus on "how professions are defined and structured in specific social-historical contexts" (66). See Tracey L. Adams, "Profession: A Useful Concept for Sociological Analysis?" *Canadian Review of Sociology/Revue canadienne de sociologie* 47, no. 1 (February 2010): 49–70. More broadly, on the development of professions and an ethos of professionalism, see, especially, Burton J. Bledstein, *Culture of Professionalism: The Middle Class and the Development of Higher Education in America* (New York: W. W. Norton, 1978); and Tracey L. Adams, *Regulating Professions: The Emergence of Professional Self-Regulation in Four Canadian Provinces* (Toronto, ON: University of Toronto Press, 2018).

9. As Law and Kim emphasize, libertarian economists Milton Friedman and Simon Kuznets largely inaugurated modern debates within economics on regulatory capture in their famous 1945 text, "Income from Independent Professional Practice." See Law and Kim, "Specialization and Regulation," 724. Others who have followed, adapted, and expanded their framework include Walter Gellhorn, "The Abuse of Occupational Licensing," *University of Chicago Law Review* 44, no. 1 (Autumn 1976): 6–27; Hayne E. Leland, "Quacks, Lemons, and Licensing: A Theory of Minimum Quality Standards," *Journal of Political Economy* 87, no. 6 (December 1979): 1328–46; and Peterson, Pandya, and Leblang, "Doctors with Borders." On the widespread exclusion of Jewish and Black applicants from early-twentieth-century medical schools, see Edward C. Halperin, "The Jewish Problem in U.S. Medical Education, 1920–1955," *Journal of the History of Medicine and Allied Sciences* 56, no. 2 (April 2001): 140–67; Michael H. Rubin, "Immigration, Quotas, and Its Impact on Medical Education" (master's thesis, Wake Forest University, 2013); and Kendall M. Campbell et al., "Projected Estimates of African American Medical Graduates of Closed Historically Black Medical Schools," *JAMA Network Open* 3, no. 8 (2020): 1–10. On the displacement of female midwives in obstetrics and gynecology by mostly male doctors, see Frances E. Kobrin, "The American Midwife Controversy: A Crisis of Professionalization," in *The Medicalization of Obstetrics: Personnel, Practice, and Instruments*, ed. Philip K. Wilson, vol. 2, *Childbirth: Changing Ideas and Practices in Britain and America, 1600 to the Present* (New York: Garland, 1996), 96–109; Charles R. King, "The New York Maternal Mortality Study: A Conflict of Professionalization," in *Medicalization of Obstetrics*, vol. 2, 110–36; Anne Witz, "Patriarchy and the Professions: The Gendered Politics of Occupational Closure," *Sociology* 24, no. 4 (November 1990): 675–90; and Alice Kessler-Harris, *Out to Work: A History of Wage-Earning Women in the United States* (New York: Oxford University Press, 2003), 117.

10. Halperin, "Jewish Problem"; Rubin, "Immigration, Quotas"; see also, broadly, Jerome Karabel, *The Chosen: The Hidden History of Admission and Exclusion at Harvard, Yale, and Princeton* (Boston: Houghton Mifflin, 2005).

11. Reciprocal recognition restrictions were (and are) particularly common in the field of medicine. See Irene Butter and Rebecca G. Sweet, "Licensure of Foreign Medical Graduates: An Historical Perspective," *The Milbank Memorial Fund Quarterly. Health and Society* 55, no. 2 (Spring 1977): 315–40; and Peterson, Pandya, and Leblang, "Doctors with Borders."

12. See, especially, Chapter 4, "The State and Immigrant Professionals: Restrictions on High-End Alien Workers," in Filindra, "E Pluribus Unum?" 128–52. Professor Irene Bloemraad generously shared with me her unpublished database of state citizenship requirements for licensure (which she draws from early to mid-twentieth-century scholarship on the topic). Though I have not reproduced those findings, they were very helpful in framing my initial research and identifying potential case studies. See also Bloemraad, "Citizenship Lessons." On the importance of state anti-alien restrictions in broader US immigration historiography, see also Linda C. Noel, "New Paths in Immigration History," *Journal of American Ethnic History* 37, no. 3 (Spring 2018): 55–60; Jacobson and Tichenor, "States of Immigration"; and Tirres, "Exclusion from Within."

13. Konvitz, *Alien and the Asiatic*, 172, 208–9.

14. Since the Progressive Era, legal scholarship has dominated academic studies of professional anti-alien licensing restrictions. See, among others, "Prohibition of Employment of Aliens in Construction of Public Works"; J. P. Chamberlain, "Aliens and the Right to Work," *American Bar Association Journal* 18, no. 6 (June 1932): 379–82; David Fellman, "The Alien's Right to Work," *Minnesota Law Review* 22, no. 2 (January 1938): 137–76; Vernier, *American Family Laws*; Konvitz, *Alien and the Asiatic*; Shyameshwar Das, "Discrimination in Employment against Aliens—the Impact of the Constitution and Federal Civil Rights Laws," *University of*

226   NOTES TO PAGES 122–3

Pittsburgh Law Review 35, no. 3 (Spring 1974): 499–555; Denny Chin, "Aliens' Right to Work: State and Federal Discrimination," *Fordham Law Review* 45, no. 4 (February 1977): 835–59; David Carliner, *The Rights of Aliens: The Basic ACLU Guide to an Alien's Rights* (New York: Avon Books, 1977); Jessye Leigh Scott, "Alien Teachers: Suspect Class or Subversive Influence?" *Mercer Law Review* 31, no. 3 (Spring 1980): 815–24; Kelly, "Wavering Course," 701–42; and Chin, "Nation of White Immigrants."

15. The plaintiffs in the 1977 US Supreme Court case *Nyquist v. Mauclet* provided a comprehensive list of New York state laws restricting noncitizens' economic rights on the basis of alienage from the time of the Civil War to the (then) present. This information was reproduced in Plascencia, Freeman, and Setzler, "Decline of Barriers," 9. See also Nyquist v. Mauclet, 432 U.S. 1 (1977); and Luis F. B. Plascencia, *Disenchanting Citizenship: Mexican Migrants and the Boundaries of Belonging* (New Brunswick, NJ: Rutgers University Press, 2012), 104–5.

16. See, in real time, Powell, "Right to Work"; and subsequently, among others, Das, "Discrimination in Employment"; and Chin, "Aliens' Right to Work."

17. On immigrant peddlers and antipeddler hostility, see Sarah M. A. Gualtieri, *Between Arab and White: Race and Ethnicity in the Early Syrian American Diaspora* (Berkeley: University of California Press, 2009); and Hasia R. Diner, *Roads Taken: The Great Jewish Migrations to the New World and the Peddlers Who Forged the Way* (New Haven, CT: Yale University Press, 2015).

18. Plascencia, Freeman, and Setzler, "Decline of Barriers," 9.

19. Chapter 2 contextualizes this political development. See also Shanahan, "'Practically American' Canadian Woman," 621–47.

20. My recounting of this important (but oft-forgotten) New York noncitizen public schoolteacher hiring controversy builds on political scientist Alexandra Filindra's discovery and succinct analysis of it in "E Pluribus Unum?" 132.

21. "No Enemy Alien Teachers," *New York Times*, December 17, 1917, 12. Filindra cites (but does not quote) from this article in "E Pluribus Unum?" 132.

22. The New York anti-alien public schoolteacher law did permit noncitizen teachers to retain their jobs if they filed their first papers within a year of the act taking effect and promptly naturalized "within the time thereafter prescribed by law." All other immigrants seeking future employment as teachers, however, had to already be US citizens. See "An Act to Amend the Education Law, in Relation to Qualifications of Teachers," New York—141st Legislature (1918 Vol. 1), Ch. 158: 749.

23. Filindra, "E Pluribus Unum?" 132. As historian Hasia Diner finds in her classic study on Irish immigrant and Irish American women, by the turn of the twentieth century, "daughters of Irish parents made up the largest group of schoolteachers in New York City, with over two thousand out of a total teaching population of seven thousand women" (97). See, more broadly, Hasia Diner, *Erin's Daughters in America: Irish Immigrant Women in the Nineteenth Century* (Baltimore: Johns Hopkins University Press, 1983), 96–98. See also Bronwen Walter, *Outsiders Inside: Whiteness, Place and Irish Women* (New York: Routledge, 2000), 56. Historians of labor disputes in American education have largely omitted the New York 1918 anti-alien public schoolteacher law from broad syntheses. But many narratives have highlighted how antiradical hysteria during and shortly after World War I led to investigations and dismissals of (mostly leftist, often Jewish) immigrant or second-generation teachers in New York City. See, especially, Diane Ravitch, *The Great School Wars: A History of the New York City Public Schools* (Baltimore: Johns Hopkins University Press, 2000), 229–30; Marjorie Murphy, *Blackboard Unions: The AFT and the NEA, 1900–1980* (Ithaca, NY: Cornell University Press, 1991), 90–98; and Dana Goldstein, *The Teacher Wars: A History of America's Most Embattled Profession* (New York: Doubleday, 2015), 91–96. For contemporaneous news coverage of New York anti-alien public schoolteacher legislation, see "Would Bar Alien Teachers," *New York Times*, March 29, 1917, 8; "Bars Alien Teachers," *New York Times*, March 27, 1918, 7; "Signs Bill to Bar Alien School Teachers," *New York Times*, April 6, 1918, 13; and "To Aid Alien School Teachers," *New York Times*, February 27, 1919, 12.

24. This plan seems to have been dropped at the end of the war, however, because no such investigation appears in the California Commission on Teacher Credentials files. See Minutes of May 20, 1918, Meeting: California Board of Education, "Commission on Credentials Minutes, 1918–1929," Files 359.01 (1–2) C3609, California State Archives, Sacramento, CA.

25. "Poison in the Spring," *Los Angeles Times*, November 23, 1919, II4.

NOTES TO PAGES 123–4   227

26. For examples, see Alvan Macauley, "What Part Should Industry Take in Naturalization Work?" (read by Mr. W. J. Schultz), *Proceedings of the National Conference on Americanization in Industries*, 91–96; and "Clothing Factory Bars Alien Workers," *New York Times*, December 31, 1920, 6. More broadly, see Robert F. Zeidel, *Robber Barons and Wretched Refuse: Ethnic and Class Dynamics during the Era of American Industrialization* (Ithaca, NY: Cornell University Press, 2020), 160–203.

27. The 1923 Wisconsin statute granted broad powers to the state Board of Control to reallocate and expend taxpayer funds on public works projects in times of "extraordinary unemployment." State and then US citizens were to receive preference before resident noncitizens could be hired on such work relief projects in Wisconsin. See "An Act to Create Sections 46.23 to 46.26, Inclusive, of the Statutes, Relating to the Extension of Public Works of the State during Periods of Extraordinary Unemployment Caused by Temporary Industrial Depression, and Regulating Employment Therein," Wisconsin Session Laws—Biennial Session (1923), Ch. 76: 69–70. See also "Blaine Signs Bill to Relieve Unemployment," *Madison Capital Times*, May 1, 1923, 3; and "State Board of Control Given Powder [*sic*] to Extend Public Work by New Bill," *Eau Claire Leader*, May 2, 1923, 5.

28. When Massachusetts hosted a conference on "Americanization in Industries" in 1919, social workers, employers, and politicians from across the country debated, among other topics, whether companies should compel their workers to become US citizens. Coercive naturalization policies proved unpopular. One of only four resolutions adopted by conference attendees was their "disapprov[al of] making naturalization a condition of employment." See "Resolutions" (page before "Program"), *Proceedings of the National Conference on Americanization in Industries*, i.

29. On the defeated 1919 bill in Texas, see HB 54: "Requiring the Employment of Citizens of the United States on Public Work," *Journal of the Texas House of Representatives*, Vol. 36, Regular session (1919), 1166. Though Texas lawmakers rejected legislation for a statewide anti-alien public works hiring law, similar demands made greater headway at the local level. Most infamously, both white and Black laborers in Fort Worth clamored successfully for the mass firing of noncitizen workers, mostly Mexican nationals, on hitherto undesirable city public works jobs during the post–World War I recession. See Emilio Zamora, *The World of the Mexican Worker in Texas* (College Station: Texas A&M University Press, 2000), 44–45, 49–50, 68; John Oscar Davis, "Anti-Depression Public Works: Federal-Aid Roadbuilding, 1920–1922" (PhD diss., Iowa State University, 2002), 194–95; and Clare Sheridan, "Contested Citizenship: National Identity and the Mexican Immigration Debates of the 1920s," *Journal of American Ethnic History* 21, no. 3 (Spring 2002): 5–6.

30. William M. Leiserson, *Adjusting Immigrant and Industry* (New York: Harper, 1924), 42. See also, more broadly, on anti-alien hiring rhetoric and employment practices in interwar Michigan, Bavery, *Bootlegged Aliens*, 136–37.

31. On previous literacy test battles and the ultimate passage of the Literacy Test Act in 1917, see, among many others, Hans P. Vought, *The Bully Pulpit and the Melting Pot: American Presidents and the Immigrant, 1897–1933* (Macon, GA: Mercer University Press, 2004), 113–19; and Jeanne D. Petit, *The Men and Women We Want: Gender, Race, and the Progressive Era Literacy Test Debate* (Rochester, NY: University of Rochester Press, 2010).

32. Southwestern business interests actively promoted the image of Mexican workers as temporary migrants to argue that their alienage was actually beneficial to Anglo residents. They warned that if businesses were unable to hire Mexican noncitizen laborers, they would be compelled to recruit other nonwhite (US citizen) workers, such as African Americans and Puerto Ricans, who could not be forcibly removed if white residents suddenly wanted hitherto undesirable jobs in the context of a recession. Such attitudes were explicitly expressed in the context of proposed California legislation to restrict hiring on publicly funded construction work to US citizens in 1929. The *Los Angeles Times* blasted the proposal, derogatorily calling it "an act to swat taxpayers, to prevent public work, to encourage the importation of Porto Rican negroes and for other undesirable purposes." See "An Act to Swat Taxpayers," *Los Angeles Times*, April 20, 1929, A4. On this juxtaposition more broadly, see, especially, Natalia Molina, *How Race Is Made in America* (Berkeley: University of California Press, 2013), 19–42. On the passage of the quota acts of 1921 and 1924, the development of the quota regime, and the Western Hemisphere "exception," see, among many others, Mae Ngai, "The Architecture of Race in American

228 NOTES TO PAGES 124–5

Immigration Law: A Reexamination of the Immigration Act of 1924," *Journal of American History* 86, no. 1 (June 1999): 67–92; Tichenor, *Dividing Lines*, 114–49; and S. Deborah Kang, *The INS on the Line: Making Immigration Law on the US–Mexico Border, 1917–1954* (New York: Oxford University Press, 2017), 36–42.

33. Marian Schibsby, *Handbook for Immigrants to the United States* (New York: Foreign Language Information Service, 1927), 95–96.

34. National American Red Cross, *The Work of the Foreign Language Information Service of the American Red Cross* (Washington, DC: Bureau of Foreign Language Information Service, 1920).

35. Quotation in main text from Schneider, *Crossing Borders*, 166. The importance of the FLIS has not gone unnoticed by historians. In addition to Schneider's study, works that discuss and/or demonstrate its power as an advocacy organization include Richard W. Steele, "The War on Intolerance: The Reformulation of American Nationalism, 1939–1941," *Journal of American Ethnic History* 9, no. 1 (Fall 1989): 9–35; Thatcher, *Immigrants and the 1930's*; Bénédicte Deschamps, "L'épreuve/les preuves de la loyauté: la presse italo-américaine face à la citoyenneté (1910–1935)," *Revue française d'études américaines* 75, no. 1 (January 1998): 47–61; Bénédicte Deschamps, "'Shall I Become a Citizen?' The FLIS and the Foreign Language Press, 1919–1939," in *Federalism, Citizenship, and Collective Identities in U.S. History*, ed. Cornelis A. van Minnen, Sylvia L. Hilton, and Colin Bonwick (Amsterdam, The Netherlands: Vrije Universiteit Press, 2000), 165–76; Gardner, *Qualities of a Citizen*; and Fox, *Three Worlds of Relief*. Historian John McClymer contends that scholars should also grapple more with the implications of the FLIS's origins in wartime, arguing that the organization proved too often averse to assertive, radical defenses of immigrant rights, especially during the first Red Scare and the early 1920s. See John F. McClymer, *War and Welfare: Social Engineering in America, 1890–1925* (Westport, CT: Praeger, 1980), 129–40, 224–25.

36. "Little Men Who Were Once Big," *The Interpreter* 4, no. 9 (November 1925): 11.

37. "Little Men," 10.

38. "Little Men," 12.

39. "Selecting Our Immigrants," *The Interpreter* 8, no. 10 (December 1929): 147.

40. "Needs of the Educated Immigrant," *The Interpreter* 4, no. 8 (October 1925): 8.

41. Schibsby, *Handbook for Immigrants*, 94.

42. Schibsby, 98–100.

43. Schibsby, 97–98.

44. Unfortunately for immigrants who used her *Handbook* (and historians who might use it as a primary source), Schibsby did not comprehensively list these policies in force on a state-by-state basis. She did, however, identify increasingly common anti-alien legislation in "California, Illinois, Massachusetts, Michigan, New York, New Jersey and Pennsylvania," when possible, because those states possessed "the largest foreign-born populations" in the country during the mid-1920s (97–98). I believe her work to be the first attempt to encapsulate the breadth of anti-alien licensing restrictions across the country. Designed as a practical handbook, Schibsby did not discuss sources or methods for her chapter. It is, however, clearly derived from the internal work (largely her own) of the FLIS. See, generally, Chapter 11: "Finding Work in the United States," in Schibsby, *Handbook for Immigrants*, 88–103. It is likely that this Danish-born naturalized citizen had been well aware of the potential power of anti-alien hiring and licensure laws in California even before her time with the FLIS. In a remarkable coincidence, she had served as a high school teacher in Mendocino in the early 1910s (the same small northern California city where Katharine Short's job became imperiled in 1915). While contemporaneous evidence suggests Schibsby was no longer teaching in Mendocino amid the California Alien Teachers Controversy, it does appear that she was still living and working in the state (most likely as a private-school instructor in San Francisco) when the dispute broke out in early 1915. See "New High School Teachers," *Ukiah Daily Journal*, July 22, 1910, 1; "Program Is Announced," *Ukiah Dispatch Democrat*, March 31, 1911, 1; "Teachers Will Meet at Ukiah," *Mendocino Beacon*, April 15, 1911, 1; "Educational," *San Francisco Examiner*, September 2, 1917, 28; and "First Editor Service Publication Retiring," *Monthly Review—Immigration and Naturalization Service* 4, no. 4 (October 1946): 50. Schibsby would be at the forefront of the FLIS's immigrant rights advocacy research and outreach from the 1920s to the early 1940s. On recent scholarship that engages her own work, see, especially, Fox, *Three Worlds of Relief*; and Cybelle Fox, "Save Our Senior Noncitizens: Extending Old Age Assistance to Immigrants in the United States, 1935–71," *Social Science History* 45, no. 1 (Spring 2021): 55–81.

NOTES TO PAGES 125–7   229

45. Schibsby, *Handbook for Immigrants*, 88–103.
46. On challenges of documentation and nationality arising from the collapse of the Russian Empire, see Christopher A. Casey, *Nationals Abroad: Globalization, Individual Rights, and the Making of Modern International Law* (New York: Cambridge University Press, 2020), 105–33; S. Deborah Kang, "Sovereign Mercy: The Legalization of the White Russian Refugees and the Politics of Immigration Relief," *Journal of American Ethnic History* 43, no. 1 (Fall 2023): 5–42; and, broadly, Mira L. Siegelberg, *Statelessness: A Modern History* (Cambridge, MA: Harvard University Press, 2020).
47. Minutes from January 7, 1924; July 5, 1927: California Board of Pharmacy, "Proceedings of the California State Board of Pharmacy," File F3888, California State Archives, Sacramento, CA.
48. "An Act to Amend Sections Two, Three, Four, Eleven and Fifteen of an Act Entitled 'An Act to Regulate the Practice of Pharmacy in the State of California…,'" California Legislature—47th Session (1927), Ch. 90: 154–160.
49. Minutes from July 25, 1927: California Board of Pharmacy, "Proceedings of the California State Board of Pharmacy," File F3888, California State Archives, Sacramento, CA.
50. Minutes from April 9, 1928: California Board of Pharmacy, "Proceedings of the California State Board of Pharmacy," File F3888, California State Archives, Sacramento, CA.
51. Minutes from July 7, 1930: California Board of Pharmacy, "Proceedings of the California State Board of Pharmacy," File F3888, California State Archives, Sacramento, CA.
52. While the board voted on July 7, 1930, to have "the matter…deferred" until the next round of meetings later that month, its members did not take up the topic (at least formally on the record) when they reassembled on July 21. Subsequently, immigrant pharmacists continued to have to "furnish" or "secure" evidence of citizenship or first papers to obtain licensure. However, references to the board asking for petitioners to submit (real or copied) citizenship papers for their records seem to have ceased thereafter. See, specifically, Minutes from July 7, 1930; July 21, 1930. See also, for subsequent context, July 29, 1931; October 5, 1931; October 27, 1931: California Board of Pharmacy, "Proceedings of the California State Board of Pharmacy," File F3888, California State Archives, Sacramento, CA.
53. Quotations in main text from Konvitz, *Alien and the Asiatic*, 172. In a rare study of the comparative political development behind such laws (though among Canadian provinces as opposed to US states), Adams finds that both "social closure theory" (which in practice largely amounts to "professional lobbying") and "state-centred explanations which hold that states regulate professions to facilitate governance" help explain the rise of citizenship requirements in professional licensing regimes in Canada (550). See, more broadly, Tracey L. Adams, "When 'Citizenship Is Indispensable to the Practice of a Profession': Citizenship Requirements for Entry to Practise Professions in Canada," *Journal of Historical Sociology* 29, no. 4 (2016): 550–77.
54. Minutes from June 17–19, 1924 (quotation in main text from 373, policy adopted 367): Texas Board of Medicine, "Medical Examiners Minutes," Box 1981/207-1, Texas State Archives, Austin, Texas. On Colwell's role, see American Medical Association, "Seventy-Fourth Annual Session of the American Medical Association House of Delegates Proceedings" (San Francisco, CA, 1923); American Medical Association, "Seventy-Fifth Annual Session of the American Medical Association House of Delegates Proceedings" (Chicago, IL, 1924); and American Medical Association, "Seventy-Seventh Annual Session of the American Medical Association House of Delegates Proceedings" (Dallas, TX, 1926).
55. American Medical Association, "Seventy-Seventh Annual Session," 30.
56. American Medical Association, 30.
57. See, especially, Halperin, "Jewish Problem," 141–43.
58. Blue-collar nativists in southern California were especially vocal in their demands to exclude (largely Mexican) noncitizen immigrants from public works jobs during the mid- to late 1920s. Authorities in Los Angeles responded to their entreaties in January 1925 by demanding that "all heads of city departments" henceforth "rigidly enforce" state and municipal policies requiring US citizenship for public employment. See "Must Hire Citizens," *Los Angeles Times*, January 24, 1925, A6. Building trades unions in Los Angeles were not satisfied, demanding that an anti-alien hiring policy be extended to publicly contracted construction projects as well. In 1926, they succeeded in pressing for and winning a citywide referendum that required workers on publicly contracted projects in the city be US citizens or immigrants who held first papers. See "Council Orders Alien Ban Vote," *Los Angeles Times*, September 18, 1926, A1; "Barring

230   NOTES TO PAGES 127-8

Alien Labor Opposed," *Los Angeles Times*, October 26, 1926, A10; "Twenty-Five Proposals on the City's Ballot," *Los Angeles Times*, October 31, 1926, A1, A2, A8; and "Record Voting Mark Expected," *Los Angeles Times*, November 2, 1926, A1, A7. The measure's passage was noted (despite seemingly contradictory headlines) by the *Los Angeles Times* several times in "Voters Frown on Bonds: Flood Control and All County and City Issues Except for Hospitals Lose," *Los Angeles Times*, November 4, 1926, 1; "Election Returns," *Los Angeles Times*, November 4, 1926, 1-2; and "State Saves Wright Act; Both Road Plans Lose," *Los Angeles Times*, November 5, 1926, 1-2.

59. Sociologist Matthew Baltz describes these demands by blue-collar nativists as efforts to ostensibly "Protect[] Citizens in Hard Times." See Matthew J. Baltz, "Protecting Citizens in Hard Times: Citizenship and Repatriation Pressures in the United States and France during the 1930s," *Theory and Society* 44, no. 2 (March 2015): 101-24.

60. The 1931 California law restricted hiring on all construction projects receiving municipal, county, or state funds to US citizens. See "An Act to Prohibit the Employment of Aliens by Contractors and Subcontractors on All Public Work, Except in Certain Cases of Extraordinary Emergency...," California Legislature—49th Session (1931), Ch. 398: 913-915. This policy was later incorporated as part of the state's Labor Code in 1937. The University of California— Office of the President (which often struggled to determine whether University of California employees fell under the state's many anti-alien hiring policies) closely tracked legislative and administrative interpretations of such laws. See "Copy of Sections 1940-1944 Inclusive of the State Labor Code, 1939" and "Quotation from Statutes and Judicial Decisions Relating to the University of California," in University Archives; UC Berkeley: University of California, President, "Bound Folders" CU 5 Ser. 3 Box 30 File: 277: "Alien Employment Policy, 1915-57." The 1931 Massachusetts statute required that "citizens of the commonwealth...be given preference" in "employments and work in any branch of the service of the commonwealth, or of any county, city, town or district therein." See "An Act Extending Existing Provisions of Law Giving Citizens of the Commonwealth a Preference in Public Service and Work," Massachusetts General Court—Acts and Resolves, Extra Session (1931), Ch. 125: 100. The 1931 Texas law amounted to a hiring policy preferential to US citizens for all public construction projects. See "Minimum Wage Scale for Highway Workers," Texas State Legislature—42nd Legislature, Regular Session (1931), Ch. 46: 69-70.

61. Read Lewis, "Have We Still an Immigration Problem?" *Interpreter Releases* 10, no. 25 (June 20, 1933): 153.

62. On coverage of the 1931 California law's implementation, see "Only Americans Can Be Employed on State Public Work in the Future," *Sausalito News*, August 14, 1931, 3; "All Citizens to Have Work on Contracts," *San Bernardino Daily Sun*, August 22, 1931, 12; "Aliens Dropped from Jobs Here," *Los Angeles Times*, August 24, 1931, A1; and "Plea Made for Native Workers," *Los Angeles Times*, September 23, 1931, 1. On the enforcement of older Golden State anti-alien hiring policies, see "Ventura Fires Alien Workers," *Los Angeles Times*, March 19, 1930, 8; and "Aliens Barred from City Jobs," *Los Angeles Times*, April 17, 1931, A10. On anti-alien public and publicly funded construction work conflicts and purges in Massachusetts during the early years of the Great Depression, see "Fire Alien Labor for U.S. Citizens," *Daily Boston Globe*, July 11, 1930, 2; "Will Enforce Law on Employing Citizens," *Daily Boston Globe*, April 17, 1930, 5; "Charge Aliens Given State Highway Work," *Daily Boston Globe*, January 23, 1931, 16; "Dowd Raps All Alien City Workers," *Daily Boston Globe*, August 25, 1931, 2; "Says Federal Aid Won't Be Withheld," *Daily Boston Globe*, September 6, 1931, A1; and "House Declines Senate Changes," *Daily Boston Globe*, February 18, 1932, 9. On efforts by then-New York governor Franklin Roosevelt and his close ally, then-industrial commissioner Frances Perkins, to strictly enforce old state citizen-preference public employment laws to oust noncitizen laborers from public works projects in the early Depression years, see, among others, "Give State Jobs to Its Citizens, Roosevelt Asks," *New York Herald Tribune*, March 22, 1930, 4; "Mayors Reminded Jobs Should Go to Citizens," *New York Herald Tribune*, July 5, 1930, 1; "Miss Perkins Bids Mayors Give Citizens Employment Preference," *New York Times*, July 5, 1930, 21; and "Roosevelt Acts to Oust Aliens from State Jobs," *New York Herald Tribune*, September 16, 1930, 1. Anti-alien hiring efforts in New York were sometimes tied to drives to prevent the employment of out-of-state US citizen migrants. See "Urges State Work First for Citizens," *New York Times*, March 22, 1930, 2; and "Local Jobless to Be Preferred for Attica Prison Construction," *New York Herald Tribune*, September 2, 1931, 8. For broader context on New York public works

NOTES TO PAGE 128   231

projects in the early years of the Great Depression, see Michael R. Fein, *Paving the Way: New York Road Building and the American State, 1880–1956* (Lawrence: University Press of Kansas, 2008), 130–39. The 1931 Texas citizen-preference law did not elicit nearly as much attention in leading Lone Star State newspapers, with coverage focusing instead on wages for road construction work. See "Texas Topics," *Austin Statesman*, March 4, 1931, 4; "Road Bond Issue Again Delayed in Senate," *Austin Statesman*, March 25, 1931, 1, 12; and "Board Will Set Road Laborers Wages," *Austin Statesman*, October 10, 1931, 2. However, Mexican noncitizen immigrants' (and Mexican Americans') access to public works jobs (and broader forms of employment and social services) in Depression-era Texas remained tenuous. See, among others, Daniel Morales, "Tejas, Afuera de México: Newspapers, the Mexican Government, Mutualistas, and Migrants in San Antonio 1910–1940," *Journal of American Ethnic History* 40, no. 2 (Winter 2021): 52–91.

63. On federal debates over noncitizen immigrants' access to New Deal programs, see Thatcher, *Immigrants and the 1930's*, 202–49. Sociologist Cybelle Fox stresses that unlike African Americans and Mexican-origin workers, white immigrants—irrespective of citizenship status—usually retained access to most New Deal federal jobs programs and social services prior to the "(Short-Lived) Triumph of Nativism" in the late 1930s. See, broadly, Fox, *Three Worlds of Relief*, 188–280. In her case study of the Detroit border region, historian Ashley Johnson Bavery highlights the importance of legal status in noncitizens' efforts to access New Deal jobs and benefits prior to the Works Progress Administration purge of 1939. See, especially, Bavery, *Bootlegged Aliens*, 179–212.

64. See, broadly, Fox, *Three Worlds of Relief*, 225–249 (p. 240 for figure); and Thatcher, *Immigrants and the 1930's*, 202–49.

65. The Massachusetts Division of Immigration and Americanization reported that the adoption of new and the resuscitation of dormant citizen-preference blue-collar hiring policies in the Bay State most impacted poor, non-English-speaking, and/or illiterate noncitizens. It found in 1930 that noncitizen workers harmed by anti-alien public works employment policies were disproportionately drawn from a "day labor group," who were "mainly non-English speaking, many of them illiterate and their present attempts toward citizenship must, of course, be fruitless until they can qualify educationally for citizenship." See Department of Education, "Annual Report of the Division of Immigration and Americanization for the Year Ending November 30, 1930" (Boston: Commonwealth of Massachusetts, 1931), 6. In turn, state and local anti-alien public and publicly funded employment policies in California landed extremely harshly on Mexican workers. See, among others, Sánchez, *Becoming Mexican American*, 210–11; Pitti, *Devil in Silicon Valley*, 82–87; and Vargas, *Labor Rights*, 46.

66. Abraham Hoffman, "Stimulus to Repatriation: The 1931 Federal Deportation Drive and the Los Angeles Mexican Community," *Pacific Historical Review* 42, no. 2 (May 1973): 205–19; Francisco Balderrama and Raymond Rodríguez, *Decade of Betrayal: Mexican Repatriation in the 1930s* (Albuquerque: University of New Mexico Press, 2006); Fernando Saul Alanis Enciso, "¿Cuántos fueron? La repatriación de mexicanos en los Estados Unidos durante La Gran Depresión: Una interpretación cuantitativa 1930–1934," *Aztlán: A Journal of Chicano Studies* 32, no. 2 (Fall 2007): 65–91; Fox, *Three Worlds of Relief*, 124–55; Molina, "Deportable Citizens"; and Adam Goodman, *The Deportation Machine: America's Long History of Expelling Immigrants* (Princeton, NJ: Princeton University Press, 2020), 42–46.

67. See, especially, Romero, "War to Keep"; and Varsanyi, "Hispanic Racialization."

68. Married women faced high rates of layoffs during the Depression by private employers and governments alike. Such sexist "marriage penalties" often built on—but accelerated—long-standing patterns of employment discrimination. See, among others, Claudia Goldin, "Marriage Bars: Discrimination against Married Women Workers, 1920's to 1950's" (working paper, Cambridge, MA: National Bureau of Economic Research, October 1988), http://www.nber.org/papers/w2747; and Landon R. Y. Storrs, *The Second Red Scare and the Unmaking of the New Deal Left* (Princeton, NJ: Princeton University Press, 2013). In fact, long before Theresa Oglou successfully battled to retain her job as a San Francisco schoolteacher in 1940 following the surprise discovery of her alienage, she had defeated a previous attempted layoff owing to her status as a married woman in 1930. The *Oakland Tribune* reported on her successful defense of her job, noting that "the [San Francisco] board of education cannot withhold permanent classification from Mrs. Teresa Oglou, a Berkeley woman...because she is married, the city attorney has declared in reaffirming a former ruling." See "Marriage No Bar to

232 NOTES TO PAGES 128–9

Teaching, S.F. Told," *Oakland Tribune*, March 5, 1930, 3. African Americans, often the last hired and the first fired in many lines of work, faced far higher rates of joblessness than white workers during the Great Depression. For a specific case study, see John Hinshaw, *Steel and Steelworkers: Race and Class Struggle in Twentieth-Century Pittsburgh* (New York: SUNY Press, 2012), 42–43. More broadly, see Katznelson, *When Affirmative Action*; and Fox, *Three Worlds of Relief.*

69. Nurses and teachers also generally had less professional autonomy delegated to them by state lawmakers relative to other contemporaneous (male-dominated) professions and professional associations in the early to mid-twentieth century. See, broadly, Susan M. Reverby, *Ordered to Care: The Dilemma of American Nursing, 1850–1945* (New York: Cambridge University Press, 1987); Murphy, *Blackboard Unions*; Ravitch, *Great School Wars*; Goldstein, *Teacher Wars*; Adams, *Regulating Professions*; and Kessler-Harris, *Out to Work*, 116–18, 128.

70. On the development and underfunding of municipal hospitals in this era, such as Boston City Hospital, see, among others, Harry Filmore Dowling, *City Hospitals: The Undercare of the Underprivileged* (Cambridge, MA: Harvard University Press, 1982).

71. While Dowd's demands were influenced by the new state law, he specifically invoked the city charter in demanding the ouster of noncitizen workers, claiming it "specifies that citizens must be employed at the hospital when it is possible to obtain them" (8). See "Demand Ousting of Alien Nurses," *Daily Boston Globe*, August 18, 1931, 1, 8 (quotation in main text from p. 8). Both Democrats, Mayor Curley and Councilman Dowd had a fractious relationship. First allies, then foes, they later reconciled in the early New Deal years. See "Curley–Dowd Hatchet Buried Yesterday," *Boston Record*, August 1, 1933, in James Michael Curley Scrapbooks, Vol. 96 (1933) (Worcester, MA: College of the Holy Cross, Special Online Collections), 8. See also "Veteran, Former Councilor: Ex-Sheriff Dowd, 65, Dies in Hub Hospital," *Boston Globe*, August 16, 1961, 25.

72. Boston corporation counsel Samuel Silverman found that the state's citizen-preference employment policy compelled the "immediate[] remov[al]" of all "nurses who are not citizens, now employed by the City Hospital," warning that it was likely "a criminal offense" for city and hospital leadership not to discharge them (9). See "14 Alien Nurses Must Lose Jobs," *Daily Boston Globe*, August 20, 1931, 1, 9 (quotation in main text from p. 9). While initial reports counted fourteen nurses fired at Boston City Hospital, the *Globe* later revised that figure to eighteen. See "Stir Over Alien Nurses' Discharge," *Daily Boston Globe*, August 21, 1931, 1, 13.

73. "Five Alien Nurses Quit Quincy Hospital Posts," *Daily Boston Globe*, September 12, 1931, 12; "Nine Quincy Nurses, Aliens, Discharged," *Daily Boston Globe*, September 20, 1931, 25.

74. The *Boston Globe* ran articles specifically about inquiries into the employment of noncitizen nurses in the cities of Fall River and Haverhill. "Survey at Fall River Regarding Alien Nurses," *Daily Boston Globe*, August 22, 1931, 3; "Haverhill Mayor Asks Ruling on Alien Nurses," *Daily Boston Globe*, August 22, 1931, 3; "Case of Fall River Alien Nurse Going before Board," *Daily Boston Globe*, August 26, 1931, 4; "Finds Haverhill Nurses' Discharge Not Required," *Daily Boston Globe*, August 26, 1931, 4. The *Globe* also reported on the rise of similar queries in Greater Boston–area city hospitals in Cambridge and Lynn. See "Stir over Alien Nurses,'" 1, 13.

75. Goodwin had participated in debates over the passage of the 1931 citizen-preference public employment law (which he wanted to be a strict citizen-only hiring law). See "Would Limit State Employes to Citizens," *Daily Boston Globe*, February 6, 1931, 19. On Goodwin's lobbying against the employment of noncitizens in state hospitals, see "Ely Opposed to Ousting Nurses," *Daily Boston Globe*, August 22, 1931, 1, 3; "Need Not Discharge Aliens, Says Ely," *Daily Boston Globe*, August 26, 1931, 1, 4; and "Ely Won't Yield on Alien Nurses," *Daily Boston Globe*, August 27, 1931, 1–2. Goodwin had recently (and unsuccessfully) aspired to the gubernatorial office in 1928. See "Boston Rum Scandal in State Campaign," *New York Times*, July 8, 1928, 21.

76. Indeed, the *Boston Globe* increasingly entitled the conflict an "alien nurse squabble" (1). See "Ely Opposed to Ousting Nurses," 1, 3. Elsewhere it described it as "the alien nurse controversy" (1). See "Ely Won't Yield," 1–2.

77. Quotations in main text from "Stir over Alien Nurses,'" 1, 13. The Massachusetts Alien Nurses Controversy was covered extensively on the "Woman Page" of the *Montreal Gazette*. See "Nurses to Lose Jobs," *Montreal Gazette*, August 19, 1931, 9; "Canadian Nurses to Be Dismissed," *Montreal Gazette*, August 21, 1931, 9; "5 More Canadian Nurses Lose Jobs," *Montreal Gazette*, August 22, 1931, 9; "Governor Disapproves," *Montreal Gazette*, August 24, 1931, 9; "Nurses Championed," *Montreal Gazette*, August 26, 1931, 9; and "Hospital Welfare

NOTES TO PAGES 129–31   233

Considered First," *Montreal Gazette*, August 28, 1931, 9. On high rates of Maritime-born nurses working in early- to mid-twentieth-century Massachusetts, see Betsy Beattie, "'Going up to Lynn': Single, Maritime-Born Women in Lynn, Massachusetts, 1879–1930," *Acadiensis* 22, no. 1 (Autumn 1992): 65–86; and Reverby, *Ordered to Care*, 80–84.

78. "Finds Haverhill Nurses' Discharge," 4.

79. For news coverage of Ely's actions during the nurses controversy, see "Ely Opposed," 1, 3; "Need Not Discharge Aliens, Says Ely," 1, 4; "Ely Won't Yield," 1–2; "Ely Welcomes Test on Nurses," *Daily Boston Globe*, August 28, 1931, 17; and "Dolan Asks Ely Take up Charge against Bigelow," *Daily Boston Globe*, September 15, 1931, 6. Ely was then also vacillating widely between embracing and eschewing deficit spending to finance public works relief programs. See Huthmacher, *Massachusetts People and Politics, 1919–1933*, 222–24.

80. "Is It Wise?" *Daily Boston Globe*, August 22, 1931, 12.

81. Quotations in main text from "City Hospital Jobs Closed to Aliens," *New York Times*, December 24, 1931, 16. On Greeff's appointment by Tammany Hall–backed mayor Jimmy Walker, see Jamie Wilson, *Building a Healthy Black Harlem* (Amherst, NY: Cambria Press, 2009), 77, 80. On the frequent practice of nurses living on hospital property (sometimes even receiving room and board in lieu of pay amid the worsening Depression) see, among others, Deborah Judd, "Chpt. 6, 'Nursing in the United States from the 1920s to the Early 1940s: Education Rather Than Training for Nurses,'" in *A History of American Nursing: Trends and Eras*, ed. Deborah Judd, Kathleen Sitzman, and G. Megan Davis (Sudbury, MA: Jones & Bartlett Learning, 2009), 109; and Philip Arthur Kalisch and Beatrice J. Kalisch, *American Nursing: A History*, 4th ed. (Philadelphia: Lippincott Williams & Wilkins, 2003), 271–74.

82. Karin Mueller to FLIS, n.d. (but from context likely late 1931), 9, in Folder 1, "Discrimination against Aliens—Correspondence, Clippings, etc." (Foreign Language Information Service, Nov. 1927–April 1936), Box 36, IHRC 1013. Immigration and Refugee Services of America Foreign Language Information Service, University of Minnesota, Immigration History Research Center.

83. Exceptions were permitted to military veterans, (some) women married to US citizens, nurses whose naturalization was pending, "persons who have been members of the city pension system for ten years or more," nursing school instructors, and, most broadly, those granted relief at Greeff's discretion. See "Acts to Oust Aliens from Hospital Jobs," *New York Times*, December 6, 1932, 23. See also "Greeff Drops 50 Aliens Employed in Hospitals: Begins Task of Weeding Out 1,000 Who Are Not Citizens," *New York Herald Tribune*, December 16, 1932, 13.

84. "City Hospitals to Oust 800 Alien Employes; Citizens Will Replace Them at Lower Wages," *New York Times*, December 4, 1932, 1.

85. "Greeff Drops 50 Aliens," 13.

86. "Dismissed to the Breadline," *New York Times*, December 17, 1932, 16.

87. Lewis, "Have We Still?" 153; "1,415 Alien Employes Dismissed from New York Hospitals," *Jewish Advocate*, December 30, 1932, 4. As historian Steven Erie has shown, such purges were not isolated incidents. They instead formed part of a broader response by (mostly Irish American) Tammany Hall–backed Democratic municipal officials in the early 1930s to "cut back in ways least harmful to the machine and to the payroll Irish" by targeting their "most draconian economy measures…at the public school system, the hospitals, and relief agencies" where Tammany patronage networks were less interwoven than in other departments (114). Tammany politicians soon lost control of the city government in large part because of growing opposition to their handling of austerity budgets. See Erie, *Rainbow's End*, 107–28. See also Ester R. Fuchs, *Mayors and Money: Fiscal Policy in New York and Chicago* (Chicago: University of Chicago Press, 2010), 57–73; Aaron Gurwitz, *Atlantic Metropolis: An Economic History of New York City* (New York: Palgrave Macmillan, 2019), 401–48; and Williams, *City of Ambition*, 90–174.

88. On the limitations of citizenship documentation in an era before the universal use of birth certificates and during a time of widespread naturalization (and expatriation) by derivation, see, among others, Smith, "'Any Woman Who Is Now . . .'"; Lawrence DiStasi, "Derived Aliens," *Italian Americana* 29, no. 1 (Winter 2011): 23–33; Schneider, *Crossing Borders*, 196–232; Landrum, "State's Big Family Bible"; Robertson, *Passport in America*; and Susan J. Pearson, "'Age Ought to Be a Fact': The Campaign against Child Labor and the Rise of the Birth Certificate," *Journal of American History* 101, no. 4 (March 2015): 1144–65.

89. Under the (stymied) Michigan law, immigrants who could prove their authorized entry into the country would have received an identification card that would then serve as their work

234   NOTES TO PAGES 131–3

permit. Any noncitizen who did not have the card was to be denied employment. Not all Michiganders supported the proposal. Jewish organizations, the American Civil Liberties Union, and left-wing union activists argued that the proposal was intrusive, dangerous, and unconstitutional. See, among others, Thomas A. Klug, "Labor Market Politics in Detroit: The Curious Case of the 'Spolansky Act' of 1931," *Michigan Historical Review* 14, no. 1 (April 1988): 1–32; Libby Garland, "Fighting to Be Insiders," *American Jewish History* 96, no. 2 (June 2010): 109–40; and Bavery, *Bootlegged Aliens*, 124–49, 206–12. On the similarly struck-down Pennsylvania law, see, among others, Alan Reeve Hunt, "Federal Supremacy and State Anti-subversive Legislation," *Michigan Law Review* 53, no. 3 (January 1955): 407–38.

90. Blue-collar nativist demands for "alien registration" gained steam in the 1920s as a means of ostensibly combatting undocumented immigration. They acquired further traction amid rising unemployment during the Great Depression. Opponents—immigrant rights organizations, civil liberties groups, some unions, and religious, often Jewish, organizations—denounced such proposals as draconian and ineffective. Opponents successfully stymied proposed national legislation throughout the late 1920s and the 1930s before the eventual adoption of the federal Alien Registration Act of 1940 amid a national security panic. See, among many others, Thatcher, *Immigrants and the 1930's*, 227–37; Schneider, *Crossing Borders*, 232–33; Libby Garland, *After They Closed the Gates: Jewish Illegal Immigration to the United States, 1921–1965* (Chicago: University of Chicago Press, 2014), 197; Krajewska, *Documenting Americans*, 49–65; and Bavery, *Bootlegged Aliens*, 180–81, 206–12.

91. Four years earlier, governor Herbert Lehman had vetoed a strict citizen-only nurses licensing bill because it did not contain a grace period for immigrant nurses to become US citizens before losing licensure. See "Governor Signs 2 and Vetoes 6 Bills," *New York Times*, May 19, 1934, 14. The legislation Lehman signed in 1938 (with such a provision) was "An Act to Amend the Education Law, in Relation to the Practice of Nursing," New York—161st Legislature (1938), Ch. 472: 1221–33.

92. "Alien Nurses Advised," *New York Times*, December 12, 1938, 15.

93. On the proliferation of such demands and their success in the Great Depression, see also Filindra, "E Pluribus Unum?" 145.

94. Schibsby, *Handbook for Immigrants*, 88–103; Fields, "Where Shall," 213–21.

95. Quotations in main text from Fields, "Where Shall," 214. While this particular article examined a host of anti-alien hiring and licensure practices, Fields underscored "that the most common form of prohibition lies in the field of professions" (214). This was but one of many studies conducted by Fields into the impact of anti-alien hiring and licensure practices. Fields, who served as head of the National League for American Citizenship, also published other studies: Harold Fields, "Unemployment and the Alien," *South Atlantic Quarterly* 30, no. 1 (1931): 60–78; Harold Fields, "Closing Immigration throughout the World," *American Journal of International Law* 26, no. 4 (October 1932): 671–99; and Harold Fields, "The Unemployed Foreign-Born," *The Quarterly Journal of Economics* 49, no. 3 (May 1935): 533–41. Fields was also active in publicizing these warnings in the press. See Harold Fields, "Unemployment Opens a New Alien Problem," *New York Times*, October 19, 1930, 129; "Finds Bar against Alien," *New York Times*, November 15, 1930, 7; "Employment Curb on Aliens Scored," *New York Times*, December 28, 1930, N3; "Industries' Ban on Alien Decried," *New York Times*, January 25, 1931, 30; and "Jobs Barred to Alien Held Grave Problem," *New York Times*, June 9, 1935, 19. His work has often been cited by many subsequent scholars. They include Donald Peterson Kent, *The Refugee Intellectual: The Americanization of the Immigrants of 1933–1941* (New York: Columbia University Press, 1953); Thatcher, *Immigrants and the 1930's*; Richard W. Steele, " 'No Racials': Discrimination against Ethnics in American Defense Industry, 1940–42," *Labor History* 32, no. 1 (Winter 1991): 66–90; Baltz, "Protecting Citizens"; Catron, "Citizenship Advantage"; and Noel, "New Paths."

96. For a rare non-FLIS work on the subject published during the 1920s, see Charles M. Kneier, "Discrimination against Aliens by Municipal Ordinances," *Georgetown Law Journal* 16, no. 2 (February 1928): 143–64.

97. Though only the author's initials are listed on the note (L. H.), his name can be deduced from the journal issue's front cover. See Helfenstein, "Constitutionality of Legislative Discrimination," 74.

98. Vernier, *American Family Laws*, 375.

99. These law review articles have since served as crucial sources of data for historical analyses of state anti-alien licensing restrictions. Filindra's work on interwar-era licensing restrictions

NOTES TO PAGES 133–4   235

relies on the *Pennsylvania Law Review* note, while Bloemraad's scholarship employs the work of Vernier. Early- to mid-twentieth-century law reviews—and work published by Fields—did exhibit some inconsistencies as a result of constantly evolving legislation. Moreover, some licensing boards adopted their own anti-alien licensing rules that were not widely known. For instance, while Fields's article identified nine state medical boards operating their own licensing policies in 1933, he did not know that the Texas Medical Board required first papers from immigrants to receive a license. For these reasons, real-time scholarly attempts to document all anti-alien licensing policies likely undercounted their breadth. See Bloemraad, "Citizenship Lessons from the Past"; and Filindra, "E Pluribus Unum?" 128–53. See also Fields, "Where Shall," 215.

100. Though uncommon, litigation against anti-alien public and publicly funded employment laws was not unheard of during the Great Depression. In 1939, following the Works Progress Administration purge of noncitizen workers, Los Angeles resident Edward Rok challenged his dismissal in US District Court. Judge Leon Yankwich ruled against him, finding that "Acts of Legislatures forbidding employment of non-citizens, whether it is done by the public body itself or by a contractor, are not considered to infringe upon an alien's right to employment." Yankwich made clear, however, that he believed such laws to be "objectionable...from the standpoint of sound government" for "encouraging hatred rather than amity between the citizen and the non-citizen." See "Alien Relief Purge Upheld: Injunction Denied to Angeleno, Dismissed from Theater Project," *Los Angeles Times*, April 18, 1939, 1-A.

101. Vernier, *American Family Laws*, 375–76.

102. This definition of state police powers actually appeared in the US Supreme Court's ruling in the 1915 *Truax* case, finding that the Arizona 80 percent law was too broad of an infringement of noncitizen immigrants' rights and federal powers under the national constitution. See Truax v. Raich, 239 U.S. 33, 41, as quoted in Kelly, "Wavering Course," 707.

103. Quotation in main text from Rt. Rev. Msgr. John A. Ryan, "Is the Alien Entitled to an Equal Chance in Getting a Job?" (presented at the Conference on the Alien in America, New York, May 2, 1936), 24. Ryan's speech was reported on in "Blaming Alien for Ills of U.S. Held Old Trick," *Washington Post*, May 3, 1936, M14. On Ryan's broader immigrant rights and labor activism, see Maggie Elmore, "Fighting for Hemispheric Solidarity: The National Catholic Welfare Conference and the Quest to Secure Mexican American Employment Rights during World War II," *U.S. Catholic Historian* 35, no. 2 (Spring 2017): 125–49.

104. Basil O'Connor, "Constitutional Protection of the Alien's Right to Work," *New York University Law Quarterly Review* 18, no. 4 (May 1941): 486–87.

105. O'Connor, 487.

106. Fellman, "Alien's Right to Work," 158.

107. Fellman, 174.

108. Department of Education, "Annual Report of the Division of Immigration and Americanization, 1930," 6.

109. Department of Education, "Annual Report of the Division of Immigration and Americanization for the Year Ending November 30, 1938" (Boston: Commonwealth of Massachusetts, 1939), 8.

110. Minutes from July 6, 1931: California Board of Pharmacy, "Proceedings of the California State Board of Pharmacy," File F3888, California State Archives, Sacramento, CA.

111. Quotation in main text from Minutes from July 29, 1931. Sandhu continued to challenge his exclusion and appeared before the board in October 1931 and was told to return, again, with his first papers later in January 1932. Sandhu did not appear in the records from the January meetings, however. See, broadly, Minutes from July 6, 1931; July 25, 1931; July 27, 1931; July 28, 1931; July 29, 1931; October 5, 1931; January 18, 1932; January 19, 1932; January 20, 1932: California Board of Pharmacy, "Proceedings of the California State Board of Pharmacy," File F3888, California State Archives, Sacramento, CA. On the (sometimes successful) efforts of elite South Asian immigrants to claim whiteness and eligibility to US citizenship in court even after the early 1920s racial prerequisite cases, see, especially, Dhillon, "Making of Modern US."

112. See Minutes from October 9, 1931; October 26, 1931: California Board of Pharmacy, "Proceedings of the California State Board of Pharmacy," File F3888, California State Archives, Sacramento, CA. As legal scholar Sidney Kanazawa highlights, Fujii was posthumously admitted to the California Bar in 2017 following the advocacy of the Little Tokyo Historical Society and the Japanese American Bar Association, among other organizations and activists.

236 NOTES TO PAGES 135–8

See Sidney Kanazawa, "Sei Fujii: An Alien-American Patriot," *California Legal History* 13 (2018): 387–409.

113. Minutes from October 26, 1932: California Board of Pharmacy, "Proceedings of the California State Board of Pharmacy," File F3888, California State Archives, Sacramento, CA.

114. Minutes from November 1, 1933: California Board of Pharmacy, "Proceedings of the California State Board of Pharmacy," File F3888, California State Archives, Sacramento, CA.

115. Quotations in main text from Sashihara et al. v. California State Board of Pharmacy, 7 Cal. App. 2d 563, 564–565 (1935); No. 46 P.2d 804. On news coverage of the first case, see "Pharmacy Ban against Aliens Wins in Court," *Los Angeles Times*, February 26, 1934, A5. See also Pharmacists §4089 "Moral Character Requirement" in *Deering's California Codes Annotated of the State of California: Adopted June 15, 1937, with Amendments through the End of the 1975 Sessions of the 1975–76 Legislature*, Business and Professions (San Francisco, CA: Bancroft–Whitney, 1975), 400; Alan Reeve Hunt, "International Law: Reservations to Commercial Treaties Dealing with Aliens' Rights to Engage in the Professions," *Michigan Law Review* 52, no. 8 (June 1954): 1184–98; and Susan Bass Levin, "The Constitutionality of Employment Restrictions on Resident Aliens in the United States," *Buffalo Law Review* 24, no. 1 (Fall 1974): 211–38.

116. See "Mr. and Mrs. Thomas T. Sashihara with their daughters, Diane, 12; and Maureen, 11; and son, Tom Jr. Their former ..." in War Relocation Authority Photographs of Japanese-American Evacuation and Resettlement, UC Berkeley: Bancroft Library and Archives/Online Archives of California; http://oac-upstream.cdlib.org/ark:/13030/ft8779p13p/?&brand=oac4.

117. Minutes from Meeting August 14, 1934: Wisconsin Board of Accountancy, "Wisconsin Accounting Examining Board Minutes," Series 2641, Box 1, Vol. 1, Wisconsin Historical Society Archives, Madison.

118. Minutes from October 9, 1939: California Board of Pharmacy, "Proceedings of the California State Board of Pharmacy," File F3888, California State Archives, Sacramento, CA.

119. The AMA had two meetings in 1935 (the first being a "special" session). The Board of Trustees reported on widespread concerns about a supposed "influx" of foreign doctors at its regular annual session. See American Medical Association, "Eighty-Sixth Annual Session of the American Medical Association House of Delegates Proceedings" (Atlantic City, NJ, 1935). Quotations in main text from p. 18. See also pp. 39–40.

120. American Medical Association, "Eighty-Ninth Annual Session of the American Medical Association House of Delegates Proceedings" (San Francisco, CA, 1938), 57. Fields's 1932 study of anti-alien licensure and employment requirements in other parts of the globe suggest that Molony's comparative claim was either significantly exaggerated or uninformed. See Fields, "Closing Immigration," 671–99.

121. American Medical Association, "Eighty-Ninth Annual Session," 61. In the 1970s, two groups of public health scholars examined the breadth and history of licensing restrictions aimed at foreign medical graduates in the United States. Both characterize the 1938 anti-alien announcement as a major restrictionist shift in AMA policy toward immigrant doctors. While I agree that Molony's measure was a major intensification of the organization's anti-immigrant attitudes, the private lobbying of Colwell in the 1920s paints a longer history of AMA support for anti-alien licensure measures. See Rosemary Stevens and Joan Vermeulen, "Foreign Trained Physicians and American Medicine" (Bethesda, MD: National Institutes of Health; Bureau of Health Manpower Education, June 1972), xiv; and Butter and Sweet, "Licensure of Foreign Medical Graduates," 315.

122. "Citizenship as a Condition Precedent to Medical Licensure in the United States," *Journal of the American Medical Association* 113, no. 16 (October 14, 1939): 1496.

123. "21 Alien Physicians Denied Texas Permit," *Austin Statesman*, June 21, 1938, 3.

124. Minutes from October 16, 1938, 264, Texas Board of Medicine, "Medical Examiners Minutes," Box 1981/207–2, Texas State Archives, Austin.

125. Minutes from November 14–16, 1938, 265–267 (quotation in main text from 267), Texas Board of Medicine, "Medical Examiners Minutes," Box 1981/207–2, Texas State Archives, Austin.

126. "Subdivision II: State Boards, Chapter 3 Medicine—Licenses and Examination," Texas State Legislature—46th Legislature, Regular Session (1939), General Laws: 352–60.

127. Garcia-Godoy's lawsuit drew substantial news coverage. The presiding judge in the case, Ralph Yarborough, was a well-known politician who would later be elected to the US Senate. See "Mexican Launches Attack on Medical Practice Act: Constitutionality of Amendment Put

NOTES TO PAGES 138–9   237

under Fire in Mandamus Suit Filed Here," *Austin Statesman*, June 21, 1939, 2; "Alien Doctor Suit Is Set," *Austin Statesman*, June 23, 1939, 15; "Doctor's Suit in Second Day: Juarez Man Asks State Examination," *Austin Statesman*, September 8, 1939, 15; "Judge Hears Medical Head," *Austin Statesman*, September 9, 1939, 1; "Godoy Suit Is Resumed," *Austin Statesman*, September 11, 1939, 9; and "Exam Rights Are Upheld," *Austin Statesman*, September 12, 1939, 9. On Yarborough's lengthy legal and judicial career prior to his election as a progressive Democratic senator, see, especially, Patrick Cox, *Ralph W. Yarborough, the People's Senator* (Austin: University of Texas Press, 2002).

128. The case was Manuel Garcia-Godoy v. Texas State Board of Medical Examiners, District Court of Travis County 53 Jud. Dis., No. 61938 (1939). More broadly, see Minutes from May 7, 1939; May 21, 1939; June 19–21, 1939; September 7, 1939; November 20–22, 1939; December 3, 1939. While several other doctors facing the same predicament soon thereafter obtained licensure thanks to his litigation, Garcia-Godoy would continue to encounter administrative roadblocks for several years. Garcia-Godoy was recorded as having been marked as having "failed to make a passing grade" at previous examinations in the minutes of the meeting on June 26–28, 1944: Texas Board of Medicine, "Medical Examiners Minutes," Boxes 1981/207-2 & 1981/207-3, Texas State Archives, Austin; Texas lawmakers and nativist doctors were not unique for their time. Filindra similarly finds that the New York Medical Society (another state branch of the AMA) also campaigned for greater licensing restrictions in 1939. See Filindra, "E Pluribus Unum?" 131.

129. Quotation in main text from American Medical Association, "Ninety-First Annual Session of the American Medical Association House of Delegates Proceedings" (New York, 1940), 24. See also "District Court in Texas Rules State May Require Citizenship in Licensure of Physicians," *Journal of the American Medical Association* 113, no. 16 (October 14, 1939): 1495–96.

130. See, especially, "The Alien Registration Act of 1940, an Address by Earl Harrison, Director of Registration, Bureau of Immigration and Naturalization, Department of Justice" (NBC, August 7, 1940), AFL Papers, Files of the Economist of the AFL, General File, Mss. 177A/5C, Box 1, Folder, "Alien Registration," Wisconsin Historical Society Archives, Madison; and Earl G. Harrison, "Our Alien Population" (Current Citizenship Problems: Eleventh Annual Conference of the National Council on Naturalization and Citizenship, New York, February 28, 1941), AFL Papers, Files of the Economist of the AFL, General File, Mss. 177A/5C, Box 1, Folder, "Alien Registration, 1941–1942," Wisconsin Historical Society Archives, Madison. On Harrison's broader career and immigrant rights advocacy, see, among others, Lewis M. Stevens, "The Life and Character of Earl G. Harrison," *University of Pennsylvania Law Review* 104, no. 5 (March 1956): 591–602. More broadly, on the Roosevelt administration's efforts to mobilize largely European and Canadian immigrants for the war effort so as to avoid the anti-German crusades of the World War I years (and its diametrically opposite attitudes toward Japanese immigrants and Japanese Americans), see Steele, "War on Intolerance"; and Steele, "No Racials."

131. Earl G. Harrison, "Present Day Attitudes toward Alienage—a Constructive Program (National Conference on Social Work, Atlantic City, NJ, June 5, 1941)," 1, AFL Papers, Files of the Economist of the AFL, General File, Mss. 177A/5C, Box 1, Folder, "Alien Registration, 1941–1942," Wisconsin Historical Society Archives, Madison.

132. Harrison, "Present Day Attitudes," 4.

133. "The Alien Registration Act of 1940, an Address by Earl Harrison, Director of Registration, Bureau of Immigration and Naturalization, Department of Justice"; "Registration of Aliens, an Address by Francis Biddle, Solicitor General of the United States" (Washington, DC: CBS, August 25, 1940); Earl G. Harrison, "Suggestions to Employers Regarding Alien Registration Act of 1940," n.d., AFL Papers, Files of the Economist of the AFL, General File, Mss. 177A/5C, Box 1, Folder, "Alien Registration," Wisconsin Historical Society Archives, Madison; and "Die Registrierung der Auslaender und die Deutschen von Herrn Frank W. Kuehl," Frank W. Kuehl Papers, Mss 617, Box 73, Folder, "German-American Alien Registration, 1940," Wisconsin Historical Society Archives, Madison.

134. His lengthy address before the National Conference of Social Work, New York Regional Meeting, was reproduced as Earl G. Harrison, "The Problems of the Alien in Wartime," *Interpreter Releases* 20, no. 7 (March 10, 1943): 53.

135. Harrison, 52–59.

238 NOTES TO PAGES 140–3

136. Harrison, 57.
137. Minutes of February 17, 1942, Meeting: California Board of Education, "Teacher Preparation and Licensing Commission—Credentials Commission, 1/19/1932–9/7/1960," Files R359.01, Box 1, California State Archives, Sacramento, CA.
138. Earl Warren, Attorney General (by T. A. Westphal Jr., Deputy) to Department of Education, Attention Mr. Alfred E. Lentz, Administrative Adviser, April 28, 1942, 4, "Teacher Preparation and Licensing Commission—Credentials Commission, 1/19/1932–9/7/1960," Files R359.01, Box 1, California State Archives, Sacramento, CA.
139. California State Department of Education, Division of Credentials, October 23, 1943, "Regulations Governing the Issuance of Emergency Credentials Authorizing Public School Service in California, Plan II," Commission for Teacher Preparation & Licensing Commission of Credentials, Subject Files, California Department of Education, Folder 1 of 2, "1942–1943," Files R359.04, California State Archives, Sacramento, CA.
140. Minutes from November 17–19, 1941; January 9, 1944: Texas Board of Medicine, "Medical Examiners Minutes," Box 1981/207–3, Texas State Archives, Austin (quotation in main text from November 18, 1941, p. 77).
141. Minutes from March 22–24, 1944; June 4–6, 1945; June 5–7, 1947; June 16–18, 1949; December 8–10, 1949; December 3–5, 1951: Texas Board of Medicine, "Medical Examiners Minutes," Box 1981/207–3; Binder, Texas State Archives, Austin.
142. Konvitz recognized this contradiction in 1946. He particularly noted that New York's "Fair Employment Practice Law" of 1945 made it illegal to "discriminat[e] against individuals because of their race, color, creed, or national origin," but it "d[id] not protect persons discriminated against because they are aliens." Konvitz hoped that state legislators would amend the law "to repeal the many statutes which discriminate against aliens by excluding them from professions and various callings." But no such legislation was forthcoming in the immediate postwar era. See Konvitz, *Alien and the Asiatic,* 189.
143. Filindra employs a 1957 article from the *Columbia Law Review* to construct her calculations of the development of anti-alien licensing laws. As in previous eras, I believe it likely undercounts the number of anti-alien licensing policies in force. See Filindra, "E Pluribus Unum?" 146–50; and "Constitutionality of Restrictions on Aliens' Right to Work," *Columbia Law Review* 57, no. 7 (November 1957): 1012–28.
144. Kent, *Refugee Intellectual,* 33.
145. Kent, 127.
146. E. P. Prass, "General Correspondence" October 17, 1947, Texas Board of Public Accountancy, Folder: "Obsolete Rulings," Box 1993/206–9, Texas State Archives, Austin.
147. Minutes of June 16, 1946; July 17, 1946; October 16, 1946; December 4, 1946: Massachusetts Board of Dentistry, "Board of Dentistry Minutes," Massachusetts Commonwealth Archives, Boston.
148. Konvitz, *Alien and the Asiatic,* viii.
149. Konvitz, 171.
150. Brilliant, *Color of America,* 28–57.
151. Demonstrating proof of legal entry into the United States was not always possible for Chinese immigrants, because many had entered as undocumented immigrant "Paper Sons" in the early twentieth century. See, broadly, Lucy E. Salyer, *Laws Harsh as Tigers: Chinese Immigrants and the Shaping of Modern Immigration Law* (Chapel Hill: University of North Carolina Press, 1995); Lee, *At America's Gates*; and Ngai, *Impossible Subjects,* 202–24.
152. Truman tried to prevent the enactment of the McCarran–Walter Act not because he sought to retain racist anti-Asian naturalization provisions. On the contrary, he felt it did not go far enough in reforming the nation's immigration laws, especially the quota system. Legal scholar Hiroshi Motomura explores the repeal of the era of first papers and aliens racially ineligible to citizenship in Motomura, *Americans in Waiting.* See also Daniels, *Coming to America,* 328–49; and Roger Daniels, *Guarding the Golden Door: American Immigration Policy and Immigrants since 1882* (New York: Macmillan, 2005), 113–28.
153. Kelly, "Wavering Course," 720–40; Plascencia, Freeman, and Setzler, "Decline of Barriers," 11–15.
154. Sugarman v. Dougall, 413 U.S. 634 (1973); *In re* Griffiths, 413 U.S. 717 (1973); Examining Board v. Flores de Otero, 426 U.S. 572 (1976). See also, especially, Plascencia, Freeman, and Setzler, "Decline of Barriers," 13.

NOTES TO PAGES 143–5   239

155. Ambach v. Norwick, 441 U.S. 68 (1979); Kelly, "Wavering Course," 731–72.

156. As political scientists Brenton D. Peterson et al. demonstrate, requirements for "lengthier US medical residency training prior to licensure" were increasingly directed at foreign medical graduates beginning in the early 1970s (46). This occurred just as state citizenship requirements were struck down in court. See Peterson, Pandya, and Leblang, "Doctors with Borders," 46, 50. Other scholars noted this phenomenon—as new licensing requirements replaced alienage bans—in real time. See Stevens and Vermeulen, "Foreign Trained Physicians"; and Butter and Sweet, "Licensure."

Chapter 6

1. Quotation in main text from Mackenzie v. Hare, No. 239 U.S. 299, 300 (1915). Ethel Mackenzie's ordeal has been studied by many previous scholars, most notably Bredbenner, *Nationality of Her Own*, 65–70; Cott, *Public Vows*, 143–44; Kerber, *No Constitutional Right*, 40–42; and Amanda Frost, *You Are Not American: Citizenship Stripping from Dred Scott to the Dreamers* (Boston: Beacon Press, 2022), 74–91.

2. See, broadly, among others, Bredbenner, *Nationality of Her Own*; Kerber, *No Constitutional Right*; Ann Marie Nicolosi, "Female Sexuality, Citizenship and Law: The Strange Case of Louise Comacho," *Journal of Contemporary Criminal Justice* 18, no. 3 (August 2002): 329–38; Ann Marie Nicolosi, "'We Do Not Want Our Girls to Marry Foreigners': Gender, Race, and American Citizenship," *NWSA Journal* 13, no. 3 (Fall 2001): 1–21; Cott, *Public Vows*; and Gardner, *Qualities of a Citizen*.

3. Bredbenner, *Nationality of Her Own*, 183–94; and Susan Goodier, "The Price of Pacifism: Rebecca Shelley and Her Struggle for Citizenship," *Michigan Historical Review* 36, no. 1 (2010): 71–101.

4. "An Act to Repatriate Native-Born Women Who Have Heretofore Lost Their Citizenship by Marriage to an Alien," 54 Stat. 715 (1940).

5. Other scholars who have noted this anomalous phenomenon include Bredbenner, *Nationality of Her Own*, 192; Volpp, "Divesting Citizenship," 447n192; and DiStasi, "Derived Aliens," 27.

6. Quotation in main text from Shelley v. United States, No. 120 F. 2d 734, 735 (US Court of Appeals for the District of Columbia, 1941). Shelley only later regained her US citizenship after coming to an accommodation with federal authorities that her oath would not entail a commitment to personally arm herself in defense of the state. See Bredbenner, *Nationality of Her Own*, 192.

7. I identify and examine all marital expatriates' naturalization petitions filed in federal district court in the cities of San Francisco, San Antonio, and Providence between FY 1923 and FY 1940 and federal repatriation petitions filed between FY 1936 and FY 1975 in San Francisco and San Antonio. (Providence repatriation files were not systematically organized at the time.)

8. The Alien Registration Act (also known as the Smith Act) of 1940 was formally titled "An Act to Prohibit Certain Subversive Activities; to Amend Certain Provisions of Law with Respect to the Admission and Deportation of Aliens; to Require the Fingerprinting and Registration of Aliens; and for Other Purposes," 54 Stat. 670 (1940). See also Gardner, *Qualities of a Citizen*, 203. The formal title of the Nationality Act of 1940 is "An Act to Revise and Codify the Nationality Laws of the United States into a Comprehensive Nationality Code," 54 Stat. 1137 (1940). See also George S. Knight, "Nationality Act of 1940," *American Bar Association Journal* 26, no. 12 (1940): 938–40.

9. Marital expatriation has not gone unnoticed by scholars. Marital repatriation, by contrast, has been less studied. Migration historians have incorporated marital expatriates into their analyses of discrete immigrant communities. See, for instance, Mark Paul Richard, *Loyal but French: The Negotiation of Identity by French-Canadian Descendants in the United States* (East Lansing: Michigan State University Press, 2008), 167; and DiStasi, "Derived Aliens." Others have contextualized marital expatriation law within broader US citizenship policymaking. See, among others, Smith, "'Any Woman'"; Nancy Green, "Expatriation, Expatriates, and Expats: The American Transformation of a Concept," *American Historical Review* 114, no. 2 (April 2009): 307–28; and Schneider, *Crossing Borders*, 208, 215. Many scholars have importantly emphasized how marital expatriation especially harmed the lives of Asian American women who became "aliens ineligible to citizenship" in their own country. See, among others, Megumi Dick Osumi, "Asians and California's Anti-Miscegenation Laws," in *Asian and Pacific American Experiences: Women's Perspectives*, ed. Nobuya Tsuchida,

240   NOTES TO PAGE 146

Linda M. Mealey, and Gail Thoen (Minneapolis: Asian/Pacific American Learning Resource Center and General College, University of Minnesota, 1982), 15; Leonard, *Making Ethnic Choices*, 56–57, 135, 154, 269n61; Judy Yung, *Unbound Feet: A Social History of Chinese Women in San Francisco* (Berkeley: University of California Press, 1995), 168–72; Salyer, *Laws Harsh as Tigers*, 212; Allison Varzally, "Romantic Crossings: Making Love, Family, and Non-Whiteness in California, 1925–1950," *Journal of American Ethnic History* 23, no. 1 (Fall 2003): 3–54; Lee, *At America's Gates*, 238; Volpp, "Divesting Citizenship"; Erika Lee and Judy Yung, *Angel Island: Immigrant Gateway to America* (New York: Oxford University Press, 2010), 288; Nayan Shah, *Stranger Intimacy: Contesting Race, Sexuality, and the Law in the North American West* (Berkeley: University of California Press, 2011), 251–54; Shiori Yamamoto, "Beyond Suffrage: Intermarriage, Land, and Meanings of Citizenship and Marital Naturalization/Expatriation in the United States" (PhD diss., University of Nevada, Las Vegas, 2019); and Michael R. Jin, *Citizens, Immigrants, and the Stateless: A Japanese American Diaspora in the Pacific* (Stanford, CA: Stanford University Press, 2022), 38–55. Numerous gender historians, in turn, have studied how early-twentieth-century women's rights activists fought to overturn the Expatriation Act. See Bredbenner, *Nationality of Her Own*; Nancy F. Cott, "Marriage and Women's Citizenship in the United States, 1830–1934," *American Historical Review* 103, no. 5 (December 1998): 1440–74; Kerber, *No Constitutional Right*; Nicolosi, "We Do Not Want"; Nicolosi, "Female Sexuality"; Cott, *Public Vows*; Gardner, *Qualities of a Citizen*; Stephanie Anne McIntyre, "A Study in Married Women's Rights and Repatriation in the United States, the United Kingdom, and Latin America: Citizenship, Gender and the Law in Transatlantic Context" (PhD diss., University of Texas at Arlington, 2014); Yoosun Park, "'A Curious Inconsistency': The Discourse of Social Work on the 1922 Married Women's Independent Nationality Act and the Intersecting Dynamics of Race and Gender in the Laws of Immigration and Citizenship," *Affilia* 30, no. 4 (2015): 560–79; Irving, *Citizenship, Alienage*; Diane Sainsbury, "Gender Differentiation and Citizenship Acquisition: Nationality Reforms in Comparative and Historical Perspective," *Women's Studies International Forum* 68 (June 2018): 28–35; and Felice Batlan, "'She Was Surprised and Furious': Expatriation, Suffrage, Immigration, and the Fragility of Women's Citizenship, 1907–1940," *Stanford Journal of Civil Rights & Civil Liberties* 15, no. 3 (2020): 315–50.

10. It is not possible to identify or explore all marital expatriates' efforts to regain their citizenship since federal authorities did not track their petitions as a distinct category until the mid-1940s. Candice Bredbenner is one of the few scholars to contextualize how many women lost their citizenship through marriage. She cites sociologist Niles Carpenter's 1927 work to highlight that native-born women and foreign-born fathers were responsible for nearly 9 percent of Caucasian births in the United States to illustrate how widespread marriages were between native-born women and noncitizen men during the 1910s and 1920s. See Bredbenner, *Nationality of Her Own*, 4. Indeed, Carpenter argued in 1927 that "the number of foreign-born men who have married native women is particularly impressive." He stressed that "whereas 138.9 out of 1,000 foreign-born mothers in the birth statistics as of 1920 had married native fathers, 237.6 foreign-born fathers had married native mothers. Clearly the bulk of mixed marriages is between immigrant men and American women." See Niles Carpenter, *Immigrants and Their Children, 1920: A Study Based on Census Statistics Relative to the Foreign Born and the Native White of Foreign or Mixed Parentage* (Washington, DC: US Government Printing Office, 1927), 233. I thank Marian Smith of the US Citizenship and Immigration Services History Office who advised me numerous times on ways to find sources and calculate annual numbers of repatriations both at the local and at the national level. My estimates are explained in both Sections 1 and 3 of this chapter and are elaborated on in their accompanying notes.

11. The citizenship status of native-born women marrying noncitizen men had long been nebulous in nineteenth-century federal legislation, court precedent, and administrative policy. While state coverture laws then usually constrained the rights of American wives by, in the words of historian Linda Kerber, "treating married women as 'covered' by their husbands' civic identity," nineteenth-century federal married women's nationality laws were often less precise (xxiii). See, especially, Kerber, *No Constitutional Right*, xxiii, 34–35. In *Shanks v. Dupont* (1830), the US Supreme Court explicitly rejected the notion that an American-born woman's citizenship automatically transferred to her husband's status upon marriage. In turn, the federal Naturalization Act of 1855, which conferred American citizenship upon the wives of immigrant men who became naturalized citizens, said nothing about American-born women who

NOTES TO PAGES 146-8   241

married foreigners. See also Bredbenner, *Nationality of Her Own*, 40–41; Nicolosi, "We Do Not Want," 7–8; Cott, *Public Vows*, 143; and Irving, *Citizenship, Alienage*, 66–69.

12. "An Act in Reference to the Expatriation of Citizens and Their Protection Abroad," 34 Stat. 1228 (1907).

13. "An Act Relative to the Naturalization and Citizenship of Married Women," 42 Stat. 1021 (1922). On this history, see, especially, Bredbenner, *Nationality of Her Own*, 81–112; Kristi Andersen, *After Suffrage: Women in Partisan and Electoral Politics before the New Deal* (Chicago: University of Chicago, 1996), 7, 28; and Galloway Kruse, "Independent Citizenship."

14. Gardner, *Qualities of a Citizen*, 121–56. See also, broadly, Volpp, "Divesting Citizenship."

15. Petition Number 5142, Amalia Bertha Stratton, December 28, 1922, Petition and Record of Naturalization, 1903–1991, US District Court for the Southern (San Francisco) Division of the Northern District of California, Vol. 48, Box 26, RG 21, NARA–Pacific (San Bruno).

16. On these mechanics, see, specifically, US Bureau of Naturalization, "Annual Report of the Commissioner of Naturalization, 1923" (Washington, DC: US Government Printing Office, 1923), 2–3; Darrell Smith, *The Bureau of Naturalization: Its History, Activities, and Organization* (Baltimore: Johns Hopkins University Press, 1926), 21–29; Henry B. Hazard, "The Trend toward Administrative Naturalization," *American Political Science Review* 21, no. 2 (May 1927): 345–49. More broadly, see Bredbenner, *Nationality of Her Own*, 113–50; and Gardner, *Qualities of a Citizen*, 121–56.

17. Quotation in main text from Sophonisba Preston Breckinridge, *Marriage and the Civic Rights of Women; Separate Domicil and Independent Citizenship* (Chicago: University of Chicago Press, 1931), 22. See also, more broadly, 21–41.

18. Schneider, *Crossing Borders*, 208.

19. Petition and Record of Naturalization, 1903–1991, SF, Vols. 46–73, Boxes 26–39, RG 21, NARA–Pacific (San Bruno).

20. All data are drawn from Petition and Record of Naturalization, 1903–1991, SF, Vols. 46–73, Boxes 26–196, RG 21, NARA–Pacific (San Bruno).

21. So numerous were such petitioners that just over a third of all naturalization applications in Honolulu's federal district court during FY 1931 (49 of 143) were filed by marital expatriates. In FY 1932, marital expatriates represented slightly more than half of all naturalization petitioners (70 of 139). All data drawn from Petition and Record of Naturalization, 1903–1991, US District Court for the District of Hawaii, Honolulu, HI, Boxes 14–15, RG 21, NARA–Pacific (San Bruno).

22. United States, *Fourteenth Census of the United States, 1920*, 22; United States, *Fourteenth Census of the United States—Population: 1920: Color or Race, Nativity and Parentage* (Washington, DC: US Government Printing Office, 1922), 26. See, especially, on these intergenerational demographics and the politics of immigration and immigrant rights in Rhode Island, Sterne, *Ballots & Bibles*.

23. Petition and Record of Naturalization, 1842–1991, US District Court for the District of Rhode Island, Vols. 63–100, RG 21, NARA–Northeast (Waltham).

24. Though Smith was crushed by Hoover nationally, his gains among immigrant and second-generation Catholic voters helped him flip Massachusetts and Rhode Island into the Democratic column, presaging Roosevelt's further inroads among such voters and within the region four years later. See, especially, Sterne, *Ballots & Bibles*, 230–35; and see, broadly, Allan J. Lichtman, *Prejudice and the Old Politics: The Presidential Election of 1928* (Lanham, MD: Lexington Books, 2000).

25. Most of the FY 1928 petitions (58) occurred between March and June, before the 1928 election. See, broadly, Petition and Record of Naturalization, 1842–1991, RI, Vol. 100–118, RG 21, NARA–Northeast (Waltham).

26. See, among others, Lewis, "Have We Still?" 150–57.

27. All data are drawn from Petition and Record of Naturalization, 1842–1991, RI, Vol. 63–189, RG 21, NARA–Northeast (Waltham).

28. All data are drawn from Petition and Record of Naturalization, US District Court for the Southern District of Texas at Houston, Vol. 14–24, Boxes 1–7, RG 21, NARA–Southwest (Fort Worth).

29. All data are drawn from Petition and Record of Naturalization, US District Court for the Southern District of Texas at Laredo, Vol. 2–3, Boxes 1–2, RG 21, NARA–Southwest (Fort Worth).

242 NOTES TO PAGES 149–50

30. On San Antonio's population in this era, see, among others, Edward Telles and Vilma Ortiz, *Generations of Exclusion: Mexican Americans, Assimilation, and Race* (New York: Russell Sage Foundation, 2008); and Morales, "Tejas, Afuera de México."

31. All data are drawn from Petition and Record of Naturalization, US District Court for the Western District of Texas at San Antonio, Vol. 17–23, Boxes 1–10, RG 21, NARA–Southwest (Fort Worth).

32. Those told they were already citizens were P.N. 6910 Sofia de la Vega Flores, February 20, 1940, SA, Box 10, RG 21, NARA–Southwest (Fort Worth); P.N. 6914 Rosa Diaz Garcia, February 23, 1940, SA, Box 10, ibid; P.N. 6924 Nettie Sigrid Brynston, March 4, 1940, SA, Box 10, ibid.

33. While some of these rejections were technically "continued" (with most then later outright denied for failure to prosecute), none of these petitions would ultimately succeed. Rejected women were P.N. 4157 Laura Grice Maverick, August 24, 1925, SA, Vol. 21, ibid; P.N. 5278, Josefa Gutierrez Andrade de Ayala, January 24, 1935, SA, Box 3, ibid; P.N. 5410 Ermina Garcia Lopez, December 18, 1935, SA, Box 4, ibid; P.N. 5660 Margarita Garza Mendoza, October 27, 1936, SA, Box 5, ibid; P.N. 6024 Felicitas Tarin Tellez, March 21, 1938, SA, Box 7, ibid; P.N. 6327 Apolonia Granado Duarte, January 3, 1939, SA, Box 8, ibid; P.N. 6433 Cecilia Chavez Gonzalez, March 8, 1939, SA, Box 8, ibid; P.N. 6532 Cruz Mireles Moran, April 26, 1939, SA, Box 9, ibid; P.N. 6643 Viviana Posos Ortiz, July 5, 1939, SA, Box 9, ibid; and P.N. 6724 Otila Castanon Suarez, September 7, 1939, SA, Box 9, ibid. One other petition was not denied, dismissed, or completed: P.N. 6125 Stella Kalteyer Weinzheimer, July 1, 1938, SA; Box 7; ibid. By contrast, unsuccessful naturalization petitions (those denied, withdrawn, or continued but never completed), in addition to instances where women learned that they were already US citizens, amounted to less than 2 percent of all marital expatriate applications filed in San Francisco's federal district court between FY 1923 and FY 1940. See, broadly, Petition and Record of Naturalization, 1903–1991, US District Court for the Southern (San Francisco) Division of the Northern District of California, Vols. 46–73, Boxes 26–196, RG 21, NARA–Pacific (San Bruno).

34. Representatives of the Bureau of Naturalization (1923–1932) and the INS (1933–1940) frequently adjusted how much information they provided within their annual reports. In some years, they calculated how many immigrants became citizens on the basis of prior nationality. In others, they broke their data down on the basis of regional patterns. And during the early years of the INS, they provided little more than national tallies. Between FY 1924 and FY 1932, the Bureau of Naturalization did report on how many "repatriated Americans" petitioned to become citizens (29,142 of 1,637,473 naturalization petitions [or 1.78 percent of the total]). While this number likely includes many of the tens of thousands of marital expatriates who became citizens once more during these years, this category is not a sufficient basis to estimate marital expatriate naturalization figures. In this era, only American men who had joined Allied armies in World War I could be formally repatriated by fast-track procedure. It is impossible to know how many of those men are included in this tally. Moreover, there was no box to mark a woman as a "marital expatriate" or a "repatriate" on the standard naturalization forms (though sometimes clerks did annotate this information on their naturalization petitions). Instead, marital expatriate petitioners were listed as possessing the nationality of their husbands or former spouses. Therefore, even if this repatriated Americans number includes some marital expatriates, it would have highly undercounted them. See "Annual Reports of the Bureau of Naturalization/Immigration and Naturalization Service, FY 1923–1940" (Washington, DC: US Government Printing Office); District Court Records cited above. See also "Series B: 337-349— Naturalization of Aliens—Sex and Former Allegiance, 1907–1945," *Historical Statistics of the United States, 1789–1945*, 38.

35. See P.N. 5033, Maria de Vacas Amaral, October 20, 1922, SF, Vol. 47, Box 25, RG 21, NARA–Pacific (San Bruno); P.N. 5129 Helen Mercedes Gilliland, December 14, 1922, SF, Vol. 48, Box 26, ibid; P.N. 5514 Erma Schwab Mosseri, August 8, 1923, SF, Vol. 52, Box 28, ibid; P.N. 5640 Ernestine Irene Welden, October 4, 1923, SF, Vol. 53, Box 28, ibid; P.N. 6484 Gertrude Sarah Ord, March 25, 1925, SF, Vol. 61, Box 38, ibid; P.N. 6630 Anna Carolina Guthrie, June 4, 1925, SF, Vol. 63, Box 32, ibid; P.N. 19367 Diana Ledoux, October 30, 1924, RI, Vol. 79, RG 21, NARA–Northeast (Waltham); P.N. 19404 Teresina Formicola, November 10, 1924, RI, Vol. 79, ibid; and P.N. 21401 Vincenzina Scotti, June 22, 1926, RI, Vol. 99, ibid. Failure to prosecute was the most common reason immigrant petitioners were denied during the Progressive Era as well. See Catron, "Citizenship Advantage," 1004n3.

NOTES TO PAGES 151–3   243

36. P.N. 5129 Helen Mercedes Gilliland, December 14, 1922, SF, Vol. 48, Box 26, NARA–Pacific (San Bruno).
37. See, for instance, P.N. 5033 Maria de Vacas Amaral, October 20, 1922, SF, Vol. 47, Box 25, RG 21, NARA–Pacific (San Bruno); and P.N. 6630 Anna Carolina Guthrie, June 4, 1925, Vol. 63, Box 32, ibid. Maria de Vacas Amaral's petition was thrown out after thirteen months. Guthrie's petition was discarded after only eleven.
38. P. N. 18478 Anna Patricia McKeen, May 7, 1924, RI, Vol. 74, RG 21, NARA–Northeast (Waltham).
39. All three of these petitions were denied on September 24, 1928. See P.N. 19367 Diana Ledoux, October 30, 1924, RI, Vol. 79, RG 21, NARA–Northeast (Waltham); P.N. 19404 Teresina Formicola, November 10, 1924, RI, Vol. 79, ibid; and P.N. 21401 Vincenzina Scotti, June 22, 1926, RI, Vol. 99, ibid.
40. Blumer likely received at least one more extension before July 6, 1925. The clerk's office stapled a postcard written by Blumer to her application, stamped June 3, 1925, which read, "I shall do my best to get in one Monday before July 6th. Or if I do not succeed I must again ask for an extension as my baby is still too young to leave alone." See, broadly, her file P.N. 5435 Alfhild Johanna Blumer, June 27, 1923, SF, Vol. 51, Box 27, RG 21, NARA–Pacific (San Bruno).
41. P.N. 5640 Ernestine Irene Welden, October 4, 1923, SF, Vol. 53, Box 28, RG 21, NARA–Pacific (San Bruno).
42. P.N. 5720, Dorothy Chamorro, December 27, 1923, SF, Vol. 54, Box 29, RG 21, NARA–Pacific (San Bruno). The petitioner's last name was variously spelled Chamorro and Chamorra in legal filings. See *In re* Chamorra, 298 Fed. 669 (1924).
43. *In re* Chamorra, No. 5720, (undated) May 1924, M. R. Bevington, State and Brief Submitted on Behalf of the United States, Contested Naturalization and Repatriation Case Files, 1924–1992, US District Court for the Southern (San Francisco) Division of the Northern District of California, Box 1, RG 21, NARA–Pacific (San Bruno).
44. *In re* Chamorra, No. 5720, (undated) May 1924, Milton Schmitt, Petitioner's Closing Brief, May 17, 1924, Judge Frank Kerrigan, Petition Denied, without Prejudice, Contested Naturalization and Repatriation Case Files, 1924–1992, SF, Box 1, RG 21, NARA–Pacific (San Bruno).
45. See *In re* Chamorra, No. 5720, May 17, 1924, Judge Frank Kerrigan, Petition Denied, without Prejudice, Contested Naturalization and Repatriation Case Files, 1924–1992, SF, Box 1, RG 21, NARA–Pacific (San Bruno) (emphasis in the original).
46. P.N. 20952 Molly Di Rita, March 29, 1926, RI, Vol. 95, RG 21, NARA–Northeast (Waltham). Breckinridge emphasizes, however, that the federal district court of Delaware came to the opposite conclusion in the case: *Petition of Fortunato*, 8 Fed. (2d) 508 (1925). See Breckinridge, *Marriage*, 29.
47. Quotation in main text from Breckinridge, *Marriage*, 39. See also, more broadly, 29–39. Recent works that explore the intersection of Breckinridge's scholarship and activism include Anya Jabour, *Sophonisba Breckinridge: Championing Women's Activism in Modern America* (Champaign: University of Illinois Press, 2019); and Batlan, "She Was Surprised." See also, on the importance of residency requirements in marital expatriates' legal encounters, Bredbenner, *Nationality of Her Own*, 80–112, 144–48; and, broadly, Gardner, *Qualities of a Citizen*, 121–56.
48. The Johnson–Reed Act of 1924 often conflicted with naturalization statutes governing marital expatriates' access to citizenship. Prior to 1930, if a marital expatriate who had been out of the country wanted to naturalize, her eligibility hinged on whether her time abroad counted as an official residence. Owing to a lack of clarity in the language of the laws governing residency status (and what the Bureau of Naturalization found as excessively generous judicial interpretations), it argued in its 1924 annual report that "the question of what is continuous residence in the United States and what constitutes a break of the continuity of residence by absence from the United States should be settled by legislation." See US Bureau of Naturalization, "Annual Report of the Commissioner of Naturalization, 1924" (Washington, DC: US Government Printing Office, 1924), 13; "An Act Relative to the Naturalization and Citizenship of Married Women" (1922); and "An Act to Amend the Law Relative to the Citizenship and Naturalization of Married Women, and for Other Purposes," 46 Stat. 854 (1930).
49. *In re* Jeanette Anderson Haas, No. 17228, July 18, 1929, Paul Armstrong, District Director of Naturalization, Brief for the United States, Contested Naturalization and Repatriation Case Files, 1924–1992, US District Court for the Southern (San Francisco) Division of the Northern District of California, Box 2, RG 21, NARA–Pacific (San Bruno).

244   NOTES TO PAGES 153–4

50. P.N. 17228 Jeanette Anderson Haas, March 23, 1929, P.R. Naturalization, 1903–1991, SF, Box 62, RG 21, NARA–Pacific (San Bruno).

51. *In re* Jeanette Anderson Haas, No. 17228, July 18, 1929, Paul Armstrong, Brief for the United States, Contested Naturalization and Repatriation Case Files, 1924–1992, SF, Box 2, RG 21, NARA–Pacific (San Bruno).

52. P.N. 17228 Jeanette Anderson Haas, March 23, 1929, SF, Box 62, RG 21, NARA–Pacific (San Bruno); *In re* Jeanette Anderson Haas, No. 17228, July 9, 1929, Everett J. Brown, Thomas J. Sedwick, and Stephen M. White, Brief for the Petitioner, Contested Naturalization and Repatriation Case Files, 1924–1992, SF, Box 2, RG 21, NARA–Pacific (San Bruno).

53. P.N. 5278, Josefa Gutierrez Andrade de Ayala, January 24, 1935, SA, Box 3, RG 21, NARA–Southwest (Fort Worth); P.N. 5410 Ermina Garcia Lopez, December 18, 1935, SA, Box 4, ibid; P.N. 5660 Margarita Garza Mendoza, October 27, 1936, SA, Box 5, ibid; P.N. 6024 Felicitas Tarin Tellez, March 21, 1938, SA, Box 7, ibid; P.N. 6327 Apolonia Granado Duarte, January 3, 1939, SA, Box 8, ibid; P.N. 6433 Cecilia Chavez Gonzalez, March 8, 1939, SA, Box 8, ibid; P.N. 6532 Cruz Mireles Moran, April 26, 1939, SA, Box 9, ibid; P.N. 6643 Viviana Posos Ortiz, July 5, 1939, SA, Box 9, ibid; and P.N. 6724 Otila Castanon Suarez, September 7, 1939, SA, Box 9, ibid.

54. See, broadly, Menchaca, *Naturalizing Mexican Immigrants*; Gunter, "More Than Black"; Martinez, *Injustice Never Leaves You*; and Max Krochmal and Todd Moye, eds., *Civil Rights in Black and Brown: Histories of Resistance and Struggle in Texas* (Austin: University of Texas Press, 2021).

55. Blumer demanded to know how "any law" could "take away my *constitutional* right for no wrong cause what so ever." See P.N. 5435 Alfhild Johanna Blumer, June 27, 1923, SF, Vol. 51, Box 27, RG 21, NARA–Pacific (San Bruno) (emphasis in original). Jeannette Anderson Haas's lawyers reminded the court that Haas "is a member of a pioneer California family" and "by birth, by family tradition, by education, by environment and by position, she is truly an American." See *In re* Jeanette Anderson Haas, No. 17228, July 9, 1929, Everett J. Brown, Thomas J. Sedwick, and Stephen M. White, Brief for the Petitioner, Contested Naturalization and Repatriation Case Files, 1924–1992, SF, Box 2, RG 21, NARA–Pacific (San Bruno). Bredbenner similarly finds that appeals to American identity and constitutional rights were commonplace among American-born marital expatriates and their allies. See Bredbenner, *Nationality of Her Own*, 65–70, 183–194.

56. Department of Education, "Annual Report of the Division of Immigration and Americanization for the Year Ending November 30, 1924" (Boston: Commonwealth of Massachusetts, 1925), 4.

57. Department of Education, "Annual Report of the Division of Immigration and Americanization for the Year Ending November 30, 1925" (Boston: Commonwealth of Massachusetts, 1926), 4.

58. See, broadly, Andersen, *After Suffrage*; and, specifically, Schneider, *Crossing Borders*, 214–22.

59. Local newspapers often reported on marital expatriates' sudden discovery of their alienage in brief exposés. See, among others, "Citizenship: Native of Austin Finds She's a Spanish Subject, Seeks U.S. Papers," *Austin Statesman*, June 10, 1929, 1. One such marital expatriate, Angelina Salese, "was not aware" for twenty-three years that she was a noncitizen "until she went to vote," as the *Baltimore Sun* reported. Salese told her interviewer that "they [election officials] stopped me…I argued that I was as much a citizen as them—I was born here, but that didn't do no good." She could not believe that her immigrant husband was now a citizen, but she had lost her citizenship decades earlier owing to their marriage. See "D'Alesandro Measure Is Magic to 'Women without Country,'" *Baltimore Sun*, April 20, 1941, 21. Some women "were unaware" of their marital expatriation as late as 1956, as the *New York Herald* reported, and had "proceeded to vote, as native-born Americans, with no repercussions." See Judith Crist, "4 Women Get U.S. Citizenship Back," *New York Herald Tribune*, May 12, 1956, A1.

60. This particular teacher was aware of the Expatriation Act of 1907 at the time of her marriage, however. The *Woman Citizen* reported that "she explained to her husband that he must take his papers out at the earliest possible moment or her sudden technical lack of citizenship would jeopardize her position in the schools." See "Alien-by-Marriage," *The Woman Citizen*, October 8, 1921, 13. Though the *Woman Citizen* article did not name this teacher, she was almost certainly Florence Bain Gaul, whose correspondence historian Candice Bredbenner first uncovers in *Nationality of Her Own*, 83.

61. "Alien Women Ignorant of Cable Law's Demand," *New York Times*, June 28, 1925, XX16.

NOTES TO PAGES 154–6 245

62. On the experiences of Asian American marital expatriates, see, especially, Volpp, "Divesting Citizenship"; Yamamoto, "Beyond Suffrage." See also Leonard, *Making Ethnic Choices*, 56–57; Gardner, *Qualities of a Citizen*, 121–56; and Shah, *Stranger Intimacy*, 251–54. Louise Comacho, a sex worker, barely escaped deportation by convincing her judge that she no longer was of "immoral character." Lillian Larch, a poor, illiterate widow, was deported to Ontario in 1931. See, respectively, Nicolosi, "Female Sexuality, Citizenship"; and Bredbenner, *Nationality of Her Own*, 172–75. Legal historian Felice Batlan has similarly and recently underscored the varied impacts of marital expatriation on women's political and economic lives in "She Was Surprised and Furious."

63. As historian Martha Gardner highlights, despite naturalization officers and judges referring to marital expatriates reacquiring citizenship as "repatriating," such women were not technically repatriated under the Cable Act. Since an act of repatriation refers to the reacquisition of citizenship through special provisions not afforded under standard naturalization laws, marital expatriates are better described as having been "renaturalized." See Gardner, *Qualities of a Citizen*, 155.

64. Yamamoto similarly emphasizes this disparate treatment in "Beyond Suffrage," 241–52.

65. Though Crist recognized that many marital expatriates found naturalizing alongside immigrant men to be insulting and expressed limited sympathy for their plight, he did not recommend creating a separate repatriation process for marital expatriates among his numerous formal legislative recommendations that year. See US Bureau of Naturalization, "Annual Report, 1923." Quotations in main text from p. 14. See, more broadly, 13–14, 27–31.

66. See, for instance, Leigh H. Nettleton, "Lecture No. 27: Loss of Citizenship (Expatriation) and Presumptive Loss of Citizenship," *Lectures: Immigration and Naturalization Service*, (Washington, DC: December 17, 1934), 3–4.

67. Quotation in main text from "An Act to Repatriate Native-Born Women Who Have Heretofore Lost Their Citizenship by Marriage to an Alien, and for Other Purposes," 49 Stat. 1917 (1936). The new law was not widely covered by the press. The *New York Times*, for instance, briefly discussed its legislative evolution in a lengthy mid-June 1936 article focused on other congressional debates. See "Congress Ready to Enact the Compromise Tax Bill and Adjourn Tomorrow," *New York Times*, June 19, 1936, 1, 5. The *Los Angeles Times* only noted its enactment in passing. See "Strike Aid Bill Signed: Planes for Army Assured," *Los Angeles Times*, June 26, 1936, 12. In practice, the INS quickly made it a policy to require "preliminary hearings" of marital expatriates to mitigate fraud. See Deputy Commissioner Edward J. Shaughnessy to All Districts, Circular No. 39, November 2, 1936; Bureau of Naturalization, Records of the Central Office: Administrative Files Relating to Naturalization, 1906–1940, Folder 1, Box No. 408, 20/154, Entry No. 26, RG 85, NARA–DC. See also Gardner, *Qualities of a Citizen*, 202n9.

68. "An Act to Repatriate Native-Born Women Who Have Heretofore Lost Their Citizenship by Marriage to an Alien, and for Other Purposes" (1936).

69. Fred Schlotfeldt to Commissioner of Immigration and Naturalization Service, July 8, 1936, Bureau of Naturalization, Records of the Central Office: Administrative Files Relating to Naturalization, 1906–1940, Folder 1, Box No. 408, 20/154, Entry No. 26, RG 85, NARA–DC.

70. Commissioner D. W. MacCormack to Solicitor of Labor Charles Gregory, July 29, 1936, Bureau of Naturalization, Records of the Central Office: Administrative Files Relating to Naturalization, 1906–1940, Folder 1, Box No. 408, 20/154, Entry No. 26, RG 85, NARA–DC.

71. Solicitor of Labor Charles Gregory to Commissioner D. W. MacCormack, Memorandum for the Commissioner of Immigration and Naturalization, August 10, 1936, Bureau of Naturalization, Records of the Central Office: Administrative Files Relating to Naturalization, 1906–1940, Folder 2, Box No. 408, 20/154, Entry No. 26, RG 85, NARA–DC.

72. Henry Hazard to District Director, Chicago, August 5, 1938, Bureau of Naturalization, Records of the Central Office: Administrative Files Relating to Naturalization, 1906–1940, Folder 3, Box No. 408, 20/154, Entry No. 26, RG 85, NARA–DC.

73. Martha Gardner highlights this discriminatory treatment toward Puerto Rican marital expatriates in *Qualities of a Citizen*, 155. On the evolving nationality status of persons born in Puerto Rico during the early twentieth century, more broadly, see Erman, *Almost Citizens*; and McGreevey, *Borderline Citizens*.

74. "An Act to Amend the Law Relative to Citizenship and Naturalization, and for Other Purposes," 48 Stat. 797 (1934). For histories of battles over this act (and related legislation), see Gardner, *Qualities of a Citizen*, 156n62, 171–75; and, broadly, Bredbenner, *Nationality of Her Own*.

246 NOTES TO PAGES 156–7

75. Deputy Commissioner T. B. Shoemaker and L. Paul Winnings, Chairman of the Board of Review, Interpretation of the Act of June 25, 1936, August 22, 1936, Bureau of Naturalization, Records of the Central Office: Administrative Files Relating to Naturalization, 1906–1940, Folder 2, Box No. 408, 20/154, Entry No. 26, RG 85, NARA–DC.

76. Deputy Commissioner T. B. Shoemaker and L. Paul Winnings, Chairman of the Board of Review, Interpretation of the Act of June 25, 1936, August 22, 1936, Bureau of Naturalization, Records of the Central Office: Administrative Files Relating to Naturalization, 1906–1940, Folder 2, Box No. 408, 20/154, Entry No. 26, RG 85, NARA–DC; Assistant Secretary of Labor C. V. McLaughlin, Interpretation of the Act of June 25, 1936, November 9, 1939, Bureau of Naturalization, Records of the Central Office: Administrative Files Relating to Naturalization, 1906–1940, Folder 3, Box No. 408, 20/154, Entry No. 26, RG 85, NARA–DC.

77. Assistant Secretary of Labor C. V. McLaughlin, Interpretation of the Act of June 25, 1936, November 9, 1939, Bureau of Naturalization, Records of the Central Office: Administrative Files Relating to Naturalization, 1906–1940, Folder 3, Box No. 408, 20/154, Entry No. 26, RG 85, NARA–DC.

78. See Applications for Repatriation, 1936–1969, US District Court for the Southern (San Francisco) Division of the Northern District of California, RG 21, NARA–Pacific (San Bruno).

79. Data drawn from Petition and Record of Naturalization, 1903–1991, SF, Boxes 137–196, RG 21, NARA–Pacific (San Bruno).

80. Solicitor of Labor Charles Gregory to Commissioner D. W. MacCormack, Memorandum for the Commissioner of Immigration and Naturalization, August 10, 1936, 8, Bureau of Naturalization, Records of the Central Office: Administrative Files Relating to Naturalization, 1906–1940, Folder 2, Box No. 408, 20/154, Entry No. 26, RG 85, NARA–DC.

81. Shortly after commencing his first term in Congress, D'Alesandro sponsored legislation seeking to exempt longtime resident noncitizens (those who had lived in the country since at least 1918) from strict educational requirements to naturalize. See "D'Alesandro Supported on Naturalization Bill," *Baltimore Sun*, April 21, 1939, 5; "Would Cure Flaws in Naturalization," *Baltimore Sun*, June 19, 1939, 5; and "Backs D'Alesandro Bill Covering Naturalization," *Baltimore Sun*, July 20, 1939, 4. D'Alesandro continued to sponsor bills to facilitate the naturalization of older immigrants in subsequent congressional terms. See, for instance, "D'Alesandro Reoffers Naturalization Bills," *Baltimore Sun*, January 13, 1943, 6. On D'Alesandro's rise to Congress as a rare freshman New Deal Democrat in 1938 (and his subsequent mayoral career) see, among others, Michael Olesker, *Journeys to the Heart of Baltimore* (Baltimore: Johns Hopkins University Press, 2001), 12–13, 32–38; and Miriam Jiménez, *Inventive Politicians and Ethnic Ascent in American Politics: The Uphill Elections of Italians and Mexicans to the U.S. Congress* (New York: Routledge, 2015), 3–4, 86–89.

82. "Would Cure Flaws," 5.

83. "An Act to Repatriate Native-Born Women Who Have Heretofore Lost Their Citizenship by Marriage to an Alien," (1940).

84. "Roosevelt Signs Bill D'Alesandro Sponsored," *Baltimore Sun*, July 9, 1940, 6. The passage of D'Alesandro's amendment in early July 1940 was treated as a minor story by national newspapers. Four short paragraphs on page 3 of the *Los Angeles Times* and four sentences on page 8 of the *Chicago Tribune* were typical. See "President Signs Repatriation Bill," *Los Angeles Times*, July 4, 1940, 3; and "Aliens' Wives May Regain Citizenship under New Law," *Chicago Daily Tribune*, July 4, 1940, 8.

85. "Yesterday Not His Birthday but D'Alesandro Was Kissed," *Baltimore Sun*, November 19, 1940, 7.

86. The *Baltimore Sun* made sure to rib D'Alesandro in its news coverage of the event, noting that some marital expatriates were so grateful that he was flooded with "hugging and kissing" and "still had lipstick reminders of enthusiastic appreciation on his cheek" when "he returned" home "to face Mrs. D'Alesandro." See "Yesterday Not His Birthday," 7. That story (and recognition of D'Alesandro's sponsorship of the bill) was picked up by several other major national newspapers. See "Congressman Becomes Popular with Women," *Indianapolis Star*, December 15, 1940, 10; and "Too Patriotic, Eh? Sponsor Repatriation Bill Wins Gushy Thanks," *Cincinnati Enquirer*, December 29, 1940, 5. The congressman even received the pen President Roosevelt had used to bring the amendment into law as a gift. It would not be the last received by a member of the D'Alesandro family from an American president. His youngest child, born just a few months earlier in 1940, would go on to serve as the first female Speaker of the US House of Representatives: Nancy (D'Alesandro) Pelosi. "Roosevelt Signs Bill," 6.

NOTES TO PAGES 157–9   247

87. Charles P. Muller, Assistant District Director INS–New York to Mr. T. B. Shoemaker, September 12, 1940, INS File 56173–496, Box 19375, RG 85, NARA–DC.

88. Gardner first highlighted INS difficulties keeping up with forms and lobbying by constituents for assistance, particularly the efforts of Highland Park residents, in Gardner, *Qualities of a Citizen*, 201–2. For the petition, see Mrs. Flora Robinson to Solicitor General Francis Biddle, November 25, 1940, INS File 56173–496, Box 19375, RG 85, NARA–DC. Other examples of outreach to INS leaders for assistance and/or clarification include Barney Sokolowski to Congressman A. F. Maciejewski, July 23, 1940, INS File 56173–496, Box 19375, RG 85, NARA–DC; Chemical Bank and Trust Company to the Naturalization Bureau, July 26, 1940, INS File 56173–496, Box 19375, RG 85, NARA–DC.

89. "Wives Regain Lost Citizenship—Ice Coats Freighter—Ruins of Tower of London," *Detroit Free Press*, December 4, 1940, 32.

90. Justice Henry Kimball to Attorney General Robert Jackson, December 20, 1940, INS File 56173–496, Box 19375, RG 85, NARA–DC. Kimball's numbers—which certainly seem high—could have been exaggerated or passed on to him by someone else. Kimball, a western New York judge, wrote to the nation's attorney general in December 1940 because the INS had been transferred from the Labor Department to the Justice Department earlier in the year. On its move from the purview of immigrant-friendly labor secretary Frances Perkins to the Justice Department as a wartime national security measure (which itself grew out of the anti–New Deal backlash of the late 1930s), see, among others, Jennifer S. Breen, "Labor, Law Enforcement, and 'Normal Times': The Origins of Immigration's Home within the Department of Justice and the Evolution of Attorney General Control over Immigration Adjudications," *University of Hawai'i Law Review* 42, no. 1 (Winter 2019): 1–71.

91. "An Act to Prohibit Certain Subversive Activities; to Amend Certain Provisions of Law with Respect to the Admission and Deportation of Aliens; to Require the Fingerprinting and Registration of Aliens; and for Other Purposes," (1940). See also, on the importance of the Alien Registration Act to immigrant women and marital expatriates, Gardner, *Qualities of a Citizen*, 203, 203n10; DiStasi, "Derived Aliens"; and Schneider, *Crossing Borders*, 232–33.

92. Quotation from "Naturalizations Up," *Chicago Daily Tribune*, December 28, 1940, 4. Immigrant rights advocates Francis Kalnay and Richard Collins hyperbolized in 1941 that the Alien Registration Act amounted to "probably the most important piece of legislation affecting aliens ever passed in the United States." See Francis Kalnay and Richard Collins, *The New American* (New York: Greenberg, 1941), ix. Contemporaneous media coverage of the law's administration included "Aliens Will Start Registering Today," *New York Times*, August 27, 1940, 6; and "Citizenship Loss in War Clarified," *New York Times*, October 5, 1940, 6. See also United States, *Regulations and Instructions for Alien Registration* (Washington, DC: US Government Printing Office, 1940).

93. Donald R. Perry, Assistant Director of Registration, to Naomi M. Gresser, September 11, 1940, INS File 56173–496, Box 19375, RG 85, NARA–DC.

94. Charles Muller, Assistant District Director, New York to Mr. T. B. Shoemaker, October 14, 1940, INS File 56173–496, Box 19375, RG 85, NARA–DC.

95. The reform, codification, and clarification of US nationality laws had been a major aim of the Roosevelt administration since its earliest days in 1933. On the tortuous evolution of the omnibus bill, see Richard W. Flournoy, "Revision of Nationality Laws of the United States," *American Journal of International Law* 34, no. 1 (January 1940): 36–46; and "An Act to Revise and Codify the Nationality Laws of the United States into a Comprehensive Nationality Code" (1940).

96. On the "omission" of the Repatriation Act's July 1940 amendment in the Nationality Code adopted just months later in October of the same year, see, especially, Marian Schibsby, "Some Naturalization Issues," *Interpreter Releases* 19, no. 34 (July 6, 1942): 235–36 (b); and "An Act to Revise and Codify the Nationality Laws of the United States into a Comprehensive Nationality Code" (1940).

97. Michigan petitioners wrote to the solicitor general that marital expatriates had been "advised and believe that under the provisions of the new naturalization law, they will not have the benefits of the simple method provided for their repatriation after January 15, 1941, when said law goes into effect." See Mrs. Flora Robinson to Solicitor General Francis Biddle, November 25, 1940, INS File 56173–496, Box 19375, RG 85, NARA–DC. In turn, New York's Justice Kimball wrote to the nation's attorney general in haste because "it appear[ed] that repatriation of women, as provided in the amendment of July 2, 1940 by reason of continuous residence in the United States, will no longer be possible after January 12, 1941." See Justice Henry Kimball to

248 NOTES TO PAGES 159–61

Attorney General Robert Jackson, December 20, 1940, INS File 56173–496, Box 19375, RG 85, NARA–DC.

98. Henry Nicolls, Assistant District Director, Boston, to Commissioner of Immigration and Naturalization, December 6, 1940, INS File 56173–496, Box 19375, RG 85, NARA–DC.

99. Charles Muller, Assistant Director, New York, to Mr. T. B. Shoemaker, November 30, 1940, INS File 56173–496, Box 19375, RG 85, NARA–DC; O. B. Holton, District Director, Saint Paul, to Commissioner of Immigration and Naturalization, December 10, 1940, INS File 56173–496, Box 19375, RG 85, NARA–DC.

100. Deputy Commissioner T. B. Shoemaker, The Status of Women within the Purview of the Act prior to Taking the Oath of Allegiance, October 3, 1940, INS File 56173–496, Box 19375, RG 85, NARA–DC; Lemuel B. Schofield, Circular 482, Rulings by the Central Office concerning the Act of June 25, 1936, as amended by the Act of July 2, 1940, October 12, 1940, INS File 56173–496, Box 19375, RG 85, NARA–DC.

101. "An Act to Repatriate Native-Born Women Who Have Heretofore Lost Their Citizenship by Marriage to an Alien, and for Other Purposes," (1936).

102. Deputy Commissioner T. B. Shoemaker, The Status of Women within the Purview of the Act prior to Taking the Oath of Allegiance, October 3, 1940, INS File 56173–496, Box 19375, RG 85, NARA–DC.

103. Deputy Commissioner T. B. Shoemaker, The Status of Women within the Purview of the Act prior to Taking the Oath of Allegiance, October 3, 1940, INS File 56173–496, Box 19375, RG 85, NARA–DC.

104. The *New York Times* did not help to clarify matters, however. Its reporter buried news that most marital expatriates did not have to register below the confusing headline "Women Who Remain Aliens Because of Marriage Are Warned to Register." Though this referred only to the relatively few women who did not regain citizenship under the recent INS reinterpretation of the Repatriation Acts of 1936 and 1940, the prominent location of this headline likely led to renewed confusion. The paper did not get around to letting the vast majority of marital expatriates know that "they are nevertheless citizens and as such are not required to register" until the end of the article. See "Citizenship Loss," 6.

105. "An Act to Prohibit Certain Subversive Activities; to Amend Certain Provisions of Law with Respect to the Admission and Deportation of Aliens; to Require the Fingerprinting and Registration of Aliens; and for Other Purposes," (1940); Applications for Repatriation, 1936–1969, US District Court for the Southern (San Francisco) Division of the Northern District of California, RG 21, NARA–Pacific (San Bruno); Applications to Regain Citizenship and Repatriation Oaths, 1937–1970, US District Court for the Western (San Antonio) District of Texas, RG 21, NARA–Southwest (Fort Worth). See also Gardner, *Qualities of a Citizen,* 203; and, more broadly, Krajewska, *Documenting Americans,* 49–65.

106. On how INS leaders sought to communicate this new complicated status to marital expatriates and how local officials often struggled to interpret what that meant, see also DiStasi, "Derived Aliens."

107. Quotation in main text from "3,000 U.S.-Born Women Seek Repatriation," *New York Times,* January 14, 1941, 23. This was but one example of major news coverage on the topic by the *Times.* See also "Becomes an American Again," *New York Times,* April 7, 1942, 6; and "Loses Repatriation Plea," *New York Times,* August 27, 1942, 21.

108. "Steve Vasilakos," *Washington Post,* October 2, 1940, 3.

109. "49 Become U.S. Citizens, 19 Repatriated," *Washington Post,* November 6, 1940, 24.

110. "79 Granted U.S. Itizenship [*sic*]; 5 Nuns in Group," *Washington Post,* January 8, 1941, 21.

111. The *New York Times* described the inundation of repatriation petitions in January 1941 as a "flood." See "3,000 U.S.-Born Women," 23.

112. All data drawn from Applications for Repatriation, 1936–1969, US District Court for the Southern (San Francisco) Division of the Northern District of California, RG 21, NARA–Pacific (San Bruno).

113. Applications to Regain Citizenship and Repatriation Oaths, 1937–1970, US District Court for the Western (San Antonio) District of Texas, RG 21, NARA–Southwest (Fort Worth).

114. Applications to Regain Citizenship, 1937–1969, US District Court for the Western (El Paso) Division of Texas, RG 21, NARA–Southwest (Fort Worth).

115. US Immigration and Naturalization Service, "Annual Report of the Immigration and Naturalization Service, FY 1944–1975" (Washington, DC: US Government Printing Office).

NOTES TO PAGES 161–5   249

116. These figures do not even account for marital expatriates who continued to regain their citizenship via the Cable Act's naturalization provisions after D'Alesandro's 1940 amendment to the Repatriation Act came into force. In San Francisco's federal district court, a sizeable number of marital expatriates continued to apply for citizenship via naturalization. In FY 1941, seventy-two women regained their citizenship in this manner. See Petition and Record of Naturalization, 1903–1991, Boxes 196–210, SF, RG 21, NARA–Pacific (San Bruno).
117. Celestine Sibley, "Local Women, Now Aliens, to Be Repatriated," *Atlanta Constitution*, January 23, 1942, 2.
118. Schneider, *Crossing Borders*, 233. So many noncitizens sought US citizenship in FY 1944 that a then–"all-time high of over 450,000" naturalizations was reached that year, an annual record that would not be surpassed for half a century (64). See Dorothee Schneider, "Naturalization and United States Citizenship in Two Periods of Mass Migration: 1894–1930, 1965–2000," *Journal of American Ethnic History* 21, no. 1 (October 2001): 64, 68.
119. Bredbenner, *Nationality of Her Own*, 183–94; Goodier, "Price of Pacifism."
120. Shelley v. United States.
121. T. B. Shoemaker to District Director, Kansas City, November 28, 1941; INS File 56173–496, Box 19375; RG 85; NARA–DC.
122. "Ruling to Be Given on Nationality Act," *Baltimore Sun*, March 10, 1942, 24.
123. The Foreign Language Information Service reported that D'Alesandro maintained that "the Act of July 2, 1940 [had] conferred on" them these rights, but his (ultimately unsuccessful) clarifying legislation was necessary because "certain courts h[ad held] that this right was cancelled by section 37 (b) (1) of the Nationality Act of 1940." See Marian Schibsby, "Legislative Bulletin No. 1," *Interpreter Releases* 20, no. 3 (January 25, 1943): 21. See also Schibsby, "Some Naturalization Issues," 235–36 (b). D'Alesandro tried—and failed—to pass similar legislation in the subsequent Congress. See Elizabeth Eastman, "Legislative Bulletin No. 5," *Interpreter Releases* 23, no. 31 (August 5, 1946): 181.
124. *In re* Watson's Repatriation, 42 F. Supp. 163, 166 (US District Court for the Eastern District of Illinois, 1941). See also, on *In re* Watson, Volpp, "Divesting Citizenship," 426n104, 447n192.
125. See, especially, Memorandum, Subject: Construction and Application of the Act of June 25, 1936, as Amended by the Act of July 2, 1940, August 23, 1948, 13, INS File 56173–496, Box 19375, RG 85, NARA–DC; John. P. Boyd, Acting Commissioner of Immigration and Naturalization to George T. Washington, Assistant Solicitor General, Interpretation of the Act of June 25, 1936, September 2, 1948, INS File 56173–496, Box 19375, RG 85, NARA–DC.
126. T. B. Shoemaker to District Director, Kansas City, March 18, 1941, INS File 56173–496, Box 19375, RG 85, NARA–DC; T. B. Shoemaker to District Director, Seattle, March 18, 1941, INS File 56173–496, Box 19375, RG 85, NARA–DC.
127. *In re* Davies, 53 F. Supp. 426 (US District Court for the Middle District of Pennsylvania, 1944).
128. *In re* Portner, 56 F. Supp. 103 (US District Court for the Eastern District of Pennsylvania, 1944); Petition of Dattilio, 66 F. Supp. 912 (US District Court for the Eastern District of Pennsylvania, 1946); Petition of Norbeck, 65 F. Supp. 748 (US District Court for the District Court of Oregon, 1946).
129. Fee also attacked the marital expatriate involved in the case. In his view, she "has been in a position to have citizenship restored to her since 1922" but "has not seen fit so to qualify herself." Fee argued that he saw "no reason to weaken the belief that citizenship in the United States is a great gift by allowing the naturalization department to foster the idea that persons who have shown no desire to assume the duties of citizenship should be given the benefits thereof." See Petition of Norbeck, 749.
130. *In re* Shee Mui Chong Yuen's Repatriation, No. 73 F. Supp. 12, 14 (US District Court for the District of Hawaii, 1944).
131. I. F. Wixon, District Director, San Francisco, California to Commissioner, Central Office, Attention: Assistant Commissioner for Adjudications, August 21, 1946, INS File 56173–496, Box 19375, RG 85, NARA–DC.
132. *In re* Shee Mui Chong Yuen's Repatriation, 14.
133. In the Matter of the Application for Naturalization of Yuen Loo Wong, No. 73 F. Supp. 16 (US District Court for the District of Hawaii, 1947).
134. Ernest A. Gross, Legal Advisor, State Department to Hon. Thomas C. Clark, Attorney General, July 23, 1948, 3, INS File 56173–496, Box 19375, RG 85, NARA–DC.

250 NOTES TO PAGES 165-9

135. Edward Rudnick, Supervisor, Citizenship Certificate Unit to Joseph Savoretti, Assistant Commissioner, Adjudications Division, November 15, 1948, INS File 56173–496, Box 19375, RG 85, NARA–DC.
136. The memorandum noted, however, that "were the question one for original determination, a different view might find support." See Memorandum, Subject: Construction and Application of the Act of June 25, 1936, as Amended by the Act of July 2, 1940, August 23, 1948, 16, INS File 56173–496, Box 19375, RG 85, NARA–DC; John. P. Boyd, Acting Commissioner of Immigration and Naturalization to George T. Washington, Assistant Solicitor General, Interpretation of the Act of June 25, 1936, September 2, 1948, INS File 56173–496, Box 19375, RG 85, NARA–DC.
137. Joseph Savoretti, Assistant Commissioner, *In re*: Elma Aretta Rombach, November 15, 1948, INS File 56173–496, Box 19375, RG 85, NARA–DC; Joseph Savoretti, Assistant Commissioner, Adjudications Division to District Director, San Francisco, November 15, 1948, INS File 56173–496, Box 19375, RG 85, NARA–DC.
138. Joseph Savoretti, Assistant Commissioner, *In re*: Elma Aretta Rombach, November 15, 1948, INS File 56173–496, Box 19375, RG 85, NARA–DC; 547-R Emma Line Jarrett, August 1, 1949, Contested Naturalization Final Hearing Reports, 1949–1982, US District Court for the Southern (San Francisco) Division of the Northern District of California, RG 21, NARA–Pacific (San Bruno); 566-R Maria del R. Fierro, October 14, 1949, Contested Naturalization Final Hearing Reports, 1949–1982, SF, RG 21, NARA–Pacific (San Bruno); 580-R Josephine Mary Rinaldi, June 14, 1950, Contested Naturalization Final Hearing Reports, 1949–1982, SF, RG 21, NARA–Pacific (San Bruno).
139. "An Act to Revise the Laws Relating to Immigration, Naturalization, and Nationality; and for Other Purposes," 66 Stat. 163 (1952), 246-47.
140. Indeed, to this day, the successor agency to the INS, the US Citizenship and Immigration Services, maintains that a marital expatriate (if she were still alive) has the right to take the oath of repatriation under the provisions of the 1936 law, as amended, to regain her citizenship rights. See US Citizenship and Immigration Services, "Title 8 of Code of Federal Regulations Part 324—Special Classes of Persons Who May Be Naturalized: Women Who Have Lost United States Citizenship by Marriage and Former Citizens Whose Naturalization Is Authorized by Private Law § Sec. 324.4 Women Restored to United States Citizenship by the Act of June 25, 1936, as Amended by the Act of July 2, 1940," https://www.uscis.gov/ilink/docView/SLB/HTML/SLB/0-0-0-1/0-0-0-11261/0-0-0-31866/0-0-0-31931.html#0-0-0-19975.
141. Crist, "4 Women," A1.
142. See, generally, Applications for Repatriation, 1936–1969, US District Court for the Southern (San Francisco) Division of the Northern District of California, RG 21, NARA–Pacific (San Bruno); and Applications to Regain Citizenship and Repatriation Oaths, 1937–1970, US District Court for the Western (San Antonio) District of Texas, RG 21, NARA–Southwest (Fort Worth).
143. Minor v. Happersett.
144. Mackenzie v. Hare.
145. *In re* Shee Mui Chong Yuen's Repatriation, 14.

Conclusion

1. Neuman, "Lost Century of American Immigration."
2. On the rise of state policies denying undocumented immigrants' access to social services during the 1970s, see, especially, Cybelle Fox, "Unauthorized Welfare: The Origins of Immigrant Status Restrictions in American Social Policy," *Journal of American History* 102, no. 4 (March 2016): 1051-74; and Fox, "'Line Must Be Drawn.'" Texas lawmakers adopted legislation in 1975 permitting the barring of undocumented students from public schools in the state. Their efforts were ultimately stymied by the US Supreme Court in *Plyler v. Doe*, 457 U.S. 202 (1982). See Coleman, *Walls Within*, 13–60.
3. Kelly, "Wavering Course," 726-38.
4. In the wake of his administration's defeat before the US Supreme Court in the 2019 case *Department of Commerce v. New York*, then-president Donald Trump effectively admitted that enabling state anti-alien apportionment schemes was a major goal of his erstwhile efforts. In announcing an executive order that he hoped would serve as a workaround to his legal defeat,

Trump claimed citizenship data were needed because "some states may want to draw state and local legislative districts based upon the voter-eligible population." See Jeremy Stahl, "Trump's Effort to Rig the Census Failed, but the Fight Is Far from Over," *Slate*, July 11, 2019, https://slate.com/news-and-politics/2019/07/trump-barr-census-citizenship-question-defeat.html. See, more broadly, Department of Commerce v. New York, 588 U.S. ___ (Docket No. 18–6210) (2019).

5. On news coverage of the recent Massachusetts law and its broader context, see John R. Ellement, "Question Four Approved, Upholding State Law Allowing Mass. Residents without Proof of Lawful Presence to Get Driver's Licenses," *Boston Globe*, November 9, 2022, https://www.bostonglobe.com/2022/11/09/metro/mass-question-3-and-question-4-results/. Political scientists Allan Colbern and S. Karthick Ramakrishnan have recently argued that the differing laws that noncitizens, especially undocumented immigrants, encounter today on a state-by-state basis are so great that they amount to distinct forms of state citizenship. On California's transition from "Worst to First" in immigrant rights lawmaking, more specifically, see Colbern and Ramakrishnan, *Citizenship Reimagined*, 205–62 (pp. 254–61 cover recent developments).

6. Matt Vasilogambros, "Noncitizens Are Slowly Gaining Voting Rights," *Pew*, July 1, 2021, https://pew.org/2TeJy4P. One of the foremost scholars and advocates of contemporary noncitizen voting rights is US congressman Jamie Raskin of Maryland. See Raskin, "Legal Aliens, Local Citizens."

7. Varsanyi, "Rise and Fall."

8. Political scientist Ron Hayduk has examined common arguments for and against noncitizen voting rights in recent years as part of Hayduk, *Democracy for All*, 57–86. For a similar study of the legal and political theory behind noncitizen voting, see Harper-Ho, "Noncitizen Voting Rights." Representative scholarly accounts supporting and opposing noncitizen voting policies, respectively, include Raskin, "Legal Aliens, Local Citizens"; and Renshon, *Noncitizen Voting*.

9. While the Trump administration's efforts to add a citizenship question to the 2020 enumeration and ensuing litigation over that attempt (most notably *Department of Commerce v. New York* [2019]) indirectly engaged the subject of potential state anti-alien apportionment schemes, the topic had been more directly before the Supreme Court just three years earlier in *Evenwel v. Abbott*. In that 2016 case, Texas resident Sue Evenwel argued that the Texas state legislature's total population apportionment basis artificially enhanced the power of voters in districts where nonvoters (such as children, noncitizens, persons formerly incarcerated, and felons) were a particularly sizeable percentage of the population to the detriment of voters in districts where nonvoters were not as numerous. She sought to compel Texas lawmakers to use US Census Bureau estimates of the state's citizen voting-age population as their basis of apportionment. In April 2016, all eight Supreme Court justices (justice Antonin Scalia had recently died) decided that Texas had the right to use its total resident population as the basis of its apportionment policy. Six justices noted that, in practice, all states had adopted a total population standard. However, the court did not concur with the Obama administration's claim that states had to use total population as the basis of state legislative apportionment. In her majority opinion, justice Ruth Bader Ginsburg agreed that citizen voting-age population data was an insufficient basis of state apportionment policy and strongly implied that states would need to demonstrate that they were not using citizen voting-age population information (or similar measures) as a proxy to discriminate against protected classes. But Ginsburg and her colleagues did not ban—outright—state reapportionment schemes that excluded noncitizens from the population. See both the court's ruling and the numerous briefs submitted in *Evenwel v. Abbott*.

10. See, especially, among many other scholars on the history of felon disfranchisement, Holloway, *Living in Infamy*.

11. Varsanyi, "Rise and Fall," 130.

12. I contextualized the history of past nativist apportionment provisions, the Trump administration's stymied citizenship question, and their potential impact on present and future debates over would-be state anti-alien apportionment policies in Brendan Shanahan, "Counting Everyone—Citizens and Non-Citizens—in the 2020 Census Is Crucial," *Washington Post*, March 12, 2020, sec. Made by History, https://www.washingtonpost.com/outlook/2020/03/12/counting-everyone-citizens-non-citizens-2020-census-is-crucial/.

13. On past and present eras of and legal paradigms governing the rights of "aliens ineligible to citizenship," see, especially, Motomura, *Americans in Waiting*; and Motomura, *Immigration Outside the Law*.

252   NOTES TO PAGES 171–2

14. Graham v. Richardson, 403 U.S. 365 (1971). On the evolving political development and juris-prudence culminating in the precedent-setting 1971 *Graham* case, see Fox, "Unauthorized Welfare." More broadly, on *Graham* and other cases recognizing strict scrutiny requirements for state alienage laws and their impact on noncitizens' access to employment and social services in the past half century, see Kelly, "Wavering Course," 704–8, 720–40.
15. See, especially, Plascencia, Freeman, and Setzler, "Decline of Barriers."
16. As Colbern and Ramakrishnan have shown, California policymakers have been at the forefront of recent inclusionary licensing developments. Undocumented immigrants have been able to serve as attorneys in the Golden State since 2012. Their broader access to licensure across state licensing boards was similarly recognized in 2014. See Colbern and Ramakrishnan, *Citizenship Reimagined*, 289.
17. On the rise of varying legal and/or visa statuses affording immigrants differing degrees of employment rights and protection, see, among many others, Cecilia Menjivar, "Liminal Legality: Salvadoran and Guatemalan Immigrants' Lives in the United States," *American Journal of Sociology* 111, no. 4 (2006): 999–1037; Carl Bon Tempo, *Americans at the Gate: The United States and Refugees during the Cold War* (Princeton, NJ: Princeton University Press, 2008); Motomura, *Immigration Outside the Law*; María Cristina García, *The Refugee Challenge in Post–Cold War America* (New York: Oxford University Press, 2017); and Adam B. Cox and Cristina M. Rodríguez, *The President and Immigration Law* (New York: Oxford University Press, 2020).
18. Pia M. Orrenius and Madeline Zavodny, "Do State Work Eligibility Verification Laws Reduce Unauthorized Immigration?" *IZA Journal of Migration* 5, no. 5 (2016): 1–17; Pia M. Orrenius, Madeline Zavodny, and Sarah Greer, "Who Signs Up for E-Verify? Insights from DHS Enrollment Records," *International Migration Review* 54, no. 4 (2020): 1184–211.
19. In this manner, while I see current debates over noncitizen voting rights as mostly distinct from those of prior eras, I strongly concur with Varsanyi's framework that "it was only in the mid 1960s that the territorial boundaries surrounding the nation-state and the boundaries surrounding the polity and those eligible to vote came closest to aligning. Hence, it was during the civil rights era that citizenship and suffrage came closest to being 'territorialised' at the scale of the nation-state." See Varsanyi, "Rise and Fall," 115.

Works Cited

Archival Records

Bancroft Library; University Archives (University of California, Berkeley)
Hiram Johnson Papers. MSS C-B, 581 Part II.
Office of the University President Records. CU-5, Series 2.
Office of the University President Records. CU-5, Series 3.
War Relocation Authority Photographs of Japanese-American Evacuation and Resettlement. Bancroft Library and Archives/Online Archives of California.

Beinecke Rare Book & Manuscript Library (Yale University)
The A.P.A. and C.P.A. Exposed, or, Why They Exist (Sandwich, ON: Little Benjamin, 1893).

California State Archives (Sacramento, CA)
California Board of Education. "Commission on Credentials Minutes, 1918–1929." Files 359.01 C3609.
California Board of Education. Subject Files. Files R359.04.
California Board of Education. "Teacher Preparation and Licensing Commission—Credentials Commission, 1/19/1932–9/7/1960." Files R359.01.
California Board of Pharmacy. "Proceedings of the California State Board of Pharmacy." File F3888.

College of the Holy Cross (Worcester, MA)
Special Online Collections. James Michael Curley Scrapbooks. Vol. 96 (1933).

Immigration History Research Center Archives, University of Minnesota, Minneapolis
Immigration and Refugee Services of America—Foreign Language Information Service Records. IHRC1013. Box 36.

Iowa State University (Ames, IA)
Online Archives of Women's Political Communication.

Library and Archives Canada/Bibliothèque et Archives Canada (Ottawa, ON)
"Employment of Aliens in California—State Law." RG 25 Vol. 1161. File 671.

Massachusetts Commonwealth Archives (Boston, MA)
Massachusetts Board of Dentistry. "Massachusetts Board of Dental Examiners Minutes." 6 volumes.
Metropolitan Water Board. "Correspondence." Environmental Affairs. MDC, 2095X, 313 N 119 T.
Metropolitan Water Board. "Minutes." Environmental Affairs. MDC, 2092X-2093X, 313 N 119 T-120 T.
Secretary of the Commonwealth Records. Labor. 788 X Bureau Statistics. 312 HH 57 3113.

254 WORKS CITED

National Archives and Records Administration (Multiple Locations)

Bureau of Naturalization. Records of the Central Office: Administrative Files Relating to Naturalization, 1906–1940. Box No. 408 20/154. Entry Number 26. Record Group 85. NARA–DC (Downtown Branch).

Immigration and Naturalization Service. INS File 56173-496. Box 19375. Record Group 85. NARA–DC (Downtown Branch).

US District Court for the District of Hawaii. Petition and Record of Naturalization. Boxes 14–15. Record Group 21. NARA–Pacific (San Bruno).

US District Court for the District of Rhode Island. Petition and Record of Naturalization. Volumes 63–189. Record Group 21. NARA–Northeast (Waltham).

US District Court for the Southern District of Texas at Houston. Petition and Record of Naturalization. Volumes 14–24, Boxes 1–7. Record Group 21. NARA–Southwest (Fort Worth).

US District Court for the Southern District of Texas at Laredo. Petition and Record of Naturalization. Volumes 2–3, Boxes 1–2. Record Group 21. NARA–Southwest (Fort Worth).

US District Court for the Southern (San Francisco) Division of the Northern District of California. Applications for Repatriation, 1936–1969. Record Group 21. NARA–Pacific (San Bruno).

US District Court for the Southern (San Francisco) Division of the Northern District of California. Contested Naturalization and Repatriation Case Files, 1924–1992. Record Group 21. NARA–Pacific (San Bruno).

US District Court for the Southern (San Francisco) Division of the Northern District of California. Contested Naturalization Final Hearing Reports, 1949–1982. Record Group 21. NARA–Pacific (San Bruno).

US District Court for the Southern (San Francisco) Division of the Northern District of California. Petition and Record of Naturalization. Volumes 46–73, Boxes 26–210. Record Group 21. NARA–Pacific (San Bruno).

US District Court for the Western (El Paso) Division of Texas. Applications to Regain Citizenship, 1937–1969. Record Group 21. NARA–Southwest (Fort Worth).

US District Court for the Western (San Antonio) District of Texas. Applications to Regain Citizenship and Repatriation Oaths, 1937–1970. Record Group 21. NARA–Southwest (Fort Worth).

US District Court for the Western (San Antonio) District of Texas. Petition and Record of Naturalization. Volumes 17–23, Boxes 1–10. Record Group 21. NARA–Southwest (Fort Worth).

Nebraska State Archives; History Nebraska Preservations Office (Lincoln, NE)

Governor Keith Neville Files. RG 1, SG 26. S4, F1.

Nebraska State Council of Defense Records. RG 23, S1. F3.

Papers of the National Association for the Advancement of Colored People

Special Subject Files, 1912–1939. Series B: Harding, Warren G. through YWCA. Part 11. Group I, Series C.

Texas State Archives (Austin, TX)

Texas Board of Medicine. "Medical Examiners Minutes." 1981/207-1, 1981/207-2, 1981/207-3, Binder.

Texas Board of Public Accountancy. "Obsolete Rulings." 1993/206-9.

University of Nebraska Library, Archives and Special Collections—Library Depository Retrieval Facility (Lincoln, NE)

Leon Aylsworth Papers. RG 12-19-10. Box 2.

Works Cited 255

Wisconsin State Archives/Wisconsin Historical Society Archives (University of Wisconsin, Madison)

Ada L. James Papers. Wis MSS OP. Box 24.

American Federation of Labor Papers. Files of the Economist of the AFL. General File. MSS 177A/5C. Box 1.

Frank W Kuehl Papers. MSS 617. Box 73.

Wisconsin Board of Accounting. "Wisconsin Accounting Examining Board Minutes." Series 2641. Box 1.

Wisconsin Woman's Suffrage Association Files. Wis MSS HV. Box 26.

Court Cases, Rulings, and Legal Opinions

Ade v. County Commissioners, 20 Pa. C.C. 672 (1898).

Ambach v. Norwich, 441 U.S. 68 (1979).

Attorney-General v. Suffolk County Apportionment Commissioners, 224 Mass. 598, 113 N.E. 581 (1916).

Brophy et al. v. Suffolk County Apportionment Commissioners, 225 Mass. 124, 113 N.E. 1040 (1916).

Burns v. Richardson, 384 U.S. 73 (1966).

City of Chicago v. Hulbert, 205 Ill. 346, 68 N.E. 786 (1903).

Department of Commerce v. New York, 588 U.S. ___ (No. 18-6210) (2019).

Donovan v. Suffolk County Apportionment Commissioners, 225 Mass. 55, 113 N.E. 740 (1916).

Evenwel v. Abbott, 578 U.S. ___ (No. 14-940) (2016).

Examining Board v. Flores de Otero, 426 U.S. 572 (1976).

Ex parte Case, 20 Idaho 128, 116 Pac. 1037 (1911).

Fraser v. McConway & Torley Co., 6 D.R. (Pa.) 555 (1897).

Garcia-Godoy v. Texas State Board of Medical Examiners, 53 Jud. Dis. (Tex.) 61938 (1939).

Graham v. Richardson, 403 U.S. 365 (1971).

Heim v. McCall, 239 U.S. 175 (1915).

In re Chamorra, 298 Fed. 669 (1924).

In re Davies Repatriation, 53 F. Supp. 426 (M.D. Pa. 1944).

In re Griffiths, 413 U.S. 717 (1973).

In re Portner, 56 F. Supp. 103 (E.D. Pa. 1944).

In re Shee Mui Chong Yuen's Repatriation, 73 F. Supp. 12 (D. Haw. 1944).

In re Watson's Repatriation, 42 F. Supp. 163 (E.D. Ill. 1941).

In the Matter of the Application for Naturalization of Yuen Loo Wong, 7953 (D. Haw. 1947).

Juniata Limestone Co. v. Blair County Commissioners, 7 D.R. (Pa.) 201 (1898).

Juniata Limestone Co. v. Fagley, 187 Pa. 193 (1898).

Mackenzie v. Hare, 239 U.S. 299 (1915).

Meyers v. City of New York, 58 App. Div. 534, 69 N.Y.S. 529 (1901).

Minor v. Happersett, 88 U.S. 162 (1875).

Nyquist v. Mauclet, 432 U.S. 1 (1977).

Opinion of the Justices to the Senate, 353 (Mass. 1967).

People ex rel. Rodgers v. Coler, 166 N.Y. 1, 59 N.E. 716 (1901).

People v. Crane, 214 N.Y. 154, 108 N.E. 427 (1915).

People v. Warren 13 Misc. 615, 34 N.Y.S. 942 (1895).

Petition of Dattilio, 66 F. Supp. 912 (E.D. Pa. 1946).

Petition of Fortunato, 8 Fed. 2d 508 (1925).

Petition of Norbeck, 65 F. Supp. 748 (D. Or. 1946).

Plyler v. Doe, 457 U.S. 202 (1982).

Sashihara v. State Board of Pharmacy, 7 Cal. App. 2d 563, 46 P. 2d 804 (1935).

Shelley v. United States, 120 F. 2d 734 (D.C. Cir. 1941).

Sugarman v. Dougall, 413 U.S. 634 (1973).

256   WORKS CITED

Truax v. Raich, 239 U.S. 33 (1915).
Williams v. Moorhead, 96 Neb. 559, 148 N.W. 552 (1914).
WMCA, Inc. v. Lomenzo, 377 U.S. 633 (1964).

Legislation—Federal

34 Stat. 1228 (1907). ("An Act in Reference to the Expatriation of Citizens and Their Protection Abroad").

42 Stat. 1021 (1922). ("An Act Relative to the Naturalization and Citizenship of Married Women").

46 Stat. 854 (1930). ("An Act to Amend the Law Relative to the Citizenship and Naturalization of Married Women, and for Other Purposes").

48 Stat. 797 (1934). ("An Act to Amend the Law Relative to Citizenship and Naturalization, and for Other Purposes").

49 Stat. 1917 (1936). ("An Act to Repatriate Native-Born Women Who Have Heretofore Lost Their Citizenship by Marriage to an Alien, and for Other Purposes").

54 Stat. 670 (1940). ("An Act to Prohibit Certain Subversive Activities; to Amend Certain Provisions of Law with Respect to the Admission and Deportation of Aliens; to Require the Fingerprinting and Registration of Aliens; and for Other Purposes").

54 Stat. 715 (1940). ("An Act to Repatriate Native-Born Women Who Have Heretofore Lost Their Citizenship by Marriage to an Alien").

54 Stat. 1137 (1940). ("An Act to Revise and Codify the Nationality Laws of the United States into a Comprehensive Nationality Code").

66 Stat. 163 (1952). ("An Act to Revise the Laws Relating to Immigration, Naturalization, and Nationality; and for Other Purposes").

Legislation—State

Arizona. 1st State Legislature. Special Session: Ch. 66: 188–194 (1912).
California Legislature. 34th Session. Ch. 185: 589 (1901).
California Legislature. 41st Session. Ch. 417: 690–91 (1915).
California Legislature. 47th Session. Ch. 90: 154–160 (1927).
California Legislature. 49th Session. Ch. 398: 913–915 (1931).
Florida Statutes. 5th Regular Session 56. Pub. L. Ch. 4328 No. 7 (1895).
Illinois. 36th General Assembly. Regular Session: 19–216 (1889).
Louisiana. General Assembly. Act No. 271: 398–399 (1908).
Massachusetts General Court. Acts and Resolves. Ch. 474: 413–414 (1914).
Massachusetts General Court. Acts and Resolves. Ch. 600: 546 (1914).
Massachusetts General Court. Acts and Resolves. Extra Session: Ch. 125: 100 (1931).
Massachusetts General Court. Acts and Resolves. January Session Act No. 347: 389–390 (1895).
Massachusetts General Court. Acts and Resolves. January Session Act No. 488: 565–582 (1895).
Massachusetts General Court. Acts and Resolves. January Session Act No. 494: 492 (1896).
New Jersey Legislature. 123rd Session. Ch. 202: 524–525 (1899).
New York. 112nd Legislature. Ch. 380: 508 (1889).
New York. 117th Legislature. Ch. 622: 1569 (1894).
New York. 120th Legislature. Ch. 415: 461–502 (1897).
New York. 125th Legislature. Ch. 454: 1098–1099 (1902).
New York. 132nd Legislature. Ch. 36: 2037–2106 (1909).
New York. 138th Legislature. Ch. 51: 101–103 (1915).
New York. 141st Legislature. Vol. 1, Ch. 158: 749 (1918).
New York. 161st Legislature. Ch. 472: 1221–1233 (1938).
Pennsylvania. General Assembly. Regular Session Act No. 139: 166–168 (1897).
Pennsylvania. General Assembly. Regular Session Act No. 182: 269 (1895).

WORKS CITED 257

Texas State Legislature. 42nd Legislature. Regular Session, Ch. 46: 69–70 (1931).
Texas State Legislature. 46th Legislature. Regular Session, General Laws: 352–360 (1939).
Wisconsin Session Laws. Biennial Session. Ch. 76: 69–70 (1923).

Newspapers

Anaconda Standard.
Arizona Republican.
Ashland Tidings.
Atlanta Constitution.
Austin Statesman.
Baltimore Sun.
Banner–Democrat [Lake Providence, LA].
Bay City Times.
Beatrice Daily Sun.
Bismarck Tribune [also *Bismarck Weekly Tribune*].
Boston Globe [also *Daily Boston Globe; Boston Daily Globe*].
Boston Herald.
Boston Record.
Buffalo Evening Herald.
Butte Miner.
Caledonian–Record [St. Johnsbury, VT].
Cameron Sun.
Canon City Avalanche.
Chicago Daily Tribune.
Christian Science Monitor.
Cincinnati Enquirer.
Colorado Free Press.
Colorado Springs Gazette [also *Colorado Springs Weekly Gazette*].
Coos Bay Times.
County Record [Kingstree, SC].
Daily Colusa Sun.
Daily Free Democrat [Milwaukee, WI].
Daily Independent [Helena, MT].
Dakota County Herald.
Detroit Free Press.
East Oregonian.
El Paso Herald.
Evening Herald [Klamath Falls, OR].
Evening Star [Washington, DC].
Fair Play [St. Genevieve, MO].
Farmington Times.
Fort Scott Republican.
Free Press [London, ON].
Fresno Morning Republican.
Greenfield Vidette.
Hanford Journal.
Hays Free Press.
Hazleton Standard–Sentinel.
Helena Weekly Herald.
Indianapolis Star.
Jewish Advocate [Boston, MA].
Kalamazoo Gazette.
Kenosha Democrat.

258 WORKS CITED

La Crosse Tribune.
La Grande Observer.
L'Anse Sentinel.
Lawrence Chieftain.
Lincoln Journal Star.
Livingston Enterprise.
Lompoc Journal.
Los Angeles Herald.
Los Angeles Times.
Mendocino Beacon.
Milwaukee Daily Sentinel.
Minneapolis Journal.
Minneapolis Tribune.
Montreal Gazette.
Morning Press [Santa Barbara, CA].
Morning Register [Eugene, OR].
Morning Tribune [San Luis Obispo, CA].
Mower County Transcript.
Nebraska State Journal.
New Orleans Picayune.
New York American.
New York Amsterdam News.
New York Herald Tribune [also *New York Tribune*].
New York Times.
North Platte Semi-weekly Tribune.
Oakland Tribune.
Omaha Daily Bee.
O'Neil Frontier.
Oregon Daily Journal.
Ottawa Citizen.
Patriotic American [Detroit, MI].
Philadelphia Inquirer.
Philadelphia Press.
Pittsburgh Commercial Gazette.
Pittsburgh Gazette Times.
Plattsmouth Semi-weekly Journal.
Portsmouth Herald.
Potosi Journal.
Press Democrat [Santa Rosa, CA].
Princeton Union.
The Progress [Clearfield, PA].
Red Bluff Daily News.
The Representative [Minneapolis, MN].
Republican Banner [Nashville, TN].
Riverside Daily Press.
Rochester Democrat and Chronicle.
Sacramento Union.
Saint Paul Globe.
San Bernardino Daily Sun.
San Francisco Call.
San Francisco Chronicle.
San Francisco Examiner.
Sausalito News.

WORKS CITED 259

The Scotsman.
Sheboygan Daily Press.
South Bend News-Times.
South China Morning Post.
St. Louis Post-Dispatch [also *St. Louis Dispatch*].
St. Paul Daily Globe.
Stockton Independent.
Tägliche Omaha Tribüne.
Tazwell Republican.
Times-Democrat [New Orleans, LA].
Topeka State Journal.
Toronto Globe [also *The Globe*].
True Northerner [Paw Paw, MI].
Tucson Citizen.
Ukiah Daily Journal.
Ukiah Dispatch Democrat.
Wall Street Journal.
Washington Post.
Wisconsin Democrat [Green Bay].
Wisconsin State Journal [Madison].
Worcester Palladium.

Works of Scholarship and Other Publications

Abel, Richard. *American Lawyers.* New York: Oxford University Press, 1989.

Abrams, Kerry. "Plenary Power Preemption." *Virginia Law Review* 99, no. 3 (2013): 601–40.

Adams, Tracey L. "Profession: A Useful Concept for Sociological Analysis?" *Canadian Review of Sociology/Revue canadienne de sociologie* 47, no. 1 (February 2010): 49–70.

Adams, Tracey L. *Regulating Professions: The Emergence of Professional Self-Regulation in Four Canadian Provinces.* Toronto, ON: University of Toronto Press, 2018.

Adams, Tracey L. "When 'Citizenship Is Indispensable to the Practice of a Profession': Citizenship Requirements for Entry to Practise Professions in Canada." *Journal of Historical Sociology* 29, no. 4 (2016): 550–77.

Advisory Commission on Intergovernmental Relations. *A Commission Report: Apportionment of State Legislatures.* Washington, DC, December 1962.

Aistrup, Joseph. *The Southern Strategy Revisited: Republican Top-Down Advancement in the South.* Lexington: University Press of Kentucky, 2015.

Alanis Enciso, Fernando Saul. "¿Cuántos fueron? La repatriación de mexicanos en los Estados Unidos durante La Gran Depresión: Una interpretación cuantitativa 1930–1934." *Aztlán: A Journal of Chicano Studies* 32, no. 2 (Fall 2007): 65–91.

Albert, Isaiah Lafayette. "English in Nebraska Schools." *North American Review* 216, no. 800 (July 1922): 143–44.

Aleinikoff, T. Alexander. *Semblances of Sovereignty: The Constitution, the State, and American Citizenship.* Cambridge, MA: Harvard University Press, 2009.

Alexander, Norman. "New Hampshire—the State with the Largest Legislative Body." *National Municipal Review* 13, no. 5 (May 1924): 306–13.

"The Alien Labor Decision." *The Bulletin of the General Contractors Association* 6, no. 3 (March 1915): 67–68.

"Aliens and Women." *The Woman's Column,* September 10, 1892, 4.

Almaguer, Tomás. *Racial Fault Lines: The Historical Origins of White Supremacy in California.* Berkeley: University of California Press, 1994.

"The Amended Alien Labor Law." *The Bulletin of the General Contractors Association* 6, no. 3 (March 1915): 68–70.

260 WORKS CITED

American Medical Association. "Eighty-Ninth Annual Session of the American Medical Association House of Delegates Proceedings." San Francisco, CA, 1938.

American Medical Association. "Eighty-Sixth Annual Session of the American Medical Association House of Delegates Proceedings." Atlantic City, NJ, 1935.

American Medical Association. "Ninety-First Annual Session of the American Medical Association House of Delegates Proceedings." New York, NY, 1940.

American Medical Association. "Seventy-Fifth Annual Session of the American Medical Association House of Delegates Proceedings." Chicago, IL, 1924.

American Medical Association. "Seventy-Fourth Annual Session of the American Medical Association House of Delegates Proceedings." San Francisco, CA, 1923.

American Medical Association. "Seventy-Seventh Annual Session of the American Medical Association House of Delegates Proceedings." Dallas, TX, 1926.

Amsterdam, Daniel. "Before the Roar: US Unemployment Relief after World War I and the Long History of a Paternalist Welfare Policy." *Journal of American History* 101, no. 4 (2015): 1123–43.

Anbinder, Tyler. *City of Dreams: The 400-Year Epic History of Immigrant New York*. New York: Mariner Books, 2016.

Anctil, Pierre. "L'identité de l'immigrant québécois en Nouvelle-Angleterre. Le rapport Wright de 1882." *Recherches Sociographiques* 22, no. 3 (1981): 331–59.

Anders, Evan. *Boss Rule in South Texas: The Progressive Era*. Austin: University of Texas Press, 1979.

Andersen, Kristi. *After Suffrage: Women in Partisan and Electoral Politics before the New Deal*. Chicago: University of Chicago Press, 1996.

Anderson, Glenn F. "The Social Effects of the Construction of the Wachusett Reservoir on Boylston and West Boylston." *Historical Journal of Massachusetts* 3, no. 1 (Spring 1974): 51–58.

Anderson, Margo. *The American Census: A Social History*. New Haven, CT: Yale University Press, 1988.

Anderson, William, and Albert James Lobb. *A History of the Constitution of Minnesota: With the First Verified Text*. Minneapolis: University of Minnesota, 1921.

Ansolabehere, Stephen, and James M. Snyder Jr. "Reapportionment and Party Realignment in the American States." *University of Pennsylvania Law Review* 153, no. 1 (November 2004): 433–58.

Anthony, Susan B., and Ida Husted Harper. *History of Woman Suffrage*. Vol. 4. New York: Fowler & Wells, 1902.

Argersinger, Peter H. "Electoral Reform and Partisan Jugglery." *Political Science Quarterly* 119, no. 3 (2004): 499–520.

Argersinger, Peter H. " 'A Place on the Ballot': Fusion Politics and Antifusion Laws." *American Historical Review* 85, no. 2 (April 1980): 287–306.

Argersinger, Peter H. *Representation and Inequality in Late Nineteenth-Century America: The Politics of Apportionment*. New York: Cambridge University Press, 2012.

Argersinger, Peter H. "The Value of the Vote: Political Representation in the Gilded Age." *Journal of American History* 76, no. 1 (1989): 59–90.

Arguments of the Woman-Suffrage Delegates before the Committee on the Judiciary of the United States Senate. Senate Misc. Doc. No. 74, 47th Cong., 1st Sess. January 23, 1880.

Asher, Robert. "Union Nativism and the Immigrant Response." *Labor History* 23, no. 3 (1982): 325–48.

Aylsworth, Leon. "The Passing of Alien Suffrage." *American Political Science Review* 25, no. 1 (1931): 114–16.

Azzi, Stephen. *Reconcilable Differences: A History of Canada–US Relations*. New York: Oxford University Press, 2014.

Baker, Gordon E. "Reapportionment by Initiative in Oregon." *Western Political Quarterly* 13, no. 2 (1960): 508–19.

WORKS CITED 261

Baker, Gordon E. *State Constitutions: Reapportionment.* New York: National Municipal League, 1960.

Bakken, Gordon Morris. *Rocky Mountain Constitution Making, 1850–1912.* New York: Greenwood Press, 1987.

Balderrama, Francisco, and Raymond Rodríguez. *Decade of Betrayal: Mexican Repatriation in the 1930s.* Albuquerque: University of New Mexico Press, 2006.

Balinski, M. L., and H. Peyton Young. *Fair Representation: Meeting the Ideal of One Man, One Vote.* Washington, DC: Brookings Institution Press, 2001.

Baltz, Matthew J. "Protecting Citizens in Hard Times: Citizenship and Repatriation Pressures in the United States and France during the 1930s." *Theory and Society* 44, no. 2 (March 2015): 101–24.

Barrett, James R. *The Irish Way: Becoming American in the Multiethnic City.* New York: Penguin Books, 2013.

Bateman, David A. *Disenfranchising Democracy: Constructing the Electorate in the United States, the United Kingdom, and France.* New York: Cambridge University Press, 2018.

Batlan, Felice. "'She Was Surprised and Furious': Expatriation, Suffrage, Immigration, and the Fragility of Women's Citizenship, 1907–1940." *Stanford Journal of Civil Rights & Civil Liberties* 15, no. 3 (2020): 315–50.

Battisti, Danielle. *Whom We Shall Welcome: Italian Americans and Immigration Reform, 1945–1965.* New York: Fordham University Press, 2019.

Baum, Dale. "Know-Nothingism and the Republican Majority in Massachusetts: The Political Realignment of the 1850s." *Journal of American History* 64, no. 4 (1978): 959–86.

Baumle, Amanda K., and Dudley L. Poston. "Apportionment of the US House of Representatives in 2020 under Alternative Immigration-Based Scenarios." *Population and Development Review* 45, no. 2 (June 2019): 379–400.

Bavery, Ashley Johnson. *Bootlegged Aliens: Immigration Politics on America's Northern Border.* Philadelphia: University of Pennsylvania Press, 2020.

Beales, Le Verne. "The Negro Enumeration of 1920: A Reply to Dr. Kelly Miller." *The Scientific Monthly* 14, no. 4 (April 1922): 352–60.

Beattie, Betsy. "'Going Up to Lynn': Single, Maritime-Born Women in Lynn, Massachusetts, 1879–1930." *Acadiensis* 22, no. 1 (Autumn 1992): 65–86.

Beck, J. D., ed. *The Blue Book of the State of Wisconsin.* Madison, WI: Democrat Printing, State Printer, 1909.

Becker, Charles. *Official Manual of the State of Missouri 1923–1924: The Blue Book.* Columbia: Office of the Missouri Secretary of State, 1924.

Benton-Cohen, Katherine. *Borderline Americans: Racial Division and Labor War in the Arizona Borderlands.* Cambridge, MA: Harvard University Press, 2011.

Berman, Ari. *Give Us the Ballot: The Modern Struggle for Voting Rights in America.* New York: Picador, 2015.

Berry, Peter Neil. "Nineteenth Century Constitutional Amendment in Maine." Master's thesis, University of Maine, 1965.

Biographical Directory of the United States Congress. https://bioguide.congress.gov/.

Blackhawk, Ned. *The Rediscovery of America: Native Peoples and the Unmaking of U.S. History.* New Haven, CT: Yale University Press, 2023.

Blackmon, Douglas A. *Slavery by Another Name: The Re-enslavement of Black Americans from the Civil War to World War II.* New York: Anchor Books, 2009.

Blackwell, Alice Stone. "Alice Stone Blackwell's Page." *The Woman Citizen,* August 31, 1918, 272.

Blatz, Perry K. *Democratic Miners: Work and Labor Relations in the Anthracite Coal Industry, 1875–1925.* Albany: SUNY Press, 1994.

Bledstein, Burton J. *Culture of Professionalism: The Middle Class and the Development of Higher Education in America.* New York: W. W. Norton, 1978.

262   WORKS CITED

Bloemraad, Irene. "Citizenship Lessons from the Past: The Contours of Immigrant Naturalization in the Early 20th Century." *Social Science Quarterly* 87, no. 5 (2006): 927-53.

Bloemraad, Irene. "Does Citizenship Matter?" In *The Oxford Handbook of Citizenship*, edited by Ayelet Shachar, Rainer Bauböck, Irene Bloemraad, and Maarten Vink, 524-50. New York: Oxford University Press, 2017.

Bone, Hugh A. "States Attempting to Comply with Reapportionment Requirements." *Law and Contemporary Problems* 17, no. 2 (Spring 1952): 387-416.

Bon Tempo, Carl. *Americans at the Gate: The United States and Refugees during the Cold War*. Princeton, NJ: Princeton University Press, 2008.

Boochever, Louis Charles. "A Study of the Factors Involved in the Passage of the 1929 Bill for Reapportionment of the House of Representatives." Master's thesis, Cornell University, 1942.

Bosniak, Linda. *The Citizen and the Alien: Dilemmas of Contemporary Membership*. Princeton, NJ: Princeton University Press, 2006.

Bosniak, Linda. "'Nativism' The Concept: Some Reflections." In *Immigrants Out! The New Nativism and the Anti-immigrant Impulse in the United States*, edited by Juan F. Perea, 279-99. New York: New York University Press, 1996.

Bouk, Dan. *Democracy's Data: The Hidden Stories in the U.S. Census and How to Read Them*. New York: Farrar, Straus and Giroux, 2022.

Breckinridge, Sophonisba Preston. *Marriage and the Civic Rights of Women; Separate Domicil and Independent Citizenship*. Chicago: University of Chicago Press, 1931.

Bredbenner, Candice Lewis. "A Duty to Defend? The Evolution of Aliens' Military Obligations to the United States, 1792 to 1946." *Journal of Policy History* 24, no. 2 (April 2012): 224-62.

Bredbenner, Candice Lewis. *A Nationality of Her Own: Women, Marriage, and the Law of Citizenship*. Berkeley: University of California Press, 1998.

Breen, Jennifer S. "Labor, Law Enforcement, and 'Normal Times': The Origins of Immigration's Home within the Department of Justice and the Evolution of Attorney General Control over Immigration Adjudications." *University of Hawai'i Law Review* 42, no. 1 (Winter 2019): 1-71.

Bridges, Amy. *Democratic Beginnings: Founding the Western States*. Lawrence: University Press of Kansas, 2015.

Brilliant, Mark. *The Color of America Has Changed: How Racial Diversity Shaped Civil Rights Reform in California, 1941-1978*. New York: Oxford University Press, 2010.

Brown, Ray A. "The Making of the Wisconsin Constitution." *Wisconsin Law Review*, no. 4 (July 1949): 648-94.

Buenker, John D. *The History of Wisconsin: The Progressive Era, 1893-1914*. Vol. 4. Madison: Wisconsin Historical Society, 1998.

Buenker, John D. "The Mahatma and Progressive Reform: Martin Lomasney as Lawmaker, 1911-1917." *The New England Quarterly* 44, no. 3 (1971): 397-419.

Buenker, John D. "The Politics of Resistance: The Rural-Based Yankee Republican Machines of Connecticut and Rhode Island." *New England Quarterly* 47, no. 2 (1974): 212-37.

Butter, Irene, and Rebecca G. Sweet. "Licensure of Foreign Medical Graduates: An Historical Perspective." *The Milbank Memorial Fund Quarterly. Health and Society* 55, no. 2 (Spring 1977): 315-40.

Cahill, Cathleen D. *Recasting the Vote: How Women of Color Transformed the Suffrage Movement*. Chapel Hill: University of North Carolina Press, 2021.

Campbell, Kendall M., Irma Corral, Jhojana L. Infante Linares, and Dmitry Tumin. "Projected Estimates of African American Medical Graduates of Closed Historically Black Medical Schools." *JAMA Network Open* 3, no. 8 (2020): 1-10.

Cantrell, Gregg. "'Our Very Pronounced Theory of Equal Rights to All': Race, Citizenship, and Populism in the South Texas Borderlands." *Journal of American History* 100, no. 3 (December 2013): 663-90.

WORKS CITED 263

Cantrell, Gregg. *The People's Revolt: Texas Populists and the Roots of American Liberalism.* New Haven, CT: Yale University Press, 2020.

Capozzola, Christopher. *Bound by War: How the United States and the Philippines Built America's First Pacific Century.* New York: Basic Books, 2020.

Capozzola, Christopher. "The Only Badge Needed Is Your Patriotic Fervor: Vigilance, Coercion, and the Law in World War I America." *Journal of American History* 88, no. 4 (March 2002): 1354–82.

Capozzola, Christopher. *Uncle Sam Wants You: World War I and the Making of the Modern American Citizen.* New York: Oxford University Press, 2008.

Carliner, David. *The Rights of Aliens: The Basic ACLU Guide to an Alien's Rights.* New York: Avon Books, 1977.

Carpenter, Niles. *Immigrants and Their Children, 1920: A Study Based on Census Statistics Relative to the Foreign Born and the Native White of Foreign or Mixed Parentage.* Washington, DC: US Government Printing Office, 1927.

Casey, Christopher A. *Nationals Abroad: Globalization, Individual Rights, and the Making of Modern International Law.* New York: Cambridge University Press, 2020.

Castellanos Canales, Arturo. "The Right of Suffrage of Shosics (Noncitizens) in the United States." JSD diss., Cornell University, 2020.

Catron, Peter. "The Citizenship Advantage: Immigrant Socioeconomic Attainment in the Age of Mass Migration." *American Journal of Sociology* 124, no. 4 (January 2019): 999–1042.

Catt, Carrie Chapman. "The Carrie Chapman Catt Citizenship Course: How the Vote Came to Men." *The Woman Citizen*, October 30, 1920, 610–13.

Catt, Carrie Chapman. "The Citizen and the Vote." *The Woman Citizen*, April 6, 1918, 366.

Census of the State of New York for 1875. Albany, NY: Weed, Parsons, 1877.

Chacón, Mario, and Jeffrey Jensen. "Direct Democracy, Constitutional Reform, and Political Inequality in Post-colonial America." *Studies in American Political Development* 34, no. 1 (April 2020): 148–69.

Chafee, Zechariah. "Congressional Reapportionment." *Harvard Law Review* 42, no. 8 (June 1929): 1015–47.

Chamberlain, J. P. "Aliens and the Right to Work." *American Bar Association Journal* 18, no. 6 (June 1932): 379–82.

Chaney, Henry A. "Alien Suffrage." *Michigan Political Science Association* 1, no. 2 (1894): 130–39.

Cheng, Cindy I-Fen. *Citizens of Asian America: Democracy and Race during the Cold War.* New York: New York University Press, 2013.

Chin, Denny. "Aliens' Right to Work: State and Federal Discrimination." *Fordham Law Review* 45, no. 4 (February 1977): 835–59.

Chin, Gabriel J. "A Nation of White Immigrants: State and Federal Racial Preferences for White Noncitizens." *Boston University Law Review* 100, no. 4 (2020): 1271–314.

"Citizenship as a Condition Precedent to Medical Licensure in the United States." *Journal of the American Medical Association* 113, no. 16 (October 14, 1939): 1496–97.

Clark, Lindley. "Labor Laws Declared Unconstitutional." *Bulletin of the Bureau of Labor* 21, no. 91 (November 1910): 916–64.

Clements, Kendrick A. "Manifest Destiny and Canadian Reciprocity in 1911." *Pacific Historical Review* 42, no. 1 (1973): 32–52.

Closson, Carlos C. "The Unemployed in American Cities." *Quarterly Journal of Economics* 8, no. 2 (January 1, 1894): 168–217.

Colbern, Allan, and S. Karthick Ramakrishnan. *Citizenship Reimagined: A New Framework for States Rights in the United States.* New York: Cambridge University Press, 2020.

Coleman, Sarah. *The Walls Within: The Politics of Immigration in Modern America.* Princeton, NJ: Princeton University Press, 2021.

Collomp, Catherine. "Unions, Civics, and National Identity: Organized Labor's Reaction to Immigration, 1881–1897." *Labor History* 29, no. 4 (1988): 450–74.

264 WORKS CITED

"Colonel Francis 'Frank' Charles Zacharie (1839–1910)," Louisiana Digital Library, https://louisianadigitallibrary.org/islandora/object/lasc-nonjusticesportraits:58

Commission on Intergovernmental Relations and Meyer Kestnbaum. *A Report to the President for Transmittal to the Congress.* Washington, DC, June 1955.

Congressional Globe of the Fortieth Congress. Washington, DC: Blair & Rives, 1834–1873.

Congressional Globe of the Thirty-Ninth Congress. Washington, DC: Blair & Rives, 1834–1873.

Connolly, James J. *The Triumph of Ethnic Progressivism: Urban Political Culture in Boston, 1900–1925.* Cambridge, MA: Harvard University Press, 2009.

"Constitutionality of Restrictions on Aliens' Right to Work." *Columbia Law Review* 57, no. 7 (November 1957): 1012–28.

Constitution of Michigan of 1850. https://www.legislature.mi.gov/documents/historical/miconstitution1850.htm.

Constitution of the State of Idaho: Adopted by a Constitutional Convention Held at Boise City in the Territory of Idaho, August 6, 1889. Caldwell, ID, 1907.

Constitution of the State of Indiana, 1851. https://www.in.gov/history/about-indiana-history-and-trivia/explore-indiana-history-by-topic/indiana-documents-leading-to-statehood/constitution-of-1851/.

Constitution of the State of North-Carolina: Together with the Ordinances and Resolutions of the Constitutional Convention, Assembled in the City of Raleigh, Jan. 14th, 1868. Raleigh, NC: Joseph W. Holden, Convention Printer, 1868.

Constitution of the State of Washington, 1889. https://www2.sos.wa.gov/_assets/legacy/1889-constitution-color.pdf.

Constitution of the State of Wyoming: Adopted by the People at a General Election Held November 5th, 1889. Laramie, WY, 1908.

"Contractors' Statement on the Alien Labor Difficulty." *The Bulletin of the General Contractors Association* 5, no. 11 (November 1914): 338–41.

Cornyn, John. "The Roots of the Texas Constitution: Settlement to Statehood." *Texas Tech Law Review* 26, no. 4 (1995): 1089–218.

Cott, Nancy F. "Marriage and Women's Citizenship in the United States, 1830–1934." *American Historical Review* 103, no. 5 (December 1998): 1440–74.

Cott, Nancy F. *Public Vows: A History of Marriage and the Nation.* Cambridge, MA: Harvard University Press, 2002.

Coulibaly, Sylvie. "Kelly Miller, 1895–1939: Portrait of an African American Intellectual." PhD diss., Emory University, 2006.

Coulter, Thomas Chalmer. "A History of Woman Suffrage in Nebraska, 1856–1920." PhD diss., The Ohio State University, 1967.

Cowan, Sarah K. "Periodic Discordance between Vote Equality and Representational Equality in the United States." *Sociological Science* 2 (August 2015): 442–53.

Cox, Adam B., and Cristina M. Rodríguez. *The President and Immigration Law.* New York: Oxford University Press, 2020.

Cox, Patrick. *Ralph W. Yarborough, the People's Senator.* Austin: University of Texas Press, 2002.

Daniels, Roger. *Coming to America: A History of Immigration and Ethnicity in American Life.* New York: Perennial, 2002.

Daniels, Roger. *Guarding the Golden Door: American Immigration Policy and Immigrants since 1882.* New York: Macmillan, 2005.

Das, Shyameshwar. "Discrimination in Employment against Aliens—the Impact of the Constitution and Federal Civil Rights Laws." *University of Pittsburgh Law Review* 35, no. 3 (Spring 1974): 499–555.

Davis, John Oscar. "Anti-Depression Public Works: Federal-Aid Roadbuilding, 1920–1922." PhD diss., Iowa State University, 2002.

Davis, Winfield J. *History of Political Conventions in California: 1849–1892.* Sacramento: California State Library, 1893.

WORKS CITED 265

The Debates and Journal of the Constitutional Convention of the State of Maine, 1819-'20. Augusta: Maine Farmers' Almanac Press, 1894.

Debates and Proceedings of the Constitutional Convention of the State of California, Convened at the City of Sacramento, Saturday, September 28, 1878. Vol. 2. Sacramento, CA: J. D. Young, Supt. State Printing, 1881.

Debates and Proceedings of the Constitutional Convention of the State of California, Convened at the City of Sacramento, Saturday, September 28, 1878. Vol. 3. Sacramento, CA: J. D. Young, Supt. State Printing, 1881.

Debates in the Massachusetts Constitutional Convention, 1917-1918. Vol. 3. Boston: Wright and Potter, State Printers, 1920.

Deering's California Codes Annotated of the State of California: Adopted June 15, 1937, with Amendments through the End of the 1975 Sessions of the 1975-76 Legislature. Business and Professions. San Francisco, CA: Bancroft-Whitney, 1975.

Derieux, Adriel I. Cepeda, Jonathan S. Topaz, and Dale E. Ho. "'Contrived': The Voting Rights Act Pretext for the Trump Administration's Failed Attempt to Add a Citizenship Question to the 2020 Census." *Yale Law and Policy Review* 38, no. 2 (Spring 2020): 322–59.

Deschamps, Bénédicte. "L'épreuve/les preuves de la loyauté: la presse italo-américaine face à la citoyenneté (1910-1935)." *Revue française d'études américaines* 75, no. 1 (January 1998): 47–61.

Deschamps, Bénédicte. "'Shall I Become a Citizen': The FLIS and the Foreign Language Press, 1919-1939." In *Federalism, Citizenship, and Collective Identities in U.S. History*, edited by Cornelis A. van Minnen, Sylvia L. Hilton, and Colin Bonwick, 165–76. Amsterdam, The Netherlands: Vrije Universiteit Press, 2000.

Deskins, Donald Richard, Hanes Walton, and Sherman C. Puckett. *Presidential Elections, 1789-2008: County, State, and National Mapping of Election Data.* Ann Arbor: University of Michigan Press, 2010.

DeWitt, Petra. *Degrees of Allegiance: Harassment and Loyalty in Missouri's German-American Community during World War I.* Athens, OH: Ohio University Press, 2012.

DeWolf, Rebecca. *Gendered Citizenship: The Original Conflict over the Equal Rights Amendment, 1920-1963.* Lincoln: University of Nebraska Press, 2021.

Dhillon, Hardeep. "The Making of Modern US Citizenship and Alienage: The History of Asian Immigration, Racial Capital, and US Law." *Law and History Review* 41, no. 1 (February 2023): 1–42.

Dinan, John. *The American State Constitutional Tradition.* Lawrence: University Press of Kansas, 2006.

Dinan, John. "Explaining the Prevalence of State Constitutional Conventions in the Nineteenth and Twentieth Centuries." *Journal of Policy History* 34, no. 3 (July 2022): 297–335.

Diner, Hasia. *Erin's Daughters in America: Irish Immigrant Women in the Nineteenth Century.* Baltimore: Johns Hopkins University Press, 1983.

Diner, Hasia. *Roads Taken: The Great Jewish Migrations to the New World and the Peddlers Who Forged the Way.* New Haven, CT: Yale University Press, 2015.

DiStasi, Lawrence. "Derived Aliens." *Italian Americana* 29, no. 1 (Winter 2011): 23–33.

"District Court in Texas Rules State May Require Citizenship in Licensure of Physicians." *Journal of the American Medical Association* 113, no. 16 (October 14, 1939): 1495–96.

Dodd, Walter F. "Illinois Rejects New Constitution." *American Political Science Review* 17, no. 1 (1923): 70–72.

Donovan, Todd, and Shaun Bowler. "An Overview of Direct Democracy in the American States." In *Citizens as Legislators: Direct Democracy in the United States*, edited by Shaun Bowler, Todd Donovan, and Caroline J. Tolbert, 1–26. Columbus: Ohio State University Press, 1998.

Dowling, Harry Filmore. *City Hospitals: The Undercare of the Underprivileged.* Cambridge, MA: Harvard University Press, 1982.

266 WORKS CITED

Dubin, Michael J. *Party Affiliations in the State Legislatures: A Year by Year Summary, 1796–2006*. Jefferson, NC: McFarland, 2015.

Dubofsky, Melvyn. "The Lattimer Massacre and the Meaning of Citizenship." *Pennsylvania History* 69, no. 1 (Winter 2002): 52–57.

Dullea, Henrik N. *Charter Revision in the Empire State: The Politics of New York's 1967 Constitutional Convention*. New York: SUNY Press, 1997.

Durfee, Elizabeth. "Apportionment of Representation in the Legislature: A Study of State Constitutions." *Michigan Law Review* 43, no. 6 (1945): 1091–112.

Eagles, Charles. *Democracy Delayed: Congressional Reapportionment and Urban–Rural Conflict in the 1920s*. Athens, GA: University of Georgia Press, 1990.

Earls, Eamon McCarthy. *Wachusett: How Boston's 19th Century Quest for Water Changed Four Towns and a Way of Life*. Franklin, MA: Via Appia Press, 2012.

Eastman, Elizabeth. "Legislative Bulletin No. 5." *Interpreter Releases* 23, no. 31 (August 5, 1946): 175–87.

Eastman, Frank Marshall. *The Law of Taxation in Pennsylvania*. Newark, NJ: Soney & Sage, 1909.

Easton, Patricia O'Keefe. "Woman Suffrage in South Dakota: The Final Decade, 1911–1920." *South Dakota History* 13, no. 3 (Fall 1983): 206–26.

Egge, Sara. *Woman Suffrage and Citizenship in the Midwest, 1870–1920*. Iowa City: University of Iowa Press, 2018.

1875 Census of Massachusetts. Boston: Albert J. Wright, State Printer, 1876.

1895 Laws of Minnesota. St. Paul, MN: 1895.

Elkind, Sarah S. *Bay Cities and Water Politics: The Battle for Resources in Boston and Oakland*. Lawrence: University Press of Kansas, 1998.

Elkind, Sarah S. "Building a Better Jungle: Anti-urban Sentiment, Public Works, and Political Reform in American Cities, 1880–1930." *Journal of Urban History* 24, no. 1 (1997): 53–78.

Elmore, Maggie. "Fighting for Hemispheric Solidarity: The National Catholic Welfare Conference and the Quest to Secure Mexican American Employment Rights during World War II." *U.S. Catholic Historian* 35, no. 2 (Spring 2017): 125–49.

Epps, Garrett. *Democracy Reborn: The Fourteenth Amendment and the Fight for Equal Rights in Post–Civil War America*. New York: Holt Paperbacks, 2007.

Erickson, Charlotte. *American Industry and the European Immigrant, 1860–1885*. Cambridge, MA: Harvard University Press, 1957.

Erie, Steven. *Rainbow's End: Irish-Americans and the Dilemmas of Urban Machine Politics, 1840–1985*. Berkeley: University of California Press, 1990.

Erman, Sam. *Almost Citizens: Puerto Rico, the U.S. Constitution, and Empire*. New York: Cambridge University Press, 2018.

Fairfield, Marion Woolworth. "Correspondence." *The Woman Citizen*, August 25, 1917, 231.

Feagin, Joe R., and Harlan Hahn. "The Second Reconstruction: Black Political Strength in the South." *Social Science Quarterly* 51, no. 1 (1970): 42–56.

Feder, Leah Hannah. *Unemployment Relief in Periods of Depression: A Study of Measures Adopted in Certain American Cities, 1857 through 1922*. New York: Russell Sage Foundation, 1936.

Fehr, Russell MacKenzie. "Anxious Electorate: City Politics in Mid-1920s America." PhD diss., University of California, Riverside, 2016.

Fein, Michael R. *Paving the Way: New York Road Building and the American State, 1880–1956*. Lawrence: University Press of Kansas, 2008.

Feldberg, Michael. "Urbanization as a Cause of Violence: Philadelphia as a Test Case." In *The Peoples of Philadelphia: A History of Ethnic Groups and Lower-Class Life, 1790–1940*, edited by Allen F. Davis and Mark H. Haller, 53–69. Philadelphia: University of Pennsylvania Press, 1998.

Fellman, David. "The Alien's Right to Work." *Minnesota Law Review* 22, no. 2 (January 1938): 137–76.

WORKS CITED 267

Fields, Harold. "Closing Immigration throughout the World." *American Journal of International Law* 26, no. 4 (October 1932): 671–99.

Fields, Harold. "The Unemployed Foreign-Born." *The Quarterly Journal of Economics* 49, no. 3 (May 1935): 533–41.

Fields, Harold. "Unemployment and the Alien." *South Atlantic Quarterly* 30, no. 1 (1931): 60–78.

Fields, Harold. "Where Shall the Alien Work?" *Social Forces* 12, no. 2 (1933): 213–21.

"Fifth Annual Report of the New York Commissioner of Labor." Albany, NY: Brandow Printing, 1906.

Filindra, Alexandra. "E Pluribus Unum? Federalism, Immigration and the Role of the American States." PhD diss., Rutgers University, 2009.

"First Editor Service Publication Retiring." *Monthly Review—Immigration and Naturalization Service* 4, no. 4 (October 1946): 50.

Flournoy, Richard W. "Revision of Nationality Laws of the United States." *American Journal of International Law* 34, no. 1 (January 1940): 36–46.

Foley, Edward. *Ballot Battles: The History of Disputed Elections in the United States.* New York: Oxford University Press, 2015.

Folsom, Burton W. *No More Free Markets or Free Beer: The Progressive Era in Nebraska, 1900–1924.* Lanham, MD: Lexington Books, 1999.

Folsom, Burton W. "Tinkerers, Tipplers, and Traitors: Ethnicity and Democratic Reform in Nebraska during the Progressive Era." *Pacific Historical Review* 50, no. 1 (February 1981): 53–75.

Foner, Eric. "Reconstruction Revisited." *Reviews in American History* 10, no. 4 (1982): 82–100.

Foner, Eric. *The Second Founding: How the Civil War and Reconstruction Remade the Constitution.* New York: W. W. Norton, 2019.

Foner, Nancy. *From Ellis Island to JFK: New York's Two Great Waves of Immigration.* New Haven, CT: Yale University Press, 2000.

Forbath, William E. *Law and the Shaping of the American Labor Movement.* Cambridge, MA: Harvard University Press, 2009.

"Fourth Annual Report of the New York Commissioner of Labor." Albany, NY: Brandow Printing, 1905.

Fox, Cybelle. "'The Line Must Be Drawn Somewhere': The Rise of Legal Status Restrictions in State Welfare Policy in the 1970s." *Studies in American Political Development* 33, no. 2 (October 2019): 275–304.

Fox, Cybelle. "Save Our Senior Noncitizens: Extending Old Age Assistance to Immigrants in the United States, 1935–71." *Social Science History* 45, no. 1 (Spring 2021): 55–81.

Fox, Cybelle. *Three Worlds of Relief: Race, Immigration, and the American Welfare State from the Progressive Era to the New Deal.* Princeton, NJ: Princeton University Press, 2012.

Fox, Cybelle. "Unauthorized Welfare: The Origins of Immigrant Status Restrictions in American Social Policy." *Journal of American History* 102, no. 4 (March 2016): 1051–74.

Fox, Cybelle, and Irene Bloemraad. "Beyond 'White by Law': Explaining the Gulf in Citizenship Acquisition between Mexican and European Immigrants, 1930." *Social Forces* 94, no. 1 (September 2015): 181–207.

Free, Laura E. *Suffrage Reconstructed: Gender, Race, and Voting Rights in the Civil War Era.* Ithaca, NY: Cornell University Press, 2015.

Friedman, Lawrence. *The New Hampshire State Constitution.* New York: Oxford University Press, 2015.

Friedman, Lawrence M., and Lynnea Thody. *The Massachusetts State Constitution.* New York: Oxford University Press, 2011.

Frost, Amanda. *You Are Not American: Citizenship Stripping from Dred Scott to the Dreamers.* Boston: Beacon Press, 2022.

Fuchs, Ester R. *Mayors and Money: Fiscal Policy in New York and Chicago.* Chicago: University of Chicago Press, 2010.

268 WORKS CITED

Gabaccia, Donna. "The 'Yellow Peril' and the 'Chinese of Europe': Global Perspectives on Race and Labor, 1815–1930." In *Migration, Migration History, History: Old Paradigms and New Perspectives*, edited by Leo Lucassen and Jan Lucassen, 177–96. New York: Peter Lang, 1997.

Galie, Peter J., and Christopher Bopst. *The New York State Constitution*. 2nd ed. New York: Oxford University Press, 2012.

Galloway Kruse, Sarah. "Independent Citizenship: Marriage, Expatriation, and the Cable Act, 1907–1936." Master's thesis, Texas Women's University, 1998.

García, María Cristina. *The Refugee Challenge in Post–Cold War America*. New York: Oxford University Press, 2017.

Gardner, Martha. *The Qualities of a Citizen: Women, Immigration, and Citizenship, 1870–1965*. Princeton, NJ: Princeton University Press, 2005.

Garland, Libby. *After They Closed the Gates: Jewish Illegal Immigration to the United States, 1921–1965*. Chicago: University of Chicago Press, 2014.

Garland, Libby. "Fighting to Be Insiders." *American Jewish History* 96, no. 2 (June 2010): 109–40.

Garner, J. W., and Alpheus Snow. "Participation of the Alien in the Political Life of the Community." *Proceedings of the American Society of International Law* 5 (1911): 172–92.

Gellhorn, Walter. "The Abuse of Occupational Licensing." *University of Chicago Law Review* 44, no. 1 (Autumn 1976): 6–27.

Gettemy, Charles. *An Historical Survey of Census-Taking in Massachusetts: Including a Sketch of the Various Methods Adopted from Time to Time since 1780 for Determining and Apportioning the Membership of the House of Representatives and the Senate and the Council (1919–22)*. Boston: Wright & Potter, State Printers, 1919.

Gettemy, Charles. *The Massachusetts Decennial Census, 1915*. Boston: Wright & Potter, State Printers, 1918.

Gibson, Campbell J., and Emily Lennon. "Nativity of the Population, for Regions, Divisions, and States: 1850 to 1990." In *Historical Census Statistics on the Foreign-Born Population of the United States: 1850–1990*. Working paper: POP-WP029. February 1999. https://www.census.gov/library/working-papers/1999/demo/POP-twps0029.html.

Glenn, Evelyn Nakano. *Unequal Freedom: How Race and Gender Shaped American Citizenship and Labor*. Cambridge, MA: Harvard University Press, 2002.

Goebel, Thomas. *A Government by the People: Direct Democracy in America, 1890–1940*. Chapel Hill: University of North Carolina Press, 2003.

Goldin, Claudia. "Marriage Bars: Discrimination against Married Women Workers, 1920's to 1950's." Working paper. Cambridge, MA: National Bureau of Economic Research, October 1988. http://www.nber.org/papers/w2747.

Goldstein, Dana. *The Teacher Wars: A History of America's Most Embattled Profession*. New York: Doubleday, 2015.

Goluboff, Risa L. *The Lost Promise of Civil Rights*. Cambridge, MA: Harvard University Press, 2007.

Goodier, Susan. "The Price of Pacifism: Rebecca Shelley and Her Struggle for Citizenship." *Michigan Historical Review* 36, no. 1 (2010): 71–101.

Goodman, Adam. *The Deportation Machine: America's Long History of Expelling Immigrants*. Princeton, NJ: Princeton University Press, 2020.

"The Governors Speak." *Everybody's Magazine* 39, no. 5 (November 1918): 4.

Graham, Sara Hunter. *Woman Suffrage and the New Democracy*. New Haven, CT: Yale University Press, 1996.

Grant, Marilyn. "The 1912 Suffrage Referendum: An Exercise in Political Action." *The Wisconsin Magazine of History* 64, no. 2 (1980): 107–18.

Green, Nancy. "Expatriation, Expatriates, and Expats: The American Transformation of a Concept." *American Historical Review* 114, no. 2 (April 2009): 307–28.

WORKS CITED 269

Greene, Victor. *The Slavic Community on Strike: Immigrant Labor in Pennsylvania Anthracite.* Notre Dame, IN: University of Notre Dame Press, 1968.

Grimes, Alan Pendleton. *The Puritan Ethic and Woman Suffrage.* New York: Oxford University Press, 1967.

Grodin, Joseph, Calvin Massey, and Richard Cunningham. *The California State Constitution: A Reference Guide.* Westport, CN: Greenwood Press, 1993.

Grube-Gaurkee, Tracie. "Women Desire the Ballot: Wisconsin Woman Suffrage Association, World War I, and Suffrage as a War Measure." Master's thesis, University of Nebraska at Kearney, 2020.

Gualtieri, Sarah M. A. *Between Arab and White: Race and Ethnicity in the Early Syrian American Diaspora.* Berkeley: University of California Press, 2009.

Guglielmo, Thomas A. *White on Arrival: Italians, Race, Color, and Power in Chicago, 1890-1945.* New York: Oxford University Press, 2003.

Gulasekaram, Pratheepan, and S. Karthick Ramakrishnan. *The New Immigration Federalism.* New York: Cambridge University Press, 2015.

Gunter, Rachel Michelle. "Immigrant Declarants and Loyal American Women: How Suffragists Helped Redefine the Rights of Citizens." *The Journal of the Gilded Age and Progressive Era* 19, no. 4 (October 2020): 591-606.

Gunter, Rachel Michelle. "More Than Black and White: Woman Suffrage and Voting Rights in Texas, 1918-1923." PhD diss., Texas A&M University, 2017.

Gurwitz, Aaron. *Atlantic Metropolis: An Economic History of New York City.* New York: Palgrave Macmillan, 2019.

Hachey, R. Lawrence. "Jacksonian Democracy and the Wisconsin Constitution." *Marquette Law Review* 62, no. 4 (1979): 485-530.

Hague, John Allen. "The Massachusetts Constitutional Convention: 1917-1919. A Study of Dogmatism in an Age of Transition." *The New England Quarterly* 27, no. 2 (1954): 147-67.

Halperin, Edward C. "The Jewish Problem in U.S. Medical Education, 1920-1955." *Journal of the History of Medicine and Allied Sciences* 56, no. 2 (April 2001): 140-67.

Hamilton, Howard D., Joseph E. Beardsley, and Carleton C. Coats. "Legislative Reapportionment in Indiana: Some Observations and a Suggestion." *Notre Dame Law Review* 35, no. 3 (1960): 368-404.

Haney-López, Ian. *White by Law: The Legal Construction of Race.* New York: New York University Press, 1996.

Hareven, Tamara K., and Randolph Langenbach. *Amoskeag: Life and Work in an American Factory-City.* New York: Pantheon Books, 1978.

Harney, Robert F. "Montreal's King of Italian Labour: A Case Study of Padronism." *Labour/ Le Travail* 4 (January 1979): 57-84.

Harper-Ho, Virginia. "Noncitizen Voting Rights: The History, the Law and Current Prospects for Change." *Immigration and Nationality Law Review* 21 (2000): 477-528.

Harrison, Earl G. "The Problems of the Alien in Wartime." *Interpreter Releases* 20, no. 7 (March 10, 1943): 52-59.

Hattam, Victoria. *In the Shadow of Race: Jews, Latinos, and Immigrant Politics in the United States.* Chicago: University of Chicago Press, 2007.

Hatton, Timothy J., and Jeffrey G. Williamson. "Unemployment, Employment Contracts, and Compensating Wage Differentials: Michigan in the 1890s." *Journal of Economic History* 51, no. 3 (September 1991): 605-32.

Hayduk, Ron. *Democracy for All: Restoring Immigrant Voting Rights in the United States.* New York: Routledge, 2006.

Hayduk, Ron. "Political Rights in the Age of Migration: Lessons from the United States." *Journal of International Migration and Integration* 16, no. 1 (2015): 99-118.

Hayduk, Ron, Marcela Garcia-Castañon, and Vedika Bhaumik. "Exploring the Complexities of 'Alien Suffrage' in American Political History." *Journal of American Ethnic History* 43, no. 2 (2024): 70-118.

270 WORKS CITED

Hazard, Henry B. "The Trend toward Administrative Naturalization." *American Political Science Review* 21, no. 2 (May 1927): 342–49.

Helfenstein, Leonard. "Constitutionality of Legislative Discrimination against the Alien in His Right to Work." *University of Pennsylvania Law Review* 83, no. 1 (November 1934): 74–82.

Heltzel, Kate, ed. *Nebraska Blue Book: 56th Edition*. Lincoln: Nebraska Legislature, 2022.

Henretta, James A. "The Rise and Decline of Democratic Republicanism: Political Rights in New York and the Several States, 1800–1915." *Albany Law Review* 53, no. 2 (1989): 357–402.

Hernández, Kelly Lytle. *City of Inmates: Conquest, Rebellion, and the Rise of Human Caging in Los Angeles, 1771–1965*. Chapel Hill: University of North Carolina Press, 2017.

Herron, Paul E. *Framing the Solid South: The State Constitutional Conventions of Secession, Reconstruction, and Redemption, 1860–1902*. Lawrence: University Press of Kansas, 2017.

Hickey, Donald R., Susan A. Wunder, and John R. Wunder. *Nebraska Moments*. 2nd ed. Lincoln, NE: Bison Books, 2007.

Hicks, John D. "The People's Party in Minnesota." *Minnesota History Bulletin* 5, no. 8 (1924): 531–60.

Higham, John. *Strangers in the Land: Patterns of American Nativism, 1860–1925*. New York: Atheneum, 1963.

Hinshaw, John. *Steel and Steelworkers: Race and Class Struggle in Twentieth-Century Pittsburgh*. New York: SUNY Press, 2012.

Hirota, Hidetaka. *Expelling the Poor: Atlantic Seaboard States and the Nineteenth-Century Origins of American Immigration Policy*. New York: Oxford University Press, 2017.

Hoffman, Abraham. "Stimulus to Repatriation: The 1931 Federal Deportation Drive and the Los Angeles Mexican Community." *Pacific Historical Review* 42, no. 2 (May 1973): 205–19.

Holloway, Pippa. *Living in Infamy: Felon Disfranchisement and the History of American Citizenship*. New York: Oxford University Press, 2013.

Horwitz, Robert. "Reapportionment in the State of Hawaii—Considerations on the Reynolds Decision." In *Representation and Misrepresentation: Legislative Reapportionment in Theory and Practice*, edited by C. Herman Pritchett and Robert A Goldwin, 21–52. Chicago: Rand McNally, 1968.

Houghton, N. D. "The Legal Status of Indian Suffrage in the United States." *California Law Review* 19, no. 5 (1931): 507–20.

House of Commons Debates. Twelfth Parliament, Fifth Session, Vol. 2. 1915.

Hughes Rollings, Willard. "Citizenship and Suffrage: The Native American Struggle for Civil Rights in the American West, 1830–1965." *Nevada Law Journal* 5, no. 1 (Fall 2004): 126–40.

Hunt, Alan Reeve. "Federal Supremacy and State Anti-subversive Legislation." *Michigan Law Review* 53, no. 3 (January 1955): 407–38.

Hunt, Alan Reeve. "International Law: Reservations to Commercial Treaties Dealing with Aliens' Rights to Engage in the Professions." *Michigan Law Review* 52, no. 8 (June 1954): 1184–98.

Huthmacher, J. Joseph. *Massachusetts People and Politics, 1919–1933*. New York: Atheneum, 1969.

Industrial Commission, ed. *The Wisconsin Blue Book*. Madison, WI: Democrat Printing, State Printer, 1913.

Innamorati, Jean, Dennis DeWitt, and Tracy Lindboe. "Workers of Wachusett." *Journal of the New England Water Works Association* 133, no. 3 (September 2019): 159–67.

Irvin Painter, Nell. *The History of White People*. New York: W. W. Norton, 2010.

Irving, Helen. *Citizenship, Alienage, and the Modern Constitutional State: A Gendered History*. New York: Cambridge University Press, 2016.

Jabour, Anya. *Sophonisba Breckinridge: Championing Women's Activism in Modern America*. Champaign: University of Illinois Press, 2019.

Jackson, Jessica Barbata. *Dixie's Italians: Sicilians, Race, and Citizenship in the Jim Crow Gulf South*. Baton Rouge: Louisiana State University Press, 2020.

WORKS CITED 271

Jackson, Justin F. "Labor and Chinese Exclusion in US History." *Oxford Research Encyclopedia of American History*, November 29, 2021. https://oxfordre.com/americanhistory/view/10.1093/acrefore/9780199329175.001.0001/acrefore-9780199329175-e-545.

Jacobson, Matthew Frye. *Whiteness of a Different Color: European Immigrants and the Alchemy of Race*. Cambridge, MA: Harvard University Press, 1998.

Jacobson, Robin Dale, and Daniel Tichenor. "States of Immigration: Making Immigration Policy from Above and Below, 1875–1924." *Journal of Policy History* 35, no. 1 (January 2023): 1–32.

Jacobson, Robin Dale, Daniel Tichenor, and T. Elizabeth Durden. "The Southwest's Uneven Welcome: Immigrant Inclusion and Exclusion in Arizona and New Mexico." *Journal of American Ethnic History* 37, no. 3 (Spring 2018): 5–36.

Jensen, Kimberly. "'Neither Head nor Tail to the Campaign': Esther Pohl Lovejoy and the Oregon Woman Suffrage Victory of 1912." *Oregon Historical Quarterly* 108, no. 3 (2007): 350–83.

Jensen, Richard J. *The Winning of the Midwest: Social and Political Conflict, 1888–1896*. Chicago: University of Chicago Press, 1971.

Jenson, Jane. "Afterword: Thinking about the Citizenship Regime Then and Now." In *Citizenship as a Regime: Canadian and International Perspectives*, edited by Mireille Paquet, Nora Nagels, and Aude-Claire Fourot, 255–70. Montreal, QC: McGill-Queen's University Press, 2018.

Jenson, Jane. "Fated to Live in Interesting Times: Canada's Changing Citizenship Regimes." *Canadian Journal of Political Science/Revue canadienne de science politique* 30, no. 4 (1997): 627–44.

Jenson, Jane, and Susan Phillips. "Redesigning the Canadian Citizenship Regime: Remaking the Institutions of Representation." In *Citizenship, Markets, and the State*, edited by Colin Crouch, Klau Eder, and Damian Tambini, 69–89. New York: Oxford University Press, 2000.

Jewell, Malcolm, ed. *The Politics of Reapportionment*. New York: Transaction Publishers, 1962.

Jiménez, Miriam. *Inventive Politicians and Ethnic Ascent in American Politics: The Uphill Elections of Italians and Mexicans to the U.S. Congress*. New York: Routledge, 2015.

Jin, Michael R. *Citizens, Immigrants, and the Stateless: A Japanese American Diaspora in the Pacific*. Stanford, CA: Stanford University Press, 2022.

Jones, Martha S. *Birthright Citizens: A History of Race and Rights in Antebellum America*. New York: Cambridge University Press, 2018.

Jones, Martha S. *Vanguard: How Black Women Broke Barriers, Won the Vote, and Insisted on Equality for All*. New York: Basic Books, 2020.

Joo, Thomas Wuil. "New Conspiracy Theory of the Fourteenth Amendment: Nineteenth Century Chinese Civil Rights Cases and the Development of Substantive Due Process Jurisprudence." *University of San Francisco Law Review* 29, no. 2 (Winter 1995): 353–88.

Journal and Debates of the Constitutional Convention of the State of Wyoming, Begun at the City of Cheyenne on September 2, 1889, and Concluded September 30, 1889. Cheyenne, WY: The Daily Sun, 1893.

Journal of Select Council of the City of Philadelphia, from October 1, 1896 to April 1, 1897. Vol. 2. Philadelphia: George F. Lasher, Printer and Binder, 1897.

Journal of the Assembly, 32nd Session, State of California. Sacramento, CA: State Printing Office, 1897.

Journal of the Committee of the Whole of the Constitutional Convention, 1920–1922, of the State of Illinois. Convened at the Capitol in Springfield, January 6, 1920, and Adjourned Sine Die October 10, 1922. Springfield: Illinois State Journal Co., 1922.

Journal of the Common Council, of the City of Philadelphia, from October 6, 1898 to March 30, 1899. Vol. 2. Philadelphia: Dunlap Printing, 1899.

Journal of the Constitutional Convention for North Dakota Held at Bismarck, Thursday, July 4 to Aug. 17, 1889. Bismarck, ND: Tribune, State Printers and Binders, 1889.

272 WORKS CITED

Journal of the Constitutional Convention of South Dakota, July, 1889. Sioux Falls, SD: Brown and Saenger, Printers and Binders, 1889.

Journal of the Constitutional Convention of the People of Georgia, Held in the City of Atlanta in the Months of July and August, 1877. Atlanta, GA: Jas. P. Harrison, 1877.

Journal of the Convention to Form a Constitution for the State of Wisconsin: With a Sketch of the Debates, Begun and Held at Madison, on the Fifteenth Day of December, Eighteen Hundred and Forty-Seven. Madison, WI: Tenney, Smith, and Holt, 1848.

Journal of the House of Representatives of the State of Michigan, 1893, Vol. 3. Lansing, MI: Robert Smith, State Printers and Binders, 1893.

Journal of the Nebraska Constitutional Convention: Convened in Lincoln December 2, 1919. Vol. 2. Lincoln, NE: Kline Publishing, 1920.

Journal of the Proceedings of the Constitutional Convention of the State of Alabama, Held in the City of Montgomery, Commencing May 21st, 1901. Montgomery, AL: Brown Printing, 1901.

Journal of the Proceedings of the Convention of Delegates Elected by the People of Tennessee, to Amend, Revise, or Form and Make a New Constitution, for the State. Nashville: Jones, Purvis, Printers to the State, 1870.

Journal of the Senate, 33rd Session, State of California. Sacramento, CA: State Printing Office, 1899.

Journal of the Senate of the State of Michigan, 1893, Vol. 1. Lansing, MI: Robert Smith, State Printers and Binders, 1893.

Journal of the Senate of the Thirty-Sixth General Assembly. Springfield, IL: Phillips Brothers, State Printer, 1889.

Journal of the Senate Special Session of the Fortieth General Assembly of the State of Illinois. Springfield, IL: Phillips Brothers, State Printer, 1898.

Journal of the Texas House of Representatives. Vol. 26, Regular Session. 1919.

Judd, Deborah. "Chpt. 6, 'Nursing in the United States from the 1920s to the Early 1940s: Education Rather Than Training for Nurses.'" In *A History of American Nursing: Trends and Eras*, edited by Deborah Judd, Kathleen Sitzman, and G. Megan Davis, 94–119. Sudbury, MA: Jones & Bartlett Learning, 2009.

Kalisch, Philip Arthur, and Beatrice J. Kalisch. *American Nursing: A History.* 4th ed. Philadelphia: Lippincott Williams & Wilkins, 2003.

Kalnay, Francis, and Richard Collins. *The New American.* New York: Greenberg, 1941.

Kamphoefner, Walter D. *Germans in America: A Concise History.* Lanham, MD: Rowman & Littlefield, 2021.

Kanazawa, Mark. "Immigration, Exclusion, and Taxation: Anti-Chinese Legislation in Gold Rush California." *Journal of Economic History* 65, no. 3 (September 2005): 779–805.

Kanazawa, Sidney. "Sei Fujii: An Alien-American Patriot," *California Legal History* 13 (2018): 387–409.

Kang, S. Deborah. *The INS on the Line: Making Immigration Law on the US–Mexico Border, 1917–1954.* New York: Oxford University Press, 2017.

Kang, S. Deborah. "Sovereign Mercy: The Legalization of the White Russian Refugees and the Politics of Immigration Relief." *Journal of American Ethnic History* 43, no. 1 (Fall 2023): 5–42.

Kantrowitz, Stephen. *More Than Freedom: Fighting for Black Citizenship in a White Republic, 1829–1889.* New York: Penguin Press, 2012.

Karabel, Jerome. *The Chosen: The Hidden History of Admission and Exclusion at Harvard, Yale, and Princeton.* Boston: Houghton Mifflin, 2005.

Karlan, Pamela S. "Reapportionment, Nonapportionment, and Recovering Some Lost History of One Person, One Vote." *William & Mary Law Review* 59, no. 5 (April 2018): 1921–60.

Katznelson, Ira. *When Affirmative Action Was White: An Untold History of Racial Inequality in Twentieth-Century America.* New York: W. W. Norton, 2005.

Kauer, Ralph. "The Workingmen's Party of California." *Pacific Historical Review* 13, no. 3 (1944): 278–91.

Kazin, Michael. *Barons of Labor: The San Francisco Building Trades and Union Power in the Progressive Era*. Urbana: University of Illinois Press, 1988.

Keil, Thomas, and Jacqueline M. Keil. *Anthracite's Demise and the Post-coal Economy of Northeastern Pennsylvania*. New York: Rowman & Littlefield, 2014.

Keith, Douglas, and Eric Petry. "Apportionment of State Legislatures, 1776–1920." Brennan Center for Justice. New York: New York University School of Law, September 25, 2015.

Kellogg, Louise P. "The Alien Suffrage Provision in the Constitution of Wisconsin." *Wisconsin Magazine of History* 1, no. 4 (June 1918): 422–25.

Kelly, Michael Cornelius. "A Wavering Course: United States Supreme Court Treatment of State Laws Regarding Aliens in the Twentieth Century." *Georgetown Immigration Law Journal* 25, no. 3 (Spring 2011): 701–40.

Kennedy, Alan H. "Voters in a Foreign Land: Alien Suffrage in the United States, 1704–1926." *Journal of Policy History* 34, no. 2 (April 2022): 245–75.

Kent, Donald Peterson. *The Refugee Intellectual: The Americanization of the Immigrants of 1933–1941*. New York: Columbia University Press, 1953.

Kerber, Linda K. *No Constitutional Right to Be Ladies: Women and the Obligations of Citizenship*. New York: Hill and Wang, 1998.

Keremidchieva, Zornitsa. "The Congressional Debates on the 19th Amendment: Jurisdictional Rhetoric and the Assemblage of the US Body Politic." *Quarterly Journal of Speech* 99, no. 1 (January 2013): 51–73.

Keremidchieva, Zornitsa. "The Gendering of Legislative Rationality: Women, Immigrants, and the Nationalization of Citizenship, 1918–1922." PhD diss., University of Minnesota, 2007.

Kessler-Harris, Alice. *In Pursuit of Equity: Women, Men, and the Quest for Economic Citizenship in 20th-Century America*. New York: Oxford University Press, 2001.

Kessler-Harris, Alice. *Out to Work: A History of Wage-Earning Women in the United States*. New York: Oxford University Press, 2003.

Kettleborough, Charles. "Amendments to State Constitutions 1919–21." *American Political Science Review* 16, no. 2 (May 1922): 245–76.

Kettleborough, Charles. *Constitution Making in Indiana Vol. 1: 1780–1851*. Fort Wayne: Fort Wayne Printing Company–Indiana Historical Commission, 1916.

Kettleborough, Charles. *Constitution Making in Indiana Vol. 3: 1916–1930*. Indianapolis: Indiana Historical Bureau, 1930.

Kettner, James. *The Development of American Citizenship, 1608–1870*. Chapel Hill: University of North Carolina Press, 1978.

Key, Valdimer Orlando. "Procedures in State Legislative Apportionment." *American Political Science Review* 26, no. 6 (December 1932): 1050–58.

Keyssar, Alexander. *Out of Work: The First Century of Unemployment in Massachusetts*. New York: Cambridge University Press, 1986.

Keyssar, Alexander. *The Right to Vote: The Contested History of Democracy in the United States*. New York: Basic Books, 2000.

Kim, Claire Jean. "The Racial Triangulation of Asian Americans." *Politics & Society* 27, no. 1 (1999): 105–38.

King, Charles R. "The New York Maternal Mortality Study: A Conflict of Professionalization." In *The Medicalization of Obstetrics: Personnel, Practice, and Instruments*, edited by Philip K. Wilson, 110–36. Vol. 2 of Childbirth: Changing Ideas and Practices in Britain and America, 1600 to the Present. New York: Garland, 1996.

King, Desmond. *Making Americans: Immigration, Race, and the Origins of the Diverse Democracy*. Cambridge, MA: Harvard University Press, 2000.

Kinzer, Donald L. *An Episode in Anti-Catholicism: The American Protective Association*. Seattle: University of Washington Press, 1964.

274 WORKS CITED

Kleppner, Paul. *Continuity and Change in Electoral Politics, 1893–1928.* New York: Greenwood Press, 1987.

Kleppner, Paul. *The Cross of Culture: A Social Analysis of Midwestern Politics 1850–1900.* New York: Free Press, 1970.

Kleppner, Paul. *The Third Electoral System, 1853–1892: Parties, Voters, and Political Cultures.* Chapel Hill: University of North Carolina Press, 1979.

Klinghoffer, Judith Apter, and Lois Elkis. " 'The Petticoat Electors': Women's Suffrage in New Jersey, 1776–1807." *Journal of the Early Republic* 12, no. 2 (1992): 159–93.

Klug, Thomas A. "Labor Market Politics in Detroit: The Curious Case of the 'Spolansky Act' of 1931." *Michigan Historical Review* 14, no. 1 (April 1988): 1–32.

Klug, Thomas A. "Residents by Day, Visitors by Night: The Origins of the Alien Commuter on the U.S.–Canadian Border during the 1920s." *Michigan Historical Review* 34, no. 2 (2008): 75–98.

Kneier, Charles M. "Discrimination against Aliens by Municipal Ordinances." *Georgetown Law Journal* 16, no. 2 (February 1928): 143–64.

Knight, George S. "Nationality Act of 1940." *American Bar Association Journal* 26, no. 12 (1940): 938–40.

Knobel, Dale T. *America for the Americans: The Nativist Movement in the United States.* New York: Twayne, 1996.

Kobrin, Frances E. "The American Midwife Controversy: A Crisis of Professionalization." In *The Medicalization of Obstetrics: Personnel, Practice, and Instruments,* edited by Philip K. Wilson, 96–109. Vol. 2 of Childbirth: Changing Ideas and Practices in Britain and America, 1600 to the Present. New York: Garland, 1996.

Kociemba, Caleb Samuel. "German Americans and the Nebraska Nonpartisan League: Links of Persecution and Loyalty." Master's thesis, University of Nebraska at Kearney, 2019.

Konvitz, Milton. *The Alien and the Asiatic in American Law.* Ithaca, NY: Cornell University Press, 1946.

Kousser, J. Morgan. *The Shaping of Southern Politics: Suffrage Restriction and the Establishment of the One-Party South, 1880–1910.* New Haven, CT: Yale University Press, 1974.

Krajewska, Magdalena. *Documenting Americans: A Political History of National ID Card Proposals in the United States.* New York: Cambridge University Press, 2017.

Krochmal, Max, and Todd Moye, eds. *Civil Rights in Black and Brown: Histories of Resistance and Struggle in Texas.* Austin: University of Texas Press, 2021.

Kromkowski, Charles A. *Recreating the American Republic: Rules of Apportionment, Constitutional Change, and American Political Development, 1700–1870.* New York: Cambridge University Press, 2002.

Lafleur, Normand. *Les « Chinois » de l'Est ou la vie quotidienne des Québécois émigrés aux États-Unis de 1840 à nos jours.* Montréal, QC: Leméac, 1981.

Lamar, Howard Roberts. *The Far Southwest, 1846–1912: A Territorial History.* Rev. ed. Albuquerque: University of New Mexico Press, 2000.

Landrum, Shane. "The State's Big Family Bible: Birth Certificates, Personal Identity, and Citizenship in the United States, 1840–1950." PhD diss., Brandeis University, 2014.

Larson, Erik. *The Devil in the White City.* New York: Vintage Books, 2003.

"Latest Subway News." *The Bulletin of the General Contractors Association* 5, no. 11 (November 1914): 335–38.

Law, Anna O. "Lunatics, Idiots, Paupers, and Negro Seamen—Immigration Federalism and the Early American State." *Studies in American Political Development* 28, no. 2 (October 2014): 107–28.

Law, Marc T., and Sukkoo Kim. "Specialization and Regulation: The Rise of Professionals and the Emergence of Occupational Licensing Regulation." *Journal of Economic History* 65, no. 3 (September 2005): 723–56.

Laws of the Territory of Idaho, 1874–1875. "An Act Relative to Elections," 683–95.

WORKS CITED 275

Lee, Catherine. *Fictive Kinship: Family Reunification and the Meaning of Race and Nation in American Migration*. New York: Russell Sage Foundation, 2013.

Lee, Erika. *America for Americans: A History of Xenophobia in the United States*. New York: Basic Books, 2019.

Lee, Erika. *At America's Gates: Chinese Immigration during the Exclusion Era, 1882–1943*. Chapel Hill: University of North Carolina Press, 2003.

Lee, Erika. "The Chinese Exclusion Example: Race, Immigration, and American Gatekeeping, 1882–1924." *Journal of American Ethnic History* 21, no. 3 (Spring 2002): 36–62.

Lee, Erika. *The Making of Asian America: A History*. New York: Simon & Schuster, 2015.

Lee, Erika, and Judy Yung. *Angel Island: Immigrant Gateway to America*. New York: Oxford University Press, 2010.

"Legislative Reapportionment." *Law and Contemporary Problems* 17, no. 2 (Spring 1952): 253–470.

Leiserson, William M. *Adjusting Immigrant and Industry*. New York: Harper, 1924.

Leland, Hayne E. "Quacks, Lemons, and Licensing: A Theory of Minimum Quality Standards." *Journal of Political Economy* 87, no. 6 (December 1979): 1328–46.

Leonard, Karen Isaksen. *Making Ethnic Choices: California's Punjabi Mexican Americans*. Philadelphia: Temple University Press, 1992.

LePore, Herbert. "Prelude to Prejudice: Hiram Johnson, Woodrow Wilson, and the California Alien Land Law Controversy of 1913." *Southern California Quarterly* 61, no. 1 (1979): 99–110.

Lepore, Jill. "Resistance, Reform, and Repression: Italian Immigrant Laborers in Clinton, 1896–1906." In *Labor in Massachusetts: Selected Essays*, edited by Kenneth Fones-Wolf and Martin Kaufman, 138–67. Westfield, MA: Westfield State College, 1990.

Levin, Susan Bass. "The Constitutionality of Employment Restrictions on Resident Aliens in the United States." *Buffalo Law Review* 24, no. 1 (Fall 1974): 211–38.

Levitt, Justin. "Citizenship and the Census." *Columbia Law Review* 119, no. 5 (June 2019): 1355–98.

Lewis, Read. "Have We Still an Immigration Problem?" *Interpreter Releases* 10, no. 25 (June 20, 1933): 150–57.

Lew-Williams, Beth. *The Chinese Must Go: Violence, Exclusion, and the Making of the Alien in America*. Cambridge, MA: Harvard University Press, 2018.

Lew-Williams, Beth. "Chinese Naturalization, Voting, and Other Impossible Acts." *The Journal of the Civil War Era* 13, no. 4 (2023): 515–36.

Lichtman, Allan J. *The Embattled Vote in America: From the Founding to the Present*. Cambridge, MA: Harvard University Press, 2018.

Lichtman, Allan J. *Prejudice and the Old Politics: The Presidential Election of 1928*. Lanham, MD: Lexington Books, 2000.

"Little Men Who Were Once Big." *The Interpreter* 4, no. 9 (November 1925): 9–12.

Lockridge, Ross Franklin. *How Government Functions in Indiana: An Indiana Supplement to Thomas Harrison Reed's Form and Function of American Government*. Yonkers, NY: World Book, 1918.

Loeb, Isidor. *Constitutions and Constitutional Conventions in Missouri*. Columbia: State Historical Society of Missouri, 1920.

Longo, Peter, and Robert Miewald. *The Nebraska State Constitution: A Reference Guide*. Westport, CT: Greenwood, 1993.

Loring, Augustus Peabody. "A Short Account of the Massachusetts Constitutional Convention 1917–1919." *The New England Quarterly* 6, no. 1 (1933): 1–99.

Lozano, Rosina. *An American Language: The History of Spanish in the United States*. Berkeley: University of California Press, 2018.

Lublin, David, and D. Stephen Voss. "Racial Redistricting and Realignment in Southern State Legislatures." *American Journal of Political Science* 44, no. 4 (October 2000): 792–810.

Luconi, Stefano. "Black Dagoes? Italian Immigrants' Racial Status in the United States: An Ecological View." *Journal of Transatlantic Studies* 14, no. 2 (2016): 188–99.

276 WORKS CITED

Luebke, Frederick. *Bonds of Loyalty: German Americans and World War I.* DeKalb: Northern Illinois University Press, 1974.

Luebke, Frederick. "The German–American Alliance in Nebraska, 1910–1917." *Nebraska History* 49, no. 2 (Summer 1968): 165–86.

Lukens, Patrick D. *A Quiet Victory for Latino Rights: FDR and the Controversy over "Whiteness."* Tucson: University of Arizona Press, 2012.

Lyman, J. Chester. "Our Inequalities of Suffrage." *North American Review* 144, no. 364 (1887): 298–306.

MacLean, Nancy. *Freedom Is Not Enough: The Opening of the American Workplace.* Cambridge, MA: Harvard University Press, 2006.

Madison, James H. *Indiana through Tradition and Change: A History of the Hoosier State and Its People, 1920–1945.* Indianapolis: Indiana Historical Society, 1982.

Madison, James H. *The Ku Klux Klan in the Heartland.* Bloomington: Indiana University Press, 2020.

Magnaghi, Russell M. *Upper Peninsula of Michigan: A History.* Marquette, MI: 906 Heritage Press, 2017.

Maltz, Earl M. "The Fourteenth Amendment and Native American Citizenship." *Immigration and Nationality Law Review* 22 (2001): 625–46.

Marable, Manning. *Race, Reform and Rebellion: The Second Reconstruction in Black America, 1945–1982.* Jackson: University Press of Mississippi, 1984.

Marinari, Maddalena. *Unwanted: Italian and Jewish Mobilization against Restrictive Immigration Laws, 1882–1965.* Chapel Hill: University of North Carolina Press, 2020.

Marshall, Thomas. "Misunderstood America." *The Forum,* 59 (January 1918): 1–12.

Martinez, Monica Muñoz. *The Injustice Never Leaves You: Anti-Mexican Violence in Texas.* Cambridge, MA: Harvard University Press, 2018.

Martinez HoSang, Daniel. *Racial Propositions: Ballot Initiatives and the Making of Postwar California.* Berkeley: University of California Press, 2010.

Massachusetts Bureau of Statistics of Labor. *Fortieth Annual Report on the Statistics of Labor, 1909.* Boston: Wright & Potter Printing, State Printers, 1911.

Massachusetts Bureau of Statistics of Labor. *Twelfth Annual Report of the Massachusetts Bureau of Statistics of Labor.* Boston: Rand, Avery, Printers to the Commonwealth, January 1881.

Massachusetts Department of Education. *Annual Report of the Division of Immigration and Americanization for the Year Ending November 30, 1924.* Boston: Commonwealth of Massachusetts, 1925.

Massachusetts Department of Education. *Annual Report of the Division of Immigration and Americanization for the Year Ending November 30, 1925.* Boston: Commonwealth of Massachusetts, 1926.

Massachusetts Department of Education. *Annual Report of the Division of Immigration and Americanization for the Year Ending November 30, 1930.* Boston: Commonwealth of Massachusetts, 1931.

Massachusetts Department of Education. *Annual Report of the Division of Immigration and Americanization for the Year Ending November 30, 1938.* Boston: Commonwealth of Massachusetts, 1939.

Massachusetts General Court, House of Representatives. *Journal of the House of Representatives for the Year 1900.* Boston: Commonwealth of Massachusetts, 1900.

Massachusetts General Court, Senate. *Journal of the Senate for the Year 1896.* Boston: Commonwealth of Massachusetts, 1896.

Matthews, J. A. *The Alger Republican Club: Our Trip to Washington: Including a Synopsis of the Organization, History and Object of the Alger Republican Club.* Detroit, MI, 1889.

Mayer, David N. "The Jurisprudence of Christopher G. Tiedeman: A Study in the Failure of Laissez-Faire Constitutionalism." *Missouri Law Review* 55, no. 1 (Winter 1990): 93–162.

McArthur, Judith N., and Harold L. Smith. *Minnie Fisher Cunningham: A Suffragist's Life in Politics.* New York: Oxford University Press, 2005.

WORKS CITED   277

McBride, Genevieve C. *On Wisconsin Women: Working for Their Rights from Settlement to Suffrage*. Madison: University of Wisconsin Press, 1993.

McClain, Charles J. *In Search of Equality: The Chinese Struggle against Discrimination in Nineteenth-Century America*. Berkeley: University of California Press, 1994.

McClymer, John F. *War and Welfare: Social Engineering in America, 1890–1925*. Westport, CT: Praeger, 1980.

McDonagh, Eileen L., and H. Douglas Price. "Woman Suffrage in the Progressive Era: Patterns of Opposition and Support in Referenda Voting, 1910–1918." *American Political Science Review* 79, no. 2 (1985): 415–35.

McDonald, Laughlin. *A Voting Rights Odyssey: Black Enfranchisement in Georgia*. New York: Cambridge University Press, 2003.

McGreevey, Robert C. *Borderline Citizens: The United States, Puerto Rico, and the Politics of Colonial Migration*. Ithaca, NY: Cornell University Press, 2018.

McIntyre, Stephanie Anne. "A Study in Married Women's Rights and Repatriation in the United States, the United Kingdom, and Latin America: Citizenship, Gender and the Law in Transatlantic Context." PhD diss., University of Texas at Arlington, 2014.

McKay, Robert B. *Reapportionment: The Law and Politics of Equal Representation*. New York: Simon & Schuster, 1970.

McKee Hickman, Laura. "Thou Shalt Not Vote: The Struggle for Woman's Suffrage in Nebraska." Master's thesis, University of Nebraska, Omaha, 1997.

McKinney, William, ed. *McKinney's Consolidated Laws of New York Annotated*. Northport, NY: Edward Thompson, 1917.

McLaughlin, William. *The Indiana State Constitution*. New York: Oxford University Press, 2011.

McNickle, Chris. *To Be Mayor of New York: Ethnic Politics in the City*. New York: Columbia University Press, 1993.

McSeveney, Samuel T. *The Politics of Depression: Political Behavior in the Northeast, 1893–1896*. New York: Oxford University Press, 1972.

Mead, Rebecca. *How the Vote Was Won: Woman Suffrage in the Western United States, 1868–1914*. New York: New York University Press, 2006.

Meeks, Eric V. *Border Citizens: The Making of Indians, Mexicans, and Anglos in Arizona*. Austin: University of Texas Press, 2007.

Menchaca, Martha. *Naturalizing Mexican Immigrants: A Texas History*. Austin: University of Texas Press, 2011.

Menjivar, Cecilia. "Liminal Legality: Salvadoran and Guatemalan Immigrants' Lives in the United States." *American Journal of Sociology* 111, no. 4 (2006): 999–1037.

Mettler, Suzanne. *Dividing Citizens: Gender and Federalism in New Deal Public Policy*. Ithaca, NY: Cornell University Press, 1998.

Michigan Manual. "Summary of Vote for Governor, 1835–2006." http://www.legislature.mi.gov/documents/publications/MichiganManual/2009-2010/09-10_MM_IX_pp_08-12_Votes4Gov.pdf.

Miller, Gary, and Norman Schofield. "The Transformation of the Republican and Democratic Party Coalitions in the US." *Perspectives on Politics* 6, no. 3 (September 2008): 433–50.

Miller, Kelly. "Enumeration Errors in Negro Population." *The Scientific Monthly* 14, no. 2 (February 1922): 168–77.

Mink, Gwendolyn. *Old Labor and New Immigrants in American Political Development: Union, Party, and State, 1875–1920*. Ithaca, NY: Cornell University Press, 1986.

Minnesota Secretary of State. "Minnesota Elections." https://www.sos.state.mn.us/media/1364/chapter_10-minnesota_votes.pdf.

Molina, Natalia. "Deportable Citizens: The Decoupling of Race and Citizenship in the Construction of the 'Anchor Baby.'" In *Deportation in the Americas: Histories of Exclusion and Resistance*, edited by Kenyon Zimmer and Cristina Salinas, 164–91. College Station: Texas A&M University Press, 2018.

278   WORKS CITED

Molina, Natalia. *How Race Is Made in America*. Berkeley: University of California Press, 2013.

Montgomery, David. *The Fall of the House of Labor: The Workplace, the State, and American Labor Activism, 1865–1925*. New York: Cambridge University Press, 1989.

Moore, Leonard J. *Citizen Klansmen: The Ku Klux Klan in Indiana, 1921–1928*. Chapel Hill: University of North Carolina Press, 1997.

Morales, Daniel. "Tejas, Afuera de México: Newspapers, the Mexican Government, Mutualistas, and Migrants in San Antonio 1910–1940." *Journal of American Ethnic History* 40, no. 2 (Winter 2021): 52–91.

Moscow, Warren. *Politics in the Empire State*. New York: Alfred A. Knopf, 1948.

Moses, Paul. *An Unlikely Union: The Love–Hate Story of New York's Irish and Italians*. New York: New York University Press, 2015.

Moss, Laura-Eve. "Democracy, Citizenship and Constitution-Making in New York, 1777–1894." PhD diss., University of Connecticut, 1999.

Motomura, Hiroshi. *Americans in Waiting: The Lost Story of Immigration and Citizenship in the United States*. New York: Oxford University Press, 2006.

Motomura, Hiroshi. *Immigration Outside the Law*. New York: Oxford University Press, 2014.

"Much-Needed Amendment in New Hampshire." *The Sacred Heart Review* 48, no. 20 (November 2, 1912): 308.

Murphy, Marjorie. *Blackboard Unions: The AFT and the NEA, 1900–1980*. Ithaca, NY: Cornell University Press, 1991.

Murray, Damien. *Irish Nationalists in Boston: Catholicism and Conflict, 1900–1928*. Washington, DC: Catholic University of America Press, 2018.

Napolio, Nicholas G., and Jeffery A. Jenkins. "Conflict over Congressional Reapportionment: The Deadlock of the 1920s." *Journal of Policy History* 35, no. 1 (January 2023): 91–117.

National American Red Cross. *The Work of the Foreign Language Information Service of the American Red Cross*. Washington, DC: Bureau of Foreign Language Information Service, 1920.

"Needs of the Educated Immigrant." *The Interpreter* 4, no. 8 (October 1925): 8–9.

Nettleton, Leigh H. *Lecture No. 27: Loss of Citizenship (Expatriation) and Presumptive Loss of Citizenship*. Lectures: Immigration and Naturalization Service. Washington, DC, December 17, 1934.

Neu, Charles E. "Olympia Brown and the Woman's Suffrage Movement." *Wisconsin Magazine of History* 43, no. 4 (Summer 1960): 277–87.

Neuman, Gerald L. "The Lost Century of American Immigration Law (1776–1875)." *Columbia Law Review* 93, no. 8 (1993): 1833–901.

Neuman, Gerald L. "We Are the People: Alien Suffrage in German and American Perspective." *Michigan Journal of International Law* 13, no. 2 (Winter 1992): 259–335.

Newman, Roger K. *Hugo Black: A Biography*. New York: Pantheon Books, 1994.

New York Department of State. "Votes Cast for and against Proposed Constitutional Conventions and Also Proposed Constitutional Amendments." Excerpted from the *Manual for the Use of the Legislature of the State of New York*. Albany, NY, 2019. https://history.nycourts.gov/wp-content/uploads/2019/01/Publications_Votes-Cast-Conventions-Amendments-compressed.pdf.

New York Supplement Volume 45, May 27, 1897–July 22, 1897. St. Paul, MN: West Publishing, 1897.

Ngai, Mae. "The Architecture of Race in American Immigration Law: A Reexamination of the Immigration Act of 1924." *Journal of American History* 86, no. 1 (June 1999): 67–92.

Ngai, Mae. "Birthright Citizenship and the Alien Citizen." *Fordham Law Review* 75, no. 5 (2007): 2521–30.

Ngai, Mae. *Impossible Subjects: Illegal Aliens and the Making of Modern America*. Princeton, NJ: Princeton University Press, 2004.

Ngai, Mae. *The Lucky Ones: One Family and the Extraordinary Invention of Chinese America*. Boston: Houghton Mifflin Harcourt, 2010.

WORKS CITED

Nicolosi, Ann Marie. "Female Sexuality, Citizenship and Law: The Strange Case of Louise Comacho." *Journal of Contemporary Criminal Justice* 18, no. 3 (August 2002): 329–38.

Nicolosi, Ann Marie. "'We Do Not Want Our Girls to Marry Foreigners': Gender, Race, and American Citizenship." *NWSA Journal* 13, no. 3 (Fall 2001): 1–21.

Noel, Linda C. *Debating American Identity: Southwestern Statehood and Mexican Immigration.* Tucson: University of Arizona Press, 2014.

Noel, Linda C. "New Paths in Immigration History." *Journal of American Ethnic History* 37, no. 3 (Spring 2018): 55–60.

Norvelle, Astrid J. "80 Percent Bill, Court Injunctions, and Arizona Labor: Billy Truax's Two Supreme Court Cases." *Western Legal History* 17, no. 2 (Summer/Fall 2004): 163–210.

Novak, Michael. *Guns of Lattimer.* New York: Basic Books, 1978.

Novak, William J. "The Legal Transformation of Citizenship in Nineteenth-Century America." In *The Democratic Experiment: New Directions in American Political History*, edited by Meg Jacobs, William J. Novak, and Julian E. Zelizer, 85–119. Princeton, NJ: Princeton University Press, 2009.

Number of Assessed Polls, Registered Voters, and Persons Who Voted in Each Voting Precinct at the State, City, and Town Elections, 1918. Boston: Wright & Potter, State Printers, 1919.

O'Connor, Basil. "Constitutional Protection of the Alien's Right to Work." *New York University Law Quarterly Review* 18, no. 4 (May 1941): 483–97.

O'Connor, Thomas H. *The Boston Irish: A Political History.* Boston: Back Bay Books, 1997.

O'Connor, Thomas H. "Irish Votes and Yankee Cotton: The Constitution of 1853." *Proceedings of the Massachusetts Historical Society* 95 (1983): 88–99.

Official Journal of the Proceedings of the Constitutional Convention of the State of Louisiana, Held in New Orleans, Monday, April 21, 1879. New Orleans, LA: Jas. H. Cosgrove, 1879.

Official Journal of the Proceedings of the Constitutional Convention of the State of Louisiana: Held in New Orleans, Tuesday, February 8, 1898. And Calendar. New Orleans, LA: H. J. Hearsey, 1898.

Official Report of the Proceedings and Debates of the Third Constitutional Convention of Ohio: Assembled in the City of Columbus, on Tuesday, December 2, 1873, Volume II—Part 2. Cleveland, OH: W. S. Robison, 1874.

Olcott, Ben W. *Blue Book and Official Directory: Oregon 1915–1916.* Salem, OR: State Printing Department, 1915.

Olesker, Michael. *Journeys to the Heart of Baltimore.* Baltimore: Johns Hopkins University Press, 2001.

Orrenius, Pia M., and Madeline Zavodny. "Do State Work Eligibility Verification Laws Reduce Unauthorized Immigration?" *IZA Journal of Migration* 5, no. 5 (2016): 1–17.

Orrenius, Pia M., Madeline Zavodny, and Sarah Greer. "Who Signs Up for E-Verify? Insights from DHS Enrollment Records." *International Migration Review* 54, no. 4 (2020): 1184–211.

Osumi, Megumi Dick. "Asians and California's Anti-miscegenation Laws." In *Asian and Pacific American Experiences: Women's Perspectives*, edited by Nobuya Tsuchida, Linda M. Mealey, and Gail Thoen, 1–37. Minneapolis: Asian/Pacific American Learning Resource Center and General College, University of Minnesota, 1982.

"Our Annual Dinner." *The Bulletin of the General Contractors Association* 5, no. 12 (December 1914): 401–4.

Paquet, Mireille, Nora Nagels, and Aude-Claire Fourot. "Introduction: Citizenship as a Regime." In *Citizenship as a Regime: Canadian and International Perspectives*, edited by Mireille Paquet, Nora Nagels, and Aude-Claire Fourot, 3–23. Montreal, QC: McGill-Queen's University Press, 2018.

Park, Yoosun. "'A Curious Inconsistency': The Discourse of Social Work on the 1922 Married Women's Independent Nationality Act and the Intersecting Dynamics of Race and Gender in the Laws of Immigration and Citizenship." *Affilia* 30, no. 4 (2015): 560–79.

Parker, Kunal. *Making Foreigners: Immigration and Citizenship Law in America, 1600–2000.* New York: Cambridge University Press, 2015.

280 WORKS CITED

Parker, Kunal. "State, Citizenship, and Territory: The Legal Construction of Immigrants in Antebellum Massachusetts." *Law and History Review* 19, no. 3 (Fall 2001): 583–643.

"Party Statistics." Michigan Legislative Biography. https://mdoe.state.mi.us/legislators/session/PartyStatistics?sortOrder=startDate&page=4.

Paxson, Frederic L. "A Constitution of Democracy—Wisconsin, 1847." *Mississippi Valley Historical Review* 2, no. 1 (1915): 3–24.

Pearson, Harlan C. *Biographical Sketches of the Members of the New Hampshire Constitutional Convention of 1912*. Concord, NH: T. J. Twomey, 1912.

Pearson, Susan J. "'Age Ought to Be a Fact': The Campaign against Child Labor and the Rise of the Birth Certificate." *Journal of American History* 101, no. 4 (March 2015): 1144–65.

Peck, Gunther. *Reinventing Free Labor: Padrones and Immigrant Workers in the North American West, 1880-1930*. New York: Cambridge University Press, 2000.

Pepper, George Wharton, and William Draper Lewis. *A Digest of the Laws of Pennsylvania from 1897 to 1901*. Philadelphia: T. & J. W. Johnson, 1903.

Perlmann, Joel. *America Classifies the Immigrants: From Ellis Island to the 2020 Census*. Cambridge, MA: Harvard University Press, 2018.

Perman, Michael. *Struggle for Mastery: Disfranchisement in the South, 1888-1908*. Chapel Hill: University of North Carolina Press, 2001.

Peter, Carolyn. "California Welcomes the World: International Expositions, 1894–1940 and the Selling of the State." In *Reading California: Art, Image, and Identity, 1900-2000*, edited by Stephanie Barron, Sheri Bernstein, and Ilene Susan Fort, 69–84. Berkeley: University of California Press, 2000.

Peterson, Brenton D., Sonal S. Pandya, and David Leblang. "Doctors with Borders: Occupational Licensing as an Implicit Barrier to High Skill Migration." *Public Choice* 160 (July 2014): 45–63.

Peterson, Dan, and Carol Rooney. *Allegheny City: A History of Pittsburgh's North Side*. Pittsburgh, PA: University of Pittsburgh Press, 2013.

Petit, Jeanne D. *The Men and Women We Want: Gender, Race, and the Progressive Era Literacy Test Debate*. Rochester, NY: University Rochester Press, 2010.

Phillips, G. W. *Past and Present of Platte County, Nebraska: A Record of Settlement, Organization, Progress and Achievement, Vol. II*. Chicago: S. J. Clarke , 1915.

Pitti, Stephen J. *The Devil in Silicon Valley: Northern California, Race, and Mexican Americans*. Princeton, NJ: Princeton University Press, 2004.

Plascencia, Luis F. B. *Disenchanting Citizenship: Mexican Migrants and the Boundaries of Belonging*. New Brunswick, NJ: Rutgers University Press, 2012.

Plascencia, Luis, Gary P. Freeman, and Mark Setzler. "The Decline of Barriers to Immigrant Economic and Political Rights in the American States: 1977–2001." *International Migration Review* 37, no. 1 (2003): 5–23.

Porter, Kirk Harold. *A History of Suffrage in the United States*. Chicago: University of Chicago Press, 1918.

Potter, Simon J. "The Imperial Significance of the Canadian–American Reciprocity Proposals of 1911." *The Historical Journal* 47, no. 1 (March 2004): 81–100.

Powell, Thomas Reed. "The Right to Work for the State." *Columbia Law Review* 16, no. 2 (February 1916): 99–114.

Proceedings and Debates of the Constitutional Convention: Held in the City of Helena, Montana, July 4th, 1889, August 17th, 1889. Helena, MT: State Publishing, 1921.

Proceedings of the Constitutional Convention Held in Denver, December 20, 1875, to Frame a Constitution for the State of Colorado Together with the Enabling Act. Denver, CO: Smith–Brooks Press, 1907.

Proceedings of the National Conference on Americanization in Industries, Held at the Atlantic House, Nantasket Beach, Massachusetts, June 22, 23 and 24, 1919. New York, NY, 1919.

"Prohibition of Employment of Aliens in Construction of Public Works." *Columbia Law Review* 15, no. 3 (March 1915): 263–65.

WORKS CITED 281

Proposed Amendments to the Constitution, Laws Passed at the Fifth Session of the Legislative Assembly of the State of North Dakota. Grand Forks, ND: Herald, State Printers and Binders, 1897.

The Proposed New Constitution of Illinois, 1922 with Explanatory Notes and Address to the People: For Submission to the People at a Special Election on Tuesday, December 12, 1922, 1922.

Rakove, Jack N. *Original Meanings: Politics and Ideas in the Making of the Constitution.* New York: Vintage Books, 1997.

Ramirez, Bruno. *On the Move: French-Canadian and Italian Migrants in the North Atlantic Economy, 1860–1914.* Toronto, ON: McClelland & Stewart, 1991.

Rana, Aziz. *The Two Faces of American Freedom.* Cambridge, MA: Harvard University Press, 2010.

Raskin, Jamin B. "Legal Aliens, Local Citizens: The Historical, Constitutional and Theoretical Meanings of Alien Suffrage." *University of Pennsylvania Law Review* 141, no. 4 (April 1993): 1391–470.

Ravitch, Diane. *The Great School Wars: A History of the New York City Public Schools.* Baltimore: Johns Hopkins University Press, 2000.

Renshon, Stanley. *Noncitizen Voting and American Democracy.* New York: Rowman & Littlefield, 2009.

Report of the Public Service Commission for the First District of the State of New York for the Year Ending December 31, 1914. Albany: New York Public Service Commission, 1915.

Reverby, Susan M. *Ordered to Care: The Dilemma of American Nursing, 1850–1945.* New York: Cambridge University Press, 1987.

Rezneck, Samuel. "Unemployment, Unrest, and Relief in the United States during the Depression of 1893–97." *Journal of Political Economy* 61, no. 4 (August 1953): 324–45.

Richard, Mark Paul. *Loyal but French: The Negotiation of Identity by French-Canadian Descendants in the United States.* East Lansing: Michigan State University Press, 2008.

Richard, Mark Paul. *Not a Catholic Nation: The Ku Klux Klan Confronts New England in the 1920s.* Amherst: University of Massachusetts Press, 2015.

Rickard, Louise. "The Politics of Reform in Omaha, 1918–1921." *Nebraska History* 53 (1972): 419–45.

Riessen-Reed, Dorinda. *The Woman Suffrage Movement in South Dakota.* Pierre: South Dakota Commission on the Status of Women, 1975.

Ritter, Luke. "Immigration, Crime, and the Economic Origins of Political Nativism in the Antebellum West." *Journal of American Ethnic History* 39, no. 2 (Winter 2020): 62–91.

Robertson, Craig. *The Passport in America: The History of a Document.* New York: Oxford University Press, 2012.

Roby, Yves. *Les Franco-Américains de la Nouvelle-Angleterre: Rêves et réalités.* Sillery, QC: Septentrion, 2000.

Roediger, David. *Working toward Whiteness: How America's Immigrants Became White: The Strange Journey from Ellis Island to the Suburbs.* New York: Basic Books, 2005.

Roediger, David, and James Barrett. "Making New Immigrants 'Inbetween': Irish Hosts and White Panethnicity, 1890 to 1930." In *Not Just Black and White: Historical and Contemporary Perspectives on Immigration, Race, and Ethnicity in the United States,* edited by Nancy Foner and George M. Fredrickson, 167–96. New York: Russell Sage Foundation, 2004.

Roller, Michael P. "Rewriting Narratives of Labor Violence: A Transnational Perspective of the Lattimer Massacre." *Historical Archaeology* 47, no. 3 (2013): 109–23.

Romer, Christina. "Spurious Volatility in Historical Unemployment Data." *Journal of Political Economy* 94, no. 1 (February 1986): 1–37.

Romero, Thomas. "A War to Keep Alien Labor out of Colorado: The 'Mexican Menace' and the Historical Origins of Local and State Anti-Immigration Initiatives." In *Strange Neighbors: The Role of States in Immigration Policy,* edited by Carissa Byrne Hessick and Gabriel J. Chin, 63–96. New York: New York University Press, 2014.

282 WORKS CITED

Rosberg, Gerald M. "Aliens and Equal Protection: Why Not the Right to Vote?" *Michigan Law Review* 75, no. 5–6 (May 1977): 1092–136.

Ross, Robert B. "Scales and Skills of Monopoly Power: Labor Geographies of the 1890–1891 Chicago Carpenters' Strike." *Antipode* 43, no. 4 (2011): 1281–304.

Ross, William G. *Forging New Freedoms: Nativism, Education, and the Constitution, 1917–1927.* Lincoln: University of Nebraska Press, 1994.

Rubin, Michael H. "Immigration, Quotas, and Its Impact on Medical Education." Master's thesis, Wake Forest University, 2013.

Rutkowski, Conrad P. "State Politics and Apportionment: The Case of New York." PhD diss., Fordham University, 1971.

Ryan, Rt. Rev. Msgr. John A. "Is the Alien Entitled to an Equal Chance in Getting a Job?" Presented at the Conference on the Alien in America, New York, NY, May 2, 1936.

Sainsbury, Diane. "Gender Differentiation and Citizenship Acquisition: Nationality Reforms in Comparative and Historical Perspective." *Women's Studies International Forum* 68 (June 2018): 28–35.

Salyer, Lucy E. *Laws Harsh as Tigers: Chinese Immigrants and the Shaping of Modern Immigration Law.* Chapel Hill: University of North Carolina Press, 1995.

Sánchez, George. *Becoming Mexican American: Ethnicity, Culture, and Identity in Chicano Los Angeles, 1900–1945.* New York: Oxford University Press, 1993.

Sargent, Noel. "The California Constitutional Convention of 1878–9." *California Law Review* 6, no. 1 (1917): 1–22.

Sautter, Udo. *Three Cheers for the Unemployed: Government and Unemployment before the New Deal.* New York: Cambridge University Press, 1991.

Savage, Sean J. *Roosevelt: The Party Leader, 1932–1945.* Lexington: University Press of Kentucky, 2014.

Saxton, Alexander. *The Indispensable Enemy: Labor and the Anti-Chinese Movement in California.* Berkeley: University of California Press, 1971.

Scarrow, Howard A. "One Voter, One Vote: The Apportionment of Congressional Seats Reconsidered." *Polity* 22, no. 2 (Winter 1989): 253–68.

Scheiber, Harry N. "Race, Radicalism, and Reform: Historical Perspective on the 1879 California Constitution." *Hastings Constitutional Law Quarterly* 17, no. 1 (Fall 1989): 35–80.

Schibsby, Marian. *Handbook for Immigrants to the United States.* New York: Foreign Language Information Service, 1927.

Schibsby, Marian. "Legislative Bulletin No. 1." *Interpreter Releases* 20, no. 3 (January 25, 1943): 17–25.

Schibsby, Marian. "Some Naturalization Issues." *Interpreter Releases* 19, no. 34 (July 6, 1942): 235–36 (b).

Schneider, Dorothee. *Crossing Borders: Migration and Citizenship in the Twentieth-Century United States.* Cambridge, MA: Harvard University Press, 2011.

Schneider, Dorothee. "Naturalization and United States Citizenship in Two Periods of Mass Migration: 1894–1930, 1965–2000." *Journal of American Ethnic History* 21, no. 1 (October 2001): 50–82.

Schneirov, Richard, and Thomas J. Suhrbur. *Union Brotherhood, Union Town: The History of the Carpenters' Union of Chicago, 1863–1987.* Carbondale: Southern Illinois University Press, 1988.

Scott, Jessye Leigh. "Alien Teachers: Suspect Class or Subversive Influence?" *Mercer Law Review* 31, no. 3 (Spring 1980): 815–24.

Searcy, Hubert. "Problems of Congressional Reapportionment." *The Southwestern Social Science Quarterly* 16, no. 1 (June 1935): 58–68.

"Selecting Our Immigrants." *The Interpreter* 8, no. 10 (December 1929): 147–49.

Self, Robert O. *American Babylon: Race and the Struggle for Postwar Oakland.* Princeton, NJ: Princeton University Press, 2005.

WORKS CITED 283

Shackel, Paul A. *Remembering Lattimer: Labor, Migration, and Race in Pennsylvania Anthracite Country*. Urbana: University of Illinois Press, 2018.

Shackel, Paul A., and Michael Roller. "The Gilded Age Wasn't So Gilded in the Anthracite Region of Pennsylvania." *International Journal of Historical Archaeology* 16, no. 4 (December 2012): 761–75.

Shah, Nayan. *Stranger Intimacy: Contesting Race, Sexuality, and the Law in the North American West*. Berkeley: University of California Press, 2011.

Shanahan, Brendan A. "Counting Everyone—Citizens and Non-citizens—in the 2020 Census Is Crucial." *Washington Post*, March 12, 2020, sec. Made by History. https://www.washingtonpost.com/outlook/2020/03/12/counting-everyone-citizens-non-citizens-2020-census-is-crucial/.

Shanahan, Brendan A. "Enforcing the Colorline and Counting White Races: Race and the Census in North America, 1900–1941." *American Review of Canadian Studies* 44, no. 3 (2014): 293–307.

Shanahan, Brendan A. "The Late Nineteenth-Century North American Catholic Schools Question: Tangled Disputes over Catholic Public Education in Manitoba and Minnesota." *The Catholic Historical Review* 110, no. 1 (Winter 2024): 47–71.

Shanahan, Brendan A. "A 'Practically American' Canadian Woman Confronts a United States Citizen-Only Hiring Law: Katharine Short and the California Alien Teachers Controversy of 1915." *Law and History Review* 39, no. 4 (November 2021): 621–47.

Shapiro, Samuel. "The Conservative Dilemma: The Massachusetts Constitutional Convention of 1853." *The New England Quarterly* 33, no. 2 (1960): 207–24.

Shattuck, Henry L. "Martin Lomasney in the Constitutional Convention of 1917–1919." *Proceedings of the Massachusetts Historical Society* 71 (October 1953): 299–310.

Sheldon, Addison E. "The Nebraska Constitutional Convention, 1919–1920." *American Political Science Review* 15, no. 3 (1921): 391–400.

Sheridan, Clare. "Contested Citizenship: National Identity and the Mexican Immigration Debates of the 1920s." *Journal of American Ethnic History* 21, no. 3 (Spring 2002): 3–35.

Shklar, Judith. *American Citizenship: The Quest for Inclusion*. Cambridge, MA: Harvard University Press, 1991.

Shull, Charles W. "Legislative Apportionment and the Law." *Temple Law Quarterly* 18, no. 3 (1944): 388–405.

Shumsky, Neil Larry. "'Let No Man Stop to Plunder!' American Hostility to Return Migration, 1890–1924." *Journal of American Ethnic History* 11, no. 2 (1992): 56–75.

Siegelberg, Mira L. *Statelessness: A Modern History*. Cambridge, MA: Harvard University Press, 2020.

Silva, Ruth C. "Apportionment of the New York Assembly." *Fordham Law Review* 31, no. 1 (October 1962): 1–72.

Silva, Ruth C. "Apportionment of the New York State Legislature." *American Political Science Review* 55, no. 4 (1961): 870–81.

Silva, Ruth C. "Legislative Representation: With Special Reference to New York." *Law and Contemporary Problems* 27, no. 3 (Summer 1962): 408–33.

Silva, Ruth C. "One Man, One Vote and the Population Base." In *Representation and Misrepresentation: Legislative Reapportionment in Theory and Practice*, edited by C. Herman Pritchett and Robert A. Goldwin, 53–70. Chicago: Rand McNally, 1968.

Silva, Ruth C. "The Population Base for Apportionment of the New York Legislature." *Fordham Law Review* 32, no. 1 (October 1963): 1–50.

Silva, Ruth C. "Reapportionment and Redistricting." *Scientific American* 213, no. 5 (1965): 20–27.

SJR 1, 37th Regular Session. Legislative Reference Library of Texas. https://lrl.texas.gov/legis/billsearch/amendmentDetails.cfm?amendmentID=88&legSession=37-0&billTypedetail=SJR&billNumberDetail=1.

284   WORKS CITED

Skrentny, John David. *The Minority Rights Revolution*. Cambridge, MA: Harvard University Press, 2002.

Smith, Darrell. *The Bureau of Naturalization: Its History, Activities, and Organization*. Baltimore: Johns Hopkins University Press, 1926.

Smith, Marian. "'Any Woman Who Is Now or May Hereafter Be Married . . .': Women and Naturalization, ca. 1802–1940." *Prologue* 30, no. 2 (Summer 1998): 146–53.

Smith, Marian. "Immigration and Naturalization Service." In *A Historical Guide to the U.S. Government*, edited by George Kurian, 305–8. New York: Oxford University Press, 1998.

Smith, Rogers. *Civic Ideals: Conflicting Visions of Citizenship in U.S. History*. New Haven, CT: Yale University Press, 1997.

Song, Sarah. "Democracy and Noncitizen Voting Rights." *Citizenship Studies* 13, no. 6 (December 2009): 607–20.

Sparrow, Bartholomew H. *The Insular Cases and the Emergence of American Empire*. Lawrence: University Press of Kansas, 2006.

Stahl, Jeremy. "Trump's Effort to Rig the Census Failed, but the Fight Is Far from Over." *Slate*, July 11, 2019. https://slate.com/news-and-politics/2019/07/trump-barr-census-citizenship-question-defeat.html.

Stanley, Amy Dru. *From Bondage to Contract: Wage Labor, Marriage, and the Market in the Age of Slave Emancipation*. New York: Cambridge University Press, 1998.

Stanton, Elizabeth Cady, Susan B. Anthony, Matilda Joslyn Gage, and Ida Husted Harper. *History of Woman Suffrage*. Vol. 6. New York: Fowler & Wells, 1922.

Starr, Paul. *The Social Transformation of American Medicine: The Rise of a Sovereign Profession and the Making of a Vast Industry*. New York: Basic Books, 1982.

State of New Hampshire Convention to Revise the Constitution June 5, 1918, January 13, 1920, January 28, 1921. 3 vols. Manchester, NH: John B. Clarke, 1921.

State of New Hampshire: Manual for the General Court, 1911 (No. 12). Concord, NH, 1911.

State of New Hampshire: Manual for the General Court, 1921 (No. 17). Concord, NH, 1921.

"Status of the Alien Labor Cases." *The Bulletin of the General Contractors Association* 5, no. 12 (December 1914): 367–88.

Steele, Richard W. "'No Racials': Discrimination against Ethnics in American Defense Industry, 1940–42." *Labor History* 32, no. 1 (Winter 1991): 66–90.

Steele, Richard W. "The War on Intolerance: The Reformulation of American Nationalism, 1939–1941." *Journal of American Ethnic History* 9, no. 1 (Fall 1989): 9–35.

Steeples, Douglas, and David O. Whitten. *Democracy in Desperation: The Depression of 1893*. Westport, CT: Greenwood Press, 1998.

Steffens, Lincoln. *The Shame of the Cities*. New York: McClure, Phillips, 1904.

Sterne, Evelyn Savidge. *Ballots & Bibles: Ethnic Politics and the Catholic Church in Providence*. Ithaca, NY: Cornell University Press, 2004.

Stevens, Lewis M. "The Life and Character of Earl G. Harrison." *University of Pennsylvania Law Review* 104, no. 5 (March 1956): 591–602.

Stevens, Rosemary, and Joan Vermeulen. "Foreign Trained Physicians and American Medicine." Bethesda, MD: National Institutes of Health; Bureau of Health Manpower Education, June 1972.

Stone, Wilbur Fisk, ed. *History of Colorado Illustrated*. Vol. 2. Chicago: S. J. Clark, 1918.

Storrs, Landon R. Y. *The Second Red Scare and the Unmaking of the New Deal Left*. Princeton, NJ: Princeton University Press, 2013.

Sugrue, Thomas J. *The Origins of the Urban Crisis: Race and Inequality in Postwar Detroit*. Princeton, NJ: Princeton University Press, 1996.

Sugrue, Thomas J. *Sweet Land of Liberty: The Forgotten Struggle for Civil Rights in the North*. New York: Random House, 2008.

Sullivan, Teresa A. *Census 2020: Understanding the Issues*. Cham, Switzerland: Springer International, 2020.

WORKS CITED 285

Summers, Mark Wahlgren. *Party Games: Getting, Keeping, and Using Power in Gilded Age Politics*. Chapel Hill: University of North Carolina Press, 2005.

Suzuki, Masao. "Important or Impotent? Taking Another Look at the 1920 California Alien Land Law." *Journal of Economic History* 64, no. 1 (March 2004): 125–43.

Sweet, Jameson. "Native Suffrage: Race, Citizenship, and Dakota Indians in the Upper Midwest." *Journal of the Early Republic* 39, no. 1 (2019): 99–109.

Sweeting, Orville J. "John Q. Tilson and the Reapportionment Act of 1929." *Western Political Quarterly* 9, no. 2 (June 1956): 434–53.

Swindler, William F. "Missouri Constitutions: History, Theory and Practice." *Missouri Law Review* 23, no. 1 (January 1958): 32–62.

Swindler, William F. "Missouri Constitutions: History, Theory and Practice (Continued)." *Missouri Law Review* 23, no. 2 (April 1958): 157–79.

"Symposium: Baker v. Carr." *Yale Law Journal* 72, no. 1 (November 1962): 1–222.

Tarr, George Alan. "State Constitutional Politics: An Historical Perspective." In *Constitutional Politics in the States: Contemporary Controversies and Historical Patterns*, edited by George Alan Tarr, 3–23. Westport, CT: Greenwood, 1996.

Taylor, A. Elizabeth. "The Woman Suffrage Movement in Arkansas." *The Arkansas Historical Quarterly* 15, no. 1 (1956): 17–52.

Taylor, A. Elizabeth. "The Woman Suffrage Movement in Texas." *The Journal of Southern History* 17, no. 2 (May 1951): 194–215.

Taylor, E. L. "Richard Plantaganet Llewellyn Baber." *Ohio History Journal* 19, no. 4 (October 1910): 370–81.

Teaford, Jon. *The Unheralded Triumph: City Government in America, 1870–1900*. Baltimore: Johns Hopkins University Press, 1984.

Telles, Edward, and Vilma Ortiz. *Generations of Exclusion: Mexican Americans, Assimilation, and Race*. New York: Russell Sage Foundation, 2008.

Thatcher, Mary Anne. *Immigrants and the 1930s: Ethnicity and Alienage in Depression and On-Coming War*. New York: Garland, 1990.

Thirteenth Annual Report of the New York Bureau of Statistics of Labor for the Year 1895, Vol. 1. Albany, NY: Wynkoop Hallenbeck Crawford, State Printers, 1896.

"Thomas Barkworth." *Michigan Legislative Biography*. https://mdoe.state.mi.us/legislators/Legislator/LegislatorDetail/3425.

Thompson, John Herd, and Stephen J. Randall. *Canada and the United States: Ambivalent Allies*. Athens, GA: University of Georgia Press, 2002.

Tichenor, Daniel. *Dividing Lines: The Politics of Immigration Control in America*. Princeton, NJ: Princeton University Press, 2002.

Tiedeman, Christopher Gustavus. *A Treatise on State and Federal Control of Persons and Property in the United States: Considered from both a Civil and Criminal Standpoint*. St. Louis, MO: F. H. Thomas Law Book, 1900.

Tienda, Marta. "Demography and the Social Contract." *Demography* 39, no. 4 (November 2002): 587–616.

Tinkle, Marshall J. *The Maine State Constitution*. New York: Oxford University Press, 2013.

Tirres, Allison Brownell. "Exclusion from Within: Noncitizens and the Rise of Discriminatory Licensing Laws." *Law & Social Inquiry* 49, no. 3 (2024): 1783–811.

Tirres, Allison Brownell. "Ownership without Citizenship: The Creation of Noncitizen Property Rights." *Michigan Journal of Race & Law* 19 (Fall 2013): 1–52.

Tirres, Allison Brownell. "Property Outliers: Non-citizens, Property Rights and State Power." *Georgetown Immigration Law Journal* 27 (2012): 77–133.

Traynor, W. J. H. "The Aims and Methods of the A.P.A." *North American Review* 159, no. 452 (July 1894): 67–76.

Traynor, W. J. H. "Policy and Power of the A.P.A." *North American Review* 162, no. 475 (June 1896): 658–66.

286 WORKS CITED

Trimpi, Helen P. *Crimson Confederates: Harvard Men Who Fought for the South*. Knoxville: University of Tennessee Press, 2010.

Tweton, D. Jerome. "Considering Why Populism Succeeded in South Dakota and Failed in North Dakota." *South Dakota History* 22, no. 4 (1993): 330–44.

Tyler, Gus, and David I. Wells. "New York 'Constitutionally Republican.'" In *The Politics of Reapportionment*, edited by Malcolm Edwin Jewell, 221–48. New Brunswick, NJ: Transaction Publishers, 1962.

Tyler, Jacki Hedlund. *Leveraging an Empire: Settler Colonialism and the Legalities of Citizenship in the Pacific Northwest*. Lincoln: University of Nebraska Press, 2021.

Ueda, Reed. "The Changing Path to Citizenship: Ethnicity and Naturalization during World War II." In *The War in American Culture: Society and Consciousness during World War II*, edited by Lewis A. Erenberg and Susan E. Hirsch, 202–16. Chicago: University of Chicago Press, 1996.

US Bureau of Naturalization. *Annual Report of the Commissioner of Naturalization*. Washington, DC: US Government Printing Office, 1923–1932.

US Census Bureau. *Fourteenth Census of the United States, 1920*. Washington, DC: US Government Printing Office, 1921.

US Census Bureau. *Fourteenth Census of the United States—Population: 1920: Color or Race, Nativity and Parentage*. Washington, DC: US Government Printing Office, 1922.

US Census Bureau. *Historical Statistics of the United States, 1789–1945; A Supplement to the Statistical Abstract of the United States, Prepared with the Cooperation of the Social Science Research Council*. Washington, DC: US Government Printing Office, 1949.

US Census Bureau. *Thirteenth Census of the United States, 1910*. Washington, DC: US Government Printing Office, 1911.

US Census Office. *Eleventh Census of the United States, 1890*. Washington, DC: US Government Printing Office, 1896.

US Census Office. *Ninth Census of the United States, 1870*. Washington, DC: US Government Printing Office, 1872.

US Census Office. *Twelfth Census of the United States, 1900*. Washington, DC: US Government Printing Office, 1901.

US Citizenship and Immigration Services. "Title 8 of the Code of Federal Regulations Part 324." https://www.uscis.gov/ilink/docView/SLB/HTML/SLB/0-0-0-1/0-0-0-11261/0-0-0-31866/0-0-0-31931.html#0-0-0-19975.

US Immigration and Naturalization Service. *Annual Report of the Immigration and Naturalization Service*. Washington, DC: US Government Printing Office, 1933–1975.

US Immigration and Naturalization Service. *Regulations and Instructions for Alien Registration*. Washington, DC: US Government Printing Office, 1940.

Valentine, David C. "Constitutional Amendments, Statutory Revision and Referenda Submitted to the Voters by the General Assembly or by Initiative Petition, 1910–2010." Columbia: Missouri Legislative Academy, December 2010.

VanBurkleo, Sandra F. *Gender Remade: Citizenship, Suffrage, and Public Power in the New Northwest, 1879–1912*. New York: Cambridge University Press, 2015.

Vargas, Zaragosa. *Labor Rights Are Civil Rights: Mexican American Workers in Twentieth-Century America*. Princeton, NJ: Princeton University Press, 2013.

Varsanyi, Monica W. "Fighting for the Vote: The Struggle against Felon and Immigrant Disfranchisement." In *Beyond Walls and Cages: Prisons, Borders, and Global Crisis*, edited by Andrew Burridge, Jenna M. Loyd, and Matthew Mitchelson, 266–76. Athens, GA: University of Georgia Press, 2013.

Varsanyi, Monica W. "Hispanic Racialization, Citizenship, and the Colorado Border Blockade of 1936." *Journal of American Ethnic History* 40, no. 1 (2020): 5–39.

Varsanyi, Monica W. "The Rise and Fall (and Rise?) of Non-citizen Voting: Immigration and the Shifting Scales of Citizenship and Suffrage in the United States." *Space and Polity* 9, no. 2 (2005): 113–34.

WORKS CITED   287

Varzally, Allison. "Romantic Crossings: Making Love, Family, and Non-whiteness in California, 1925–1950." *Journal of American Ethnic History* 23, no. 1 (Fall 2003): 3–54.

Vasilogambros, Matt. "Noncitizens Are Slowly Gaining Voting Rights." *Pew*, July 1, 2021. https://pew.org/2TeJy4P.

Vecoli, Rudolph. "Chicago's Italians prior to World War I: A Study of Their Social and Economic Adjustment." PhD diss., University of Wisconsin, 1963.

Vernier, Chester Garfield. *American Family Laws: A Comparative Study of the Family Law of the Forty-Eight American States, Alaska, the District of Columbia, and Hawaii (to Jan. 1, 1937)*. Stanford, CA: Stanford University Press, 1938.

Volpp, Leti. "Divesting Citizenship: On Asian American History and the Loss of Citizenship through Marriage." *UCLA Law Review* 53, no. 2 (December 2005): 405–83.

Vought, Hans P. *The Bully Pulpit and the Melting Pot: American Presidents and the Immigrant, 1897–1933*. Macon, GA: Mercer University Press, 2004.

Waldman, Michael. *The Fight to Vote*. New York: Simon & Schuster, 2016.

Waldron, FlorenceMae. "Gender and the Quebecois Migration to New England, 1870–1930: A Comparative Case Study." PhD diss., University of Minnesota, 2003.

Walker, Francis Amasa. *A Compendium of the Ninth Census*. Washington, DC: US Government Printing Office, 1872.

Walter, Bronwen. *Outsiders Inside: Whiteness, Place and Irish Women*. New York: Routledge, 2000.

Walter, David O. "Reapportionment of State Legislative Districts." *Illinois Law Review* 37, no. 1 (1942): 20–42.

Waugh, Joan. "'Give This Man Work!': Josephine Shaw Lowell, the Charity Organization Society of the City of New York, and the Depression of 1893." *Social Science History* 25, no. 2 (2001): 217–46.

Weaver, Oren W. *The Census System of Massachusetts*. Boston: Albert J. Wright, State Printer, 1876.

Weil, Patrick. *The Sovereign Citizen: Denaturalization and the Origins of the American Republic*. Philadelphia: University of Pennsylvania Press, 2013.

Wells, Cory D. "'Tie the Flags Together': Migration, Nativism, and the Orange Order in the United States, 1840–1930." PhD diss., University of Texas at Arlington, 2018.

Wells, David. *Legislative Representation in New York State: A Discussion of Inequitable Representation of the Citizens of New York in the State Legislature and Congress*. New York: International Ladies' Garment Workers' Union, 1963.

"What Our Organizers Are Doing." *The American Federationist* 18 (July 1911): 550–56.

White, Leonard D. "The New Hampshire Constitutional Convention." *Michigan Law Review* 19, no. 4 (1921): 383–94.

White, Leonard D. "The Tenth New Hampshire Convention." *American Political Science Review* 15, no. 3 (August 1921): 400–403.

Wiitala, Stephen. "Election Law Turmoil in Nebraska." Master's thesis, University of Nebraska, Omaha, 1991.

"William Gray." Parliament of Canada. https://lop.parl.ca/sites/ParlInfo/default/en_CA/People/Profile?personId=13112.

Williams, Hattie Plum. "The Road to Citizenship." *Political Science Quarterly* 27, no. 3 (September 1912): 399–427.

Williams, Mason B. *City of Ambition: FDR, La Guardia, and the Making of Modern New York*. New York: W. W. Norton, 2013.

Williamson, Leland M., Richard A. Foley, Henry H. Colclazer, Louis Nanna Megargee, Jay Henry Mowbray, and William R. Antisdel, eds. *Prominent and Progressive Pennsylvanians of the Nineteenth Century*. Vol. 2. Philadelphia: Record Publishing, 1898.

Wilson, Jamie. *Building a Healthy Black Harlem*. Amherst, NY: Cambria Press, 2009.

Wirls, Daniel. "Regionalism, Rotten Boroughs, Race, and Realignment: The Seventeenth Amendment and the Politics of Representation." *Studies in American Political Development* 13, no. 1 (April 1999): 1–30.

288   WORKS CITED

Wisconsin Historical Society, Dictionary of Wisconsin History. https://www.wisconsinhistory.org/Records/Article/CS7222.

Witgen, Michael J. *Seeing Red: Indigenous Land, American Expansion, and the Political Economy of Plunder in North America.* Chapel Hill: University of North Carolina Press, 2022.

Witz, Anne. "Patriarchy and the Professions: The Gendered Politics of Occupational Closure." *Sociology* 24, no. 4 (November 1990): 675–90.

Wolf, Thomas P., and Brianna Cea. "A Critical History of the United States Census and Citizenship Questions." *Georgetown Law Journal Online* 108, no. 1 (2019): 1–36.

Wolfe, French Eugene. *Admission to American Trade Unions.* Baltimore: Johns Hopkins University Press, 1912.

The Woman Citizen. "Alien-by-Marriage." October 8, 1921, 13.

The Woman Citizen. "The Alien in Equal Suffrage States." April 27, 1918, 438.

The Woman Citizen. "Amending the Amendment." July 13, 1918, 125.

The Woman Citizen. "Catching Up with Indiana Women." December 14, 1918, 592.

The Woman Citizen. "Citizenship in Nebraska." February 2, 1918, 189.

The Woman Citizen. "Hearings before House Committee." January 12, 1918, 130–31, 136–37.

The Woman Citizen. "How to Win a State." November 16, 1918, 508–9.

The Woman Citizen. "Justice in Nebraska." February 23, 1918, 249.

The Woman Citizen. "Should Aliens Vote?" September 10, 1921, 18.

The Woman Citizen. "South Dakota's Citizenship Measure." July 20, 1918, 148, 158.

The Woman Citizen. "South Dakota to the Fore." April 6, 1918, 369.

The Woman Citizen. "Southern Suffragists Roused over Slacker Vote." January 12, 1918, 132, 137.

The Woman Citizen. "Texas's Women Voters." July 20, 1918, 156.

The Woman Citizen. "The Teutonic Touch in Nebraska." August 25, 1917, 230.

The Woman Citizen. "To Get Back Beer." June 15, 1918, 45.

The Woman Citizen. "What Happened to Texas?" August 27, 1921, 18.

The Woman Citizen. "William E. Borah." October 26, 1918, 429.

The Woman's Tribune. "Voters Who Are Not Citizens." January 25, 1896, 1.

Woodward, C. Vann. "The Political Legacy of Reconstruction." *The Journal of Negro Education* 26, no. 3 (1957): 231–40.

Wright, Deil S. "The Advisory Commission on Intergovernmental Relations: Unique Features and Policy Orientation." *Public Administration Review* 25, no. 3 (September 1965): 193–202.

Wroble, Susan. "Agapito Vigil." In *Colorado Encyclopedia.* https://coloradoencyclopedia.org/article/agapito-vigil.

Wyman, Mark. *Round-Trip to America: The Immigrants Return to Europe, 1880–1930.* Ithaca, NY: Cornell University Press, 2018.

Yamamoto, Shiori. "Beyond Suffrage: Intermarriage, Land, and Meanings of Citizenship and Marital Naturalization/Expatriation in the United States." PhD diss., University of Nevada, Las Vegas, 2019.

Yung, Judy. *Unbound Feet: A Social History of Chinese Women in San Francisco.* Berkeley: University of California Press, 1995.

Zamora, Emilio. *The World of the Mexican Worker in Texas.* College Station: Texas A&M University Press, 2000.

Zeidel, Robert F. *Robber Barons and Wretched Refuse: Ethnic and Class Dynamics during the Era of American Industrialization.* Ithaca, NY: Cornell University Press, 2020.

Zelden, Charles L. *The Battle for the Black Ballot: Smith v. Allwright and the Defeat of the Texas All White Primary.* Lawrence: University Press of Kansas, 2004.

Ziegler-McPherson, Christina A. *Americanization in the States: Immigrant Social Welfare Policy, Citizenship, & National Identity in the United States, 1908–1929.* Gainesville: University Press of Florida, 2009.

Ziegler-McPherson, Christina A. *Selling America: Immigration Promotion and the Settlement of the American Continent, 1607–1914*. Santa Barbara, CA: Praeger, 2017.

Zolberg, Aristide R. *A Nation by Design: Immigration Policy in the Fashioning of America*. New York: Russell Sage Foundation, 2006.

Zuckerman, George David. "A Consideration of the History and Present Status of Section 2 of the Fourteenth Amendment." *Fordham Law Review* 30, no. 1 (October 1961): 93–136.

Index

accountants, licensure laws and 122, 136, 141

African Americans
apportionment and 18, 106–8
disfranchisement of 29
enfranchisement of 18–20
Jim Crow regime, under 29, 167
public works projects and 51
racism directed toward 2, 18–20, 26–29, 51,
69, 106–8, 110, 231–232n68, 233n81
Reconstruction, during 18–20
suffrage and 18–20
trades, exclusion from 195n87

Alabama
apportionment (federal) 106
disfranchisement of noncitizens in 26
immigrants in 104
voting restrictions in 29

Albert, Isaiah Lafayette 103, 218nn58–59

Alger Club 77

alienage laws
generally 1–2
blue-collar nativist hiring laws
(*see* blue-collar nativist hiring laws)
differences in 5–8, 168
licensure laws (*see* licensure laws)

Alien Registration Act of 1940
generally 120, 139, 234n90
enactment of 131
marital repatriation and 145, 158, 160,
163, 166–67

Alien Tax Act of 1897 (Pennsylvania
law) 43–45

Ambach v. Norwick (1979) 143

American Federation of Labor 39, 198n128

American Legion 123

American Medical Association (AMA) 126–27,
136–39, 236nn119–21

American Party. *See* Know-Nothing Party

American Protective Association (APA) 74, 76,
206nn42–45

antebellum period
apportionment during 15–17
citizenship, political rights during 12–17, 37
suffrage during 12–15

Anthony, Susan B. 20, 71, 82, 205n25

apportionment. See also *specific state*
generally 6–7, 95–97, 116
African Americans and 18, 106–8
antebellum period, during 15–17
citizen-only rights and 116
constitutional conventions and 11, 15–16,
23–24, 95–103, 114–15
contemporary debates 170
current status 172
equal protection and 112–13
exclusion of noncitizens from (debated and/
or adopted) 15–16, 18–20, 23–24, 95–103,
105–8, 111–16, 214n10
federal constitution, under 15
Fourteenth Amendment and 18–20, 106
gridlock and 104–11
malapportionment 100, 104–11, 113–15
"one man, one vote" and 111–16
political self-interest and 219n86
Reconstruction, during 18
reform proposals 111–16
unions and 96, 111
votes-cast proposals 101–3, 106, 214n9,
217n50, 223n132

architects, licensure laws and 122, 143

Arizona
anti-alien public hiring laws in 36, 52
apportionment in 102, 115
blue-collar nativist hiring laws in 52, 54–55,
197–98n124
80 percent citizen hiring law 54–55, 61, 63
malapportionment in 214n9, 223n132
public works projects, anti-alien hiring
laws and 200n145
statehood of 30, 186–87n135

Arizona Territory, disfranchisement of
noncitizens in 30

Arkansas
alien suffrage in 21, 28–29
disfranchisement of noncitizens in 85–86,
91, 93–94, 186n128

Armstrong, Paul 153

Arthur (Prince, also known as the Duke of
Connaught) 59, 202n183

Ashbridge, Samuel 52, 198n126

292 INDEX

Asian immigrants
  alienage laws and, generally 4, see also
    specific state
  anti-Chinese laws 37–39
  licensure laws and repeal of "aliens ineligible
    to citizenship" status 141–142
  marital repatriation and 147, 154, 166
  racialization of 3, 37–39
  racism directed toward 2–3, 23–24, 30,
    37–39, 104–5, 134–36, 141–42

Baber, R. P. L. 22
Baker, Gordon 113–14
Baker v. Carr (1962) 112, 114
Bane, Francis 113
Barber Asphalt Paving Company 46
Barkworth, Thomas 75–76, 206nn49, 52
Beall, Samuel 13
Beck, James 105–6
Benton, J. H. 50–51
Biddle, Francis 157
Bigelow, George H. 129
birthright citizenship 2, 19, 144
Black, Hugo 104, 112
Black Codes 18
Blackwell, Alice Stone 72
Blaine, James 18–19
blue-collar nativist hiring laws. See also
    specific state
  generally 6, 35–37, 62–63, 168
  anti-Chinese laws 37–39
  anti-temporary immigrant worker
    laws 39–41
  challenges to 168–169
  current status 171–72
  "dead letter" laws, as 36
  first papers laws and 40
  Fourteenth Amendment and 61
  Great Depression, during 128
  judicial intervention and 62–63, 143
  public employment and 45, 52, 56–63,
    119–20, 123, 128–32, 140,
    229–30n58, 230n60
  public works projects and 40–43,
    45–52, 123, 128, 229–30n58, 230n60,
    230–31n62
  unemployment and 41–45, 53–63,
    123, 128–32
  weakness of, as often portrayed in
    historiography 188n9
Blumer, Alfhild Johanna 151–52, 154,
  243n40, 244n55
Bobb, Emma 92

Bone, Hugh 96
Borden, Robert 59, 202n182
Born, John A. 193n58
Breckinridge, Sophonisba 153, 243n47
Brennan, James 98–100, 216n26
Brock, Nathan 50
Bromwell, H. P. H. 22
Brown, Olympia 71, 80–81, 81f
Bryan, William Jennings 59–60
Bureau of Naturalization 146, 149, 151, 155,
  242n34, 243n48
Burke, Walter James 27
Burns v. Richardson (1966) 112–13

Cable Act of 1922 146–47, 150–51, 153–56,
  245n63, 249n116
California
  Alien Land Act of 1913 54–55, 142
  Alien Land Act of 1920 97, 142
  alien suffrage in 169–70
  anti-Chinese laws in 37–39
  apportionment in 23–24, 104–5, 223n134
  blue-collar nativist hiring laws in 35, 37–39,
    45, 54–55, 128, 194–95n77, 203n201,
    230n60, 230–31n62
  Board of Pharmacy 125–26, 136
  disfranchisement of noncitizens
    in 23–24, 30
  exclusion of persons ineligible to citizenship
    from apportionment in 23–24,
    214n9, 223n134
  immigrants in 104–5
  licensure laws in 119–20, 122–23, 134–36,
    140, 252n16
  marital repatriation in 146–51, 160–62,
    162t, 165
  pharmacists in 125–26, 134–36
  public employment, anti-alien hiring laws
    and 45, 56–63, 119–20, 140, 194–95n77,
    203n201, 229–30n58
  public works projects, anti-alien hiring laws
    and 198n128, 229–30n58, 230n60,
    230–31n62
  "sanctuary" status of 169
  social assistance in 169
  Teacher Preparation and Licensing
    Commission 140
  teachers in 56–63, 119–20, 122–23, 140
California Teachers' Association 57–58
Cameron, Simon 20
Campbell, Lewis 22
Canada
  comparative example, as 70

INDEX 293

Department of External Affairs 59
Ministry of Justice 59–60
Canadian immigrants
blue-collar nativist hiring laws and 39–40
licensure laws and 129–30
marital repatriation and 146–47
nurses 129–31
teacher controversy in California and 58–61
Cannon, James Jr. 105
Cardozo, Benjamin 53, 55
Carmody, Henry 191n38
Carpenter, Niles 240n10
Castleman, Alfred L. 14
Catholics
marital repatriation and 148
political opposition to 16–17, 74
Catt, Carrie Chapman 67, 71–72
Cavanaugh, John 102
Celler, Emanuel 108, 158
Census Bureau 106–8, 110–11, 114
Census citizenship question 110, 114, 169–71,
250–51n4, 251n9
Chamorro, Dorothy 151, 153–54
Chaney, Henry 70, 204n20
Chee, Toy 193–94n68
Chicago v. Hulbert (1903) 48
Chicago World's Fair (1893). *See* Columbian
Exposition (1893)
Childs, Curtis 101
Chinese Exclusion Act of 1882 38, 142
Chinese immigrants
Alien Tax Act of 1897 (Pennsylvania
law) and 44
apportionment and 23–24, 214n9, 223n134
blue-collar nativist hiring laws and 37–39
due process and 38
equal protection and 38
licensure laws and 142
marital repatriation and 147, 164–65
"Paper Sons" 238n151
racism directed toward 23–24, 37–39, 189n18
Chipman, John 40
citizen-only rights
generally 4–5, 168, 172
apportionment and 116
state level, at 7
World War I, during 85–94, 97–103
citizenship, political rights
generally 5–6, 11–12
antebellum period, during 12–17, 33
apportionment (*see* apportionment)
constitutional conventions and 33
Gilded Age, during 25–33

historical evolution of 11–12
Jim Crow regime, under 25–33
Reconstruction, during 17–25, 33
state-by-state differences in 12, 33, 168
suffrage (*see* suffrage)
citizenship regime 177n28
Civil Rights Act of 1964 3
Civil War 2, 173n2, 179–80n23
Clark, Thomas 165
Clay, Henry (Pennsylvania politician) 43
Cleveland, Grover 40, 42, 74, 77, 95
Closson, Carlos 42
Cold War, licensure laws during 141–42
Coleman, William C. 163
Colorado
alienage laws in 1
alien suffrage in 21, 82
constitutional conventions in 21–22,
182–83n72
immigrants in 72
statehood of 30
suffrage in 1
women's suffrage in 21–22, 71, 82,
205n25, 208n95
Colorado Territory, alien suffrage in 30, 180n27
Columbian Exposition (1893) 41, 70–71,
191 nn.36, 38
Colwell, N. P. 126–27
Comacho, Louise 245n62
Committee on Public Information 124
Connecticut, malapportionment in 100
Constitutional Convention, United States
(1787) 12, 15
constitutional conventions. See also *specific state*
apportionment and 11, 15–16, 23–24,
95–103, 114–15
suffrage and 13, 21–23, 26–27, 29, 31–33
contemporary debates 170
Conway, P. J. 57–58
Corliss, John 40
coverture 3, 240n11
Coxey, Jacob 42
Crane, Clarence A. 53, 55–56, 56*f*
Crawford, Andrew 83
Crist, Judith 166
Crist, Raymond 155–56, 245n65
Curley, James Michael 129

Dahlman, James 84
Dakota Territory, alien suffrage in 21, 30,
32, 180n27
D'Alesandro, Thomas 157–59, 163, 246nn81,
86, 249n123

294 INDEX

Decker, C. J. 129
decree, marital repatriation by 157–66
Deferred Action for Childhood Arrivals
 (DACA) 171
Delaney, John 48
Delaware, immigrants in 182n69
Democratic Party
 alien suffrage and 13–14, 28, 31, 75–76, 80
 apportionment and 95–96, 98–101, 103–6,
  108–11, 114–15
 blue-collar nativist hiring laws and 47
 disfranchisement of noncitizens
  and 87–88, 93
 women's suffrage and 89
dentists, licensure laws and 141
Department of Commerce v. New York (2019)
 250–51n4, 251n9
Dewey, Thomas 111
Dickinson, E. M. 105
doctors, licensure laws and 125–27, 134, 136–38,
 140–41, 239n156
Donovan, James 98
Doran, John L. 13–14
Douglass, Frederick 204–5n24
Dowd, John F. 129, 232n71
Doyle, Jeremiah 101–2
due process 38
Dunn, Charles 14

Eisenhower, Dwight D. 111
Electoral College 30, 71, 73–74
Emergency Quota Act of 1921 123
Equal Nationality Act of 1934 156
equal protection
 Alien Tax Act of 1897 (Pennsylvania
  law) and 45
 apportionment and 112–13
 Chinese immigrants and 38
 licensure laws and 133, 136, 143
 national citizenship and 2
Evenwel, Sue 251n9
Evenwel v. Abbott (2016) 170, 251n9
E-Verify 172
Examining Board v. Flores de Otero (1976) 143
Expatriation Act of 1907 58, 82, 144, 146,
 161, 244n60

Fahy, John 43
federal law, relative predominance of in
 contemporary era 170–72
Fee, James A. 164, 249n129
Fellman, David 133–34
Ferguson, James 211n147

Fields, Harold 132, 234n95
Fifer, Joseph 40–41
Fifteenth Amendment 20–21, 28, 82, 84,
 211n136
first papers laws
 generally 44f
 blue-collar nativist hiring laws and 40
 licensure laws and 135–36, 142
 marital repatriation and 83
 suffrage and 14–15, 69, 84, 90
Fitzpatrick, John 27
Florida
 alien suffrage in 21, 186n129
 disfranchisement of noncitizens in 26, 29
Flower, Roswell 42
Flynn, Edward 109–10
Foran Act (Alien Contract Labor Act)
 of 1885 39
Ford, Melbourne 39–40, 190nn25–26
Foreign Language Information Service
 (FLIS) 124–25, 132–33, 228nn35,
 44, 249n123
Fourteenth Amendment
 Alien Tax Act of 1897 (Pennsylvania
  law) and 45
 anti-Chinese laws and 24, 38
 apportionment and 18–20, 106
 birthright citizenship 144
 blue-collar nativist hiring laws and 61
 equal protection under (*see* equal
  protection)
 licensure laws and 136
 "one man, one vote" and 112–13
 "penalty clause" 106
Frelinghuysen, Joseph 89
Friedman, Milton 225n9
Fujii, Sei 134, 235–36n112
Fujita, Haruko 135f
Fukushima, Fusuichi 135
Fuller, Arthur 209n115

Garcia-Godoy, Manuel 138, 138f,
 236–37 nn.127–28
*Garcia-Godoy v. Texas State Board of Medical
 Examiners* (1939) 138
Gardner, Frederick 91–92
Gardner, Henry 17
Gatliff, G. J. 62
Geary Act of 1892 38
Georgia
 alien suffrage in 21
 disfranchisement of noncitizens in 26
German–American Alliance 87

INDEX   295

German immigrants and refugees
    from Germany
    Nazi period, during 131–32, 136–37
    public works projects and 47
    World War I, anti-German sentiment
        during 85–90, 98, 102–3
Gerwig, C. W. 193n59
Gifford, Peter D. 14
Gilded Age
    blue-collar nativist hiring laws during
        (see blue-collar nativist hiring laws)
    citizenship, political rights during 25–33
Gill, John 53, 198n131
Gilliand, Helen Mercedes 150–51
Ginsburg, Ruth Bader 251n9
Gonzalez, Cecilia Chavez 153–54
Goodrich, James P. 91
Goodwin, Frank 129, 232n75
Goolin, Peter 125
Gordon, Frank 198n127
Gore, Thomas 89
Graham v. Richardson (1971) 252n14
Grange, the (agricultural organization) 22, 54
Grant, Madison 123
Gray, William 58–59, 202n182
"Great Compromise" (of 1787) 15
Great Depression
    generally 109
    blue-collar nativist hiring laws
        during 128–32
    licensure laws during 127–139
    marital repatriation during 146–55
    New York legislative apportionment debates
        during 109–11
Greeff, J. G. William 130–31
Gregory, Charles 155–56
Gresser, Naomi 158
Griffiths, In re (1973) 143
Gross, Ernest A. 165

Haas, Jeanette Anderson 153, 244n55
Hagle, D. C. 40–41
Halverson, Gunder 79
Harris, Franklin 43, 192n55, 193nn58, 61
Harrison, Earl 139–40
Hart, William 27
Hawaii
    apportionment in 112–13
    marital repatriation in 147, 164–65, 241n21
Hayes, Rutherford B. 30
Heim, William 53
Heim v. McCall (1915) 53, 61–63, 171, 198n134
Helfenstein, Leonard 132

Hill, William 218n67
hiring laws. See blue-collar nativist hiring laws
Hobby, William 211n147
Hoch, Homer 105, 108
Hogan, Joseph 31
Holden, C. W. 32
Homeland Security, US Department of 167
Hoover, Herbert 148, 241n24
House of Representatives, US
    apportionment of 15–20, 104–8, 116
    exclusion of noncitizens from
        apportionment debated and
        rejected 15–20, 104–8, 169
    failure to reapportion 104–8, 214n10
    "penalty clause" and 19, 106–8
Hulshof, John 122
Hyatt, Edward 56–57

Idaho
    apportionment in 102
    blue-collar nativist hiring laws
        in 191n32, 198n128
    first papers laws in 40
    malapportionment in 214n9
    statehood of 30
Idaho Territory, alien suffrage
    in 180n27, 182n70
Illinois
    apportionment in 102
    blue-collar nativist hiring laws in 35,
        40–41, 191n32
    first papers laws in 1, 40–41
    public works projects, anti-alien hiring
        laws and 48
Immigration and Nationality Act of 1952.
    See McCarran–Walter Act of 1952
Immigration and Naturalization Service (INS)
    Annual Reports 242n34
    generally 247n90
    licensure laws and 139–140
    marital repatriation and 7, 144–46, 149,
        155–66, 248n104
immigration quota system
    generally 3–4
    licensure laws and 123–27
Indiana
    alien suffrage in 15
    apportionment in 102
    disfranchisement of noncitizens
        in 85–86, 91–94
    immigrants in 93, 104
    male-only apportionment in 214n9, 217n50
Indian Citizenship Act of 1924 2

296 INDEX

Indian immigrants
    licensure laws and 134, 136, 235n111
    marital repatriation and 147
Irish immigrants
    apportionment and 16–17
    marital repatriation and 147
    public works projects and 46–49
    Tammany Hall and 122, 233n87
    teachers, as 226n23
Italian immigrants
    blue-collar nativist hiring laws and 39
    marital repatriation and 147
    public works projects and 41, 43, 46–47,
        50–51, 191n34

Jackson, Robert 158
James, Ada Lois 80–81
Japanese immigrants
    alienage laws, generally, and 97
    licensure laws and 134–36, 141
    limitation of property rights 54
    marital repatriation and 147, 167
Jester, Beauford H. 140–41
Jews, licensure laws and 127, 136
Jim Crow regime
    African Americans under 29, 167
    citizenship, political rights under 25–33
    institutionalization of 143
    literacy tests under 69
    marital repatriation under 153–54
    Mexican immigrants under 90
    poll taxes under 69
    voting restrictions under 106
Johnson, Andrew 18
Johnson, Ed 128
Johnson, Hiram 59–61
Johnson, Reverdy 182n58
Johnson, Stanley B. 119–20, 224n4
Johnson–Reed Act of 1924 123–24, 243n48
Jones, Herbert 61
Justice, US Department of 165, 247n90

Kalodner, Harry 164
Kamalian, A. 125
Kansas
    alien suffrage in 15, 21, 30, 209nn107, 115
    apportionment in 102
    disfranchisement of noncitizens in 85, 88
    malapportionment in 214n9
    women's suffrage in 88
Kato, Shigeo 134
Kearney, Denis 23

Kennedy, Arthur 42
Kent, Donald Peterson 141
Kentucky
    exclusion of noncitizens from
        apportionment in 17
    immigrants in 182n69
Keppel, Mark 58, 200n157, 201n169
Kernan, T. J. 27–28
Kerrigan, Frank 151, 153
Kestnbaum, Meyer 111
Kestnbaum Commission 111–12
Kimball, Henry 158, 247n90, 247–48n97
Kinney, William 100
Knights of Labor 26, 39, 46
Know-Nothing Party 16–17, 37, 100,
        181 nn.40, 42
Konvitz, Milton 126, 141–42, 238n142
Kruger, David 126
Ku Klux Klan 93, 123
Kuznets, Simon 225n9

Labor, US Department of 247n90
La Guardia, Fiorello 105, 108–9
Lansing, Robert 60–61
Larch, Lillian 245n62
Latino immigrants, see also *Mexican*
        immigrants
    racialization of 3
    racism directed toward 2
Lattimer Massacre (1897) 45
lawyers, licensure laws and 122, 125, 132
League of Women Voters 68, 92–93, 146
Lehman, Herbert 109–10, 234n91
Levick, Marjorie 161, 163
licensure laws. See also *specific state*
    generally 6–7, 119–21, 143, 168
    accountants and 122, 136, 141
    architects and 122, 143
    challenges to 132–133, 142, 168–69
    Cold War, during 141–43
    current status 171–72
    dentists and 141
    doctors and 125–27, 136–38, 140–41, 239n156
    equal protection and 133, 136, 143
    first papers laws and 135–36, 142
    Fourteenth Amendment and 136
    Great Depression, during 127–39
    immigration quotas and 123–27
    INS and 139–40
    lawyers and 122, 125, 132
    nurses and 128–32
    origins of anti-alien licensure laws 121–23

INDEX 297

pharmacists and 125–26, 134–36
teachers and 119–20, 122–23, 140,
143, 226n22
World War II, during 139–41
Lincoln, Abraham 30
Literacy Test Act of 1917 123
literacy tests 69, 123
Lockridge, Ross Franklin 92–93
Lodge, Henry Cabot 40
Lodge–Corliss Bill 40
Lomasney, Martin 98–100, 216n27
Looney, B. F. 90
"lost century" 169
Louisiana
alien suffrage in 21, 184n98
blue-collar nativist hiring laws in 52,
197–98n124
Cajuns in 185n120
constitutional conventions in 26–28
disfranchisement of noncitizens in
26–28, 184n98
immigrants in 182n69
voting restrictions in 29
Lowell, A. Lawrence 127
Lyford, James 101
Lyman, J. Chester 69–70

MacCormack, D. W. 155
Mackenzie, Ethel 144–45
Mackenzie, Gordon 144
Maginnis, Martin 31
Maine
apportionment in 116
exclusion of noncitizens from
apportionment in 16, 19, 214n9, 223n133
malapportionment 100, 104–11, 113–15
marital repatriation. See also *specific state patterns*
generally 5–7, 144–46, 166–67
Alien Registration Act of 1940 and 145, 158, 160, 163, 166–67
decree, by 157–66
first papers laws and 83
INS and 7, 144–46, 149, 155–66, 248n104
Jim Crow regime, under 153–54
less scholarly study of than marital expatriation 239–40n9
naturalization, as 146–55
nebulous nature of citizenship 240–41n11
Nineteenth Amendment and 144, 146, 154
oath, by 155–64, 161f–62f, 162t
petitions 148f–50f, 152f

"marriage penalties" 231–32n68
Marshall, George 165
Marshall, Thomas 92–93
Martin, Grant 84
Martin, James 45
Marvin, Earl 103
Maryland
alien suffrage in 169–70
immigrants in 182n69
Massachusetts
apportionment in 16–17, 19, 24–25, 24f,
98–100, 113, 216n38, 222n118
blue-collar nativist hiring laws in 1, 45,
48–51, 128–30, 194nn74–75, 200n145,
230n60, 230–31n62, 231n65
Bureau of Statistics of Labor 25, 38, 98
census in 24–25, 24f
dentists in 141
disfranchisement of noncitizens in 13
Division of Immigration and
Americanization 134, 154, 231n65
drivers' licenses in 169
exclusion of noncitizens from
apportionment in 7, 16–17, 19, 24–25,
98–100, 113, 180–81nn37–38
licensure laws in 128–30, 141
malapportionment in 113, 214n9
marital repatriation in 159
Metropolitan Water Board 49–51,
196–97n110, 197n119
nurses in 128–30
public works projects, anti-alien hiring laws
and 45, 48–51, 230n60, 230–31n62
McArthur Brothers 41
McCarran–Walter Act (Immigration and
Nationality Act) of 1952 142–143,
165–166, 238n152
McHarg, Ormsby 79–80
McIsaac, Daniel 48–49, 51, 196n102
McKeen, Patricia 151
McLaughlin, Frank 164–65
Metcalf, Henry H. 101
Mexican immigrants
blue-collar nativist hiring laws
and 39, 62, 128
Jim Crow regime, under 90
marital repatriation and 149, 153–54, 166
public employment, anti-alien hiring laws
and 62, 128, 227n29, 230–31n62
temporary migrants, framed as
227–28n32
Mexican Revolution 54

298 INDEX

Michigan
alien suffrage in 15, 72
disfranchisement of noncitizens in 33,
73–78, 75f
identification documents in 131, 233–34n89
immigrants in 73, 104
Miner Law 74
Michigan Political Science Association 70
Middleton, C. R. 31
Miles, James 192–93n57
military voters 210n125
Miller, Kelly 107–8, 107f
Miner, John 74
Minnesota
alien suffrage in 15
disfranchisement of noncitizens
in 33, 78–79
immigrants in 73
marital repatriation in 159
Minor, Virginia 20–21
Minor v. Happersett (1875) 20–21, 167
Minton, Maurice 47
Mississippi
apportionment (federal) 106
voting restrictions in 29
Missouri
alien suffrage in 21, 28–29
constitutional conventions in 91–92
disfranchisement of noncitizens
in 85–86, 91–92
immigrants in 182n69
Missouri Council of Defense 91
Mitchel, John 54
Molony, William R. 137
Montana
constitutional conventions in 31–32
disfranchisement of noncitizens in 31–32
immigrants in 31, 182n71
statehood of 30
Montana Territory, alien suffrage in 21, 30
Moorhead, Harley 84
Moses, Robert 109
Mueller, Karin 130
Muirhead, A. S. 68–69, 204n10
Muller, Charles 158

National American Woman Suffrage
Association (NAWSA) 67–68, 71,
88–89, 208n95
National Association for the Advancement of
Colored People (NAACP) 106, 219n82
Nationality Act of 1940 145, 158–60, 165, 167
National Municipal League 111, 113

Native Americans
disfranchisement of 15, 186n132
racism directed toward 2, 15, 30
Native Sons of the Golden West 54
nativist hiring laws. See blue-collar nativist
hiring laws
Naturalization Act of 1855 201n168, 240n11
Naturalization Act of 1870 62
Naturalization Act of 1906 69, 84, 209n115
Nawn and Brock 50
Nebraska
alien suffrage in 21, 30, 72, 84–85, 180n27
apportionment in 98, 102–3, 116
disfranchisement of noncitizens
in 85–88, 88f, 94
exclusion of noncitizens from
apportionment in 98, 102–3, 214n9,
218n64, 223n133
immigrants in 73, 104
Siman Act 102–3
women's suffrage in 86–88
Nebraska Council of Defense 86–87
Neuman, Gerald 169
Nevada
alien suffrage in 180n27
statehood of 30
Neville, Keith 87–88
Newcombe, E. L. 202n194
New Deal 109–10, 120, 128, 157
New Hampshire
apportionment in 98
exclusion of noncitizens from
apportionment proposed in 100–2, 169
New Jersey
blue-collar nativist hiring laws in 35, 194n76
public works projects, anti-alien hiring
laws and 45
women's suffrage in 12
New Mexico, statehood of 30, 186–87n135
New Mexico Territory, disfranchisement of
noncitizens in 30
New York
alienage laws, generally, in 1
Alien Labor Law 46–48, 53, 55
blue-collar nativist hiring laws in 35,
46–48, 53–55, 190n31, 192n50, 199n138,
230–31n62
Bureau of Statistics of Labor 45–46
census (state) in 24–25, 110
constitutional conventions in 11, 16,
95, 114–15
Department of Labor 47–48
disfranchisement of noncitizens in 13

exclusion of noncitizens from
apportionment in 7, 15–16, 95–96, 108–11,
114–15, 214n9
immigrants in 104–5
licensure laws in 1, 121–22, 130–32,
143, 226n22
malapportionment in 100, 105, 108–11,
113–15
marital repatriation in 158–60
nurses in 130–32
public employment, anti-alien hiring laws
and 61, 63, 130–32, 230–31n62
Public Service Commission 53, 55
public works projects, anti-alien hiring laws
and 42, 45–48, 53–55, 230–31n62
reapportionment proposals
in 220n95, 222n122
social assistance in 169
subway hiring controversy 53–55, 61
suffrage requirements in 11
teachers in 122, 143, 226n22
New York Central Labor Union 46
New York City Brotherhood of Carpenters and
Joiners 46
New York General Contractors
Association 53, 199n139
New York State Nurses Association 131
New York State Women's Republican Club 105
Nicolls, Henry 159
Nineteenth Amendment
generally 211n136
alien suffrage and 89
approval of 91
coverture and 3
marital repatriation and 144, 146, 154
Noji, Yohei 141
Norbeck, Peter 89
Norcop, Maurice 135–36
North Carolina
apportionment in 115
exclusion of noncitizens from
apportionment in 96, 214n9
malapportionment in 223n132
North Dakota
alien suffrage in 33, 184n98
disfranchisement of noncitizens in 33,
79–80, 184n98, 187n152, 207n81
immigrants in 73, 183n87, 205n33
statehood of 30
Northwest Ordinance (1787) 13
Nourse, Joseph 119
nurses, licensure laws and 128–32
Nyquist v. Mauclet (1977) 226n15

oath, marital repatriation by 155–62, 164
Obama, Barack 251n9
O'Brien, William J. 46–47
O'Connor, Basil 133–34
O'Donnell, Charles C. 23
Oglou, Theresa 119–20, 224n4, 231–32n68
O'Hara, James 76
Ohio
constitutional conventions in 22, 183n84
disfranchisement of noncitizens in 22
Oklahoma, disfranchisement of noncitizens
in 187n151
Oklahoma Territory, alien suffrage in 184n98
Oleson, A. R. 103, 218n62
"one man, one vote" 111–16
Oregon
alien suffrage in 15, 21, 30, 82–83
apportionment in 116, 181n46
immigrants in 72, 182n71
marital expatriation and repatriation
in 82–83, 164
white-only apportionment in 116,
214n9, 223n134
Oyama v. California (1948) 142

Pacelli, Tito 47
Panama Canal 83
Panama Exhibition (1915) 58–59
Panic of 1893 41–45
Panic of 1907 80, 197n124, 199n141
Panic of 1913 54
Parker, Kunal 3
Partridge, John S. 150–151
Patton, Edward 52
Pelosi, Nancy 246n86
Pennsylvania
Alien Tax Act of 1897 and 43–45
anti-alien public hiring laws in 36, 52
blue-collar nativist hiring laws in 35, 42–43,
193nn60–63
first papers in 193n66
identification documents in 131
Panic of 1893 in 42
public works projects, anti-alien hiring laws
and 42–43, 52
People v. Crane (1915) 61–63, 171, 198n134
People v. Warren (1895) 46–47
Perkins, Frances 230–231n62, 247n90
Perry, Donald R. 158
pharmacists, licensure laws and 125–26,
134–36
Plyler v. Doe (1982) 250n2
poll taxes 26–27, 29, 69, 90

300 INDEX

Portuguese immigrants, marital repatriation and 147
Presley, C. A. 27
Prince, Ethel 131–32
Progressive Era
demographic contrast of alien suffrage states during 73*t*
suffrage during 72–85
public employment. See also *specific state*
blue-collar nativist hiring laws and 45, 52, 56–63, 122–23, 128–32
public works projects. See also *specific state*
blue-collar nativist hiring laws and 40–43, 45–52, 61–62, 123, 128
Puerto Ricans, marital repatriation and 156, 245n73

Quinn, Timothy 100

racialization
Asian immigrants, of 3, 23–24, 37–39, 189n18
Latino immigrants, of 3, 62, 227–28n32
southern and eastern Europeans, of 190n22
racism, relation to alienage 3, 5
Radical Republicans 18–19, 182n58
Raich, Mike 54
Rankin, John 104–5
Rauf, M. A. 136
Reconstruction
generally 2, 173n2
African Americans during 18–20
apportionment during 18–20
citizenship, political rights during 17–25, 33
suffrage during 18–25
Redeemer period 26, 182n68
Red Scare (first) 123
Reed, James 92
regulatory capture 225n9
Repatriation Act of 1936 (and amended in 1940) 144, 155–59, 164, 166, 248n104, 249n116
Republican Party
alien suffrage and 17–19, 28, 31
apportionment and 95–96, 98–106, 110–11
Census citizenship question and 170–71
disfranchisement of noncitizens and 73–80, 84, 93
elite opposition to alien suffrage 68–69
women's suffrage and 89
Reynolds v. Sims (1964) 112–14
Rhode Island
malapportionment in 96, 100
marital repatriation in 147–51

Rich, John 77
Richardson, William 14–15
Rockefeller, Nelson 114
Rok, Edward 235n100
Roosevelt, Franklin D.
generally 139
apportionment and 110, 220n95
electoral performance of 109, 241n24
Nationality Act of 1940 and 157–58, 246n86
nationality laws and 247n95
New Deal and 120, 128
Repatriation Act of 1936 and 155
Supreme Court and 112
Tammany Hall and 109–10
World War II and 237n130
Ryan, John A. 133

Sackett, Frederic 104
Sakuda, Kesanosuke 135
Salese, Angelina 244n59
Sanders, H. T. 13
Sandhu, Makhan Singh 134
Sargent, Francis 32
Sashihara, Thomas T. 135, 135*f*
Sashihara et al. v. California State Board of Pharmacy (1935) 136, 171
Schafer, John 105–6
Schenck, Robert 19
Schibsby, Marian 124–25, 132, 228n44
Schlotfeldt, Fred 155
Scott Act of 1888 38
Second Reconstruction (civil rights era as) 3, 174–75n10
sexism, relation to alienage 5
Shanks v. Dupont (1830) 240–41n11
Shelley, Rebecca 144–45, 163, 239n6
Shelley v. United States (1941) 144–45, 163–64
Shklar, Judith 5
Shoemaker, T. B. 159–60, 163
Short, Katharine 35, 58–62, 187n1, 228n44
Short, William 58
Sibley, Celestine 161–62
Silva, Ruth 114–15, 115*f*
Silverman, Samuel 232n72
Slack, L. Ert 93
Smith, Al 96, 148, 241n24
Socialist Labor Party 44
Socialist Party 122
South Carolina, voting restrictions in 29
South Dakota
alien suffrage in 26, 33, 71, 184n98
disfranchisement of noncitizens in 85, 89, 94

INDEX 301

statehood of 30
women's suffrage in 71, 89
Soviet Union, licensure of immigrants
 from 125–26
Spring Rice, Cecil 59
Stainback, Ingram 165
Stanton, Elizabeth Cady 20
Stapleton, George 31
State, US Department of 54, 60–61, 165
Steffens, Lincoln 198n126
Stevens, Thaddeus 18–19
Stewart, Anna 57–58
Stratton, Amalia Bertha 146–47
Stratton, Harry D'Arcy 146
suffrage. See also *specific state*
 generally 6, 67–68, 94, 168
 African Americans and 18–20
 antebellum period, during 12–15
 constitutional conventions and 13, 21–23,
  26–27, 29, 31–33, 67–68
 contemporary debates 170
 demographics, effect of 203–4n8
 elite opposition to alien suffrage 68–72
 erosion of noncitizen suffrage at Gilded Age
  constitutional conventions 33–34
 first papers laws and 14–15, 69, 84, 90
 Jim Crow regime, under 25–33
 literacy tests and 17, 26, 29, 32, 69
 military voters 210n125
 poll taxes and 26–27, 29, 69, 90
 Progressive Era, during 72–85
 Reconstruction, during 18–25
 women and 12, 20–22, 30, 67–68,
  71–72, 86–90
 World War I, during 85–94
Sugarman v. Dougall (1973) 143
Sumner, Charles 20
suspect class, alienage as 4, 143, 171
Sutherst, W. E. 57
Sweeting, Orville 107
Swift, Morrison I. 42

Takahashi v. Fish & Game Commission
 (1948) 142
Tammany Hall 47, 68–69, 109–10, 233n87
Tate, Thomas 197n112
teachers, licensure laws and 119–20, 122–23,
 140, 143, 226n22
Tennessee
 apportionment in 17, 115
 disfranchisement of noncitizens in 23
 exclusion of noncitizens from
  apportionment in 17

immigrants in 183n87
malapportionment in 112, 214n9, 223n132
terminology xvii–xviii
Texas
 accountants in 141
 alien suffrage in 21, 28–29, 85
 apportionment in 17, 115, 170, 223n132, 251n9
 blue-collar nativist hiring laws in 45, 128,
  230n60, 230–31n62
 Board of Medical Examiners 127, 137–41
 Board of Public Accountancy 141
 disfranchisement of noncitizens
  in 89–91, 94
 doctors in 127, 137–41
 exclusion of noncitizens (in part) from
  apportionment in 17
 immigrants in 182n69
 licensure laws in 137–38, 140–41
 malapportionment in 214n9
 marital repatriation in 148–50, 153–54,
  160, 162t
 public works projects, anti-alien hiring laws
  and 45, 227n29
 schools in 169
 women's suffrage in 89–91
Thatcher, Henry C. 182–83n72
Thirteenth Amendment 18
Three-Fifths Compromise 15, 18
Tiedeman, Christopher 48, 196n100
Tilson, John 106–7
Tin, Sheet Iron and Cornice Makers' Union 46
Tinkham, George 106, 219n82
Tinnin, W. J. 23
Traynor, W. J. H. 74
Truax, Billy 54
Truax v. Raich (1915) 61
Truman, Harry S. 142, 238n152
Trump, Donald 169, 250–51n4, 251n9

Underhill, Charles 100
unemployment 41–45, 53–62, 127–39
union membership, barriers to
 noncitizens 188n3
Universidad Nacional Autónoma de
 México 138, 140–41
University of California 58
US Citizenship and Immigration
 Services 250n140
Utah Territory, women's suffrage in 21–22

Vandenberg, Arthur 106, 108, 219n82
Vernier, Charles 132–33
Vigil, Agapito 22

302 INDEX

voting rights. *See* suffrage
Voting Rights Act of 1965 3

Wachusett Dam 49–51, 49*f*
Wagner, Robert 53, 199n139
Walsh, David 49–51, 196n108, 197n123, 200n145
Warren, Charles 31–32
Warren, Earl 112, 140, 143
Warren, Henry 46
Washington, D.C., immigrants and noncitizens
 in 160, 182n69
Washington, statehood of 30
Washington Territory, alien suffrage in 21, 30,
 180n27, 187n150
Webb, Ulysses S. 35, 56–57
Welden, Ernestine 151
Wellin, Patrick 23
Westphal, T. A. Jr. 140
West Virginia, immigrants in 182n69
Wheeler, Benjamin Ide 57
Whig Party 14, 16
White, Truman C. 46
Williams, Hattie Plum 92–93
Wilson, Henry 19–20
Wilson, Woodrow 55, 61, 89, 123–24
Wisconsin
 alien suffrage in 13–15
 blue-collar nativist hiring laws in 1, 45,
  123, 227n27
 Board of Accountancy 136
 Board of Control 227n27
 disfranchisement of noncitizens in 80–81
 immigrants in 73
 licensure laws in 136
 public employment, anti-alien hiring
  laws and 123
Wisconsin Political Equality League 80–81
Wisconsin Woman's Suffrage Association 80
WMCA, Inc. v. Lomenzo (1964) 114
women
 alien suffrage, ties to women's suffrage 1, 32,
  67–68, 71–72, 80–82, 86–90, 186n126

loss of citizenship 3
 marital expatriation and repatriation
  (*see* marital repatriation)
 "marriage penalties" 231–32n68
 suffrage and 12, 20–22, 30, 67–68, 71–72,
  86–90, 144, 154, 161, 163
Wong, Yuen Loo 165
Workingmen's Party 23, 37
Workingmen's State Trade Assembly 46
Works Progress Administration (later
  Works Projects Administration) 128,
  235n100
World War I
 generally 54
 citizen-only rights during 85–94, 97–103
 demographic contrast of alien suffrage states
  during 86*t*
 suffrage during 85–94
World War II
 immigrants and 237n130
 licensure laws during 139–41
 marital repatriation during 157–67
Wright, Carroll D. 25, 38–39
Wyoming
 blue-collar nativist hiring laws in 40,
  191n32
 constitutional conventions in 32
 disfranchisement of noncitizens in 32
 first papers laws in 40
 immigrants in 31
 statehood of 30
 women' suffrage in 30
Wyoming Territory
 alien suffrage in 21, 30
 women's suffrage in 21–22, 30

Yankwich, Leon 235n100
Yarborough, Ralph 236–37n127
Yick Wo v. Hopkins (1886) 38
Yuen, Shee Mui Chong 164–65

Zacharie, Frank 26, 185n104